The Essential Guide to Storage Area Networks

ISBN 0-13-093575-1

90000

9 780130 935755

Prentice Hall PTR
Essential Guide Series

THE ESSENTIAL GUIDE TO DATA WAREHOUSING

Agosta

THE ESSENTIAL GUIDE TO WEB STRATEGY FOR ENTREPRENEURS

Bergman

THE ESSENTIAL GUIDE TO THE BUSINESS OF U.S. MOBILE WIRELESS COMMUNICATIONS

Burnham

THE ESSENTIAL GUIDE TO TELECOMMUNICATIONS, THIRD EDITION

Dodd

THE ESSENTIAL GUIDE TO WIRELESS COMMUNICATIONS APPLICATIONS: FROM CELLULAR SYSTEMS TO WAP AND M-COMMERCE

Dornan

THE ESSENTIAL GUIDE TO COMPUTER HARDWARE

Keogh

THE ESSENTIAL GUIDE TO NETWORKING

Keogh

THE ESSENTIAL GUIDE TO COMPUTER DATA STORAGE: FROM FLOPPY TO DVD

Khurshudov

THE ESSENTIAL GUIDE TO DIGITAL SET-TOP BOXES AND INTERACTIVE TV

O'Driscoll

THE ESSENTIAL GUIDE TO HOME NETWORKING TECHNOLOGIES

O'Driscoll

THE ESSENTIAL GUIDE TO KNOWLEDGE MANAGEMENT: E-BUSINESS AND CRM APPLICATIONS

Tiwana

THE ESSENTIAL GUIDE TO APPLICATION SERVICE PROVIDERS

Toigo

THE ESSENTIAL GUIDE TO STORAGE AREA NETWORKS

Vacca

THE ESSENTIAL GUIDE TO MOBILE BUSINESS

Vos & deKlein

THE ESSENTIAL GUIDE TO COMPUTING: THE STORY OF INFORMATION TECHNOLOGY

Walters

THE ESSENTIAL GUIDE TO RF AND WIRELESS

Weisman

The
Essential
Guide to
Storage Area Networks

JOHN VACCA

Prentice Hall PTR, Upper Saddle River, NJ 07458
http://www.phptr.com

A CIP catalog record for this book can be obtained from the Library of Congress

Editorial/Production Supervision: *MetroVoice Publishing Services*
Acquisitions Editor: *Mary Franz*
Marketing Manager: *Dan DePasquale*
Editorial Assistant: *Noreen Regina*
Cover Design: *Bruce Kenselaar*
Cover Design Direction: *Jerry Votta*
Art Director: *Gail Cocker-Bogusz*
Project Coordinator: *Anne R. Garcia*

© 2002 Prentice Hall PTR
Prentice-Hall, Inc.
Upper Saddle River, NJ 07458

The publisher offers discounts on this book when ordered in bulk quantities.
For more information, contact: Corporate Sales Department, Phone: 800-382-3419;
FAX: 201-236-7141; E-mail: corpsales@prenhall.com; or write: Prentice Hall PTR,
Corp. Sales Dept., One Lake Street, Upper Saddle River, NJ 07458.

10   9   8   7   6   5   4   3   2   1

ISBN 0-13-093575-1

Pearson Education LTD.
Pearson Education Australia PTY, Limited
Pearson Education Singapore, Pte. Ltd.
Pearson Education North Asia Ltd.
Pearson Education Canada, Ltd.
Pearson Educación de Mexico, S.A. de C.V.
Pearson Education—Japan
Pearson Education Malaysia, Pte. Ltd.
Pearson Education, Upper Saddle River, New Jersey

To Joseph Dosio, for not only being my cousin, but for being a very valued and respected friend.

Contents

Part 1
Overview of SANs Technology

Part 6
SAN Solutions and Future Directions

Foreword

Storage Area Networks (SANs) are becoming part of IT architectures around the world. Like many new technologies that have emerged in the past, SANs present new opportunities for convenience, ease of use, reliability, and cost reduction. But as with all new technologies, SANs also pose many challenges in implementation, competing standards, confusing product offerings, and uncertain product development strategies on the part of many vendors entering the field.

This book is written for people who need to cut through the confusion about SANs and get down to product selection, acquisition, and deployment. The book starts with the basic concepts and takes readers through all of the necessary learning steps to enable them to implement a SAN.

Vacca has captured more information about SANs in this book than readers will find spread out over dozens of white papers and reports that have been published about SANs. Readers will save thousands of hours of research time and will be able to move ahead on their SAN project in two days instead of two months.

Another challenge in implementing new technologies is being able to cut through vendor hype and work toward a solid product selection. The knowledge that readers will gain from this book will help them slice through the vendor fog and collect information about products necessary to make a more informed product selection. More importantly, readers will be able to select the best SANs product for their environment.

This book also provides essential guidance during the installation and implementation of SANs technology. Vacca is the first writer to give the process of testing SANs solutions before they go on line. This testing approach will assure that end users are not beating down the door of the IT department in revolt because a SANs project is not living up to its promise.

—Michael Erbschloe
Vice President of Research
Computer Economics
Carlsbad, CA

Introduction

The increasingly sophisticated and prolific world of IT has dramatically altered the demand for data storage and enhanced its value to the enterprise. Desktop, department, and enterprise environments have all evolved to the point where data that was once viewed as a static resource is now viewed as a mission-critical company asset. In this highly competitive environment, the IT community has come to realize how the capabilities of online storage management and the presence of a standard operating system such as Windows NT can significantly enhance data storage systems.

At the desktop level, office applications such as spreadsheets, word processors, database programs, multimedia, and imaging software have driven the most recent generation of PCs to the point where they feature hard drives with multiple gigabytes of storage and random access memory (RAM) of up to 1 gigabyte. Moving up to the department and workgroup levels, the demands on data storage have increased exponentially as users have begun working collaboratively on projects that generate terabytes of data and span not only departments and workgroups, but nations and continents.

IMPORTANCE OF STORAGE ....

Storage was once a peripheral—a mere feature of the server. Those days are long gone, and that's a good thing because information shouldn't always be hidden behind, or bottled up inside, a single server. It should be positioned so that it can be made quickly but securely available to other applications and/or departments within the enterprise. So, now that storage is out from behind the server's shadow, we need to recognize its true value. Here's why:

First, the value of data as a corporate asset has risen dramatically over the last few years. Maintaining its availability, integrity, and security is now a matter of life or death for many enterprises.

Second, with the advent of storage networking, data storage as an enterprise core competency has become demanding and complex. And with new technologies reaching the market at a torrid pace, it becomes harder and harder to understand and make judgments about all the alternatives.

Finally, there is currently a critical shortage of the trained staff required to manage the new enterprise storage environment. As a result, expertise in recruiting, training, and retaining storage management staff is now a vital enterprise IT function.

Value of Data

Data (translated by applications and infrastructure into information) has grown in value to the point where, for many enterprises, it is the most valuable corporate asset. It's a competitive differentiator—the underpinning of all customer-facing applications like CRM and CSM. And with the advent of the Web, it has expanded in importance to become mission-critical to the very enterprise as viewed through the portal. In this environment, storage is now the single most important IT resource for assuring:

- Data Availability
- Data Integrity
- Disaster Recoverability

Data Availability

The persistent availability of data as defined by the storage utility model which basically assures that enterprise data will always be accessible, will always be *on*—just like electricity. Lost access to data can be severely damaging and possibly fatal to the enterprise. For example, in a health care setting, continuous access to data could make the difference between life and death.

Data Integrity

The protection and preservation of data from corruption, loss, and outside attack is known as data integrity. Storage can also be thought of as a vault. When you retrieve data, you expect to retrieve exactly what was deposited. Storage and storage management personnel are the guardians of data.

Disaster Recoverability

The ability of storage networks and storage management applications to play a critical role in recovering from the inevitable disaster is known as disaster recoverability. Disaster scenarios include anything from the loss of a server running a critical application, to the loss of an entire data center due to fire, flood, earthquake, etc.

Enterprise Core Competency

It would be a gross oversimplification to say that storage was once a simple matter of plugging an array into a SCSI port. Then again, compared to the array of alternatives available now from FC-AL to FC Fabric, the IP derivatives and soon InfiniBand and beyond, the days of one-size-fits-all SCSI are also long gone. Data storage as an enterprise core competency is becoming exceeding complex. Here's a brief, and by no means exhaustive, list of the technologies now directly involved in or significantly touching upon data storage as covered in this book:

- Fibre Channel-Arbitrated Loop and fabric architectures
- Ethernet and IP
- Server clustering
- Data backup and restoration
- SCSI
- Wide and Metropolitan Area Networking protocols
- Bridging, routing, and switching
- Host bus adapters and drivers
- Broadband communications
- Enterprise management applications
- Database and file system architectures
- Operating systems

PROS AND CONS OF STORAGE ....

As companies grapple to store and protect vast (and growing) amounts of data, Storage Area Networks (SAN) are gaining momentum. A SAN is a dedicated configuration of multiple servers connected to peripheral storage devices using high-speed fiber and special routers, switches, and hubs. A SAN, usually part of an enterprise's overall computing resources, enables enterprises to consolidate data from disparate servers onto a centrally managed storage network.

Storage Area Networks offer certain key advantages over file serving and Network Attached Storage (NAS) boxes, namely improved data sharing, convenient storage expansion, remote backup and recovery, and increased uptime. But the adoption rate of SANs has been slowed by drawbacks such as high cost; interoperability of software; hardware and components; and data security concerns.

The Pros

Some companies see Storage Area Networks as a solution. The following are the pros:

- Data sharing
- Live expansion capacity
- Remote backup and recovery

Data Sharing

A SAN makes stored data available to multiple users simultaneously, without disrupting productivity. A SAN provides high-speed access to data among a number of system servers, thus enabling data to be retrieved faster when used by a large number of users. This is critical for efficient company operations and for Web storage where millions of users may need to access data.

Individual computers in a SAN see each data-storage device as a shared resource, eliminating data bottlenecks common to NAS and file serving environments. You might have 30 computers, but each one sees the storage as one big pool.

Live Expansion Capacity

A SAN allows network administrators to expand storage capacity without shutting down critical file servers. Instead, new storage devices are plugged directly into the fiber connecting the various servers to existing storage capacity. With the Internet, system administrators have to make sure their data is available all the time—and keep it safe to boot.

Remote Backup and Recovery

Since it's a separate network, a SAN enables automatic data backup, meaning IT administrators don't need to swap out backup tapes each day. Backup occurs without interrupting users on other company computer networks. One of the complaints of companies using NAS boxes is that backup traffic is consuming too much bandwidth from their production networks.

A SAN also makes data migration more manageable. Data is transported across high-speed fiber and stored on a remote server. This eliminates the need to store data on the hard drive of individual machines. It also makes data recovery easier if there's a disaster.

The Cons

The information age presents network managers with a daunting challenge: store ever-increasing amounts of business-critical data, keep it secure but accessible at high speeds to multiple users, and ensure timely, regular backup—all without increasing IT costs. The following are the cons:

- Cost
- Interoperability
- Network Security

Cost

Industry experts say a comprehensive SAN could cost hundreds of thousands of dollars, putting them beyond the reach of most small enterprises. Although a SAN could yield savings through the need for fewer IT professionals, the upfront cost intimidates most companies.

Some small- and medium-size enterprises might want to build miniature SANs, consisting of a few switches on the network, for specific departments and applications. These smaller networks give them a head start and can be expanded later to accommodate their computing needs.

Interoperability

Interoperability also is a drawback. Companies implementing a SAN often buy hardware from one company, software from another company, while a third company supplies the components needed to connect everything together. There is no overarching standard for SANs right now. A lot of vendors make a single component, so companies need to be careful that the components they select are compatible with their system.

The Storage Networking Industry Association (SNIA) of Mountain View, California, is promoting open standards to ensure that different vendors' storage networking products work compatibly. But the association concedes open standards are at least a year or two away.

Network Security

The lack of industry standards also heightens concern about security and the ability to prevent unauthorized access to data. Several workable options exist, including hybrid systems that use newer technology with more established architectures. Concern about security is the chief impediment to widespread implementation of SANs.

Security safeguards should be built into a SAN. A SAN really is no different than any other computer network. The same need to separate different kinds of machines so that they can't be used to leverage each other's access still exists.

MULTIPLE DATA STORAGE OPTIONS......................

The question for today's enterprise then, is how to manage the myriad aspects of storing and controlling this data in all of its new forms across not only the local and departmental levels, but also the divisional and corporate levels. The most obvious facet of this question is the quantity of data which must be managed and its storage requirement. However, simply providing enough storage capacity is not sufficient. Organizations today must also worry about the performance of the devices relative to the needs of the users, the cost-per-megabyte of that storage, the reliability of the different devices (which directly relates to the concept of system availability), and the ease with which an organization can ensure that data read from the storage media is identical to that written (data integrity). Different storage devices have different profiles in terms of the dimensions described in the preceding. Some are slower but cheaper, some have very high capacity but are expensive, and so on. Users, too, have different needs in terms of these same dimensions, so most enterprises today attempt to mix and match the technologies and their profiles to the specific needs of their users and their corporate bottom lines.

Planning for and architecting an online storage management approach has become a required exercise in prudent IT operations. A good online storage management plan is one that understands user profiles and makes use of the various storage alternatives. This sound approach will avoid the traps many organizations fall into, where the misapplication of technology to a storage need results in overly expensive solutions, poorly performing solutions, and, almost always, in dissatisfied customers.

Not surprisingly, storage technology is typically categorized according to the different profile dimensions described earlier: availability, capacity, performance, and economics. The availability of data is directly related to its logical location. *Online* data is immediately available to users. *Nearline* data is a term that applies to data accessible to the user after a noticeable delay, but which is still completely automated by the storage device. Because it is either no longer available or has been archived to lower-cost media, *offline* data (sometimes referred to as *farline data*) is typically housed in libraries not connected to any storage device, and which must be manually handled and mounted on the device in order to be delivered to the user. Tape libraries are good examples of offline or farline storage. In developing software systems, there is an old joke that goes *One can get software systems built that are good, fast, or cheap; pick any two.* Similarly, there are tradeoffs in the combinations of attributes of different systems. You can get high capacity and fast access time only at very expensive prices; you can get lower prices by sacrificing either access time or capacity, and so on.

A well-conceived online storage management system optimizes all three of these data storage categories by automatically ensuring that they each contain prioritized data available at access speeds that correlate to the data's value. This approach requires that the most frequently used data be stored on magnetic disks and available online, while less active data is maintained in nearline mode on optical disks or tape. This logical approach to prioritizing and accessing data streamlines business processes and maximizes the productivity of users, while controlling the costs of storage.

MANAGING THE ARSENAL......................................

The good news is that there is an arsenal of storage devices that can be deployed in response to an organization's needs. In fact, most organizations typically rely on a variety of storage devices in order to satisfy all of their needs. Optical drives, jukeboxes, fixed and removable magnetic disks, tape drives, and RAID (Redundant Arrays of Independent Disks) are all deployed in varying configurations across enterprises today. The bad news is that you now have to manage a set of repositories that have very different physical and operational characteristics, and your core computer systems don't do nearly as much as you'd like them to do with regards to managing all of this.

While some other operating systems, such as UNIX, support the concept of removable devices in the core operating system, PCs and PC-based servers have implemented a storage model that presumes a single platter per drive. Device drivers are used to associate the physical devices to the operating system functions, but as long as the operating system itself only issues commands based on the notion of fixed media, additional software is needed to circumvent this problem. Therefore, any device that features removable or replaceable media, such as the popular Iomega series of drives, the newer optical 120 MB floppy media, or the older Bernoulli boxes, may be physically attached to a computer system, and the operating system will be able to identify it by a letter of the alphabet. If you can assume a system in which there are two floppy drives and two logical partitions of hard drives, the new removable drive might be referred to as drive "E." The operating system will therefore recognize the fact that there is a storage device, but since it assumes that the device is a fixed drive, it will be unaware that the drive is capable of accommodating removable media and, as such, has no mechanism for dealing with multiple, disparate *volumes*. Therefore, a different and supplementary set of software is needed to help applications recognize the insertion and extraction of removable media. To avoid attempts to write to a device whose media has been changed or removed, ancillary layers of software are designed to impart the concept of volumes, allowing applications to work with removable media even if the application sees each drive as a fixed device.

There are three dimensions to the problem of optimizing the plethora of storage media and technologies available on the market today. First and foremost is integrity of the stored information. The system is expected to help the user maintain that integrity through functions such as backup and restore, and the use of cyclic redundancy checks, error correcting codes, or parity checks to make sure the data is not corrupted.

Secondly, the system must help the user track and locate where the data is in logical terms and map that location to the physical devices. This entails the management of sectors and tracks on different media and the logical and methodical layout of the data across those sectors and tracks, including correlating those physical locations to a hierarchical or network filing system devised by the users. Finally, you have to be able to handle the multiple technologies used in data management, including optical, magnetic, disk, tape, and so forth.

GROWING STORAGE STAFF ....

There are benefits to be realized today from implementing storage networks, but because of the shortage of IT personnel with storage expertise, enterprises are hesitant to move forward. Recruiting, training, and retaining skilled storage management staff must become a core IT competency if the real benefits from storage innovation are to be realized.

WHO'S USING SANS?...

Despite the economies of scale they offer, cost and technical complexity have kept adoption rates of SANs low. It is estimated only 6 to 11% of Fortune 500 companies have installed SANs. The rate among smaller and medium-size enterprises is much lower. In a few years, however, SANs could become a necessity for all organizations with growing data storage demands, especially given the projected growth of e-commerce.

Before SANs, the choice was to add more storage capacity to a single server. But no longer it is enough to throw more space at a storage problem. The key is to manage space more effectively, because the one thing companies can't afford to be is *down*.

Finally, the nature of the storage environment has changed radically in the last few years. It is now characterized by unprecedented growth in the volume of data to be managed; a quantum leap in complexity; and the sheer number of available combinations and permutations. Add to that the growing value of data to the enterprise, and the overwhelming importance of storage—storage networking becomes obvious.

WHO THIS BOOK IS FOR ....

This book can be used by domestic and international system administrators, government computer security officials, network administrators, senior managers, engineers, sales engineers, marketing staff, WWW developers, military senior top brass, network designers and technicians, SAN project managers, SAN installers, LAN and PBX administrators, and other SAN personnel. This book is also valuable for systems analysts, design engineers, programmers, technical managers, and all dataprocessing, telecommunications, and office automation professionals involved in designing, configuring, or implementing SANs. In short, the book is targeted for all types of people and organizations around the globe who have responsibility for managing and maintaining the SAN service continuity of organizational systems including line and project managers; team members, consultants; software and security engineers; and other IT professionals who manage SAN cost justification, investments, and standards. Others who may find it useful are scientists, engineers, educators, top-level executives, information technology and department managers, technical staff, and the more than 900 million Internet, intranet, and extranet users around the world. Some previous experience with SAN installation is required.

WHAT'S SO SPECIAL ABOUT THIS BOOK? ....

The Essential Guide to Storage Area Networks (SANs) is unique in its comprehensive coverage of SAN installation, cost justification and investments, and the latest standards. The book is a thorough, up-to-the-minute professional's guide to every aspect of SAN and disaster recovery, from planning through installation and management.

The high availability of mission-critical systems and communications is a major requirement for the viability of the modern organization. A SAN disaster could negate the capability of the organization to provide uninterrupted service to its internal and external customers.

Furthermore, the proliferation of powerful workstations and PCs, together with a vast installed base of minicomputers and mainframes, has produced immense pressure to link these resources. Local Area Networks allow the sharing of programs, data, and peripherals by providing common access to local and remote SAN resources.

This book provides you with the fundamental knowledge you need to design, configure, and implement SANs. The book emphasizes the integration of available software and hardware.

In this book, you also learn to identify vulnerabilities and implement appropriate countermeasures to prevent and mitigate failure risks. You learn techniques for creating a continuity plan and the methodology for building a SAN infrastructure that supports its effective implementation. Key features include, but are not limited to:

- Understanding basic SAN terminology, technology, and protocols
- Selecting SAN technology based on application requirements
- Configuring SANs to help interconnect the computing resources of your organization
- Supporting LAN storage
- Creating, documenting, and testing a successful SAN and disaster recovery plan for your organization
- Performing a risk analysis and Business Impact Assessment (BIA) to identify vulnerabilities in core processes
- Selecting and deploying an alternate SAN site for processing mission-critical applications
- Recovering SAN infrastructure, systems, networks, data, and user access
- Organizing and managing SAN and disaster recovery teams
- Testing and maintaining an effective recovery plan in a rapidly changing IT environment

- Performing threat and impact analysis
- Selecting alternative SAN and disaster recovery (DR) sites and equipment
- Planning your SAN and DR project
- Developing strategies for SAN systems and communications recovery
- Organizing team structures for use in an emergency
- Creating a SAN and disaster recovery plan from an existing template

The book is organized into seven parts and includes appendixes as well as an extensive glossary of SAN terms and acronyms at the back. It provides a step-by-step approach to everything you need to know about SANs as well as information about many topics relevant to the planning, design, and implementation of them. The book gives an in-depth overview of the latest structured SAN technology and emerging open standards. It discusses what background work needs to be done, such as developing a SAN technology plan, and shows how to develop SAN plans for organizations and educational institutions. More importantly, this book shows how to install a SAN system, along with the techniques used to test the system, as well as the certification of system performance. It covers many of the common pieces of SAN equipment used in the maintenance of the system, as well as the ongoing maintenance issues. The book concludes with a discussion about future planning, standards development, and the SAN industry.

Part I: Overview of SANs Technology

This part of the book coveres types of SAN operating systems software and hardware; the driving forces behind SAN; SAN market demand and projections; the evolution of the SAN market; and the value of information. Next, it discusses disaster recovery; I/O performance; high scalability and flexibility; technology platform, techniques, and alternatives; breaking tradition in video distribution; and SAP R/3 storage management. Part I also covers evolving standards for SANs and SANs standard organizations. Furthermore, this part discusses self-service SAN, outsourcing with service providers, high-speed data sharing among multiple computer platforms; Storage Area Networks: opportunity for the indirect channel, end-to-end services for multivendor enterprise Storage Area Networks and storage subsystems for video services. Finally, this part shows you how to reduce or eliminate single points of failure in enterprise environments—Storage Area Networks (SANs) can help improve the overall availability of business applications. High availability is achieved not through a single product, but rather through a comprehensive system design that includes all the components in the SAN. By utilizing highly available components and solutions (as well as a fault-tolerant design), enterprises can achieve the availability needed to support 24×7 uptime requirements.

Part II: Designing SANs

Part II begins by giving you an overview of how to design Storage Networks with Fibre Channel switches, switching hubs, and hubs; components; installation planning, and practices; application testing and SAN certification design issues; and SAN design documentation issues. This part covers the financial impact of a SAN, justification of SAN operating costs, and financial considerations and acquisitions. It also shows you how to design distributed SAN standards and discusses new standards design issues. Finally, Part II discusses traditional captive storage architecture, SAN architecture, and SAN design considerations.

Part III: Planning for SANs

Part III opens up by showing you how to make SANs a reality in your environment with your infrastructure; why Internet-based exchange pours resources into a SAN infrastructure; and how to prepare for a Storage Area Network. Next, Part III shows how SAN clustering technologies are an essential component of this new era of mission-critical web-based commerce. It also shows why sole reliance on industry-standard benchmarks for selecting the right hardware can be detrimental to the SAN architecture design. Finally, you'll learn how SAN simulation techniques can be used to understand the impact of your users, networks, and applications on the clustering requirements to ensure that your virtual doors are never closed.

Part IV: Installing and Deploying SANs

Part IV discusses physical layer testing, application layer testing, management layer testing, why you should use SAN Testing, and the SANmark Revision TestSuite. This part shows you how to deploy a SAN, get started on a SAN, use storage switch technology to accelerate the next phase of SAN deployment, and put data to work for e-businesses. Finally, this part covers SAN testing and troubleshooting; documenting and testing SANs; and certifying SAN performance.

Part V: Maintaining SANs

This part begins by taking a look at the data management solution, virtual Storage Area Networks, and a management strategy for the Fibre Channel-Arbitrated Loop. This part discusses the facts about SAN software; documentation standards; and increasing efficiency in the prepress market. Finally, this part covers present and future SAN management standards.

Part VI: SAN Solutions and Future Directions

Opening up with a discussion on the causes of data unavailability, cost tradeoffs, high availability objectives, and the SAN—including the single building, campus cluster, and metro cluster—this part examines solutions to making SAN work. This part also examines the role of SANs in computer forensics with regards to computer and data storage of evidence collection and forensic analysis. Finally, this part presents a summary, current conclusions, and recommendations for the future of SAN development and implementation.

Part VII: Appendices

Seven appendices provide direction to additional resources available for SANs. Appendix A is an online storage management checklist. Appendix B is a list of top SANs implementation and deployment companies. Appendix C contains SAN product offerings. Appendix D consists of standards for SANs. Appendix E is a discussion of SCSI versus Fibre Channel Storage. Appendix F is a list of miscellaneous SAN resources; and, Appendix G is a glossary of SAN terms and acronyms.

CONVENTIONS...

This book has several conventions to help your way around and to help you find important facts, notes, cautions and warnings:

Sidebars: We use sidebars to highlight related information, give an example, discuss an item in greater detail, or help you make sense of the swirl of terms, acronyms, and abbreviations so abundant to this subject. The sidebars are meant to supplement each chapter's topic. If you're in a hurry on the cover-to-cover read, skip the sidebars. If you're quickly flipping through the book looking for juicy information, read only the sidebars.

Notes: A note highlights a special point of interest about the SAN topic.

Caution: A caution tells you to watch your step to avoid any SAN-related problems (safety or security, etc.).

Warning: A warning alerts you to the fact that a SAN-related problem is imminent or will probably occur (safety, security, etc.).

—John R. Vacca
34679 TR 382
Pomeroy, Ohio 45769
jvacca@hti.net

Acknowledgments

There are many people whose efforts on this book have contributed to its successful completion. I owe each a debt of gratitude and want to take this opportunity to offer my sincere thanks.

A very special thanks to my editor Mary Franz, without whose continued interest and support would not have made this book possible. And editorial assistant Noreen Regina, who provided staunch support and encouragement when it was most needed. Special thanks to my technical editor, Vi Chau, who ensured the technical accuracy of the book and whose expertise in SAN system technology was indispensable. Thanks to my production editor, Anne Garcia; project manager, Scott Suckling (MetroVoice); and copyeditor Ann Salinger whose fine editorial work has been invaluable. Thanks also to my marketing manager, whose efforts on this book have been greatly appreciated. And, a special thanks to Michael Erbschloe who wrote the foreword for this book. Finally, thanks to all of the other people at Prentice Hall whose many talents and skills are essential to a finished book.

Thanks to my wife, Bee Vacca, for her love, her help, and her understanding of my long work hours.

I wish to thank the organizations and individuals who granted me permission to use the research material and information necessary for the completion of this book.

Finally, a very special thanks to my publisher, Jeff Pepper, without whose initial interest and support would not have made this book possible; and, for his guidance and encouragement over and above the business of being a publisher.

Part 1

Overview of SANs Technology

1 SANs Fundamentals

Network and server downtime is costing companies hundreds of millions of dollars in business and productivity losses. At the same time, the amount of information to be managed and stored is increasing dramatically every year.

A new concept called the Storage Area Network (SAN) could offer an answer to the increasing amount of data that needs to be stored in an enterprise network environment. By implementing a SAN, users can offload storage traffic from daily network operations while establishing a direct connection between storage elements and servers.

Basically, a SAN is a specialized network that enables fast, reliable access among servers and external or independent storage resources. In a SAN, a storage device is not the exclusive property of any one server. Rather, storage devices are shared among all networked servers as peer resources. Just as a Local Area Network (LAN) can be used to connect clients to servers, a SAN can be used to connect servers to storage, servers to each other, and storage to storage.

A SAN does not need to be a physically separate network, either. It can be a dedicated subnetwork, carrying only the business-critical I/O traffic between servers and storage devices. A SAN, for example, would not carry general-purpose traffic such as email or other end-user applications. This type of net avoids the unacceptable trade-offs inherent in a single network for all applications, such as dedicating storage devices for each server and burdening a LAN with storage and archival activity.

Furthermore, as distributed networks are re-engineered to achieve continuous operations and to host mission critical applications, a common data-center technology is being applied to them. Data centers use a network storage interface called Enterprise System Connection (ESCON) to connect mainframes to multiple storage systems and distributed networks. This type of network is also called a SAN. In other words, SANs are employed by mainframe data centers and account for approximately 58% of all network traffic. What is new is that SAN architectures are now being adopted in distributed networks out of low cost SAN technologies such as Small Computer System Interface (SCSI), Serial Storage Architecture (SSA), and Fibre Channel.

BUT WHAT IS A SAN—REALLY?..............................

As previously mentioned, a SAN is a high speed network, similar to a LAN, that establishes a direct connection between storage elements and servers or clients. The SAN is an extended storage bus which can be interconnected using similar interconnect technologies as LANs or Wide Area Networks (WANs): routers, hubs, switches, and gateways. A SAN can be local or remote; shared or dedicated; and includes unique externalized and central storage and SAN interconnect components. SAN interfaces are generally ESCON, SCSI, SSA, High-Performance Parallel Interface (HIPPI), or Fibre Channel, rather than Ethernet. It doesn't matter whether a SAN is called a Storage Area Network or System Area Network, the architecture is the same in either case.

SANs create a method of attaching storage that is revolutionizing the network because of the improvements in availability and performance. SANs are currently used to connect shared storage arrays; clustered servers for failover; interconnect mainframe disk or tape resources to distributed network servers and clients; and to create parallel or alternate data paths for high performance computing environments. In essence, a SAN is nothing more than another network, like a subnet, but constructed from storage interfaces.

SANs enable storage to be externalized from the server and in doing so, allow storage to be shared among multiple *host* servers without impacting system performance or the primary network. The benefits are well proven as this architecture emerges from mainframe Direct Access Storage Device (DASD). It is nothing new. In fact, the DEC VMS network environment is based on SAN architectures and clustered servers. For example, EMC already has a large installed base of SAN attached disk arrays (for example, EMC's disk array product: Symmetrix) and has achieved such a high level of customer confidence that they are the standard of comparison [1]. So, what's new? This important technology is moving into the mainstream in distributed networking and is now the normal, adopted way of attaching and sharing storage.

Often referred to as the *network behind the server*, SANs represents a new model that has evolved with the advent of shared, multi-host connected enterprise storage. A SAN bypasses traditional network bottlenecks and supports direct, high-speed data transfer in three different ways:

- Server-to-storage
- Server-to-server
- Storage-to-storage [2]

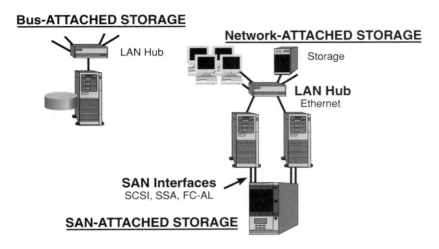

Figure 1.1
Storage attachments.

SAN architecture and terminology is getting confused as each product camp goes about praising the merits of their solutions. The following discussion is aimed at providing a simple set of definitions and terms that should be adopted by the industry. To begin, storage can be attached to the network in one of three ways. According to Strategic Research Corporation [2], ninety-nine percent of today's server storage connections are *bus-attached* via a form of SCSI or Integrated Development Environment (IDE) as shown in Figure 1.1 [2]. Bus attached storage operates through the server. Availability and performance are limited to the server's capabilities and loading. Storage is externalized from the server via Network Attached Storage (NAS) or SAN Attached Storage (SAS). NAS and SAS are very similar from an engineering standpoint, but it is essential to differentiate them to help the customer understand the differences in implementations.

Network Attached Storage (NAS)

NAS is a disk array that connects directly to the messaging network via a LAN interface such as Ethernet using common communications protocols (see sidebar, "Storage Sorting"). It functions as a server in a client/server relationship, has a processor, an OS or microkernel, and processes file I/O protocols such as Server Message Block (SMB) and Network File System (NFS).

STORAGE SORTING

Storage area networks are fast becoming part of the IT lexicon, but the abundance of other storage management acronyms is making things a bit confusing. As previously explained, a SAN is a collection of networked storage devices that can automatically communicate with each other.

Note: A SAN doesn't have to use Fibre Channel as its underpinnings. For example, the mainframe environment's Enterprise Systems Connection channels could form the SAN interface.

The key to understanding what makes a SAN is understanding that the goal is to divorce all users and network administrators from storage management. Storage, retrieval, and file transfers are automatically managed in a true SAN.

OK, so what is network attached storage? SANs may include NAS-enabled devices, but they aren't the same thing.

A NAS system is connected to application servers via the network. But unlike a SAN, with NAS users can directly access stored data without server intervention. A SAN will automate management of storage systems, while NAS devices don't have this capability.

And when it comes to automated management in a SAN, there's yet another definition floating around: hierarchical storage management (HSM). HSM is simply managing data movement from online to offline storage, such as to tape devices.

SAN Attached Storage (SAS)

A shared storage repository attached to multiple host servers via a storage interface such as SCSI, Fibre Channel-Arbitrated Loop (FC-AL), or ESCON. The SAN is an extended, shared storage bus which can be interconnected using similar interconnect technologies as LANs or WANs, routers, switches, and gateways.

Note

FC-AL is not the only fibre channel interconnect used in "SAN." More and more fibre channel users use switched fibre channel as an interconnect. Fibre channel can be used by itself, and *arbitrated loop* can be removed.

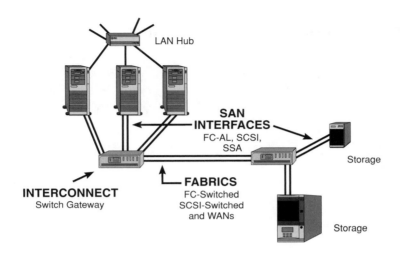

Figure 1.2
SAN network terminology.

The next key terminology point deals directly with SAN architectures. The three SAN components are the SAN interfaces, the SAN interconnects, and the SAN fabric as shown in Figure 1.2 [2]. These are often mixed together, but really are distinct elements of the SAN. Think of the relationship between these three fitting together in a chained sequence, server-to-interface-to-interconnect-to-fabric-to-interconnect-to-interface-to-storage array.

SAN Interfaces

SCSI, FC-AL, SSA, ESCON, bus-and-tag, and HIPPI are common SAN interfaces. All allow storage to be externalized from the server and can host shared storage configurations for clustering. Multiple channels can be installed or loops built to provide increased performance and redundancy. It is incorrect to say that SCSI cannot be extended, multiplexed, switched, and connected via gateways to WANs like serial interfaces.

SAN Interconnects

Extenders, Multiplexors (Mux), Hubs, Routers, Gateways, Switches, and Directors are the SAN interconnects. Sounds just like a LAN or WAN, and it is. SAN interconnects tie storage interfaces together into many network configurations and across large distances. Interconnects also link SAN interfaces to SAN Fabrics. One common misconception is that FC-AL, a SAN interface, is a SAN Fabric, Fibre Channel Switched (FCS). It is not (see sidebar, "SAN Myths").

SAN MYTHS

Anyone considering a storage area network quickly encounters a number of myths. Like most technology myths, SAN myths contain a grain of truth, but the reality is often quite different. The following are the top five common SAN myths:

The Fibre Channel Myth

When first conceived, SAN technology was specified on Fibre Channel as the preferred communications link. Fibre Channel was able to provide the speed and the distance SAN required. Today, the majority of SANs are being implemented with Fibre Channel, either arbitrated loop or switched topologies. However, the SAN is not locked into Fibre Channel. Rapid developments are occurring with SCSI over Internet Protocol (IP) for use in SANs. The Fibre Channel SAN will continue to have a place in the enterprise data center, but protocols using SCSI commands are emerging, and vendors will introduce SAN products using the SCSI protocol over the next few quarters.

The Interoperability Myth

Early SANs indeed suffered from a lack of interoperability among components from different vendors. However, interoperability is improving, especially within the switch, hub, and host bus adapter market. Through a number of interoperability events, dubbed Plug Fests, competing vendors come together to iron out many of the interoperability issues. Observers expect any remaining interoperability issues to completely fade away within 12 months.

The Skills Barrier Myth

Certainly SANs introduce new technologies into the enterprise storage world, particularly fibre and networking, which require new skills. Information technology (IT) storage experts groomed for directly attached SCSI storage now must learn new protocols and new configurations. Switched fibre SANs, in particular, require advanced networking skills. There is no getting around it; SANs require an understanding of networking. However, new tools, new products, and new service offerings from the vendors are making SANs easier. And, service providers increasingly have a solid stable of trained people who can help any organization implement a SAN.

The Management Myth

Early SAN adopters complained that SANs were hard to manage and administer. And they were, due mainly to a lack of tools. Today, however, SAN administrators are finding a growing selection of tools to manage the SAN, perform backup, create virtual storage pools, monitor resources, manage the topology, and more. Storage vendors are responding with tools to manage the various SAN components, and more and better tools are in the pipeline.

The Cost Myth

SANs entail a large, initial capital outlay, but the long-term benefits are significant. While it is cheaper initially to attach low-cost disk storage to a server, the cost of administering storage attached to multiple servers and the inefficiency that results from underutilized pools of storage, shift to the overall total cost of ownership advantage clearly to the SAN. Recent studies suggest that half of all server-attached storage goes unused because it can't be shared. With a SAN, storage utilization increases to 70% and, ultimately, can hit 90%. And with a SAN, each administrator can manage far more storage.

The trouble with technology myths is that technology keeps changing. Even if a SAN myth was true once, it probably isn't today.

SAN Fabrics

Switched SCSI, FCS, and Switched SSA form the most common SAN fabrics. With gateways, SANs can be extended across WAN networks as well. Switches allow many advantages in building centralized, centrally managed, consolidated storage repositories shared across a number of applications.

Building A SAN

Building a SAN requires network technologies with high scalability, performance, and reliability in order to marry the robustness and speed of a traditional storage environment with the connectivity of a network. As the SAN concept has developed, it has grown beyond identification with any one technology. In fact, just as LANs use a diverse mix of technologies, so can SANs. This mix can include Fiber Distributed Data Interface (FDDI), Asynchronous Transfer Mode (ATM), and IBM's Serial Storage Architecture, as well as Fibre Channel. SAN architectures also allow for the use of a number of underlying protocols, including Transmission Control Protocol/Internet Protocol (TCP/IP) and variants of SCSI.

A SAN allows different kinds of storage (mainframe disk, tape, and Redundant Array of Inexpensive Disk [RAID]) to be shared by different kinds of servers, such as Windows NT, UNIX, and OS/390. With this shared capacity, organizations can acquire, deploy, and use storage devices more cost-effectively. SANs let users with heterogeneous storage platforms utilize all of its storage resources. This means that within a SAN, users can backup or archive data from different servers to the same storage system; allow stored information to be accessed by all servers; create and store a mirror image of data as it is created; and share data between different environments.

By externalizing storage and taking storage traffic off the operations network, companies gain a high-performance storage network, shared yet dedicated networks for the SAN and LAN, and improved network management. These features reduce network downtime and productivity losses while extending current storage resources.

In effect, the SAN does in a network environment what traditionally has been done in a back-end I/O environment between a server and its own private storage subsystem. The result is high speed, high fault tolerance, and high reliability.

With a SAN, there is no need for a physically separate network because the SAN can function as a virtual subnet operating on a shared network infrastructure, provided that different priorities or classes of service are established. Fibre Channel and ATM allow for these different classes of service. Early implementations of SANs have been local or campus-based.

But as new WAN technologies such as ATM mature, and especially as class-of-service capabilities improve, the SAN can be extended over a much wider area. Despite the hype about the coming of unlimited bandwidth, WAN services remain costly today. However, as WAN technologies improve their quality of service, they will provide (even over public WANs) the robustness needed for each application, including networked I/O.

SAN Tools

In addition to reliability and performance, SANs promise easier and less costly network administration. Today, administrative functions are labor-intensive and IT organizations typically have to replicate management tools across multiple server environments. With a SAN, there is just one set of tools, and replication costs can be avoided. The traditional software functions of security management, access control, data management, and storage management will be mapped into the SAN architecture and performed differently than they have been in the past. For example, different security strategies have to be pursued when storage devices are more widely available.

Specialized I/O protocols such as Network Data Management Protocol (NDMP) are emerging, and the software functions will evolve much as LAN functionality has progressed in recent years.

Why Are SANs Important?

SANs will enable almost any application that moves data around the network to perform better. Just like conventional *subnets*, SANs add bandwidth for specific functions without placing a load on the primary network. In this fashion, SANs compliment LANs and WANs. SANs also enable higher performance solutions such as data warehousing. In fact, as Figure 1.2 shows, SANs are really pervasive and applicable to many networking environments [2].

SAN technology enables the network architecture of shared multihost storage, connecting all storage devices as well as interconnecting remote sites. This will soon be the standard configuration for centralized networks running mission-critical applications. Both disk and tape operations are centralized, attached via the SAN, and more resilient, as well as operating faster. As the IT community has learned in the database market, the key to application performance is usually the I/O network, not the disk drives themselves. SAN architecture holds the keys to the future.

The benefits of a SAN network architecture are huge and will cause many sites to adopt this methodology of attaching storage and transferring data. This list is indicative of the types of benefits seen in sites operating with SANs (see sidebar, "SAN Benefits").

SAN BENEFITS

Higher Application Availability

Storage is externalized, independent of the application, and accessible through alternate data paths such as found in clustered systems.

Higher Application Performance

Server and bus overhead degrades performance. Independent SAS arrays will outperform bus-attached arrays, as well as be compatible with performance clusters.

Easier Centralized Management

SAS configurations encourage centralization and the ensuing large management benefits.

Centralized and Consolidated Storage

Storage centralization and consolidation result in higher performance, lower cost of management, more scalability, flexibility, reliability, availability, and serviceability.

Practical Data Transfer, Vaulting, and Exchange with Remote Sites

Cost effective implementations provide high availability disaster protection (remote clusters and remote mirrored arrays)[2].

SAN Applications

Now look at SANs from an application viewpoint. At a high level, for example, Strategic Research Corporation has identified six application areas currently utilizing SAN architectures for data transfer as shown in Figure 1.3 [2]. This is not to mean there won't be more in the future. The purpose of Figure 1.3 is to explain how pervasive the technology is already [2].

As previously discussed, in the changing network architecture, externalized storage is a generic application, fitting a myriad of network-hosted applications with many benefits. Next, is clustering. Clustering is usually thought of as a server process

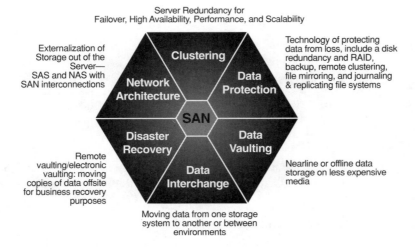

Figure 1.3
Applications utilizing SANs.

providing failover to a redundant server or scalable processing through using multiple servers in parallel. In a cluster, the SAN provides the data pipe, allowing storage to be shared. For example, Microsoft's ClusterServer, which is an availability cluster, shares a single array between two servers attached via a SCSI SAN. Next, data protection architectures operate through creating redundancy of storage on a dynamic basis. SANs provide the best interconnects, allowing storage mirroring, remote clustered storage, and other high availability (HA) data protection solutions because of the performance and independence as a secondary data path. SANs do not impact the primary network or the servers and they provide redundancy. Data vaulting is the process of transferring data, usually for the purpose of archive or logging, to a remote site. SANs make a very efficient transmission medium. Interchange and disaster recovery operations are very similar and use SANs the same way, whether local or remote, just for different purposes. SANs provide a very efficient pipe for moving data offsite or between sites. Disaster protection systems can be built on remote vaulting (backup) processes or with high availability remote array mirroring or clustering.

TYPES OF SAN OPERATING SYSTEMS SOFTWARE AND HARDWARE COMPONENTS ....

Recently, for example, EMC Corporation announced that their SAN software that's designed to manage storage devices made by some of its rivals, is a mixed-vendor support that is being done in reaction to pressure from systems administrators [1]. Users have been pushing for the ability to manage EMC's Symmetrix and Clariion disk arrays along with other storage products and connectivity devices. To start with, disk storage systems made by Compaq Computer, Hewlett-Packard, and Hitachi; and tape devices from Storage Technology have been qualified to work with the new software.

Network switches and other connectivity devices made by companies such as San Jose-based Brocade Communications Systems, and Broomfield, Colorado-based McData Corporation, can also be controlled. An addition to EMC's Enterprise Storage Network (ESN) product line, the new ESN Manager tool provides a single point of control for administrators to use in managing multiple *zones* of interconnected storage devices.

The development of ESN Manager should scare the hell out of other vendors. EMC is already clearly the storage king. All of a sudden, if EMC actually lives up to what they say and becomes an open systems management provider, they are really a lethal weapon.

EMC hopes to prompt users that don't have its devices now to migrate from single-vendor storage setups to mixed SANs that include Symmetrix and Clariion arrays. People claim EMC is proprietary, but they really are not.

EMC's announcement follows one made recently in which Sun Microsystems said it was teaming up with former rival Brocade. Sun said it would start selling Brocade's Silkworm switches, which act as data traffic directors in a SAN. Brocade in turn announced that it would begin using Sun's Jiro SAN management software with its devices.

EMC's increased spending on software research and development is a sign that the company is *genuinely interested* in doing more than selling disk arrays. EMC executives want to be more accessible to users who haven't fully committed to Symmetrix and Clariion.

Management tasks supported by ESN Manager include setting limits on which end users can access different devices on a SAN, and configuring logical pathways between various servers and storage subsystems. The software's base price is $24,000 per Symmetrix box, making it a relatively high-end offering in the storage management market.

Sharing Data in a SAN

EMC, for example, has also rolled out software which it claims will unite the competing worlds of NAS and SANs. EMC's HighRoad integrates new software processes into its Celerra File Server and other servers to improve file-sharing capabilities.

The software is aimed at web hosting, image processing and simulation, and modeling applications. It uses separate mechanisms for control actions and data delivery. HighRoad brings together SANs and NAS by routing files and other data directly from the SAN to the user without the intervention of a NAS server.

Customers need all their information to work together. It's about creating one unified infrastructure that builds on the individual and combined strengths of their data and storage networks.

Recently, EMC bought NAS software developer CrosStor, which was working on combining the two storage technologies. EMC also unveiled its latest Clariion IP4700 product, which is aimed at the low-end market dominated by rival Network Appliance. EMC claimed its product will be more reliable than Network Appliance's NAS clusters and cost half the price.

The storage industry has been very busy lately. Coinciding with EMC's announcement, IBM recently pledged to offer a universal storage system that works with all software and hardware systems. Sun Microsystems also announced plans to boost its storage unit by acquiring data storage management software maker High Ground Systems for $500 million.

Tools to Unlock SAN Promise

SAN software tools could bring IT managers closer to the data sharing they thought they were getting when they first bought SANs. People thought when they got a SAN, they'd be getting the ability to share data. And it's true, but they need management tools for that sharing to happen.

SAN resource management starts with knowing what components you have—a process that should be automated. BMC Software in Houston, Texas; Computer Associates International in Islandia, New York; and IBM's Tivoli Systems in Austin, Texas, all claim that their new tools offer varying degrees of *autodiscovery* capabilities.

Autodiscovery in theory does the same thing that Windows 98 does on your machine at home. Plug in some new equipment, and your system automatically sees it and understands how to manage it.

But, most people who have SANs are still working to put together and monitor all the pieces of the infrastructure. The promise of SANs runs far ahead of what users should expect today. It's rare to see anyone start from a SAN and go straight to application-level management. You have to crawl before you walk, and there's still some crawling to be done to get to interoperability and management at the component level. Underlying the success of the SAN concept is the key assumption that standards will be developed.

In an International Data Corporation (IDC) survey in 2000, more than half of IT managers responding indicated that they were considering purchasing a SAN. But 80% indicated that open standards are critical for any SAN implementation they would consider. See Chapter 3, "Standards," for more information.

We're still a long way off from having universal standards in SANs. However, SANs are following a path similar to what happened in the LAN environment.

The Case for SAN Hardware

Storage hardware is about as exciting to most IT and business managers as watching pet rocks sunbathe. But it's rapidly becoming the single most important element of e-business innovation. Just look at your company's e-business infrastructure.

There's only one proprietary component: the enterprise customer data. Never put that at risk in terms of availability, security, ability to scale customer relationship management (CRM) systems, speed of access, backup and archiving, or server consolidation.

Almost every other platform component is now a commodity; a company can substitute one excellent vendor's products for another's—low-end and mid-range servers, PCs, and Internet hosting services, for example. Or a company has some wiggle room: It can call in systems integrators and C++/Java wizards, or build front-end links to legacy systems. This is by no means easy, but none of these areas is the *giant bottleneck* that storage is now.

Here's the problem for IT: For decades, storage has been handled as just an add-on to IT strategy and as JBOD—storage professionals' acronym for *just a bunch of disks*. Whoever handles JBOD purchases says, "Your data warehouse is exploding again? Buy two clusters and call back next month."

Even the NAS versus SAN debates about how to best manage networked storage are typically handled in nonbusiness terms, centering on such concerns as response times and operating costs. In IT, there's often a wide gap in thought and knowledge between network and storage professionals.

Try asking your best telecommunications experts about Fibre Channel or backup and archiving. Then talk to the storage people about IP-based SANs. In most instances, you'll see blank stares. Look at the network architecture plans. See if you can find the storage architecture plans. Good luck. Then look at your company's many CRM activities and see if there's any discussion of their implications for storage beyond JBOD and *aspirin*. Again, good luck.

IT needs to raise the strategic discussion of storage in the same way, and to the same degree, that telecommunications moved in the 1990s from cables and boxes to e-business architecture; and in the same way that databases have moved from software to CRM. Storage vendors and buyers need to build an entirely new dialogue.

In the JBOD world, vendors are box salespeople, and IT organizations are box buyers. Both are in a commodity transaction, not partners in enterprise storage strategy. The JBOD suppliers come in with feature lists, prices, and service promises. That's fine for semicommodities such as low-end servers, PCs, and Internet hosting. But, it's inappropriate when the discussion is about the architecture for the firm's customer data resources or its e-business strategy and platform architecture—and recognizing the importance of never putting either at risk.

As the storage issue rises above JBOD, IT must redefine the vendor dialogue, and vice versa. Will EMC's powerful sales force and aggressive selling be the basis for your company's dialogue? Will Hitachi Data Systems' increasing dominance in pure technology and product leadership translate into architecture leadership? Will Sun be able to turn its e-business server strengths into comparable networked storage strengths? Until a year ago, $3 of sales in servers meant $1 of storage sales for Sun.

Now, it's the reverse. Dell, Compaq, Network Storage Solutions and Hewlett-Packard (which is mostly Hitachi with a different logo) all have good boxes.

Which will be the platform partner? That would be the next IT e-business agenda. Which would you choose? Probably Hitachi, because if your firm's customer data is your proprietary business edge, you would want the best hardware. But, don't take anyone's word for it. IT professionals must have their own opinions, shaped in their companies' best interests.

SAN MARKET DEMAND AND PROJECTIONS BY REGION AND COUNTRY ....

Japanese businesses, buffeted by a decade of economic anemia and suffused with the conservatism that permeates IT investment strategies, are cautiously coming around to the use of SANs. But new evidence that the economy may be slipping back into recession and centralized corporate bureaucracies may dampen adoption of SANs on a large scale.

Research institutes and educational customers are early movers to SANs. Central Tokyo University is using a SAN because they have an immediate need for more storage. But currently, SAN users remain a minority in Japan, where many companies use centralized storage and backup methods such as tape drives and hard drives.

Nevertheless, according to Gartner Group's Dataquest unit, the storage market in Japan is the fastest growing market in the Asia-Pacific region, where it is projected to grow at nearly 17% per year and reach $4.2 billion by 2003. That growth is being driven by the rapid expansion of communications infrastructure throughout Japan. Japan currently has nearly 61 million wireless subscribers; and, according to Dataquest, the country is Asia's biggest Internet market with total subscribers expected to hit 64.5 million by 2004.

One touted benefit of SANs is that they give users the ability to add more storage capacity without burdening the corporate data center. But some Japanese companies view SANs as the outsourcing of key business functions and remain reluctant to make that move.

Traditionally, Japanese companies like to make centralized decisions, and so moving small parts of a business to a SAN is not always feasible. This kind of change for a company is very complex.

There are some real cultural differences in the way business decisions about IT get made, and you have to respect them. And, while another factor in the slow adoption of SANs is cost, Japanese companies are being confronted by a unique twist on the need for more storage.

First there is the double-byte issue—referring to the need for added storage when using *kanji* characters. Each letter of their (Roman) alphabet takes a single byte of memory, but with Japanese (and Chinese or Korean) characters, you need twice as much storage capacity.

The second driving force for SANs are Internet service providers. With the explosion of Internet usage, service providers have to offer customers around-the-clock storage and remote backup. That wasn't something companies had to think about before. Tokyo-based ASAHI Net uses a Network Appliance. SAN provided by ITFOR to serve more than 200,000 subscribers and 190 domestic access points. But, current business and technology conditions continue to slow the growth of SANs in the region.

Business spending on capital equipment, one of the bright spots in 2000, as Japanese companies scrambled to buy technology, is sagging. The government projects a 2.1% decline in capital spending for the fiscal year, following a 9.4% jump in 2001.

EVOLUTION OF THE SAN MARKET ....

Thanks to the Internet and the rapid global expansion of computing, humans and their machines will create and store more information in the next three years than in the 300,000 years of history dating to the earliest cave paintings and beyond [1]. That was what researchers at the School of Information Management and Systems at the University of California at Berkeley forecasted late in 2000, much to the delight of EMC Corporation, the data storage giant that sponsored their work.

EMC was quick to pitch the study to Wall Street, adding it to analysts' projections that spending on data storage products is drawing even with spending on computers themselves and that it will account for 70% of information technology budgets by 2005. EMC also included its own projection that an individual (EMC likes to call him "Tommy" in its advertisements) could easily have a terabyte (the equivalent of 250 million pages of text) of stored personal records, photos, and other data by 2005.

The obvious outcome of such trends, of course, would be mind-boggling growth for data storage products and, more to EMC's point, full-scale storage systems intelligent enough to support the Internet's need for constant access to data. Data needs to live someplace. There's almost no value if it's just put away.

EMC's need to keep Wall Street awed is directly linked to its track record. It became the biggest gainer on the New York Stock Exchange in the 1990s by grabbing leadership of the market from IBM, producing both astonishing profits and sizzling growth. Then, as other technology giants stumbled in 2000, its shares gained another 10% to finish the year at $66.50. From such a pinnacle, convincing the Street the best is yet to come will be no mean feat. But, there are plenty of other companies beating the same drum, from giants like IBM, Compaq Computer, and Sun Microsystems, to fast-growing newcomers like Network Appliance, Brocade Communications, and Veritas Software.

Storage is becoming the heart and soul of all business. What you know about your customers, suppliers, and partners will differentiate you at the end of the day.

Trouble is, even if the vendors and analysts are right about the growth, investors may well have become unrealistically optimistic about how easily it will translate into profits. The publicly traded industry leaders tumbled in 2000, but are still trading at nosebleed levels that leave little room for earnings disappointments.

The impact on data storage of a general slowdown in technology spending is Wall Street's current fear, but storage companies also have to contend with tougher competition. New technology is driving down prices, just as in traditional computer markets. In addition, networking giants like Cisco Systems and discount computer specialists like Dell Computer are moving in, while rising interest from venture capital firms is spawning a steady stream of start-ups scrambling to define niches. They are fighting over a rapidly shifting landscape that International Data Corporation estimates was worth at least $70 billion in 2000, depending on which technologies and services are included.

Storage is getting to be as complex as servers and networks. One sector of the storage market focuses on data used in computations that are stored in caches on microprocessors, on memory chips, or inches away on disks inside a computer. At the other end of the technology spectrum is tape-based storage, which provides a low-cost if somewhat less convenient alternative to disk storage.

But the heart of the action these days revolves around disk-based storage systems outside the computer. The newest hardware building blocks are specialized file servers. Some, not much bigger than a VCR, allow users to add storage capacity directly to Internet networks without buying full-scale server computers. The workhorses for big enterprises, though, are refrigerator-size storage arrays of disks that support one or more mainframes or networks of smaller computers.

Steady advances in the disks and the software that manages them are producing astonishing performance gains. Remember Moore's Law, the longstanding rule that shrinking circuitry allows chip companies like Intel to double the processing power of processors every 18 months? Well, that amazing progression (from the room-size computing monsters of the 1950s to far more powerful fingernail-size chips) pales in comparison with advances in data storage. EMC, for example, says that the volumes of data it will stuff into shoebox-size devices by 2005 would have required covering an area the size of Argentina if 1950s technology were still in use.

For all that, the hottest storage battleground is not storage hardware but software, switches, and other components that meld the storage devices into intelligent networks and keep them online. Brocade Communications' market leadership in Fibre Channel, a specialized protocol for designing such storage networks, drove its shares from an initial public offering price in May 1999 of $2.38, adjusted for splits, to $133.72 in October 2000, though it has since retreated. Veritas's strength in software to manage incompatible storage products from numerous different vendors helped its shares climb from a split-adjusted initial price of 53 cents a share in 1993, to a secondary offering in August 1999 at $22.14 and a peak of $174 in March 2000.

Storage services are also booming as big data users hire consultants, rent outside capacity, or simply turn over the entire problem to technology management experts like IBM Global Services or new specialists like StorageNetworks, a two-year-old start-up based in Waltham, Massachusetts. International Data estimates that the service sector had revenues of more than $24 billion in 2000 and indicates its sales should top $40 billion in 2003.

If there is anyplace where the sometimes conflicting visions of storage's future intersect, it has to be the headquarters of EMC in the Boston suburb of Hopkinton. EMC, like IBM in the past, strives to design equipment that performs best with EMC software, so that customers become locked into it as a vendor. And, like IBM's mainframe business in the 1960s, EMC counts on its reputation for reliability and service support to make it the safe, if premium-price, choice for information managers. But, company officials say, any resemblance ends there and that no one will catch EMC off guard as EMC itself caught IBM in the storage business.

EMC's strategy assumes that information pipelines (bandwidth in the industry's jargon) will become so huge and fast that it will no longer be necessary to store data locally to ensure quick access. Such bandwidth, in EMC's estimate, will allow as much as 90% of data to be centralized in the kind of big businesses that have been EMC's prime customers. From medical files, to movies, to financial records, data consumers would download what they need when they need it, but would not necessarily store it on their own computers.

The best architecture for such data reservoirs is still up for grabs, however. Some data will reside in dedicated, maximum-security systems linked to particular computers. Some will be in cheap file servers (NAS) attached to the Internet. A lot of it is likely to end up in networks of storage devices (SANs) that would be linked to the Internet, computers, and tape storage systems through specialized servers.

How things develop depends on evolving network equipment and software as much as on the storage devices themselves. In areas where the landscape isn't as clear as EMC likes, they're placing multiple bets.

Big bets, too, judging from EMC's vow to invest $2.5 billion over the next two years in research and development, more than 75% of it in software. But what if projections like the Berkeley study prove to be wildly inflated? What if people become smarter about saving only what they really need? The industry's answer is another question: why would they bother? With storage prices headed from about 40 cents a megabyte today to less than a cent in 2005; and the industry moving toward making access to storage as easy as the universal dial tone on the telephone, it's going to take too much energy to throw things away. Besides, the Berkeley figures may well be too conservative, since they exclude any estimates for duplicate storage of information once it is created, one of the fastest-growing segments of the business.

THE VALUE OF INFORMATION ....

Finally, people have always placed a high value on information and knowledge. From the first cuneiform characters pressed into clay tablets to today's petabytes of data held on magnetic media, information has been protected and valued. Because it was valuable and hard to acquire or store, information was kept in the hands of a few experts for thousands of years. It was only with the advent of printing in the fifteenth century that an information explosion began that led to thriving new nations and burgeoning societies, such as those of North America and Europe.

As information and knowledge became more available from 1500 onwards, it became essential to learn to read. At first, only the rich and privileged had the time and the means to learn to read and access new information. However, as the need for skilled labor to build and maintain societies evolved, governments realized that an educated workforce was essential to national prosperity. An association of schools, libraries, vocational training establishments, and colleges appeared almost overnight in the newly industrialized countries, and created a knowledge and information system that catapulted its developers into the twentieth century, laying the foundation for today's astonishingly successful, connected world.

The lesson learned from these information-based developments is that sharing knowledge and data makes a society and its individuals and organizations better able to communicate and work together for mutual benefit. Just as money is much more useful when it is invested and in circulation, so is information a much more useful tool and broader resource when it is shared. The opening months of the twenty-first century show global business poised to benefit from shared electronic information in the same way that society was just beginning to see the real advantages of universal education around 1900.

The Business Information Landscape Today

The profusion of storage technology advances available now or soon to come to market is guaranteed to confuse IT professionals and leave business executives bewildered. While the objective is simple (to provide the best possible information systems), the method and technologies to be used are anything but simple.

For example, Tivoli Systems has refined the various available components into what it calls the Information Grid [3]. This combination of components consists of: SAN topology; new technologies, such as fiber channel hubs; switches and interconnects; new disk and tape technologies; and resource and data sharing techniques. The Information Grid promises extraordinary opportunities if organizations can deal with the inherent challenges.

Today's business information environment still consists largely of islands of information within an organization that have limited contact with each other and very little in the way of effective links and conduits across which information and data can flow to the people who need them. These islands may be in the form of large existing corporate systems that are based on mainframe architecture. They may be simple LANs that link the PCs or Microsoft Windows NT systems of a branch office or remote facility, or perhaps UNIX technology-based departmental systems in engineering, research, or accounting functions. Whatever form information takes, it has always been difficult, if not impossible, to share—and it is even more difficult to achieve the powerful benefits of harnessing information into a single, seamless environment.

Preparing for Storage Area Networking

By 2002, most experts expect the first complete implementations of SANs to be in place and running successfully (see Chapter 2, "Types of SAN Technology"). A large number of IT vendors are actively pursuing this goal. However, for the IT user community, deciding which company or companies to form successful relationships with will be critical.

SAN technology is part of the larger challenge of establishing a full storage networking management strategy. Careful consideration should be given to choosing a vendor or partner that is capable of implementing the full range of benefits of storage management. These benefits include:

- $24 \times 7 \times 365$ availability
- Scalability
- Data sharing across different architectures
- Storage access at all times and from all locations
- Better performance
- Cost reductions
- Improved security
- Significantly better data protection
- Verifiable and consistent data integrity
- Easy-to-use, consistent data management tools [3]

For example, Tivoli, in partnership with many of the leading storage management and SAN vendors, has developed and planned for the technology required to ensure successful, full implementation of SANs. Tivoli is developing new products that will be essential to exploit the Information Grid in all its capabilities. As highly IT-dependent companies develop increased competitive advantage through adept management of their information and data, they are turning to Information Integrity Initiatives (checking the reliability and quality of information) to provide the structure for their storage strategies. The key areas where installations must be prepared for SAN implementation and also for storage management fulfillment are:

- Application management
- Data management
- Resource management
- Network management
- Element management

Application Management

Application management is a vital component of the relationship between business systems and IT capabilities. It is also the obvious point at which strategic business goals can be furthered by the skillful implementation of enterprise applications. However, there are some considerations that affect application management in an enterprise environment. Large-scale business applications are usually very complex, involve custom and off-the-shelf software, and are linked to the three most common architectures—mainframe, open systems, and desktop environments. The picture is further complicated because all of these enterprise applications are essential to the financial health of a business.

Data Management

Data is the lifeblood of business. Just as governments and business discovered that money was an engine for economic growth only when it was available, so are businesses rapidly realizing that data assets are many times more effective and valuable when widely accessible. For example, in the Tivoli Information Grid, data management assures that data is available and accessible for applications; that data meets the specifications for application use; and that data is recoverable in case of a failure. Data management functions with all types of storage, whether remote, centralized, or removable. Data management functions at all levels, from large system servers to desktops.

Resource Management

Business executives who are intimately involved with IT are sometimes puzzled by decreases in the unit cost of processors, storage, communication, and the increased total cost of IT. Storage management, in general, and storage area networking, in particular, should provide some relief from this conundrum by managing pooled, fixed disk, and tape resources, as well as all removable media and the implementation of just-in-time storage management.

Network Management

Network management is probably the most critical part of the SAN and storage management challenge, in terms of the burgeoning e-commerce market. LAN and WAN resources already form part of every large enterprise and are familiar to all business executives. SANs are the logical extension of these proven networks and bring the same, or greater, value to the companies that deploy them. SANs will be as critical to business success in the future as LANs and WANs are today. SAN capabilities in the network management space include predictive capacity planning, connectivity mapping, performance, and error mapping, largely in the Fibre Channel area.

Element Management

Element management is the most detailed of the layers of storage management, and is usually overlooked by business planning. It involves the management and interaction of individual hardware elements within the SAN from different storage manufacturers, which enables SANs to integrate different storage architectures from different manufacturers.

The Challenge of Implementing SAN Technology

Although rapid strides have been made in SAN technology, and a great deal of implementation work is underway, knowledgeable IT watchers do not expect to see genuine SAN solutions up and running until the last quarter of 2002. To achieve a genuine SAN solution, the following are the basic conditions that a network must meet:

- Any-to-any interconnection of servers and storage systems
- Speed of recovery and magnitude of data loss after disaster
- Universal access and sharing of resources

- Centralized resource management
- Excellent information protection and disaster tolerance
- High levels of security and data integrity in system architectures
- Massive scalability to cope with the future explosive growth in information technology deployment [3]

SAN is not the ultimate cure for the challenges executives face due to the exponential growth of e-business and corresponding requirements for high storage capacity and data protection. However, SAN is an essential component in the future of business IT. Terms like multivendor tape resource sharing and LAN-free data transfer over established IP and Fibre Channel networks will soon become commonplace, as companies encounter the challenge of using SAN technology to provide business advantage.

Implementing SAN environments will consume many resources in the coming years. The selection of trading partners, such as IBM, Tivoli, or one of the other experienced technology creation and deployment companies, will be an essential prerequisite for success. As further enhancements (such as disk and data sharing) become common, the more important it will be to have a broad spectrum of experience and capability with technology integration.

The essential characteristics to look for in a SAN vendor or trading partner are not found in any one capability. It is immaterial whether that capability is in volume mapping, tape management software, or any other point. The key criteria for selecting a company to build a SAN or storage network management system is its ability to help make the best-of-breed technologies from all sources work together for the best total system. Most of the proven, smaller vendors have excellent products that can be considered at the element-management stage of creating a SAN.

The Storage Networking Management Vision

The future vision of storage area networking management is one that exploits both the Information Grid and customers to create storage solutions and networks that build business advantage (see Chapter 19, "SAN Solutions for Consideration"). By taking the best technologies and combining them with those from various integrators, it will be possible to assemble e-business, manufacturing, retail, banking, healthcare, or any other type of business IT solution that an enterprise will need. Islands of data will become transformed into a united resource that shares information and multiplies its worth to each organization. Storage area networks will vault their users through the twenty-first century by enabling the sharing of data and information, and multiplying their worth far beyond their value as discrete resources.

FROM HERE..

This chapter covered types of SAN operating systems software and hardware, the driving forces behind SAN, SAN market demands and projections, the evolution of the SAN market, and the value of information. The next chapter discusses disaster recovery; I/O performance; high scalability and flexibility; technology platform, techniques, and alternatives; breaking tradition in video distribution; and SAP R/3 storage management.

END NOTES..

[1] EMC Corporation, 35 Parkwood Drive, Hopkinton, Massachusetts, 01748, 2001.

[2] Michael Peterson, "Storage Area Networking: The Next Network," Strategic Research Corp., 350 So. Hope Ave. #A103, Santa Barbara, CA. 93105, 2001.

[3] "The Value of Information," Tivoli Systems Inc., 9442 Capital of Texas Highway North, Arboretum Plaza One, Austin, Texas 78759, USA, 2001.

2 Types of SAN Technology

Storage area networks technology holds great promise, but the lack of workable automation software currently stands in the way of deployment. So, imagine if all your storage devices were attached to a switch and could communicate with each other. And imagine all storage administration and management was totally automated. With no need to guide storage and retrieval traffic, manage backups, or worry about the performance strain on your network, you could become the Maytag repairman of storage management (see Figure 2.1) [1].

SAN structure

A storage area network provides centralized management of storage devices from anywhere on the network. The idea is to untie storage tasks from specific servers and enable a shared storage facility that uses high-speed network technologies as a backbone.

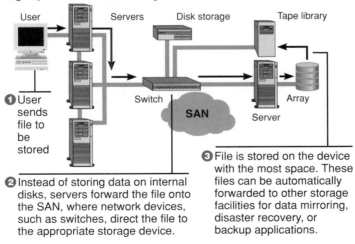

1 User sends file to be stored

2 Instead of storing data on internal disks, servers forward the file onto the SAN, where network devices, such as switches, direct the file to the appropriate storage device.

3 File is stored on the device with the most space. These files can be automatically forwarded to other storage facilities for data mirroring, disaster recovery, or backup applications.

Figure 2.1
How the SAN structure works.

This isn't an impossible dream—it's all part of the promise of SANs. As defined in Chapter 1, a SAN is a collection of networked storage devices, such as server hard drives, tape libraries, RAID, and CD jukeboxes, which are able to communicate with each other automatically.

The automated management software required to make SANs a reality isn't yet available. However, the underpinnings of SANs are maturing (see sidebar, "Update: Fujitsu Sets Up U.S.-Based Storage Software Unit"), providing the technology for some useful, cost-effective applications that you can start using today.

UPDATE: FUJITSU SETS UP U.S.-BASED STORAGE SOFTWARE UNIT

Fujitsu Ltd. recently launched a new U.S.-based company that will develop and market open storage software products with the aim of competing against the likes of heavyweight vendors such as IBM and EMC Corp. The new Fujitsu Software Technology Corporation unit, which is being referred to more informally as Fujitsu Softek, is based in Sunnyvale, California, and will operate as a part of Fujitsu's Amdahl Corporation subsidiary. Fujitsu Softek combines products from the former Amdahl Software division with new storage management software that's now in the works.

Fujitsu indicated that the new company is being organized along five lines of business, including storage management software, storage infrastructure, storage resource management, quality-of-service monitoring, and consulting. The upcoming storage management software, a version of a storage networking package developed by DataCore Software Corporation in Fort Lauderdale, Florida, is due for release in 2002. Other new products, including one for monitoring quality of service, are available now as additions to existing Amdahl Software tools for migrating data between storage devices and other uses.

Nevertheless, software for managing storage area networks is still in its infancy. But, it's quickly becoming a necessity for users who have hundreds of terabytes of data stored on networks made up of devices from multiple storage vendors.

Amdahl was looking for a way to reallocate some of its resources after disclosing a plan to exit the mainframe business in 2000. The new unit's software will work across multiple operating systems and support storage devices from different vendors.

FC-AL: A FIRST STEP...

Fibre Channel-Arbitrated Loop transport protocol supports 200 MBps throughput, dual-port channels, and hot-pluggable drives. Storage vendors are positioning FC-AL as the leading interface for SANs.

Think of FC-AL as SCSI on steroids. While SCSI can only connect up to 15 devices, FC-AL lets you connect as many as 125 devices to a single host adapter. And while SCSI requires hundreds of wires to attach devices, FC-AL's loop architecture lets you use one cable to create a loop among the attached devices.

For example, Paramount Pictures in Hollywood, California, recently implemented the FC-AL transport protocol as the company's first step toward a SAN. The company has eight high-end servers and scores of workstations on a FC-AL loop that's used to transfer video for the TV show *Entertainment Tonight*. The ample throughput allows editors to send video to the production crew for live news feeds and makes the editing process much faster. It used to take a few minutes to pull up video; now it happens in real time.

Paramount went with Fibre Channel because they had a 17-year-old video editing system in place that was totally inefficient and obsolete. When they researched the options, FC-AL was easiest to implement and integrate with their existing editing software and production systems.

FC-AL is attractive because it's a dual-port technology. This means a server can simultaneously send and retrieve documents to the same tape drive with no waiting.

FC-AL is also built for distance, which is useful in an environment such as Unisys' in which tape libraries are scattered throughout the building. While SCSI only allows a 25-meter stretch between machines, FC-AL supports spans of up to 10 kilometers.

Moreover, FC-AL is less expensive to implement than SCSI. FC-AL host adapters cost between $900 and $1,400; SCSI adapters only cost about $170, but you need to buy one SCSI adapter for every seven to 15 drives. And, because FC-AL requires fewer adapters, there's less maintenance and upkeep.

One of the most striking differences between it and SCSI is network availability during daily backups. Backups used to push the network to its limit and usually took the entire night. During a backup, many telecommuters were unable to log on because the network was so bogged down.

Now that the SAN routes backup traffic for the best performance, it takes about one hour, and even during that hour, accessing the network is no problem. Telecommuters can be a lot more productive.

The implementation of FC-AL itself is usually a no-brainer. Everything gets wired into the backplane of the circuit board with very few software changes.

However, interoperability must be considered when choosing a SAN. Pay attention to the details and compatibility with existing systems, and you won't have much trouble.

SAN SETBACKS ....

Although companies such as Paramount and Unisys are already reaping the benefits of FC-AL, it will be some time before they'll be able to fully realize the benefit of SANs. Several limitations of Fibre Channel technology are holding back the development of automated SANs.

Instead of relying on the loop architecture, full Fibre Channel implementations use switches to route traffic (see sidebar, "Inrange Releases 128-Port Fibre Channel Fabric Switch")—this requires a major software overhaul. Four years into Unisys' deployment, they're still working on rewriting the software code in order to make switching work. It's expensive, labor-intensive, and requires a lot of expertise.

> **Note**
> ────
> **It is possible to build a small SAN with FC-AL (loop). People use "full" or switched FC for larger-scale networks or for future scalability.**

INRANGE RELEASES 128-PORT FIBRE CHANNEL FABRIC SWITCH

Banking on the accelerated adoption of Fibre Channel SANs in the enterprise marketplace, Inrange Technologies has released the 128-port model of its IN-VSN FC/9000 Fibre Channel Director, a switching infrastructure, which enables users to centrally manage and add storage resources in SANs.

A Fibre Channel director provides a central point of connectivity and manageability for SAN infrastructures. According to Inrange, based in Lumberton, New Jersey, the director is the "traffic cop" that servers and storage systems connect to in order to speak to one another. For scale, it is generally accepted that a director must support at least 32 concurrent devices.

Inrange's customers, and the market, don't want to rely upon dozens or hundreds of discrete little devices, all stitched together with cables. Too tough to manage, too tough to plan, and very high risk.

Since directors are one logical switching element that can accommodate 128 devices, they do not require cables between little switches (called inter-switch links, or ISLs). Directors provide a way to aggregate and scale SAN infrastructure and improve manageability. Directors simplify, fundamentally, the deployment and management of infrastructure.

The FC/9000-128 has no single point of failure protecting the network from outage danger due to a failure in the switching element. With little switches stitched together, there is a real risk of downtime if one or more of the switches that are cabled together have a problem.

Directors have what is known as a nonblocking architecture, which means that all devices in the SAN can speak through the network at full speed, without having their traffic *blocked* due to network traffic jams. Networks of smaller switches normally are prone to over subscription, a bad thing that can be associated with overbooking in the airline industry. In an over subscription environment, there are more devices attached to the network than their is internal network bandwidth, which means that someone is going to just have to wait for network resources to be freed up.

Inrange introduced the industry's first 64-port fibre channel director in early 2000, in response to this emerging market need for users to build SANs that could expand easily and maintain performance levels as ports were added, that were simpler to manage than weaving together a mesh of smaller switches, and that offered bullet-proof levels of redundancy to protect businesses with no tolerance for downtime.

The 128-port FC Director is available immediately for factory orders. Users of the 64-port FC/9000 systems can migrate to 128-port models through simple field upgrades.

According to Inrange, more than 98% of the traffic directed by its FC/9000 technology is for UNIX, NT, Linux, and other open systems platforms. The technology has no server or storage platform bias. The design allows SAN switching to scale from 24 to 256 ports, where the performance per port does not degrade.

With its technology partner QLogic, Inrange will provide 2 GB and 256-port director technologies later in 2002. In the Fibre Channel space, Inrange competes with the likes of Brocade and McData, but only McData is producing another director-class product. List pricing for the FC/9000-128 range from about $200,000 for a 48-port unit to just over $500,000 for a fully configured 128-port unit.

The key problem Unisys has encountered is with the drivers. There are big software changes as soon as you start expanding the availability of different storage devices.

Note

A switched network might include as many as 16 million disk drives.

Moreover, while Fibre Channel provides more centralized management, servers don't automatically route data where it belongs. The instructions must still come from the multiple host adapters, and the management software to automate those instructions, needs to be improved.

Interoperability, reliable chip sets, and compatibility with Windows NT are other thorny issues that need to be addressed before switched Fibre Channel is ready for prime time. One vendor's device doesn't necessarily work with another's, and you can't ignore incompatibility with a platform like NT. Today's SANs support UNIX.

Not surprisingly, vendors are singing a slightly different tune. Most host bus manufacturers are developing the enabling drivers for Fibre Channel-ready switches.

NT compatibility will exist soon, and companies such as Compaq and StorageTek are integrating drivers into Fibre Channel network devices such as hubs and switches. Even though the driver issue isn't solved, switched Fibre Channel is so superior to FC-AL, that it's worth the implementation hassles. The real issue of switches versus the hub loop is that the loop is not reliable. When the loop fails, the whole thing goes down. With the switch approach, there is fault tolerance.

Nevertheless, hot-pluggable drives allow administrators to replace a failed drive without bringing the whole looped network down. Besides, vendors such as Ancor, Brocade, and Vixel are pricing their Fibre Channel switches at $19,000 and up. When you're spending that kind of money, the programming costs associated with switched Fibre Channel won't look so expensive.

Nothing is easy, and Fibre Channel is no exception. It is, however, a viable mechanism, and despite its glitches, it's the only candidate out there at present.

Companies with extensive testing capabilities have the best chance of success with Fibre Channel switching rollouts. If you're thinking of becoming an early adopter, consider buying all your Fibre Channel products from the same vendor because the technology is hard to debug and troubleshoot. People tend to forget that new technologies just take time to work themselves out. Until then, the expense and labor associated with true SANs will go with the territory of being an early adopter.

TECHNOLOGY AND CONFIGURATION ....

To help companies design and deploy world-class SAN solutions, companies like Brocade have developed a series of certified, interoperable enterprise SAN configurations along with step-by-step implementation guides. The entire library of these *pre-tested* SAN configuration guides includes more than 30 popular SAN environment and application configurations.

For example, Brocade's SOLUTIONware configurations simplify SAN implementation by providing a *recipe for success* for addressing today's most challenging data storage management, resource management, and business continuance requirements (see Figure 2.2) [1].

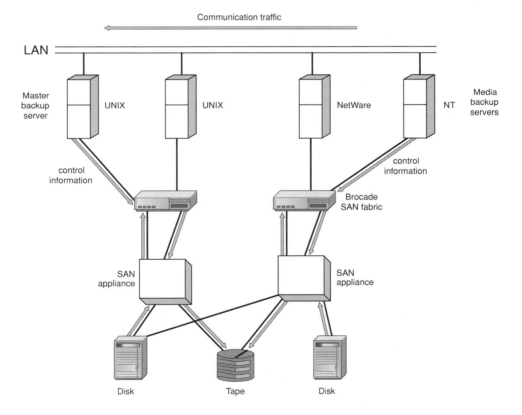

Figure 2.2
A server-free backup and recovery SOLUTIONware configuration designed to offload all backup traffic from the production network.

These certified SAN configurations provide the advantages of:

- Scaling server and storage resources quickly and independently aiming to meet fast-paced data growth
- Improving resource utilization throughout the enterprise
- Reducing the data backup window and improving data recovery times
- Increasing application availability to support 24×7 business requirements
- Improving the efficiency of storage management to help lower overall operating costs [1]

HIGH SCALABILITY AND FLEXIBILITY ....

For providers of Web-based services, it is the best of times and the worst of times. The best of times because customers are spending more than ever on services. The worst of times because with traditional architectures, no matter how much capacity sites allocate, end-user demand outstrips the horsepower and storage capacity of the server plant. The most important problem faced by Web infrastructure designers is how to provision the systems to cope with the incredibly rapid growth in the number of users and storage capacity.

SANs, based on Fibre Channel switched fabrics, provide a powerful framework for building and managing a server plant that is flexible, cost-effective, and future-proof. In this part of the chapter, an analysis of several scaling problems are presented in order to show how SAN technology can address these issues—allowing the administrator to create Web infrastructure with unprecedented management, flexibility, performance, and scaling characteristics.

Current Web server design has severe limitations in the ability to scale the storage component of the installation. These issues arise from storage directly attached over I/O channels to each server (Direct Attached Storage [DAS]).

Switched Fibre Channel networks SANs provide a solution to these storage scaling problems. Among the benefits of SAN Attached Storage are:

- Open Systems Model for Networked Storage provides best price/performance through level playing field
- Enhanced Storage Management monitors the entire storage asset within a single framework; flexibility to add or reconfigure storage as needed without downtime
- Independent Scaling of CPU and Storage capacity decouples servers and storage so that either can be scaled separately

- Easy Migration—where current applications run without software changes; incremental deployment allows flexible adoption

Web Service Scaling Factors

In capacity planning for Web services, there are several factors to be considered:

- Number of hits per minute (measure of number of clients)
- Outbound bandwidth
- Storage capacity (number and size of Web data to offer to end users)

Number of Hits per Minute

This is the overall summary capacity metric for a site, the number of hits per minute that can be provided to the user population. This is dependent on the number of servers and the outbound bandwidth (and the size of the delivered content). An important, closely related metric is the average time to deliver a URL. Maintainers of a site usually track these numbers and take action if the time to deliver a URL gets too long (site is too slow as it becomes busier).

Outbound Bandwidth

The outbound bandwidth capacity is the size in bits per second of the first network hop between the server plant and the Internet (or the network between the users and servers). In Internet-based services, the server plant designer has, in general, no control over the quality of the users' network connections, but this first hop is a first order consideration in providing a given hit per second rate because every request and reply is pushed through this pipe (see Figure 2.3) [1]. The fatter the pipe, the more requests and replies can be pushed through it in a given time.

The importance of this variable has given rise to the Web Hosting segment of the Internet space (see Figure 2.4) [1]. This is because Web hosting facilities (such as Exodus, Level 3, Abovenet, etc.) provide very fast connectivity to the Internet. Locating the servers on a corporate site requires purchasing a high capacity leased line to the Internet. Generally speaking, it is more cost effective for a given Internet access rate to locate the server equipment at the Web Hoster (this service is also called *colocation*).

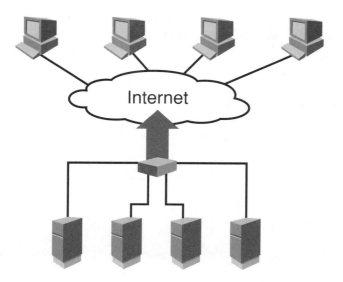

Figure 2.3
Internet service scaling factors.

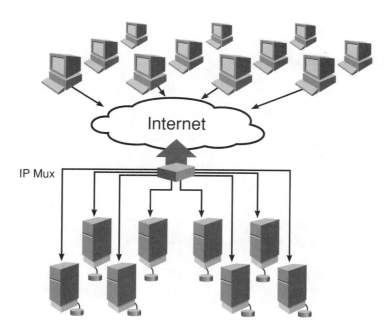

Figure 2.4
Current Web server architecture.

In the following discussions, let's assume that neither the outbound bandwidth nor user networks are an issue. If these are a problem, they must be addressed in the network, not in the server plant.

Storage Capacity

Storage capacity is, on the surface, a straightforward issue, but with current server plant design, scaling the amount of storage becomes problematic since server scaling and storage scaling are tightly coupled. The next part of the chapter provides a description of modern designs for Web server installations. An analysis is then provided of current storage practices in the Web server plant.

Current Web Server Practice

Web sites need to provide scalable capacity for servicing user requests. Most large installations utilize *load balancing* to achieve CPU capacity scaling. Load balancing can be done in several different ways but the most prominent and highest performance method is to use a server load balancing hardware device (see Figure 2.5) [1], often a Layer 4 network switch.

> **Note**
>
> The Layer 4 (network intelligence bar levels 1 to 7) network switch looks at URL and Web content, not just computer and server addresses. Wire-speed performance is achieved on all LAN and WAN interfaces, making the switch well suited for customers who rely on high-concentration server farms for their intranets or e-commerce presence. The switch acts as a front end for network cache server clusters, or farms, maximizing server resources by providing enhanced delivery of content between the server farms and users in the public or private Internet. This is done by directing Web flows to the optimal local or remote server farms interconnected with the switch, based on server loading, content distribution, and network conditions. Equally important are their quality of service capabilities that monitor content for per-flow provisioning and policing of bandwidth, as well as built-in firewalls that police unauthorized access through intelligent denial-of-service prevention.

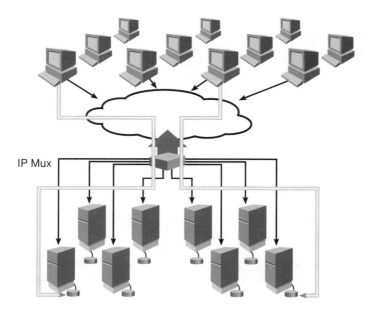

Figure 2.5
Server load balancing.

The load balancing switch sits between the delivery network (Internet) and the servers. As requests come for a URL (such as: *www.my_company.com*), the Load Balancer intercepts the connection request and selects a particular server from among a pool of servers to handle the request.

Figure 2.5 shows two different clients requesting the same URL from the server plant. A different server is selected for each client. The paths through the network are shown for the two different clients.

This scheme works extremely well for scaling the CPU capacity of the site. As more CPU cycles are needed, the site administrator purchases and deploys new server hardware to keep pace with the increased demand.

A key point here is that the same data (the URL) is delivered to each client. That implies that each server has a local copy of all of the Web data to be delivered. This is the crux of the storage scaling problem.

Storage in the Web Server Plant

Figures 2.4 and 2.5 depict the Web data storage directly attached to the servers. This is how most Web servers begin. The implication of DAS is that all servers must have copies of the data (see Figure 2.6) [1].

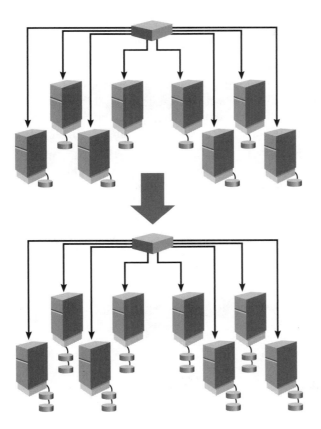

Figure 2.6
Adding storage to DAS Web servers.

This gives rise to three issues:

- How to keep all copies of the Web data synchronized for all servers: As Web data is updated, added, or removed, it is necessary to make the changes on every server's local disk.

- How to expand storage capacity of the entire site: If more storage capacity is needed, every server needs to add disk storage. When the storage capacity of the servers is reached, no more data can be added. Each server must be taken down to add disk storage.

- How to grow servers when more CPU capacity is needed: The load balancing hardware allows more CPU to be added, but doesn't solve the problem of storage replication or growth. When servers are added, it is necessary to purchase additional disk storage for each server [1].

Revisiting the SAN

In this part of the chapter, the concept of the SAN is explored in more detail to lay the groundwork for application of SAN principles to Web server architecture. A Fibre Channel switched network or fabric provides a high-performance any-to-any interconnect for server-to-server or server-to-storage traffic. Fibre Channel combines the characteristics of networks (large address space, scalability) and I/O channels (high speed, low latency, hardware error detection) on a single infrastructure.

Fibre Channel allows multiple protocols for networking (IP), storage (SCSI), and messaging (VIA) over a single infrastructure. This infrastructure can be used to create a Storage Area Network in which peripheral devices such as disk storage and tape libraries are attached to the Fibre Channel network and shared among attached nodes (see Figure 2.7) [1].

Some of the desirable features of this manner of organizing servers and storage are:

- Storage Management
- Cost Effective Open Systems Model
- High Performance
- Scalability
- Distance
- Storage Consolidation
- Decoupling Servers and Storage
- Pay-As-You-Go Model for Advanced Features
- Storage Efficiency

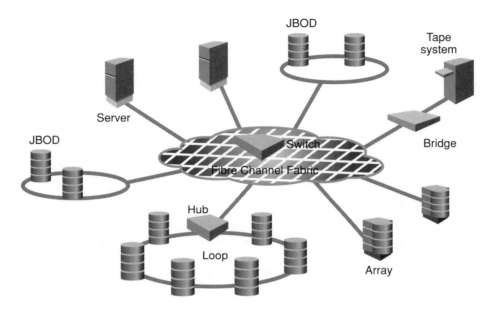

Figure 2.7
A Storage Area Network.

Storage Management

SAN attached storage allows the entire investment in storage to be managed in a uniform way. For example, software tools exist that allow storage to be allocated to the hosts, replicated, backed-up, and monitored on an ongoing basis. This is in contrast to direct attached storage, where each host's storage must be managed separately.

Cost Effective Open Systems Model

SANs provide an Open Systems model for the server and storage infrastructure that ensures that the site administrators will be able to choose best-of-breed price/performance server and storage equipment. In addition, as hardware price and performance improve, the administrator can evolve the site gracefully while continuing to make full use of existing equipment.

High Performance

Fibre Channel fabrics provide a switched 100 MBps full duplex interconnect. In addition, block-level I/O is handled with remarkable efficiency compared to networking traffic. A single SCSI command can transfer many megabytes of data with very little protocol overhead (including CPU interrupts). As a result, relatively inexpensive hosts and storage devices can achieve very good utilization and throughput on the network.

Scalability

Fibre Channel fabrics use a 24-bit address allowing 16 million devices to be addressed. In addition, Fibre Channel networks allow the number of attached nodes to increase without loss of performance because as switches are added, switching capacity grows. The limitations on the number of attached devices typical of channel interconnects disappears.

Distance

Traditional storage interconnects are limited in the length of cable that can attach hosts and storage units. Fibre Channel allows links up to 10 kilometers, which vastly increases the options for the server administrator.

Storage Consolidation

SANs allow a number of servers to utilize sections of SAN attached storage devices. This allows for cost efficiencies that come from purchasing storage in large units. In addition, this arrangement makes it possible to ensure consistent quality and support across the entire server population.

Decoupling Servers and Storage

Externalizing the storage from the server makes it a first class asset in its own right. Servers can now be upgraded while leaving storage in place. Storage can be added at will and dynamically allocated to servers without downtime.

Pay-As-You-Go Model for Advanced Features

Because the SAN is extensible, it allows incremental deployment of features such as fault tolerance and hot backup sites. There is no need to pay for these features until the economic justification has been demonstrated.

Storage Efficiency

In the SAN, since all servers can, in principle, access any storage device, the potential exists to enhance the server software to *share* storage devices (see Figure 2.8) [1]. This has profound implications for any application in which data is now replicated or shared via traditional networking techniques.

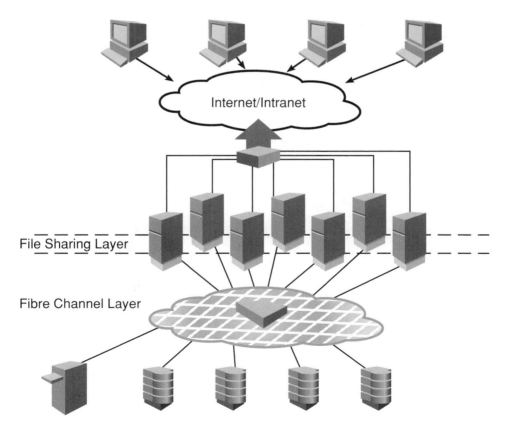

Figure 2.8
SAN back-end server architecture.

Current network-based approaches to sharing peripheral devices suffer from severe protocol inefficiencies. For example, in NFS shared storage, to deliver 1 MB from server to client, the server must:

1. Perform the I/O to the disk.
2. Marshal 667 (1,000,000/1500) data frames onto the Ethernet through the IP stack.

The client must:

3. Receive 667 data frames on interrupts from the Ethernet card through the IP stack.
4. Reassemble the data into application format [1].

In contrast, in a SAN with shared (or cluster) file system, no NFS server is required. The CPU which needs the data, simply retrieves it from the storage device in one interrupt through the SCSI stack.

SANs for Web Servers: A Scalable Alternative

Having discussed the benefits of Storage Area Networks, let's explore the application of SAN technology to Web servers with particular attention to the issues of scaling mentioned earlier.

Figure 2.8 depicts a Web server plant with the addition of a SAN with SAN attached storage and a shared file system. This organization of the server infrastructure retains all the benefits of the previous architecture while addressing its storage scaling limitations. The next part of the chapter elaborates on the specific benefits of the SAN for an application and explains how the limitations are removed and scalability is enhanced.

Storage Management

Storage is a significant portion of the investment in the server infrastructure. In the Web space, storage requirements are growing at least 100% per year. As this investment grows, managing this resource becomes more important.

The SAN provides a management framework in which storage is not viewed as subordinate to servers but as a first-class asset that can be managed in its own right. A growing number of software tools (BROCADE ZONING, Veritas Volume Manager, Transoft SANManager, etc.) provide a principled methodology for:

• Partitioning storage

- Allocating storage to hosts
- Replicating data
- Storage health monitoring
- Backup [1]

These capabilities are key in allowing for the growth of storage and maintaining the site uptime targets while controlling administrative costs.

Hot-Pluggability and Rapid Reaction to Success

One of the key ingredients in planning Internet infrastructure is the ability to scale rapidly as a site becomes popular. If a new site is successful in attracting users, it is not unusual to find that the number of hits per day increases by three or four orders of magnitude in 60 days or less.

Switched Fibre Channel SANs allow the site administrator to bring the site on-line with a modest investment in infrastructure without committing to expensive custom configured servers with built-in limits on storage or number of clients. New storage can be installed, configured, and brought online without server downtime.

Independent Scaling of Servers and Storage

Traditional server design binds storage to individual CPUs. Servers with large storage capacity are more expensive because of additional controllers, chassis, and power supply requirements.

Since the SAN allows storage and servers to be added on an as-needed basis, relatively modest server configurations can be used for the initial implementation (see Figures 2.9 and 2.10) [1]. If more server CPU cycles are necessary to meet a user load, servers can be easily added with or without associated storage. Also, if more storage is needed across a server plant (to accommodate more content), it can be easily added by attaching to the SAN and associating it with the existing servers.

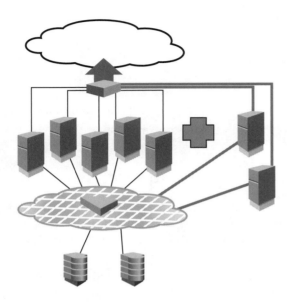

Figure 2.9
Adding servers.

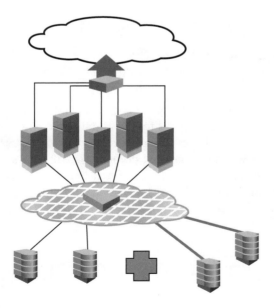

Figure 2.10
Adding storage.

SAN Scaling

Switched Fibre Channel SANs provide a framework in which the server/storage infrastructure can be scaled up indefinitely as the number of users increases without downtime for forklift upgrades.

Switching Capacity Increases As Number Of Switches Grows • One reason switched SANs can continue to scale is that, like other switched networks, switching capacity increases as switches are added to the network. In contrast, in shared medium networks (such as Fibre Channel-Arbitrated Loop and shared Ethernet), performance degrades as the available bandwidth is shared among an increasing number of attached nodes.

Advanced Routing Allows the SAN to Grow Indefinitely • As the number of nodes in the network grows, the administrator simply adds switches to the network. There is typically no user configuration necessary; the fabric automatically learns the topology of the network as switches and nodes are added.

For example, Brocade's switches allow the Storage Network administrator to build large meshed networks of switches that may have multiple paths between attached nodes. The Fabric Operating System (Fabric OS™) software automatically routes around any failed links. This makes it possible to create SANs that have no single point of failure. In addition, the Fabric OS™ allows for multiple links between switches to add bandwidth in the network, should a bottleneck exist.

Easy Migration

It is not at all difficult to migrate from existing infrastructure to the SAN. To configure a SAN, the following components are needed:

- Host Bus Adapters (HBAs) connect servers to the SAN
- Fibre Channel storage connects directly to the SAN
- SCSI-FC bridge allows SCSI (disks and tape) components to be attached to the SAN
- SAN Network Components—Fibre Channel switches [1]

Since current Fibre Channel HBAs for Windows NT and UNIX make SAN-attached storage look like locally attached SCSI resources, there are no operating system or application software upgrades required to get started with SANs. It is straightforward to begin with one or two hosts and a single SAN attached storage device, either JBOD, FC-AL disk drives, or Fibre Channel RAID.

Many storage network administrators contemplating implementing SANs in their Web site begin with a focus on SAN attachment for tape libraries. SAN attached tape allows backup to be done faster and with less contention than network-based backup. Many of the enterprise tape backup vendors have programs in place to support this configuration.

Shared Storage

In principle, in the SAN, all servers may share a pool of storage using a software layer known as a cluster file system or shared file system. As of this writing, software is under development at several vendors.

In traditional approaches, content is replicated from one server's disk to the other servers' disks. With cluster file systems, the potential exists to coalesce all storage to create a much larger shared pool of SAN attached storage that all the servers can share.

Figure 2.11 shows two different clients requesting the same URL from the site [1]. The load balancing hardware selects a server for each client. The paths show that both servers access the URL from the same disk storage. This is in contrast to the scheme shown previously, where each server must have its own copy of the Web data.

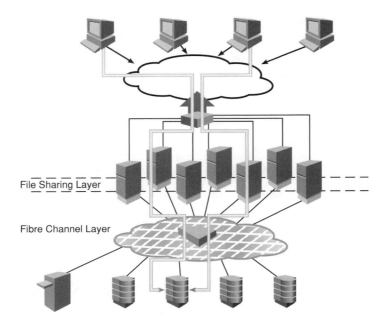

Figure 2.11
Shared file system access to data.

Pay-As-You-Go Model for Advanced Features

Because the SAN is extensible, it allows incremental deployment of features such as fault tolerance and hot backup sites. There is no need to pay for these features until the economic need has been demonstrated.

For example, with this architecture, a hot backup site can be readily constructed by distributing the server and storage plant across two physical sites (see Figure 2.12) [1]. By utilizing dark fiber, where available, this can be done in a straightforward manner and the sites can be separated by as much as 10 kilometers (up to 120 kilometers with link extenders). Without dark fiber, ATM connectivity will be utilized to extend the Fibre Channel fabric across two or more widely separated sites.

Another example would be to create a fault tolerant disk subsystem. Again this is a straightforward extension of the initial architecture. The administrator would add a second adapter to each server and connect to another switch. The disks are already dual-ported so the only expense for adding a second connection to the disks is the second switch port.

This configuration can then seamlessly tolerate the loss of any host adapter, switch, or port on storage units (see Figure 2.13) [1]. Software or hardware mirroring precludes downtime caused by failure of any single storage device.

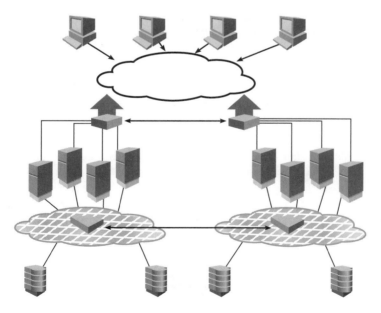

Figure 2.12
Hot backup site at up to 10 kilometers.

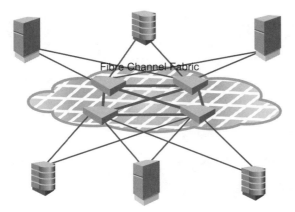

Figure 2.13
Fault tolerant disk subsystem.

TECHNOLOGY PLATFORM, TECHNIQUES, AND ALTERNATIVES ....

It wasn't long ago that IT professionals shrugged off storage as a straightforward, albeit very boring, aspect of maintaining a computing infrastructure. But in the last few years, a push towards shared enterprise storage (see Figure 2.11) has given rise to several deployment options.

For instance, when does an NAS device do a better job storing hordes of enterprise data than a SAN? And, how do these newer technologies compare with local storage, where a hard disk is directly accessed by a server via a SCSI cable connection?

Recently, switch maker McData [2], leading server vendor Compaq, and partner MierCom (forever known from this point on as the Global Test Alliance [GTA]), kicked the competitive tires of these storage technology alternatives to see how performance (see Chapter 14, "Certification of SAN Performance") varied across several common storage scenarios [3]. Their test bed (see Chapter 12, "Testing Techniques"), was set up to loosely emulate file Servers, Web servers, video servers, and other application servers with regard to the data they routinely transfer to and from a storage location. The GTA varied the storage location between a local SCSI attached disk drive, a disk drive on a storage server across a Gigabit Ethernet LAN, and a disk drive in a SAN disk array connected over a Fibre Channel SAN.

Which setup worked best? It depends. The GTA tests show the right storage route to take depends on the storage network environment, the size of the files being stored or retrieved, the type of Peripheral Component Interconnect (PCI) bus connection, and how your users access the stored data. Specifically, their tests indicate that:

- The NAS environment (where data moves between a server *initiator* and a storage *target* over a Gigabit Ethernet network) can deliver better data-transfer performance than a SAN in certain cases, such as when file sizes are small.

- SANs really outperform the NAS alternative when data reads or writes are sequential and file sizes are large, such as when a server is delivering streaming video, or when a server is backing up large data volumes.

- When connecting a server to a SAN, performance is virtually the same whether the SAN adapter uses a 32-bit or 64-bit PCI bus connection.

- For a Gigabit Ethernet network interface card (NIC) in their NAS environment, performance was typically better via a 64-bit PCI bus connection than a 32-bit PCI bus connection. But the difference isn't much—only about 10% in tests.

- In all cases, writing data to a storage device takes more time and resources than reading it, and subsequently yields much lower data-transfer performance.

- With random data reads (when there's no correlation between data from one read to the next) data-transfer performance is much lower than sequential reads of large data files in all scenarios they tested.

- With random reads, data-transfer performance over a Gigabit Ethernet NAS is nearly as good as reading data from a local disk drive on a SCSI bus [3].

The data presented is, among the first such published storage comparison results. Still, readers are cautioned to keep two points in mind.

First, these results are based on the particular equipment the GTA deployed. A SAN disk array other than the Hitachi 5800 that they used, for example, might exhibit different performance characteristics.

Second, due to the broad differences between SAN, NAS, and SCSI environments, the results should not necessarily be viewed as perfect apples-to-apples comparisons. For example, while direct SCSI data storage exhibits the best data-transfer performance in some scenarios, it is not generally accessible by multiple servers concurrently, as stand-alone storage nodes in the NAS or SAN environments are.

Also, while the GTA used an off-the-shelf Compaq server as a NAS storage target, they employed a specialized Hitachi Disk Storage Array as the target node in the SAN environment (see Figure 2.14) [3]. There are specialized NAS storage nodes available, too, but their attempts to procure one for this testing were unsuccessful.

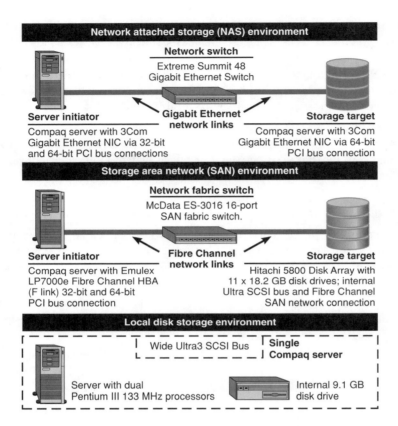

Figure 2.14
In GTA's comparison of competing storage technologies, they set up three
test beds to measure the effectiveness of each deployment option.

How the GTA Did It

The test scenarios GTA created involved an application-processing server, which, depending on the application, could be an email server, Web server, database server, or video server. This server was the initiator of each storage operation, meaning that it issued all disk read and/or write requests.

Those requests were sent to and processed by a storage target, which varied depending on the environment. In the NAS environment, the storage target was a Compaq ProLiant server, accessed via an IP-based Gigabit Ethernet network. In the SAN environment, the storage target was a Hitachi 5800 Disk Array, which was built for the purpose of being a SAN node. In the SCSI environment, the storage target was one of the application server's internal disk drives.

GTA used the same Compaq server configuration as the initiator in all the scenarios. This was a fairly robust Compaq ProLiant ML370, with dual 866-MHz Pentium III processors and 1 GB of RAM.

GTA only changed the initiator server configuration when they changed from a NAS to a SAN environment. Then they replaced the 3Com Gigabit Ethernet NIC with an Emulex LP7000e host bus adapter Fibre Channel.

In the SAN and NAS environments, GTA also compared data-transfer performance between 32-bit and 64-bit PCI bus connections. This was the connection inside the application server used by the Gigabit NIC and the SAN host bus adapter. The 3Com Gigabit NIC they used, model 3C985B-SX, can be plugged into a 32-bit PCI slot or 64-bit PCI slot within the Compaq server. The Emulex LP7000e HBA comes in different models for 32-bit and 64-bit PCI bus connections.

The SCSI environment is not affected by whether a Gigabit Ethernet or Fibre Channel storage network is in place. The internal disk drive was a SCSI bus connected directly to the processor motherboard of the Compaq server. No network I/O or NICs were involved.

Another key component to this testing was a sophisticated, public domain software test tool from Intel called Iometer. This software is well suited for this mixed-technology environment because it measures and reports average data transfer in megabytes per seconds—whether the data is being sent to a local SCSI-connected disk, out over a Gigabit Ethernet network via a NIC, or out over a SAN via a host bus adapter. Iometer issues disk reads and/or writes to any defined disk drive, which can be a local drive or a network drive mapped to a NAS node, or a drive on a remote SAN disk array. Iometer, which consists of client and server software components, can also perform the same tests across multiple platforms concurrently and consolidate the results, or it can perform a test via multiple *threads* (instances of the same software process running concurrently and independently) on the same processor. This was the method GTA used for running two and five servers against the same storage target at the same time.

Scenarios

In GTA's research on how to characterize different real-world storage applications, they found that storage scenarios vary in three regards: the relative percentage of storage requests that are reads versus writes; whether disk access is random or sequential; and the typical file size. Based on this information, they developed five scenarios for this comparative testing.

In GTA's first file-server scenario, they designed the server to imitate an application server, such as an email or file server, that conducts many, typically small, reads and writes continuously. This scenario is characterized by 80% reads, 20% writes.

File size is fixed at 4 KB, and disk access is random in all cases. This scenario tests how well small files can be served across a Gigabit Ethernet network versus a Fibre Channel SAN.

The cumulative data-transfer rates achieved in this scenario (see Figure 2.15) are relatively scant—less than 1 MBps [3]. This is the impact of moving fairly small files, running a mix of reads and writes, and using random disk access, all of which tend to slow things down. In this scenario, data-transfer performance for all three storage environments is fairly comparable. It is only when five or more servers are collectively accessing the disk storage that the SAN environment provides slightly greater aggregate throughput. A SAN might be a slightly better choice in this type of scenario, but only if you expect to have multiple servers concurrently accessing the same disk storage.

GTA's second file-server scenario (see Figure 2.16) was similar to the first with one exception [3]. Rather than fixing all the file sizes at 4 KB, they also included larger file sizes as 10% were 8 KB and another 10% were 16 KB. This scenario tested how the storage alternatives compared with some larger file sizes added in.

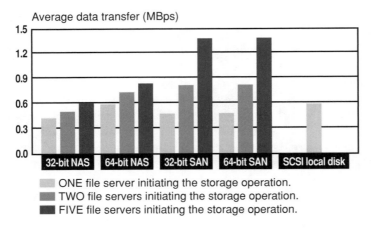

Figure 2.15
In this series of tests, GTA measured how different storage technologies handle an application server reading and writing small files (4 KB) to a target storage device. They ran tests with one, two, and five servers initiating the storage operation.

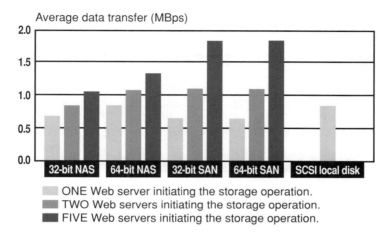

Average data transfer (MBps)

ONE Web server initiating the storage operation.
TWO Web servers initiating the storage operation.
FIVE Web servers initiating the storage operation.

Figure 2.16
In this series of tests, GTA measured how different storage technologies handled an application server reading and writing a mix of small and large files (4 KB, 8 KB, and 16 KB) to a target storage device. They ran tests with one, two, and five servers initiating the storage operation.

GTA's tests with this scenario showed that, as file sizes increased, data-transfer throughput also increased. As with the first file-server scenario, though, there was no clear winner between NAS, SAN, or local SCSI disk. It's noteworthy that, even with five servers collectively accessing the same disk storage, only 1% to 2% of the Gigabit Ethernet or Fibre Channel bandwidth was used. This means the transport capacity of Fibre Channel and Gigabit Ethernet is huge.

In GTA's third scenario, one, two, and then five Web servers were serving the same set of Web pages and files. All disk operations are reads; all disk access is random. File sizes were variable, ranging from 20% very small (512 bytes) to 10% fairly large (128 KB). This scenario showed how well Web pages can be served over the different storage/transport options.

GTA was surprised with the results of their testing with this scenario (see Figure 2.17) [3]. Given random-access retrieval of a range of file sizes, data-transfer rates achieved in the NAS environment clearly outperformed the SAN. Indeed, the NAS throughput was roughly double the SAN throughput in all cases. And despite the hype concerning the throughput speed offered by SANs, it was surprising to see Gigabit Ethernet perform so much better than Fibre Channel SANs in any situation.

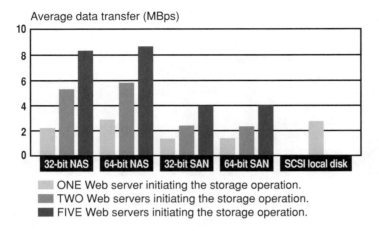

Figure 2.17

Figure 2.17
In this series of tests, GTA measured how different storage technologies handle a Web server randomly reading and writing files of various sizes to and from a target storage device. They ran tests with one, two, and five servers initiating the storage operation.

In GTA's fourth scenario, one, two, and five video servers delivered streaming video. As with the previous scenario, all disk operations were reads. However, all disk access here is sequential. The same 64 KB file size was used in all cases. This scenario tested the relative performance of serving streaming video over the different storage/transport options.

When comparing the video server scenario with the results of the Web server scenario, GTA saw the opposite result (see Figure 2.18) [3]. With sequential disk access to large files, and consistent, fairly sizable files, the SAN environment outperformed the NAS alternative by a considerable margin—from more than double for a single video server, to nearly four times the throughput when five video servers were reading the same disk files across the SAN or NAS. In the case of five video servers, the cumulative SAN throughput, 47 MBps, tapped roughly half the Fibre Channel SAN's bandwidth. These tests indicated that if you are going to serve large amounts of video from a shared-storage node, your best bet is a SAN deployment.

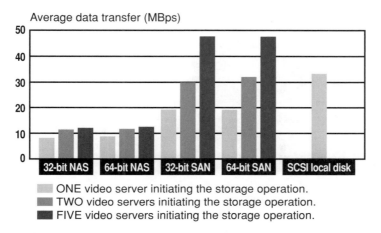

Average data transfer (MBps)

ONE video server initiating the storage operation.
TWO video servers initiating the storage operation.
FIVE video servers initiating the storage operation.

Figure 2.18
In this series of tests, GTA measured how the different storage technologies handled a video server sequentially reading large video files (64 KB) from a target storage device. They ran tests with one, two, and five servers initiating the storage operation.

In GTA's final scenario, one, two, and five application servers were writing folders and directories to the storage target in large, 1 MB files. All disk operations were writes, and disk access was 100% sequential. This scenario tests how well large files are transported and written sequentially to a backup storage disk, emulating server backup to tape.

In this scenario, applications servers were writing massive amounts of sequential data to a storage target's disk (see Figure 2.19) [3]. In the NAS and SAN environments, it seemed the maximum disk-write-throughput point might have been reached because the storage data-transfer rate did not increase with two or more servers, compared with a single-server initiator. With the Hitachi 5800 disk array in the SAN environment, the peak GTA reached was about 30 MBps; with the Compaq NAS server the write capacity to a single disk peaked at about 5 MBps. The specialized SAN storage node clearly outperformed the off-the-shelf server acting as a NAS node in their test bed. They didn't know how well a specialized NAS device would have fared by comparison, but given these two storage nodes, the SAN alternative delivers much better performance.

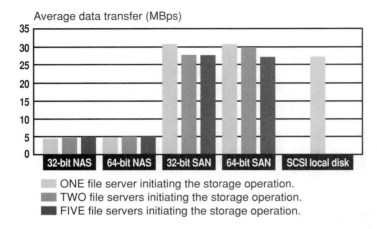

ONE file server initiating the storage operation.
TWO file servers initiating the storage operation.
FIVE file servers initiating the storage operation.

Figure 2.19
In this series of tests, GTA measured how the different storage technologies reacted when an application server wrote files to specified directories on a target storage device. They ran tests with one, two, and five servers initiating the storage operation.

The SCSI option did well here, for backing up a single server. Indeed, performance was comparable to doing backup over a SAN. However, a key motivation to doing a backup in the first place was to create and maintain a copy of a server's data in a location where it would be safe if something took out the server. Local SCSI doesn't accomplish that end.

Other Scenarios

There are many other scenarios that could still be tested. For example, it would be interesting to see how data-transfer performance compares if disk storage was striped across multiple target disk drives, instead of just one. It would also be interesting to see how different, specialized storage nodes (such as those from Network Appliance in the case of NAS, or EMC in the case of SANs) perform by comparison. However, neither vendor was willing to participate in this novel test bed.

> **Note**
>
> **A stripe (striped) is a set of strips at corresponding locations of each member extent of a disk array which uses striped data mapping. The strips in a stripe are associated with each other in a way (relative extent block addresses) that allows membership in the stripe to be quickly and uniquely determined by using stripes to map virtual disk block addresses to member extent block addresses. Also, a striped array or**

striped disk is a disk array with data mapping, but no redundancy for failure protection. Striped arrays are usually used to improve I/O performance on data that is of low value or easily replaced.

The data presented represents a first step toward quantifying which of the various storage alternatives does the best job for a particular set of requirements. As GTA's testing shows, there are cases in which each delivers the best relative data-transfer performance. Therefore, it is clear that, as far as storage technologies go, one size does not fit all. Indeed, the moral of this story may be that users need to gain a better understanding of their storage needs before they sign on the bottom line for a SAN or NAS-based storage network.

BREAKING TRADITION IN VIDEO DISTRIBUTION......

Today's workstation-based video creation and manipulation tools allow users to treat video as discrete chunks of images and sounds that can be manipulated in various ways. This abstraction provides the freedom to focus on content generation rather than the tools used to create the content. Yet, while the latest video tools allow far more creativity and functionality, the way video is distributed among these tools remains unchanged.

SANs are the basis for a new video distribution system. They allow the video moving between the tools to be treated in the same way as the video inside the tools— as discrete chunks of images and sounds. SANs empower entire teams of people to focus on the process of creation and creative collaboration rather than on how to best move materials between workstations.

Purely Analog Video

To the video pro of the 1970s, video seemed as if it was a constant flow or stream of information. Thus, it was natural to develop a method of distributing analog video throughout a video creation or manipulation facility (TV station, production facility, post house, and others) that resembled standard water plumbing. Video coaxial cables (pipes) connected video tape recorders (water tanks) with mixers (faucets), monitors (sinks or tubs), and cameras (artesian wells). A video tape recorder (VTR) would continue to play or record (much like an open faucet), even with no mixer or monitor or camera connected—blindly spraying video into the ether or recording only the Brownian motion of magnetic particles.

In most video facilities, a crossbar switch installed within this equipment essentially allowed a temporary replumbing of the many pipes connecting the various video devices. With this crossbar, or *video routing* switch, a temporary connection could be made between any of the inputs and outputs of the switch. Video poured into the plumbing system at one end would be guaranteed to spray out the other in common— they add an abstraction layer that insulates users from the complex technology that makes them work.

Today's dominant operating paradigm of the nonlinear editing system strives to remove any trace of the linearity of videotape or the complexity of video digitization and manipulation. Instead it presents only a time line on which to place various-sized chunks of video. Any video tool using the nonlinear paradigm works roughly the same way. Video does not seem to *flow* in today's video workstation; instead, the flow has been frozen into chunks that are simply stacked end-to-end along the time line.

The video distribution systems in most facilities, however, were meant to handle flowing video, not frozen chunks. To move frozen chunks of video between worksta-tions, they must first be melted back into a liquid stream and refrozen at the next workstation. While serial digital video in SDI and SDTI formats is an attempt to keep video in its *frozen* state, or at least in a slush, some customers are still less than satis-fied. At best, just the conversion from the 4:2:2 YUV format used in SDI to the 4:4:4 RGB used by many computer-based workstations concerns some high-end post facili-ties. At worst, there is a question as to why video must be moved or copied at all.

In an effort to come up with something better, some video creation and manipu-lation facilities have explored the use of standard computer LAN technologies like Ethernet and ATM. But LANs are not quite fast enough to give every video worksta-tion an uninterrupted supply of video as needed. LANs do, however, provide a view of a better way video could be distributed in a facility.

The Introduction of Digital to Video

By the mid-1980s, the video *frame buffer* forced many in the video business to realize that video is not really a stream of flowing information but a collection of discrete chunks of information in time that can be controlled and manipulated as desired (something the film industry had known all along). Initially, the most flexible and af-fordably sized *chunk* of video was a frame, or actually, two fields. It was quickly dis-covered that with the proper hardware and software, frames of video could be manipulated individually and even reordered to convey a different message, tell a dif-ferent story, or alter video reality.

By the end of the decade, video manipulation functions were performed in soft-ware running on standard off-the-shelf computers enhanced with specialized video in-put/output boards. These new *video workstations* were a normal evolutionary development. The designers of the next-generation video equipment determined that to remain competitive, expertise must lie not in building special-purpose computers for video, but in building special-purpose video boards and software to work with general-purpose computers.

The Video Creation and Manipulation Workstation

From a distance, video workstations and the applications that run on them all have one characteristic in common—they add an abstraction layer that insulates users from the complex technology that makes them work.

A Faster Network

A close examination of a video facility with multiple video workstations connected together with a LAN reveals a commonly overlooked solution to the lack of speed provided by LANs when used for video. Most video workstations have not only a relatively low-bandwidth connection to the LAN, but also a relatively high-bandwidth connection to their local storage. This connection to local storage, whether it is through a disk media channel like SCSI, SSA, or Fibre Channel, provides data to the video workstation at speeds many times greater than the LAN can provide.

From the perspective of a wiring diagram, a SAN is very similar to the traditional streaming video and routing switcher system. But a look just beneath the surface reveals that the two diagrams represent completely opposite operating paradigms. For example:

- Instead of a highly intelligent and expensive data storage device—a VCR, a SAN uses a dumb and relatively inexpensive data storage device—a disk drive.
- Instead of a dumb, manually operated and slow central circuit switch—a video routing switcher, a SAN uses a very intelligent, automatic and extremely fast central packet switch—a Fibre Channel switch.
- Instead of passive manipulation devices that perform actions on whatever is fed into them—DVEs, mixers, monitors, and others, a SAN uses extremely active and intelligent manipulation devices that must request the data on which an action is to be performed—like video workstations.
- Instead of data being blindly pumped down a pipe by a storage device with no knowledge of what is on the other end of that pipe, a SAN *sends* data only to the manipulation devices that request the data [4].

Push versus Pull

To date, video distribution in facilities has employed a *push* metaphor, like water pumped out of a tank, a fine example of the classic mid-20th century centralized command operating paradigm—the way our grandfathers liked to build things. Video distribution with a SAN uses a *pull* metaphor, similar to the World Wide Web. Intelligent clients request data from distributed storage, and the data flows to them as bursts of data packets that they assemble and use as they desire. This is a good example of an early 21st century object-oriented, distributed local intelligence operating paradigm. Yet, this 21st century operating paradigm, using a SAN for distributing media throughout a video facility and a file-level SAN O/S such as Tivoli SANergy File Sharing, allows many capabilities that are impossible with the existing method of distributing video in a facility. For example:

- *No More Sneaker-Net:* SAN users can access all video materials on shared storage; thus, the need to carry disks or tapes between workstations for reconnection or redigitization is eliminated.

- *No More Copying—Sharing Instead:* SAN users avoid the need to copy materials from a server or other workstation to their local workstation, and thus the time spent waiting for those copies to occur. A workstation connected to a properly designed SAN can read and write the same files on the shared storage simultaneously with every other workstation.

- *Increased Reliability:* Fault-tolerant RAIDs guarantee that if a single disk in the RAID fails, none of the data is lost.

- *Increased Work Flexibility:* With multiple identical or similar workstations running the same applications all connected to the SAN, there is no reason a job could not be started on one workstation and finished on another. Moreover, if one workstation fails, the job can be continued from any other workstation on the SAN.

- *Increased Application Flexibility:* If the latest and greatest application happens to run only on the Windows NT® platform, files can still be shared between it and all the existing Macintosh® and SGI™ workstations.

- *Increased Storage Efficiency:* With the centralized shared storage possible with a SAN; each workstation can use as much storage as needed for each job. With more than enough gigabytes shared between a few workstations, everyone has all the storage they need, and no one has leftover storage being wasted.

- *Decreased Overall Storage:* Because multiple workstations can use the same materials at the same time, the volume of online materials is reduced; thus, the total storage requirements are reduced.

- *Quieter Edit Suites:* A Fibre Channel-based SAN allows up to six miles between devices. This allows many SAN users to move their storage into a soundproof, climate-controlled room separate from the edit suite.

- *Simultaneous Backup and Restores:* It is possible to backup and restore files from and to the shared storage while other users are accessing the storage. This capability eliminates middle-of-the-night backups and emergency *everyone stay off the network* restores.

- *Easier Segregation of Tasks, Reduced Number of VCRs:* Some facilities find it more efficient to have a single Networked Learning Environment (NLE) devoted to digitizing materials and outputting finished programs to tape. If the collaboration on jobs at a facility allows this type of work flow, it is possible to save the cost of a VCR for each edit bay. Also, the creative staff can focus on their work and leave the repetitive tasks to other personnel.

- *Simultaneous Viewing of the Same Work:* Similarly, some facilities find that having an additional NLE for client viewing improves efficiency by reducing interruptions. With a viewing station, clients can essentially look over the shoulder of an editor at work-in-progress, without interruption to the creative staff; in fact, even without their knowledge.

- *Improved Visual Quality:* The near-perfect form of video is as frozen chunks. A SAN linking video workstations minimizes the number of freeze and thaw cycles and helps preserve the visual quality of the video.

- *Overlapping and Pipelining Processes for Faster Job Completion:* With a SAN, it is no longer necessary to wait for an entire chunk of video to be processed before starting another process on that video. As soon as one frame has finished the first process, it can be used on a workstation located elsewhere on the SAN.

- *Better Collaboration, Better Productivity:* The speed up in work flow enabled by a SAN allows people to collaborate more easily to create better projects or to reduce the time a single project takes to complete [4].

SANs in Video

SANs are the basis for a new video distribution system that seamlessly matches the recent advancements in video creation and manipulation systems. SANs provide many advantages over the traditional streaming and routing switch distribution systems. Using a SAN with a SAN O/S such as Tivoli® SANergy File Sharing, today's video post production facilities can complete the transformation begun by modern video creation and manipulation tools, and become highly efficient, collaborative environments designed to maximize creativity, profitability, and system availability.

Recent new products such as Systeme, Anwendungen, Produkte's (SAP's) Business to Business Procurement, E-Commerce Portals, and the emerging SAP Application Service Provider markets, require an ever increasing need for continuous system availability. This last part of the chapter provides information on an essential component of required advanced infrastructure solutions—the High Availability Split Mirror Backup/Recovery.

Note

Systeme, Anwendungen, Produkte (SAP) in der Datenverarbeitung (German: Systems, Applications, and Products in Data Processing; SAP AG). SAP is the German software company, SAP AG. SAP's R/3 integrated suite of applications and its ABAP/4 Development Workbench became popular starting around 1993.

The described Split Mirror solution delivers a backup with no impact on the live R/3 System (*serverless*) using advanced functions of IBM's Enterprise Storage Server (ESS). This *zero* downtime for the live R/3 System means that SAP users do not miss a beat while the backup takes place. No transactions are canceled during the copy/backup process.

Instant availability of consistent copies of the database provides the ability to place an emergency system at the user's disposal while recovering the live database from a disaster. Beyond Backup/Recovery, a consistent copy of the live database may be used for various purposes, such as the creation of a Business Warehouse (BW) system.

SAP R/3 STORAGE MANAGEMENT ....

Service level agreements increasingly have to reflect that in case of planned downtime such as backup, hardware/software maintenance, and R/3 upgrade, and unplanned downtime such as error analysis and restore, the system has to be available again within minutes. Figure 2.20 shows a combination of advanced infrastructure solutions developed by SAP's Advanced Technology Group (ATG) in cooperation with their storage partners. In this scenario they constantly copy the live data and allow business continuation during split (and resynchronization) of the mirror [5].

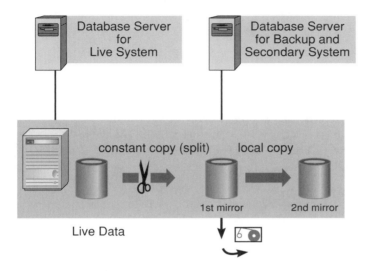

constant copy (split)   local copy

1st mirror   2nd mirror

Live Data

Figure 2.20
Split mirror backup and standby R/3 System.

Once the mirror is split, ATG creates additional copies for backup and a standby SAP R/3 System. With this solution they are minimizing the impact on the live environment and offloading the backup activity from the live database server.

The split mirror solution was successfully implemented for a SAP R/3 database managed by DB2/390 stored on one IBM Enterprise Storage Server (ESS) using ESS's advanced functions—the local FlashCopy and synchronous Peer-to-Peer Remote Copy (PPRC).

Customers that require remote data vaulting or need to scale to a larger database size can simply extend this split mirror solution to an additional ESS. The split mirror solution described in this part of the chapter is an exact repetition of the solution implemented on IBM's RAMAC Virtual Array (RVA).

In this implementation, only logical volumes that contain DB2 LOGs, Bootstrap Dataset (BSDS), and ICF catalog are constantly mirrored and all other logical volumes used by the R/3 database are synchronized only for backup and refresh of the standby system. With this setup, ATG assures that user or application logical errors are not copied immediately to the mirror. In case of a disaster, ATG can recover the database to a certain point in time, starting with the last backup and applying the LOGs of the live system. This process (called DB2 Conditional Restart) may be very time consuming.

Business continuation in a split mirror implementation (described later) that also supports remote data vaulting (two storage subsystems), will be significantly reduced if the live storage subsystem is completely lost. To avoid having to perform a DB2

Conditional Restart in this situation, you need to perform constant PPRC of all logical volumes that belong to the R/3 database.

Environment Setup

Because split mirror backup/recovery is a high availability solution, ATG highly recommends the use of two physically separated database hosts and two ESS storage systems. Each database host manages its own ESS storage system, and the fast resynchronization of the live database with a remote copy is managed by the ESS systems.

In ATG's tests, they used two LPARs running in a SYSPLEX environment instead of the two physically separated database hosts. The R/3 live database was stored in one *ESS cluster*, the mirror and an additional copy in the other *ESS cluster* (an overview of the ESS structure is discussed later in the chapter).

For the fast synchronization of the mirror, ATG used the synchronous Peer-to-Peer Copy (PPRC) function. To adjust these commands for a certain environment, it is necessary to know the parameters used by the PPRC commands and how to value them as shown in Table 2.1 [5].

Table 2.1   PPRC Parameters

Parameter	Description
ser#	The serial number is a unique number given to each ESS at the plant.
Ssid	Subsystem ID of a logical subsystem (LSS)
lss ID	Two digit number of an LSS—last 2 digits of SSID
linkaddr	Physical link to/from the storage system Format: **aaaa bb cc** **aaaa** primary volume's 3990 Cluster/Interface (System Adapter ID "SAID") **bb** ESCON director "DESTINATION" address. "00" if directly attached pair of DASD control units, or with static ESCON switch. **cc** reserved address; always "00" for a 3990-06
ccuu	Address (4 digits) of a device (logical volume) inside the ESS
cca	Channel connection address of a logical volume (last 2 digits of ccuu)
serial	Name of a logical volume

The logical volume addresses and names are defined by the customer's storage administrator, who provides those that fit the customer's naming conventions.

ESS Structure and Connections

The ESS is divided into two symmetrically structured units called clusters. Each cluster can take over the workload of the other, should one be unavailable.

Host and PPRC Connections • The ESS is equipped with 16 Host Adapters (HA) located in four HA bays. Each bay contains four HAs and each HA consists of two ports. In ATG's OS/390 test environment, they only used ESCON connections for the host and PPRC connections.

Figure 2.21 shows the SAIDs of the ESCON ports of ATG's test ESS (from the front) [5]. The highlighted ports are used for PPRC between the two ESS clusters. The primary Logical Partition on the Host Mainframe (LPAR) and ESS cluster 1, and the secondary LPAR and ESS cluster 2, are connected by 8 ESCON connections each.

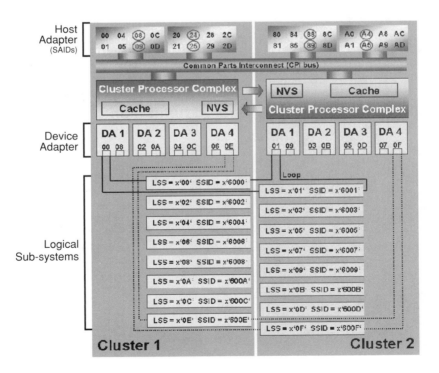

Figure 2.21
Overview of test ESS.

ATG chose this configuration to treat their test ESS as two separate storage systems. This is, however, not the recommended configuration.

In general, a host is connected to ports located in all four HA bays. This configuration will increase the availability. Should one connection, a HA bay or even a cluster, not be available, the CPI (Common Parts Interconnect) bus will give access to the data.

From the host or ESS storage system point of view, data will be transferred on logical paths. The maximum logical paths per ESCON port is 64. To maximize the PPRC I/O throughput, ATG used 4 ESCON connections (corresponding to 256 logical paths) between the two ESS clusters.

Volume Layout and Definition of the Mirror

ATG's live database which consists of

- B2 BSDS, LOGs, catalog, and directory

- all R/3 pagesets (table and index spaces)

- ICFCAT and user catalog is spread across 48 logical volumes (3390-3). They named this set of volumes DBt2 as shown in Figure 2.22 [5].

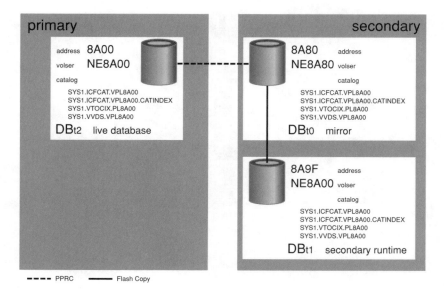

Figure 2.22
Volume layout.

Volume set DBt0 is the mirror of the live database, created by PPRC. Since PPRC copies tracks from one volume to another, the copy will only differ from the original in the device address. During the PPRC process that makes the DBt0 volumes accessible on the secondary side (RECOVER), ATG renames the volumes to their original names. In the end, names and contents of the catalog datasets are unchanged and still reflect the volumes used by DBt2. Volume set DBt1 is a local FlashCopy (on the same cluster or storage system) of the mirror—their secondary runtime instance.

To maximize I/O throughput, it is recommended to spread the volumes evenly across all available logical subsystems (LSSs). In ATG's environment, they have 8 LSSs on each cluster (see Figure 2.21). Every LSS in cluster 1 contains 6 DBt2 volumes and every LSS in cluster 2 contains 6 DBt0 and 6 DBt1 volumes.

Split Mirror Backup

The live system is in normal READ/WRITE operation. Only the LOG-volumes (DB2 LOGs, BSDS, ICFCAT, and user catalog) are in a constant synchronous PPRC connection. After the last resynchronization (BACKUP), all other PPRC volume pairs were suspended and they are now accessible as usual simplex volumes as shown in Figure 2.23 [5].

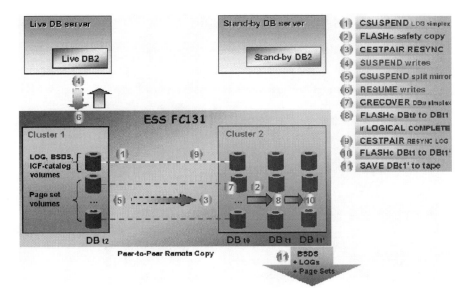

Figure 2.23
Split mirror backup solution.

Split Mirror Backup Process

On the primary side, ATG suspends the LOG-volume pairs. This allows them to operate on the primary and secondary side without any mutual influence. On the secondary side, they make the LOG-volumes simplex and vary them together with all other DBt0 and DBt1 volumes online (step 1).

The next step is to FlashCopy the DBt0 volumes to the DBt1 volumes (step 2). This safety copy will help ATG to recover from a disaster that may happen during the resynchronization of their mirror. A user or application logical error during the resynchronization would immediately make their mirror also inconsistent. The safety copy DBt1 will enable them to recover the database with a DB2 conditional restart on the secondary side, while the live system is available for error analysis.

At this point in time, ATG is ready for the resynchronization of the mirror. They again establish all PPRC pairs in RESYNC mode, which copies only those tracks updated during the period of suspension (step 3).

As soon as this process is 99% finished, ATG causes DB2 to suspend all writes (step 4) coming from the R/3 application. This DB2 function throttles down application writes, but no R/3 application process will recognize this—they will only slow down as long as ATG causes DB2 to resume write operations.

Once the remaining 1% of updated tracks is also synchronized, ATG suspends all PPRC pairs (step 5). Immediately after the mirror is split, they cause DB2 to resume all write operations (step 6).

Note

Only in the short period between step 4 and step 6 were application writes slowed down.

The Live System Is Now Back To Normal READ/ WRITE Operation

On the secondary side, ATG now makes all DBt0 volumes simplex and varies them together with all other DBt0 and DBt1 volumes online (step 7). Because they need the DBt0 volumes back as fast as possible to establish the PPRC pair between the LOG-volumes, they copy with FlashCopy all DBt0 volumes to DBt1 (step 8). As soon as the FlashCopy relationship is established (LOGICAL COMPLETE), FlashCopy allows READ/WRITE access although the tracks are not yet physically copied.

Note

Before a task can update a track on the source that has not yet been copied, FlashCopy copies the track to the target volume. The following reads to this *old* track on the target volume will be satisfied from the target volume. After some time, all tracks will have been copied to the target volume, and the FlashCopy relationship will end.

Immediately after the *logical complete* message, ATG again establishes the PPRC pairs in RESYNC mode (step 9) for the LOG volumes.

The Environment Is Now Back To Normal Processing

In ATG's test scenario, they assumed that the standby system also has to be available as soon as possible. Therefore, after the first FlashCopy is physically completed, they start a second FlashCopy from DBt1 to DBt1' (step 10). They have to wait for the physical completion of the FlashCopy started in step 8, because a source and target volume can be involved in only one FlashCopy relationship at a time.

As soon as this second FlashCopy is logically completed, ATG restarts their standby system and, after the copy is physically completed, they move the contents of the DBt1' volumes to tape (step 11).

Process Automation

The detailed description of the split mirror backup shows the complexity of this process. Of course the process can be managed by system administrators, but to avoid additional points of failures, ATG has to concentrate on the automation of this process.

A single PPRC command is actually synchronous, but if a set of commands (for example, RECOVER for all volume pairs that contain the live database) is started under ICKDSF or TSO BATCH (IKJEFT01), ATG is not sure if all commands finished successfully at the point in time their process gets back control. The same is true for MVS commands, such as VARY, which varies volumes ONLINE or OFFLINE.

ATG solved the latter problem with a WAIT loop that runs a certain amount of time to ensure that the command successfully finished. PPRC offers the QUERY command to get information about the progress of a command. This information is presented formatted or unformatted on an output screen (in the SYSLOG or in a dataset).

From the operations point of view, this is not handy, because for every QUERY call, ATG gets a huge message output in the MVS system log. To find out if, for example, all paired volumes are synchronized, they will need a program that scans this output.

Suspension of Application Writes

For a recovery, DB2 on OS/390 needs consistency points (checkpoints identified by a high written RBA) that are established by the commands QUIESCE or ARCHIVE LOG, but these commands wait for COMMIT. With SAPs recommended DB2 parameter settings, the commands will wait 15 seconds less than the resource timeout. This means, if there is continuous activity in the SAP R/3 System, the commands may never finish successfully.

Be aware that the SUSPEND log write command is not a DB2 checkpoint. This means pages modified in DB2 buffers will not be flushed out to disk. But, all log buffers will be written to disk and, due to the log-write latch, all application writes will be suspended. After the successful execution of this command, all PGLOGRBAs (in the table) and indexspaces are less than or equal the RBA achieved by this command. The latter will enable a normal DB2 restart on the copied DBt1 volume set to get a consistent SAP R/3 database image.

Recovery

The backup process described earlier will provide a physical dump of the live database achieved at the moment of application write suspension. This dump will be on tape and on the DBt1' volumes of the secondary storage system.

The contents of the DBt1 volumes differ from the DBt1' volumes in that after the restart of the standby system all modifications done by transactions open at the moment of write suspension are rolled back. The LOG volumes of the DBt0 volumes contain the contents of the live system's LOG volumes and all other DBt0 volumes have the same contents as their corresponding DBt1' volumes. Immediately after the moment where application writes are resumed, the contents of all DBt0, DBt1, and DBt1' volumes (with the exception of the DBt0 LOG volumes) will go out of date.

The kind of recovery scenario a customer will apply depends on his or her service level agreements. He or she may decide to temporarily offer the users a read-only system (DBt1) or he or she might try to find a reverse engineering process that will recover a consistent live system.

If the error analysis or the reverse engineering process takes too long, the customer may decide to go back to the last backup. In this case, the DBt1' image will be copied back to DBt2, and DB2 will be restarted. In the latter scenario, the customer may lose too much work, therefore he or she may decide to recover to a point in time closer to the disaster. In this case, the DBt0 image will be copied back to DBt2 and the DB2 LOGs will be applied. This DB2 Conditional Restart process can be very time-consuming.

FROM HERE ....

This chapter covered technology and configuration; high scalability and flexibility; technology platform, techniques, and alternatives; breaking tradition in video distribution; and SAP R/3 storage management. The next chapter discusses evolving standards for SANs and SANs standards organizations.

END NOTES...

[1] Mark Sausville, "The Web and Storage Area Networks: Scalable Storage for the Web," Brocade Communications Systems, Inc., 1745 Technology Drive, San Jose, CA 95110, 2001.

[2] McDATA Corporate Headquarters, 310 Interlocken Parkway, Broomfield, CO 80021, 2001.

[3] MIER Communications, Inc., 410 Hightstown Road, Princeton Junction, NJ 08550, 2001.

[4] "Storage Area Networking: Breaking Tradition in Video Distribution," Tivoli Systems Inc., 9442 Capital of Texas Highway North, Arboretum Plaza One, Austin, Texas 78759, USA, 2001.

[5] Siegfried Schmidt, "SAP R/3 Storage Management: Split Mirror Backup Recovery on IBM's Enterprise Storage Server (ESS)," SAP AG, Neurottstr. 16, 69190 Walldorf, Deutschland (Germany), 2001.

3 Standards

The SAN, with its promise of ubiquitous data access and reduced storage management costs, has captured the attention of IT managers and vendors alike. SANs are evolving to provide a flexible, scalable infrastructure for data storage that delivers any-to-any connectivity between host systems and storage devices. Visionaries hope to build on this robust infrastructure to deliver a storage utility that will simplify and automate the provisioning and maintenance of data storage resources.

Behind the scenes, SAN standards have been evolving, as well. It should come as little surprise that the initial discussion of SANs coincided with the formalization of standards for the Fibre Channel interface (see sidebar, "Freedom through SAN Standards"). Fibre Channel standards, ratified by the American National Standards Institute (ANSI X.3230-1994), provided the first viable interconnect suitable, in terms of bandwidth and throughput, for disk input and output. The standard introduced three potential deployment options for Fibre Channel including a switched fabric, which has become the basis for current thinking about SANs.

FREEDOM THROUGH SAN STANDARDS

Historically, in the computer industry, the best of technical ideas can fizzle amid the chaos that reigns until standards are established. UNIX and LANs, are two cases that immediately come to mind.

In the case of UNIX, applications written under a UNIX operating system from one company could not run under UNIX developed by another company. Once a Unix standard was ratified, software applications became portable; that is, applications could move from one UNIX platform to another without modification. Similarly, departments within an enterprise that had LANs manufactured by one vendor could not communicate with other departments that had LANs from a different vendor until standards were developed and implemented by all LAN vendors. A similar situation exists today with SANs.

Conceptually, the SAN is the answer to the storage problems that have arisen with the advent of e-business and its attendant needs for 24×7 availability, quick response to user demands, 99.999% uptime, and rapid nondisruptive backup of data. However, the lack of standards has resulted in incompatibility problems that have delayed the acceptance of SANs. But that is about to change. Industry organizations have been working diligently to develop such standards and their efforts are about to come to fruition.

In the past, the SAN standards effort has been chaotic, to say the least. To prevent this chaos from continuing into the future, the Fibre Channel Industry Alliance (FCIA) and the Storage Networking Industry Association (SNIA) (the two leading storage networking industry groups) have organized working groups to work on standards in their areas of expertise. The FCIA consists of several working groups developing Fibre Channel standards, and the SNIA working groups are developing standards for areas such as SAN management and SAN security.

Both organizations keep abreast of what the other is doing and have specific members that act as liaisons with the other organization. These changes should eliminate the delays that have occurred in the past, when formal processes were nonexistent and ad hoc bodies were needed to kick start the standards process. Once the working groups in these two organizations have developed a proposal for a standard, they will submit it to the appropriate standards body for ratification, or formal acceptance.

There are two major standards bodies involved with SANs: the American National Standards Institute (ANSI) Technical Committee T11, which defines all of the protocols for Fibre Channel technology; and the Internet Engineering Task Force (IETF), which defines the management standards for SANs. Once the standards have been ratified by one of these bodies, they are circulated to the Fibre Channel vendors and implemented in those vendors' Fibre Channel devices or management software.

Fibre Channel Standard

Today, two major standards are imminent: a Fibre Channel standard called FC-SW2 that will ensure compatibility among Fibre Channel switches, and a Management Information Base (MIB) management standard that will permit Fibre Channel devices such as switches to be managed by any vendor's software that uses the Simple Network Management Protocol (SNMP).

Note: FC standard documents like Fibre Channel-Generic Services (FC-GS) specifies "generic services" for FC switches.

An ad hoc committee called the Open Switch Fabric Initiative (OSFI) developed the FC-SW2 standard over a two-year period. Five major switch vendors (Ancor, Brocade, Gadzoox, McData, and Vixel formed the OSFI) contributed ideas and, in some cases, intellectual property to the standard. The OSFI worked closely with the SNIA and the FCIA; they reviewed and provided input to the standard.

The FC-SW2 interoperability standard should be ratified soon. ANSI's Technical Committee T11 is planning to have a letter ballot in October 2001, and when it goes out to letter ballot you don't usually get too many technical comments. After they finish that step, they will submit it for review and that's when it becomes a standard.

The switches made by the Fibre Channel vendors that implement the standard will be able to communicate and interoperate with those made by other vendors that also implement the standard. Users will no longer have to be concerned about being locked into one switch vendor; they can now feel free to change vendors to take advantage of lower prices and new technology without the fear of interoperability issues.

MIB Standard

The other important standard that is close to ratification is the management MIB. This standard has been developed and proposed to the IETF by another ad hoc group called the Fibre Alliance, which was formed under the leadership of EMC Corporation and consists of 50 storage networking vendors. The standard is presently being reviewed by the IETF, and should be ratified by that body very soon.

The goal of these SAN standards is to assure users that they can take advantage of new technological developments or lower prices by switching from one vendor's product to another without being concerned about interoperability problems. As it stands today, users must purchase SANs that are pretested and preconfigured to be assured that their SANs are free from interoperability problems. This situation keeps prices high and slows the acceptance of the technology because potential

> users fear they will become locked into a particular vendor if they purchase a SAN that is not built to an industry standard. Once the standards are implemented, users will be free to purchase without fear and vendors will be free to enjoy the fruits of their labor [1].

To support the deployment of SANs and to move the technology closer to its *storage utility* vision, standards-making efforts are moving forward on several fronts. The Technical Committee NCITS/T11—which is a subcommittee of the National Committee for Information Technology Standards (NCITS) and a part of ANSI—is responsible for the development of Fibre Channel standards. The IETF, SNIA, FCIA, and other industry groups are also working out the details on a number of SAN-related issues. Their efforts are helping to evolve the SAN from an interconnect technique toward a true network infrastructure.

Note

The SNIA definition specifically does not identify the term SAN with Fibre Channel technology. When the term SAN is used in connection with Fibre Channel technology, use of a qualified phrase such as "Fibre Channel SAN" is encouraged. According to this definition, an Ethernet-based network whose primary purpose is to provide access to storage elements, would be considered a SAN. SANs are sometimes also used for system interconnection in clusters.

LIKE ETHERNET, SANS STANDARDS ARE EVOLVING..

According to Brocade Communications Systems. SAN standards development is following the same pattern as Ethernet in the 1970s and 1980s. Ethernet standards originally specified a technology for moving data, reliably and fast, over a network interconnect. The earliest standards defined low-level functions such as wiring and signaling and identified the parameters of message headers and frame sizes—in short, the basic requirements for successfully moving data from point A to point B. Over time, the standards evolved to support the requirements of effective management of the network, and ultimately the integration of numerous LANs into the enterprise networks of today.

SAN standards development is following a very similar pattern. The basic work for data movement has been done and Fibre Channel standards covering interconnect, data transport, and basic management are complete, allowing critical SAN deployment. Brocade is now refining the areas of management, discovery, WAN connectivity, and other requirements to make the Fibre Channel SAN an integral part of the enterprise management framework.

Note

Brocade is one of the FC SAN equipment vendors participating in the refinement of SAN standards.

This is necessary work, to ensure that the products of vendors are able not only to interoperate, but to integrate—enabling simplified and cost-effective storage management and, ultimately, the universal, intelligent, self-provisioning storage infrastructure that the IT world is seeking.

A PHASED APPROACH ....

From an evolutionary point of view, three discrete phases in standards development are seen—the data movement phase, the discovery and management phase, and the interoperable solutions phase. While work is proceeding concurrently in many of these phases, the completion of standards for each phase may be viewed as an enabler for the subsequent phase.

Phase one, covering data movement standards, is complete. The NCITS/T11 committee has worked out the details of basic data movement across an interconnect by specifying devices, topologies, generic services, basic management services, and basic name services. Standards for Fibre Channel have been defined to the extent that devices can be configured into a SAN, identified and named—and can exchange data.

The current work of the T11 committee is focused on phase two: discovery and advanced services. The T11 committee is seeking to standardize a method for automatically discovering the topology of a SAN and identifying what devices are connected, including their attributes and characteristics.

Of importance to this effort is the definition of a MIB for devices connected in a SAN. Familiar to many from the world of Ethernet networking, MIBs provide a common format for identifying devices, their capabilities and characteristics, and their operational status. In the management of a network, MIBs are often polled to auto discover network topology and to facilitate the management of a network.

The Internet Engineering Task Force oversees much of the work currently being done on MIB structure standards. The IETF is working with proposals submitted jointly by the Fibre Alliance, a vendor consortium led by EMC Corporation (Hopkinton, Massachusetts) and the SNIA in 1999. The work of the IETF is being coordinated with the T11 committee. SNIA is very active in the area of SAN management, security, and applications. They are already working in cooperation with the standards-making bodies (NCITS/T11 and IETF) on issues that fall under the second phase of standards evolution. The purpose of SNIA is to develop standards for the definition and testing of interoperable and well-managed systems to accelerate the adoption of storage networking.

The Storage Networking Industry Association, an international nonprofit industry group comprising more than 80 companies interested in promoting standards and technology for storage and SANs, might be described as a *lobby* within phases two and three of the standards-making effort. Many SNIA members, including Brocade, also sit on the standards-making committees, such as T11.

SNIA's working groups cover a broad range of issues. One focus is to draft standards recommendations that will enable policy-based management of SANs themselves.

SNIA is working to find a common way for discovering more detailed information about SAN-connected devices. There needs to be some method to identify what type of device—tape library, disk array, and such—is connected, the vendor and model of the device, its RAID level, and so forth, before policy-based management can be used to manage the SAN as a platform.

As for the mechanism of management, SNIA is also working to draft proposals for submission to standards bodies covering the mechanism for monitoring and managing storage devices, SAN network switches and hubs, and server host-bus adapters (the network interface cards of the SAN world). Current SANs must be monitored through an out of band mechanism—usually a secondary Ethernet network interconnecting devices that uses the well-defined SNMP to collect and report device status to a management tool. SNIA is endeavoring to define alternative management approaches, including an *in-band* management scheme that will enable the management of the SAN through the same Fibre Channel interconnect that is used for data transport.

Security is another important area being explored by SNIA. Once SNIA has succeeded in distributing storage access, they will need to come up with ways to make the stored data available only to authorized individuals, to protect its integrity and authenticity, and to protect it from hostile attacks.

GETTING TO THE THIRD PHASE ....

Ultimately, the efforts of SNIA accomplish two important tasks. For one, recommendations of the organization, which represent the tacit or explicit agreement of vendors on techniques and methods, help to expedite the standards-making process. When major vendors lock horns over proposed standards, the standards process often bogs down.

Proof of this assertion can be found by reviewing the history of the evolution of Ethernet within Institute of Electrical and Electronics Engineering (IEEE), as well as the development of Internet standards within IETF. Articulating standards that run contrary to the approach of a dominant vendor can lead to a bifurcation between the formal standard of an official body and a de facto standard of an industry vendor, which is also undesirable for many reasons.

Early in the evolution of standards for SANs, there was some fear that proprietary proposals of system, network, or storage vendors would compete with the proposals of SNIA (see sidebar, "SANs Standards Organizations"). In retrospect, there has been considerable cooperation among vendors in SAN standards-making efforts. This has contributed much to the efficiency of the process to date.

SANs Standards Organizations

Storage Networking Standards-Related Web Sites:

1. Fibre Channel Industry Association: *www.fibrechannel.com*
2. Fibre Alliance: *www.fibrealliance.org*
3. Storage Networking Industry Association: *www.snia.org/*

NCITS/T11 sites:

4. *www.t11.org*—Technical Committee NCITS/T11, part of NCITS
5. *www.ncits.org*—National Committee for Information Technology Standards and part of ANSI
6. *www.ansi.org*—American National Standards Institute [1]

The second benefit of having the input of SNIA to standards-making bodies derives from the pragmatic interest of member vendors to move standards closer to the user (see sidebar, "Storage Users Endorse Push on Standards"). SNIA members are working to further standards as a means to an end. Ultimately, they want to realize profitable shares of the market that is growing around SANs. As they test their own approaches and receive customer feedback, they are able to glean better insights into what users want from SANs. This is reflected in their work within SNIA, making the recommendations of the group a more accurate reflection of market demands.

STORAGE USERS ENDORSE PUSH ON STANDARDS

Kohler, Wisconsin-based manufacturing conglomerate Kohler Company, hopes installing a SAN will let them create tape backups without disrupting the company's normal course of back-office operations.

Tewksbury, Massachusetts-based Avid Technology wants to upgrade their SAN by removing single points of failure, adding clustering capabilities, and installing new middleware that can control all the storage devices on the network. Ultimately, Avid sees it as an excellent step on the road to disaster recovery.

Multiple vendors have acknowledged that they have to work together to create interoperability standards for what are now disparate storage systems. One result of a lack of cooperation among vendors is that security is almost nonexistent in storage installations.

As technology becomes more complex, CIOs care less about the guts of their storage infrastructure and more about the ease with which it runs and their companies' return on investment. More and more, those investments are being eaten up by network management costs, as opposed to the purchase of raw-data storage capacity.

While different storage vendors may make claims of interoperability, no one is ready to bet his job on such promises. You'd really love for it to be any-to-any (storage) technology, but that doesn't seem to be here right now.

Interoperability standards are expected to support storage virtualization—the ability for users to pool together physical storage on devices made by different vendors. Virtualization is the next technology block to watch over the next 18 months. The virtues of virtualization are:

- Increased interoperability between different types of storage devices from different vendors
- Lower network management costs, which lead to greater return on investment for storage networks
- Increased security for stored data [1].

In the third phase, standards are being developed for mapping SAN resources so they can be provisioned to applications automatically. Examples of these applications include storage consolidation, serverless and LAN-free backup, and disaster recovery. There will also be standards to enable resource management and utilization efficiency, and quality of service. You see similar standards appearing in the Ethernet world today for bandwidth management, bandwidth allocation, and quality of service guarantees. In the third phase of the standards effort, let's look at the same sorts of issues with respect to SANs.

OTHER PLAYERS ....

The evolution of SAN standards is not necessarily a linear path through the three phases. The process can be affected by technological breakthroughs, new vendor directions or initiatives, and by changes in the industry brought about by consolidations and mergers.

For example, the 2000 merger of the Fibre Channel Loop Community, an industry organization fostering awareness of the use of Fibre Channel's loop topology as a storage interconnect, and the Fibre Channel Association (FCA), another industry organization promoting Fibre Channel technology and awareness generally, created a new organization, the FCIA. An important outcome of the merger, which brought together those seeking SANs based on the arbitrated loop topology and advocates of Fibre Channel switched fabric topologies, was a unified voice to promote Fibre Channel-based SAN implementation and solutions.

Note

Fibre Channel Industry Association (FCIA): Its mission is to nurture and help develop the broadest market for fibre channel products.

As a result, the FCIA has become the *caretaker of the road map for Fibre Channel* and serves as a collection point of input from the vendor and end-user communities. They relay the input to the NCITS/T11 committee, which, in turn, serves as the official monitoring body of the Plug Fest interoperability demonstration and conference held annually by the organization.

FCIA is the caretaker of the Fibre Channel roadmap, and SNIA is the caretaker of the storage networking roadmap. SNIA differs from FCIA because it looks at storage networking generally, while FCIA is dedicated to Fibre Channel technology. SNIA caters to all kinds of technologies, including the SCSI, Fibre Channel, Gigabit Ethernet, and others.

In addition to mergers of standards advisory groups, standards-making activity has also been affected by issues discovered following the implementation of existing standards. For example, the NCITS/T11 committee and ANSI have already formalized standards that describe a basic level of interoperability between Fibre Channel SAN switches. However, as in the early days of Ethernet, vendors have implemented standards-compliant technologies that, in some cases, will not allow their switches to interoperate with those of other vendors whose products are also standards-based.

Note

ANSI is a standard-setting, nongovernmental organization which develops and publishes standards for "voluntary" use in the United States. American Standard Code for Information Interchange (ASCII) sort. ANSI is also a means of alphabetizing, which accounts for capital letters and numbers. To arrange something in an ASCII sort, numbers (digits) come first in numerical order, followed by capital letters in alphabetical order, followed by lower case characters in alphabetical order.

Now, additional requirements for interoperation that relate to zoning philosophies and interswitch routing have been identified and are being addressed in the NCITS/T11 committee. Rather than a setback or reversal of the standards-making process, the committee prefers to view such activity as standards refinement. The experience of other standards-making efforts, notably Ethernet, evidenced similar standards refinement requirements as the technology matured.

THE FUTURE OF SAN STANDARDS ....

Today, most of the interface and data movement standards for Fibre Channel SANs are well established. The next phases of the evolution of SAN standards will require the complementary work of NCITS/T11 and IETF, which is concerned with MIBs, discovery, and IP-related issues (see sidebar, "Storage Standoff"). The NCITS/T11 committee is largely beyond the interface issues now and are hard at work on the management requirements of larger fabric networks, where complementary standards are being developed.

Note

IETF is short for Internet Engineering Task Force, the main standards organization for the Internet. The IETF is a large open international community of network designers, operators, vendors, and researchers concerned with the evolution of the Internet architecture and the smooth operation of the Internet. It is open to any interested individual.

STORAGE STANDOFF

A slew of storage-over-IP proposals have obsessed storage vendors for the last year, dislodging conventional ideas of direct-attached storage and splitting partners and competitors alike. Heavy-hitting storage and network infrastructure players are sparring over four proposals for transporting storage data across IP networks. Observers indicate the battle will probably end in a standoff between three: the draft for SCSI over TCP (iSCSI) submitted to the Internet Engineering Task Force; the Fibre Channel over IP draft submitted to the IETF and ANSI; and the Fibre Channel Backbone proposal before ANSI. A storage network start-up's proposal, yet to be submitted in full to a standards body, doesn't have a chance.

Amid the storage-over-IP standards wrangling, vendors that have partnered to deliver end-to-end storage solutions often find themselves at odds. Some are ready to adopt iSCSI, others favor Fibre Channel over IP and some, such as Dell Computer, have thrown their money into upstart camps or haven't committed at all. Users are left sorting through the confusion.

The iSCSI Camp

Backers of the iSCSI proposal include its originators Adaptec, Cisco, Hewlett-Packard, IBM, Quantum, and SANgate. iSCSI specifies a way to transport data residing on SCSI devices natively over TCP. Until the arrival of Gigabit Ethernet, LAN speeds have been woefully inadequate for transporting this type of block data. Now that 10 Gigabit Ethernet looms on the horizon, the idea of moving block data over IP is even more attractive.

iSCSI makes no changes to standard communications or network infrastructure gear, but does require the addition of a Fibre Channel-to-Gigabit Ethernet router and intricate router software to take SCSI data from the storage device and transport it as IP data across the network. The IETF is expected to adopt the iSCSI draft by the end of 2001. Adaptec and Cisco are also planning to ship iSCSI-based products by the end of 2001.

But Adaptec and a few other companies indicate that iSCSI needs more. They've extended the specification with SNMP management information bases, IP Security, or an ATM transport protocol called the SCSI Encapsulation Protocol (SEP). For example, Adaptec plans to support the SEP-enhanced iSCSI specification. It and other companies undertaking similar developments are confident the products will work with iSCSI when it becomes a standard.

Down the Fibre Channel

The opposing specification, Fibre Channel over IP, comes from Brocade Communications Systems, Gadzoox Networks, Lucent Technologies, McData, and QLogic. In this scheme, Fibre Channel frames are encapsulated in IP frames for movement over a Gigabit Ethernet, SONET or ATM LAN, WAN, or metropolitan area network (MAN).

Note: FC backbone is a specification to link geographically distributed FC SAN islands with WAN connections such as ATM and SONET. It doesn't provide better or worse performance than FC over IP.

Some vendors are selling prestandard Fibre Channel-over-IP products for joining geographically disconnected SANs, and are claiming that the equipment will be software-upgradable to the standard when it appears in mid-2002. Brocade and Gadzoox also are among a group of vendors that have submitted the Fibre Channel Backbone proposal to ANSI. Fibre Channel Backbone allows greater distance and higher performance than Fibre Channel over IP.

Each of these three proposals complements the others. For instance, a user might use Fibre Channel over IP to connect SANs located in the New York boroughs of Queens and Brooklyn; Fibre Channel Backbone to extend the distance to Rochester, New York; and iSCSI to transport storage data within a small office in New Jersey. However, only Entrada Networks has announced a switch that will incorporate all three specifications.

Odd Spec Out

The fourth proposal flies in the face of the rest. The proposal, called storage over IP, is a superset of iSCSI and Fibre Channel over IP. It comes from Nishan Systems, a start-up funded by Dell Computer, Quantum, Siemens and Sun. Nishan indicates it will win the standards game, claiming that giants such as Cisco, IBM, and Lucent just don't realize it yet.

Most competitive vendors won't comment publicly on Nishan's proposal, but indicate the company has alienated itself with its bluster. There's a large degree of wishful thinking on Nishan's part. It's not realistic to assume that any of the standards bodies are looking to create a single, unified standard for three effectively disparate topics. It is completely unrealistic to assume that one relative neophyte is going to change the way those bodies operate.

There is little doubt that iSCSI will ultimately win the storage battle. But it's not a battle over what is best. It's about what vendor has the market swing to make it happen (see Table 3.1) [1]. Right now, that's Cisco.

Standardizing Fibre Channel over IP would be superfluous. There are point solutions to solve specific problems that don't need a standards verification. CNT (a Minneapolis storage infrastructure company) sells Fibre Channel over IP and ATM.

At least one user agrees. EchoStar, a broadband satellite TV company in Denver, shuttles storage data across an IP MAN using CNT technology every day [1].

Table 3.1
How storage companies stack up on supporting storage-over-IP proposals

Company Name	Fibre Channel over IP (ANSI and IETF draft)	iSCSI (IETF draft)	Fibre Channel Backbone (ANSI draft)	Nishan SoIP (portion submitted to IETF)
Adaptec		X		
Agilent Technologies		X		
Brocade Communications	X		X	
Cisco	X	X		
CNT	X	X	X	
Crossroads Systems	X	X	X	
Dell	Uncomm.	Uncomm.	Uncomm.	X
EMC	X	X		
Entrada Networks	X	X	X	
Gadzoox Networks	X		X	
Hewlett-Packard		X		
IBM		X		
Lightsand Communications	X			

Table 3.1
How storage companies stack up on supporting storage-over-IP proposals (Continued)

Company Name	Fibre Channel over IP (ANSI and IETF draft)	iSCSI (IETF draft)	Fibre Channel Backbone (ANSI draft)	Nishan SoIP (portion submitted to IETF)
Lucent	X		X	
McData	X		X	
Nishan Systems	X	X		X
Nortel Networks	X			
Pirus Networks		X		
Qlogic	X		X	
Quantum/ATL	X			X
SANGate		X		
SANRAD		X		
Siemens				X
Sun Microsystems				X
Vixel	X	X	X	

Standards will continue to precede requirements in the area of SANs, making the course to the universal storage utility a standards-driven one. Storage on demand, virtualized storage, and device-independent capacity management are the exciting, up-and-coming benefits of SANs. Even before these "killer applications" arrive, SANs will provide a secure storage infrastructure that can be managed efficiently.

Cost-benefits and performance, flexibility, and scalability, rather than killer applications, may ultimately drive SAN development. Standards-based SANs enable interoperability of SAN components, which in turn prevents IT managers from falling prey to *vendor lock-ins* and proprietary solutions. Moreover, standards reduce the cost of implementation for SANs and SANs themselves reduce the costs to maintain and manage storage used by a company. In a world where data storage requirements are doubling on an annual basis, standards-based SANs offer the only intelligent and cost-effective solution.

Once a standards-based storage infrastructure is established within an organization, advanced applications can be developed to make use of the infrastructure. Considerable attention is already being paid to creating a virtual storage repository that will respond with the right kinds of storage to the requirements of a *SAN-aware application*. The potential benefits of such a capability are enormous, provided that a standards-based SAN enables them.

FROM HERE ....

This chapter covered evolving standards for SANs and SANs standard organizations. The next chapter discusses self-service SAN, outsourcing with service providers, and high-speed data sharing among multiple computer platforms. It also looks into other aspects of SANs, including: opportunity for the indirect channel, end-to-end services for multivendor enterprise SANs, and storage subsystems for video services.

END NOTES...

[1] Jon William Toigo, "Standards Evolving for Storage Area Networks," Brocade Communications Systems, Inc., 1745 Technology Drive, San Jose, CA 95110, 2001.

4 Types of Vendor and SANs Service Providers

IT leaders have long been evaluating various build versus buy and lease versus buy scenarios. Soon after the first mainframe was sold, almost any asset (from software to hardware to human resources) could be leased, rented, or contracted. As demand for storage has started skyrocketing, the application service provider (ASP) model has spawned storage service providers (SSPs) and vendors that specialize in helping organizations manage their enterprise storage requirements. Leading SSPs and vendors such as Articulent [1], ManagedStorage International [2], Storability [3], StorageNetworks [4], and StorageWay [5] seek to transform complex storage systems into simple, pay-for-use services.

SSPs and vendors evaluate your needs, provide advice, and recommend, implement, and manage data-storage solutions for you. SSPs typically provide services to resolve the three principle problem areas of data storage: primary online-data storage, backup and restorability, and availability and accessibility.

To address primary data storage, SSPs design and implement systems that serve as your online-data store. The storage devices may reside locally at your data center or at a remote co-location facility. Either way, the SSP monitors the data-storage infrastructure for you and resolves any issues that arise.

In terms of backup and restorability, SSPs optimize archival procedures, and increasingly they perform this function for you off site. Finally, to help ensure constant data availability and to avoid disasters, SSPs also offer real-time data replication services.

Almost half of the respondents to a recent industry survey reported that their organizations' storage requirements would increase 49% over the next 12 months, and five out of 10 respondents cited data-storage needs as a business-critical priority. With so much riding on their data-storage solutions, chief technology officers (CTOs) should consider the benefits of hiring external storage-management expertise.

SSPs understand how to design, implement, and manage secure, scalable, highly available data-storage infrastructures. Few organizations can afford to hire employees who focus solely on the vagaries of SANs, Fibre Channel networking, NAS devices, and other enterprise technologies.

If you design an enterprise storage solution inhouse, you risk considerable exposure should it fail to meet scalability and availability requirements. The costs of unplanned downtime, obsolescent equipment, and inadequate capacity can be devastating.

Because SSPs can implement storage solutions quickly, they can reduce the time to market required for critical new e-commerce and electronic customer relationship management (e-CRM) initiatives. By hiring an SSP to design storage solutions for these systems, organizations can reap the associated benefits immediately.

What's more, SSPs can manage these solutions around-the-clock, even if the storage devices reside at the customer's data center. Because SSPs have technicians available on call, they can resolve issues as soon as they become problems.

A key reason to consider an SSP is the high cost and relative scarcity of qualified personnel. Purchasing storage is not expensive—the price per gigabyte seems to drop every day. However, the cost of installing, configuring, managing, and backing up data is considerable. By providing you with experienced technicians, an SSP alleviates these personnel and financial burdens.

Storage Area Network vendors have also made progress toward solving interoperability woes, but analysts caution do-it-yourselfers to consider the turnkey approach. With that in mind, let's take a look at the self-service SAN.

SAN SELF-SERVICE ....

More than two years after storage vendors introduced the concept of the SAN as a high-performance alternative to server-based storage, interoperability remains the major implementation problem. Customers who were swept up by the initial SAN hype discovered that while off-loading storage functions from data network servers onto a specially designed, high-speed, high-availability storage net made sense in theory, in real-world conditions it was extremely difficult.

First of all, no standards existed for the SAN itself, particularly in the area of management. While standards did exist for Fibre Channel technology, those standards were interpreted differently by vendors and a virtual sandstorm of interoperability resulted.

Some SAN vendors began working on standards through organizations such as the SNIA, the FCIA, the FCA, and the OSFI. Others began to invest heavily in interoperability labs to pretest SANs before delivery, and they embarked on an educational program in the form of seminars, white papers, and so-called Plug Fests, where vendors could see how well their equipment worked with components from other vendors.

Note

According to IDC, the total worldwide SAN market is $4.5 billion and will grow to $24.9 billion by 2004. Dataquest predicts the Fibre Channel SAN component market (switches, hubs, directors, and host-bus adapters) will grow from $140 million in 1998 to $4.6 billion in 2004.

To some extent, these efforts have paid off. We're not past interoperability issues; we're not at plug-and-play. It's better than it was, and it's getting better steadily.

The promise of a SAN and the theory behind it are sound, but the reality of putting one together (especially with the person who is not very familiar with high-speed technologies and setting up complex systems) is just not there. But progress is being made on the standards front.

For example, the OSFI has defined the standard for interoperability between Fibre Channel switches manufactured by different vendors. Brocade donated its protocol to the group to hasten the acceptance of the standard, which is now with the Internet Engineering Task Force awaiting ratification.

Note

OSFI was formed to create a way to make larger SAN a reality and to make standards for Fibre Channel switch interoperability. Brocade had to open its previously proprietary switching protocol because the other FC switch vendors were close to inventing a competing protocol, and Brocade was going to be the only FC switch vendor with a proprietary protocol. The "donation" of its protocol to OSFI was a move necessitated by the need to maintain its lead in the market and to continue to claim openness.

The Fibre Channel Alliance is working on an MIB specification for SAN management. Substantial progress has been made on the SAN MIB. Pathlight Technology in Ithaca, New York recently announced it will implement the MIB in several of its products, hoping other SAN vendors such as Veritas and Legato will follow. Both of those vendors currently have products implementing the MIB on their product roadmap.

Note
The SNIA, the major SAN standards body, currently has 11 working groups addressing standards relating to Fibre Channel storage, discovery, policy-based management, and security.

The Interoperability Labs

In addition, the largest SAN vendors have invested in interoperability labs. EMC has devoted 160,000 square feet, more than $3 billion in equipment and 1.5 petabytes of storage to its interoperability lab in Hopkinton, Massachusetts. Being a storage-only company requires EMC to have all major vendors' equipment in its lab. As a result, the company has 2,000 systems for testing and reproducing customer environments and 860 open systems hosts.

A typical operation that takes place in the lab is the qualification of new products. EMC brings in new products and runs them through their testing procedures. If EMC detects a problem, they return the product to the vendor that supplied it. The vendor then upgrades EMC's firmware or code and gives it back to them to retest. If EMC finds no other issues during the retest, they qualify it.

Like EMC, IBM has invested heavily in interoperability. It has dedicated 90,000 square feet of space and $600 million worth of equipment to its interoperability lab in Gaithersburg, Maryland. The lab includes equipment from all major server vendors including Compaq, IBM, and Sun; switch vendors such as Ancor, Brocade, Gadzoox, and Vixel; routers from Chaparral and Crossroads; and software from Computer Associates, Hewlett-Packard, Legato, and Veritas.

IBM's role is to get the interoperability team together with their skills so that they can help clients design, do proof of concept, and test their planned solutions. The team creates customer environments within the lab and conducts presale briefings using typical configurations.

The IBM lab goes beyond simple interoperability. It also looks at the application level to help companies improve the management of their business through better availability of information.

Mass Mutual Insurance in Springfield, Massachusetts, recently made use of the IBM interoperability lab while planning its SAN implementation. Their intention was twofold: First, they wanted to validate their design assumptions, and second, they wanted to get a first-hand look at the technology that IBM had implemented in the lab, because a lot of the equipment that IBM has is equivalent to the equipment that Mass Mutual Insurance has. Mass Mutual wanted to make the storage environment a utility, so that it would be available on demand and movable among applications.

By using the IBM Global Services Lab, Mass Mutual found it could skip the pilot stage (and the expenses associated with it) that many other companies had experienced in the course of deploying SAN technology. They didn't have to go through the trouble and investment of bringing the components in-house to find out if they worked together. They were able to go to Gaithersburg and kick the tires, which was very beneficial to them. It made the whole process a lot easier.

Recently, Compaq began building a large interoperability lab on its campus in Colorado Springs, Colorado. But, this interoperability lab has a new twist. Compaq has built the lab in cooperation with SNIA and is making it available to all SNIA members. According to Compaq, this will make its interoperability lab the first large-scale commercial lab to be *open to the public*. The lab is scheduled to be completed in 2002.

The Turnkey Solution

Another approach vendors have taken to eliminate interoperability problems is the turnkey SAN. McData's FabricPaks [6] is an example of this approach.

A typical McData FabricPak consists of the McData ED-5000 Fibre Channel Director, JNI host bus adapter, EMC or Hitachi data arrays, Chaparral or Crossroads bridges, and tape libraries from a variety of vendors, including ADIC, ATL, StorageTek, and Exabyte. Recently, McData has expanded on this core concept by adding services and applications such as NetBackup 3.2 from Veritas. The company also plans to add database and enterprise resource planning configurations.

By investing heavily in interoperability labs, coming together to develop SAN standards, and sticking with turnkey solutions that they knew would work, SAN vendors have survived the interoperability SANstorm that at one point threatened to bury them. They have found an oasis of success in the first phase of the SAN life cycle. This means users can purchase pretested SANs without fear of running into major problems.

But the struggle is far from over. Customers still can't mix and match switches and hubs from various vendors. And there are still problems at the storage-management level.

SERVICE PROVIDER OUTSOURCING ....

If you don't feel like becoming a SAN do-it-yourselfer, you can opt for a relatively new alternative—outsourcing your SAN to an SSP. The SSP handles the whole shooting match, from design and installation to management. Working with this business model, customers are freed from huge capital investments that a modern storage infrastructure requires and the difficult task of recruiting qualified personnel to run the storage facility. End-user customers are going to absolutely flock to SSPs because building a SAN, building an enterprise-class storage network for an internal IT shop, is a huge undertaking, which most companies do not have the skill sets to tackle.

StorageNetworks in Waltham, Massachusetts, is an SSP. The company has a Virtual Private Network (VPN) called the Global Data Storage Network, which has more than 200 terabytes of storage, most of which has been implemented as a SAN. The SANs consist of storage arrays with fabric switches connected to 28 points-of-presence (POP) throughout the United States and in London. Each of the POPs has its own data center and is interconnected. The network is monitored from a network operations center in Waltham.

In building its SANs, StorageNetworks tries to remain vendor neutral, using equipment from several vendors, including EMC, Finisar, Nortel Networks, Brocade, and StorageTek on the hardware side, and Legato and Veritas on the software side. StorageNetworks maintains its own interoperability lab where it qualifies these components, and then the SAN is deployed by the company's own personnel.

The company's Global Data Storage Network permits customers to obtain an unlimited amount of storage, replicate data, and back up and restore data from the network rather than from their own data center. The services are delivered in the form of protection, availability, continuity, and scalability (PACS), which are turnkey service packages. The PACS fall into three categories: DataPACS for primary data storage; the BackPACS for backup and restore; and SafePACS for data replication.

TechTarget.com, a Web start-up in Dedham, Massachusetts, considered installing its own storage, but decided to outsource that function to StorageNetworks. They decided to outsource for two reasons: First, they determined that StorageNetworks could handle the job better and faster. Second, while managing a storage farm is important, it's not anything that's going to add to their market cap, so they decided to outsource it.

Now, let's look at why the modern enterprise is a mixture of platforms and computer systems of various capabilities with a range of specific functions. New servers are added routinely to departmental, back-office, and enterprise-wide locations. This internal *web* of systems demands sharing of material between these servers, and at speeds never before possible.

MULTIPLE COMPUTER PLATFORMS HIGH-SPEED DATA SHARING ....

The day of a single site being controlled by a single platform architecture is long since gone. Now it is routine to have high-end UNIX systems mixed into the same network as specific-function Microsoft Windows NT servers, along with an expectation that these two platforms, and others, can seamlessly integrate each other's data. Once upon a time, services such as FTP and occasional email messages were considered *normal* interconnection technologies. Today, the expectation is for direct file system-level interaction that completely masks which server is providing the data—and even masks which type of server.

Applications have matured to embrace such cross-platform capabilities. For example, opening a PhotoShop document in a shared repository on a UNIX system and changing it on a Windows NT system is now possible, even though the basic machine architectures could be the reverse-end. Text documents, pictures, movies, audio files, and many other media formats have matured to a level of heterogeneity. The challenge now is to provide such transparent sharing services at the high-speed user's demand.

Deficiency of LAN Solutions

Perhaps the most popular idea for cross-platform, server-to-server sharing is to introduce gigabit-type technology between the servers and run a protocol-rich layer on top. Many players in the industry are adopting gigabit Ethernet running TCP/IP between systems. It offers all the value of Ethernet/IP communication; namely, superb application history, cross-platform capability, transparent mounts (for example, SMB/Internet File System (CIFS)/Samba, or NFS), and a range of tools. There is, however, a very fundamental problem with TCP/IP: performance. While the technology is sufficient for today's 10BaseT and 100BaseT applications, the protocol processing overhead makes realizing speeds above 100BaseT nearly impossible. Most gigabit installations, especially on a Windows NT platform, run at a small fraction of their technical bandwidth. Worse still, when achieving high throughput, the protocol processing swamps the processors at both endpoints, rendering serious challenges for the remaining server tasks.

Note

The biggest difference between LAN protocols and storage protocols in general is that storage protocols are executed mostly in hardware as opposed to software execution of LAN protocols. Hardware execution gives magnitudes of improvements over software execution.

It is often assumed that each server is required to talk to other servers, especially if the goal is to retrieve data owned by the other server. If it turns out that the primary goal is to share the data between heterogeneous servers, a more simplistic approach is to wire each server directly to the storage elements.

The SAN Revolution

A SAN typically conjures a picture of several RAIDs or other storage systems knitted together with a new wiring technology. While this certainly is a SAN, this type of network becomes far more valuable once there are more computers attached to it. The common view of attaching multiple computers to a SAN, unfortunately, is for the purpose of partitioning, or amortizing central storage costs over several servers, with each logical partition dedicated to particular servers.

More and more, storage-purchase decisions are being made separately from server-purchase decisions. This is largely because of enormous storage requirements and expected growth per server. While it may have been acceptable to have 2 to 4 gigabytes of server storage non-RAIDed in the past, servers now routinely control 50 to 100 gigabytes, and IT managers demand more reliability for their data. RAID systems can be expensive; thus, it is a welcome efficiency to have multiple servers amortize the cost of a higher-end RAID. This is *partitioning* and perhaps the first exposure to a SAN in a typical server room. Partitioning is indeed useful, but what if the servers could actually reach out and address any part of the storage pool regardless of who or what the primary server is or what type of platform is employed?

True SAN-Based Data Sharing

There is a strong desire to *share* the storage data among the connecting servers. If possible, this would allow the scaling of servers to unprecedented levels and the off-loading of the pedestrian duties of backup and off site mirroring on the primary LAN. Servers aside, workstations could also be directly connected to the SAN fabric and have LAN-like sharing at SAN speeds—an invaluable capability for the insatiably bandwidth-hungry worlds of movie making and graphics processing.

Physically wiring a SAN with multiple computers and a pool of storage technically allows the computers to touch any and all data. However, the hard mounting of volumes by multiple servers leads to instant trouble. Computer operating systems were never designed to allow the direct, unmanaged mounting of a volume by multiple servers. Allocation of new storage extents, cache coherency among systems, and a range of other issues immediately arise. A single *bit* out of place on a storage system can result in a payroll database blending into the corporate logo. In short, it will not work.

Yet, the power of directly connecting servers to storage is too enormous to overlook. Each server would literally have full-bandwidth access to any storage element at hundreds of megabytes per second and would not be encumbering any other server to deliver that data, unlike traditional protocol-based serving. In the rapidly growing world of enterprise data, such value cannot be ignored.

There have been numerous approaches and attempts to solve the *operating system challenge* introduced by SANs. Some early approaches were similar to partitioning, but allowed multiple machines to mount some volumes in a read-only fashion, thus severely limiting the overall utility of the SAN. More typically, software vendors would attempt to create a new file system to handle the complexities of multiple machines. While some were moderately successful, they were always homogeneous in nature, not cross-platform.

Attempts at true cross-platform global file systems have been lackluster and have left managers leery with regard to stability. A new file-system type is nothing to be taken lightly in the Information Age; it takes about 10 years for a file system with a valid track record to gain acceptance. Add to that the challenge of connecting various types of operating systems and platforms, as well as attaining data integrity. To date, there are no successful cross-platform global file-system solutions in the marketplace. All attempts have performed poorly and are extremely risky with regard to data stability.

The Future Is Sharing

SAN technology is valuable on numerous fronts. The initial desire to exploit SANs for centralized administration, the amortization of external storage, and off-load of backup and mirroring needs from LANs, is well recognized. SAN-aware equipment is being sold in ever-increasing numbers as a follow-on to existing storage interface technologies, such as SCSI. Back-office and server rooms are now routinely equipped with SAN-ready servers and storage. There is a natural desire to wire together multiple servers and storage elements. The real value is in the ability to share data between elements at will, at high speed, and without compromise.

Now, let's look at why the storage market is experiencing significant growth. From 1998 through 2001, the disk storage systems market increased at a healthy 11.6% compound annual growth rate (CAGR). The key driver of this growth was the deployment of large database applications, enterprise data warehouses, and data marts. New data-intensive applications, such as the Internet and e-business, will drive the market to triple-digit growth. Internet and e-business applications often grow much faster than legacy applications and have caused many companies to grow to multiterabyte installations within months.

INDIRECT CHANNEL OPPORTUNITY ....

Over the last four years, the indirect channel has been the primary beneficiary of storage market growth with revenue through the indirect channel increasing at 42.6% CAGR. This represents $10.5 billion in additional revenue through the indirect channel. Over the same period, the direct channel increased revenue only $4 billion or 4.9% compounded annually. With the storage market forecast to grow more than 43% from 2001 through 2006, combined with the increasingly important role of the indirect channel, the opportunity for the indirect channel is substantial.

The Changing Role of the Channel

Customers demand more sophisticated solutions, such as SANs, that require a more consultative sales model and a better understanding of the customers' applications and business needs. These solutions require more than simple system configuration, and, because of its close customer relationships, the indirect channel is well positioned to deliver these solutions.

Although the indirect channel has only begun to see the benefits of SAN growth, the long-term growth opportunity for this channel is significant. This change comes at an ideal time. Research from IDC [7] shows that the indirect channel's revenue from other technology areas, such as servers, will grow at a slower rate. The server-centric channel will be the primary beneficiary of the growth in indirect sales of storage because the channel that delivers server solutions is more data-focused than the channel that delivers communications solutions.

Large customers increasingly make storage decisions independent of server decisions. As this trend continues to penetrate the base of large customers, it will spread to small and mid-tier accounts. The indirect channel is well positioned to take advantage of this trend because customers view the indirect channel as more objective and more supplier-neutral. This neutrality allows the channel to recommend the best solutions for a customer's application.

Note

Customer perception is that the indirect channel is more objective when recommending storage solutions best suited for the customer's applications.

From the perspective of a server supplier, the storage market can be divided into two segments: the captive storage market and the noncaptive storage market. In the captive market, the server and storage solutions are of the same brand. In the noncaptive market, the server and storage solutions are of different brands. As storage and server decisions become more independent, storage suppliers will need to focus both on protecting the captive base to maintain market share and expanding into the non-captive base to grow market share.

Note

While the direct channel within the storage market increased a modest 4.9% CAGR from 1997 to 2001, the indirect channel experienced a robust 42.6% increase.

Storage divisions of server suppliers seek to grow their storage business independent of their server business. These suppliers realize the importance of the indirect channel in capturing noncaptive storage opportunities. The direct sales force of server suppliers is less successful in selling noncaptive storage than independent, third-party channel partners.

Note

SAN solutions will require close customer relationships, which the indirect channel is well positioned to deliver.

Drivers of Storage Market Growth

Historically, customers viewed data from a single-application perspective. Thus data was important only if the application it supported was critical. Furthermore, data was only valuable as long as that single application still needed the data. If the application was properly managed, the data was deleted soon after the application's requirement for the data was complete. Typical data retention periods were measured in days, weeks, or months, except in the instance of specific regulatory requirements. Only the smallest possible subset of the total available data was retained. Customers that view data this way place their emphasis on storage cost, data protection, and storage management. They also view storage primarily as an expense.

Increasingly, however, companies view data separate from any single application and more as a strategic corporate asset that should be leveraged. Now, the emphasis shifts from protection and management to providing information access, and from storing data to transformation of raw data into actionable information. Key components of this data-access model include network connectivity, data replication, data transformation, and rapid data delivery. With this model comes the desire to keep more atomic-level data for a longer period of time. This data can be used as input for high-value applications, such as data mining and data marts that allow companies to spot new opportunities and react quickly to new trends. Data marts and data analysis tools are key components of an e-business strategy because they allow suppliers to recommend products based on the previous buying behavior of either the customer or the profiles of similar customers. Therefore, e-businesses have significantly greater needs for storage capacity and storage system performance. Fortunately for companies, the market has responded.

> **Note**
>
> **Increasingly, corporations view data as a strategic asset, rather than an application-specific requirement. Key components in this emerging data-access model include network connectivity, data replication and transformation, and rapid data delivery.**

Identifying and Creating Opportunities in the SAN Market

The key to success in the SAN market is identifying the customers that will benefit from its solutions today. Certain characteristic user environments will immediately benefit from a SAN. Any e-business is dependent on the customer's ability to store and process data. The data is the heart of e-business solutions, all of which require rapid and reliable access to large amounts of storage. SAN solutions provide the framework and the speed to build these large complex systems.

SANs, an evolving technology, are generally considered new to the market. The SAN concept is more likely to be well received by early technology adopters, rather than the companies that take a wait-and-see approach to IT investments. With these customers, it is important to stress that SANs can be built in phases and that each phase offers value. Over time, these solutions will evolve into a more robust SAN according to the customers' time schedule. SANs are most effective for certain types of applications and, in fact, initially most SAN implementations will be installed to address a specific operational or business requirement, as noted previously.

Companies involved in transaction-based applications, such as e-commerce, customer service, or even financial applications, are good candidates for a SAN. These companies require quick access to data, and the transaction volume is often unpredictable. The SAN provides both high-speed interconnect and scalable connectivity that allows these companies to respond quickly to changing requirements. Customers that require 24 × 7 availability may benefit from a SAN solution. It is not surprising that SANs frequently support UNIX and mainframe operating systems. These operating systems offer the reliability required for 24 × 7 availability. The need for a SAN is based on the workload, not the operating system, however, and with the increasing use of NT for enterprise applications, SANs will ultimately be found supporting many Windows NT applications.

Note
─────

SAN technology customers will probably be early technology adopters and companies involved in transaction-based applications, such as e-commerce, customer service, and financial applications. Customers requiring 24×7 availability are also strong candidates for a SAN solution.

Storage Suppliers Respond to Growing Customer Demand

Over the years, suppliers have delivered higher disk capacities and better performance in traditional server-attached storage systems. Customers can meet their growing capacity demands at an affordable price because of rapidly declining disk prices. However, these solutions typically fail to adequately address the information management and data-delivery requirements for this growing mountain of data. Thus, more users are demanding the next generation of storage solutions, SANs. SANs are not new, but their application of Storage Area Networks to heterogeneous operating environments, including open systems (UNIX and Windows NT), is new.

Indirect Channel A Critical Component of SAN Solutions

SANs bring with them not only tremendous market potential but exceptional opportunities for the indirect channel. Although most major suppliers have announced SAN strategies and can ship SAN-enabled products today, many are constrained by the lack of resources to design and implement the customer's unique SAN solutions. In order to maximize the market share, vendors must have a comprehensive coverage model. In most situations, indirect partners provide the direct customer relationships required for market dominance. Recognizing this, many SAN component suppliers rely solely on indirect partners for sales.

SANs are to storage what LANs and WANs were to networking. Both of these markets remain significant opportunities for the indirect channel. SANs are an ideal fit for the indirect channel. As network-enabled storage solutions, each SAN requires some degree of uniqueness. For the foreseeable future, these solutions will require both consulting and face-to-face selling. Unlike low-end, server-attached storage, these technologies are not likely in the near term to become commodities and fall prey to direct-over-the-Internet sales.

Timing Is Critical

The time is now for the indirect channel to aggressively develop a competency in SANs. Those who hesitate are likely to lose, a sentiment that is echoing through the channel. While SANs provide a lot of value add for the channel, they also provide a built-in return. SANs are an evolving technology with market demand and increased opportunity for adding value. From an enterprise storage perspective, storage-focused partners will have to be in this business or will find themselves at a decided disadvantage as resellers.

Note

Although component suppliers have SAN products, most rely on indirect channel partners for sales. This presents a tremendous opening for the indirect channel in the rapidly emerging SAN market.

Customers seek knowledgeable advice, and the size of the opportunity is increasing significantly. Resellers that choose not to develop SAN competency should form partnerships with others that have. Those that fail to either develop or partner for SAN competency are inviting competitors into their accounts.

A growing number of channel members are developing SAN expertise. Early predictions were that these would be partners with a networking background, but time has shown that it is in fact the server and storage, or data experts that are making the transition.

Sharing Information

Today customers are challenged with sharing information. With single-server storage, only users of that server can easily access the information on that server. To alleviate this situation, many customers use consolidated enterprise storage for easier sharing of data. Many of these solutions are limited because they support a single operating system, and all are limited by the number of servers they can simultaneously support.

SANs virtually eliminate the limitation on connectivity by utilizing a switch and are rapidly evolving to eliminate limitations on heterogeneous operating system support. Currently, most SAN implementations support multiple servers but only a single operating system. However, an increasing number of SANs can support multiple operating systems and a variety of storage products, both disk and tape (see Figure 4.1) [7].

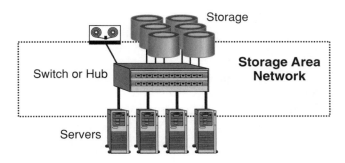

Figure 4.1
Storage Area Network.

Two components, storage systems and a logically isolated network, make up SANs. The storage systems may include both disk and tape as well as SAN-management software, and they must be SAN-capable. The network includes adapters, wiring, bridges, hubs, switches, and directors. Adapters attach servers and peripherals to the wiring in the network; bridges convert from one protocol to another (typically SCSI to Fibre Channel); and hubs, switches, and directors provide the central connection point and routing capability (much like a LAN hub or switch).

The SAN market is a subset of the overall storage market. To fully understand how and where SANs fit, it is important to look at the market as a whole. Approximately 30% of disk storage sold is internal to a server. Therefore, anyone selling servers is in the storage business. About half of the disk storage market is external storage connected to a single server. The remaining 20% of the storage market is capable of simultaneously supporting multiple servers and is often referred to as enterprise storage. Little or no growth is expected in the market for internal storage and single-server solutions through 2005. Virtually all of the growth will come from networked storage solutions that support the storage requirements for multiple servers.

> **Note**
>
> **Little or no growth is expected for the internal storage or single-server solutions through 2005. However, networked storage solutions are expected to ramp aggressively.**

SANs Are Not a New Technology

Although industry talk of SANs has only recently emerged, SANs are not a new technology. They have existed for many years as a solution, but were not labeled SANs. Today, they are found predominantly in mainframe environments supported by suppliers such as IBM, Hitachi Data Systems, and Amdahl.

Note

Today, SANs are found today primarily in mainframe environments. However, they are now expanding into the open systems market.

IBM was among the companies that delivered first-generation SANs with its ESCON director providing the switching capability. ESCON directors, ESCON converters (the mainframe equivalent of a bridge), ESCON channels (the mainframe equivalent of a Fibre-Channel adapter), and ESCON cabling is still prevalent today. Today, the vast majority of mainframe disk and tape is deployed in a SAN. And because it has entered the mainframe market, the indirect channel has likely sold and installed many SANs, as well.

Expanding SANs into Open Systems

Recently, SANs supporting open systems, such as UNIX, Windows NT, and NetWare, have entered the market. Some are robust SANs that support multiple operating systems and servers, and provide highly scaleable switching through Fibre-Channel directors; but, to date, most implementations are for a single-server brand and single OS.

Although some suppliers may claim that single-OS, single-server SANs are not true SANs because they lack multioperating system support, the true beauty of a SAN installation is that it can be built over time. A SAN is best thought of as a series of building blocks, as shown in Figure 4.2 [8].

SAN Building Blocks

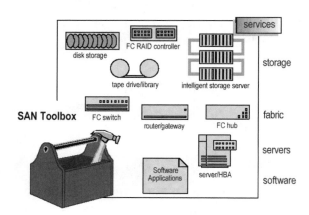

Figure 4.2
SAN component toolkit.

Note

SAN development can occur in phases, with each level of completion having value to the customer.

A SAN can be delivered and implemented in one step, but it does not have to be. Rather it can be constructed over time. Most customers move slowly and build up to a more robust SAN solution. Fortunately for customers, each phase of implementation provides a SAN solution of its own. Customers begin receiving benefits immediately without waiting for future technology that will leverage the current investment. Even at the lowest level, implementing point-to-point Fibre-Channel connections may provide performance benefits, particularly over older SCSI and SCSI2 technologies. Many customers already have components that are supported in a SAN. Without having to be replaced, the components become building blocks that can be combined to create a SAN.

Note

Most customers build in steps toward a robust SAN solution. Additionally, most potential customers are SAN-ready, with installed components that can be utilized to create a SAN environment.

This building block approach allows both suppliers and business partners to grow their capabilities over time. While the channel is building its expertise, they can follow a road map in which the investments are made over time and as customer demand requires. Another advantage exists for those that have already begun to invest in SANs—they have found success in the additional consulting and services opportunity. Since most SANs are built over time, someone has to stay involved and help put the pieces together. Many times, these components come from different vendors or various divisions within one company. The channel allows for one-stop shopping and a single point of contact.

Translating SANs into Opportunity for Partners

This is a tremendous opportunity for indirect channels, not only because of the consulting and service involved with a SAN, but because it provides an opportunity to continually revisit and work with the customer to develop a solution that may in fact take months or years to fully implement. Having the opportunity to schedule time with the customer on an ongoing basis ensures account control. Many indirect partners have already learned the annuity value of storage and schedule regular customer meetings to increase disk sales.

Note

Since SANs are a long-term, often revisited investment, they represent a significant consulting and service opportunity for the indirect channel. Many partners have already learned the annuity value of storage.

SANs go beyond just repeat sales, however, by allowing the indirect partner to enhance his position as a trusted advisor. SANs provide a great deal of service opportunity. Nobody understands how to set a SAN up so there is service opportunity just to explain it, which translates to upfront consulting revenue. Following that, there is revenue for the installation, and then in skills transfer. As many suppliers and partners move toward an increased service model, SANs provide a very viable foundation for this transition.

The market has seen many indirect partners build extremely successful and viable businesses with LANs and WANs. The same will be true of SANs. The hardware and installation are only the tip of the iceberg. With a SAN, there is connectivity services, then switching equipment, then fiber, and then software. Taking this one step at a time, the user is able to grow his or her SAN expertise and leverage it across a variety of individual customers as the situation dictates.

Business Value of SAN

One of the key challenges in selling a SAN, helping customers understand what a SAN can do for their business, is also an opportunity. SANs have many additional benefits for the end-user. They offer a viable method for delivering highly available, high-performance storage for the full complement of servers in an enterprise. SANs provide a flexible, scalable infrastructure that can support rapid unplanned growth. This is especially true for emerging Internet businesses, where exponential growth is rampant, as well as for more established businesses, as a result of frequent mergers and acquisitions. However, while customers implement SANs to support growth, companies are challenged to use their technical staff more efficiently. The high demand for skilled technical staff has resulted in a skills shortage, particularly in the high growth areas of UNIX and NT. In fact, this was exactly the driver for one SAN implementation at a large insurance company in the Midwest. By implementing a SAN, the customer was able to manage the storage from a single location and balance storage requirements across multiple systems. This centralized management approach reduced the requirements for additional staff at multiple sites.

Note

SANs represent a strong business value, allowing customers to manage storage from single location and balance storage requirements across multiple systems.

The move to a 24 × 7 operating environment has created another driver for SANs. Continuous storage availability is an absolute must for the new generation of 24 × 7 applications. Companies frequently use the Web as a business tool to expand the trading day and global reach, but the cost of becoming Web-enabled is that downtime, whether planned or unplanned, costs business. Many SAN-based utilities reduce downtime and significantly improve application recovery time.

What Will Drive SAN Sales?

There are several factors that will drive initial SAN sales: one is operational, the other is application-oriented. On the operational side, server and storage consolidation will drive SANs because today's point-to-point storage-server solutions are limited in terms of server connectivity.

> **Note**
>
> **Many factors will drive SAN growth. Initially, server and storage consolidation will increase SAN opportunities, while the escalating demand for both additional data and rapid data access will sustain the long-term growth prospects of the technology.**

The increasing demand for additional data is also driving the need for SANs. Customers seeking high growth of data volumes, as can be found in the e-world, has been a key identifier of a SAN prospect.

A SAN provides the infrastructure to reduce the negative impact on application servers and networks that results from doing LAN-based backups. This LAN-free (or serverless) backup is important to users that back up data frequently or have high transaction activity throughout a day and cannot afford to impact the performance of the application server. Backups do not slow down LAN performance because the SAN puts the storage on its own network.

> **Note**
>
> **A SAN provides the infrastructure to reduce the negative impact on application servers and networks that results from doing LAN-based backups. Furthermore, LAN-free backup still uses servers to move data across the SAN. Serverless backup uses equipment in the SAN infrastructure to move data in the SAN, so that the servers can continue to serve applications instead of having to spend processing cycles for backups. The state of the art today is LAN-free backup. All of the SAN vendors are working on serverless backup and need more time to take this operation to maturity.**

SANs can be implemented over a fiber network, providing the foundation for data replication over distances. Customers value this feature because it provides a higher degree of disaster tolerance and another level of security to their data. Having data replicated between sites also ensures faster recovery in the event that one site fails.

The enhanced distance capabilities of fiber-optic cabling also provide benefits to companies that are experiencing high growth and physical space constraints. One SAN user indicated that the rapid deployment of additional servers had caused a space limitation, yet storage requirements dictated a need for additional storage. Through the implementation of a SAN, this customer was able to locate the storage on a separate floor from the servers using fiber connections and switches, thereby relieving the physical space concern.

While data replication drives some customers to SANs, the ability to reduce the amount of data replication drives others. One SAN user indicated that the main driver for implementing a SAN was the ability to do true data sharing. They were tired of replicating the data 17 times. They want everyone to be able to access the data at the same time, but were uneasy with the idea of all their applications going after the same data simultaneously. They were sick of making tons of copies and moving the data from one place to another, so the SAN made a lot of sense for them.

Overcoming Users' Concerns about SANs

SANs are new to many customers and are therefore causing some hesitation to be the first to implement. Early SAN implementations can be kept simple and do not have to be a disruptive installation. In fact, it is likely that many customers already have some form of SAN in their data center, most likely found in their IBM and compatible mainframe environments. However, in the UNIX and NT markets where SANs are less broadly adopted, some segments and components exist that can be easily adapted to a SAN. Some have SAN-ready storage systems in place already, meaning that the storage already supports Fibre Channel connectivity and the manufacturer has tested the storage system in a SAN configuration.

Customers can start with a departmental solution before deploying a SAN across the enterprise. Others may simply purchase SAN-ready components that later can be connected in a SAN, thereby protecting the customer's investment. Once the value of a SAN is clearly established, it can be expanded across multiple departments, building to an enterprise-wide installation.

Note

To ease customer apprehension over a SAN investment, the network can be developed over time and built up on the customer's request. To this end, the greatest customer acceptance of SANs has been in initially focusing on departmental or small group requirements for SAN implementation.

What SANs Mean to the Channel: Road Map for Exploiting SAN Opportunities

SANs provide the channel with an opportunity to work directly with the end-user to customize and design a SAN strategy. Partners can participate in the audit, design, and implementation of the customer's storage strategies, moving beyond the traditional application, server, or hardware solution provider. In fact, Champion Computer [9] built an entire business around SANs. Customers are becoming aware of the importance of storage and are looking for trusted neutral advisors—a key opportunity for the indirect channel.

With every server and independent storage supplier coming to market with a SAN solution, it is critical for users to have someone to guide them through this barrage of new products. Partners that help them navigate to an appropriate solution are well positioned to increase customer loyalty and gain entrance to new accounts as well.

Building Up to SAN

Storage Area Networks begin with hardware and services and end with applications. It's not a one shot deal, and it's more than just fulfillment. The channel should begin by building or partnering for expertise in storage audits, SAN design, SAN implementation, and SAN management as well as SAN-enabled storage applications, such as LAN-free backup and data replication. These are the SAN opportunities that exist today.

Note

SANs begin with hardware and services and end with applications. It's not a one shot deal.

Initially, it is not necessary for the channel to possess all of the knowledge or absorb all the cost associated with building SAN expertise. The channel should begin by talking to their customers about SANs and work with a supplier that is willing and has the capacity to augment and support the channel, allowing the channel to match its investment with the opportunity.

Choosing a SAN Supplier

Most SAN suppliers are diving into the indirect channel to capture mindshare and market share. This situation allows the indirect channel to be very selective in choosing its suppliers. Indirect partners should seek suppliers that will complement and not compete with them.

A strong SAN supplier will provide the foundation and the support for a successful SAN implementation. It will value the channel's customer relationships and allow the partner to continue these relationships through value-added services and consulting, not limit the relationships to fulfillment. The best SAN suppliers will work with the indirect partners as a team, not a competitor. They will seek partnerships that allow each to leverage the other in a flexible manner, acknowledging that the channel's success is not their loss but rather their gain. In other words, they will seek a partnership based on the desire for mutual success, one that supports the channel when and where it is necessary, allowing the channel partner to grow its expertise over time, and rely on the supplier as it grows. True SAN partners will also invest in creating a healthy noncaptive market for its channel partners.

SAN solutions contain many components. In choosing a SAN supplier, channel partners should choose a supplier with as many of the pieces as possible. These components include SAN software; SAN-ready disk and tape storage; networking products; professional services; and, a significant investment in SAN interoperability testing. This allows the channel a broader range of internal resources and expertise, an additional pool of potential complementary partners, and some insulation from the rampant acquisitions that may cause some of the third-party products within a SAN to be unavailable after such an acquisition.

Note

Channel partners should choose a supplier with a broad range of SAN components including SAN software; SAN-ready disk and tape storage; networking products; professional services; and a supplier that has made a significant investment in SAN interoperability testing.

The channel should also look to suppliers who will enable complementary partner engagements. Partners will develop expertise in a specific application. Few partners will have expertise in all areas. Therefore it is wise to work with a vendor who has both the breadth of products required for a SAN as well as a broad range of channel partners that will facilitate the joint-engagement model.

IBM Business Partners: Opportunities in Storage Area Networks—The Sum is Greater than the Whole

IBM owns the majority of the components required for a complete SAN implementation. IBM offers components such as disks, and RAID controllers, complete disk storage systems, tape drives, tape automation and storage management, network management, and SAN management software sold under the Tivoli brand name. IBM also brings a strong global presence and the ability to deliver all of the services and certification necessary for a successful SAN implementation.

Note

IBM has rapidly developed its SAN business partnering relationships.

The IBM SAN solution also includes options for third-party products, if the customer or partner prefers. Its interoperability facility in Gaithersburg, Maryland, is designed for just this reason. Customers are welcome to visit the site where IBM maintains an extensive lab to test various suppliers' parts in a true SAN environment. There are no penalties for incorporating third-party products. From a partnering perspective, IBM has come a long way in a very short amount of time. Each one of the IBM customers found business partner involvement, something that would not have been found just a short time ago. The company has been recognized by the industry as a leader in its channel programs. The recent enhancements to its PartnerWorld program signal a sincere interest in a long-term relationship with the indirect channel for all products.

Note

IBM is in position to be a long-term leader in the SAN market.

IBM has made some strategic changes in its internal organization, including the indirect partners in all accounts, leveraging their value add. The once direct, true-blue IBM has recognized the value of the indirect channel, and this has filtered across all divisions. IBM services will subcontract for the channel partners and has been known to subcontract to the channel or engage in whatever model is most suitable for the partner. Investments are being made in field resources to drive storage solutions for the indirect channel, with the company taking a much more proactive partnering role than it had in the past. In fact, the company has dedicated field resources specifically to the SAN initiative for the indirect channel.

But, winning in the market and with the channel will not be without challenges. IBM is not alone in its ability to provide scalable, reliable, and interoperable storage products. It is not the only vendor with an extensive interoperability storage lab, and it is not the only supplier with a keen eye on the indirect channel. The company will have to continue to invest in its products and services, as well as maintain a balance between its various direct sales programs and the channel partners, always keeping this balance (across all product and service offerings) to ensure that it does not sacrifice one for another. IBM will face competition on two fronts: competition with product offerings and competition for its channel.

As SANs storm into the market, partners should closely examine what suppliers bring to the table, beyond just the hardware or the software components. IBM's ability to supply and test an entire solution combined with a strong commitment to indirect channels is a recipe for success. In the case of IBM, the sum is truly greater than the parts. The growth projections for the storage market overall are significant. This rare and strategic opportunity for indirect partners is not likely to be replicated any time soon. With points of entry from many angles, the race to solution will soon heat up. Business partners from a variety of areas of expertise are poised to take advantage of the opportunity. Only those that start down the path to delivering fully functional SANs will be the beneficiaries. The time to act is now.

Note

IBM's ability to supply, test, and support an entire SAN solution, combined with a strong commitment to indirect channels, is a successful strategy.

So, driven by the explosive growth of data-intensive applications and businesses' escalating reliance on information as a competitive differentiator, storage is rapidly becoming a central component of corporate technology strategies. The new storagecentric infrastructure that companies envision includes an open, modular, scalable storage network not tied to any one server or application. The objective is a single, massive data repository accessible by any person, application or system across the entire organization. Emerging technologies such as NAS and the SAN promise both a single source of data and improved performance and availability.

Although this concept of centralized storage is simple, getting there today is not easy. While industry organizations contend with standards issues and leading vendors bring forth first-generation SAN offerings, companies face the dual challenge of managing their current storage resources and choosing the approach to networked storage that best meets their requirements. IBM has the unbiased expertise and broad scope of design, planning, and implementation services to help companies leverage current IT investments and achieve a vendor-neutral, integrated storage solution with an open path to the future.

MULTIVENDOR ENTERPRISE STORAGE AREA NETWORKS END-TO-END SERVICES........................

One of the most significant challenges facing IT executives today is data management. Companies across all industries are launching new business-critical applications (for example, electronic business [e-business], enterprise resource planning, and business intelligence) turning information into a strategic corporate asset. Its value to the organization and the bottom line is often directly related to how easily this information can be shared across the entire enterprise and beyond, including customers, suppliers, and other trusted trading partners.

With information taking center stage as a competitive differentiator, storage has moved from supporting player to a leading role in a company's IT strategy and budget. More than 500 IT managers were recently surveyed as they identified SANs, along with application and transaction servers, as the three most important product areas for their organizations in 2001. In many cases, the storage system (from disk to tape, and the management that goes along with it) becomes a much bigger investment than the server itself. According to the Boston-based consultancy The Yankee Group [10], 95 cents of every hardware dollar spent by companies from now until the year 2002 will be spent on storage.

The immediate tactical issue is how to accommodate the sheer volumes of data produced by new core business applications, new data-intensive technologies such as data warehousing and multimedia, and the commercialization of the Internet. Storage capacity has been doubling annually for several years running—with no end in sight. The San Diego-based National Storage Industry Consortium projects that the amount of data stored on the world's networks will reach 4,000 petabytes (or 4 million terabytes) in 2002.

Steadily increasing disk capacity and declining prices are fueling further growth by enabling projects that require even more vast volumes of data. The money that bought 40 megabytes of storage in 1989 can buy 10 gigabytes today. At these prices, it begins to look reasonable for a broadcast company, for example, to begin digitizing 500,000 hours of video archives. This single application would require 60 million terabytes—60 times more than the sum total of stored data that exists in the world today.

Storage Management Challenges

Capacity alone is only part of the total storage equation. More critical are the storage management requirements to protect business-critical data and make it available to a wider range of users and applications, all while delivering minimum downtime and maximum performance. Yet, managing these vast volumes of data across networks and disparate systems is increasingly difficult and costly.

In today's distributed IT environment, each hardware storage system and storage management software product is tied to an individual server, creating islands of data that are hard to bridge. Data is frequently duplicated from one isolated storage system to another, so it can be accessed from different applications. From a business perspective, this can result in decisions based on inaccurate, out-of-date information. Assembling the *big picture* in a timely fashion is often impossible.

Managing these disparate systems is a labor-intensive process, often requiring more staff. Different user interfaces and limited integration between products mean that storage resources must be configured, monitored, and managed individually and locally—requiring skills that are specific to the products and platforms involved. Flexibility and scalability are limited. The perpetual question that storage managers supporting a dynamic and rapidly changing business must face is, *Do I have enough of the right kind of storage attached to the right server and application?*

Networked Storage: The New Paradigm

Storage is rapidly evolving from a cost center to a strategic IT infrastructure that supports key business goals and increased customer satisfaction by providing *any time, anywhere* access to crucial business data. Enabled by new and emerging technologies, these storagecentric infrastructures go beyond online hard disk systems and offline storage archives to include special storage servers, new storage networks, and the management software to make it all appear as a seamless whole to enterprise applications.

The two key storage innovations aimed at enabling wide-open data sharing are NAS and SANs. Both technologies liberate storage devices from their servers and make data generally available to a variety of users across multiple operating systems. The two technologies also share key advantages over traditional storage architectures:

- Capacity and performance are both scalable, allowing incremental expansion as the needs for greater storage and faster access arise
- Companies can make storage decisions independent of server considerations
- Storage management is removed from the server, freeing up CPU resources for running business applications
- Data duplication can be substantially eliminated
- Data availability is no longer tied to the availability of a single server
- Centralized storage management can simplify administration, reduce long-term operating costs, and allow storage personnel to focus on strategy and planning rather than day-to-day problem solving [8]

Both NAS and SAN are expected to gain a wide following. International Data Corporation [7], projects that expenditures for NAS systems will grow from $900 million in 1998 to $10.5 billion in 2002, while SAN expenditures will increase from $3 billion in 1998 to $11.4 billion by 2002. But here the similarities end.

The key element of a NAS system is a storage *appliance* that manages the flow of data across a LAN or WAN. Directly attached to the network rather than an application server, the NAS device is itself a *thin* server that manages storage operations and an array of disks. Because NAS uses standard LAN/WAN connections and supports multiple communications protocols, it can support data from a wide range of UNIX and Windows NT servers. Gateways can extend availability to mainframe systems.

SANs are separate, centrally managed, high-speed storage networks consisting of multivendor storage systems, storage management software, and network hardware. SANs are based on a *fabric* of Fibre Channel hubs, switches, and gateways connecting storage devices and servers on a many-to-many basis. Application and transaction servers are attached both to the SAN and to a LAN or WAN, providing the link between client systems and single, massive *pool* of enterprise data. SANs can be configured to provide hundreds of servers in many locations with direct access to hundreds of terabytes of shared storage resources. A SAN can also enable direct storage-to-storage connectivity, allowing management activities such as mirroring, backup, and archiving to take place independent of any server. This storagecentric Fibre Channel network architecture provides the additional benefits of:

- Increasing uptime by off-loading backup functions from the server
- Boosting performance by releasing LAN/WAN capacity for users
- Enabling near real-time updates of remote disaster recovery sites
- Supporting advanced multiserver clustering solutions for new levels of availability and business continuity [8].

Implementation Challenges

The good news for IT executives envisioning an open storagecentric infrastructure for their organizations is that they don't have to make an either/or choice today between NAS and SAN solutions. In fact, many companies consider NAS a first-step toward an eventual SAN deployment. Other companies are looking to move ahead quickly with SAN technology to achieve early and sustainable competitive advantage by leveraging their information resources. And, industry-leading vendors are rolling out SAN-ready products with great fanfare.

Although the implications of falling behind (not keeping pace with technology) can be devastating to a business's ability to compete, the impact of a major architecture change can be huge and potentially disruptive. The margin for error is thin, the technology is still largely unproven (standards are not fully ratified and many interoperability issues have yet to be resolved), and the data management is complex.

However, if a company chooses to proceed (from *test the waters* to *full speed ahead*), success will depend in large part on a carefully defined strategy and detailed planning. Listed in the sidebar, "Implementation Strategy and Planning Steps," are the steps required and many of the factors that need to be taken into consideration.

IMPLEMENTATION STRATEGY AND PLANNING STEPS

Assessment and Strategy

1. Inventory and analyze current data and storage environment.
2. Understand business climate and objectives, and their impact on future storage requirements.
3. Define the overall approach for storage utilization and deployment across the enterprise.
4. Define the overall approach for data access design and implementation for the enterprise.
5. Determine a strategy for phasing in new technology and integrating with the existing investments and infrastructure.

Planning and Design

Define the tactical and operational plans for different aspects of storage operations, including:

- Reliability management
- Network availability management
- Fault detection and recovery planning, covering hardware, firmware, and software
- Failure isolation and failure modes management
- Dynamic reallocation of network resources
- Data migration

Design a storage, data, and network solution that supports business goals, addressing:

- Storage system software
- Operating system software

- I/O control system
- Database architecture
- Database administration, redundancy, error recovery, backup, and restoration
- System interoperability
- Storage capacity
- Performance
- Connectivity issues
- Network protocol interfaces
- Physical network infrastructure
- Standards
- Scalability

Implementation and Execution

Develop objectives, time frame, resources, measurements, and reporting for implementation.

- Install and test necessary environmental (temperature, humidity) and/or mechanical (shock, vibration, floor loading) modifications to new or existing IT facilities.
- Install and test power supply and power protection systems.
- Upgrade wiring and cabling infrastructure as required, including generating cabling plans and defining cabling and hardware interconnections.
- Install and test hardware, software, and database systems.
- Migrate data from old infrastructure to new.
- Ensure that all installations meet design goals, comply with standards, and attain performance goals.
- Monitor systems and measure service levels.
- Plan for continuous improvement [8].

A Service-Driven SAN Strategy, from IBM

As a technology marrying storage, servers, and network disciplines, SAN requires an unprecedented level of cross-discipline expertise. In most IT organizations, the skills and the level of expertise required to tackle a SAN project remain in short supply. As

NAS and SAN evolve and eventually enter the mainstream, companies will increasingly look outside the IT department for help in understanding and exploiting storage technology for competitive advantage.

IBM Global Services, one of the world's leading services providers, offers solutions that can transform your current storage hardware into a well-managed, information-driven IT infrastructure. IBM's commitment is to providing open, vendor-neutral solutions that fit a company's technology profile (from conservative to early adopter) and address short- and long-term business objectives.

From early consulting, planning, and design through integration and testing, IBM offers end-to-end services solutions for SAN deployment designed to maximize the benefits of information sharing across the enterprise. Plus, their business and technology consultants understand the key role that a storage infrastructure must play to enable business-critical applications such as enterprise resource planning, e-business, business intelligence, customer relationship management, and supply chain reengineering. Leveraging their extensive experience, knowledge base, and lessons learned in IT planning, design, and implementation, IBM Global Services people can help you:

- Protect your current investments in people skills, hardware, and software.
- Enable the integration of new technologies as they emerge, mature, and become more affordable by deploying a building block infrastructure.
- Apply experience and lessons learned from the mainframe arena, like systems managed storage concepts and switched fabric management, to the open systems environment.
- Support multiplatform interoperability.
- Minimize the risks of unproven technology by providing the *mix 'n match* freedom of choice to deploy what makes most sense for your unique environment [8].

In addition, IBM Global Services will provide the services and education required to support multivendor SAN implementations, allowing companies to manage their technology resources (application servers, storage servers, network hardware, and storage management software) and share information across storage networks regardless of vendor computing systems and software applications.

Finally, with the unprecedented proliferation of high-speed communication services, many people will have high-speed access to virtually unlimited amounts of information in many forms of media. A tremendous amount of research effort is being applied to the problems of how to provide these multimedia services to tens and hundreds of thousands of concurrent users. The I/O problems alone are significant and represent a form of data intensive computing. This part of the chapter attempts to place analytical boundaries on the problems of designing and building a scalable multimedia storage server. The result is a compelling case for NAS as well as a set of equations that can be used to estimate the hardware requirements for such a system.

STORAGE SUBSYSTEMS FOR VIDEO SERVICES.........

Information exists in many forms: text, images, sound, and movies (also referred to as multimedia). Computer systems have reached the capacity and performance levels where it is practical to store and retrieve these kinds of information in digital form. A prime example of this is the World Wide Web (WWW). In the not-to-distant future feature-length movies will be available to the general public on-demand via telephone and/or cable service. Such a service implies very large numbers of concurrent users per provider-node. Emerging disk and network technologies are beginning to reach the point where it is possible to construct cost effective systems to support these endeavors. This part of the chapter focuses on the storage systems necessary to support video server applications and is intended to present some of the basic design considerations and challenges faced in the construction of such systems.

Related Work

There is a great deal of research in both the commercial and academic sectors related to multimedia systems. Most notably, there are a number of groups at the University of California, Berkeley working on many of the storage management related issues. There is also the Multi-Media Research Center at the University of Minnesota Department of Computer Science that is focusing on the wide-area distribution of multimedia in a learning environment. Furthermore, there are many corporate sponsored projects currently under development to build test systems for video server applications.

An important aspect of this research is that it deals with problems associated with the storage and movement of large amounts of time-critical data between storage systems and the end-users. It so happens that these types of systems are also used to process and view results of simulations performed on supercomputers where the amounts of data are so large that existing storage and networking technologies are not adequate to handle such tasks. Therefore, this research directly benefits both the commercial and scientific communities equally well.

Research on high performance storage subsystems is being conducted in the Laboratory for Computational Science and Engineering (LCSE) at the University of Minnesota, Minneapolis, Minnesota, (*www.lcse.umn.edu*). Due to the similarities between scientific visual computing and video server application performance requirements, it seemed appropriate to apply the same techniques used to design and build the scientific storage servers to that of designing and building large scale video servers.

Overview

The video server paradigm was chosen because real-time, multiuser, interactive video has one of the most intense I/O requirements of any data intensive application. First, the quantity of data is enormous as are the number of possible concurrent users. Second, the real-time aspect contributes a degree of complexity by requiring jitter-free delivery of all the data to all the users. Finally, allowing the user to interact with the delivery system causes unpredictable changes in the data flow (pause, rewind, fast-forward, etc.). These three elements define the underlying design criteria.

The basic concept behind a video server is a large digital video repository located within a community that would service many thousands of customers. This service will most likely be available 24 hours a day, 7 days a week to all customers. Therefore, a single installation has the potential of being accessed simultaneously by all customers at any given time. Modeling and forecasting user loads is beyond the scope of this chapter. However, it is necessary to make some assumptions about user loads in order to set the design criteria.

Therefore, the entire design spectrum is presented—including worst-case, average, and best-case scenarios for disk subsystem performance. A worst-case design philosophy is taken that guarantees a minimum level of performance from such a system. For example, in order to support a given number of users, the worst-case performance specifications is assumed for the disk subsystems. The actual performance will most likely be higher, but the important point is that the worst-case scenario represents the lower bound of system performance.

In order to quantify and describe a system, an analytical model is developed that is intended to put the majority of the design parameters into perspective relative to each other (how many users, how many disks, how much memory, etc.). This model is then verified to some extent by empirical studies performed at the LCSE. The equipment available at the LCSE is used principally for visualizing large time-dependent scientific data sets by a single user. It so happens that this same hardware forms the essential components of a video server from a storage systems point of view. The only differences are application and (possibly) configuration issues. Even so, this equipment allows for empirical modeling of a video server on a smaller scale than the ultimate system. Scaling these analytical models up, after empirical modeling, can then proceed with a higher level of confidence.

Overall System Requirements

A video server is basically an intelligent storage system that has the following components (See Figure 4.3) [11]:

- Storage server(s)
- Storage subsystems
- Network(s)
- Software

These systems must have a high degree of reliability and availability as well as being cost effective. It is important to show how each of these components are interrelated so that systems are not over designed with hardware that cannot be effectively utilized or underdesigned causing systems to become stressed due to a weak link in the component chain. However, before such interrelationships can be shown, it is necessary to outline the requirements for each of the components in more detail.

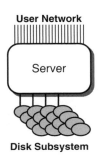

User Network

Server

Disk Subsystem

Figure 4.3
The basic server configuration consists of a server with a disk subsystem connected to one side and the user network connected to the other side. Data flows from the disk subsystem through the server to the user network.

Storage Server Requirements

The storage servers are the computers that mediate data flow between the user network and the storage subsystem. These machines have the following characteristics:

- Large main memories for caching or speed-matching to the user network
- Many I/O channels for streaming data between storage subsystems and memory
- Multiple processors to manage time-critical processing of I/O requests

Issues involving the storage server are:

- Size of main memory

- Number of I/O channels
- Number of processors or processing elements
- The underlying architecture (bus-based interconnect, hyper-cube, etc.) [11]

Storage Subsystem Requirements

The storage subsystems considered in this part of the chapter are entirely disk based. However, the disk interfaces discussed are parallel SCSI and Fibre Channel, with emphasis placed on the latter. Issues involving the storage subsystems are:

- Performance limits of disks, RAIDs
- The kinds of disks that can be used
- Tradeoffs between disks and RAIDs
- Factors that determine the overall disk capacity limits
- Disk interfaces (Parallel SCSI, Fibre Channel, HIPPI, etc.) [11]

User and Storage Area Network Requirements

It should be noted that the networks considered in this part of the chapter pertain primarily to the storage subsystems (otherwise known as SANs) and interserver communication. Analysis of the external *user network* is beyond the scope of this chapter and is mentioned only to the extent that its operational parameters are outlined (it can consume whatever data rate it is fed by the server).

Software Requirements

The software required to manage an information server of this type is vast and complex. It is beyond the scope of this chapter to describe the data base management and scheduling techniques used in such a system. Instead, certain behavioral characteristics are assumed that lead to worst-case scenarios in terms of the frequency of requests and locality of reference. The general behavioral characteristics will be considered for things such as:

- Device Drivers
- Cache management
- Stream scheduling, prediction
- Filesystem and data layout [11]

Configuration Issues

A video server would service communities of varying sizes which implies a wide spectrum of system requirements to handle user loads. These system requirements translate to system configuration issues. These issues are driven by things such as:

- The number of movie titles kept *online* on primary storage
- The number of users that can access the system concurrently
- Physical connectivity
- The level of interactivity (start/stop, pause, reverse, play only, etc.)
- How to maximize the number of users while minimizing costs
- How to deal with advances in technology (system upgradeability)
- Serviceability, reliability, availability [11]

The performance of the system as a whole is determined by the configuration. The configuration of the system is in turn determined by the storage subsystem and server requirements. Therefore, you need to model these systems based on reasonable assumptions about the *operational parameters*. This part of the chapter discusses system configuration issues that arise as a result of varying these parameters and presents example configurations.

The Basic Server Configuration

The basic system configuration can be thought of as a server with a user network and a disk subsystem. The server is a computer that has the ability to move data from the disk subsystem to the user network in a time-dependent manner under the direction of a scheduling program. Figure 4.3 shows many logical user connections into the server. The actual connection into the server could be many individual slow-speed physical connections, one high-speed physical connection with many virtual connections, or some combination of the two. This is an implementation detail of the user network and is, again, beyond the scope of this chapter.

The point of interest lies in the disk subsystem and its connection to the server. However, the first question to address is the real I/O bandwidth of the server. Most computer companies advertise peak I/O bandwidth which can be much higher than the realized I/O bandwidth in an actual system configuration. The real I/O bandwidth must be arrived at empirically under actual system loads in order to be reasonably accurate and believable.

Once the total I/O bandwidth is obtained, it must be divided equally between the user network and the disk subsystem due to conservation of bandwidth. This basically states that the rate at which data flows into a system plus the rate at which the data flows out of the system cannot exceed the total bandwidth of the system. For example, a server with a total real I/O bandwidth of 400 MBps cannot exceed 200 MBps in plus 200 MBps out during the same period of time.

The real bandwidth of a server therefore determines the number of users that can be serviced by the server assuming a constant (or average) data transfer rate required per user. This can be simply stated as [11]:

$$N_{users} = \frac{\text{Total Real I/O Bandwith}}{2 * R_{user}}$$

where R_{user} is the transfer rate required per user.

To put this into perspective, extend the previous example of a server that has a real I/O bandwidth of 400 MBps. The number of users (N_{users}) this server could support is given by [11]:

$$N_{users} = \frac{400 \times 106}{2 \times 200\ 103} = 1000\ users$$

using a standard transfer rate per user (R_{user}) of 200 KBps. It should be noted that examples throughout this part of the chapter make the assumption that the data transfer rate per user (R_{user}) is constant. This also implies that the data transfer rate from the disk subsystem and subsequently the data request size from the disk subsystem is constant as well. Now that the number of users has been estimated purely from bandwidth considerations, it is necessary to determine the number of disks required to support this user load.

The Disk Subsystem

In terms of performance, the disk subsystem must match the user network I/O requirements under a worst-case scenario. This means that each subsequent I/O request to the disk subsystem will incur the maximum latency (seek, rotational delay, etc.) of the disk subsystem. Designing a disk subsystem this way insures that the actual performance of the subsystem will most likely be somewhat better.

Let's begin with the basic component of the disk storage subsystem: the disk drive. The performance of a disk drive has several components of overhead that vary widely depending on the specific manufacturer and model of drive used and whether they are used individually or in disk arrays. For simplicity let's examine the use of individual disk drives. Furthermore, the time it takes to transfer the data from the disk to the server is critical and depends on two factors: the amount of data requested per transfer (request size) and the data transfer rate from the disk.

The request size is the most obvious. The more data requested, the longer it will take to transfer at a given data transfer rate. But the data transfer rate is more complicated because it is not a fixed value. Rather it depends on several factors including:

- The location of the data on the disk (inner versus outer cylinders)
- On-drive data caching
- The speed of the host interface (slow SCSI, fast SCSI, fast and wide SCSI, HiPPI, Fibre Channel, etc.) [11]

The reason the data transfer rate varies according to the location of the data on the disk is a result of Zoned-Bit-Recording (ZBR). This is a common technique whereby more data is placed on the outer tracks than the inner tracks while the disk maintains a constant angular velocity. The net result of ZBR is the data transfer rate from the outer tracks is significantly higher than from the inner tracks. For the purposes of this analysis, the inner-track (slowest) transfer rate will be used to determine the time to transfer the data.

For all scenarios, on-drive data caching is simply assumed to be off. It is assumed that there is zero time between any two successive requests to a disk and that successive requests are at opposite ends of the disk. Hence the disk cannot perform any read-ahead operations into the cache because there is no locality of reference in the request stream. It is also not permissible to let the disk drive reorder the request stream. Even in the unlikely event there is some locality of reference within the request stream, because the request stream is time critical, it must be performed in the order given. The task of managing the request stream is the responsibility of the scheduling process in the server and is beyond the scope of this chapter.

Finally, another less frequent source of overhead is bad sector management. Bad sectors do not occur on every access, but they will occur periodically. The periodicity of hitting a bad sector is purely random from disk to disk and is difficult to generalize. However, the techniques for managing bad sectors are such that the effect of bad sectors is usually one to two orders of magnitude smaller than the rotational latency or seek time. Therefore, it is reasonably safe to ignore this effect for the purposes of estimating configuration parameters.

The overhead associated with traversing the device driver(s) software as well as the host-bus adapters (hardware and firmware) are also considered to be part of the disk subsystem even though they are not on the disk itself. This is principally a function of the server rather than the disk, but must be included in the overall time it takes to process an I/O request. For simplicity, it is safe to assume a fixed amount of time for the operating system and the host-bus adapter to process a request since there are no moving parts in either the server or host-bus adapters. These times are usually small, but can become a significant percentage of the total time it takes to process an I/O request particularly when the request size is small. To summarize the disk subsystem, the time it takes to process an I/O request can be characterized as follows [11]:

$$T_{request} = T_{os} + T_{cmd} + T_{seek} + T_{rot} + T_{xfer}$$

where:

- T_{os} is the time it takes the operating system to process a request.
- T_{cmd} is the time it takes the disk to process the command to execute (read data).
- T_{seek} is the time it takes the disk to seek from one end to the other.
- T_{rot} is the time to complete one rotation of the disk.
- T_{xfer} is the time it takes to transfer the requested number of bytes using the inner track transfer rate.
- $T_{xfer} = N_{bytes/req} / R_{disk}$ where R_{disk} is the inner track transfer rate.

Once the data transfer time is known, the number of users that a single disk can support is given by the following argument. First, the number of seconds of video data that can fit into one request of $N_{bytes/req}$, is denoted by $S_{video/req}$ (Seconds of video per request) and is given by the following equation [11]:

$$S_{video/req} = \frac{N_{bytes/req}}{R_{user}}$$

which is just the request size divided by the rate at which the user requires the data. Once the request for $N_{bytes/req}$ bytes of data has been satisfied, that particular user will not need to re-access the disk for $S_{video/req}$ seconds. Therefore, the number of users that can be supported per disk is simply the number of additional requests that can be fit into $S_{video/req}$ seconds [11]:

$$N_{users/disk} = \frac{S_{video/req}}{T_{request}}$$

given that each request takes $T_{request}$ seconds.

To further extend the previous example, assume the request size to be 1 megabyte (or 1024*1024 bytes) and a constant data transfer rate to the user of 187,500 bytes per second. This yields a value for $S_{video/req}$ of 5.59 seconds. The number of users per disk can then be calculated from the $T_{request}$ values (given in Table 4.1 below) for worst, average, and best-case scenarios [11].

Table 4.1 *Values are given for a Seagate Baracuda 9 disk drive under worst, aver- age, and best-case scenarios. The T_{xfer} assumes a request size of 1 MB. All values are in seconds unless otherwise noted.*

Baracuda 9	Worst	Average	Best
T_{os}	0.0005	0.0005	0.0005
T_{cmd}	0.0010	0.0010	0.0010
T_{seek}	0.0190	0.0080	0.0000
T_{rot}	0.0083	0.0042	0.0000
T_{xfer}	0.1498	0.1049	0.0874
R_{disk} (bytes/sec)	7000000	10000000	12000000
$T_{request}$	0.1786	0.1185	0.0889
$N_{users/disk}$	31.3	47.2	62.9

There is a significant difference between the worst and best-case number of us- ers that a single disk can support, but it is still only a factor of two. Furthermore, this bounds the number of uses that a single disk can support. It is now a problem of scal- ing up the number of disks to match the assumed user load.

Now that the number of users supported by a single disk is known, the minimum number of disks required to support N_{users} on the server is given by [11]:

$$N_{disks} = \frac{N_{users}}{N_{users/disk}}$$

This of course is further constrained by physical factors such as number of I/O channels available, disks per channel, and so forth.

Previously, it was determined that the number of users the hypothetical server could support (N_{users}) was 1000. Therefore, using the equation, the number of disks required to support 1000 users is 34.1, 22.6, and 17.0 for the worst, average, and best- case scenarios. Again, this example shows how the problem of scaling up the disk subsystem is at least bounded. Finally, it must be determined how to connect these disks to the I/O channels without over running the bandwidth on each I/O channel. Given that each disk has a transfer rate of R_{disk} bytes per second (see Table 4.1) and the channel has a bandwidth of $B_{channel}$ bytes per second, the number of disks per channel is conservatively given by [11]:

$$N_{disk/channel} = \frac{B_{channel}}{R_{disk}}$$

Care must be taken however, when choosing the value of R_{disk} to use, because if the worst case, R_{disk} value is used, then the number of disks per channel may be too large. The reason is that the worst-case assumption creates a channel filled to capacity with slow disks. However, the performance of each disk will most likely be better than the worst-case scenario in which case the total bandwidth requirements of all the disks on the channel exceed the available bandwidth on the channel. Conversely, if the best-case value for R_{disk} is used, there may not be enough disks on the channel, but it should never exceed the channel bandwidth. At this point, it may be appropriate to use the average-case value for R_{disk} to arrive at a number of disks that can *comfortably* reside on a single channel. In this example, the value for $B_{channel} = 100 \times 106$ Bps and R_{disk} is taken from Table 4.1 as the average data rate of 10×106 Bps. Therefore, you could connect 10 disks per channel.

$N_{disk/channel}$ is then rounded down to the nearest integer because you cannot have half a disk on a channel. If on the other hand, this number is rounded up, then it could be thought of as using the fractional bandwidth of the last drive rather than the entire bandwidth of the drive. This is something the upper level software would need to know so as not to overdrive the I/O channel. By restricting the number of drives to the lower number however, the overdrive problem cannot occur. The number of channels required to support N_{disks} is then given by [11]:

$$N_{chan} = \frac{\text{Total number of disks}}{\text{Number of disks per channel}} = \frac{N_{disks}}{N_{disk/channel}}$$

It is known from the previous steps that anywhere from 17 to 34 disks are required to support 1000 users (best to worst-case scenarios). Using a value of 10 disks per channel and the previous equation, it is easy to see that the server would need between 2 and 4 channels.

To summarize briefly, the number of users (N_{users}) is given by the ratio of the total I/O bandwidth of the server to the continuous data rate required by each user (R_{user}) divided by two. The number of users that one disk can support is given by dividing the number of seconds of video per request ($S_{video/req}$) by the maximum time it takes to process any request on a storage subsystem ($T_{request}$).

Next, the number of disks required to support the maximum number of users (N_{users}) on the server is N_{users} divided by the number of users per disk ($N_{users/disk}$). And finally, the number of I/O channels is given by dividing the total number of disks (N_{disks}) by the number of disks per channel ($N_{disk/channel}$).

At this point, the design and configuration of the disk subsystem has been estimated and bounded. It is now necessary to address the storage server requirements.

The Video Storage Server

The storage server controls the data flow from the storage subsystem through the server to the user network. It must have a certain amount of memory to buffer the incoming data long enough to send it out to the users. The server is effectively performing the function of a speed-matching buffer between the high-speed disks and the slower user network. It must also have enough processing power to handle the computational aspects of request scheduling and data movement across many hundreds or thousands of users per server machine. This part of the chapter discusses the memory and processing requirements as well as addressing the issues pertaining to multiple-server configurations.

Server Memory Requirements

A single server under a maximum load of N_{users} requires a certain minimum amount of main memory on the server to act as a buffer between the disk subsystem and the user network. The reason for this is that the data being fed to the user network is done so in a highly controlled, jitter-free isochronous flow. The data coming in from the disk subsystem is far more bursty, being transferred in large chunks so as to maximize the efficiency of the disk devices. Therefore, the memory in the server is used to smooth out the data flow between the disk subsystem and the user network. The question is, how much memory is needed? The following equation estimates the memory size as [11]:

$$M = N_{users/disk} \times N_{disks} \times N_{bytes/req}$$

where M is the amount of memory (in bytes) required for buffer space.

In the example server with 63 users per disk (best-case scenario), 17 disks per server, and a request size of 1.05×106 bytes, the minimum memory size would be $63 \times 17 \times 1.05 \times 106$ or 1,125 MB of memory buffer space plus whatever is needed for the operating system. Anything beyond this amount could be used as a cache for data with a high degree of temporal locality, but upon close examination, this is impractical. Given a typical 100 minute movie (6,000 seconds), any two users on the server would have to be within a few seconds of each other on the same movie in order to avoid a disk access. With the number of different titles accessed and the number of users, times of access, and so forth, the probability of this happening is quite small; and it takes quite a bit more memory in order to increase this probability only to avoid a disk access.

Server Processing Requirements

The storage server processing requirements can be generalized into a few basic categories such as disk management, network management, buffer management, stream scheduling, and the user network interface. In general the disk device drivers consume a small percentage of CPU resources to process an I/O request. However, certain implementations of controllers can require the device driver to handle multiple interrupts per I/O operation which can seriously affect the time-critical nature of video server storage systems. This generally is not a problem for a small number of devices and/or a small number of I/O requests, but can be a significant problem on a fully configured server where each disk is being accessed to its limit in a continuous manner.

The network hardware is similar to that of the storage subsystem in that it consists of a relatively few controllers, each with a finite bandwidth that must be parceled out amongst the users in some fashion. The network I/O drivers are also similar to the disk device drivers, but it is beyond the scope of this chapter to describe them in any detail. For the sake of discussion though, it is estimated that the network device drivers can take at least the same amount of time to process an I/O request as the disk driver. Furthermore, network protocols may require a certain amount of data copy operations to move pieces of data from the user buffers into buffers that will ultimately be sent to the user over the network. These data copy operations can consume a significant amount of processing power as well as internal memory bandwidth and need to be considered when designing the server software and hardware. There are techniques used by the file system to avoid unnecessary data copy operations that may be applied to the network drivers; however, that is an issue that is beyond the scope of this chapter but deserves mention nonetheless. The buffer management, file system management, and I/O scheduling software is also beyond the scope of this chapter, but they have the potential for consuming a significant amount of processing power and internal memory bandwidth that will compete with the memory bandwidth needed to support the video data streams.

Multiple Server Configurations

An important aspect of video servers is that the number of users that a typical server installation would need to serve would most likely be much larger than any one server could support. Therefore, it is necessary to employ multiple servers. But, this raises the questions of data placement and duplication of data.

Given a large number of user connections coming into an installation, does a single user connection get dedicated to a single server for the life of the connection (the length of the movie being watched); or, does the user connection float across the servers, accessing a different server, each with a sequential piece of the movie? The answer to this question dictates the layout of the data across the servers. If any one user were restricted to a single server, then all the movies on that server would have to be duplicated on the other servers for access by other users.

To avoid the duplication of large amounts of movie data, it would be necessary to put all the "A" titles on one server, "B" titles on a second server, and so on. This avoids duplication but runs into serious contention when every 6-year-old in the area wants to watch *Aladdin* from the "A" server all at the same time, and nobody is watching anything on the "B" server. The "A" server is overwhelmed while the other servers sit idle—a serious load balancing problem.

If, on the other hand, the movies are distributed across all the servers and the user network connection floats across the servers (accessing the data it needs at the required times), then the load is distributed across all the servers as well as the disk subsystems. However, if any one server fails, the data on the disks attached to that server becomes inaccessible.

The answer is, of course, give all servers access to all the disks. This way the load is balanced across the entire array of disks and there is no unnecessary duplication of data.

The traditional way to do this is shown in Figure 4.4 [11]. Assuming a user remains connected to a specific server for the entire length of the movie, each server would be connected together with a high-speed network (HIPPI). All the file systems on all the servers would then be cross mounted so that any server would be able to access data on any other server indirectly via the high-speed interconnect. This is possible, but not a scalable configuration because the bandwidth required to support the server intercommunication is subtracted from the total real I/O bandwidth, leaving less for the disk subsystem to use. Secondly, as the number of servers grows, the amount of interconnection traffic grows exponentially and intercommunication bandwidth requirements soon exceed reasonable limits. This may work for two or three servers, but not many more than that.

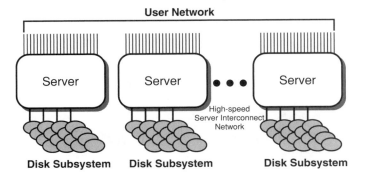

Figure 4.4
Multiple Server Configuration with high-speed server interconnect network.

The Server Interconnect Problem: A Case for Fibre Channel

Given the problems with having multiple servers simultaneously accessing multiple disk drives or arrays, it is necessary to look beyond traditional disk storage interface technologies to solve this problem in a more scalable way. Fibre Channel is an ANSI standard interface technology that is now available and being actively implemented by a wide variety of hardware vendors. It is a hybrid of channel and networking technology that has the performance of a channel and the flexibility of a network. A configuration using Fibre Channel as the primary interconnect to the disk subsystems is shown in Figure 4.5 [11]. The advantage of this configuration is that each of the servers can have a direct path to each of the storage devices without having to communicate with any other server. Secondly, the Fibre Channel path is very high performance (100 MBps), low latency, and very reliable. Finally, a Fibre Channel-based server provides a level of availability that the more traditional configurations cannot.

An effective use of Fibre Channel would be to define a storage network that consists of the servers and the disks. There would be one scheduling server that maintains a coherent view of all the disks and schedules all I/O operations for each of the servers. The actual I/O operations however, take place directly between the requesting server and a specific disk. This storage network topology allows both server-to-server communication and server-to-disk communication. A Fibre Channel switch or fabric is used to make the connections between the servers and disks. The fabric is similar to a crossbar switch and allows for N simultaneous transfers to occur where N is half the number of ports on the switch.

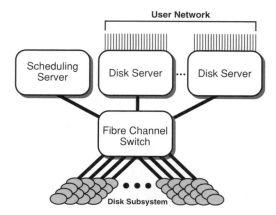

Figure 4.5
A Fibre Channel server configuration. The scheduling server communicates with all other storage servers and tape subsystem servers.

Getting the Server out of the Data Path

The goal of a video server is to deliver movie data from a central location to a large number of users in a time-critical fashion. Previously mentioned configurations required the server to *stage* the data in order to speed match the disk subsystem to the user network. This staging process is limited by the bandwidth of the servers and the efficient utilization of the I/O channels.

An alternative approach would be to move the speed-matching function into the disk and give each disk a Fibre Channel interface. The disk could be instructed by the scheduling server to read a piece of data into the disk's own cache and subsequently transfer it to a destination switching element directly on the user network, thereby bypassing the server entirely. The data would be routed directly to the user through a series of switches and routers that would take care of the different network protocol. This is the most efficient configuration, but also the most specialized. One nice feature of this approach is that the performance of the system is more easily estimated because there is no longer a storage server component to throttle the data flow between the disks and the user network (see Figure 4.6) [11]. Therefore, the performance of this system is based almost entirely on the performance characteristics of the disk devices.

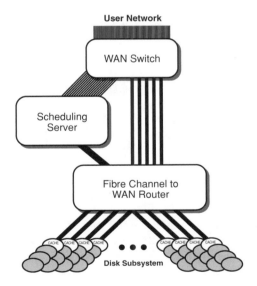

Figure 4.6
Third-party transfers used to send the movie data directly to the user via the user network. The data is buffered by each of the recipients. Timing and control is performed by the server which need only accept commands from the user network. Data rates are speed matched by caches on each disk array.

Scheduling Software

The task of scheduling is somewhat beyond the scope of this chapter, but there are some issues that deserve mention. Scheduling in general can be thought of from three different perspectives: User scheduling, Disk scheduling, and User Network scheduling. It isn't clear at this point what sort of request comes in from the user, but a reasonable assumption would be something like *select a movie title* followed by *play*, and occasionally *stop*, *pause*, *reverse*, and so forth. Once the *play* command is received, the main scheduler can determine the number and location of all the frames the user needs to be given as well as the order and times in which to deliver them. The challenge is to apply these scheduling needs to the current disk scheduler. If the user at some point pushes *pause* or *reverse* or some such function, then that user's current schedule must be revised accordingly. The question is can it be done in real-time and what are the consequences of such actions?

Disk Scheduling

The disk scheduler must maintain a consistent view of all the disks in terms of what requests are needed and when they are needed. In normal computing environments, the disk scheduling is not necessarily time critical, and requests are submitted, queued, and returned according to some algorithm that tries to maximize the efficient use of the disk subsystem, but does not guarantee delivery times. This disk scheduler must be able to start operations at specific times and guarantee the arrival of data by specific times. In order to do this, it must be able to manage the individual disk request queues and detect and compensate for *hot spots*.

Hot spots occur when many users require access to a single resource (a disk or a channel) at the same time. This phenomena deserves serious attention, because it can cause delays in the delivery of data. There are two aspects of hot spots to be considered: detection and compensation. Hot spots can be detected by the disk scheduling software when the user schedule is composited with the overall disk schedules. At this point in time, the disk scheduler should be able to discover points in time when any particular disk queue may be overloaded. To compensate for this, the requests can be moved up to occur earlier than they would normally. However, this requires more memory for additional buffers to hold this early data. Another way to handle this is to have duplicate data blocks on other disks, with the hope that the other disk will have room in its queue to accommodate the request at the specified time. A combination of both these methods would probably suffice.

The application of a Fibre Channel-based storage network to a video server allows the disk scheduling process to view and control access to all the disks in the entire subsystem. There is also a higher degree of reliability by using a network attached storage model, because if no single server *owns* any set of disks or disk subsystems, then any server can be brought on or offline without affecting the disk subsystem. Furthermore, disks can be added to the subsystem to increase the capacity, performance, or accessibility independently of the servers that access them.

Nevertheless, this chapter presented a simple set of equations that sufficiently bound the configuration requirements for a video server and disk subsystem. The video server requirements indicate a significant memory size for speed matching as well as a large number of low-speed or a small number of high-speed I/O channels. There is also a substantial requirement for processing, and multiprocessing is a must. The I/O problems become more complex when multiple servers are interconnected in order to support a growing user network.

Multiple interconnected video server systems need to have a large degree of connectivity. NAS is a significant contribution in such systems because it allows for a much higher degree of data accessibility as well as greater scalability in performance, capacity, and interconnectivity. The internal bandwidth of the individual video server systems is more efficiently utilized by having all the storage directly accessible to any server in the *cluster*.

Thus, the scheduling software is key to an efficient video server system. Combined with Network Attached Storage and the appropriate storage network switching devices, ultimately, a video server can act more as a *traffic cop* rather than a *shipping company*.

Finally, your affinity for a SAN Service Provider (SSP) will depend largely on your organization. Fortune 500 businesses, that have spent years building internal data centers, are not likely to consider SSPs, at least not for legacy data management. These companies have already made a sizeable investment in facilities, systems, and people and can capably predict and manage their storage needs. In other cases, regulatory requirements may preclude the use of remote data storage facilities; banks, pharmaceutical companies, and certain federal agencies are less likely to employ an SSP. For example, businesses that maintain internal data centers, but that have not had the resources to accommodate unusual growth, are ripe for an SSP that can manage storage solutions onsite.

IS THERE AN SSP IN YOUR FUTURE?

Although SSPs offer many benefits, entering this young market is not for everyone (see sidebar, "Vendors and SAN Service Providers"). A variety of factors, including type of business, security needs, and budget, must be considered when evaluating a data-storage outsourcer.

VENDORS AND SAN SERVICE PROVIDERS

Business Case

SSPs implement enterprise storage infrastructures and ensure scalability and high availability. Outsourcing this responsibility allows businesses to focus on their core competencies instead of on data management.

Technology Case

Deploying an enterprise storage system requires experience with network topologies, OSes, protocols, and combinations of disk units, communication equipment, servers, and more. For many companies, it is best to leave it to the experts.

Pros

- Already know and understand top-notch solutions
- Provide systems that satisfy client requirements
- Monitor systems and resolve issues quickly
- Help get new systems online in less time

Cons

- Increased security risk when moving data storage off-site
- Young, potentially risky market [11]

Companies such as ASPs and ISPs and others that already use off-site data centers are excellent candidates for public-utility SSPs that maintain enterprise storage facilities in co-located data centers (see Figure 4.7) [11].

Young companies may not be able to predict how quickly their storage needs will grow. Rather than making a substantial investment in an infrastructure that may fail to meet future requirements, they may be better off with an outsourced, offsite storage solution.

But, if your primary data-storage system resides off-site, security concerns may limit the appeal of an SSP. For security reasons, more SSPs are adopting a premises-neutral strategy to accommodate customers who insist that their data-storage systems reside under their direct control.

To address security issues unique to co-location facilities, public-utility SSPs rely on logical unit number (LUN) masking, LUN zoning, or port zoning to secure primary data. For traditional backups across common communication channels, these SSPs can put managed storage switches in front of backup systems to maintain security.

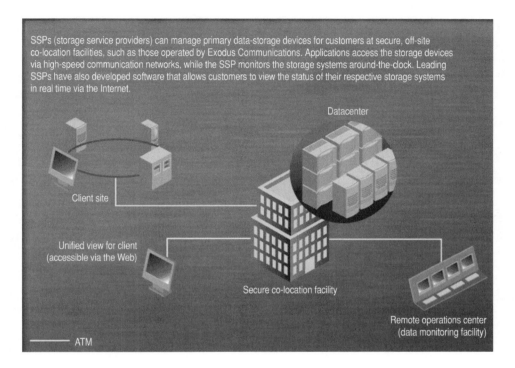

SSPs (storage service providers) can manage primary data-storage devices for customers at secure, off-site co-location facilities, such as those operated by Exodus Communications. Applications access the storage devices via high-speed communication networks, while the SSP monitors the storage systems around-the-clock. Leading SSPs have also developed software that allows customers to view the status of their respective storage systems in real time via the Internet.

Datacenter

Client site

Unified view for client
(accessible via the Web)

Secure co-location facility

Remote operations center
(data monitoring facility)

ATM

Figure 4.7
Public-utility SSP model.

Economic factors influence every lease versus buy decision. SSPs cite several factors in their favor, including reduced downtime and fewer employees. By downgrading data-storage costs to just another business expense, SSPs can help insulate customers from technical obsolescence and capital asset depreciation. Of course, the relative costs and benefits of using an SSP are situational. Like all cost-benefit analyses, your calculations will depend on your subjective estimates as they relate to your particular operating environment.

Given that the SSP market is in its infancy, it's no surprise that a good deal of misconception exists in this market—especially concerning the location of primary data stores. Many IT managers erroneously believe that to use an SSP, they must relinquish their data to an off-site facility. That's simply not true. Unlike many consultants, SSPs are vendor agnostic, and they implement the solutions they recommend. In the right environment, the SSP value proposition is very attractive indeed.

FROM HERE...

This chapter covered the self-service SAN, outsourcing with service providers, and high-speed data sharing among multiple computer platforms. It also looks into other aspects of SANs including: opportunity for the indirect channel, end-to-end services for multivendor enterprise SANs and storage subsystems for video services. The next chapter discusses growth demand for Internet-based SAN services, DNS, and how organizations can build upon the existing DNS infrastructure to deliver scalability, reliability, and dynamic allocation of SAN traffic based on real-time network conditions.

END NOTES...

[1] Articulent, 45 South Street, Hopkinton, MA 01748, 2001.

[2] ManagedStorage International, 10075 Westmoor Drive, Suite 100, Broomfield, Colorado 80021, 2001.

[3] Storability, Inc., Corporate Headquarters, 118 Turnpike Road, Southborough, Massachusetts 01772, 2001.

[4] StorageNetworks, 225 Wyman Street, Waltham, Massachusetts 02451, 2001.

[5] StorageWay, Inc., Corporate Headquarters, 3501 W. Warren Ave., Fremont, CA 94538, 2001.

[6] McDATA, Corporate Headquarters, 310 Interlocken Parkway, Broomfield, CO 80021, 2001.

[7] Janet Waxman and John McArthur, "Storage Area Networks: Opportunity for Indirect Channel," International Data Corporation, 5 Speen Street, Framingham, MA 01701, 2001.

[8] "End-to-End Services for Multivendor Storage Area Networks (SANs)," IBM Corporation, 1133 Westchester Avenue, White Plains, NY 10604, 2001.

[9] Champion Computer Systems, 433 Stewart St., Champion, Ohio 44483, 2001.

[10] The Yankee Group, 31 St. James Avenue, Boston, MA 02116-4114, 2001.

[11] Thomas M. Ruwart, "Storage Subsystems for Video Services," Brocade Communications Systems, Inc., 1745 Technology Drive, San Jose, CA 95110, 2001.

5 Providing SAN Scalability and High Availability

In networked systems such as SANs (with their associated servers, fabric, and storage components, as well as software applications), downtime can occur even if parts of the system are highly available or fault tolerant. To improve business continuance under a variety of circumstances, SANs can incorporate redundant components, connections, software, and configurations to minimize or eliminate single points of failure.

THE INCREASED NEED FOR HIGHER AVAILABILITY...

With the emergence of the Internet and the proliferation of global e-business applications, more and more companies are implementing computing infrastructures specifically designed for continuous data and system availability. Today, even applications such as company email have become critical for ongoing business operations. Faced with increased customer and internal user expectations, companies are currently striving to achieve at least 99.999% (the "five nines") availability in their computing systems—a figure equivalent to less than 5.3 minutes of downtime a year. Additional downtime can severely impact business operations and cost valuable time, money, and resources.

To ensure the highest level of system uptime, companies are implementing reliable storage networks capable of boosting the availability of data for all the users and applications that need it. These companies typically represent the industries that demand the highest levels of system and data availability—the utilities and telecommunications sector, brokerages and financial service institutions, and a wide variety of service providers, for example.

HIGH-LEVEL AVAILABILITY OBJECTIVES ....

System availability is less the result of individual products or devices than it is an overall philosophy of system design. Developing highly available networks involves identifying specific availability requirements and predicting what potential failures might cause outages. The first step is to clearly define availability objectives, which can vary widely from company to company and even within segments of the same company. In some environments, no disruption can be tolerated while other environments might be only minimally affected by short outages. As a result, availability is a function of the frequency of outages (caused by unplanned failures or scheduled maintenance and upgrades) and the time to recover from such outages.

Many companies are addressing their availability requirements by implementing networked fabrics of Fibre Channel devices designed to provide a high-performance storage environment. These flexible SANs are based on the following principles:

- A thorough understanding of availability requirements throughout the enterprise
- A flexible design that incorporates fault tolerance through redundancy and mirroring
- Simplified fault monitoring, diagnostics, and repair capabilities to ensure fast recovery
- A minimal amount of human intervention required during failover event
- A reliable backup and recovery plan to account for a wide variety of contingencies [1]

To make sure systems can avoid or withstand a variety of failures, SANs incorporate a wide range of capabilities, including:

- Highly available components with built-in redundancy and hot-plugging capabilities
- No single points of failure
- Intelligent routing and rerouting
- Dynamic failover protection
- Nondisruptive server and storage maintenance
- Hardware zoning for creating safe and secure environments
- Predictive fabric management [1]

SYSTEM AVAILABILITY THROUGH REDUNDANCY ....

One of the simplest ways to increase availability is to implement fully redundant SAN environments to help ensure that alternate devices, data paths, and configurations can support enterprise applications during failures or other problems. A critical aspect of any high-availability system, redundancy helps prevent isolated failures from causing widespread outages. It also enables nondisruptive maintenance and upgrades—minimizing disruption to system operations.

Implementing multiple levels of redundancy throughout a SAN environment can reduce downtime by orders of magnitude. For instance, hardware components, servers, storage devices, network connections, and even the storage network itself can be completely redundant. A fundamental rule for improving fault tolerance is to ensure dual paths through separate components regardless of a vendor's assurances of high availability. This is especially true when physical location and disaster tolerance are a concern, or when a complex device can become a single point of failure.

APPLICATIONS...

One of the keys to improving availability is shifting the focus from server availability and recovery to application availability and recovery. Mission-critical applications should be supported on clustered or highly available servers and storage devices to ensure the applications' ability to access data when they need it—even in the midst of a failure. Sophisticated software applications can enable application or host failover, in which a secondary server assumes the workload if a failure occurs on the primary server. Other types of software, such as many database applications, enable workload sharing by multiple servers—adding to continuous data availability where any one of several servers can assume the tasks of a failed server.

In addition, many server vendors and value-added software providers offer clustering technology to keep server-based applications highly available, regardless of individual component failures. The clustering software is designed to transfer workload among active servers without disrupting data flow. As a result, clustering helps companies guard against equipment failures, keep critical systems online, and meet increased data access expectations.

Some clustering software, such as Veritas Cluster Server, enables application failover on an application-by-application basis. This capability enables administrators to prioritize the order of application failover. Fibre Channel SANs facilitate high-availability clustering by simplifying storage and server connectivity. Moreover, SANs can provide one of the most reliable infrastructures for server clustering, particularly when clustered servers are distributed throughout the enterprise to achieve higher levels of disaster tolerance, a practice known as *stretched clusters*.

SERVERS AND HOST BUS ADAPTERS......................

To ensure high availability, servers should include redundant hardware components with the dual power supplies, dual network connections, and mirrored system disks typically used in enterprise environments. Servers should also have multiple connections to alternate storage devices through Fibre Channel switches and a minimum of two independent connections to the SAN. In most cases, servers should feature dual-active or hot-standby configurations with automatic failover capabilities.

The next single point of failure to consider after the server is the path between the server and the storage. Potential points of failure on this path might include HBA failures, cable issues, fabric issues, or storage connection problems. The HBA is the Fibre Channel interconnect between the server and the SAN (replacing the traditional SCSI card for storage connectivity). Using a dual-redundant HBA, configuration helps ensure that a path is always available. In addition to providing redundancy, this configuration might enable overall higher performance due to the additional SAN connectivity.

To achieve fault tolerance, multiple paths are connected to alternate locations within the SAN or even to a completely redundant SAN. Server-based software for path failover enables the use of multiple HBAs, and typically allows a dual-active configuration that can divide workload between multiple HBAs—thus improving performance. The software monitors the *health* of available storage, servers, and physical paths and automatically reroutes data traffic to an alternate path if a failure occurs.

In the event of an HBA failure, host server software detects that the data path is no longer available and transfers the failed HBA's workload to an active one. The remaining HBA then assumes the workload until the failed HBA is repaired or replaced. After identifying failed paths or failed-over storage devices and resolving the problem, the software automatically initiates failback and restores the dual path without impacting applications. If desired, an administrator can manually perform the failback to verify the process.

The software that performs this failover is typically provided by system vendors, storage vendors, or value-added software developers. Software solutions (such as Compaq SecurePath, Veritas Dynamic Multi-Path, and EMC PowerPath) help ensure that data traffic can continue despite a path failure. These types of software products effectively remove connections, components, and devices as single points of failure in the SAN to improve availability of enterprise applications.

To help eliminate unnecessary failover, the software distinguishes between actual failures and other network events that might appear to be failures. By recognizing false failures, the software can help prevent unnecessary failover/failback effects caused by marginal or intermittent conditions. After detecting an actual failure, the software typically waits to determine whether the event is an actual failure. The typical delay in the failover process can range from an instant failover (when a loss of signal light is detected) up to a minute (if the light signal is still available and the path failure is in another part of the network). These delays are typically adjustable to allow for a variety of configurations and to allow other, more rapid recovery mechanisms such as path rerouting in the SAN.

STORAGE ....

To improve performance and fault tolerance, many of today's storage devices feature multiple connections to the SAN. Multiple connections help guard against failures that might result from a damaged cable, failed controller, or failed SAN component, such as a Gigabit Interface Converter (GBIC) optical module. The failover process for storage connections typically follows one of the following methods.

One method is transparent failover, in which a secondary standby connection comes online if the primary connection fails. Because the new connection has the same address as the original failed connection, failover is transparent to the server connection, and application performance is not affected. After the primary connection is repaired, it assumes the workload.

Another method is to use dual or multiple active connections with each connection dedicated for certain logical volumes within a given storage system. If one connection fails, the other active connections automatically assume its logical volume workload until it comes back online. During this time, the alternate connections support all logical volumes, so there might be a slight performance impact depending on workload and traffic patterns.

A third method used for storage path failover also utilizes dual or multiple active connections. In this case, however, both connections can simultaneously access the logical volumes. This design can improve performance through load balancing, but typically requires host-based software. During a storage connection failure, the alternate active connection continues to access the logical volumes. After the failed connection is repaired, the other path becomes active and load balancing resumes.

All of these failover methods are designed to ensure the availability of the enterprise applications that use them. In addition, failover generally is coordinated with server software to ensure an active path to data, transparent to the application.

MIRRORING ....

Another effective way to achieve high availability in a SAN environment is by mirroring storage subsystems. SANs enable the efficient mirroring of data on a peer-to-peer basis across the fabric. These mirroring functions contribute tremendous fault tolerance and availability characteristics to SAN-based data. Combining the mirroring functions with switch-based routing algorithms (which enable traffic to be routed around path breaks within the SAN fabric) creates a resilient, self-healing environment to support the most demanding enterprise storage requirements (see sidebar, "Demand for Data Storage in Enterprises"). The mirrored subsystems can provide an alternate access point to data regardless of path conditions.

DEMAND FOR DATA STORAGE IN ENTERPRISES

Storage ought to be one of those things that IT managers can deal with out of their back pockets. Need more? Just buy more disks.

Are there trusty rules of thumb for this? Not on your life. It's a complex equation that drives demand for data storage in enterprises, and all the old rules of thumb are changing.

Because the growth of disk capacity is outpacing that of speed to access the disk, the system *cost* of access is rising. Data engineers are working on schemes where the disks are accessed sequentially, like tape drives, rather than randomly, to keep the cost of these *fetches* down.

Tape drives are being relegated to use as data archives because it can take days to reload all the information in a multiterabyte tape drive. Automated tape libraries help, turning off-line storage into near-line storage, but disk drives are almost as economical. Many companies now keep an entire set of duplicate disk systems at remote locations as backups.

RAM costs are falling faster than the costs of magnetic storage. A megabyte of RAM used to cost 10 times as much as a megabyte of disk RAM and 1,000 times as much as tape RAM. Now, 1 MB of RAM costs only three times as much as 1 MB of disk RAM and 10 times as much as tape RAM. So when in doubt, put it in RAM.

To net it out, processor speed improvements are outpacing main memory improvements, which are outpacing magnetic media access-time improvements. More information on disk must be cached so that the information on the disk can be read sequentially, and the caches themselves must get bigger in order to keep memory full.

Put anything over a network, and the storage equation grows even more complex. The overhead of sending messages around wide area networks is so much more than sending a message from a computer to a disk drive, that it pays to cache any Web page that will ever be called up again.

There are four implications for IT professionals. One is that the performance of tomorrow's systems will be at least as dependent on the data transfer and caching software running on them as on the hardware itself. Second, the proliferation of caches in and around the network will stress current system management tools.

Third, storage dynamics and optimal system design will vary from application to application with, say, scientific computing and Internet commerce representing two extremes. Fourth, no one but you will understand this.

Designing multiple, complex applications will be tough enough in the next few years. Deciding how to optimize performance by implementing storage management systems will add to the challenge. How much do you cache? Where do you locate proxy servers? Do you go with RAID 5 (efficient with space) or mirroring (efficient with access)? And so on.

This is the rocket science of IT systems management. It's not something others in your organization care to know about or are even capable of appreciating. But, you should [2].

A common use of mirroring involves the deployment of remote sites within the enterprise. Implementing SANs through Fibre Channel switches enables the distribution of storage and servers throughout a campus, metropolitan area, and beyond. Fibre Channel overcomes many of the distance limitations of traditional SCSI connections, enabling devices to be extended over much longer distances for remote mirroring, tape backup, and disaster recovery operations.

Native Fibre Channel supports server and storage connections at distances up to 10 kilometers, which is adequate for most large campus applications. For higher availability solutions that require disaster tolerance, even longer distances might be required to connect disaster recovery sites.

This capability enables SANs to use existing long-distance optical connections or to connect to MANs that employ Dense Wave Division Multiplexing (DWDM) technology. In addition, tunneling technologies can be used to connect SANs to existing WAN IP infrastructures—increasing distances between remote sites well beyond 100 kilometers.

SWITCHES ....

The SAN infrastructure itself is typically one of the highest availability components of storage networks. Fibre Channel switches are capable of extremely high reliability—thus providing much better than five nines of availability on the only nonredundant component (the motherboard). Availability improves with switches that feature hot-pluggable, redundant power supplies and cooling, as well as hot-pluggable GBIC modules that enable single-port replacement of optics without impacting other working devices.

The ability to upgrade switches efficiently is important for testing new firmware within specific environments. Because a network of switches can provide alternate paths within a SAN (path failure can be handled transparent to applications), administrators can upgrade switches in the network without interrupting operations. Upgrades on switches with device connections are performed in conjunction with the dual-path capabilities of servers and storage. However, with the switch *fastboot* option, failover is often transparent to any server-based failover software, depending on the delay configured into the software.

After an administrator has tested the new firmware, it can be downloaded to other portions of the SAN. The ability to upgrade selected parts of the network or run different firmware versions within the SAN, is a key advantage over single monolithic switch designs. For instance, a particular capability or fix for a device might need to be loaded onto only the applicable switch. Also, switch resellers often standardize into a particular version of switch firmware. As the SAN grows, it might include switches from many different resellers. As a result, administrators have the choice of continuing to use the supported firmware versions on particular switches instead of being forced to upgrade the entire system.

In contrast, upgrading a director-class product typically involves a *fast code load* that requires a brief interrupt as control is transferred from the director's primary CPU to the secondary CPU. During this transfer, certain critical functions are unavailable—although the process is usually transparent to applications. However, devices attached to the director are disconnected for a brief period and are required to log back into the fabric. This additional step can lead to path failure during the switchover if there are any problems logging back into the fabric. This potential problem is one of the reasons system designers do not generally use a single product for high availability, unless it has two completely separate systems within the device (such as nonshared CPUs or memory).

One of the most common points of failure on a switch-based SAN is the port optics. Because of the physical nature of the connection and various environmental factors, port optics and copper interfaces are typically more susceptible to failure. Dust, physical damage, and heat can cause these connections or components to fail. To ensure higher availability in the event of a failure, the media components of the switches (as well as the HBA and storage) should feature hot-pluggable devices such as GBICs or Small Form-factor Pluggable (SFP) devices. These devices enable hot replacement of just the failed port. In contrast, director-class switch designs that incorporate multi-port cards with fixed media, require all the connections on the associated card to be taken offline along with the failed port—causing unnecessary path failure.

NETWORKING IN THE FABRIC ....

Although redundancy provides an excellent way to enhance availability, it does not protect against all types of outages. Just as companies have embraced client/server networking to overcome the limitations of the mainframecentric IT infrastructure, many are taking a similar approach to SANs. A networked SAN is a flexible architecture that can be easily implemented and quickly adapted to changing requirements—extending the availability characteristics of hardware and software components into the SAN fabric itself.

Redundancy in the SAN fabric is built through a network of switches—each with its own redundant components and separate processors—to provide a robust mission-critical SAN solution. With connected servers, switches, and storage ensuring high availability, the networked fabric provides a more resilient infrastructure than a single-point product (such as a director-class switch) that can become a single point of failure. With an infrastructure of switches, administrators can grow their network to meet high port count needs. As future products provide actual core networking capabilities (such as 2 Gb support and trunking) administrators can build a higher speed core to meet future SAN requirements.

Networking a fabric of switches not only increases availability, but also enables design flexibility and *pay-as-you-grow* scalability. No matter how many ports it has, no single product can always meet every storage need. Networks are the only way to achieve steady SAN growth. Utilizing 16-port switches as the building block of the fabric, enables SAN designers to continue a smooth pattern of growth without being forced to make large incremental purchases when the N+1 port threshold is reached, as would be the case with a director-based product (see Figure 5.1) [1].

Today's SAN infrastructures require port aggregation to solve problems such as backup and storage consolidation. For port aggregation large noncongestive directors are overkill, since Inter-Switch Links (ISLs) are not a limiting factor in current devices or applications. A network of smaller switches enables the SAN to support the appropriate level of bandwidth by increasing the number of switches.

With future SAN technologies such as virtualization and global file systems, bandwidth requirements might increase and require a higher bandwidth core back-

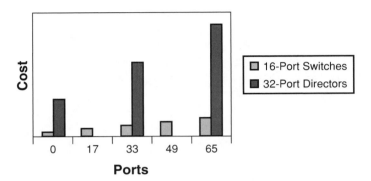

Figure 5.1
Scaling with switches enables pay-as-you-grow networking.

bone. As 2 Gb core switches become available, a true core 2 Gb backbone can support the higher bandwidth requirements and still be compatible with the 1 Gb SAN infrastructures implemented today.

MESHED TREE TOPOLOGY FOR SWITCHES.............

One of the easiest ways to increase availability in a SAN is to network switches in a meshed tree topology. This topology connects devices to edge switches, which then connect to central interconnecting switches that in turn connect to other parts of the SAN or other devices (see Figure 5.2) [1]. This approach enables easy scaling of the network around a meshed infrastructure and works well as long as there is a high degree of interoperability among the switches.

> **Note**
>
> **FC switches versus "meshed-tree" SANs built from multiple small switches: Meshed trees are good for redundancy, but above a certain SAN size, they may cost more than the single directory class switch; and, they suffer from longer data latency because the data must traverse more switch hops to get to their destinations.**

Some vendors believe that a single-point product approach is better than a networked fabric of multiple switches. However, the single-point model has several limitations. As soon as storage requirements surpass the number of available ports, the single-point product must be replaced or additional switches must be added. Either option typically entails a redesign of the enterprise SAN, which can disrupt operations. Moreover, the single-point model introduces a single point of failure into the

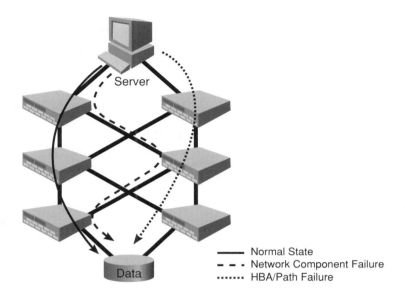

Figure 5.2
Failover in a single fabric with dual connectivity.

SAN, while limiting connectivity options for various server and storage device types. Because of these limitations, companies are usually better served by scaling the fabric of the SAN with multiple high-availability switches in a networked configuration.

A SINGLE FABRIC WITH DUAL CONNECTIVITY ....

Although high-availability devices within an enterprise SAN contribute to the overall availability of the entire system, they do not guarantee it. True high availability can be achieved only through an end-to-end system composed of highly available components and devices—as well as fault-tolerant capabilities. This type of solution can help ensure business continuance regardless of failures.

Dual attachment of servers and storage devices to a single fabric can produce a highly available system through the inherent reliability of the network itself. Each high-availability switch within a networked fabric combines with the other switches to provide distributed functions, such as error detection, login requests, state change notification, and management. The sharing of fabric functions enables workload sharing while helping to ensure that no single failure can disrupt the entire system. Because the switches run their own independent firmware and do not share memory like director-class products do, there is a much lower chance of a single switch impacting the entire network.

For instance, if a director-class switch experiences a firmware problem, it is likely to occur when the first CPU goes down and the secondary CPU comes online—a situation that might bring down the director itself. If there were a problem within the firmware, it would likely occur on both CPUs, possibly introducing a single point of failure within the SAN.

In contrast, a network of independent switches continues to provide connectivity if a non-redundant component fails or is taken offline in a single fabric. The high availability of the fabric stems from the near-statistical impossibility of experiencing a second failure during the repair of the first failure. The probability of two simultaneous hardware failures in the same fabric is extremely low, well into eleven nines of availability.

A Fibre Channel switched fabric can handle changes to the network (such as a link, optical, or switch failure) with minimal impact on all the connected devices. For example, if a central switch providing interconnectivity to other switches fails, the neighboring switches immediately detect the failure and inform other switches and devices within the fabric. Fabric Shortest Path First (FSPF), the standard routing protocol for Fibre Channel, detects the failed route, determines the next shortest route for data traffic, and updates the routing table. This change typically occurs within two seconds or less (the error timeout for frames within the fabric). By utilizing redundant links and alternate paths within the network, FSPF provides an effective way to cope with failed links as well as switch and SAN device outages (see Figure 5.2).

After a new route is established, data flow continues without requiring path failover from the storage or servers. From an application perspective, there is no downtime—just a brief pause for rerouting. This process is less intrusive than the failover of a CPU in a director-class product, when the secondary CPU comes online. Because the director has only one processor handling all operations during this period, all devices must log out and back into the director. Networked fabrics do not require this step, because any remaining switches keep their devices logged in, so all traffic continues around the failed switch. Other switches in the fabric send out SNMP traps, alerting the management software that the failed switch should be replaced. In addition, optic failures on a director might affect more than the failed port due to the types of port cards used in these products.

Another example of a failed switch in a single networked fabric might involve an edge switch directly attached to storage or servers. If the failure is a redundant component, such as a power supply or fan, it does not affect the fabric or devices. If the failure is a port optic (GBIC) failure, only the single port is affected and the storage or servers' dual connection failover process occurs. Because the GBIC can be hot-swapped, replacement does not impact the switch or fabric. In contrast, optic failures on some director-class products require the replacement of a four-port card, which potentially takes three working ports offline during the repair period and increases the likelihood of problems during path failback.

If a motherboard fails on an edge switch in a networked fabric, the attached storage and server devices utilize their dual-path failover process. This process can be almost instantaneous, depending on several factors—such as the type of failure, the path failover software used, and the type of storage used. Just like the motherboard on an edge switch, a port card failure on a director-class product initiates the path failover capabilities of the storage or server. This occurs because the card is not one of the redundant components of the system. The possible result is an optical failure or other internal hardware failure that requires all ports on the card to fail over during the replacement procedure.

Some storage and failover software applications immediately fail over if they detect a loss of light in the port optics, since it would be an obvious failure. Other failures in which the light is not lost might take longer to detect. This delay is typically used to filter out a thrashing event (such as repeated failover/failback attempts), due to intermittent or marginal conditions. After the failover occurs, an alternate path is used. This path might already be active, since most dual-connected devices support dual-active connections for load balancing and redundancy. As a result, the storage or server might detect only an increase in traffic rather than a change of state.

In dual-path configurations, only one side (server or storage) needs to initiate a path failover. For example, if a failure affects the storage, only the storage (not the server side) needs to alter paths. The fabric reroutes data from the server to the new storage connection. To minimize repair time, all fabric switches should support auto-discovery. This capability enables a replacement switch to be added to the existing network and powered up, where it can then automatically discover the fabric and learn fabric-wide information such as zoning and name services. In addition, automatic recovery features can minimize recovery time and limit potential errors. These features provide easy scalability of the SAN when new switches are being added for increased connectivity.

Note

Zoning is equivalent to the concept of "virtual LAN" and is meant to provide the ability to limit access to resources, but can be used in the context of redundancy to prevent troubles from starting and spreading.

A DUAL FABRIC WITH DUAL CONNECTIVITY..........

An even higher level of availability can be achieved with the use of dual paths and a dual-fabric design. Compared to single fabrics, dual-redundant fabrics simplify the concept of high availability and fault tolerance, because all components are redundant and parallel—from the server connections to the fabric itself. Any edge switch failure within one of the fabrics causes the redundant fabric to assume the additional data flow. The remote possibility of subsequent failures during any repair sequence means that the system can easily achieve much better than five nines of availability. Because the port counts are generally the same for a single large fabric and two smaller dual fabrics, the differentiating factor in availability levels is typically based on management capabilities and overall system design.

A primary difference between a single fabric and a dual fabric is the reaction during a failover. Because storage and server connections are typically split between dual fabrics, connections for both the source and destination paths might need to fail over to the alternate fabric (rather than just one side within a single fabric). In either case, failover is transparent to applications. Again, because most devices support dual-active paths, failover might involve only an increase of data flow to the alternate path rather than a state change from inactive to active. Any failures to a central switch within each fabric are routed around—enabling continuous operation without any failover on the storage or servers (see Figure 5.3) [1].

Many companies use dual fabrics in a geographically separate SAN-based disaster-ready environment to ensure that operations can continue if a disaster disrupts operations at one of the locations. To ensure true high availability, the switchover from the primary site to the backup site must occur within a company's defined parameters of allowable downtime.

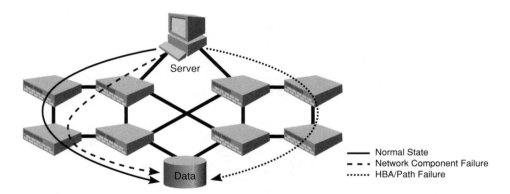

Figure 5.3
Failover in a dual fabric with dual connectivity.

RELIABILITY CALCULATIONS FOR SINGLE AND DUAL FABRICS...

The reliability and high availability of either a dual fabric or a single fabric with dual connections is based on the same principles used to measure other network or RAID storage systems. Although the probability of a single failure is very low, the probability of another failure within the repair period of the first is nearly statistically impossible. Reliability is further increased by the fact that in a RAID system or a SAN fabric, downtime must be caused by a specific component failure—not just any component failure. Because the likelihood of another failure is so remote, the following calculation is often used as a conservative model for determining overall system reliability.

For example, in a six-switch fabric with dual connections between devices, the availability during a single switch or port failure is 99.9995%. The probability of any secondary failure within the remaining five-switch fabric is nearly eleven nines in this conservative calculation. Refer to Figure 5.4 to see this calculation using the Markov probability modeling analysis [1].

For dual-redundant fabrics, only a failure in the other fabric needs to be considered since the active path would be in the active fabric. For example, in a three-switch dual-redundant configuration (which provides approximately the same port count as a single six-switch configuration), the model would be as shown in Figure 5.5 [1]. The probability of a single switch failure within the dual three-switch fabrics is similar to a single fabric. Availability would be 99.9995%. The probability of a second failure in

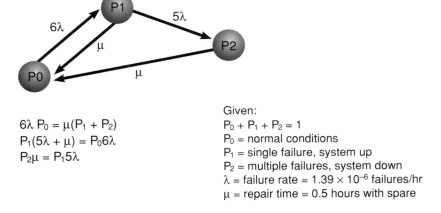

$6\lambda\,P_0 = \mu(P_1 + P_2)$
$P_1(5\lambda + \mu) = P_0 6\lambda$
$P_2\mu = P_1 5\lambda$

Given:
$P_0 + P_1 + P_2 = 1$
P_0 = normal conditions
P_1 = single failure, system up
P_2 = multiple failures, system down
λ = failure rate = 1.39×10^{-6} failures/hr
μ = repair time = 0.5 hours with spare

Figure 5.4
Availability model for a six-switch redundant fabric.

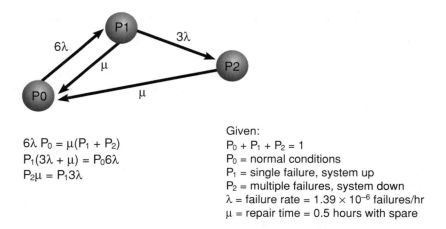

$6\lambda P_0 = \mu(P_1 + P_2)$
$P_1(3\lambda + \mu) = P_06\lambda$
$P_2\mu = P_13\lambda$

Given:
$P_0 + P_1 + P_2 = 1$
P_0 = normal conditions
P_1 = single failure, system up
P_2 = multiple failures, system down
λ = failure rate = 1.39×10^{-6} failures/hr
μ = repair time = 0.5 hours with spare

Figure 5.5
Availability model for a three-switch dual-redundant fabric.

the other three-switch fabric during this repair cycle is only fractionally higher than in the single fabric—into the eleven nines. This difference is due to a fewer number of switches that can potentially fail.

These examples help demonstrate why companies rely on highly available SANs to ensure business continuance. The fact that a single fabric has nearly the same availability rate as a dual-redundant fabric means that configuration decisions can be based solely on design philosophy, management infrastructure, and physical location requirements, rather than availability concerns.

ZONING ....

The easiest way to increase system availability is to prevent failures from ever occurring—typically by monitoring fabric activity and performing corrective actions prior to an actual failure. By leveraging advanced SAN features such as zoning and predictive management, companies can deploy a much more reliable and resilient SAN environment.

To help prevent localized failures from impacting the entire fabric, specific parts of SANs can be isolated through the use of zoning—in which defined zones limit access between devices within the SAN fabric. Companies can specify different availability criteria at the connection, node, and network level to address the potential impact of certain types of outages. For instance, several minor outages in one environment might be much less destructive than a single large outage in another environment—even if the total amount of downtime is the same. The use of zoning helps limit the types of interactions between devices that might cause failures, and thus prevents outages.

Especially as companies build larger SANs with heterogeneous operating systems and storage systems, zoning is an effective way to prevent failures. Although zoning can be implemented through either software or hardware techniques, hardware zoning provides the most secure method, with software zoning providing a more flexible but less secure approach.

Software zoning in a Fibre Channel SAN fabric is enabled by the use of the Simple Name Server (SNS), a list of devices allowed in the zone. Devices within the zone need only check the list to learn what other devices are allowed. Only the absence of knowing about the other devices prevents a zoned device from communicating with them. Because software zoning does not physically block unauthorized data from being sent, it works under the assumption that all devices are well behaved and that they have no malicious intentions.

Hardware zoning in a Fibre Channel SAN fabric provides an additional level of protection (see Figure 5.6) [1]. After a hardware zone is established, a switch creates a table of devices that can communicate with other devices in the fabric. Only traffic from devices in this zoned list are passed to the destination. All nonauthorized devices are blocked and dropped by the actual switch Application Specific Integrated Circuit (ASIC) hardware. Overlapping hardware zones allows devices to share resources such as a tape library or RAID connection, but not be in the same zone, thus increasing the security within the SAN.

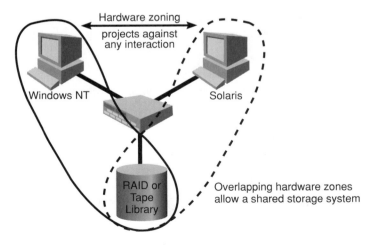

Figure 5.6
Hardware zoning to ensure reliability in a heterogeneous SAN.

By blocking the flow of unauthorized data and control information, hardware zoning can restrict interaction between devices within the fabric. For example, a server in a heterogeneous environment might attempt to log in to all devices within the fabric, whether those devices represent other servers or storage. If the server resides in a zone with all the other servers, it could cause unnecessary and potentially erroneous data flow when attempting to communicate with them. If login attempts occur repeatedly, they could disrupt operations or even cause a failure in other server connections. As a result, zoning servers (especially heterogeneous servers) provide an additional level of assurance against potential failures.

Without zoning, failing devices that are no longer following the defined rules might attempt to interact with other devices in the fabric. With zoning, these failing devices cannot affect devices outside of their zone.

Note

This type of event would be similar to an Ethernet device causing collisions on only a segment of a network.

Other critical requirements for zoning are the ability to overlap hardware zones and to implement fabric-wide hardware zoning. The ability to overlap hardware zones is essential for secure storage resource sharing. The ability to share storage resources through logical volume allocation requires that multiple servers share a physical path into the storage. If hardware zones cannot overlap, all devices that utilize this physical path must reside in the same zone-creating potential interaction and disruption between devices. Overlapping hardware zones enable each server (or groups of servers) to reside in a zone with the storage connection while another hardware zone can also see the storage connection. The two distinct zones and all their devices cannot communicate with each other—only with the shared storage system.

To be truly effective, hardware zoning must be available across the enterprise fabric. Hard zones should be able to transcend physical switch products and allow devices to be securely zoned, regardless of their location in the fabric. Fabric-wide zoning, which enables information to be distributed to all switches in the fabric, can be accessed and managed from any switch in the fabric. In addition, the flexibility to locate devices at the most appropriate place within the fabric, can help ensure reliability by enabling remote physical placement of devices and connections.

FABRIC MANAGEMENT......................................

As the network grows and interconnectivity expands across the enterprise, SAN manageability plays a greater role in ensuring high availability. Comprehensive management tools can simplify administrator tasks while helping to alert them to potential failures. One of the most effective ways to ensure the availability of the SAN, is to use predictive threshold monitoring systems that enable administrators to predict and monitor basic environmental levels, as well as fabric-level events and errors over time.

Advanced fabric-wide switch monitoring and diagnostics enable both reactive and proactive servicing—helping to ensure rapid identification of failed components. Brocade Fabric Watch®, a robust fabric-monitoring software tool, enables each switch in the SAN to constantly monitor the network and its attached nodes for potential faults—automatically detecting potential problems before they create costly outages. This innovative tool enables administrators to:

- Receive event notifications when switch and fabric elements exceed thresholds
- Quickly identify and isolate faults
- Utilize a single comprehensive fabric monitoring solution rather than multiple, vendor-specific software solutions [1]

For example, Fabric Watch enables administrators to set thresholds to alert them to performance issues within the fabric (see Figure 5.7) [1]. The threshold could be set for a particular device or a connection between switches, for example. This technique enables administrators to potentially add a server or a new connection prior to impacting application performance or potentially taxing the server and causing a failure. Threshold monitoring could also include error statistics or link status information to alert administrators to a possible cable or optics problem prior to that problem impacting operations. As a result, predictive failure capabilities can help administrators resolve a situation before a failure occurs.

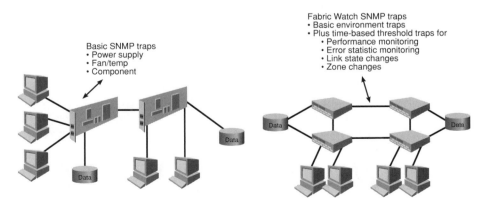

Figure 5.7
Visibility into the SAN from Fabric Watch.

THE KEY TO HIGH AVAILABILITY.............................

Achieving higher availability through redundancy and fault tolerance begins with a thorough understanding of specific system uptime requirements. True high availability stems from the use of highly available components in a networked infrastructure designed to tolerate a variety of failures.

Key points to consider in fault-tolerant design are how much of the system would be affected by a certain type of failure, and how long it would take to repair the problem. Proper system design (as well as the use of management software and zoning techniques) can help ensure that an isolated failure at one location does not lead to multiple failures in other areas of the network.

A critical factor in eliminating the possibility of a complete system outage is avoiding all potential single points of failure—through redundancy of components, devices, connections, and paths. In addition, physically separating devices can help build fault tolerance by protecting against localized physical disasters. Because director-class products cannot be distributed like a network of switches, they are more vulnerable to localized disasters, and represent a potential single point of failure that might impact the fault tolerance of the entire system.

Finally, the ability to tolerate failures and ensure continuous system operation is the key factor in providing high availability for the overall system. Multiple connectivity paths, clustering techniques, and dual fabrics all contribute to a fault-tolerant solution. In addition, the use of redundant paths, components, and software can lower the mean time between failures (MTBF) rate to a point where large networked systems can achieve true high availability.

FROM HERE...

This chapter showed how reducing or eliminating single points of failure in enterprise environments—SANs—can help improve the overall availability of business applications. High availability is achieved not through a single product, but rather through a comprehensive system design that includes all the components in the SAN. By utilizing highly available components and solutions (as well as a fault-tolerant design), enterprises can achieve the availability needed to support 24 × 7 uptime requirements. The next chapter opens up Part II, "Designing SANs," and discusses how to design Storage Networks with Fibre Channel switches, switching hubs, and hubs; components; installation planning and practices; application testing and SAN certification design issues; and SAN design documentation issues.

END NOTES..

[1] "Improving System Availability with Storage Area Networks," Brocade Communications Systems, Inc., 1745 Technology Drive, San Jose, CA 95110, 2001.

[2] John Gantz, "The Changing Rules of the Storage Game," International Data Corporation, 5 Speen Street, Framingham, MA 01701, 2001.

Part 2

Designing SANs

6 SAN Design Issues

Server and storage technology is undergoing a fundamental change that promises significant increases in processing power, availability, and distributed access to massive amounts of data. Multiprocessor servers, high performance backplanes, server clustering applications, the physical separation of storage from servers, and multiterabyte capacity of storage arrays are rapidly exceeding the capabilities of the traditional SCSI architecture that previously bound servers and storage together.

Fortunately, technical innovations in server and storage products have not occurred in isolation. Interconnect technology has undergone its own metamorphosis, with SCSI protocol over parallel bus reemerging as a serial transport over Fibre Channel. This convergence of new server designs, server clustering, autonomous gigabyte storage arrays, and Fibre Channel architecture, is raising the server/storage paradigm to a higher plateau: storage networking. From the vantage point of storage networking, managers of Enterprise networks can now envision and implement innovative designs to enhance data availability and accommodate the growing demands of their users.

FIBRE CHANNEL TOPOLOGIES ....

Fibre Channel architecture offers three topologies for SAN design: point-to-point, Arbitrated Loop, and switched fabric. All are based on gigabit speeds, with effective 100 megabyte per second throughput (200 megabyte full duplex). All allow for both copper and fiber optic cable plant, with maximum distances appropriate to the media (30 meters for copper, 500 meters for short-wave laser over multimode fiber, 10 kilometers for long-wave laser over singlemode fiber).

Point-to-point is a simple dedicated connection between two devices, and is used for minimal server/storage configurations. Point-to-point cabling typically runs directly from one device to another without an intervening hub using a subset of Fibre Channel protocol between the two devices. For additional devices, storage managers can extend the point-to-point cabling scheme, but since the media is no longer under the exclusive control of two nodes, Arbitrated Loop protocol must be used to negotiate access.

FC-AL is a shared gigabit media for up to 127 nodes (one of which may be attached to a switched fabric). Arbitrated Loop is analogous to Token Ring or FDDI, in that two communicating nodes possess the shared media only for the duration of a transaction, and then yield control to other nodes. Arbitrated Loop uses an additional subset of Fibre Channel commands to handle negotiating access to the loop, and specific sequences for assigning loop addresses (Arbitrated Loop Port Address, or ALPA) to the nodes.

Arbitrated Loops originally connected transmit and receive interfaces between multiple nodes creating an extended ring topology, similar to early Token Ring implementations. This configuration, however, was vulnerable to the same issues that surfaced in point-to-point LAN topologies. A break anywhere along the point-to-point chain would bring down the entire segment and would be very difficult to troubleshoot.

Arbitrated Loop hubs facilitate loop implementation by aggregating loop ports via a physical star configuration. Loop hubs typically provide 7 to 12 ports, and can be used to build larger loops via cascading. As with hubs in Ethernet and Token Ring LAN environments, Arbitrated Loop hubs provide greater control and reliability. Arbitrated Loop hubs employ bypass circuitry at each port to keep dysfunctional nodes from disrupting loop traffic. Other hubs provide status and diagnostic light emitting diodes (LEDs) at each port.

Since one of the Arbitrated Loop node addresses is reserved for attachment to a Fibre Channel switch, a loop can participate in a broader network or fabric built with multiple switches and loops. The combination of Arbitrated Loop hubs and switches provides flexibility in allocating bandwidth and designing storage network segmentation.

A Fibre Channel switch typically provides 8 to 16 ports, with full gigabit speeds available at each port. Following the model previously established by Ethernet switches, a Fibre Channel switch port may be configured to support a single node or a shared segment of multiple nodes (a loop). Because a switch requires more processing power (memory and microcode at each port to properly route frames), switch-per-port costs are usually greater than six times Arbitrated Loop hub-per-port costs.

A Fibre Channel switching hub is a hybrid technology that offers the advantages of both Arbitrated Loop and fabric switching. A switching hub manages the address space of two or more Arbitrated Loop segments to create a larger, logical loop. This allows nodes on physically separate loops to transparently communicate with one another, while maintaining higher available bandwidth on each physical loop. Switching hub products optimize extended Arbitrated Loop performance. They also give some of the benefits of fabric switching at a favorable price point.

CUSTOMER SELECTION OF FIBRE CHANNEL PRODUCTS ....

Anyone with experience with storage interconnects will instantly see applications appropriate for Fibre Channel switches, switching hubs, and hubs. A single Arbitrated Loop hub is a viable and cost-effective solution for 2-to-12 node configurations of one or more servers and associated storage arrays. Multiple Arbitrated Loop hubs can be cascaded to build 10 to more than 60 node networks with reasonable bandwidth. Storage managers can design a combination of Arbitrated Loop hubs and switching hubs to balance individual loop performance with high availability between loops. Managers can also position a fabric switch to provide a combination of dedicated gigabit access with shared gigabit access via hubs and/or switching hubs.

Unfortunately, vendor positioning of Fibre Channel products is sometimes misleading. A vendor that only manufactures Arbitrated Loop hubs may be tempted to complain that Fibre Channel switches are far too expensive and complex to deploy. A vendor who only supplies switches may attempt to counter objections to the higher per-port cost with denigrating remarks against Arbitrated Loop hubs. While healthy competition between vendors is essential for driving technology to higher levels, misinformation will not aid the adoption of Fibre Channel solutions for storage networking.

Just as today's Enterprise networks continue to deploy a diversity of products and topologies for LAN and WAN solutions (scaling each component according to performance, application, and cost), storage networking will extend on the basis of diverse products, including coexistence with legacy SCSI devices. Fibre Channel switches, switching hubs, hubs, and Fibre Channel-to-SCSI bridges are not competing solutions to the same problem, but integral components of a single, more comprehensive solution.

DESIGNING STORAGE NETWORKS ....

There are a number of design considerations for a storage network that effect the initial selection of products and their deployment:

- Application requirements
- Protocol support
- Cable plant
- Distance between devices
- Number of devices
- Accommodation of legacy devices

- Anticipated growth
- Traffic volumes
- Departmental segmentation
- Redundancy
- Disaster recovery
- SNMP management
- Cost/performance ratio
- All of these factors are interrelated and should be balanced for optimum use and cost savings

Application Requirements

The first question that you should ask when designing a storage network is: *What is the application?* Full motion video, prepress graphics processing, relational database queries, data mining, server clustering, tape backup, disaster recovery, and so forth— each have significantly different bandwidth, port population, segmentation, and distance requirements.

A single storage network design, moreover, may have to accommodate multiple applications concurrently (data mining plus tape backup plus disaster recovery). Designing for present and future storage applications (see sidebar, "Applications and Storage Links") requires an analysis of ongoing transaction needs and an understanding of what combination of Fibre Channel products can fulfill them. Fabric switches, switching hubs, and hubs, plus cabling options for short and long wave laser and copper, offer a rich toolset for building to both simple and complex storage application specifications.

APPLICATIONS AND STORAGE LINKS

BMC Software (Palm Desert, CA) is offering up a new solution that helps users get the most out of their applications and storage devices. BMC recently launched the Patrol Application Storage Resource Manager (AS-RM), the final component of BMC's Application-Centric Storage Management solution, which identifies and correlates which storage assets support individual business applications. The goal of the Resource Manager is to extract specific application information and associate it with all of its related storage, down to where information is located on a particular disk. The ASRM tells you which applications are consuming data at what rate.

Products weren't the only news coming out of BMC. To support the completion of the full ACSM solution, BMC has formed the ACSM Consortium Partner Program. The consortium is made up of vendors that will partner to test and integrate their systems with the Patrol products, according to BMC. Brocade, Cisco Systems, Crossroads Systems, EMC, Gadzoox Networks, Hitachi Data Systems, Inrange, JNI, McData, Network Appliance, Nishan Systems, OTG Software, and QLogic have all been named as members of the consortium. The partners will work with BMC to develop storage management solutions.

The ACSM is the partner consortium that helps BMC bring these products to market. The full ACSM solution is made up of BMC's Knowledge Modules, Patrol Storage Network Manager, Patrol Storage Resource Manager, and Patrol Application Storage Resource Manager.

Rounding out BMC's slew of storage announcements was the addition of four new Storage Knowledge Modules: Patrol for Brocade Silk-Worm, conXsan, McData Directors, and Patrol for Nishan IP Storage Switches. These join the modules already in place for EMC's Symmetrix, Network Appliance Filers, and Compaq StorageWorks, bringing the total number of Knowledge Modules to seven. Knowledge Modules are the parts of BMC's Patrol solution that discover, capture, store, and report physical attributes and event information for storage systems and storage network interconnect devices including disks, bridges, hubs, routers, and host bus adapters. While the ASCM solution has a dedicated sales team that has been *immersed* in the technology, BMC indicated that the solution is also available through its regular worldwide sales force [1].

Protocol Support

The most common protocol for storage networks is SCSI-3 over Fibre Channel. Vendors of host bus adapters (HBAs) and storage arrays rely on SCSI-3 to seamlessly replace parallel SCSI with Fibre Channel and universally provide device drivers for upper layer SCSI application support. It may also be desirable to run other storage protocols (HIPPI) or IP over Fibre Channel. Support of IP and other protocol stacks vary among HBA vendors, so you should select a particular HBA with both current and future protocol requirements in mind (see sidebar, "iSCSI to Let Businesses Move Large Amounts of Data Long Distances via an IP Network"). In Arbitrated Loop, the upper level protocol is transparent to the hub or switching hub and so is not a consideration in hub selection.

iSCSI to Let Businesses Move Large Amounts of Data Long Distances via an IP Network

Technology managers still trying to understand the difference between NAS and SANs have a new development to learn: iSCSI. More than 300 vendors are working to finalize a standard for the Small Computer Systems Interface over IP protocol, which they say will revolutionize storage networking by letting businesses move large amounts of data in and out of storage over long distances via low-cost IP networks. It will compete with more expensive Fibre Channel networks, currently the leading method of handling storage networks.

Even without a final standard, products are beginning to appear. Cisco Systems recently unveiled the SN 5420 Storage Router, which is designed to move data between Fibre Channel SANs and an IP network, where information can travel further than Fibre Channel's 10-kilometer limit. The router is slated to be available soon for $27,000.

Startup 3Ware Inc. has shipped the Escalade 7000, the third version of its iSCSI-compliant switches, which launched in December, 2000. Brocade Communications Systems recently introduced its SilkWorm 12000 Core Fabric Switch, which will support Fibre Channel, IP, and other communications protocols such as Infiniband. And, Fibre Channel switch vendor Vixel indicates it has a modified switch that works with switches from telecom equipment maker Lucent Technologies, that will ship in volume soon and offer speeds of 200 MB per second.

Note: Vixel and Lucent are working on FC over IP module for the Lucent switch, not iSCSI.

One use for iSCSI will be to provide access to stored data from remote offices that can't be reached by Fibre Channel. For example, GX Technology, which analyzes seismic data for energy companies, uses a Fibre Channel SAN. But GX has offices in Calgary, Alberta; London; and Jakarta, Indonesia that ship data to Houston headquarters via tape. GX is open to the prospect that iSCSI could link all of the offices to the main data storage at headquarters over GX's IP network. The storage network is very flexible. It will take time for this new technology to take hold, but these IP-based SANs will be important for any company that wants the same administrator to manage both kinds of information [2].

Cable Plant

Fibre Channel supports both copper and optical fiber cabling, although fiber's immunity to EMI and support for longer distances makes it the clear choice for reliable connectivity. Fibre Channel vendors early on agreed to rename *Fiber* to *Fibre*, so as not to exclude the use of copper.

For cost considerations, some vendors of Fibre Channel storage arrays, HBAs, and even Arbitrated Loop hubs have elected to provide only copper interfaces on some products. You need to understand the distance limitations and Electromagnetic Interference (EMI) susceptibility of copper to properly provision these products, and you should take care to stay well within specified guidelines.

A passive copper interface provides no signal balancing, and should not exceed 15 meters in length. An active copper interface does provide signal balancing, and can be run as long as 30 meters. For example, Vixel's hubs provide support for mixing the use of copper and optical fiber on a port-by-port basis (via GBICs) [2].

Fibre Channel hub and switch products that offer copper-only ports may not only have EMI issues to overcome, but require external media interface adapters (MIAs) to support optical fiber. You need to be aware of this additional expense and reliability issue in the selection process.

Optical fiber cabling provides superior flexibility in storage network design. Multimode fiber can be run up to 500 meters; single-mode fiber can extend to 10 kilometers. Since optical fiber is immune to external EMI, storage managers can deploy it within or between buildings and extend storage networking across an entire campus.

Distance between Devices

The physical organization of servers and storage devices may impact both the selection of cable plant on specific ports and the number of devices on any one Fibre Channel segment. In the majority of server/storage configurations, managers will locate nodes within the same room or building. For Arbitrated Loop, the total loop length can be quite large (tens of kilometers), although propagation delay through any media should be factored into network design.

The Fibre Channel specification for Arbitrated Loop, for example, allows up to 10 kilometers for long wave, single mode fiber between nodes without retiming the signal. That does not mean, however, that you could design a network with 126 nodes separated by 10 kilometers each (a total of 1260 kilometers) and expect a robust, high bandwidth network. In practice, a 10-kilometer run might be extended on a few ports (for disaster recovery), with the majority of ports well under 500 meters.

Fabric switches and switching hubs (the Vixel Rapport 4000 and Rapport 3000, respectively) provide additional flexibility for extended distances on a per port basis. Since bandwidth is allocated per port, it would be possible to design multiple 10-kilometer runs.

Distance between nodes is a very real consideration when selecting copper or fiber interfaces. If device distance is at the threshold of copper's maximum length (30 meters on active copper), it would be advisable to install fiber instead. Storage networking is the most business-critical network space, and nothing is gained by pushing recommended specifications to the maximum limit in order to cut costs.

Number of Devices

The address space for Fibre Channel switch fabric allows for millions of devices, more than adequate for large, enterprise networks. Switch products are typically 8 to 16 port configurations, but can integrate many more devices via Fabric Loop ports attached to Arbitrated Loop hubs, and switching hubs or extensions to additional switches.

> **Note**
>
> **Another way for determining the number of devices to use in a SAN is to match disk drive bandwidth capability with the required data bandwidth. Each disk drive nowadays can sustain about 10 MBps.**

Arbitrated Loop provides 127 addresses per loop, with one address reserved for switch attachment. Theoretically, it is possible to cascade multiple hubs to create a 126 node loop. Practically, such a configuration would not support normal server/storage transactions, since each node represents a latency factor against loop performance. It would be a more efficient use of bandwidth to configure multiple loops and employ a switching hub or switch to connect them.

Typical Arbitrated Loops contain 3 to 12 nodes. You should not exceed a maximum of 50–60 nodes to insure high bandwidth and availability. If you require additional nodes within the same logical address space, a switching hub can provide transparent activity between loop segments without violating bandwidth requirements for each loop segment.

Your device count should also include the internal configuration of disk arrays. If a disk array (JBOD) uses Arbitrated Loop as an internal architecture for linking disks, and the internal loop is connected to the external loop port, then each disk within an enclosure should be counted as a node.

Accommodation of Legacy Devices

A well-conceived migration path from parallel SCSI to Fibre Channel (FC) may leverage a network's current investment in SCSI disks and tape subsystems by employing Fibre Channel-to-SCSI bridges (sometimes referred to as FC-SCSI *routers*). FC-SCSI bridges offer a means to integrate parallel SCSI into a storage network design with minimal religious warfare between old and new technology proponents.

FC-SCSI bridges provide both Fibre Channel and parallel SCSI interfaces, and handle the conversion between serial SCSI-3 and previous versions of SCSI protocol. A FC-provisioned server can therefore transparently access storage or tape regardless of the ultimate downstream interface.

Anticipated Growth

Computer networks continue to grow exponentially. Your selection of switch and hub products for current requirements should therefore accommodate projected growth and thus maximize the initial investment. Your initial storage network may require only a single 7 port Arbitrated Loop hub (3 servers + 3–4 storage arrays). Depending on anticipated bandwidth and port requirements, however, a switching hub might be a more suitable investment. Additional devices could then be accommodated with hubs without subsequently dividing the bandwidth of a single Arbitrated Loop.

Traffic Volumes

By calculating average frame size, buffer capacity on both servers and storage arrays, number of active nodes, and so forth, it is possible to determine a reasonable configuration given traffic volumes. As in LAN internetworking, however, you continually adjust Fibre Channel bandwidth provisioning in response to user application's changes. Full motion audio/video applications, for example, are better served by switching hubs or switches since each port can deliver 100 MBps throughput. You can easily support typical SQL database applications, on the other hand, with medium-to-large Arbitrated Loop configurations that would be difficult to cost justify using dedicated switch ports.

Departmental Segmentation

Fibre Channel offers a number of solutions for segmentation of storage on a departmental or workgroup basis. A fabric switch can provide a backbone for tying multiple Arbitrated Loops together. A manufacturing department and engineering workgroup may have separate servers and storage arrays, but occasionally require access to each other's data. Each department could install Arbitrated Loops, with a port on each loop connected to the fabric switch. Each would preserve a shared 100 megabyte bandwidth for their own transactions, with a switched 100 megabyte pipe between them.

In addition, Arbitrated Loop addressing provides both public and private address schemes, which allows selected devices on the same loop to operate in conjunction with or in isolation from a switched fabric. A department that requires access to the fabric (via public addresses) can share the same loop topology as a department that has only local requirements (via private addresses).

Redundancy

Traditional concepts of redundancy focus on backup (or load sharing) power supplies and multiple fans. These components, however, are rarely the cause of network disruption. Loss of network availability is more often caused by the erratic behavior of an attached node or breaks in the cable plant that either downs the segment or sends it into suspended animation.

You can achieve high availability for storage networking by configuring dual Arbitrated Loops. If one loop fails (a marginal HBA takes the loop down), the redundant loop provides an alternate path between devices. You can also implement this dual-path configuration with Fibre Channel switches.

Disaster Recovery

Disaster recovery (sometimes known under less alarming euphemisms) was at best difficult to achieve with parallel SCSI storage configurations. Typically, storage managers use servers connected to high-speed routers to periodically back up data to a remote disaster recovery site.

Fibre Channel's support for 10-kilometer lengths at 100 MBps offers a superior solution for disaster recovery. You can back up or mirror an entire storage configuration via a switch, switching hub, or Arbitrated Loop hub connection to a remote, off-campus location.

> ### Note
>
> **Fibre Channel disk drives all come with dual FC connections, so setting up a dual-redundant path to the servers is as easy as making the connection. Dual redundancy requires dual HBAs on the servers and special software to implement, but the user can expect to get this software fairly readily from the HBA suppliers or from the SAN management software vendors.**

By taking backups and disaster recovery transfers off the LAN, Fibre Channel offers a significant performance benefit: Not only is the transfer rate much higher (to 100 MBps), but data can be transferred in native SCSI protocol without the overhead of TCP/IP or LAN protocol conversion.

SNMP Management

SNMP management support is by now a given for all enterprise-level LAN/WAN devices. No vendor would offer an Ethernet switch or Frame Relay product into a business-critical environment without full MIB-II support and extensive vendor-specific MIB extensions. Although servers may provide SNMP statistics, and storage arrays may provide SCSI Enclosure Services data via SNMP platforms, storage networking is a relative newcomer to SNMP requirements.

Designing manageability into a storage network adds costs to the individual components, but significantly reduces overall operational costs. Simplifying device configuration, integrating diagnostic and rapid recovery features, and reducing support requirements, all contribute to cost savings. The greatest savings that manageability offers, however, is in maximizing system uptime. When networks go down, companies lose money. For most companies, an hour or two of downtime during business hours would have paid for manageability many times over.

If SNMP management is a mandatory requirement for an enterprise network's design criteria, you should carefully evaluate the level of SNMP support of a Fibre Channel hub or switch. If a vendor fulfills only the minimal SNMP device and enclosure status features in order to qualify as *SNMP managed*, its products will be insufficiently manageable to maintain stable operation.

Cost/Performance Ratio

The decision to implement a new technology or upgrade is always a business-based decision. A company calculates the return on investment (ROI) and cost of implementation versus the increased performance (number of business transactions/dollars per second) that the implementation provides.

Fibre Channel, as an infrastructure, has a favorable return on investment, since it is the only viable technology refresh for storage that allows faster servers and massive databases. The more transactions per second, the higher the ROI.

Within the Fibre Channel suite of products, application requirements drive the return on investment for specific configurations, cost per port, manageability, reliability, vendor support, and other factors. This is not easily determined by a simple formula, but as healthy competition between Fibre Channel vendors raises the standards for product features and concurrently lowers the overall implementation costs, designers of storage networks will have even more enviable choices to make.

Therefore, Fibre Channel provides a robust, high availability, flexible, and cost effective solution to the contradiction between server/storage innovations and legacy parallel SCSI transport. Fibre Channel switches, switching hubs, Arbitrated Loop hubs, and FC-SCSI bridges all play an essential part in storage area network design. Despite occasional excesses in vendor rhetoric, both fabric switch and loop technology will contribute to the success of this breakthrough technology.

Finally, the need to serve nonvolatile data to millions of clients worldwide continues to drive the design and deployment of storage area networks. Let's take a look.

DESIGN IT AND THEY WILL COME ....

The need to store and share data with thousands—and possibly millions—of other people continues to propel the development and deployment of SANs. Whether these Fibre Channel-based topologies are moving into relatively small environments like a small group of interconnected physicians' offices, or whether they're going into an insurance company with multiple satellite sites, the SAN industry has grown—almost overnight—into a multibillion-dollar endeavor.

And there's more good news. As SAN deployment becomes more widespread, designers have the opportunity to tackle such challenges as SAN-to-SAN connectivity, *growing* individual SANs, and adding additional features and software applications. Furthermore, as end users become increasingly educated about SANs, designers will have to meet the demand for increasingly customized features, all the while keeping costs as low as possible. Daunting challenges? Certainly. But the opportunity to develop SAN solutions for a hungry market is about as exciting as it gets.

SAN Story

As previously defined, a SAN is basically a combination of hardware and software that enables stored information to be shared by multiple users, thereby creating a *storage network*. The architecture is designed to make all storage devices available to all servers on a LAN or WAN. As more storage devices are added to a SAN, they also will be accessible from any server in the larger network. In this situation, the server acts only as a path between the end user and stored data. Because stored data does not reside directly on any of a network's servers, server power is freed up for business applications.

End-User Education

End-user education is the most important component in the long-term success of SANs. As end users begin to understand SAN technology, they will be in a better position to understand how to more effectively implement and leverage SAN topologies. That, in turn, will create additional market opportunities and drive future development.

The current state of SAN implementation is reminiscent of the design and deployment of LANs in the last decade. It took a long time before the average end-user understood that he or she could actually connect a couple of PCs and manage them as a network. That same scenario is repeating itself in storage. End-users will sharpen their skills, and SAN deployment and development will continue.

Furthermore, as end-users continue to understand how to implement and manage a SAN, they will begin using their SANs in different ways. Today, SANs are attractive because they provide such features as serverless backup, remote backup, and remote disaster recovery. Those features are requirements of today's Internet age and people understand that. But as time goes by, there will be long-term implementations of SAN topology that people haven't even thought of yet.

The world of SANs will really begin to flourish when all the management software is in place and the end-user understands the technology well enough to be able to implement it to solve their specific problems—problems that designers haven't yet imagined. It's a connected cycle. As end-users begin to understand and implement SAN technology more fully, they will begin using SANs in new ways. Those new uses will create demand for new and different SAN topologies. It's definitely a good situation, but it also makes it incumbent upon designers to keep pace with user demands.

Opportunities are ripe because these emerging storage topologies are colliding with networking technology at the perfect time. This will continue to create demand for features and applications that weren't originally thought about. Therefore, the process has moved beyond inventing a better mousetrap. Now, brand new ways of catching the mouse are being invented.

SAN-to-SAN Connectivity

Many of the basic hardware interoperability issues surrounding SANs have been solved. The next challenge, therefore, is to connect SANs to MANs. The big telecom companies—meaning Nortel, Lucent, Cisco, and some of the others—are wondering how they can more fully utilize the optical infrastructure in the MANs. And, there are certainly technical issues to be dealt with in this space. For example, are we going to see Fibre Channel over IP? SCSI over IP? Fibre Channel over SONET? In any case, everyone is wondering how to effectively utilize an optical MAN. SAN-to-SAN connectivity is a great use of the MAN.

Today, one of the most popular ways to implement SANs is a dedicated leased line. Companies can lease a DWDM wavelength on the optical metro network. That way, they have a dedicated, noninterrupted line. A dedicated line is a good idea, because the features of a SAN begin to diminish when you begin separating it and integrating it with other networking activities such as a LAN.

Some people don't like to put their heartbeat information between servers on their SAN or their LAN. They want a dedicated network for that. And when you begin to cross too much distance, you start creating latencies. That's when you start diminishing the performance of a SAN (see Figure 6.1) [3]. As SANs become too dispersed, or when you try to put too much of the storage-centric traffic over a larger geographic area, you start losing the qualities of SAN.

But, it's also important to remember the application. SAN applications are probably not going to involve some sort of an online transaction processing (OLTP) application across the MAN. Instead, it's going to be some kind of replication, some kind of backup, and some kind of disaster recovery—something that is not latency sensitive.

This is exactly what people are doing when they are connecting these clusters of SANs. They're doing it for nonlatency-sensitive kinds of operations: disaster recovery, backup, and data warehousing.

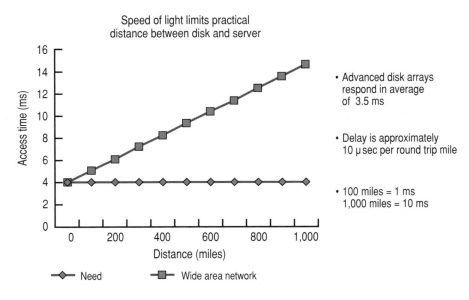

Figure 6.1
How distance affects the performance of Storage Area Networks.

At the same time, the concept of extending a SAN without losing the utility and definition of a SAN is somewhat of a misnomer. By extending the connectivity between SANs, you don't have to maintain anything about a SAN as a local entity or a consolidator of storage. You're just adding functionality that happens to be particular to the geographic and application requirement. So, you don't have to maintain anything across that MAN, you're just adding the capability to cover distance.

For example, let's say it's snowing and the road is covered. Then snowplows come along and push the snow into little piles. You can think of those piles as SANs on a network. There will be a geometric multiplication of SANs—localized SANs. Within their own group, you have scheduled storagecentric traffic that requires no geographical latency. At some point, you cache the operation or application and send the valuable data across the MAN over to the next SAN. So, you're reducing the amount of overall traffic you actually push long haul.

Cost Considerations

Cost is a major aspect involved with implementing the MAN infrastructure for SAN-to-SAN storage (see Figure 6.2) [3]. Today, it is still rather expensive to move data over SONET infrastructure or some type of MAN. Until that cost comes down, people are going to continue to do what they're doing today, and that's to keep stuff on their own wire. It hasn't changed in ten years.

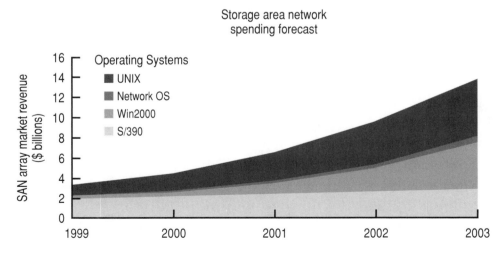

Figure 6.2
Market analyst IDC expects spending on storage area networks to grow to $14 billion by 2003.

You see, monopolies arise very quickly in this area when it comes to phone services. This is a similar model. Volume doesn't always immediately drive down costs in those kinds of markets. Monopolies hold onto their markets pretty well. It really isn't any different, unless the government gets involved.

And, what about bandwidth? All you hear about is how bandwidth is becoming plentiful. But, for this kind of application, it doesn't seem to be plentiful enough. It's not really known if anybody who wouldn't use a remote capability for storing large amounts of data wouldn't do it if it were inexpensive enough. Actually, everyone would do it. The SSPs are depending upon it, and they're coming into the market pretty quickly. But, their services are targeted at the very high end, and that's where the money is.

SAN Software

Right now, the big focus for SAN development is management software. Most of the hardware interoperability issues have been worked out. Software development continues to be the hot area.

Management software has always been the critical aspect of the SAN. The hardware and the infrastructure exist, but taking advantage of that infrastructure is another matter. If you can manage 4 Tbytes instead of 1 Tbyte with a single person, for example, you're much better off.

Basically, the idea behind SAN management software is a smart SAN topology. Over the course of the next several years, the winning topology will be the one that tends to cluster tasks under applications that are storage-traffic-centric. Those will outperform those that don't.

And, it's happening already. Companies such as Veritas, Legato, DataCore, and Compaq are all designing software that creates a file system for a SAN. The industry is in the process of taking features from the mainframe and bringing them into the SAN world. For example, DataCore *virtualizes* the SAN with their management software. Storage software companies such as Veritas, Legato, and Tivoli all have Fibre Channel SAN software products that manage SANs. You're going up the food chain and pulling fruit from the mainframe world and trying to open it up to industry standards.

While you can leverage some of the principles of the existing networking software, you can't really leverage the software itself, because it's for connectivity management, which is important, but the discussion is about data management. There's a big difference when you're talking about data management spread out over a network. That's not something existing solutions deal well with. You throttle your access to storage down to zero if you try to implement it in the same way.

It's just not the right kind of software solution. But, a lot of this is getting piped out of the original equipment manufacturer (OEM) into the integrator market and a lot of it involves end-user education going forward. In the end, the driving force is the person in the big enterprise service center who is growing his or her storage at 100% or more per year. He or she has to do something. Smart SAN software will help him or her adapt, while minimizing the need to hire more IT professionals.

OEM Involvement

Most OEMs have been involved in SAN development since the beginning. Today, most of their effort is put into developing software. They know that SANs generated a half-billion dollars in 1999 and $1.2 billion in 2000 for switches, hubs, and host adapters. The potential revenues for SAN software are much higher. People realize that data is more valuable than money at this point. That's why the SAN market will continue to grow.

A lot of companies are at this point—where they are furnishing full end-to-end finished products to OEMs. It consists of firmware, software, drivers, services software, discovery software, and management software. From the component point of view, it's the entire SAN infrastructure.

The OEMs then take that component set and combine it with application software to make it useful for an end-user as something more than just a utility. Currently, a lot of effort is going into refitting the same product for different people's platforms. There's a lot of demand for customized solutions.

FROM HERE ....

This chapter opened up Part II, "Designing SANs," and discussed how to design Storage Networks with Fibre channel switches, switching hubs, and hubs; components; installation planning and practices; application testing and SAN certification design issues; and SAN design documentation issues. The next chapter covers the financial impact of a SAN, justification of SAN operating costs, and financial considerations and acquisitions.

END NOTES...

[1] Kevin Komiega, "BMC Links Applications and Storage," searchStorage.com, c/o TechTarget.com, 117 Kendrick Street, Needham, MA 02494, 2001.

[2] Chris Lyon and Gina Calabria, "Designing Storage Networks with Fibre
     Channel Switches, Switching Hubs, and Hubs," Vixel Corporation, Cor-
     porate Headquarters, 11911 North Creek Parkway South, Bothell, WA
     98011, 2001.

[3] Mike Downing, "Designing for the SAN Market: Build It and They Will
     Come," International Data Corporation, 5 Speen Street, Framingham,
     MA 01701, 2001.

7 Cost Justification and Consideration

$\mathbf{T}$he safe but unglamorous storage system is likely to be the technology least affected by budget squeezes during the proposed economic downturn. The data of a company is the business and, therefore, where it is stored must be important.

Many companies have recently taken a conscious decision to spend a lot of money on storage systems. It will be the least affected area during the downturn. This is because organizations are waking up to the fact that managing data, even though a troublesome task, can increase productivity and save money.

By 2003, organizations will devote up to two-thirds of their IT budgets on storage, according to a report by The Butler Group. However, many businesses could save a great deal of time and money by implementing SANs.

SANs are bound to save companies money in management because they cut down on human intervention. This could be a solution to the data storage overload that many IT managers currently experience.

SANs usually pay for themselves in less than a year. They also provide businesses with a reliable way of backing up information, which is vital. The problem all IT managers face is that you just can't afford to be down for a minute.

FINANCIAL IMPACT OF A SAN...............................

Any new technology, such as SANs, has many impacts on the enterprise in which it is implemented. The SAN must make sense from an operational as well as a financial perspective. Fortunately, SANs provide significant benefits in both respects. Indeed, the financial benefits are firmly based on the operational impacts of replacing traditional storage infrastructure with a SAN. The operational benefits of a SAN include improved scalability, distance, and configuration flexibility over traditional SCSI storage architectures. The financial benefits parallel the operational benefits, and can be categorized in several ways. In order to simplify the analysis in this chapter, it will focus on three areas of SAN savings: capital, backup, and management costs. The SAN impact will be compared to the way things are done today in a SCSI environment.

Caution

This part of the chapter explores the potential impact of cost justification and consideration of implementing a SAN. Comparisons and financial projections are speculative only, and not a guarantee of savings. Actual savings depend on a number of factors not limited to the actual environment, software, and operational considerations.

Capital Savings

One of the largest potential savings of implementing a SAN is that of reduced capital expenditures. This saving comes about by separating the growth of storage from that of the servers to which they are traditionally attached. In traditional SCSI architectures, as the need for storage increases, more storage is added to a server until the server runs out of space, or if the storage is external, the server's SCSI bus runs out of space after 15 devices. These limitations are significant since a large number of servers are significantly underutilized if their primary reason to be added was just to get more storage. The growth rate of storage is so high that it is difficult to manage such growth, and the urgency to add more storage has discouraged more efficient server utilization. The operational imperative has been to just get some storage to keep functioning.

A SAN disconnects server growth from storage growth. The SAN creates a network for storage, much as a LAN is a network for messages (see Figures 7.1 to 7.3) [1]. Two different networks allow the storage to grow independently of the servers, much like the LAN allows clients to be added independent of the server. As the data storage grows, the growth rate for the server is tied to the processing power requirement, not the need to add more paths for storage. The SAN provides the scalability and configuration flexibility to allow the storage to grow independently of the server.

The magnitude of these savings is dependent on several factors, including the rate of storage growth. By knowing the utilization rate of the servers in the enterprise, and understanding the growth rate of the data required, it is possible to estimate the amount of savings from this impact. Reducing the rate of server growth by just 10%, while growing storage at 100% or even 50%, could provide enough savings to pay for the SAN in less than one year. When calculating server costs, include all of the associated costs, including the software, maintenance, floorspace, and environmental expense. Consideration should also be made for management of the servers. Systems

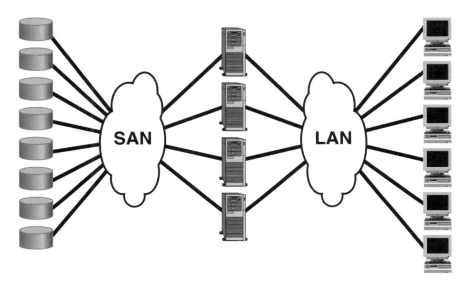

Figure 7.1
LAN and SAN structures.

programmers and administrators run the servers and, as the number of servers grow, there will be pressure to increase headcount, training, and management costs for the operation of the servers. If an enterprise is already thinking of consolidating data sites to reduce costs, a SAN should be considered to further leverage those efforts and provide additional savings.

Backup Savings

Perhaps one of the most underappreciated disciplines in information technology is backup. It is difficult to focus on backup when you are struggling with a storage growth rate of 100%. It is very easy to focus on backup after a fire, flood, or an errant backhoe operator who has destroyed the only copy of important data. SANs provide a better way of backing up data, as well as several ways to provide high availability configurations.

The most common backup configuration today means putting a tape drive with each server to protect its data. This not only costs a lot of money in tape drives and tapes, it requires a lot of human power to manage the backup process and the tape media management. To be more efficient, most IT departments put a tape library in a central location, then send the backup traffic via the LAN to a dedicated backup server which manages the tape library. This provides several benefits. There is a reduced capital cost in tape drives for every server, somewhat offset by the tape library cost, as well as more efficient use of tape media in some cases. In all cases a central tape library provides a far more efficient use of the human element to coordinate the backups and make sure they are performed on a regular basis, which assures the tape media is handled in a methodical manner. This change, however, is not for free. It does significantly impact the LAN, since the backup traffic now uses the LAN to get data from the servers to the tape library. Additionally, it creates a server that is significantly utilized for backup, and servers and their related costs are a significant impact, as you saw earlier.

A SAN provides further improvement on today's LAN backup-based model (see Figure 7.2) [1]. It creates an infrastructure independent of the LAN to move data from the server to the tape drive. The server is still involved in the data transfer, but the LAN is replaced with the SAN. In many cases, backup traffic is a significant portion of all LAN traffic. The financial impact of reducing an investment of any significant magnitude in the LAN can finance the development of the SAN. By replacing the LAN infrastructure with a SAN infrastructure, you create a dedicated resource for storage traffic that is more efficient than using the LAN for all data traffic. As you have seen, there are additional benefits of the SAN other than offloading the LAN on this one application.

The SAN also holds the promise of another category of backup saving, that of a reduced server backup. Even though the SAN offloads the LAN, the backup server is still managing the backup process—directing the movement of data from the disk where it is stored to the tape drive where it is backed up. A data mover has been demonstrated by companies like Gadzoox® Networks and Legato software that reduces the server's overhead to almost zero. This opens the door for smaller backup servers, and possibly some additional consolidation to eliminate servers, thus saving even more money.

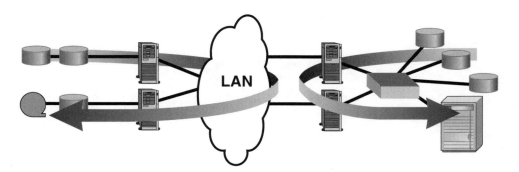

Figure 7.2
Conventional backup on left side of LAN compared to SAN backup on right.

Finally, by avoiding the need for backup, cost savings can be realized. The cost of data unavailability is high. Cost estimates range from $3 million for banks or financial corporations to about $300,000/hour for a data center in a large enterprise. As the world moves to e-commerce and increasing interconnections, those costs will surely rise. To avoid data unavailability is the best approach, but making sure it is done cost-effectively is important. The SAN provides an infrastructure that allows a high availability configuration to scale far better than traditional SCSI architectures. When the two elements of high availability and more efficient backups are combined, they can more than justify the purchase of a SAN.

Data Management

Data management in traditional SCSI architectures is mostly limited to adding new data volumes, managing storage performance, backup, and if necessary, data recovery. The limitations of a SCSI bus mean that many of the things done in the LAN network world are not possible, nor are they needed, in the SCSI data world. With the increased flexibility of the SAN storage architecture, there is more need to manage the data due to the flexibility of the networked topology. From this effort comes yet another array of savings by using a SAN.

Storage pools, or storage consolidation, are another significant impact of SAN management on costs (see Figure 7.3) [1]. A SAN provides the means to share storage

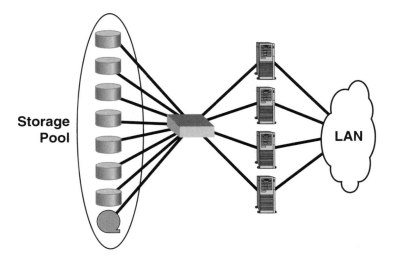

Figure 7.3
SAN showing a storage pool of disk storage and tape to be shared among servers.

among servers. With rapid storage growth, it is too difficult to accurately predict where each gigabyte of storage will be needed. As a result, guesses are made, leaving some servers with excess capacity and others under configured. Enterprises spend a lot on storage that is not optimally utilized due to inflexible storage/server configurations.

A SAN provides the infrastructure to more efficiently share storage resources. By allowing many servers to access a wide array of storage, the traditional limiting link between servers and storage is broken. This allows more efficient storage expenditures since it can easily be shared among servers. In some environments, if storage purchases can be reduced by only 12% because of this capability, the SAN infrastructure can be justified.

Asset management is another benefit of SAN management in terms of operational ease. Just keeping track of all an enterprise's storage is almost impossible in an environment where growth is 70–120% a year. SANs allow a storage topology to be created so management can see how storage assets are arranged. This can impact the amount of labor dedicated to storage and allow further productivity in the IT department.

Getting more productivity from the people already managing storage is important, and avoiding more headcount can also help defray the cost of a SAN while improving operational efficiencies. Thus, SANs, with their unique combination of operational impacts on the data center, provide many cost benefits even with simple hub-based configurations. As customer needs get more involved, the flexibility of a SAN to grow more sophisticated allows further flexibility and increased cost benefits. As the move into switching for SAN function occurs, an additional level of benefits accompanies that migration, justifying the increased cost and function.

Now, let's look at how virtualized storage offers to cut SAN operating costs, and ease the justification and administration of your data assets.

JUSTIFICATION OF SAN OPERATING COSTS ....

As today's e-business applications become increasingly datacentric, storage always seems in short supply. Add the increased capacity requirements of multimedia and on-demand video being deployed more often by human resources and marketing departments, and the task of keeping up with storage requirements and operating costs can seem insurmountable.

In today's IT landscape, it is not uncommon to find complex networks of diverse, multivendor storage technologies taking on much of the challenge. Anyone responsible for ensuring storage availability across mixed networks knows what a challenging and expensive undertaking this can be.

Although existing solutions have made local access to LAN and WAN data sources possible, the hassle of running disparate protocols for accessing storage devices remains, as does the difficulty of accurately tracking storage capacities which often results in waste. Many vendors offer to resolve the data dilemma, but you must find one that matches your needs. These options often require expensive and proprietary investments.

With a multitude of devices spanning the typical enterprise, data access can be difficult, backups are typically less than seamless, and taking full advantage of your storage capacities often remains impossible. That is where storage virtualization can be your friend.

Storage virtualization offers a means of addressing storage functionally rather than physically. Storage virtualization extracts the physical process of storing data through software (and sometimes hardware) layers that map data from the logical storage space required by applications to the actual physical storage space. Users can access storage without needing to know where a device is or how it's configured—and without incurring significant performance and operating costs overhead.

As an example, virtual storage would enable multiple, low operating cost, commodity disks across the network to appear to the user as a single, multiterabyte disk. The disks could even comprise optical storage devices or a cache management system, but the actual implementation operates in complete transparency to the end-user or application.

Furthermore, because the disk appears as a single entity to the network administrator, virtual storage disks make it easier to redistribute, reconfigure, and add to storage capacity; thus allowing for more effective management and improved performance. Because any reasonably-priced commodity storage components can comprise the actual back end, and Pentium-based servers can replace expensive proprietary boxes, the open architecture of virtualization benefits your long-term ROI. You'll enjoy lower operating costs and an improved life span for your current hardware.

Adopting storage virtualization management software has many benefits, but it carries some caveats. You often hear the terminology of storage virtualization bandied about without regard for implementations or standards. Although 2001 will likely see most SAN vendors jumping on the bandwagon and implementing some virtualization features in their product offerings, the number of storage virtualization vendors almost matches the number of implementation standards.

Currently, though, most vendors seem to be building unto their own vision: some optimized for speed, others for ease of maintenance, whereas some focus only on improving backup capabilities. Early adopters will be challenged by the fact that no standards exist among vendors. Be certain you know what your vendor's interpretation of storage virtualization is and how its implemented solution will benefit your business.

There are proposals on the table, notably from Hewlett-Packard and Sun Micro-systems, for developing an interoperability framework. These efforts aim to improve the communication capabilities of cross-management systems, and they include handling requirements for many storage devices. But full adoption by vendors is a ways off.

You can find some good starting points for storage virtualization from companies such as Veritas (*www.veritas.com*), DataCore (*www.datacore.com*), IBM, and HP, al-though most vendors with whom you work are likely to have solutions. It's time to stop putting out fires and start flooding your storage pool with a commonsense alternative like storage virtualization. As the information glut grows, adopting open, scalable ar-chitectures will be imperative to meeting capacity demands in a cost-effective manner.

Finally, let's look at how to avoid overspending on Storage Area Networks by matching features to your needs; as well as how to make smart decisions about pur-chasing storage.

FINANCIAL CONSIDERATIONS AND ACQUISITIONS...

Most IT managers know about the explosion in storage requirements that's been driven by e-commerce and other applications, and most have heard vendors extolling the vir-tues of SANs as a way of consolidating and better managing storage resources. But what's not so clear is the balance between costs and benefits.

Everyone offers the basic components—high-speed Fibre Channel hubs or switches that provide the high-speed 1 GBps SAN backbone to which vendors attach disk arrays, tape libraries, optical disks, and other resources. Servers access the SAN either through Ethernet bridges or by direct connection using a Fibre Channel host adapter.

Around this infrastructure, vendors add value by wrapping their own perfor-mance-tuning and management tools and by adding features ranging from the ability to dynamically reallocate storage among servers to fault-tolerance schemes. Each function you choose, however, adds to the total cost.

SANs are expensive, and prices vary widely. So what do you get for your mon-ey? What features do you really need (see sidebar, "SAN Features Shopping List")? And what can you really afford? The three companies profiled below each had differ-ent storage requirements. And each chose a different vendor, spending from less than $200,000 to more than $1 million. Here's what they got in return.

SAN FEATURES SHOPPING LIST

In addition to the basic hardware, SANs include a mix of features that can add considerably to overall cost. The key is to determine which features you need up front. Here's a quick rundown of common features (from the basic to high-end functions) and why you might need them.

Zoning

This basic function allows the grouping of SAN ports (and associated devices) by function or location so that many servers can share the same storage devices. While devices may be included in more than one zone, only devices in the same zone can see one another.

LUN Masking

This basic feature keeps one server from overwriting a volume used by another server. Assigning logical unit numbers (LUN) is a way for a RAID storage system to present a hard disk drive to a server. A basic SAN function, LUN masking makes specific LUNs (and hence devices) visible only to specified servers within the same zone.

LUN Mapping

This is the ability to take one LUN and map it as different LUNs to multiple servers. It allows the SAN to work with some finicky server host bus adapters (HBA) that expect LUN numbers to appear in a specific order. This is less of a problem with newer HBAs.

Dynamic Storage Allocation

This allows available physical SAN storage resources to be reallocated among servers as needed.

Storage Virtualization

This is the ability to carve up SAN storage from the physical drive pool into virtual drive volumes that can be shared to heterogeneous server environments. This level of abstraction makes volume management easier.

Nondisruptive Backups

This is software that manages SAN backup and restoration processes with minimal disruption to SAN performance. Tools are available from both SAN vendors and third-party suppliers.

Snapshot Copy

To avoid performance hits from backups, users often create off line copies of their data. But copying all blocks in a disk volume takes time. A snapshot copy takes a picture of the target volume's current state, creating a table of tracks, sectors, and volumes that can be used to start backups sooner so they can be completed earlier—an important consideration when backup times are long.

Remote Data Mirroring

This enables the creation of remote mirrored data sets for rapid disaster recovery.

Remote Data Replication

Also called remote copy; it creates off-line mirror images of active production volumes that can be used to run data integrity checks and other tasks in parallel and without affecting response time performance of live data.

Multipathing

A fault-tolerance feature that reroutes data to an alternate path when an HBA, cable, or controller fails. It may also provide dynamic load balancing by rerouting data in the SAN to improve efficiency.

Serverless Backups

This feature allows backups to take place across the SAN without server involvement. The device or software uses the Network Data Management Protocol to respond to a server agent's backup request to move data directly between SAN-attached disk arrays and SAN-attached tape storage. This feature requires special software from a tape backup vendor such as Pathlight Technology in Ithaca, NY, The relatively new, high-end feature can be expensive to implement.

Application Failover

This feature supports clustered servers that have access to one another's data volumes but don't have to be running the same applications. When Server A fails, Server B accesses Server A's volume, launches the failed server's applications, accesses the data, and takes over the function. This approach results in some downtime because the application must launch on Server B and users may need to reconnect.

Clustered Application Support

This is the ability of an application operating in a server cluster to pool multiple server resources together. When one server fails, the other keeps the application running against the same data volume. For users, the failover is seamless. Some SAN vendors offer features that enable this process to work more smoothly [2].

Mission-Critical

WorldStor Incorporated in Fairfax, VA, is a storage service provider, offering storage as a utility to companies that have elected to outsource their storage operations. The company needed very high reliability because of the nature of its business and wanted a vendor with a proven SAN architecture.

WorldStor stepped back and looked at exactly what they were trying to provide: an enterprise-class storage utility service that customers could bet their data on. The reason that they did not look too closely at some vendors, including Compaq and Xio-tech, is that they knew these companies were not far enough along in their development cycle to provide them with an architecture that was as stable and as well tested as a product from one of the big players.

WorldStor ultimately chose four EMC Symmetrix SANs for two reasons: EMC's proven architecture; and its extensive portfolio of management software. Supplying raw capacity is the easy part of their business; it's managing the availability and the performance of the data that resides on that storage that poses the challenge. And those challenges are the very things that EMC develops its software to address.

The four SANs hold between 5 and 10 terabytes (TB) of data each and use EMC's Symmetrix 8730 and 8430 storage array controllers; its Celerra File Server to make SAN volumes appear to remote clients as network-attached storage; and its Connectrix Fibre Channel switches. WorldStor makes extensive use of EMC's Control Center management software, plus Symmetrix Remote Data Facility for storage mirroring, TimeFinder for replication, Volume Logix for storage virtualization, and Symmetrix Data Recovery software.

WorldStor's Symmetrix SAN didn't come cheap. The multimillion-dollar price tag that they paid for (its four EMC SANs) is high. But, WorldStor has saved thousands of dollars in software development costs because it was able to purchase software tools from Hopkinton, Massachusetts-based EMC instead of developing them in-house. So, in the long run, WorldStor's total cost to offer the service to their customers is not any more expensive than some of the storage service providers that are attempting to use more commodity-based products.

The Middle Road

Senior managers at Hannaford Bros., a 112-store grocery chain based in Scarborough, Maine, were looking into a new SAN in 2000. They wanted a design that would tie into heterogeneous environments, including UNIX, Windows NT, and OS/390.

EMC was the only company that offered this capability, but it was unwilling to take systems responsibility for all SAN components. So Hannaford Bros. focused on building a homogeneous system to support their seven Compaq ProLiant 8500 Windows NT servers, which provide email, file, and Web services. The applications weren't as mission-critical as the core business systems, but high availability was a requirement, particularly for file sharing and messaging.

Hannaford Bros. evaluated offerings from EMC and Compaq and chose Compaq's StorageWorks in December 2000, because not only would it provide all of the equipment from the switches to servers and the disk arrays, but it would also support it.

That's the big difference between the way EMC works and the way Compaq works. EMC would point to Bus Logic or Brocade or Compaq and say, "Those guys have the problem." But EMC, whose Symmetrix SAN continues to run in Hannaford's mainframe environment, is getting better. At the time, Compaq was also cheaper. EMC's Connectrix switch was tremendously expensive compared to the cost per connection in the Compaq system.

Hannaford's StorageWorks SAN, deployed in April 2000, consists of 2.6 TB of storage, three StorageWorks RA8000 disk arrays, two eight-port Fibre Channel switches, a 16-port Fibre Channel switch, and two RAID controllers. The total price of the SAN, including the disk storage array, switches, host bus adapters, and software (but not including the servers or installation), was approximately $450,000.

The SAN improves the performance of Lotus Notes servers dramatically. Hannaford uses RAID 5 in StorageWorks, and since that's a six-channel connection to the disk, it's very, very fast. Similarly, the SAN delivers excellent file-serving performance because it provides access to a large amount of disk space.

For higher availability, Hannaford uses Compaq's multipathing utility that re-routes disk data to an alternate path when it detects a failure on the host bus adapter, cable, or controller and provides dynamic load-balancing to improve I/O efficiency. If any component fails, the SecurePath software switches the route to a different SAN path without a glitch. Hannaford can easily change paths manually with a drag-and-drop procedure.

Hannaford concedes that Compaq's variety of systems they can connect to is immature. Compaq doesn't have the wide range of offerings that EMC does. That wasn't a factor for the project, but it's one reason an EMC SAN still runs on Hannaford's mainframes.

Hannaford saved money by doing the setup in-house, but it wasn't easy. The installation really requires a typical propeller head. But once the SAN is installed, running, and documented, it works very well, and the tools do exactly what Compaq says they will do.

The Value Approach

Andersen Corporation, a manufacturer of windows in Bayport, MN, reports the data on the company's Windows NT servers has been doubling every 11 months for the past few years. As a result of this data explosion, Andersen had been experiencing server disk I/O problems on their exchange servers and problems backing up the data on those servers. By installing a SAN, Andersen hoped to solve both their backup and disk I/O problems with one product.

Andersen looked seriously at EMC, Santa Clara, CA-based Hitachi Data Systems, and Hewlett-Packard before choosing Eden Prairie, Minnesota-based Xiotech's Magnitude SAN. Andersen's technical committee reviewed proposals from all the vendors and cut the field down to finalists EMC and Xiotech before making its final choice.

The committee's criteria included interoperability, scalability, ease of use, the ability to operate in a heterogeneous environment (UNIX and Windows NT), and price. It chose Xiotech because, for Andersen's needs, it stacked up well against the competition in all of those categories and cost less. The total price tag came to less than $200,000.

Andersen uses two Xiotech SANs—one for development and a second for production. Each includes a single host bus adapter, one 16-port Fibre Channel switch and 24, 50 GB SCSI drives (for 1.2 TB of storage). The production environment services nine HP NetServers running Windows NT. Andersen also plans to add UNIX hosts to the production SAN. Software components included Xiotech's Redi Storage management software, Volume Director (for storage virtualization), and Zone Manager (for zoning).

So far, Andersen is impressed with the Magnitude SANs. Availability comes down to more than just hardware redundancy. There are lower-cost solutions that adequately provide the hardware platform. Xiotech does that very well. The storage management software has been easy to use, and setup also went smoothly thanks to the plug-and-play nature of the product.

Final Decision

Choosing the best SAN for a company's needs and budget can be daunting, but some choices are clear. For high availability in mission-critical data centers, established SAN vendors such as EMC and Hitachi offer a mature architecture, sophisticated management and support capabilities, and an established track record (although companies like Compaq and Xiotech also offer high-end configurations and are closing that gap).

For less critical needs, offerings from Compaq, Xiotech, and others may offer what you need for less. But users suggest comparison shopping, since EMC and other high-end vendors also offer lower-end configurations and all vendors tend to discount substantially below initial sticker prices. A seemingly expensive SAN may actually end up being the more economical choice.

As it turns out, you can't buy a SAN on a shoestring budget. But with some smart planning, you can get the most cost-effective SAN for your company's needs—and perhaps save hundreds of thousands of dollars in the process.

Acquisitions

Data grows, no matter what; however, with rising pressures on budgets, companies are getting nervous about purchasing more and more storage. In the past, a common practice has been to overbuy storage ahead of demand. However, with the price of storage dropping continuously, companies can save a lot of money by buying only what they need, when they need it. But to do so, you must be confident about growth. And for that, you need accurate data about your storage. To accumulate the information needed to forecast growth, it is recommended that companies invest in an application-centric storage management tool that will do the following:

- Inventory the storage devices installed on your network. Companies routinely inventory network assets. However, rarely do they have good statistics on storage usage. Find a tool that will hunt out storage devices and describe what and where they are.

- Gather application-specific usage statistics. Data is power. The tool should give you detailed statistics on how the storage is used as well as who the biggest consumers are—by function, application, and file type, not just in total gigabytes. Only when you know which applications are growing the fastest, can you manage your storage purchases wisely.

- Report information for all storage configurations. No one configuration (direct-attached, network-attached, or SAN-attached) is the right choice for every application. Consequently, the tool must be capable of gathering metrics for all configurations installed on the network [2].

Deferring expenses is smart. Gathering and analyzing historical data is the key to making smart decisions about purchasing storage and controlling your budget.

Finally, the improvements in operational and financial considerations make SANs an easy decision. Like any new technology, SANs should be implemented in a careful and methodical way to get the largest benefit. Now go out and build one!

FROM HERE ....

This chapter covered the financial impact of a SAN, justification of SAN operating costs, and financial considerations and acquisitions. The next chapter shows you how to design distributed SAN standards and discusses new standards design issues.

END NOTES...

[1] Erik Ottem, "Financial Impact of a SAN," Gadzoox Networks, 5850 Hellyer Avenue, San Jose, CA 95138, 2001.

[2] "How to Make Smart Decisions About Purchasing Storage," searchStorage.com, c/o TechTarget.com, 117 Kendrick Street, Needham, MA 02494, 2001.

8 Standards Design Issues

The demand for greater speed across network connections has been restricted by a number of bottlenecks. Arguably, the greatest restriction to data flow is the nature of the I/O architecture. While data can buzz around the world with astonishing speed, it must still have a point of orientation and delivery. In many cases, an organization may have tremendous amounts of bandwidth, yet have systems with extremely slow and primitive I/O buses.

For example, InfiniBand technology addresses the shortfall of current I/O buses. The performance gains could range from 500 Mbps to 6 Gbps per link. The implications for storage networking design standards are enormous.

Note

InfiniBand means *infinite bands*, but don't take its translation too literally. InfiniBand is a new bus technology that hopes to replace the current Peripheral Component Interconnect (PCI) bus standard that only supports up to 133 Mbps across the installed PCI slots, providing a maximum shared bandwidth of just 566 Mbps (Megabits per second).

The InfiniBand Trade Association (IBTA) [1] developed and published the specification for the InfiniBand architecture in the fall of 2000. The development of this specification had industry-wide support, with over 326 companies participating. The new point-to-point switched fabric topology network technology is expected to be transformed into a variety of interconnect and computer server commercial products by the end of 2002. Companies like Intel, for example, already have InfiniBand prototype devices in development and have established dedicated interoperability labs (see sidebar, "Intel Tries Open Source for Storage Standard").

INTEL TRIES OPEN SOURCE FOR STORAGE STANDARD

Intel will share the source code for new storage technology in hopes that freely available technology will speed the adoption of new, less expensive storage networks. The chipmaker announced recently that technology related to the Internet SCSI specification (iSCSI) is now available as open-source software. The iSCSI specification combines the popular SCSI interface with Ethernet technology to allow servers to exchange data from storage devices using IP-based networks. The iSCSI specification would reduce the need for companies to settle on more expensive technologies, such as Fibre Channel, to link storage systems.

Intel's communications standard, created by its Technology Research Lab, is specifically aimed at allowing Ethernet networks to carry data from storage devices. The chipmaker hopes that by offering the standard as open source, developers will adopt it more quickly. As a result, products built around it (such as switches, routers, and adapters) would be available sooner.

At the same time, developing technologies such as the iSCSI-based Ethernet technology plays to Intel's goal of expanding to become more than just a desktop chipmaker. One of the areas they're getting more heavily into within networking is network storage. This is a technology that would help them there. What they're trying to do is create an infrastructure that would allow the industry to create lower-cost network storage. But there's also something in it for Intel.

Note: iSCSI is not an Intel standard. It is a spec created jointly by many in the industry.

What you'll see down the road is Intel products that would allow you to support the iSCSI specification. By implementing storage devices using the iSCSI specification, organizations can add storage to any location on an Ethernet network with less complexity and expense. Also, as an extension of an Ethernet network, network administrators can use the same utilities to manage the entire network, including storage server farms.

Also, networking giant, Cisco, announced it would let any company use its iSCSI driver software, so long as it conforms to the specification. Intel's open-source iSCSI software is now available on the Web.

Intel also announced that it is leading a multicompany group to help accelerate the deployment of next-generation standards that will extend Ethernet to include networked storage. This iSCSI Group, a new group within the IP Storage Forum of the Storage Networking Industry Association, will work to accelerate the use of the iSCSI [1].

InfiniBand enables increasing data flow rates on servers, storage devices, and interconnect devices through the I/O fabric. The term fabric is used in order to illustrate the nature of the architecture that relies on communication strands or links. As with any fabric, these strands can be interwoven to provide different patterns of data flow. In theory, the I/O throughput with InfiniBand technology should be increased initially by two to four times. The simple design offers increased system performance, enhanced reliability, and greater availability. It also provides independent scalability of fabric elements.

DESIGNING DISTRIBUTED SAN STANDARDS: CRAM COURSE ON INFINIBAND ARCHITECTURE TECHNOLOGY ....

A fabric of InfiniBand switches and links is used to provide connections between servers, distributed remote storage, and networking devices. The InfiniBand fabric will both coexist with, and replace, existing I/O technology standards. While *standards* such as Ethernet, Fibre Channel, and Peripheral Component Interconnect (PCI) have existed side by side and continue to evolve, none of them effectively provide true interoperability or manageability. The InfiniBand architecture can theoretically provide operating system and hardware platform interoperability while improving system configurations (see Figure 8.1) [1].

The key to InfiniBand is switching technology that links host-channel adapters (HCA) to target channel adapters (TCP). The switch operates between the HCA and TCA to manage and direct data packets. Architecturally, the host-channel adapter typically resides near the CPU and memory. In contrast, the target channel adapter supports the storage and peripheral device I/O.

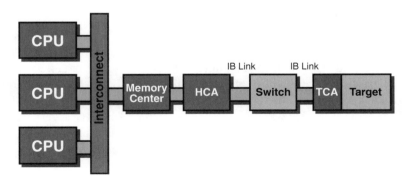

Figure 8.1
Simplified view of InfiniBand architectural model.

Note

The HCA helps the server CPU to get on to the Infiniband network while the TCA connects the Infiniband network to the I/O devices such as storage controllers.

InfiniBand switching technology offers manageability that does not exist in traditional buses. With InfiniBand, it is possible to utilize variables on data packets that include service levels and other identifiers. And through the InfiniBand fabric, it is also possible to configure InfiniBand links between multiple tiers of servers. The objective is to more appropriately allocate the resources of the entire system and connected devices.

InfiniBand was created to dramatically increase the speeds of n-tier architectures. InfiniBand links will transcend connections between first-tier Web servers, second-tier application servers, and third-tier database servers. The multiple data strands that comprise the InfiniBand fabric can be combined in 1x, 4x, and 12x strands in order to achieve higher-speed interconnects. This technology will be particularly valuable when used in clustering environments for classic failover, workload adjustments, and general manageability. Each of the three levels of fabric strands will be applied to specific technology needs:

- The 1x link will most likely be used for simple connectivity. For example, front-end devices like Web hosting, file, or print services can effectively utilize the throughput of a single 1x link (2.5 Gbps).

- The two-tier computing environment could find the 4x link particularly beneficial. On this level, it is common to find multiple processor systems on which workload balancing is an underlying requirement. Therefore, the ability to configure the data flow accordingly could dramatically impact overall performance.

- The 12x link will be best used for third-tier and n-tier environments. Latency is always a concern in heavy transactional environments and cannot be tolerated. The InfiniBand architecture helps eliminate data flow latency by virtue of the availability of multiple link strands. In other words, Infiniband is architected for very low latency communication among the hosts in a network by allowing application software to directly access the network interface. The multiple strands of data links only allow a lot of data to move, but don't necessarily contribute to low latency.

InfiniBand replaces shared bus architectures. As a result, I/O can be removed from the server chassis itself. This will enable significantly greater server chassis design density. Moreover, it will result in less physical space being needed to host more computing power. Freed from strictly confining shared I/O buses, data centers can be constructed with more scalable and flexible infrastructure configuration.

Driving Forces behind Infiniband Technology Adoption

InfiniBand technology connects servers with remote storage and networking devices, and other servers. In addition, it can be used inside servers for interprocessor communication (IPC) in parallel clusters. Internet Service Providers (ISPs) and other enterprise users that require dense server deployments will benefit from the small form factors of InfiniBand devices. Industry supporters of InfiniBand believe that many other potential benefits exist, including enhanced performance; reduced system latency; streamlined data sharing; built-in security and quality of service; and advanced usability features.

The problem InfiniBand is resolving involves mismatched technologies combined with lagging, outmoded components. With processors eclipsing 1 GHz and server farms scaling as needs require, speed is being achieved safely in peer environments. However, when these environments have to push data outside their confines, the issue of interoperability immediately raises its ugly head. Dealing with mixed equipment, operating systems, storage methodologies, and data streams all play a part in the current slowdown.

Revolutionizing Internet Data Centers

As a new server I/O technology specification, InfiniBand is expected to revolutionize Internet data centers. It simplifies and expedites server-to-server connections. It also makes links to other server-related systems such as remote storage and networking devices less cumbersome.

The InfiniBand specification is designed to overcome current interoperability limitations. In so doing, InfiniBand will address traditional bandwidth hogs like streaming video, graphics, and multimedia bandwidth like any other data transmission.

InfiniBand positively overcomes hardware bottlenecks. The speed of server virtual memory and storage memory communications has always been an issue. The bus technology in servers simply has not been up to the task. InfiniBand link-based technology will reduce this problem.

An interesting and possibly major advance made possible by InfiniBand is the innovation of remote clustering. Scalable and highly available clusters could conceivably exist through the interconnection of servers in remote locations. The current requirement to colocate all clustered servers could be eliminated.

Another important factor in the adoption of InfiniBand technology is cost. According to Framingham, Massachusetts-based, IDC, cost will play a significant role in promoting InfiniBand adoption. IDC analysts expect that InfiniBand will drive down the cost of servers, interconnects, bridges, and switches. Users of these products will need to refocus on providing highly available solutions that take full advantage of this new system architecture.

SAN Standard Design Implications

The potential for InfiniBand to transform computing is tremendous. The first significant change is that the CPU and memory can be separated from storage. This will permit the individual management of application loading on the CPU, memory, and storage. The system will no longer be a monolithic beast, but a highly configurable set of components in which data flow can move with appropriately defined speed.

The initial use of InfiniBand will probably be traditional and restricted to bus improvement within the same server. However, this should rapidly evolve into clustering environments and first-tier Web server applications. The next likely utilization will occur with SANs where data retrieval is critical. The next wave will include radical new designs of computer systems that embrace more specialized functionality and are not constrained by the current *everything-in-the-same-box* architecture.

IDC View of Infiniband

IDC is bullish on the future of InfiniBand. They have defined a number of markets in which InfiniBand should have the greatest impact. The industry's choice for I/O Architecture, IDC envisions the following computing marketplace activity:

- General Purpose Entry Server Market
- Application Server Market
- RISC Server Market
- Server Provider Adoption

General Purpose Entry Server Market

IDC foresees a substantial adoption of InfiniBand for general purpose server utilization. As a segment that constitutes 90% of all server units, it is believed that migration can occur to InfiniBand without major impacts on existing infrastructures.

Application Server Market

A rapidly growing segment of the server market (projected by IDC to top $22 billion by 2005) includes special purpose servers that are usually preconfigured and preinstalled. Since these systems have narrowly defined computing purposes, they are ideal for factory-based InfiniBand installation. Arrays of systems could be installed using InfiniBand fabric.

RISC Server Market

Vendors of proprietary Reduced Instruction Set Computer (RISC) systems will probably be slow to adopt InfiniBand technology. IDC believes that these vendors are at least in part locked into the ASIC-controlled subsystems that are *burned into* silicon. When adoption does take place, look for it on the lower end of the RISC-based offerings first.

Server Provider Adoption

The emerging service-provider segment should be among the earliest wide-scale adopters of InfiniBand. In part, this will occur because service providers do not have significant legacy system investments. They will also benefit from the flexibility, dense server designs, performances, and cost of ownership that is promised with the InfiniBand technology fabric.

The Role of the InfiniBand Trade Association

The IBTA was created to ensure that industry I/O standards could address costly computing environment bottlenecks. The IBTA has three primary objectives:

1. Plan and develop comprehensive specifications that meet current and future requirements.
2. Draw on existing technology to advance the concept of peer-to-peer interconnection.
3. Utilize its governance authority to balance the development process in an open and fair manner [1].

The goals of the IBTA are broader than mere administrative objectives. Ultimately, the group hopes the resulting technical specification will result in a number of solid benefits for the computing and networking industry. These include:

- InfiniBand technology will be initially used to connect servers with remote storage networking devices and with other peer servers. The technology will also be used within servers for IPC in parallel clusters. This will benefit organizations such as ISPs.
- Greater performance, reduced latency, enhanced built-in security and improved quality of service.
- Total cost of ownership. By addressing issues of speed, reliability, and configuration, costs can be lowered and performance increased.
- Scalability to increase in two areas. First, the fabric is designed to eliminate latency in I/O transmission. Second, the physical modularity will result in a reduced need to purchase extra capacity upfront. Scaling can occur in what the IBTA calls a *pay-as-they-grow* approach [1].

Postscript

New software and hardware industry standards appear so often that it is difficult to evaluate them all. Many standards die before giving birth to commercial products. InfiniBand will likely not fall into that category. In fact, its high level acceptance seems already assured by endorsements from Compaq, Dell, Hewlett Packard, Microsoft, and Sun Microsystems. The technology appears to have both technological and economic merits.

Challenges still lie ahead for InfiniBand. This is one of many I/O industry standards. The investment already made in bus architectures is tremendous, and therefore resistance to change could be significant. Regardless of the technical value add associated with InfiniBand, change takes time and legacy environments will not quickly be altered.

InfiniBand is an important technology. However, its commercial success is still not clear.

Now, let's look at IP storage standards. Is it still too early to determine a winner?

NEW STORAGE STANDARDS DESIGN ISSUES..........

When it comes to embarking into the relatively new uncharted waters of IP storage standards design, some users might be hesitant to take a chance on mapping out future directions. When it comes to storage standards design, good price/performance ratios, and high marks in ease-of-use/speed of implementation usually produce a winner. Right now, those criteria work against Fibre Channel. Both SCSI and IP are well established storage standards, so iSCSI will do quite well.

For example, Measurisk (an independent, New York City-based application service provider [ASP] that offers advanced risk measurement analysis to capital market participants worldwide) is a beta user of IPStor, an IP software solution for SAN and NAS environments offered by FalconStor of Melville, NY. IPStor (designed to work with iSCSI when it becomes available) allows users to construct an IP-based network storage infrastructure using off-the-shelf technologies such as Gigabit Ethernet, SCSI, and Fibre Channel.

At Measurisk [2], high-density servers are being deployed that primarily provide operating system storage. Thus, the systems are in need of external storage. They've learned from their older servers that internal or direct-attached external storage is not manageable across the enterprise and has the potential to be underutilized. These two factors led Measurisk to pursue SAN-based solutions in 2000. They soon came to learn that SANs are expensive, proprietary, and lack interoperability standards. These attributes effectively put them on the sideline in terms of implementing a SAN solution.

Measurisk can address the preceding new SAN standards design issues using IP-based storage. The company purchased its first NAS device in 2000. IPStor saves them from having to wait for SAN interoperability issues to be resolved. It also means he or she is able to leverage his or her existing investment in Gigabit Ethernet and will not have to learn about Fibre Channel.

IPStor is hardware independent and directly supports standard storage interfaces such as SCSI and Fibre Channel without converter boxes. The solution's full suite of storage services include mirroring, replication, snapshot, zero impact backup, and restore.

IP Debate Heating Up

As vendors begin to promise more IP-based storage solutions, the debate over the proposed design of IP storage standards is becoming more strident. An assortment of players in the storage industry are hard at work on a variety of specifications for IP storage. Three proposals include the draft for iSCSI submitted to the IETF; Fibre Channel over Internet Protocol (FCIP); and Internet Fibre Channel Protocol (iFCP)—a gateway-to-gateway protocol to interconnect SANs based on existing SCSI and Fibre Channel devices over TCP/IP.

> **Note**
>
> **An additional proposal, Fibre Channel Backbone, is also before ANSI. Also, iSCSI is SCSI on top of TCP which provides the flow control and congestion management.**

The SCSI protocol that appears to be strongest is iSCSI. This layers SCSI on top of IP and uses all of the IP advantages, such as flow control and congestion control to give high data integrity and traffic control. If the data is being sent over the Internet, this kind of traffic control is really necessary and will be demanded by the Internet community.

In an effort to show unity in the storage industry, the SNIA announced recently the formation of the SNIA IP Storage Forum. The purpose of the SNIA IP Storage Forum is to market and promote standards-based block storage networking solutions using IP networks.

Note

SNIA is a not-for-profit organization, made up of more than 200 companies and individuals spanning the storage and networking industry.

In addition to expanding market awareness of IP storage, the Forum will also work with standards bodies to help bring IP standards-based solutions to market. IP storage technologies will allow new storage solutions that exploit the use of the industry-standard Internet Protocol. Applications for IP storage include remote mirroring and backup; distributed Internet data centers; storage service provisioning; and transparent Local, Metropolitan, and Wide Area Network storage networks.

Industry Unity over Standards?

The SNIA IP Storage Forum itself is evidence that the industry players are working together to educate and illuminate the future customers of IP storage solutions. It is important to realize that most storage is still directly attached to servers. Many customers would like the benefits of pooled storage but don't want a second network. Everybody has an Ethernet. Everybody knows it. It's plug-and-play and incredibly affordable.

Still, not everyone is prepared or eager to travel the IP storage route. Storage buyers are trying to make sense out of what they can do in 2002 without committing to the future, where many of the wars are yet to be fought. It has more to do with preserving potential than getting it right, because what's right can change within the course of a year. Most buyers are not on the bleeding edge. They will wait for larger vendors to present them with strategies for deploying *ultimate* IP storage solutions. This is where it gets interesting. There may not be consensus among the big players, giving new definition to "*competing alternatives*."

In fact, camps do exist. Backers of iSCSI include Cisco, Hewlett-Packard, and IBM (see sidebar, "PC Storage Standards Committee Dumps Content Protection Proposal"). The FCIP proposal is backed by vendors such as Brocade Communications Systems, Gadzoox Networks, and Lucent Technologies. By 2004, 28% of an IT budget will be storage. 2002 is the year of getting it ready. The standards need to be completed (iSCSI is slated for August 2002), and proof of concept products will be available during 2002.

PC STORAGE STANDARDS COMMITTEE DUMPS CONTENT PROTECTION PROPOSAL

The latest in a line of controversial standard proposals aimed at preventing the copying and unauthorized distribution of protected data stored on removable media devices, such as flash memory, Zip drives, and DVDs, has been narrowly voted down by the technical committee that's working on the issue. The members of Technical Committee T13, which is operating under the aegis of NCITS, voted 8–7 against a surprise proposal submitted recently by San Jose-based Phoenix Technologies, Ltd. The last-minute proposal was an unexpected alternative to an encryption standard previously put forward by IBM.

Note: *The Technical Committee T13 is responsible for all interface standards relating to the popular AT Attachment (ATA) storage interface utilized as the disk drive interface on most personal and mobile computers today. The charter of Technical Committee T13 is to provide a public forum for the development and enhancement of storage interface standards for high volume personal computers. The work of T13 is open to all materially impacted individuals and organizations. T13 is a Technical Committee for the National Committee on Information Technology Standards. NCITS is accredited by, and operates under rules approved by, the American National Standards Institute. These rules are designed to ensure that voluntary standards are developed by the consensus of directly and materially affected interests. NCITS develops Information Processing System standards, while ANSI approves the process under which they are developed and publishes them. Nevertheless, the T13 decision to reject content protection does not have much to do with SAN. The content protection proposal has to do with controlling the distribution of digital entertainment content (carried in CD, DVD, or hard disks shipped inside PCs). Generally speaking, the ATA interface is not an important consideration when SANs are talked about. The NCITS web site may be accessed at http://www.ncits.org/.*

IBM and fellow proponents Intel Matsushita Electronic Components and Toshiba, withdrew their proposal in favor of the one from Phoenix

Technologies after critics contended that their submission would lead to content protection on hard drives and even create difficulties for users who simply wanted to create backup copies of their data.

The replacement proposal was said to include a more generic approach to incorporating copy-protection mechanisms into the ATA standard, which dictates the way PCs communicate with hard drives and other peripherals. The approach suggested by Phoenix Technologies would have let manufacturers program up to eight commands into a disk drive, such as privacy or audio/video streaming commands.

But through a mail-in balloting process that ended recently, the T13 committee opted not to include the *generic functionality* scheme in one of the ATA standards it's developing. The 8–7 vote, with four abstentions and four no-shows, fell far short of the two-thirds required to pass a proposed standard.

The T13 panel is responsible for all the ATA-related interface standards used on PCs and mobile computers. The proposed standard generated *a lot of interest among committee members* because of its versatility.

A company with a better approach to audio/video streaming, for example, could take advantage of such a scheme as easily as a company that wanted to implement content protection. Ultimately, though, the committee decides the merits of all proposals through voting, and the votes for this proposal were not there.

Critics of the proposals submitted by both IBM and Phoenix Technologies, considered them a threat to the civil liberties of users and charged that the two approaches would have allowed technology vendors to control what computers could read or copy. Despite the outcome of the balloting, the remainder of the ATA standards that the T13 committee is developing remain on a *steady track toward completion* in 2002. It's still possible for other proposals related to the copy protection issue to be brought before the committee [1].

Despite the various proprietary interests, there are signs of vendor cooperation and partnership. In the SAN arena, for instance, vendors continue teaming up to offer SAN-designed applications. Brocade Communications Systems, of San Jose, CA and HighGround Systems, of Marlborough, MA recently announced that they are expanding their partnership to deliver enhanced storage resource management solutions for Brocade-based SANs. HighGround is now utilizing the Brocade application programming interface (API) to achieve better interoperability with the Brocade SilkWorm infrastructure. Users will be able to use HighGround's Storage Resource Manager (SRM) solutions to proactively manage Brocade-based heterogeneous SANs. Management capabilities will include real-time *layered views* of the SAN topography.

Customer Considerations

It makes sense that vendors want to demonstrate to customers that they are getting value for their storage dollar. Most buyers are additionally hindered right now by budgetary constraints due to the slowing economy. The focus may change from easiest to deploy and manage to best ROI.

Some users are already heavily invested in Fibre Channel technology, and thus don't see a pressing need for further investments in IP storage solutions. The principle advantage of Fibre Channel technology is the ability to present disk resources to multiple servers and platforms.

For example, instead of being forced to buy proprietary IBM disks to cover that requirement, you can allocate disk to those servers from a Hewlett Packard XP256, which offers roughly 3 terabytes of storage. Once those servers are retired, the disk can be reallocated elsewhere. Along the same lines, you can allocate large amounts of disk to a given server and then take it back and allocate it to another server all via logical assignment versus physical connections. You can appreciate that flexibility.

One vendor touting the benefits of IP storage is Nishan Systems of San Jose, CA. The company's Storage over IP (SoIP) solutions encompass iFCP and iSCSI along with Internet Storage Name Service (iSNS), a companion name service protocol designed to meet the requirements of iFCP and iSCSI.

Note

Nishan's iFCP proposal does use TCP which has congestion management. The value proposition of iFCP is that the customers can use their Fibre Channel HBAs to work with an IP network (running on Ethernet) to construct a SAN. This circumvents the needs to buy FC switches, which are more expensive than Ethernet switches and may have interoperability issues.

The SoIP approach does not have the flow control and congestion control which will be necessary for transferring SCSI data over the Internet, but would be fine for use on one's own network or in a data center. Since this is the target of much of the early need for IP Storage, it is a fine protocol, but it doesn't stand up to the long term needs of allowing Internet data transfers.

FCIP (an encapsulation approach to sending data over IP) looks promising but is also not without technical hurdles. This is easier to do and to visualize than a layering scheme but has some performance and overhead drawbacks. It is also easier to understand than layering and will definitely be used by many companies. iSCSI will be dominant in layering and FCIP will be the strongest for encapsulation, and both will be widely used.

No Winning Protocol Likely

Despite early predictions for strong iSCSI acceptance, there is likely to be no single *winning* protocol in the storage standards arena. Multiple protocols will exist and the adapter cards will automatically handle all of the most popular approaches. The real winner is IP. The power of Ethernet yet again comes to bear. Tunneling, encapsulation, and layering will all be used, depending on the application, and will have edge devices (see sidebar, "Use IEEE 1394 to Boost On-the-Go Storage") that will translate as needed.

USE IEEE 1394 TO BOOST ON-THE-GO STORAGE

With rapid advances in technology, today's traveling consultants are expected to be more productive than ever and to travel with a fully loaded office stored on their laptops. One way to fortify your traveling arsenal is to invest in a storage device that utilizes the IEEE's 1394 standard interface for connecting storage, digital video, and other devices to your computer. Many peripherals helpful to the traveling type are now available in 1394-compliant versions, such as removable drives and printers.

A Technology By Any Other Name

According to About.com, the technology behind the 1394 standard was developed by Apple and was first trademarked with the name FireWire. IEEE 1394 offers data bandwidth up to 40 MBps, and with the help of one or more IEEE 1394 hubs, one IEEE 1394 port can support up to 63 peripheral devices. In addition to *FireWire*, this protocol is also known as *i.link* and *Lynx* [1].

Today's enterprise largely runs Fibre Channel and will continue to embrace it. They will use IP to tie SAN islands together and to create SAN to WAN connections. The mass market for IP storage is in the small to medium business—those that have yet to implement a Fiber Channel SAN but who want or need a storage network. They are more price sensitive and less performance sensitive, therefore making them a perfect match.

Note

IP storage also will have to face interoperability issues just as FC does. The lesson for IP storage from FC is that cooperation among vendors are critical to the success of the standard.

Of course, certain wrinkles are still being ironed out. The main technical issues in the IP storage arena currently focus around ordered messaging and the ability to deal with dropped packets. These are really TCP/IP issues, and are being worked out. In storage, like life, there is no magic bullet. There will continue to be a mix of new and legacy technologies, ad infinitum. The issue isn't one of cannibalization but how to make all these things work together cohesively.

Finally, you should keep pushing ahead on everything that you can agree on, while keeping your mind open to new ideas. Right now, this part of the industry is in its infancy. You need more of almost everything. IP storage today has limited speed and needs a higher guarantee of integrity. For these reasons, the initial implementations are going to be in areas where performance and other needs are not so critical—backup, for example. But, as the industry solves problems and increases performance for IP Storage, the potential exists to use it anywhere.

FROM HERE

This chapter covered how to design distributed SAN standards and discussed new standards design issues. The next chapter discusses traditional captive storage architecture, SAN architecture, and SAN design considerations.

END NOTES

[1] Robert Williams, "InfiniBand I/O Standard Will Enhance Storage Networking," Enterprise Certified Corporation, 180 Sunrise Lane, Boulder, CO 80302, 2001.

[2] Measurisk, 342 Madison Avenue, New York, NY 10173, 2001.

9 Architectural Design Considerations

Enterprise storage continues to grow at a phenomenal rate, with some estimates seeing a doubling in storage every 12–18 months. Although the cost of hard disk drives continues to drop, the rapid increase in the amount of data being stored creates increased management costs. The costs of providing data in terms of backup and recovery, high availability, high performance access, and storage management creates a complex web of software and hardware to support clients in the enterprise.

Many IT professionals would say the four most important things regarding their computer environments are: availability/reliability, performance, configuration flexibility, and cost. New technologies continually appear, but unless they can improve the state of these four key criteria, the technology will not be adopted. A new approach to data storage has arrived that provides these benefits. The new model is the SAN and it brings networking technology to the data storage environment. The SAN provides better availability/reliability, performance, and more configuration flexibility for improved access at a lower cost than today's traditional server-based captive storage approach.

TRADITIONAL CAPTIVE STORAGE ARCHITECTURE...

In large enterprises today, there may be thousands of servers distributed over hundreds of sites. There may be terabytes of data that contains vital information for that enterprise. Traditionally, this data resides on storage arrays that are controlled by the server that hosts the application using the data. Things get more interesting if server A needs data from storage array B as shown in Figure 9.1 [1]. To get to data today, the client request must go through server B to access the data. To get to the data on server B, the client's application running on server A accesses a LAN which connects servers and clients.

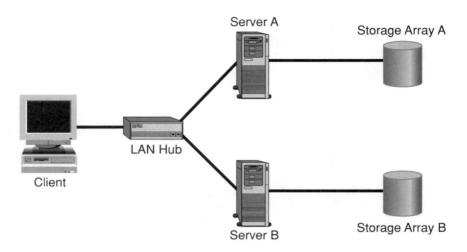

Figure 9.1
Traditional captive storage model.

The server will authenticate the client's request for data (check the authorization of the client to read or write data) and if approved, provide access to the data. The server is often doing other things as well, processing large number-crunching applications, managing a printer or modem network, and many other tasks. Due to the many roles servers play, traditional captive storage architecture design creates several issues for the use and management of data in the enterprise.

The availability of data depends upon access to the data, which involves hardware and software. In the traditional captive storage model, if the server B is broken, there is no way to access the data on storage array B, since the server controls all access to the data. In many cases, the value of the data exceeds that of the server itself. If server B is unavailable for any reason, the application on server A that needs the data on storage array B can not proceed. Availability of data is a problem with traditional captive storage (see Chapter 18, "The Role of SANs in High Availability Business Systems" for more information).

Performance is another issue for traditional captive storage. Since the server that controls the storage is doing other things, the workload of the server can affect the ability to respond to data requests from other servers. If server A needs data on storage array B, it must go through server B. If server B is busy, server A must wait. The move to enterprise resource planning will only exacerbate this situation, where more of an enterprise's operations need to coordinate efforts for maximum effectiveness. Therefore, poor performance in terms of access to data on another server can affect overall enterprise efficiencies (see Chapter 14, "Certification of SAN Performance," for more information).

Configuration flexibility in traditional captive storage is limited by the interface, SCSI. The SCSI bus has been around for years, but is severely limited by distance since it can span only 25 meters at best, and much less distance in many circumstances. This limits the ability to link together devices in the same building, not to mention the building next door. Distance limitations require extra cost and management to circumvent. Additionally, SCSI can only link 15 devices to a host, so large configurations require several buses, which require adapter cards that plug into server expansion slots which are often limited in many servers. Greater configuration flexibility could save management effort and cost.

Speaking of cost, there are three aspects of costs of storage in the enterprise: data unavailability, implementation, and management. Data unavailability is expensive. In case studies published by IDC in 2000, one user estimated data unavailability cost the enterprise $400,000 per hour while some customers such as Nation's Bank put the figure at $5 million per hour (per *www.fclc.org* Web site). Another cost is management. In the IDC case studies, the research company estimated that the cost of enterprise storage in a centralized environment was 20% lower than that of distributed storage. This advantage was entirely due to lower management costs since the study assumed that the price for enterprise storage hardware would be twice that of the distributed storage. Storage is distributed throughout the enterprise, if it could be managed more like a centralized resource, it could improve efficiencies and reduce cost (see Chapter 7, "Cost Justification and Consideration," for more information).

SAN ARCHITECTURE ....

The SAN approach is a shared storage alternative to the traditional captive storage approach. Network concepts can now be extended from the LAN to storage by using a SAN. It allows the storage and the server to grow independently of each other. SAN architecture uses the FC interface to provide flexibility that allows the SAN to do storage networking. In the traditional captive storage environment, SCSI is the legacy attachment, which requires a dedicated server to manage the connection between the storage and the rest of the world. In the captive storage model, SCSI has one way to get the data, while a SAN's FC provides a different relationship between the server and the data—a peer-to-peer topology instead of the linear topology as in captive storage use of SCSI. This means that multiple servers can access multiple peripherals creating a more flexible approach than with SCSI. This approach is less susceptible to server and network constraints than that found in traditional captive storage. It is taking LAN-type topology to the SAN as shown in Figure 9.2 [1]. Just as the LAN allows the client easy access to many servers, the SAN provides easy access for many servers to many storage devices.

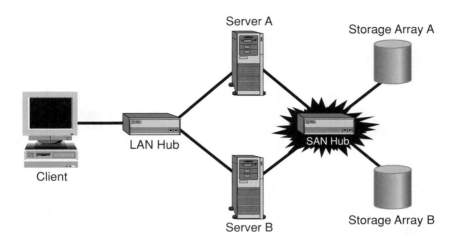

Figure 9.2
Taking LAN-type topology to the SAN.

Interface Comparison

While the SAN is a new topology, there are key differences in the interface between traditional captive storage, which uses SCSI, and the SAN, which uses Fibre Channel. Disk drives are available from IBM, Fujitsu, Quantum, and Seagate that provide direct Fibre Channel attachment that operates at speeds of up to 100 MBps. There are four categories of benefit of FC over SCSI, even though both SCSI and Fibre Channel continue to be improved:

1. Fibre Channel provides up to 126 nodes on a link, whereas SCSI is limited to 16.
2. Fibre Channel provides dual port capability on the device that can be integrated into certain topologies for improved availability or performance.
3. Fibre Channel drives provide greater distance flexibility, up to 10 kilometers between nodes.
4. Nodes can cascade so that two nodes can be linked together for 20 kilometers link or a larger number of devices [1].

The combination of distance and number of device capabilities start to make storage with Fibre Channel look more like a network device. This capability is what really provides the SAN with its advantage over traditional captive storage configurations. While SCSI may make sense as an internal interface, the vast advantages of Fibre Channel over SCSI for storage subsystem connectivity are profound.

SAN's Shared Storage versus Traditional Captive Storage

The following is a review of the four key enterprise requirements in regards to storage, availability/reliability, performance, configuration flexibility, and cost. The comparison is between the SAN and traditional captive storage (see sidebar, "Startups Challenge Traditional Captive Storage Methods"), and does not consider NAS. NAS is an easier way to add storage to the network but doesn't address the fundamental architecture of storage/servers/networks, because it plugs into the existing network. NAS does not benefit from the SAN architectural advantages detailed below and the benefits of using NAS should be considered separately. NAS and SAN are not mutually exclusive and may be used together depending on the customer environment.

STARTUPS CHALLENGE TRADITIONAL CAPTIVE STORAGE METHODS

Some of the storage industry's new kids on the block are building their products on IP storage and NAS and SAN convergence—technologies that are out to challenge the more traditional captive storage methods. For example, Pirus Networks of Acton, Massachusetts, has developed a family of switches that can handle both block-level and file-level transfers. The first model of Pirus' new switches, the PSX1000, will perform both SAN and NAS functions and support Fibre Channel, iSCSI, and Ethernet protocols.

For its part, LeftHand Networks of Boulder, Colorado, which is basing its products on an IP architecture called Network Unified Storage, is scheduled to announce its new products in the third quarter of 2002. They too are expected to handle block- and file-level transfers.

LeftHand and Pirus are two of more than a dozen new players coming into a market that many agree is the backbone of the Internet: storage. LeftHand officials describe their new device as a 1U-high storage module. It's expected to hold half a terabyte of storage and contain a controller, cache, and disk subsystem in a single package.

It can be configured to handle both block-level data or file protocols, thus combining NAS and SAN features. Each module can be placed in parallel for quick scalability, and it uses the network as a bus so the CPU does not become the bottleneck.

Pirus is targeting Storage Service Providers that have multiple *tenants* using one storage system. Each packet that moves through the Pirus device must pass through multiple security checks to ensure it has access to the right disk drive.

Pirus' switches, which will be available for beta testing in the second quarter 2002, are compatible with products from Brocade Communications Systems, McData, Vixel, and QLogic. Some analysts would argue against calling Pirus' product a switch because it performs a variety of tasks, including disk management and data pooling through virtualization and security. It works more like a traditional storage platform. To call it a switch alone is a pejorative term. It should be called a robust storage communication element that has switch attributes.

Recently, Pirus acquired software developer Blue Spruce Networks of Wichita, Kansas. As a whole, the company has 115 employees, 90 of whom are engineers [1].

Availability/Reliability

The SAN is based on a new but well tested interface: Fibre Channel. Reliability of the components of this architecture is expected to be better than that of captive storage, due to the elimination of a significant SCSI usability issue of correct termination. Fibre Channel does not suffer from termination issues like SCSI. Additionally, dual ports on the FC disk drive allow an alternate path for data; so if one port is disabled, the other port will provide continued access to data. Since SCSI only allows one port, there is no way to provide a redundant path into a disk drive in SCSI as there is in Fibre Channel.

At the subsystem level, high availability configurations are available with a SAN. This is not even possible with traditional captive storage (see Figure 9.3 [1]. SAN architecture scales much better than traditional captive storage due to the simplicity of a central SAN connection. Fault tolerant designs create problems even sooner with traditional captive storage scaling, since the connections soon look like a spider's web. SAN configurations need only two connections between components to provide two paths. In traditional captive storage, as more servers and arrays are added, N more connections will be required to provide an alternate path adding cost, reliability concerns, and management complexity. In many cases, the server and/or the array could not even support the desired number of host bus adapters to make such a configuration possible, making SAN the only reasonable alternative.

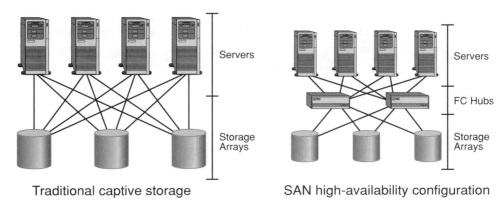

Traditional captive storage   SAN high-availability configuration

Figure 9.3
SAN high-availability configuration and traditional captive storage.

Performance

Performance of any storage configuration depends upon a number of elements. Moreover, the speed of the individual components continues to change as technology improves. For instance, the Fibre Channel interface currently operates at 100 MBps (200 MBps in full duplex), whereas the current Ultra2 SCSI interface operates at 80 MBps. Continued improvements will arrive for both SCSI and FC drives, so real performance may depend more on the architecture than just the interface speed. Even with the advent of the next generation of SCSI that should provide even higher speeds, FC not only provides increased speed over SCSI, but provides better scalability, distance, and configuration flexibility that will allow it to out perform SCSI in complex SAN configurations.

From a subsystem perspective, total throughput can be improved for a storage pool by using a SAN. Traditional captive storage architecture means that the server/storage path is linear and can easily become a bottleneck to high performance. SAN architecture doesn't allow a busy server to slow access to the data that would have been controlled by that server. Multiple servers and multiple storage devices attached to a SAN can eliminate the traditional busy server performance constraint.

Configuration Flexibility

Captive Storage architecture takes the SCSI bus into the storage device on a dedicated path. SCSI is limited to 15 devices attached to the host (16 nodes) in a connection up to 25 meters long. SAN's use of Fibre Channel allows from 126 to 16 million nodes, depending on the configuration. Fibre Channel covers distances as great as 10 kilometers per node. This is important for high availability configurations where a mirrored or backup site can provide an alternative if the primary site has problems. Fibre Channel also allows hot plugging and self-discovery, making the network dynamic easy to configure and manage. Because of the large number of nodes accommodated by Fibre Channel, it is a very scaleable architecture, providing the ability to attach terabytes of data. Finally, the dual port nature of Fibre Channel offers additional flexibility for redundancy providing improved access to individual hard drives for superior data availability and performance. The desired application will dictate the optimal configuration for performance and availability.

Cost

Storage costs are a combination of availability, implementation, and management costs. SAN can affect all three areas. Perhaps one of the largest areas of cost benefit is data availability, and backup's impact on availability. In many departmental systems, there is no consistent backup. Now, the SAN can share expensive tape unit costs and manage the backup procedures. Data that is not protected can prove very expensive to recreate in the event of data unavailability. Additionally, the SAN can facilitate high availability configurations that will allow departments to now have data protection more like traditional enterprise operations. By using the SAN to provide easy data replication, combined with traditional high availability techniques, data can be protected from power outages, unfortunate backhoe excavation, fires, and so forth.

Implementation costs on a SAN can be lower due to the configuration flexibility by making it easy to scale. FC provides easy component expansion with its true hot-plugging for easy addition of new devices. The SAN architecture, with its large number of nodes available, allows several terabytes even in simple configurations.

Finally, SAN's impact on management costs allows many enterprise storage management tools and techniques to benefit from the distributed storage environment. Part of the enterprise storage cost savings found in the 2000 case studies by IDC, as described earlier, came from more efficient management. SAN provides an ideal architecture to allow central management of storage attached to the SAN. Another source of greater efficiency is asset tracking—a SAN strength. Since SAN hubs and switches can keep track of the attached storage in a managed environment, management savings are possible. Another management aspect is capacity planning—another SAN strength. Capacity planning is limited in traditional captive storage configurations, where storage is distributed since it is hard to find and manage. With a SAN, storage is more easily shared and capacity can be added more simply (based on an overall need and not just behind one server), resulting in a more effective addition of storage and storage management.

FROM HERE ··

This chapter covered traditional captive storage architecture, SAN architecture, and SAN design considerations. The next chapter shows you how to make SANs a reality in your environment with your infrastructure, why Internet-based exchange pours resources into a SAN infrastructure, and how to prepare for a Storage Area Network.

END NOTE ··

[1] Gadzoox Networks, Inc., 5850 Hellyer Avenue, San Jose, CA 95138 USA, 2001.

Part 3

Planning for SANs

10 Implementation of Plan Development

When designing a SAN, be sure to plan for future requirements as well as current needs. The exponential growth of data—and the need to store, share, and manage that data effectively—has made the selection of a data storage infrastructure a make-or-break business decision. The once-popular method for growing storage—hauling in yet another server with a disk array attached—is losing its appeal, as server-captive storage configurations have proven too inefficient, costly, and unmanageable to meet the needs of today's storage requirements.

In place of server-attached storage, networked storage architectures such as SANs have been gaining popularity. In fact, some industry analysts estimate that more than 80% of the world's external storage will be SAN-attached by 2003. Why? Because SANs provide the scalability, accessibility, and manageability to satisfy present and future business computing requirements.

SANs are strategic investments that provide infrastructure-level solutions for data storage that can scale to meet future needs and reduce storage management costs over the long haul. However, IT managers need to consider several important factors to ensure their SAN technology choices will serve their needs today and scale to be a solid foundation for the large inter-networked SANs of the future. There are four fundamental decision points to consider when planning and implementing a SAN-based storage infrastructure:

1. How large will it scale, and can it be scaled without disrupting the storage environment?
2. How highly available will it be, and will future growth compromise availability?
3. Does the level of security in the SAN infrastructure support current and future requirements?
4. How easy will it be to manage [1]?

SCALABILITY ....

There are many issues to consider when measuring the scalability of a SAN infrastructure. Scalability is a function of how large the SAN can grow (how many hosts and storage devices it can support), how flexible it will be as it grows, and how well it will support the future technologies.

In Fibre Channel-based SANs, there are two general approaches to building a framework for storage applications: centralized and networked. The centralized model is usually based around a director, which has a larger number of ports than other switches and is usually more expensive. In a centralized SAN, once the *core* interconnection is in place, the SAN can be expanded through the interconnection of smaller switched-fabric SANs in departments and workgroups that are cabled back to the large switch, or director, to provide an enterprise SAN architecture. One drawback to the centralized model is the relatively high up-front cost of the director.

Alternatively, in the networked model, interconnection devices are cascaded, or interconnected, to create a meshed fabric. This approach provides a cost-effective entry into SANs, yet can scale to support large port counts in a *pay-as-you-grow* fashion.

Many SANs are first deployed at the workgroup or departmental level and then expanded over time throughout the data center. In an example of a networked approach, an IT organization could deploy a networked fabric of two smaller port count switches for UNIX storage consolidation in one department. The organization could then add two more switches to support NT consolidation in a separate department. When the IT organization is ready to centralize backup for the UNIX and NT systems using LAN-free backup, switches can be added as needed to the fabric to support the backup application. In this example, the SAN has scaled seamlessly from a 4 to 8 to 10-switch networked fabric. The networked model enables users to grow the SAN incrementally, optimizing the infrastructure investment.

Scalability also entails being able to grow nondisruptively and dynamically, which acknowledges another reality: growth can come in different areas, at different times, and with different technological demands. For example, an IT organization may need to grow the SAN to accommodate more servers and storage devices or to support new applications. Or, a SAN may need to grow to accommodate new technologies such as higher speeds.

With organic SAN growth, it's essential that the environment be able to scale without affecting storage operations. In the preceding example, by adding switches to an existing fabric, there was no downtime for the existing servers and storage devices, and no redesign was required to scale the fabric. However, this level of scalability and flexibility is only achievable if the switching infrastructure has the distributed intelligence to automatically detect new switches in the fabric and disseminate certain fabric-wide information, such as addressing and zoning information.

Another significant benefit of the networked model is the ability to grow the SAN by adding new switches to an existing fabric. With a centralized SAN model, expanding beyond the port capacity of a monolithic switch can often mean replacing the entire SAN infrastructure with a larger, more capable switch—what's often referred to as a forklift upgrade, which is a disruptive scaling method at best.

A networked model also has inherent advantages in accommodating technology change. For example, in moving from 1 Gbps to 2 Gbps Fibre Channel speeds, users with a networked model can upgrade devices incrementally to take full advantage of each speed increment.

Another advantage is flexibility in working within Fibre Channel's 10-kilometer distance limitation. With a networked fabric approach, the host and storage subsystems can achieve distances of up to 40 kilometers through the distributed placement of switches that support 10-kilometer inter-switch links.

HOW AVAILABLE IS IT? ....

Availability within a storage network should be considered in the context of user access to data; it is imperative that the applications deliver end-to-end availability of the entire storage environment. When selecting a SAN infrastructure, it's critical to consider both the availability of the underlying hardware and the reliability of the SAN environment.

High availability means that an application has continued access to its data. Designing a highly available SAN is a matter of designing resiliency into the underlying storage network, so that in case of failure of a connector, a link, or an entire interconnection device, the application can still access the data without interruption.

There are many types of failures that can affect data access: hardware failures; software failures; physical events such as fire, flood, and earthquakes; and operator error. A SAN design that accounts for and minimizes the possibility of human error (the most common cause of failure) will inherently be more reliable.

When selecting a SAN infrastructure, IT managers must consider the level of automation. If a new switch is added to the SAN, will the SAN automatically detect the addition and educate the switch about the rest of the SAN, such as providing zoning information? This type of autodiscovery and autoconfiguration is possible only if the fabric contains some distributed intelligence about the SAN to enable each device to self-learn the topology nondisruptively.

In addition, users should consider the resiliency of the underlying SAN infrastructure. Does the SAN heal itself in the case of a port or switch failure? Does it automatically reroute around failures? Are components such as power supplies redundant and hot swappable, or does replacing them require a complete shutdown of the device?

More importantly, consider the design of the SAN and its failure points. High availability and business continuance require duplication of servers, applications, user access to applications, storage, and more. IT managers should design resiliency into the network to achieve the highest levels of availability.

SECURITY ISSUES ....

IT managers must also consider security as a primary concern when designing and implementing a SAN. For example, zoning is a fundamental security feature of a SAN. Zoning enables users to logically segment a SAN with a visibility *firewall* to control access and visibility to servers and storage subsystems. With zoning, network administrators can arrange fabric-connected devices, servers, or workstations into virtual private SANs within the physical configuration of the SAN fabric. Zone members *see* only members in their zones and, therefore, access only one another. A device not included in any zone is not available to the devices in the zones.

There are two types of zoning: hardware and software. Whereas software zoning uses worldwide names to define membership in a zone, hardware zoning is specified by physical port. For optimal security, both types of zoning should be supported, because zone overlap enables a storage device (or server) to reside in more than one zone and to be shared among different servers, which may be in separate zones. Another important zoning factor is its scalability. How many zones are supported? As the SAN increases in size, any limitation in the number of zones can be problematic.

HOW EASY IS MANAGEMENT?

When evaluating manageability, IT managers should consider both the underlying manageability of the infrastructure and the tools that are available to access it. Companies such as Veritas [2] now offer tools that can take advantage of switching platforms to monitor device status, automatically discover a SAN topology, and perform software-controlled zoning. However, it's important to remember that the chain is only as good as the weakest link. Even the most sophisticated management tools cannot compensate for a SAN infrastructure that can't support zoning or other basic management features.

Perhaps more importantly, manageability of a SAN goes beyond passive monitoring to proactive management, which includes finding and fixing problems before they're seen. With proactive management, users can establish policies and thresholds to prevent interruption of service.

MINIMIZING TOTAL COST OF OWNERSHIP (TCO)....

One of the most important benefits of a SAN is the return on investment from the optimal use of existing storage resources. As users grow the SAN over time to support larger environments and span wider geographic areas, it's essential that the SAN infrastructure can accommodate legacy and future technologies.

For example, many legacy SAN environments are based on loops. Will your new SAN infrastructure support these loop-based environments? How easily can the loop environment be upgraded to full fabric functionality? Is it a license key upgrade, a software upgrade, or a full switch replacement?

If your SAN infrastructure is already fabric-based, are the vendor's products themselves compatible and interoperable? Will future product enhancements be accessible without a hardware upgrade? If you need to expand servers and storage, can switch port capacity be accomplished without disrupting the storage environment?

THINKING STRATEGICALLY ....

The preceding questions all point to the total cost of ownership advantages of SANs over server-attached storage. In addition to product acquisition costs, IT managers need to know what burden the SAN will place on staff and budgets as it grows beyond the workgroup or business unit. A SAN should be scalable and easily internetworked, supported by automated features such as autodiscovery and zoning information sharing. Moreover, the SAN should be highly manageable and available, with emphasis on resiliency through hot-swappable components and self-healing fabrics.

To avoid one of the greatest costs of a SAN (the need to rearchitect the entire network from scratch once a limitation is encountered), IT managers should anticipate what the limits may be for the technology under consideration. Can another switch be added easily to the SAN? Can the SAN be internetworked over IP or through fiber-optic networks in a metropolitan area via DWDM technologies? The SANs of the future will require a higher level of internetworking capability to facilitate growth and interconnection of the large fabric SAN beyond enterprise boundaries and into a global environment.

Coping with future data storage and storage management needs requires that the right choices be made for today, as well as with an eye toward the future. IT managers interested in SANs should deploy a scalable, manageable, and internetworking-ready storage technology infrastructure. Following that model in choosing the proper SAN architecture will not only ensure immediate benefits today, but will create an infrastructure designed for the future.

Now, in recovering from an IT disaster, timing is everything. Costs can mount quickly with each minute that access is denied to critical systems, networks, and data. That's why it's essential to have a plan for getting your data back—whether that means replicating your entire SAN or just the critical pieces of it, using company-owned or outside resources.

DISASTER RECOVERY PLAN ....

Downtime costs vary from industry to industry, based on dependency upon technology and typical labor costs. Companies that are the most dependent upon automated systems, such as energy and telecommunications enterprises, accrue an average of nearly $3 million in losses for every hour of downtime, based on lost revenue and employee idling, according to an October 2000 Meta Group study as shown in Table 10.1 [3]. IT-dependent manufacturing companies and financial institutions suffer per-hour revenue losses of $1.5 million to $1.6 million. Health care, media, and hospitality/travel companies, less dependent upon IT infrastructure, lose between $330,000 and $636,000 of revenue per hour (see Table 10.1).

Table 10.1 The Cost of Downtime

Industry Sector	Revenue/Hour	Revenue/Employee-Hour
Energy	$2,817,846	$569.20
Telecommunications	2,066,245	186.98
Manufacturing	1,610,654	134.24
Financial Institutions	1,495,134	1,079.89
Information technology	1,344,461	184.03
Insurance	1,202,444	370.92
Retail	1,107,274	244.37
Pharmaceuticals	1,082,252	167.53
Banking	996,802	130.52
Food/beverage processing	804,192	153.10

Table 10.1 The Cost of Downtime (Continued)

Industry Sector	Revenue/Hour	Revenue/Employee-Hour
Consumer products	785,719	127.98
Chemicals	704,101	194.53
Transportation	668,586	107.78
Utilities	643,250	380.94
Health care	636,030	142.58
Metals/natural resources	580,588	153.11
Professional services	532,510	99.59
Electronics	477,366	74.48
Construction and engineering	389,601	216.18
Media	340,432	119.74
Hospitality and travel	330,654	38.62
Average	$1,010,536	$205.55

But vulnerability is a relative thing. Dollar losses may not be your primary concern if you're in charge of, say, a utility company whose IT outages can leave customers without heat. Protracted outages also can translate into a loss of customer confidence. That's a major vulnerability for even the smallest just-in-time manufacturer or e-business.

If your organization can handle the hefty price, you can attack the problem of business continuity by replicating everything in your production environment at an alternate, company-owned backup facility. You can use high-speed networks and storage and server mirroring to provide instantaneous failover from one site to the other for hiccup-free disaster recovery.

Most companies, however, can't afford a strategy of full redundancy. For these enterprises, specialized vendors can help replace critical IT infrastructure. Traditional business recovery-service vendors, such as Comdisco Continuity Services, Hewlett-Packard Business Recovery Services, IBM Business Continuity and Recovery Services, and SunGard Recovery Services, make up one part of this market. Web-based data-center providers, such as Exodus Communications and eDeltaCom, represent a new crop. The theory is that hammering out recovery logistics before an interruption occurs will speed recovery in the wake of a lightning strike or tornado.

Modern storage-recovery requirements present a problem for conventional business-continuity planning. With the proper logistics, provisions can be made to replace system platforms, networks, and even user work areas quickly, but the real key to recovery is time to data. How rapidly data can be restored for use by business applications, decision-makers, and customers is the ultimate determinant of successful recovery. Given this fact, the proliferation both in volume of data and in the type and topology of storage platforms within a single company can create requirements that will make or break the efficacy of all other recovery plans.

Data Explosion

Like the potential for disaster, data is growing at an exponential rate in many companies. Conservative estimates from International Data Corporation place data growth at approximately 80% per year. From a not-so-measly 184,641 TB of stored data worldwide in 1999, IDC projects that new data storage will grow to almost 2,000,000 TB by 2003.

Much of that growth can be attributed to the Internet, email, and increasingly top-heavy and media-rich application software. A significant percentage of data growth can be attributed to data replication—one side effect of the lack of cost-effective data-sharing technologies. Added to the mix is an abundance of files left over from application-development work, and stale data that its creators use, forget about, and never delete from their disks.

In many organizations, real data growth, excluding replication and waste, is somewhat lower than the average cited by analysts, but not by much. Few companies have the time or staff to perform accurate analyses, and automated tools for storage management in a distributed-systems environment are in short supply.

The result is a data deluge that's difficult to segregate into critical and noncritical categories. In the absence of effective classification and management tools to separate data that must be restored immediately from data that can tolerate a lengthier downtime, all data must be included in the backup process.

Given the sheer volume of data on backup tape and the comparatively slow speed of data-restoration technologies, it's easy to see how storage recovery may lag many hours—or even days—behind the restoration of server platforms and networks in a post-disaster scenario. To make matters worse, recovery-facility vendors say that, while clients' data is increasing by more than 80% annually, requests for additional disk-storage capacity in the recovery environment are averaging less than 15% growth per year. This apparent gap in storage-recovery requirements may not be discovered, despite periodic plan tests, until it's too late.

Platform Proliferation

Topologies for storage within the corporate IT infrastructure have proliferated. SAS (server-attached storage) is out; networked storage—including NAS and SANs is in. Networked storage solutions will show a robust combined annual growth rate of 67% from 1999 through 2003, according to IDC, while the growth rate for storage solutions based on the traditional server-with-attached-storage-array model will decrease by 3% during the same period.

Of course, companies rarely mothball older, still-serviceable storage components when they bring new storage components in-house. Thus, the move to NAS and SANs merely increases the number of platforms on which data is stored—as well as the number of targets to which data must be restored following a disaster.

Networked storage solutions can pose special difficulties that significantly degrade the already-marginal speeds of most tape-based data-restoration solutions. For example, in a SAN, physical disk devices are increasingly *managed* by storage domain servers, storage routers, and/or software-based virtualization products that work to deliver virtual volumes to SAN-attached servers. These provide the real value of a SAN: They enable dynamically scalable volumes (comprising many distributed physical disks and array partitions) that can be grown or shrunk to meet changing storage demands.

In a storage-restoration situation, these SAN virtualization layers must also act as interpreters, or filters, that direct data streams back to the target disks and partitions that make up the virtual volume where data normally resides. This process introduces several thorny issues related to how data-layout records are maintained, and how the records can be interpreted efficiently by the virtualization products so that data is restored correctly and quickly.

Several storage vendors, including Veritas Software, have launched initiatives to address these issues, but solutions are not yet forthcoming. Ironically, early adopters of SAN technology often cite efficient backup as one of their primary reasons for embracing the topology. Restoration, however, is an important limitation to SAN efficacy—especially as virtualization approaches come to the fore. With newer SANs (as with many RAID 5 arrays today), data is easy to back up, but difficult and slow to restore.

Restoration Is the Issue

Many tape-backup-and-restore software vendors concede that the industry has always emphasized backup over restore capabilities. Before the advent of SANs, which provide a means of handling large-scale data movements (backups, data replication, and so on) on a network separate from the production LAN, the primary concern of end-users with respect to backups was time. As organizations demanded 24x7 operation from their applications, windows of opportunity to take systems offline to perform backups were shrinking. Backup speeds were paramount.

Tape-drive vendors began producing higher-capacity tape formats, faster drives, robotic libraries, and even parallel channels and tape RAID to support efforts to move data off disk drives and onto tape much more quickly. Restoration speed was often an afterthought in customers' purchasing decisions. Backups were viewed as a necessary burden—an insurance policy that, one hopes, would never have to be accessed.

The speed of data restoration (time to data) is affected by several factors (see Figure 10.1) [3]. Some people would include several *prequel* steps (obtaining the tapes from off-site storage, transporting them to the recovery site, configuring them into a robotic library, and verifying their data integrity) as important components of the time-to-data calculation. When a robotic library is used, time must be added for the proper tape to be identified, or *picked*, and positioned in the drive by the robot. Depending on the manufacturer, robotic picking and loading requires up to 30 seconds per tape. Getting to the data on the tape and beginning a transfer requires from 30 seconds to one minute, depending on the type of tape. All these time factors need to be considered before the actual data-transfer process is evaluated.

Once the tape is positioned for reading and data restoration, the speed at which the tape drive is capable of reading data recorded on the tape is a significant issue. In the open-systems world, rated speeds for popular tape formats range from 6 MBps for DLT8000 drives to 15 MBps for LTO Ultrium tape. A second factor is the rate at which the drive interface or interconnect (for example, SCSI or Fibre Channel) can transmit data to the destination device. Interconnects are approaching 1 GBps, but the capability of disk devices to use all that bandwidth varies widely.

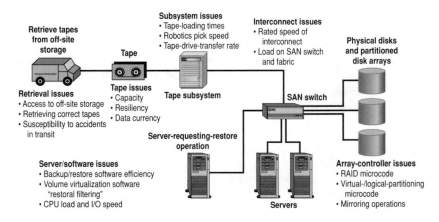

Figure 10.1
From tape to disk: Factors affecting data-restoration speed.

Many vendors rate their data-restoration capabilities on the basis of these two factors alone, creating a rather deceptive impression of the speed with which a terabyte of data can be transferred from a tape to a disk. In the real world, according to backup-and-restore software vendors, most users can consider themselves fortunate if the actual performance of their restore operation approaches 30 percent of the vendor's rated speed. To understand why, consider the following mitigating factors.

If tape data is being sent to a storage device directly, the speed at which that device can record the tape-data stream is important. While calculating the speed at which data can be written to a single disk drive is easy, determining the data-restoral speed of a RAID array can be more challenging. This is due to the operation of the RAID controller itself. A RAID 5 controller, for example, must work to ensure that parity information is recorded with data. It performs two write operations for every write command it receives, resulting in a measurable slowdown of the data-writing process. Without special workarounds, this delay can double tape transfer times in data restoral. This *write penalty* dilemma existed for nearly two decades before SANs, but it anticipated some of the potential problems with SAN virtualization schemes. In a high-end array that performs RAID tasks as well as on-array virtualization, the controller may also slow down data restoration as it directs data streams to logical partitions configured within the array.

The storage device's capacity is also a factor. Fifteen years ago, tape capacities exceeded the average disk drive capacity by a ratio of 23 to 1. By 1994, the year that Exabyte Corporation introduced its MammothTape technology, providing an unprecedented 20 GB of native capacity, Seagate Technology was just bringing its 2.1 GB Barracuda server disk drive to market. Today, the highest-capacity tape in the open-systems space is the 110 GB SuperDLT from Quantum Corporation, while a single large server disk, such as Seagate's Cheetah, holds about 74 GB, for a ratio of about 1 to .75. This practically mandates the use of tape libraries to restore even a modest amount of data and is an important consideration when calculating the time to data for a multiple-disk array.

Although direct tape-to-disk (sometimes called server-free or LAN-free) backup and restore strategies are increasing in popularity, chances are that a server will be involved in the restore process. The server will host a software application such as Veritas NetBackup, Legato NetWorker, or Computer Associates ARCserve 2000 to facilitate the data restoration, and both the server processor and the bus architecture can impose latencies in the restore process.

Moreover, software components such as the server operating system, file system, and restore application may exact a toll by limiting the number of concurrent or parallel data streams that can be supported in the restoration. Server file systems can also generate overhead in the restore process as they record and organize data that's being written to attached or tethered drives.

Note

Concurrency and parallelism have been introduced to reduce the time for backups and restores by increasing the number of connections between the tape and the disk devices.

Taken together, these factors throw several wrenches into vendor estimates regarding data-restoration speed. Without factoring in software, server, or virtualization-related overhead, vendors estimate that 24 hours is required to restore from tape to disk 5 TB of data recorded on LTO Ultrium tapes in a tape library. That estimate includes 24 minutes to swap 13 100-GB tapes. Performing the same task with DLT8000 technology requires 60 hours, with 42 minutes consumed in swapping the 40-GB tape cartridges. With virtualization schemes added to the equation, the time required to restore 5 TB of data could be much greater.

Given all the variables associated with a specific storage configuration, it's easy to see why vendors don't offer binding performance guarantees on data-restore operations. As with automobiles, your mileage will vary.

Mirror, Mirror

With all the inherent limitations of tape-restore operations, it's no surprise that many recovery-service vendors offer disk mirroring as a solution. Both traditional disaster-recovery vendors and newcomers to the high-availability market, such as SSPs (storage service providers) and Web-based hosting companies, seek to leverage the value of disk mirroring to become the guarantors of corporate survival.

Mirroring encompasses a number of strategies, ranging from symmetric, near-real-time storage replication, to asymmetric, time-delayed solutions, to site replication. All of these strategies have two things in common: they provide time-to-data advantages over tape-based storage-recovery strategies, and they usually carry a hefty price tag.

Symmetric and asymmetric mirroring are not new technologies. In a symmetric-mirroring configuration, data writes are made to two (or more) arrays at nearly the same time (see Figure 10.2) [3]. Data is written to Array 1, then further updates to that array are held in queue until the same write can be made to Array 2. In the past, symmetric mirroring was practical only within the confines of the data center, with mirrored arrays collocated with one another. Placing the secondary array a significant distance from the primary resulted in a latency delay and poor performance of the overall system. As high-speed MANs are rolled out in certain major cities, the greater bandwidth makes symmetric mirroring practical. Both SSPs and traditional recovery-site vendors report an uptick in subscriptions to their symmetric mirroring services, though the customers tend to be Fortune 1,000 companies or other enterprises that stand to realize significant losses for even a modicum of downtime.

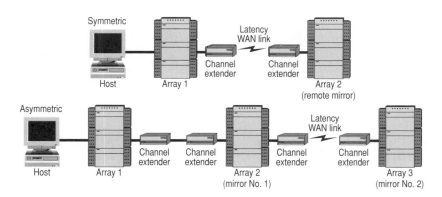

Figure 10.2
Mirroring configuration.

If a company does not have access to a fiber optic MAN operating at core carrier speeds and can't afford to *light the fiber* itself, asymmetric mirroring is an alternative. Asymmetric mirroring usually entails three arrays: Arrays 1 and 2 are collocated and symmetrically mirrored; and, Arrays 2 and 3, which are geographically remote from each other, communicate mirrored data across a slower-speed network. As a separate mirror operation, the exchanges between Arrays 2 and 3 do not impose a latency penalty on the production system and mirror.

Of course, in an asymmetric mirror, the data on Array 3 is always out of sync with Array 2. The length of the *mirror gap* (the difference in data between the arrays) is determined by the distance between the arrays and the bandwidth offered by the interconnecting network. A company considering this option must weigh the costs of some lost transactions against the advantages of having most data ready for use in the event of an unplanned interruption. Moreover, the cost for not only two but three storage arrays, and for the interstitial network, must be factored into cost-benefit analysis.

The preceding also applies to mirroring arrangements involving SANs. With a SAN, data can be routed to multiple targets via a switch. The major expenses involved include the cost for an identical (or compatible) storage infrastructure at a remote location and the bandwidth used in the solution. A growing number of recovery vendors and SSPs have introduced a menu of service offerings that provide a certain time to data at a specified price.

Not to be ignored are Web-based hosting services, the so-called new-age data centers. Increasingly, these organizations are leveraging their multilocation infrastructures, interconnected by core carrier networks, as a panacea for companies that need high-availability storage and facility-recovery strategies. If your IT infrastructure uses a rack-mount data-center model, a Web-hosting company may be able to fulfill all or part of your recovery strategy with mirrored failover services.

Mirroring, it should be stressed, is not a replacement for tape, contrary to the position adopted by some array vendors. Mirroring is prone to data downtime, particularly from corruption wrought by malicious and misbehaving software. When erroneous data is written to one mirror, it is replicated on another. Without some means of restoring data to a precorrupted form, such as via tape backups, a mirroring strategy may not provide the airtight storage-recovery mechanism that business-continuity planners expect.

No Panaceas

Mirroring is not a comprehensive solution in any environment in which multiple storage topologies are in play. Moreover, poorly managed data storage (in which a significant volume of noncritical data [or replicated data] is mixed inexorably with critical data) multiplies the cost of mirrored solutions.

In the end, a sound storage-recovery strategy must begin with a sound storage-management strategy. Companies need to take inventory of their storage, establish a migration path to a strategic storage infrastructure, and invest in the skills and technology required to put storage into a recoverable form. Even if your backup plan involves straightforward tape backups, coming up with a regular scheme and managing it actively are essential.

In the past, contingency planners were presented with a problem and told to do their best with the hand of cards they were dealt. In the modern world of storage, contingency planning and recoverability requirements must be factored into the design process.

So, what's behind the move to SANs? With that in mind, let's take a look at how SANs transcends bad economic times.

HOW TO MAKE SANS A REALITY IN YOUR ENVIRONMENT WITH YOUR INFRASTRUCTURE......

Brocade Communications Systems has good reason to be satisfied with the state of the storage networking industry. The company, which bills itself as the leading provider of SAN infrastructure, owns more than 90% of the market for Fibre Channel switches, according to International Data Corporation. In addition, Brocade has an extensive roster of systems, applications, and storage vendor partners with which it does business.

Brocade believes it is positioned to do even better, despite the trying economic times. The company believes this because data growth is exploding at triple-digit rates. This has convinced them that SANs are technological necessities regardless of the wayward economy.

Whether you're in a high growth economy or a slow growth economy, it's very hard for any company to constrain the growth of its data. Data growth will continue at a triple-digit pace just as it did in 2000. This kind of explosive growth requires companies to start implementing management tools that will help centralize their costs of administering and managing data. Such an investment is not only prudent, but cost-effective. According to a recent Gartner Group Incorporated study (Stamford, Connecticut), it costs companies five to seven times more to administer and manage data than it does to acquire the platforms on which that data resides.

So, if an IT executive has explosive data growth and has gotten headcount constraints, he or she has to find a better way. Enter SANs. By connecting progressively larger numbers of servers to storage and tape subsystems, SANs enable companies to optimize their computing environments and storage environments; improve their resource sharing; and develop a foundation upon which they can implement centralized administration, centralized management, and centralized data movement applications.

By comparison, direct-attached storage doesn't scale well, is not conducive to resource sharing, and fails to help users distribute data externally via Internet technology. Moreover, direct-attached storage does not exploit the current movement toward server consolidation, or lend itself to the development of internal service level agreements. SANs are service-level-agreement friendly because they provide a block data networking framework by direct-attached systems.

Every leading systems company on the face of the planet offers a Fibre Channel-based SAN solution. Making matters even better, the islands of technology that resulted from the installation of specialized SANs during the late 1990s are now giving way to large networks with hundreds of interoperating multivendor servers handling multiple terabytes of common storage.

As the islands of technology have gone away, the costs of SANs have gone down, because those single-vendor systems of the past frequently required the purchase of additional servers and storage subsystems. Not any more. Now, users are finding that they can dovetail their SANs with their existing IT systems. From a pure connectivity standpoint, you can deploy SAN technology today at a price that is equal to or less than Gigabit Ethernet.

For example, let's briefly look at two more recent studies. The first one, conducted by Merrill Lynch, found that CIOs have placed SANs at the top of their prioritized technology shopping lists. The second one found that prior to the coming of SANs, one systems person was able to administer a single terabyte of data, but in the age of SANs, that single person can now administer 3.7 terabytes of data—another example of doing more with less.

What about the unsettled state of standards? This brouhaha is one of the biggest confusion points in the industry. Standards are well-defined, well-understood, and that interoperability is widespread.

Note

Brocade has relationships with 21 of the world's 21 systems companies.

Brocade delivers heterogeneous block data connectivity. In no uncertain terms, that incompatibility has far less to do with protocols than it has to do with applications and operating systems revisions.

Brocade worked their way up the protocol stack and they're now dealing with application compatibility issues. Nevertheless, the benefits are well understood, and there is an increasing level of belief that the technology is ready for prime time.

In describing what users want, the CEO should first note the differences in what they need. Citing a continuum of user requirements, the CEO should note that on one end of the spectrum, there are users who have minimal system integration resources and are more inclined to satisfy storage networking needs by hiring outside help. On the other end are users with considerable internal systems integration resources who are interested in architecting their own storage network systems.

No matter what their expertise level or company size, what these users want most is willingness on the part of their vendors to sit down with their other vendors and hammer out interoperability agreements that will provide users with the comfort of knowing that they will not end up marooned on their own private islands of incompatibility.

With that in mind, users should move, but move thoughtfully toward implementing SANs. People have a tendency to over complicate things. Therefore, heterogeneous SANs can be designed without spending a lot of money and a lot of time. System shoppers should be mindful of compatibility issues and careful to stay with well understood interoperability matrices and network design topologies.

Think not about the problem you are trying to solve today, but what your environment might look like in a year or two in the future. You should approach this with a project plan, as well as try to break it down into a series of phases rather than using the big bang theory.

INTERNET-BASED WATER EXCHANGE POURS RESOURCES INTO A SAN INFRASTRUCTURE ....

Despite the well-documented problems relating to interoperability and management of SANs, many companies have successfully implemented SAN projects. For example, Azurix [4] a spinoff from energy giant Enron and a dotcom in Houston, quickly realized the importance of a robust storage infrastructure for the Internet-based water exchange it was creating. The idea behind the exchange is to treat water like any commodity, which can be bought or sold. Azurix opened its first exchange in California, where it's attempting to get farmers to move their trading of water from local coffee shops to the Internet.

Azurix considers SANs as a possible solution to their storage problem. The company initially looked at Dell, EMC, Hewlett-Packard, and Sun before narrowing the choice to Dell and EMC.

The IT department ultimately decided on EMC because it met all of the company's needs. Implementation of EMC's SAN started in mid-November 1999 and was finished by the first of December. The installation was almost flawless. The only glitch was a minor power problem that resulted from a miscommunication between the IT department and the EMC installation crew. Other than that, the installation went very smoothly.

The major reason for going to a SAN was to keep operational costs flat. At a time when skilled storage management personnel are difficult to find and expensive to hire, Azurix management was looking for technology that would minimize the number of people needed to manage the huge storage infrastructure requirements of Azurix's new e-business operations.

So far, the EMC system has exceeded expectations. If you look at what operations people do in server management, the vast majority of their time is spent in storage management. And what the EMC SAN does is create one 4-terabyte disk that you can allocate on-the-fly to any server. It's much less labor-intensive in managing disk space than the Compaq-based solutions that Azurix was using previously.

EMC also offered flexibility and scalability. Normally, with a Compaq, HP, or Sun storage array, you're limited in the total capacity that you can put on each system. With EMC, however, Azurix can tie in any number of systems for any number of projects across the board whether Windows NT or UNIX, and virtually one administrator can administer every single system from a storage perspective.

In addition, EMC's replication software makes it possible to rapidly migrate to new applications. In the past, when Azurix software developers wanted to test out a new application, they would take an archive copy of the production environment and manually push the patch into that environment—a process that typically took two to eight hours.

The process was lengthy because each development environment, whether based on a Compaq, HP, or Sun storage array, was usually tied to one storage farm. As a result, you would have to move code from server to server, by interacting with each storage farm. In some cases, you would have to hit two or three storage farms just to move one piece of code between two servers.

The new SAN and its associated software have simplified the process and substantially decreased the time involved. With the new EMC system, Azurix can take a real-time snapshot of the production code, pull that out of production, and produce the new code in a matter of milliseconds. Then with the touch of a button, you can put the production code back in place with zero business impact.

Another advantage of the EMC Symmetrix system is its high-availability software that has made possible hot online backups and snapshots for disaster recovery. The EMC backup utility lets the Azurix IT department do rapid backups that do not interrupt business operations and formulate realistic disaster-recovery procedures that don't consume inordinate amounts of time.

Because of the SAN infrastructure, Azurix customers can access the site at any time and get their questions answered quickly because the hardware ensures high availability of the system and improves response times. With the SAN, Azurix customers are not kept waiting when they urgently need water to irrigate their crops because the site is always up. Likewise, sellers can move their product where it is needed quickly because they do not have to worry about disruptions in service caused by systems maintenance.

PREPARING FOR A STORAGE AREA NETWORK ......

Finally, the concept of connecting a company's heterogeneous storage resources as part of a SAN is not a new one. It has been discussed for at least ten years, if only in theoretical terms. However, the development of information as a business tool and competitive weapon, allied to the explosive growth of e-commerce and Internet-based applications, has provided the impetus for SAN planning, development, and implementation.

In some ways, the development of the SAN in IT environments was inevitable and has occurred with other new innovations in the past. The most striking comparison is that of information to fiscal capital. Capital, or money, only becomes truly valuable when it is working and in circulation. If it sits in a bank vault or a box under the bed, it cannot work and create a return on investment. Similarly, if information is allowed to flow effortlessly around a company, it becomes infinitely more valuable and can create more fiscal and intellectual capital and so increase corporate worth.

The current and future value of stored information may be judged by the fact that more than 70% of all capital investment in the world in the year 2002 will be in IT, and the proportion will increase in the coming years. Of the capital expenditure on IT, the Yankee Group, a Boston-based consultancy, estimates that 77 cents of every dollar will be spent on storage in all its forms. For example, SAN benefits include:

- Better access to information
- Expanded business continuance capabilities
- Maximized hardware utilization
- Improved business decisions
- Upgraded disaster recovery capabilities
- Improved relationships with suppliers, business partners, and customers
- Freedom from vendor dependence
- Greater ability to implement the newer information manipulation techniques, such as data warehousing, data mining, and customer retention systems [5]

On the other side of the balance are factors that include:

- Increased costs
- Greater complexity
- Information security concerns
- Connectivity issues over long distances [5]

Any organization (private company, publicly owned corporation, or government body) should assess whether it needs a SAN and, if so, how complex and widespread it should be. Once that decision is made, the process of preparing for and building a SAN can begin.

Making the Decision for a SAN?

This sounds like a trick question but it is serious. For smaller organizations the answer will probably be no, at least in the short term, as the cost of implementation will outweigh the benefits for companies that may already have homogeneous IT systems and a limited number of locations. For large enterprises, the answer is almost certainly yes, because their information resources are spread over many locations around the world and in a variety of different storage environments from different vendors supplying everything from mainframes to laptops. Because of the information access they give, the return on investment in SANs and SAN technology is too significant to ignore.

As usual, the challenge will be for those organizations and companies that do not fall into the two previously defined categories. Key questions for SAN planners to answer are:

- What are the short, medium, and long-term business objectives of my organization?
- What is its predicted corporate growth, and in which business and geographical areas?
- What applications are in place that will give additional business benefits from creating a SAN?
- How is my company deploying current server and storage resources?
- How many locations would be part of a SAN and what are the current storage and connection parameters for remote locations?
- What is the inventory of storage and server devices?
- What are the current server and storage purchase plans?
- What is the current storage position and strategy?
- What internal personnel resources can be used to implement a SAN strategy?

Accurate answers to the preceding questions provide the basis for a SAN implementation decision. If your organization has only one or two locations, homogeneous technology, and is in a passive growth and investment mode, a SAN is probably not in its immediate future. A fast-growing company with multiple sites and diverse systems and storage resources, in a rapidly expanding business environment that involves significant customer interaction and management, had better be looking seriously at SAN implementation to maintain its business advantage.

A final decision must also be made on the philosophy of the SAN to be installed, and it is one that requires considerable thought. Will it be a company-wide, monolithic network that links all locations, or will the better option be a series of SANs, by region or business unit, linked into a super-SAN?

There are many companies offering SAN hardware and services to potential users. Most, if not all, have legitimate contributions to make. Anyone assessing SAN strategy needs to look at as many options as possible. However, this part of the chapter discusses experience with SAN solutions, services, and products available only from IBM and Tivoli and shows how they can aid in assessing an organization's SAN position and requirements.

IBM and Tivoli have Web sites that can help potential SAN implementers with the decision making process. You can find these sites (*Warning:* URLs are subject to change without notice) at: *storage.ibm.com/ibmsan* and *tivoli.com/support*.

Planning and Designing a SAN

Once a decision is made to implement a SAN, the hard work starts. Although the Y2K issue was overblown to many people outside the IT community, some real advantages to the industry and its customers have resulted. Two of these advantages relating to the decision to implement a SAN are: Every CIO should now have a complete and relatively up-to-date inventory of all the hardware and software that exists in the company; and most old and outdated hardware and software have been replaced.

Armed with the information gathered in the decision making process and generated by the system audit, it is now time to call in some external specialist to help. Unless, that is, you have an IT organization which is technically adept, and which has the time available to complete the planning and design of your SAN in-house. There are many sources for different levels of assistance in this vital task, including the well-known system integrators; server and storage manufacturers; and specialist SAN vendors. The services mentioned here are from IBM Global Services and Tivoli, but you should consider other options. Choose your SAN implementation partners for their ability to integrate a variety of technologies and applications together with the resources and intellectual capital to complete this complex task.

At the planning stage, the key is first to update the most recent audit of all your server and storage resources throughout the organization; and to examine and define the tactical plans and requirements for your soon-to-be implemented SAN. The following schedule of activities is drawn from Tivoli and IBM planning recommendations, but is applicable to all vendor hardware and software configurations.

Technical Audit

IBM and Tivoli specialists can carry out a complete audit of the disk and tape resources; channel and communication hardware; software; utilities you have installed; and assess its suitability and capability in a SAN environment. Or, they can do the review based on your existing audit.

Planning

This is the stage at which the future shape of the SAN is decided. Key areas for consideration are, first, to define the operational planning parameters for:

- Network availability
- Disaster recovery planning and fault detection plans, including failure isolation

- Data migration
- Storage network availability and recovery processes
- Dynamic reallocation of resources on the network [5]

Network Design

With the organization's business goals as the critical factor, you should design a solution that includes:

- System interoperability
- Storage capacity
- Performance
- Database architecture
- Operating and storage system software
- Database administration, including error recovery, backup and restore, and redundancy
- Connectivity and network protocols including cabling design
- Standards
- Scalability [5]

Implementation

Until now, the SAN development process has been in the nonphysical stage with all the work being done on planning, presentation, and design. With most of that work completed, it is time to turn designs into physical reality in the following stages:

- Implementation commencement with environmental and physical requirements including as necessary, but not limited to, installation of additional power supplies; extra heating, cooling, and ventilation requirements; and building changes
- Full power test of all newly installed power supply and uninterruptible power systems
- Additional wiring and cabling infrastructure installation, according to the cabling plan developed in the network design stage
- Installation and testing and parallel running of the hardware, software, and database systems

- Migration of data to new infrastructure
- Running new production systems
- Monitoring systems and service levels [5]

It will be obvious to anyone reading this part of the chapter, that planning, designing, and implementing a SAN is not a task to be undertaken lightly or without assistance. IT departments in even the largest of corporations and government departments are today staffed in a lean and economic way. It is unlikely that a sufficient array of skills and capabilities will be available without looking to outside resources. Table 10.2 provides a checklist for the critical functions listed [5].

Table 10.2 Checklist for SAN Planning, Network Design, and Implementation.

Task Technical Audit	Date started	Date completed	Comments
Planning			
1. Network availability			
2. Disaster recovery and fault detection plans			
3. Data migration			
4. Network availability and recovery processes			
Network Design			
1. System interoperability			
2. Storage capacity			
3. Performance Database architecture			
4. Operating and storage system software			
5. Database administration			
6. Connectivity and network protocols			
7. Standards			
8. Scalability			

Table 10.2 Checklist for SAN Planning, Network Design, and Implementation.

Task Technical Audit	Date started	Date completed	Comments
Implementation			
1. Environmental and physical requirements			
2. Full power test of all newly installed power supply and uninterruptable power systems			
3. Additional wiring and cabling infrastructure installation			
4. Installation and testing and parallel running.			
5. Migration of data to new infrastructure			
6. Run new production systems			
7. Monitor systems and service levels			

Additionally, a SAN implementation will, by design, affect every facet of a company's IT activities. Testing and development will not always be possible using only inhouse systems. So where do you find the resources to speed the implementation of a SAN strategy?

Getting Help

The very nature of a SAN makes the prospect of creating and implementing it daunting. Finding the help that is needed by most organizations may seem almost as difficult. For example, entering "storage area networking" into a search engine, such as Lycos, produces 12,362 Web sites and 358 news articles that provide a match, and Lycos is one of the more discriminating sites. Infoseek (now GO.COM, *beta.go.com/*) produced 25,850 matches. Just counting the companies mentioned in the first ten pages of one query response showed 103 companies that offered SAN expertise, and there were another 1,200 pages to go. So how do you decide where to go for help in the critical areas of planning, design, and implementation; and where can you test your configuration without influencing your production environment? Typical sources of support include:

- Hardware vendors
- Software vendors
- System integrators
- Niche market experts, such as disaster recovery specialists, and database providers [5]

All of these specialists may already be doing business with your organization and will have a good knowledge of your installations and the part their products play in your IT strategy. They also know something about your business and what your goals are; and they definitely belong in your SAN process. However, none of the leading players in each category is likely to have the breadth of knowledge and experience needed to manage a project of the size and nature of a heterogeneous, multivendor, multinational SAN implementation for a large enterprise. It must also be remembered that many experts are saying that the first implementation of a fully configured SAN will not be completed until the fourth quarter of 2002, simply because not all the technology will be in place until then. Your organization should look for the following capabilities in a SAN implementation partner:

- Broad market knowledge that results from having trading partnerships with multiple vendors. The Team Tivoli program is one example of this with its more than 150 Tivoli-ready solutions that enable customers to choose from a wide array of SAN-tested products. There are similar programs from other companies that can also be examined.
- Vendor-neutral policies that allow for completely open SAN deployments from the mainframe to the desktop.
- Education and training capabilities that will enable maximum return from your in-house staff.
- Cross-discipline expertise that marries storage, server, network, and application capabilities. Business expertise that matches the IT strengths of a SAN trading partner [5].

SAN implementation will have a far-reaching influence on an organization's business prospects, so IT wisdom alone is not enough to ensure business success. Table 10.3 shows a short checklist for SAN implementation partner selection [5].

Table 10.3 Checklist for SAN implementation partner selection.

Implementation Partner Criteria	Yes (names of possible partners)	No (reasons for rejection)
Broad market knowledge that results from having partnerships with multiple vendors		
Vendor-neutral policies that allow for completely open SAN deployments		
Education and training capabilities for preparing in-house staff to manage SAN		
Cross-discipline expertise that marries storage, server, network, and application capabilities		
Business expertise that matches the IT strengths of prospective SAN partners		

The final, but possibly most important, consideration should be whether your SAN implementation partner has access to a testing environment that will allow you to try out the components of your SAN without degrading your production systems.

The IBM Global Services Testing Centers in the United States and Germany are examples of what is available to customers. Designed to help IT departments meet the challenges of creating enterprise storage area networks, these Centers have more than 6,000 MIPS of processing power on IBM mainframes; open systems-based processors and desktop systems; networking devices; and storage. What makes the facilities in Gaithersburg or Mainz truly effective is that both centers also have a very wide range of non-IBM hardware and software which allows customers to create almost any configuration of products and to emulate their individual, unique corporate environments.

Judicious use of a facility, such as that at Gaithersburg or Mainz, helps SAN developers get performance analysis assistance for a proposed SAN installation and can help users decide which currently installed technology should have a place in a SAN. At the preimplementation stage, designers can establish which hardware and software is interoperable and if any additional hardware and software is required. The proposed new systems can be tested against a workload to see if they are robust enough for production testing and if parallel running of production applications eventually can be carried out.

Going Live with a SAN

The final test is the switchover to a live SAN environment. Unlike almost all significant technology improvements in recent years, SAN switchover is likely to require some sort of system closedown. While not completely certain at this time, enterprises should include the possibility in any planning.

Risks in implementing a SAN do exist. However, the risks can be mitigated by choosing a good SAN implementation partner and by selecting the right mix of existing and new hardware and software. The result can be better profits and a higher return on your organization's investment in IT.

FROM HERE ....

This chapter showed you how to make SANs a reality in your environment with your infrastructure, why Internet-based exchange pours resources into a SAN infrastructure, and how to prepare for a Storage Area Network. The next chapter shows how SAN clustering technologies are an essential component of this new era of mission-critical web-based commerce. It also shows why sole reliance on industry-standard benchmarks for selecting the right hardware can be detrimental to the SAN architecture design. Finally, you'll learn how SAN simulation techniques can be used to understand the impact of your users, networks, and applications on the clustering requirements to ensure that your virtual doors are never closed.

END NOTES...

[1] Derek Granath, "SAN Infrastructure: A Strategic Business Decision," Brocade Communications Systems, Inc., 1745 Technology Drive, San Jose, CA 95110, 2001.

[2] Veritas Software, 1600 Plymouth St., Mountain View, CA 94043, 2001.

[3] "IT Performance Engineering & Measurement Strategies: Quantifying Performance Loss," Meta Group, 208 Harbor Drive, PO Box 120061, Stamford, CT 06912-0061, 2001.

[4] Azurix, 333 Clay Street, Suite 1000, Houston, Texas 77002-7361, 2001.

[5] "Sanity Check," Tivoli Systems Inc., 9442 Capital of Texas Highway North, Arboretum Plaza One, Austin, Texas 78759, USA, 2001.

11 Virtual Storage Area Networks Planning Techniques: Making the Web Mission-Critical

There is never enough data storage. Accessing it can be complicated, using it fully is almost impossible, and making backups can be tricky. Those are just some of the problems associated with data storage, and they have increased considerably as the amount of data to be stored has ballooned.

First, there was the blurring of the distinction between networked and local resources. With an appropriate layer of hardware and software support, it was possible to make networked resources appear local, so that disks spread around the network could be accessed as if they resided on the local computer. That made it possible to more fully use the capacity of data storage spread over a LAN or a WAN (see sidebar, "Data Stored in Next Three Years Will Outstrip All in Humankind").

....

DATA STORED IN NEXT TWO YEARS WILL OUTSTRIP ALL IN HUMANKIND

Data storage hardware and software shipped by suppliers during the next three years will hold more information than all the data stored to date in the 50,000-year history of humankind. The demand is being driven by storage system costs plummeting at an annual rate of 50%, coupled with a seemingly insatiable appetite for information to be at the fingertips of Internet-savvy consumers and businesses alike.

Data storage costs are declining even faster than Moore's Law. This is in reference to a prediction first made in 1965 by Intel co-founder Gordon Moore (one that has held true ever since) that the number of transistors per square inch on integrated circuits would double every 18 months, nearly halving computing costs during the same time frame.

> The price of accessing stored information of all types has reached the point where 92 cents of every dollar spent on storage systems goes toward software needed to manage the stored data, and only 8 cents is needed for the actual media on which to store it. Companies have learned that when information flows faster outside the organization than inside, bad things happen.
>
> It's important to have stored intelligence close to the function that needs it. This trend has led toward *distributed intelligence* over networks. Networked enterprises require networked storage.
>
> Storage product sales were hard hit by corporate belt-tightening during 2000, however. Also, 60% of all customers' industry-wide existing storage is not utilized. Furthermore, corporations' insatiable need to store data has not slowed during the past year's high-tech buying slowdown, but short term, companies will be optimizing what they have.
>
> While vast storage capacity exists, industry recognizes that it will fill and eventually overflow with data. Smart switching mechanisms and fiber-optic pipes that can move huge amounts of information quickly and far more inexpensively than today are on the horizon. Global private and Internet data centers will assist one another in handling and balancing data storage levels, such that a user won't be able to tell whether the downloaded page came from up the street or out of Malaysia [3].

But making networked resources appear local didn't necessarily make it easy to use network data-storage capacity; there were still different protocols for accessing different storage devices. And there was the difficulty of keeping track of the odd megabyte here and there. With the movement toward storage virtualization, such problems may go away.

Storage virtualization is an effort to abstract the function of data storage from the procedures and physical process by which the data are actually stored. A user no longer needs to know how storage devices are configured, where they are, or what their capacity is.

For example, it could appear to a user that there is a 1 TB disk attached to his or her computer where data is being stored. In fact, that disk could be elsewhere on the network, could be composed of multiple distributed disks, or could even be part of a complicated system including cache, magnetic and optical disks, and tapes. It doesn't matter how data are actually being stored. As far as the user sees, there is just a simple, if very large, disk.

NO STANDARDS YET ....

Storage virtualization can be implemented with different schemes or standards. At present, the market hasn't settled on any preferred standard, which means that what's under the hood (or what's in that layer of software and possibly hardware) depends on which vendor you've chosen.

Though there's a drive toward standardization, it's still a way off. Right now, many vendors are focusing on individual problems, planning, designing, and building according to their ideas of a virtual storage system. One consideration for most vendors is that storage virtualization aims to provide the most complete use of storage resources without sacrificing performance. Other important vendor concerns are ease of use and maintenance.

Some of the storage virtualization systems being fielded are disk-oriented, presenting a disklike interface to users and configuring the actual storage out of multiple networked disks. A term that comes up frequently in discussions of disk-oriented systems is the storage pool.

From a user's perspective, the storage pool is a reservoir from which he or she may request any amount of disk space, up to some specified maximum. The goal of the intervening software and hardware layers is to manage the disjointed disk space so it looks and behaves like a single attached disk.

The disk-oriented paradigm offers a number of benefits beyond simplicity for users. When the interface to a series of heterogeneous networked disks is unified, it becomes possible for a systems administrator to impose a single policy that covers all the data storage. It's also easier to implement a single, comprehensive backup scheme. The virtual interface helps ensure that the full capacity of the data-storage devices spread around the network is used. And, that the system is scalable; adding more disks is invisible to users.

Some examples of disk-oriented systems are Fort Lauderdale, Florida-based DataCore Software's SANsymphony (see sidebar, "DataCore Extends Virtualization"), which sits on a SAN server; Compaq Computer's Storage Works Virtual Replicator on Windows NT and Windows 2000; and Compaq's proposed VersaStor Technology for SANs. But other possible approaches can be useful. Some virtual storage schemes are much more tape oriented—that is, primarily concerned with backing up data.

DataCore Extends Virtualization

Three-year-old start-up DataCore Software recently released version 4.0 of its SANsymphony suite, further extending the company's technology lead in the nascent storage virtualization market. New to the product is the Asynchronous IP Mirroring (AIM) option, which essentially makes network storage pooling and remote replication services (common at the enterprise level) more affordable for departments and smaller organizations.

With the new release, storage administrators now have a single way of replicating data from any storage supplier's device to off site locations over existing Fibre Channel or IP Local, Metropolitan, or Wide Area networks. The most notable benefits are more affordable disaster recovery and simplified storage administration.

DataCore has also added tertiary support to its synchronous network mirroring capability, enabling storage administrators to send mirrored data to two locations simultaneously. Destinations can be changed dynamically via a drag-and-drop graphical user interface.

Responding to user demand for increased flexibility and fault tolerance options, DataCore has also established alternate path support for mixed-operating environments (Solaris, Windows NT, and Windows 2000), dual-port array extension, enhanced Microsoft Cluster support, and on-the-fly RAID protection.

As for competing out-of-band products from Compaq and Veritas (in particular), the two are at a performance (in the case of Veritus) and pricing disadvantage to SANsymphony. Also, the SANsymphony is less expensive and easier to manage than a comparably configured Veritas configuration. There are (simply) fewer nodes to manage.

SANsymphony starts at approximately $30,000 per configured virtualization node, plus the cost of host bus adapters and/or switches. DataCore is proving that in-band is not necessarily slower and less scalable than out-of-band techniques. And, they've cleverly worked around issues with the in-band virtualization approach.

Critics of in-band, versus out-of-band, virtualization techniques versus out-of-band cite problems with performance and difficulties with scalability as potentially significant stumbling blocks, especially in larger, more-complex SAN environments. In-band models pass data and control information along the same, rather than separate, paths.

> **Note:** *DataCore is not trying to get virtualization incorporated into switches, they work with switch vendors in the area of joint marketing and on positioning virtualization as an aid to selling large SANs and hence, more switches.*
>
> DataCore discounts such statements for their particular in-band product, claiming its SANsymphony software actually improves performance, via caching, in many implementations, while providing enterprise-level scalability. Advanced caching actually boosts the performance to back-end devices without significantly driving up system costs [1].

One example is Louisville, Colorado-based Storage Technology's Virtual Storage Manager. To a host, it looks as if data is being written to a physical tape device, even though there's actually an intermediate disk buffer that handles the data before it's written onto a backup tape cartridge. This technique of staging data makes for speedy and efficient backup.

Some proposed storage-virtualization frameworks are designed to let different virtual storage management systems interoperate and also to standardize how various storage elements (such as disks, tapes, and cache) are handled. The idea here is to take best advantage of inexpensive, slower media, while still providing users with quick access to needed data. Among these systems are Hewlett-Packard's Virtual Storage Architecture Guide and Sun Microsystem's Jiro.

Now, let's look at how SAN clustering technologies are an essential component of this new era of mission-critical web-based commerce.

SAN CLUSTERING TECHNOLOGIES..........................

As requirements for computer performance, storage capacity, and network connectivity grow, it is often apparent that a single server is not sufficient to provide the desired types of computing resources demanded by businesses today. In the world of supercomputing, it was discovered that many small, inexpensive computers could be used in parallel, to provide a large aggregate computer performance. This technique for improving performance has been migrating to other computer applications. Many web hosting companies serve web pages with hundreds or thousands of small, cheap servers, not very different from a standard desktop PC. This approach is very effective in reducing the cost of a large installation, while simultaneously providing better aggregate service than can be provided even with a single, very large, expensive server.

Though some tasks can be easily divided into pieces so that data can be either divided or replicated across the cluster, others are not so easily partitioned. Serving read-only, static web pages can easily be replicated such that each server in the cluster has its own copy of all the web pages. However, if the cluster of servers is acting as an NFS or Samba server, an update on one of the servers must be updated on the entire cluster in case the next access of that file is from another server. For this type of application, storage replication is impractical for two reasons—it can become very expensive as storage needs grow, and it is impossible to copy data many times quickly and reliably. For these kinds of applications, some form of shared storage is necessary.

Note

The Samba server contains an open source software suite that provides seamless file and print services to SMB/CIFS clients. Samba is freely available under a General Public License.

The traditional approach for sharing storage is with a file server. While this works fine in some cases, the server acts as a bottleneck and as a single point of failure. To get around this, a machine in a cluster should have direct access to the storage devices and be able to concurrently access the file system on those devices.

Traditional IP Clustering and SANs

In addition to clustering for scalability, several solutions are available to provide load balancing (see Figure 11.1) [2] and failover for web-serving and other network services. Eddieware, Polyserve's Understudy, and the Linux Virtual Server, all provide basic failover for read-only services. Using GFS allows this to be extended to services that must write shared data (see sidebar, "The Global File System [GFS]").

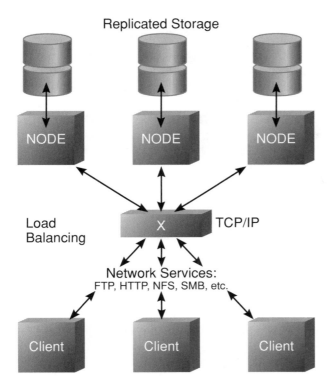

Figure 11.1
Traditional cluster applications.

THE GLOBAL FILE SYSTEM (GFS)

The Global File System (GFS) offers the ability to mount the same file system on multiple nodes in a Linux cluster. The resulting *Storage Cluster* allows high scalability of both cluster applications and clustered network services. Storage Clusters also provide high availability to compute services, and fast failure recovery. Storage Clusters also simplify data storage management, cluster node management, and increase the efficiency with which storage devices are used.

The Linux Cluster Logical Volume Manager (CLVM) allows intelligent use of storage resources, including dynamic partitioning and disk sharing for GFS or EXT2 file systems. GFS Storage Clusters can be run on a variety of hardware configurations with vastly different costs and performance levels. GFS currently runs on the Linux operating system and will be ported to FreeBSD UNIX in 2002.

For example, Sistina Software Inc. is developing several pieces of software to ease systems administration, increase storage efficiency, and protect the integrity of mission-critical data. GFS and the Linux CLVM are open source software, released under the Free Software Foundation's Gnu General Public License (GPL) [2].

Another technology often used for storage solutions is the SAN. This provides high bandwidth access from multiple computers to storage devices. While this allows sharing of block devices, it does not allow sharing of file data.

Storage Clusters

While IP-only clustering and SAN technologies are powerful enablers in the enterprise computing field, GFS and CLVM provide a powerful glue to bind them together. The Storage Cluster which is made possible by GFS and CLVM, extends these technologies to more diverse applications and further exploits their advantages (see Figure 11.2) [2].

Storage Clusters are superior to SANs and IP-clustering alone because:

- No file/storage replication is necessary.
- Machine, network, and disk failures do not stop system operation.
- No wasteful standby machines are needed.
- Load balancing is made more efficient.
- Shared system image simplifies administration [2].

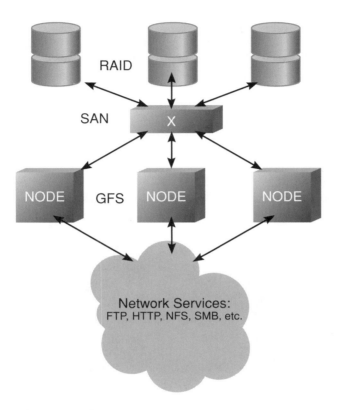

Figure 11.2
Storage cluster applications.

The Global File System

GFS allows multiple nodes in a cluster to access the same files on the same storage devices, placed in some universally addressable storage device. To the users and programs on the GFS cluster nodes, the file system looks like a local disk, but GFS keeps all the caches, and file system views, coherent across the cluster.

GFS is a solution which allows the creation of *Storage Clusters*. Like the Sun Microsystems adage *The Network is the Computer™*, Storage Clusters exist by the rule *The Data is the Cluster*. Storage Clusters allow nodes in a cluster to share data at high speeds without the restrictions of a client-server storage model. Storage Clusters are capable of a much more diverse set of tasks than a traditional cluster without shared storage. Parallel file serving, web serving, database applications, and data-intensive clustered computing can be conducted on a Storage Cluster. They offer the same benefits regular clusters offer less data intensive tasks.

Furthermore, Storage Clusters allow a much higher degree of fault tolerance and availability than other technologies. If one node within a Storage Cluster is disabled in some way, the other nodes in the cluster can see its files and complete the unfinished task. In the event a cluster node dies unexpectedly, recovery is very fast because GFS is a journaled file system.

An Overview of the GFS Storage Cluster Architecture

The GFS allows cluster nodes to share direct access to files on the SAN. For the file system to work, several factors must work together.

All of the nodes in the cluster must be able to read from and write to a shared storage device. This is accessed as a block device in Linux. This can be a Fibre Channel storage device, a shared SCSI device, or a network block device. The performance of the Storage Cluster is primarily limited by the storage characteristics of the transport medium and the underlying storage device.

Since GFS can run on a wide variety of cluster configurations, with varying performance characteristics, scalability, and cost, it can adapt to the user's changing needs. A basic configuration can be constructed using an ethernet network to connect a cluster to inexpensive disks using a Network Block Device (NBD). When higher performance or reliability is necessary, Fibre Channel can be added later. Smaller configurations can use less expensive parallel SCSI storage.

If multiple storage devices are to be used in the same GFS file system, they are either striped or concatenated together using the Pool volume manager. Pool is a very simple volume manager used only to combine disk partitions. Pools can be resized online without rebooting any nodes in the cluster. Pool is also necessary when using the SCSI Device Memory Export Protocol (DMEP) synchronization method, which will be covered later in this chapter.

The GFS file system sits logically on top of the Pool layer. GFS is a local file system with normal local file system optimizations. GFS maintains file system coherence across the cluster nodes with a cluster addressable lock space. GFS uses a generic locking layer that can use nearly any locking protocol for synchronization. The lock protocol currently used conforms to the SCSI DMEP. Some RAID manufacturers support this protocol on their controllers. However, if it is not possible to use one of those devices, DMEP is also supported by an IP server written by Sistina Software. This locking protocol allows GFS to coordinate access to the file system so that the distributed caches remain coherent.

GFS is a journaled file system which maintains an independent journal for each node in the Storage Cluster. If a node in the cluster fails, it will fail to update a *heart-*

beat lock on the DMEP device, and the other nodes in the cluster will detect the failure. The journal for that node can then be recovered. All other nodes in the cluster can continue working all the while, unless they are working on files that the failed machine had locked before the failure. To access these files, the journal must first be recovered.

> **Note**
>
> **The journal can be replayed to restore the state of the storage before the node responsible for that storage area fails. The other nodes in the cluster can continue to serve requests that would have been destined for the failed node.**

In order to prevent rogue machines from writing to the storage device after it has been deemed *failed* by the other nodes in the cluster, it must be reliably and forcibly removed from the cluster. This is achieved with one of several Shoot The Other Machine In The Head (STOMITH) methods. These methods involve returning the node to a known harmless state, which usually involves forcibly rebooting the computer. STOMITH can also be achieved by excluding the failed node from the storage with Fibre Channel zoning.

Storage Cluster Features and Advantages

While the fundamental advantages of high speed, totally coherent access to shared storage on a cluster are vividly apparent for some users and tasks, other equally advantageous possibilities are less obvious. Several are described here to give a sampling of how this technology can be used to the greatest advantage. Other benefits may be more specific to the Storage Cluster's primary task. Shared root file systems can simplify systems administration. Centralized storage increases the efficiency with which hardware resources can be used. LAN-free and parallel tape backup allow large file systems to be efficiently backed up without killing network performance. Storage Clusters can be best used for increased scalability and higher availability for these applications among others:

- NFS serving or NFS replacement
- Samba serving
- Mail serving
- Web serving, http proxy caching
- Java Servlets
- Clustered compute tasks

Shared GFS Root File Systems

A normal cluster can often provide transaction services faster and cheaper than a single large server. However, managing even a small cluster can be tedious and expensive. Competent system's administrators are difficult to find, and it is a serious waste of their time if they have to administer each node in a cluster. Some tools and scripts are available that make this less difficult, but they have limited functionality and are problematic if you ever want to undo changes, have rolling upgrades, or upgrade when not all of the nodes are available to the cluster. Storage Clusters can help this situation.

GFS can be used for the root file system of a Storage Cluster. Thus when an upgrade is made on one node of the cluster, all the nodes can use the new data, executables, etc. GFS supports context-sensitive links, which allows the nodes in the cluster to have different identities and to maintain some independent configuration files, while sharing most of their files. A Storage Cluster can have multiple shared root file systems, allowing multiple versions of the file system. This allows upgrades to be tested on a few nodes before the entire production cluster is upgraded. The simplified administration of the cluster alone can make Storage Clusters a worthwhile investment, even if the regular run-time data of the cluster does not need to be shared.

Storage Clusters and Centralized Storage

One severe problem with duplicated storage is upgrades. One rule of computer users is that when you give them some amount of storage, they will find a need for three times as much. If the storage needs of the users outgrows the available storage of an IP-only Cluster with replicated storage, each node of the cluster must be upgraded. This means buying more storage for each node, installing the hardware, and then reconfiguring the software to use the new storage.

In a Storage Cluster, upgrades are much simpler. One need only buy one new storage device, attach it to the shared storage medium, and reconfigure the software in one place. GFS also supports online growing of the file system. The file system can be enlarged without resetting any of the nodes in the cluster. This further extends the uptime of the cluster, and allows the Storage Cluster to provide services during hardware upgrades as well as software upgrades.

Centralized storage is also easier to administer. A large amount of storage is often underutilized simply because it is attached to the wrong machine, or simply forgotten about. Storage Clusters allow better utilization of available storage space and allow older devices to be well used, even when they have been migrated away from jobs now serviced by new storage.

Simple Storage Clusters can be created using only CLVM, allowing intelligent sharing of block devices but not the file system. Take, for example, the case where two

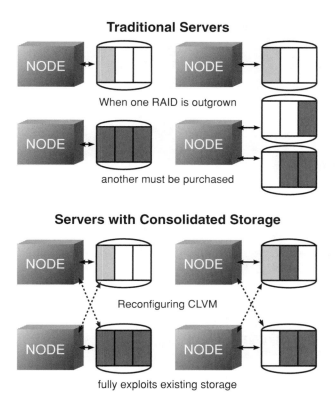

Figure 11.3
Traditional servers and servers with consolidated storage.

identical servers are attached to identical RAIDs. One server is an NFS server, while the other is an internal web server. The web server is only using 20% of its RAID, while the NFS server has filled its RAID and needs more storage. In the traditional server case (see Figure 11.3), or even the simple SAN case, a second RAID would need to be purchased for the NFS server. With CLVM, the disks can be dynamically repartitioned so that the unused storage on the web-server can be used by the NFS server. This alleviates the need to purchase another RAID box.

Storage Clusters and Parallel Tape Backup

Storage Clusters are well suited to data centers with large amounts of data. However, it is a very lengthy process to back up very large file systems. One way in which GFS Storage Clusters can ease this process is to divide up the file system among several cluster nodes and run backups in parallel across the cluster (Figure 11.4). If one of the

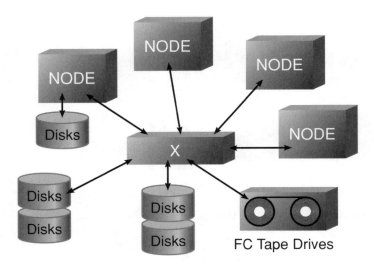

- Multiple parallel dumps
- Keeps traffic off the LAN
- Backup shared and local disks
- Centeralized media management

Figure 11.4
Parallel LAN—free backup.

nodes doing the parallel tape backup fails in the middle of the backup, then another node can be assigned to restart the backup job. If the tape drive is a shared cluster resource, then the failed backup can be resumed without restarting.

Since the entire cluster can access shared backup devices, all parts of the Storage Cluster can be backed up. Some file systems, or parts of file systems can be backed up with differing regularity. If the GFS Storage Cluster is implemented on a SAN, this can be done without filling the local area network with backup traffic, which is necessary when a centralized backup server is used.

This next part of the chapter discusses the SAN virtualization architectural planning guidelines. Five approaches will be explored with regard to sharing virtual disk capacity, citing the potential advantages and pitfalls of each. Along with detailed descriptions of each approach, this part of the chapter will break down many key issues IT managers may face while making a decision on which of the five approaches to take.

SAN VIRTUALIZATION ARCHITECTURAL PLANNING GUIDELINES ....

Now that SAN *plumbing* has matured with an ample collection of Fibre Channel products, it's time to turn our attention to fully harnessing the storage assets at the other end of the light beams. That takes us into the realm of SAN virtualization.

While SAN connections widen the pipes and stretch the distance between disks and hosts, the new plumbing alone does little to reconcile the conflicts among servers competing for scarce disk space. You can look at SAN virtualization products as capacity brokers in this chaotic environment. In their simplest form, they collect all or portions of the SAN's physical disks into a pool and hand out logical slices to needy application servers without having to recable or rezone the SAN.

Properly architected, virtualization provides many benefits, such as the ability to allocate storage resources on demand, integrate storage products from multiple vendors, configure selectively for high availability, and reduce the total cost of ownership. Choosing a virtualization product is the challenge. Now, let's look at some guidelines that customers usually use, and consequently, influence solutions.

Virtualization Schemes

At last count, five divergent approaches to sharing virtual disk capacity have emerged in the SAN market, spanning about 10 discrete implementations. Ranging broadly in price, performance, and utility, these virtualization solutions can be categorized by the methods they use to translate the physical reality to the host's logical view. The effectiveness of each technique is essentially determined by where in the SAN the mapping takes place and what platform is used to deliver the services. Thi taxonomy classes the offerings into:

- Multihost storage arrays
- Host-based LUN masking filters
- File system redirectors via outboard metadata controllers
- Specialized in-band virtualization engines
- Dedicated storage domain servers [1]

Note

Some virtualization engines are packaged versions of storage domain servers.

Selection Criteria

While virtualization suppliers' claims are often indistinguishable, there are seven criteria that determine the success and viability of each approach:

1. The degree of independence that these products provide from a host's operating system and file system
2. The broadness of support for a mixture of storage hardware
3. The ability to protect investments in legacy storage assets
4. The ability of the security policy to share virtual resources while adequately excluding uninvited guests
5. The effectiveness of the technology at minimizing losses due to planned and unplanned downtime
6. The breadth of devices consolidated into a centralized management view
7. The ability to leverage commodity hardware and storage devices for improved performance and functionality at reasonable cost

Ultimately, the best choice for virtualized SANs must provide unprecedented levels of reliability, availability, and scalability, while serving as the basis for advanced storage services and management.

Host Independence

This is a critical point. Several suppliers have elected to place virtualization software on the hosts—each and every host, that is. These vendors' engineering teams are spending a lot of time just on porting and qualifying software to every operating system. This process compromises focus and energy. History has shown that this strategy is difficult to maintain given all the version changes across many host environments. And the fact remains that this approach requires IT staff to install intrusive, processor-consuming software on each host or risk problems. Host-based solutions can mean only one thing for the system administrators: more headaches every time a system is added or updated.

Mixed Storage Support

The usual answer from many vendors is *Don't mix. It's hard. They don't interoperate.* Translation: vendor lock-in. While choosing products from a single vendor can provide a certain level of near-term comfort, in the long run, you are compromising your ability to respond to change. Fortunately, a few suppliers without allegiances to specific storage hardware are far more liberal, willing, and most importantly, able to put nearly anyone in their storage pool as long as it talks Fibre Channel.

Legacy Investment Protection

How much of your current disk population is FC-ready? If your mix includes SCSI, Enhanced Integrated Drive Electronics (EIDE), or SSA drives, the SAN virtualization choices get slim. Of course there are Fibre Channel routers and bridges that could be worked in for additional cost and complexity. It's better instead to look for storage pooling products that have built-in support for your existing interfaces. Properly done, the hosts won't know the difference between virtual devices coming from an FC drive and a native SCSI spindle (performance of the hardware aside).

Security Concerns

Security and host independence are somewhat intertwined. Depending on host-based software or hardware to implement the security layer for shared access control over a SAN is misplacing the authority. A rogue host doesn't play fair—it can read and write to any disk in the pool, unintentionally corrupting a neighbor's data. You should steer towards outboard security implementations that centralize access control and you'll sleep nights. There's another benefit: with the growing importance of personal privacy in the e-commerce world, an outboard security implementation that simplifies the auditing of data trails is recommended.

Resiliency to Outages

Buying devices in pairs to protect against failure is simply not the best way to spend the IT budget, even though it may be a common practice. The more practical (and effective) way is to amortize redundancy across many resources in an N+1 fashion. In other words, when you need five units, buy six, not 10, and you'll have a great combination of availability and cost savings. Make sure your virtualization solution supports this capability—not all of them do and can cause an unanticipated increase in cost of ownership.

Centralization

Some define centralized storage pools and storage management as limited to disks within one box, or one vendor's line of products. What is your definition? You should look for centralized administration that includes pooling all the disks across a network, regardless of where, how many, or what make or model of storage is attached.

Price-Performance Leverage of the Virtualization Platform

For reasons already discussed, the virtualization engine should be outboard, and not a burden of the hosts. In this case, the platform for the virtualization becomes extremely important. Some vendors' products use proprietary or custom hardware and software to provide virtualization and other services. Naturally, this increases the development and testing costs, which the end user must ultimately fund. In addition, the performance and reliability of the system is more of a gamble, for which the end user bears a large portion of the risk. You should also look for solutions that leverage existing, proven, high-performance technologies that are cost-efficient, familiar, easily upgradeable, and extensible. This includes processors, storage devices, and operating systems. With that in mind, now you can plan on flexibly scaling your performance, redundancy, and capacity based on your budget and business needs, rather than the other way around.

Back to the Choices

Let's compare the SAN virtualization alternatives and see how each one ranks against the criteria.

Multihost Arrays

A multihost array puts the pooling responsibility at the storage subsystem level, usually with RAID controller firmware. This implementation offers favorable performance, as well as high availability configurations. Connectivity to many flavors of hosts is supported, but you can only buy the disks that come with the array. Perhaps the biggest drawback of this approach is that the size and makeup of the pool is limited to the array's monolithic enclosures. Spilling over means running multiple pools and losing allocation freedom and centralization. Although some vendors might offer centralized management for multiple arrays, there are unanswered questions about multivendor support.

LUN Masking

One means of enabling storage pooling is to install specialized device drivers on each host to prevent that host from accessing storage resources that it doesn't *own*. These LUN Masking drivers are typically configured using a central management application that can be either host-based or outboard. Although this method might work well for small, controlled configurations, it introduces several complexities and costs in large data center and enterprise SAN operations. First, the LUN masking support must span a potentially wide spectrum of server platforms—as noted earlier, this presents a significant challenge for the vendor to adequately supply and maintain. Also, because every single host must have the LUN masking driver, there is a performance hit to the host and therefore the network. Plus, change management across numerous hosts is tedious, costly, and slow. Perhaps even more disconcerting is the ability for any *rogue* host without the proper LUN masking software to defeat the security controls of the shared resources and corrupt others' disks in the storage pool.

File System Redirectors

A third type of pooling technique involves the use of file system redirector software. Basically, file access control travels over the LAN, but disk data I/O moves over the high-speed SAN. Each host on the SAN requires software to facilitate the mapping of file names to block addresses, all brokered by an external metadata controller or file system manager. To be fair, these products are really targeted at offloading disk I/O traffic from LANs, rather than general purpose virtualized storage pooling. There is also a level of storage abstraction in the design. Like LUN masking software, file system redirection is tied to specific operating environments and components must be installed on every host. Though the file sharing services offer value, they are not the best solution for general SAN virtualization and storage management. You should overlay file redirection software on a virtualized storage pooling service to get the best of both worlds.

Specialized In-Band Virtualization Engines

These products provide virtualized storage pooling by consolidating the storage allocation and security functions on dedicated platforms that sit between the hosts and the physical storage (thus *in-band*). Typically, no additional software is required on the hosts, allowing the engines to support the diverse range of popular open systems servers. The virtualization engine can incorporate a wide range of components and features. At one end are the entry-level products that strictly address simple storage pooling needs and require the purchase of external switches and storage devices to complete the picture. Others choose to embed switching support in the *appliance* bundle. Still others include disks and appear very similar to multihost arrays, but potentially at lower price points with greater configuration flexibility. The particular components of the appliance are not necessarily measures of quality, merely options.

You should note that there is a war raging between the out-of-band (outside the data path) and the in-band virtualization camps. Some argue that in-band products slow data access down, and that the failure of the virtualization platform could compromise availability. This is only true if the product is carelessly designed. The successful, intelligent storage control suppliers have proven that you can use caching and alternate paths to achieve big performance and availability payoffs. We've all seen dramatically enhanced I/O response firsthand from JBODs and disk arrays that were supplemented with in-band virtualizations engines sporting advanced caching. As for survivability, configuring alternate paths is a long-standing, proven method for continuous availability that can be implemented for storage networks.

So, the true measure of success for these appliances lies in their ability to confront and deal with these technical challenges. Lesser implementations will expose themselves as single points of failure; intelligent ones will provide alternate paths and multinode redundancy through classical networking techniques proven in the LAN and WAN space. Weaker products will experience a significant performance hit as data travels through the appliance. Successful solutions will possess sophisticated, robust read and write caching algorithms that actually improve the performance of the physical disks under their control, while also leveraging the cache already built in to the disk arrays.

Storage Domain Servers

A storage domain server is a commercial server platform dedicated to the virtualization and allocation of disk storage to the hosts. The virtualization function is implemented in software that runs as a network storage control layer on top of the platform's native operating system. This allows it to leverage many of the operating system's networking, volume management, device interoperability, and security features. Some storage domain servers are designed to collaborate over the SAN. In this way, they distribute the load and management chores for a large storage pool while maintaining centralized administration. The hardware performance and number of storage domain servers can be optimized to meet a broad range of performance and availability requirements.

Storage domain servers are capable of adding value to the I/O stream by optionally performing host and storage device-independent caching; in-band performance and load monitoring; and snapshot and remote mirroring services, to name a few. The richer the feature set, the simpler it becomes to institute LAN-free and server-less backups, disaster recovery programs, and decision support practices across the entire storage pool without regard to the supplier of the physical SAN components. The end result is a huge reduction in acquisition, administrative, and upgrade costs with high return on investment for nearly any type of SAN environment.

The similarities to specialized virtualization engines are not coincidental; many specialized appliances are simply storage domain servers with hardware and software add-ons. While they lose some of the flexibility of a storage domain server, these appliances bundle the necessary services in a plug-and-play solution at targeted price points. In the end, just as the deployment of network domain servers delivered significant advancement for LANs, storage domain servers promise to deliver the most compelling advantages of disk virtualization for SANs.

Finally, the recent flood of storage virtualization products presents an abundance of choices—and a fair share of confusion. To cut through the chaos, this part of the chapter has tried to identify the key factors that will influence each offering's long-term success and viability for both the end user and the vendor. These are summarized in Table 11.1 [1]. Ultimately, the best product for you will provide complete freedom of choice and high performance at a reasonable cost. That way, you (not the vendor) have control over your storage environment.

Table 11.1 Assessment Summary.

Consideration	Virtualization Approach				
	Multi-Host Disk Array	LUN Masking Software	File Redirector Software	Specialized Virtualization Engine	Storage Domain Server*
Host Independence	Yes	No	No	Yes	Yes
Mixed Storage Support	No	Yes	Yes	Varies	Yes
Legacy Investment Protection	No	No	No	Some	Yes
Security	Strong	Weak	Weak	Strong	Strong
Resiliency to Outages	Good	Good	Good	Varies	Configur-able
Centralization	Good if only one box	Good	Good	Varies	Good

Table 11.1 *Assessment Summary.*

Consideration	Virtualization Approach				
	Multi-Host Disk Array	**LUN Masking Software**	**File Redirector Software**	**Specialized Virtualization Engine**	**Storage Domain Server***
Price-Performance	Poor	Good	Good	Varies	Configur-able
Virtualization Platform	Proprietary	Each host	Each host + Metadata Controller	Some proprietary	Commer-cial servers

*Powered by DataCore Software

Now, let's move on to the last part of the chapter which defines true storage virtualization and discusses how it can improve scalability, performance, availability, and manageability of data when it is embedded in SANs. Finally, the last part of the chapter will conclude by discussing nonvirtualized storage and true storage virtualization.

ENSURING THAT YOUR STORAGE VIRTUALIZATION DOORS ARE NEVER CLOSED................................

Any database administrator (DBA) will tell you that the storage configuration for a database environment is crucial to the successful operation of that database. For example, speeding up access to data from the storage device enables an increase in the number of transactions performed—and it is putting money in the bank. Increasing storage capacity, without impacting users, is vital to productivity. Because of the sheer increase in the amount of data being stored, manageability of this data has become paramount. Of course, none of the preceding matters unless users have access to the database on a 24 × 7 basis.

IT departments are turning to new storage options, such as storage area networks, to reduce the burden placed on today's overtaxed Web, ERP, and database servers, not to mention the resource constraints felt by most IT departments. SANs place storage on a separate, high-speed network, allowing numerous disparate servers to attach to centralized disk and other storage devices. In a SAN environment, each server's storage resides in one central location, easing the storage management workload for an organization's IT staff. SANs are also attractive to the enterprise because they allow data to be easily shared, moved, and protected. The organization can manipulate and analyze data to identify market trends, locate opportunities, and develop business strategies. Backup traffic is off-loaded from the data network and does not impact network performance. The user can also add storage without the expense of adding servers.

But the benefits of SANs need not stop there. A significant technology called true storage virtualization can improve scalability, performance, availability, and manageability of data when it is embedded in SANs. True storage virtualization is already being deployed and is helping to resolve real business issues today.

What Is True Storage Virtualization?

The term *virtualized storage* is not new to the industry. The ability to centrally manage storage and make it available to multiple machines has been implemented in the mainframe arena for years. In today's open systems world, however, the definition can be expanded to include having the ability to stripe across and utilize all available space in a centralized storage pool and the ability to centrally manage and share this storage with a heterogeneous server network.

Separately, each provides significant benefits to the storage system. Combined, they enable a centralized storage solution that is more easily managed, fast, highly available, and easy to scale for future database needs.

The Ability to Stripe Across and Utilize All Available Space

With true storage virtualization, a virtual disk is created by striping a user's data across all the physical disk drives in a SAN (see sidebar, "Taking True Storage Virtualization in a New Direction"). The creation of these *virtual disks* means that the time-consuming effort of managing the physical aspects of storage (the physical drives themselves) is removed. This greatly simplifies storage capacity management and it is a benefit unique to truly virtualized storage (see sidebar, "Benefits of a Truly Virtualized SAN").

TAKING TRUE STORAGE VIRTUALIZATION IN A NEW DIRECTION

The rapid increase in demand for information bandwidth and the increasing value of data residing on the Internet has created a growing dependence on storage for access to information anytime, anywhere. For example, Panasas Inc. (based in Pittsburgh, Pennsylvania, with strong ties to Carnegie Mellon University, and with facilities in Houston and in

Silicon Valley), launched less than a year ago, has developed a technology intended to help answer those needs and extend the functionality of existing storage products. It is the Object-based Network Storage (ONS). According to Panasas, ONS systems are highly scalable networked data systems that deploy *smart* data storage devices (called object storage devices [OSDs]) to eliminate the performance and capacity scaling limitations of current storage solutions. Most current solutions are built on file servers that map logical volumes of end user/server data onto fixed physical blocks of attached disk drives. According to Panasas, ONS systems are more intelligent and therefore more easily managed—which should reduce total cost of ownership for data storage.

ISVs Scramble

By providing an independent scalable global file system, Panasas has identified the next significant issue on the horizon for heterogeneous storage based on NAS or SAN. Panasas, which has not yet announced its products, will probably play on a variety of platforms, thus providing even more extensibility.

In other words, Panasas is familiar with a variety of ISVs and legacy players on both the hardware and software side that may soon offer similar products. It is a difficult and complex undertaking with the first products not likely to come on the market from any vendor before the end of the year. But going forward, this is clearly the next area of work to be done.

Maxing Out

The issues Panasas describes are real. The fact is that the NAS products from EMC and NetApp do, in fact, max out either in capacity (when the box is full) or performance, and then you have to add another box. The problem is that the two boxes do indeed look like two separate instances of NAS, with two file systems, and they have to be managed separately. It becomes a real issue when you have 100 boxes, which is not uncommon in large enterprises or search sites.

Note: *A number of other vendors are also aiming at providing true NAS virtualization [5].*

BENEFITS OF A TRULY VIRTUALIZED SAN

True storage virtualization includes both the ability to stripe across and utilize all available space in a centralized storage pool, and the ability to centrally manage and share this storage with a heterogeneous server network. A truly virtualized SAN offers the following benefits:

Simplified storage capacity management: The user can focus on his or her storage requirements instead of on the size, type, and characteristics of the physical disk drives. The user can increase storage capacity by simply adding disk drives or mixing and matching drives of any capacity or type. This can be done quickly and without bringing the system down.

Simplified configuration: The user can easily configure the storage to the specific environment. Different RAID levels can run in the box and RAID levels can be changed on the fly.

Centralized storage in a heterogeneous server environment: Different servers with different operating systems can attach to and share a massive, centralized storage pool concurrently.

Simplified allocation of storage: The user can carve out storage into *virtual disks* that can be doled out to servers when and where capacity is needed. The user can then return the capacity to the storage pool when finished.

Simplified volume expansion: The user can quickly expand virtual disks on the fly.

Simplified data management: The user can easily manage, copy, mirror, and swap data within the storage box and across the SAN.

Efficient utilization of capacity: Striping the data across any and all available disk drives allows the system greater flexibility in how the storage is configured.

Maximized system performance: All spindles and actuators are available to process read/write requests. This eliminates data access bottlenecks or hot spots. In addition, seek distances are reduced, resulting in faster access times [4].

By striping data across all available disk drives, users can perform nearly all storage management tasks quickly and easily without bringing the servers down. For example, the following tasks may take only seconds to complete while online, allowing the user to improve both scalability and availability of the storage allocated to a particular application server:

- Allocate storage to a server by creating a new virtual disk.
- Increase storage for the application server by expanding its assigned virtual disk. For example, with a few simple keystrokes, a database server could find its allotted capacity substantially increased, allowing the database to grow easily.
- Add storage capacity to the SAN by plugging in another disk drive of any capacity or speed. The system picks up the storage space and adds it to the free storage pool to be assigned as needed.
- Remove storage assigned to a specific server and return the unused space to the free storage pool by deleting the virtual disk. This frees up the unused capacity for another application.
- Create, change, or mix RAID levels without bringing the system down [4].

In addition, striping data across all available spindles effectively eliminates database hot spots—bottlenecks caused by database applications continually accessing a particular set of physical spindles. With storage virtualization, the data is striped across as many disk drives as are available, and all of the associated spindles and actuators take part in moving the data.

The Ability to Centrally Manage and Share Storage

The benefits of the second component of virtualization come from data centralization and the ability to work effectively with a wide variety of servers and operating systems. True storage virtualization simplifies storage management and allows efficient sharing of data throughout the system.

By employing virtualization technology, the user can easily perform all aspects of storage management from one central console and, as in the previous examples, the user can perform these tasks without bringing the system down (see sidebar, "The Shifting Face of Virtualization"). They can copy, swap, and mirror data between virtual disks and perform LUN masking, LUN mapping, and clustering on fibre channel devices attached to the storage platform. LUN masking and LUN mapping are particularly important in SAN configurations because they enable heterogeneous servers to share the same storage. These techniques ensure that volumes of storage are assigned to only specified servers and that the servers are able to appropriately recognize the storage volumes. Each of the following tasks can be performed online within a heterogeneous server environment:

- Change the LUN of a disk to which the user wants to attach new database servers.

- Mask out a particular LUN to prevent undesired access to storage volumes by certain servers in a heterogeneous server network.

- Copy the data from one virtual disk to another to replicate volumes of data for testing or backup.

- Mirror volumes of data from one virtual disk to another for disaster recovery and fault tolerance.

- Migrate data from one virtual disk to another for application and OS upgrades [4].

THE SHIFTING FACE OF VIRTUALIZATION

Vendors' widely varying approaches to storage technology prevent interoperability among systems. For example, in 2000, while extolling the promise of its enterprise storage server (code-named Shark), IBM officials indicated that they would later add to it virtualization capabilities.

However, recently, IBM quietly nixed plans to implement virtualization in Shark. Instead, the company plans to develop an enterprisewide virtualization technology that sits on the network close to the switch—in an area also known as the *SAN cloud*.

IBM's change of direction underscores a growing debate in the storage industry revolving around virtualization and the frustration of IT managers anxiously awaiting the technology's promise of interoperability between storage systems and networks. With storage virtualization, IT managers would have the ability to logically move terabytes of data with a few simple keystrokes, as well as more easily manage the vast and disparate storage devices they oversee.

But, there's disagreement among vendors as to just where within the storage framework the virtualization should reside—on the server, within the SAN cloud, or in the applications. As a result, IT managers are worried that storage vendors from separate camps will end up squaring off.

The result could be the same problem that plagues other areas of storage technology: one vendor that does not communicate with another vendor's products. Hopefully, these companies will start talking to the SNIA and the standards bodies as they are developing these products.

There is no single tool that virtualizes them all. That is, the virtualization Holy Grail you're looking for. Everybody wants virtualization, but then there are the Not in My Back Yard Syndromes (NIMBYS)—those who don't want to provide the hooks into other storage.

For example, Compaq Computer is working on a virtualization software piece called VersaStor, and both it and IBM's Tank are expected out by 2002. Recently, Kom Networks, of Nashua, New Hampshire, announced its Virtual Storage Works, which virtualizes storage at the file level.

Storage service providers such as NaviSite want to see virtualization done at the application level, so that the application decides to move storage based on where it is needed. In other words, you'll need to solve the problem on the software layer by making the application aware at the file level of the storage assets.

When Shark was first delivered about 18 months ago, IBM planned to put virtualization within the disk array. Now, the focus is on Tank, a policy-based management virtualization for data sharing on heterogeneous server platforms. Internally, IBM did not find a compelling reason to put virtualization in Shark, according to industry analysts. For example, the company found a different way to execute the snapshot copy feature.

Those customers that were expecting virtualization with Shark will be disappointed. But, many people did not expect Shark to live up to its initial promise because IBM was soft-pedaling it from the start.

Nonvirtualized versus Virtualized Storage in the Real World

A number of storage options in wide use today do not offer true storage virtualization. Data stored on server-attached storage, for example, is decentralized and cannot be shared, moved, or easily protected from disasters. Server-attached RAID devices provide the benefits of redundant storage, but do nothing to solve the problems associated with decentralized data. Large RAID storage devices incorporate all of the storage capacity located within a physical chassis into a potentially massive centralized storage pool and offer a variety of tools to centrally manage the storage pool. RAID devices also offer striping (RAID 0) for improved performance, but not in a manner which creates virtual disks and their resultant benefits.

SAN appliances, which have been recently introduced, aggregate the storage that is physically located on a variety of storage devices across the network. By aggregating heterogeneous storage on the SAN, they give the user a *virtualized view* of his or her storage. The user can also utilize disk drives as needed and perform LUN masking and mapping from the SAN appliance box as well.

Even though SAN appliances and large RAID storage devices provide centralized storage, as in the definition of storage virtualization, the user must still be keenly aware of the physical characteristics of the disk drives within the system to effectively utilize and manage the storage pool. These devices also suffer from a number of limitations that can be resolved by implementing a SAN with true storage virtualization. The limitations of these devices range from inefficient use and expansion of capacity, to configuration issues (the user must select the stripe size, RAID type, volume configuration, and so forth, up front, and it's difficult to change the configuration).

The scenarios that will be discussed in the final part of this chapter demonstrate the limitations of nonvirtualized storage and the benefits of opting for a truly virtualized architecture. For simplicity's sake, the scenarios will assume that there are only three available disk drives or storage devices in the system. In reality, however, there may be dozens of disk drives or even dozens of storage devices.

Nonvirtualized Storage and True Storage Virtualization

A SAN appliance is connected to a heterogeneous SAN that supports an Oracle or Informix database. The SAN is comprised of three storage devices: one with 18 GB of storage, one with 36 GB of storage and one with 73 GB of storage as shown in Figure 11.5 [4].

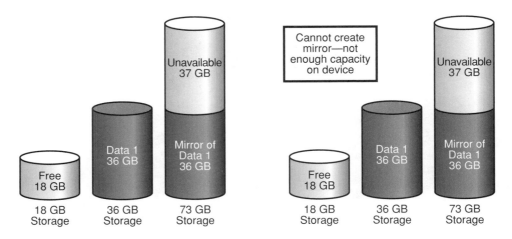

Figure 11.5
Storage in a SAN appliance environment.

Scenario #1

To get improved performance and fault tolerance, a user's wish is to create a RAID 10 volume of 36 GB. Without storage virtualization, the SAN appliance puts the data on only the 36 GB storage device and uses the 73 GB storage device to create the mirror. The additional space on the 73 GB storage device is not used and is not available for future use. In addition, the extra actuators that are available on the 18 GB storage device are not used. The user is then forced to understand the physical characteristics of the storage on the SAN to carve out the space that he or she needs.

If the user wanted to create a RAID 10 volume of 36 GB on a typical large RAID device loaded with a 36 GB drive, a 73 GB drive, and an 18 GB drive, it would be impossible (see Figure 11.6) [4]. The RAID device would only recognize 18 GB of capacity on each of the drives; thus, there would not be enough capacity to create the initial 36 GB mirrored volume (72 GB total).

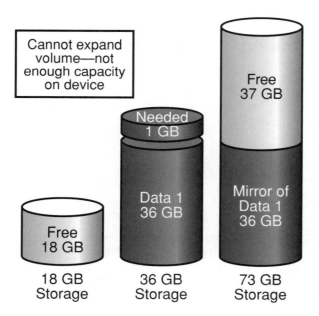

Figure 11.6
Volume cannot be expanded.

Scenario #2

After creating a RAID 10 volume of 36 GB, the user may want to create another RAID 10 volume of 9 GB. By not striping the data across all the spindles in the system, creating this volume is impossible.

Scenario #3

After creating a RAID 10 volume of 36 GB, the user may want to expand the volume to 37 GB. However, it cannot be done because with fixed RAID sets there is no additional space allotted to expand the initial volume. Again, the user is forced to understand the physical characteristics of the storage in order to allocate capacity (see Figure 11.7) [4].

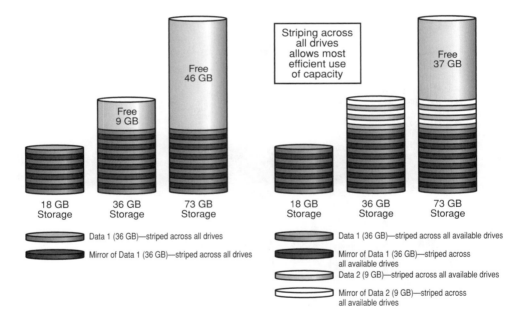

Figure 11.7
True Virtualized Storage Environment.

In these scenarios, the downfalls of nonvirtualized storage involve:

- *Complexity:* The user cannot carve out and redistribute storage without being acutely familiar with the aggregated physical devices. This makes the user's task much more difficult.

- *Reduced performance:* By not using all the spindles in the system, fewer actuators are available for data transfer which limits performance.
- *Inefficient utilization of storage capacity:* Much of the available storage capacity is not used, thwarting scalability. This can significantly increase costs, as the user must purchase additional storage to meet capacity requirements in the inefficient system.
- *Inflexibility:* The user cannot easily configure the storage to suit his or her changing needs [4].

A Better Solution: True Storage Virtualization

A SAN that offers true storage virtualization is equipped with an 18 GB disk drive, a 36 GB disk drive, and a 73 GB disk drive as shown in Figure 11.8 [4].

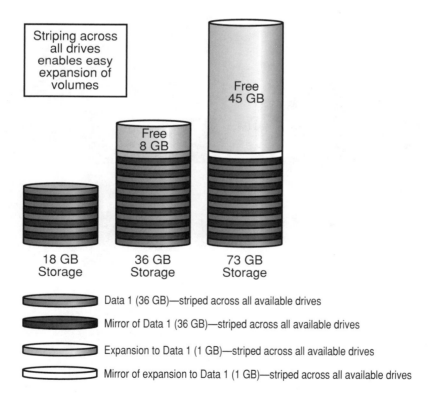

Figure 11.8
Virtualized Storage Environment.

Scenario #1

The same user wishes to create a RAID 10 volume of 36 GB for his or her database application. With storage virtualization, the device creates a virtual disk that stripes the data and the mirror across the 18 GB, 36 GB, and 73 GB disk drives, putting some of the data on each of the spindles.

The unused capacity on all the drives is managed and available to be allocated for future use. All the actuators in the system are available for data access, improving overall access time. Performance is optimized, and the user is shielded from having to understand the physical characteristics of the storage in the box.

Scenario #2

After creating a RAID 10 volume of 36 GB, the user wants to create another RAID 10 volume of 9 GB. By striping the data across all the spindles in the system, creating the second virtual disk is now possible. The capacity that is available on the 36 GB and 73 GB disk drives is used, and the virtualization software ensures the RAID 10 mirroring is met while ensuring optimal utilization of space and actuators.

Scenario #3

After creating a RAID 10 volume of 36 GB, the user may want to expand the volume to 37 GB (see Figure 11.8). With virtualization, the extra storage is simply carved out from the 36 GB and 73 GB disk drives and allocated to the server.

The free space on the partially used drives will be utilized with any new storage the user adds to the system, something that nonvirtualized storage cannot offer. By striping the data across all the spindles on the SAN, a truly virtualized storage pool is created. This provides significant benefits over nonvirtualized storage:

- *Simplicity:* The user can easily carve out and redistribute the storage capacity without knowing the characteristics of the individual disk drives.
- *Maximized performance:* All the actuators in the system are in use and available to process read/write requests.
- *Efficient utilization of storage capacity:* All the storage that is available can be utilized, eliminating the costs of purchasing unnecessary disk drives.
- *Flexibility and scalability:* The user can easily configure and expand virtual disks to meet his or her current and future database storage needs.

The preceding examples compare two cases that utilize three spindles. Imagine applying this concept to 64 drives or across the entire SAN. The differences to a user who must manage storage across the enterprise are staggering. True storage virtualization enables the user to manage storage at an enterprise level—not at the disk drive level.

In database environments, as well as other data-intensive environments, storage virtualization can significantly improve availability, scalability, performance, and storage capacity management. SANs that implement true storage virtualization are just what DBAs need to tackle their biggest challenges.

FROM HERE...

This chapter showed you how SAN clustering technologies are an essential component of this new era of mission-critical web-based commerce. It also showed why sole reliance on industry-standard benchmarks for selecting the right hardware can be detrimental to the SAN architecture design. Finally, you also learned how SAN simulation techniques can be used to understand the impact of your users, networks, and applications on the clustering requirements to ensure that your virtual doors are never closed. The next chapter discusses physical layer testing, application layer testing, management layer testing, why you should use SAN Testing, and the SANmark Revision TestSuite.

END NOTES...

[1] Heidi Biggar, "DataCore Extends Virtualization," DataCore Software Corporation, Headquarters, Corporate Park, 6261 Northwest 6th Way, Suite 110, Ft. Lauderdale, FL 33309, InforStor, PennWell, 98 Spit Brook Rd., Nashua, NH 03062, 2001.

[2] Andrew Barry, "Storage Clusters for Linux," Sistina Software Inc., 1313 5th St. S.E. Minneapolis Suite 111, Minnesota 55414, 2001.

[3] Jim Strothman, "Data Stored in Next Two Years Will Outstrip All in Humankind," ISA—The Instrumentation, Systems, and Automation Society, 67 Alexander Drive, Research Triangle Park, NC, 27709, 2001.

[4] Christopher Groh, DM Review, 240 Regency Court, Suite 100, Brookfield, WI 53045, 2001.

[5] searchStorage.com, c/o TechTarget.com, 117 Kendrick Street, Needham, MA 02494, 2001.

Part 4

Installing and Deploying SANs

12 Testing Techniques

Before implementing a costly SAN solution, you might want to test that solution by:

- Checking the physical capabilities of your Fibre Channel investment
- Seeing if your solution will work with the intended applications
- Testing the management and configuration capabilities of your solution

PHYSICAL LAYER TESTING ....

SAN solutions are designed to provide high-speed connectivity and throughput, but they don't always succeed. Like a new car, you'll probably want to test drive your SAN solution before you buy. Critical SAN solution pieces must be able to handle full and extended loads, and meet the industry's Fibre Channel technology specifications.

Physical layer testing services can take any single piece or combination of SAN technology devices and run an effective load test on them. You should have the ability to test the device at 100% utilization for a defined period of time. You should also be able to measure performance and report any failures so that you know what the device really can do. You should also be able to provide physical device layer component testing that may include:

- Availability testing designed to determine whether the device, such as a Fibre Channel switch, successfully delivers uninterrupted connectivity across the network.
- Scalability testing designed to identify whether the device will continue to be effective over time and as the SAN solution grows and changes.

- Manageability testing designed to identify whether a SAN solution device designed to manage SAN resources can effectively and safely do so.
- Usability testing designed to determine whether tools present an interface that respects the administrator's time and to determine configuration without interrupting the network [1].

APPLICATION LAYER TESTING ....

You should also be prepared to test all SAN system technology layers, but testing application layer components is also an area you should truly try to excel in. Your core expertise should also be the enterprise network. That expertise and your vigilant monitoring of the industry's pulse should make for a choice test lab. Whether you are just starting into an Enterprise Resource Planning (ERP) project, or are upgrading an existing system, you should be able to provide testing of any application layer component in an enterprise environment that includes the latest hardware, operating system software, and complementary application software; and ensures that serious Internet companies will be prepared to take full advantage of each opportunity.

MANAGEMENT LAYER TESTING............................

Testing management layer components as they fit into the enterprise may include:

- Validating that connectivity of the network's disks, once almost exclusively an integral part of the network's servers but now physically separated from those servers, is being properly tracked by the management software
- Determining whether disk response time is satisfactory
- Identifying whether the management software is adequately tracking and reporting the status and health of storage devices
- Comparing different vendor-specific MIBs to determine which one best meets a particular company's needs, interoperates successfully with legacy and planned SAN components, and provides all the bells and whistles the company needs and wants [1]

Thus, your ability to help define your own SAN solution, and your ability to then assemble and pretest the complete enterprise solution you have chosen means significant cost and time savings for you.

WHY USE SAN TESTING?..

As an integrator, implementor, consultant, or IT professional responsible for choosing or integrating a SAN system into an existing or planned company network, your primary concern is that the complete design and implementation of all SAN system pieces will successfully fulfill the mission which you chose for it, and will not disrupt the network. You should try to take advantage of the extensive SAN technology knowledge that is available, as well as facilities to help your company or your customers get the most for their money, making sure they know that's exactly what you're doing.

As an independent hardware or software vendor working to make your product the best in the industry and a financial success for your company, your product must effectively meet all the needs of any enterprise network into which it may be introduced. As previously stated, you should also try to take advantage of extensive SAN technology knowledge and facilities to prove that your product fits seamlessly into existing and planned networks, and that in comparison tests, your SAN system meets or beats your competition in many ways.

Storage Area Network system buyers want and need reliability, scalability, and interoperability in their SAN systems. SAN system and technology testing will help you to prove to yourself and your customers that your SAN system is just what they've been looking for. You should be able to rely on your ability to have available the kinds of physical, application, and management resources your SAN solution testing demands, including:

- Terabytes of fibre-attached data storage
- Fibre Channel switches from multiple leading vendors
- Enterprise-class server hardware and backup solutions
- State-of-the-art Fibre Channel frame analyzing equipment [1]

Now, let's look at how the FCIA established the SANmark program to provide implementors of Fibre Channel SANs with an objective indication of how Fibre Channel products perform against existing standards.

SANMARK REVISION "A" TEST SUITE ....

As previously stated, the FCIA established the SANmark Qualified Program to provide the industry with an objective indication of how Fibre Channel products perform against reasonable standards and to permit the use of the trademarked term *SANmark*, and any associated logo(s), in the identification and promotion of products meeting the published test indices. The SANmark Qualified Program goals are:

- Make Fibre Channel solutions easy to use, easy to install, manage, configure, diagnose, and troubleshoot.

- Ensure Fibre Channel continues to attain the highest performance and *installed base maturity* available in the market.

- Proliferate heterogeneous shared SAN resources and heterogeneous management framework over WAN connections [2].

Note

The FCIA is an international organization of manufacturers, systems integrators, developers, systems vendors, industry professionals, and end users. With more than 200 members and affiliates in the United States, Europe, and Japan, the FCIA is committed to delivering a broad base of Fibre Channel infrastructure to support a wide array of industry applications within the mass storage and IT-based arenas. FCIA Working Groups focus on specific aspects of the technology that target both vertical and horizontal markets, including storage, video, networking, and SAN Management.

The Role of the SANmark Revision "A" Test

The SANmark Revision "A" test suite is a set of tests designed to ensure that the shared Fibre Channel media is used in a nondisruptive manner. The test suite has been derived from experiences in the construction of Fibre Channel networks at the FCIA group test periods in Dallas and at the UNH Fibre Channel consortium's test center.

In other words, the SANmark Revision "A" test suite is a small set of tests that addresses problem areas noted in the past. It is not a comprehensive basis for the full certification of Fibre Channel or SAN products in and of itself. However, once basic conformance has been established to the FC-AL, Fibre Channel Physical (FC-PH), Private Loop Direct Attach (PLDA), Small Computer Systems Interface-Fibre Channel Protocol (SCSI-FCP), and Fabric Loop Attachment (FLA) documents, this test suite will help ensure that the device under test will operate as a good neighbor in Fibre Channel networks.

For example, as with cable assemblies, SFF-8410 was developed as a means to validate the electrical performance of high-speed copper cable assemblies. It is intended to reflect actual system operation and worst-case transceivers. This means that all signals that are normally active during system operation must be active at the extreme allowed stress condition during the testing and that the poorest quality compliant transmitters and compliant receivers are assumed. This scheme is needed for implementing an *open* interconnect model, where it is not known as a priori—where the High Speed Serial (HSS) cable assembly will be connected on the other end.

The FCIA will from time to time update and expand the SANmark test suite. When either more device types or additional functionality are added to the suite of tests, the version level will be incremented and the corresponding licenses will be made available. The FCIA is working to index the test suites further and host them on the FCIA site. However, until that happens, they may be downloaded from: *www.iol.unh.edu/testsuites/fc/index.html.*

Caution

URLs are subject to change without notice.

Now, let's look at another testing technique. The new SNIA technology center has recently opened for interoperability testing.

OTHER TESTING TECHNOLOGY.............................

The SNIA recently opened the doors to its new Technology Center located in Colorado Springs, Colorado. It's the largest independent storage networking complex in the world. The function of the Technology Center is to provide a place where vendors and IT professionals can test storage interoperability.

Testing the interoperability of large storage networking and server configurations is a main focus of the lab. The Technology Center enables industry players to prove and demonstrate interoperable configurations, architectures, education, and services for complete and proven storage networking solutions.

SNIA wants to build a knowledge base of information on networked storage solutions to help propel the industry into a higher value-add position. One example of how the Technology Center is going to deal with interoperability issues is events called *Plug Fests*. The purpose of these Plug Fests is to gather vendors in specific areas, such as IP Storage, and have them use their various implementations of the technologies to see if the vendors' products interoperate.

For educational purposes, the Technology Center is going to conduct workshops to teach the vendor and user communities about various standards and interoperability. These educational workgroups will be hands-on training in the labs and classrooms. To test the architectures, the Technology Center will have permanent configurations of new technologies in place that will be used to test interoperability.

SNIA also plans to hold workgroup symposiums at the Technology Center four times a year. The workgroups will facilitate the study, development, and recommendation of storage standards for various standards bodies.

According to SNIA, early adopters have found that while storage networking technology promises to be beneficial by reducing maintenance costs and providing greater data and application availability, it can be very difficult to implement. That's where the lab comes in. It's vision is to promote and accelerate the use of highly evolved, widely accepted storage network systems across the IT community and to solve real-world business problems. For the end users, the lab promises access to a multivendor networked test facility in which they can test new storage architectures in complex realistic production environments (see sidebar, "New SAN Testing Lab").

New SAN Testing Lab

Dell Computer Corporation recently indicated that it's teaming up with storage systems vendor Imation to set up a performance and interoperability testing lab for use by Dell customers who are installing SANs at their companies. The lab is one of a burgeoning number of such sites created by SAN manufacturers during the past two years, but it's the first of its kind for Round Rock, Texas-based Dell. The deal with Oakdale, Minnesota-based Imation was disclosed almost simultaneously with an announcement of new systems and services aimed at broadening Dell's appeal as an enterprise-level vendor.

According to analysts, SAN labs serve a dual purpose: They act as a showcase for users looking to buy and configure a storage network; and they serve as a proving ground for testing storage interoperability between the different servers that most companies use to run their corporate applications.

Almost every major storage company, and several independents, have set up these testing centers for both Network Attached Storage devices and SANs. Dell's shared facility with Imation is located within a SAN testing lab that the latter company opened at its headquarters site in June 2000. For Dell, the deal with Imation meant being able to set up a fully operational lab in 90 days—half the time it would have taken the computer maker on its own.

Dell is looking to set up a similar testing lab on the West Coast. They're trying to work their way across the country.

There are main technology groups SNIA wants to explore in the Technology Center. A sample of these technology groups include: Disk resource management, Fibre Channel management, storage media library management, and a Common Information Manager (CIM) demo.

The function of the Technology Center is to provide a place where people from these types of technology areas can come together and do work. SNIA is also planning on using the Technology Center as a place to validate standards it is working on—such as extended copy, Fiber Alliance MIB, and the Host Bus Adapter API. With more than 14,000 square feet, the state-of-the-art facility will include the following:

- 554 LAN connections
- 186 Fibre Channel optical cable connections
- 800 × 20 Amp circuits, with a total available power in the labs and classroom at over 2,000 Amps

So far, SNIA has received positive feedback about the Technology Center. Vendors are very excited about how far SNIA has come with interoperability.

FROM HERE

This chapter discussed physical layer testing, application layer testing, management layer testing, why you should use SAN Testing, and the SANmark Revision TestSuite. The next chapter shows you how to deploy a SAN, get started on a SAN, use storage switch technology to accelerate the next phase of SAN deployment, and put data to work for e-businesses.

END NOTES

[1] "Before Implementing a Costly SAN Solution, You Might Want To...," KeyLabs, 385 South 520 West, Lindon, Utah, 84042, 2001.

[2] "SANmark Qualified Program," Fibre Channel Industry Association, 404 Balboa Street, San Francisco, CA 94118, 2001.

13 Installation and Deployment

Storage Area Networks are being installed and deployed more frequently today, but uncertainty still exists among users about why to install them and the applications that can make the best use of them. SANs are high-speed networks, similar to LANs, that connect disk subsystems directly to servers or clients. The idea is to relieve network congestion or bypass distance limitations imposed by traditional SCSI storage connections.

Fibre Channel-based SANs can be configured in several ways and for any number of reasons. They can be installed and deployed as FC-ALs or switched fabric networks. They can be local or remote, spanning campuses and using wide-area connections.

Methods for implementing SANs may differ, but most network professionals offer the same recipe from one installation and deployment to another: start small and think globally. They recommend implementing small, simple FC-AL or switched fabric networks to share data among servers.

You need to approach SANs with a broader plan than simply dropping in more storage and seeing if it is going to be successful. You also need to plan not only where you are today, but where you want to be tomorrow and then consciously choose the applications that work in the context of a bigger picture.

LOOK TO YOUR APPLICATIONS...........................

You also look at your applications to determine which applications warrant adding a SAN and which will do just as well on server-attached RAID. It is recommended that you begin with a small, low-impact or low-budget application, such as consolidating several servers to the same storage device, before moving to full-blown implementation. From this application, users can test the *proof of concept*, and then grow the SAN to involve more of the routine tasks of the data infrastructure. For example, data replication and creating multiple active copies of data that would increase utilization or ease maintenance and testing operations.

Users also recommend dividing applications into categories based on importance. For mission-critical application data, users need to design in redundancy and fault tolerance with duplicated storage, switches, and host bus adapters, so there is no single point of failure.

PREPARE FOR FUTURE...

Not surprisingly, users have implemented SANs in different ways, but most are preparing for future growth. For example, The Motley Fool (*www.nopay-phone.com/motley.fool.htm*) and Home Depot [1] use FC-AL and will need to migrate to a switched fabric architecture before they can add any more servers, clients, or applications to their SANs.

Users agree, though, that relying on a systems vendor or integrator for your first SAN implementation is the wise route. You should also expect your vendor to guarantee interoperability between Fibre Channel and Small Computer System Interface (SCSI) devices.

It is reasonable to choose a vendor to implement a limited package. It is also unlikely a vendor would be able to completely understand business applications and where a midsize-to-large business is going.

The plan for a data infrastructure closely parallels the network and systems infrastructure. Blending the three into a single cohesive network is necessary to the planning. That way, storage becomes another infrastructure resource that users can manage. This strategy also helps ensure network, applications, and other groups in the enterprise network environment interoperate.

Successful SAN implementation also depends in large part on getting the approval of management. For example, most SAN deployments are just the start of a much larger SAN implementation that management has approved and provided the funds for.

Ensuring that you get a properly funded program and a disciplined investment plan rather than budgeting in fits and starts is important. You do not want the first application to have to bear all the cost. You need to think about planning for this, investing in it, and then allocating the cost back to the business across multiple applications.

With that in mind, companies functioning in the same vertical market with the same basic needs will often choose very different solutions, but all achieve satisfying results. Now, let us look at how to deploy a SAN by examining how three companies in the digital printing industry fulfilled similar storage needs in three distinct ways.

HOW TO DEPLOY A SAN ....

The introduction of digital technology has propelled document printing from a mechanical to a computerized function, bringing opportunities for new imaging techniques, customized documents specific to each ad campaign or promotion, and online order processing. These new functions, however, take up vast amounts of storage space. The original computer systems purchased to handle office applications were not intended to accommodate the huge imaging files that digital printing requires, nor did they have backup systems in place to protect 24-hour online transaction data. Print vendors are scrambling to find cost-effective ways to increase storage and backup capabilities yet stay competitive in a very close market. The three vendors below are very happy with their completely distinct solutions to the same basic storage problem.

Expanding Storage the SAN Way

The printing industry's data storage needs have surged since the onset of Print-On-Demand (POD) order fulfillment. The introduction of digital printing technology brought the ability to quickly change and customize printed documents on demand. Businesses no longer need to inventory printed in-stock brochures now that they've discovered how easily customized tradeshow handouts, menus, and promotional pieces can be obtained. The cost effectiveness of POD digital printing allows companies to do smaller runs of specific materials instead of ordering large amounts of generic brochures (50% of which lose relevancy before being used).

For example, MediaFlex [2] of Campbell, California, provides the e-commerce infrastructure for a number of print vendors and their customers. A user can now log on to his or her print vendor's e-business Website, connect to a Webpage of his or her own previously ordered print templates, select a product, make changes to his or her company's documents right on the screen, and place his or her order. He or she can check price quotes, get order confirmation, and view a proof copy in real time, 24×7.

To provide these benefits, the customer requires a data storage methodology with 100% file availability, large storage capacity (a single typical document template is 25 MB to 50 MB), scalability for a growing client base, and complete security for online server data. MediaFlex chose a switched-fabric SAN to meet its needs. Four existing enterprise servers were integrated with a new RAID device in a SAN Fibre Channel switching environment. Redundant hardware throughout the file delivery subsystem over a dual-switched, multiple server-to-RAID storage channel provides automatic failover protection and fault isolation, guaranteeing continual operation. In that way, the configuration assures network availability, allows centralized backup functions with quick failover disaster recovery capabilities, permits file sharing between servers, and provides scalability without online interruptions.

The SAN contains four Sun 400 MHz E450 enterprise servers running version 7 of the Solaris operating system. Each server is equipped with two Fabric cards, 124 MB of RAM, and 9 GB of hard disk space. Web traffic is funneled to two servers and the other two are reserved for network files and applications. All four are active, but a failure in one will prompt another to take over in approximately 15 seconds.

A Hitachi 5846 full Fiber Channel RAID, with 140 GB of total usable file storage space, is connected directly to the Sun servers through two Brocade Fiber Channel switches. The RAID device is equipped with two controllers and 10 drives, and is used for all storage needs, freeing up the servers' hard disks for applications. The controllers connect to each other and to the servers' Host Bus Adapter Fabric cards via redundant Fibre Channel bus paths. If one controller fails, the RAID automatically and transparently switches to the remaining controller.

In addition, a tape library allows near-online secondary storage, conserving online storage space by migrating rarely used files from the RAID through storage zoning and a continual automated backup process. Veritas Volume Manager software handles all storage management and backup tasks.

The SAN storage solution was installed and running in two days. To date, Mediaflex, their print vendors, and their customers continue to benefit from the system's speed (the SAN and RAID can read a 25 megabyte file in 1 second), enhanced file accessibility (client files must be available to several applications and both Web servers), state-of-the-art online scalability, and complete reliability (system downtime is virtually eliminated).

A Packaged Solution

Dallas-based Blanks Color Imaging [3], which specializes in printing, also found its storage capacity inadequate for its expanding business. Founded in 1940 as a letterpress shop, Blanks expanded and diversified by combining prepress, sheet-fed printing, and digital photography services into a turnkey print delivery format. The company operates seven days a week to produce brochures, advertising supplements, posters, and other marketing materials for direct mail businesses, department stores, and large national printing companies. Blanks' data storage capacity could not meet the company's growing workload.

The company had two-fold system needs. First, they were still relying on 2 GB digital audio tape and a 1.2 GB optical disk. With the large, image-based files generated by the current turnkey format, these did not meet the need. Second, too much time was used shuttling 100 MB to 150 MB high-resolution files over the 10 MB Ethernet network. Initially, the company attempted to save time by placing active files on a 2 GB removable hard drive that was hand-carried as needed between imaging workstations, but that method proved very inefficient.

After researching other options, Blanks resolved its system needs with the purchase of a Scitex Server System package. The company's 100 nodes now reside on a 100 MB Ethernet LAN. The new server is a Scitex Ripro 5000 AIX with a 640 GB RAID disk array, backed up by a Breece Hill automated tape library with four Quantum Digital Linear Tape (DLT) 7000 drives. Each cartridge holds up to 70 GB of compressed data, and the library currently holds 4.2 terabyte (TB: 1,024 gigabytes) of data in near-online storage.

Legato NetWorker software electronically manages all files, migrating them at predetermined intervals from the RAID device to the tape library. That archiving and backup software, linked with the Scitex Timna database, manages 150 DLT cartridges that replace the original 1,800 DAT. The cartridges provide ready availability to 7 TB of recent and current images, layouts, and advertisements (representing $6 million in business). Designers waited three to six hours for that same data when it was stored on DAT. Seventy-five DLT cartridges are reserved for RAID array backup; 50 are used to archive past jobs and image files.

Twice-a-day incremental backups are implemented. A full system backup, which requires eight to nine hours, is performed weekly, and files are safeguarded by storing tape copies both onsite and offsite. They maintain three sets of all files, which are rotated continuously. At any one time, one set is in the RAID device, one is in the tape library, and one is offsite. That provides excellent protection for client files, and should a large disaster ever befall, no more than six hours of work can be lost.

With the Legato and Scitex software, employees are able to track archived files. The automation software, faster network, and DLT library system have improved efficiency, increasing throughput by 30% to 40% and dramatically improving turnaround time to clients.

Using HSM Technology

Banta Digital Group's [4] expertise involves customized digital imaging and content management services. Customers' desktops are connected directly to Banta's WAN, from which they're able to manage their own documents' entire creative design, digital prepress, and digital printing processes. The company guarantees its customers 100% file availability, complete data protection, and ample storage capacity. Over 200 users may be logged on to the Banta network at any one time, resulting in an enormous number of files being updated and saved continuously. The company needed a system tailored specifically for its unique and extremely high-volume data storage and availability requirements.

Banta chose to install a hierarchical storage management (HSM) data protection and availability system consisting of an enterprise server connected to three levels of storage. The HSM software automatically, seamlessly, and transparently manages the network's three-level storage hierarchy. New and frequently used files are saved on a RAID device (online storage), while less frequently used files are migrated to a large-capacity, near-online, magneto-optical (MO) jukebox. Rarely used files are archived to a high-capacity 34 TB DLT library.

As an added protection, the HSM software package is configured to automatically mirror RAID data onto the MO library within minutes of being received. In the case of extremely large customer files, RAID space is conserved by saving only 40 GB of the file on the RAID device, automatically off-loading the overage to MO. A second copy of the entire file is immediately saved with the archived files on tape.

Banta's existing LAN has been upgraded to Fast-Ethernet/ATM. The connections coming from external nodes into the network were upgraded from T1 and frame relay to higher-capacity DS3 lines. To ensure complete file availability, redundant hardware was installed throughout the file delivery subsystem (access paths, controllers, and so forth).

The enterprise server chosen by Banta is a Sun 336 MHz E6500, containing 10 GB of RAM and running on Solaris 2.6. The E6500 has 10 CPUs, eliminating the possibility that a CPU malfunction could result in system failure or downtime.

The first tier of online data storage is a StorageTek CBNT-CO1 Fibre Channel RAID device with a 1 TB capacity and 100 MB per second access speed. Banta is currently using 60 18-GB drives, but the RAID device is scalable to 120 drives for each of its two controllers. Because each controller has its own Fibre Channel bus path, if one fails, the other (failover) controller can take over automatically.

A SCSI-attached disc El050 read/write jukebox is the second storage tier. The jukebox contains 1,000 platters (5 TB of data storage) and 16 disc drives; it's scalable to 32 drives to accommodate future needs. Offloading RAID online storage onto the near-online MO jukebox is a low-cost method of improving the performance and access speed of the RAID device while continuing to keep less frequently used files accessible.

The final tier of storage in the hierarchy is a StorageTek 9710 tape library. Banta uses 6 of the possible 10 DLT 7000 drives. The library has a total data capacity of 28 TB. Though the rarely used files are now archived, all data in the HSM-controlled tape library remain available to the user. In contrast with typical tape archives, the HSM system eliminates the need to search for and reload offline tapes.

The bulk of Banta Digital Group's customers are catalogers, advertisers, and creative designers, all of whom have benefited from the new HSM system. Besides enjoying 100% guaranteed file access and the disaster recovery safety net provided by the backup hierarchy and redundant hardware, they've seen new product introduction time drop from 32 to 19 days and the prepress production cycle shortened from 3 days to 1 day. Transparent to the clients, Banta has also been able to reduce staffing requirements by eight people, giving them another advantage in a competitive industry.

Each company's unique situation dictates the storage solution that's best for it. No one solution will work in each case. The three storage styles, though not at all alike, incorporate cutting-edge technology and state-of-the-art hardware and software, as well as advanced file availability, storage capacity, and data protection.

GETTING STARTED ON SAN ....

As with any new technology, a phased implementation is the best for several reasons. Primary reasons include risk management, maximized return on investment, improved learning of a new technology, and ease of integration. By allowing the IT staff to incorporate a new technology in a staged (in stages) and thoughtful way, not only enables (activates) the SAN architecture, but allows its optimization in each unique environment. As the staff gains experience, more components can be added with increased storage management to enjoy more advantages of the architecture. SAN deployment is no riskier than many other IT projects, but like all significant IT projects it should be carefully managed for best results. Indeed, using SAN for data replication may reduce risk for other critical IT projects like application development, testing, and migration projects.

Implementation should start with a simple configuration of a single FC hub and a few devices in a local environment. Once this is mastered and extended to greater numbers and types of devices, the next logical progression would be to link two FC hubs together with a small switch for additional benefits of distance and logical isolation. Finally, the initial small switch would be tied to a larger switch to gain a more enterprise-wide view of storage for improved storage management and cost effectiveness.

Start with Hubs

The best way to integrate any new technology is to start small, master the technology, and grow. Start the SAN topology in a department with either a managed hub connecting the existing server to the new SAN that connects either a RAID or simple disk array. This will provide a low-cost entry with great flexibility that will be used as a building block for subsequent configurations. A reasonable first step is migrating SCSI bus devices to the new Fibre Channel way of doing things. Attaching existing SCSI arrays to a protocol converter for Fibre can provide investment protection, improved management, and easy implementation. Even this initial stage of SAN will provide faster access to data, improved scalability, greater distance capability, and improved data availability. Hub implementation will greatly ease the ability to enable a LAN-free/SAN-based backup and restore capability with the appropriate application software. This results in a backup procedure that minimizes its impact on the LAN by putting the backup traffic on the SAN.

The hub stage should then be repeated in different departments or facilities as learning improves and the procedures are tailored to fit the particular installation environment (see Figure 13.1) [5]. The end result is a series of SAN hubs installed throughout the enterprise providing improved access, reliability, and performance.

The hub phase is also known as the SCSI bus migration phase. The money and time spent implementing this phase will provide immediate benefits as well as positioning for subsequent implementations.

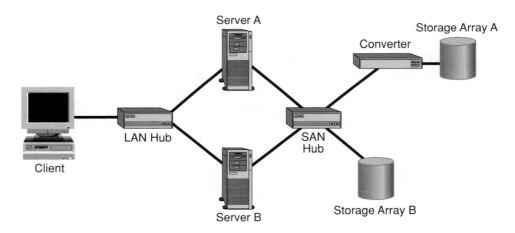

Figure 13.1
The hub stage.

Link Hubs to a Fibre Channel Switch

After the initial hubs and the storage system management software have been installed, departments or other logical groups should be linked together. This phase is called the Storage Infrastructure phase. This phase provides the first glimpse into the broader benefits of the SAN, while still protecting the investment in the hub phase and providing a smooth learning curve to ensure the enterprise gets the highest return on investment from each phase of the SAN implementation. The linking of the hubs with a small switch allows the departmental hubs to be connected with a back-up link for higher availability. In the event that one of the primary links between departments has problems, the alternate link can be utilized to provide improved availability. Additionally, it will enable the long distance connection, up to 10 km between two nodes, which provides greater disaster tolerance as shown in Figure 13.2 [5].

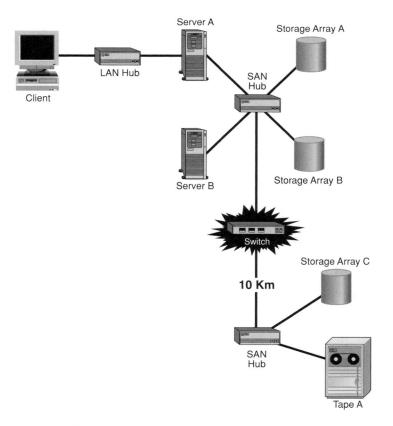

Figure 13.2
Long distance connection between two nodes.

The distance and department segmentation that are provided with a switch will allow the departments to share valuable storage resources and start to develop common management of the storage resource. One of the largest benefits of a SAN is the simple sharing of storage assets—disk arrays and tape libraries. One significant problem with traditional captive storage architecture is assuring consistent management of the data in distributed departments. The switch allows hubs to link together with fast physical connection while maintaining logical separation. The switch also allows more disaster-tolerant applications since the departmental storage can now be backed up remotely, improving the availability of important data in case of an emergency. The logical separation prevents problems in one department from spilling over to another department.

In the preceding example (see Figure 13.2), the client now has access to a valuable tape unit for backup via his or her SAN. It allows a valuable tape library to be used by more clients. This provides better protection for enterprise data with less server overhead, at less cost, and sets the stage for common management of storage assets. This can be done at distances up to 10 km to allow groups at a distance to access these resources. It also allows data replication for better disaster tolerance by mirroring data from one site to another via the switch without the distance limitations of SCSI or the overhead of traditional data networks. As the amount of critical data grows and the need for continuous access increases, data replication on the campus with the preceding configuration provides a simple way to protect your operations. This becomes even more feasible as the cost of storage continues to decline.

Note

Data replication, mirroring, and other storage management tasks require the implementation of the appropriate software to ensure data integrity is preserved.

Big Switch Phase

Once the hubs and switches are installed together with the storage management software, it is time for a larger switch. This environment will allow the enterprise to fully recognize the benefits of the SAN and it will have been implemented in an incremental way with high reliability, legacy equipment utilization, and maximum return on investment of time and capital. It is not necessary to risk the integrity of your data to incorporate a new technology, but it is necessary to manage its introduction. This final stage is referred to as the universal data center since data is now available throughout the enterprise with a variety of applications, locations, and storage devices. During the phased-in introduction, experience has already been gained in the hub and switch topologies. Experience gained with storage management software has allowed consistent storage management even in a diverse environment. The incremental implementation being recommended allows the realization of improved availability/reliability, performance, and configuration flexibility at an attractive cost. The SAN allows the enterprise to maximize the utilization of its LAN, servers, and storage by differentiating the network to provide for its different functions. It allows easier data sharing among different systems, and backup that will not impact LAN performance of the clients gaining access to their data. In this final stage, you can find consistent data management, access security, and shared access managed by the SAN in a cost-effective manner that can scale to the largest data centers.

The switch environment as shown in Figure 13.3, allows many departments to be linked together with high-capacity dedicated bandwidth for the traffic associated with a large storage network [5]. For example, large clustered environments benefit from high concurrency found in the large switch.

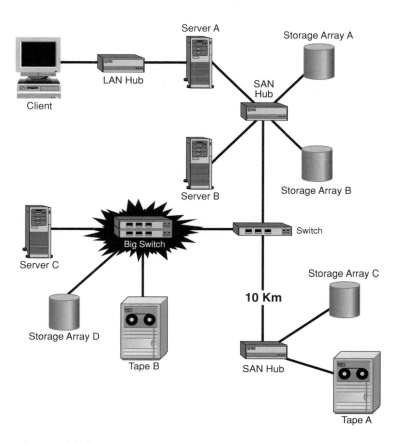

Figure 13.3
The switch environment.

Figure 13.4 shows the three phases of SAN implementation: Hubs for the SCSI bus migration phase, small fibre channel switches for building a storage infrastructure, and large switches for the universal data center [5]. By building the SAN in a well defined and thoughtfully considered plan, each element is more likely to build a low-risk, high-return implementation. SAN provides a superior solution to the concerns of traditional captive storage: reliability/availability, performance, configuration flexibility, and cost. The SAN architecture is based on Fibre Channel development that started in 1988 and a vast amount of experience has been gained since that time. It is time for your enterprise to enjoy the benefits of SAN technology. This low-risk, incremental approach preserves the investment in the equipment from the previous phase, and builds on the experience and management techniques used in each successive step. The phased approach outlined in this chapter will allow a greater opportunity for a successful adoption of the SAN technology so your enterprise can reap the rewards of better reliability, performance, and configuration flexibility at a more reasonable cost.

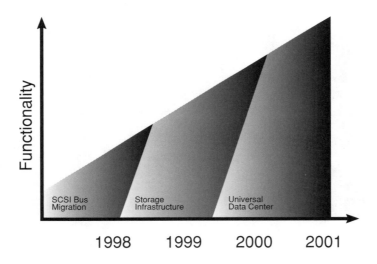

Figure 13.4
The three phases of SAN implementation.

THE NEXT PHASE OF SAN DEPLOYMENT: STORAGE SWITCH TECHNOLOGY ....

The architecture of open enterprise storage is undergoing a fundamental change. Today's model of distributed servers, each with their own private connection to storage, is rapidly transitioning to a network of storage resources shared by many heterogeneous servers. This new storage architecture has assumed its own identity as a SAN. Fibre Channel, an open industry standard, has emerged as the technology foundation for the SAN because of its suitability for storage networking. Desirable Fibre Channel attributes include high bandwidth, long distance connections, scalability, and broad industry support from major enterprise server, storage, and networking providers.

Modeling client-server LANs, the SAN environment interconnects servers and storage, using a network of high-speed connections (see Figure 13.5) [6]. SAN eliminates the performance bottlenecks, distance constraints, and scalability limitations imposed by traditional SCSI-based architectures, enabling a more distributed storage network for enterprise environments.

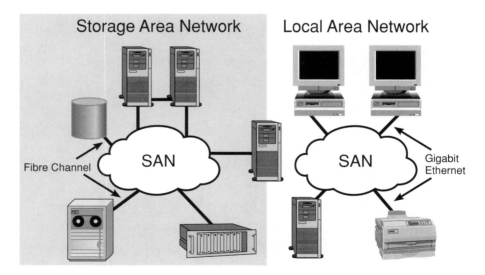

Figure 13.5
SAN–LAN environment.

What's Driving SAN Evolution?

Initial deployments of SAN have focused on displacing SCSI interconnects mainly in single server or two-node cluster environments where extended distances and higher storage scalability is required. Storage Hubs, based on Fibre Channel technology, lower total cost of ownership by consolidating connections and enabling centralized management of the expanded storage resources. According to market research firm, International Data Corporation, the total cost of managing storage can be reduced by 60% and IT administrators can effectively manage 970% more storage capacity under a centralized SAN environment as compared to the traditional distributed server and storage model. In early deployments of SAN, Storage Hubs provide the simplest and most cost-effective solution (see Figure 13.6) [6].

Based on the promise of significantly lower total cost of ownership when multiple servers share a centralized pool of storage, the industry is now preparing to broaden the application and scope of the SAN to include more complex implementations necessitating the addition of switching. As mainstream operating systems and storage devices support multiserver applications, these servers will require concurrent access to the shared storage resources. The switch provides this concurrency as well as necessary services such as *zoning*—or the ability to segment the network and bind each server to specific disk or tape storage resources (see Figure 13.7) [6]. However, although the desire to introduce switching to SANs is quite clear, it is not without its challenges.

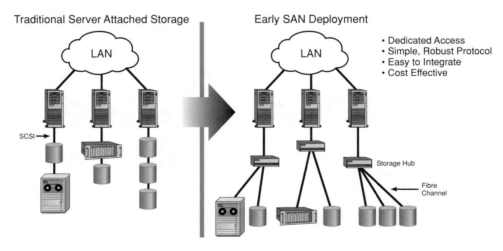

Figure 13.6
The Storage Hub replaces private SCSI interconnects.

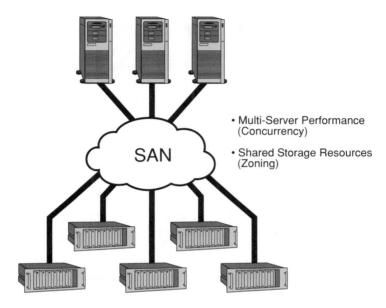

Figure 13.7
SAN switching benefit.

While all of the servers, hubs, and storage subsystems are based on the widely supported Fibre Channel protocol known as FC-AL, the early switch products are based on a newer protocol called *Fabric* and are positioned more for SAN backbone applications and less for storage consolidation applications. Although they do provide the required concurrency and switch services, these Backbone Switches have proven to be extremely problematic and costly to implement.

Note

FC-BB defines backbone switches (BBWs) that connect SAN islands across WANs.

Much of this difficulty appears to be directly related to the complexity of the Fabric protocol itself. Attempts to achieve multivendor interoperability with Backbone Switches have proven to be a daunting challenge leading some to dub the Fabric protocol as a "nonstandard standard" (see Figure 13.8) [6].

In addition to their complexity, the cost of Backbone Switches is also a barrier to their adoption. Backbone Switches are inherently expensive, typically four to eight times the cost per port of a Storage Hub. However, for many users and integrators, the transition and support costs are perhaps even more painful than the purchase price. Because the Fabric protocol does not directly connect to existing storage devices and

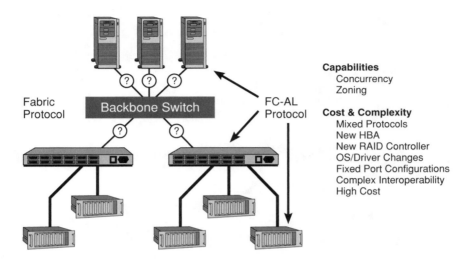

Figure 13.8
The problem with Fabric.

host adapters, implementers must reengineer the network with specialized software, firmware, and hardware on all of the host and storage connections. Extensive multi-vendor interoperability testing must also be performed to verify the stability and reliability of the Fabric-based network. These cost and complexity barriers have severely limited the addition of switching within the SAN. And until recently, SAN implementers had no alternative to the Backbone Switch.

The Storage Switch: A Simple, Cost-Effective Approach to SAN Switching

Fortunately, a new switch class was recently introduced to the SAN—the Storage Switch. The Storage Switch delivers the same concurrency and zoning services offered by the Backbone Switch while eliminating the cost and complexity of a mixed protocol environment (see Figure 13.9) [6]. How is this possible? Based on an innovative implementation of the existing industry standard FC-AL protocol, the Storage Switch maintains the same technology and characteristics of the existing installed base of Storage Hubs, storage subsystems, and servers. This approach challenges the common misconception that the FC-AL protocol is limited for use only in a shared bandwidth *loop* topology or that Fabric protocol is required for a switched topology. In truth, the FC-AL standard defines a simple and cost-effective communication protocol that is well suited for both loop and switch topologies. Embracing the FC-AL protocol, a Storage Switch eases the addition of switching and provides a flexible building block for continued SAN evolution and rapid deployment.

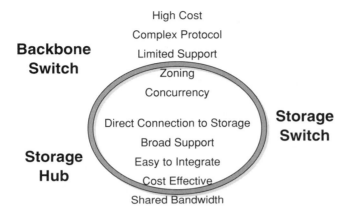

Figure 13.9
Storage Switch provides best of both worlds.

Applying Storage Switch in the SAN: One-Tier SAN

For small networks with multiple servers, a Storage Switch can immediately boost storage performance by allowing concurrent traffic between each server and the shared storage resources (see Figure 13.10) [6]. Since the Storage Switch is based on

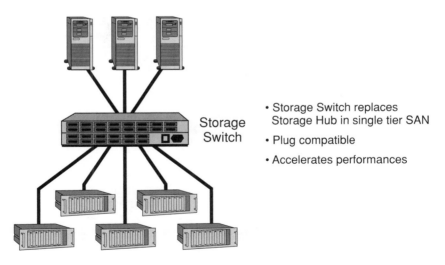

Figure 13.10
Storage Switch easily drops in place of hub to improve performance.

the same protocol as the Storage Hub and other connected devices, the hub can literally be removed and replaced with a Storage Switch without any other changes to the network. This unique attribute of the Storage Switch drastically reduces the engineering effort and completely preserves the installed base of connected end-node devices. As the network grows, it's easy to add another Storage Switch or Storage Hub to facilitate more servers or expanded storage capacity.

Two-Tier SAN

In SAN environments where higher storage scalability is a priority, a combination of hubs and switches can be utilized to construct a two-tiered SAN (see Figure 13.11) [6]. In this environment, the Storage Hub facilitates the broad, concentrated connectivity for storage while Storage Switch takes the place of the Backbone Switch to provide the needed concurrency and zoning. This network design can support scaling storage capacity to hundreds or even thousands of terabytes using existing loop protocol standards and technology without ever introducing the fabric protocol and deferring the need for a costly Backbone Switch.

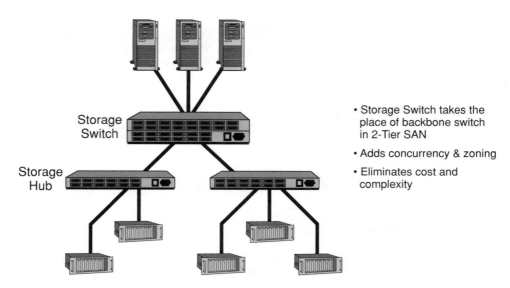

Figure 13.11
Storage Switch directly connects to existing Storage Hubs in 2-tier SAN.

Three-Tier SAN

In extremely large topologies where scalability to thousands or tens of thousands of terabytes is required, the Backbone Switch can be added at the top tier to provide the needed connectivity to thousands of host and storage devices. However, this introduces network complexities that must first be addressed. Since most Backbone Switches today only support 8 to 16 ports, building a network of this size would require a complex interswitch linking scheme and would likely introduce serious performance bottlenecks moving data from one end of the network to the other. These problems will certainly be solved in future phases of SAN deployment and the Storage Switch will complement the existing Storage Hub and future Backbone Switch in a 3-tier network hierarchy of SAN infrastructure components.

By enabling more graduated steps in multitier architecture, Storage Switch flattens out the cost of ownership curve as node count increases by providing building blocks for optimal scalability. With Storage Switch, scaling of storage to thousands of terabytes can be accomplished without ever introducing mixed protocols.

Although Backbone Switch vendors are adopting technology to allow direct connection to both FC-AL and Fabric-aware storage devices, it adds even more cost to the implementation (see Figure 13.12) [6]. In shedding the complexity of Fabric, the Storage Switch becomes a more cost-effective solution. When you consider the additional cost of transitioning to Fabric-aware host adapters and the cost of integration and support, the total cost of acquisition, integration, and support for the Storage Switch drops even further.

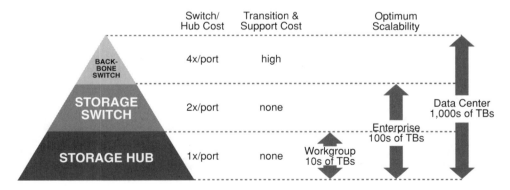

Figure 13.12
Cost and scalability comparison.

Industry Validation of the Storage Switch

Major system, storage, and networking leaders such as 3Com, Clariion, EMC, Hewlett-Packard, Hitachi Data Systems, Intel, and Seagate have endorsed the Storage Switch technology. These companies view Storage Switch as a positive step for the industry that will accelerate the migration to switching and are anticipating availability of products beginning in early 2002. Simple implementation, investment protection, and the ability to apply prior knowledge and practices will accelerate the adoption of SAN switching technology. Fibre Channel Fabric switch benefits have been limited by the complexity, cost, and interoperability issues.

One thing is clear: The technology is based on existing industry standards. SAN switch providers are free to implement a Storage Switch product today as an attractive alternative to the backbone switch.

Next, let's explore how deploying an enterprise SAN can help make the corporate information utility a reality.

PUTTING DATA TO WORK FOR E-BUSINESS IN SAN INSTALLATION AND DEPLOYMENT ....

Finally, for several years now, analysts have been saying that we have left behind the Industrial Age and entered the Information Age. Increasingly, information is the raw material for developing competitive differentiation and value add.

But in today's rapidly evolving business environment, making effective use of information is an increasingly challenging task. The pace of change is so fast (and the volume of information has become so great) that IT systems can become choke points rather than the enablers of efficient information exchange.

To flourish in the Information Age, a company must be able to make information as pervasive and easily accessible as electricity or telephone service. Such a corporate *information utility* would permit on-demand exchange of information across functional and departmental lines, forging new connections to customers and suppliers. Finding practical and affordable ways to link everyone to the flow of information has become a strategic necessity.

The Changing Environment

The advent of Internet technology has transformed today's business environment into a highly competitive, expanding, unpredictable, networked economy. Over the past few years it has become apparent that success in this new business environment depends on one thing: adaptability.

Successful businesses around the world have been transforming themselves, through a series of stages, from traditional *make-and-sell* organizations into *sense-and-respond* organizations: more responsive, more flexible, in a word, more adaptive. Ultimately, these businesses view the enterprise as a dynamic and adaptive collection of capabilities that can be quickly reconfigured to create customer value.

The key to adaptability (and delivering increased value profitably) is to become what Gartner Group calls a *zero latency* organization, one that has the ability to exchange information immediately for purposes of gaining an edge. Success in today's extremely competitive business environment depends on a company's ability to adapt (continuously and rapidly) to changing conditions by immediately accessing and processing information for driving strategic business decisions.

Unfortunately, many organizations are finding an unexpected roadblock on the way to zero latency: their information technology systems. Many corporate computing environments are built to solve specific tactical, rather than strategic, concerns. The result is separate *islands* of information that can leave a company at a competitive disadvantage.

What's required is a zero latency computing environment, one that enables the free, immediate exchange of information. But, the development of such a system poses a number of challenging technical and management questions.

The Challenges

Probably the single greatest challenge to the development of a zero latency computing environment is the enormous growth of business data. Even before the advent of electronic commerce, it was estimated that new front-office business applications (such as enterprise resource planning suites) were resulting in an annual doubling of corporate data.

With e-business, that rate of increase is compounded. Information is the currency of e-business, the elemental medium of exchange. As a result, as organizations make the transition from traditional business to static Web serving to performing actual business transactions via the Internet or extranets, they can see information volume increase eight fold. Before they can profit from this unprecedented wealth of information, most organizations face the challenge of finding an affordable way to store and manage it.

This rate of growth has serious implications across a number of other areas, as well. For example, globalization and e-business each demand 24x365 information availability. Not only does this mean investing in redundant systems to ensure critical information is available even during a hardware or software failure, it means the amount of time available for backups, updates, and maintenance is drastically reduced or eliminated.

The information explosion also can have unexpected impact on system performance. Take, for example, an e-commerce site that must retrieve information from and update a corporate inventory system. To enable the Web transactions, information must flow back and forth across the corporate LAN. As the volume of Web hits increases, the LAN can become choked, slowing response times to unacceptable levels—not just for the inventory and Web applications, but for every application that must send information across that same network.

Finally, there are the complications of managing information in a heterogeneous environment. The staff must be prepared to deal with a variety of operating systems and user interfaces. In addition, limited integration between products from different vendors will likely require separate management tools and control points. In addition to requiring investments in redundant skills and management software, the process is very labor-intensive, as staff must perform the same functions multiple times across multiple servers. The results are less efficient information management and a higher total cost of computing.

These challenges define a new set of requirements for a corporate computing environment. In order to enable a company to make efficient use of increasing volumes of information, a corporate computing system must:

1. Provide a solution that addresses strategic business needs rather than individual computing requirements
2. Be transparent to business applications
3. Reuse existing hardware, software, and skills
4. Provide centralized management of information and devices
5. Work across a heterogeneous environment
6. Provide flexibility necessary for rapid response to changing conditions while controlling costs [7]

The distributed computing environments typical in business today, which tie information to a single server, lack the flexibility to meet these needs. But a relatively new approach to information management, known as the SAN, promises to provide the foundation for the development of the corporate information utility.

The Promise of SANs

As previously explained, a SAN is a high-speed network dedicated to information management. More formally, a SAN is a combination of technologies (including hardware, software, and networking components) that provides any-to-any interconnection of server and storage elements.

By separating information management from information processing, a SAN provides the flexibility required to meet the new computing requirements defined in the preceding. More to the point, by enabling the free, immediate exchange of information, a SAN provides the foundation for a zero latency computing environment.

SANs are based on a *fabric* of Fibre Channel hubs, switches, and gateways connecting storage devices (such as disk arrays, optical disks, or tape libraries) and servers on a many-to-many basis. Application and transaction servers are attached to both the SAN and to LANs or WANs, creating what appears to be a massive pool of data.

SANs can be configured to provide servers in different locations with direct access to huge amounts of shared storage resources. A SAN also can enable direct storage-to-storage connectivity (for example, between multiple disk arrays or between a disk array and a tape library) allowing management activities such as backups and archiving to take place independent of any server.

Inherent in the promise of SANs are two compelling advantages. The first is the creation of a true information utility. By eliminating the one-to-one relationship between individual servers and critical business data to create a corporate information *bank*, a SAN can make that information readily available across the enterprise.

The second advantage is that a SAN can provide a faster, more effective way to deal with rapidly increasing volumes of information. With a separate information management network, additional capacity can be *plugged in* as needed with minimal impact on the performance of application or transaction servers, LANs or WANs.

SANs promise more responsive and robust systems, as well. For example, by reducing the amount of traffic that must travel along corporate networks, installing a SAN has the effect of increasing available bandwidth. The result is response times that are well matched to the requirements of e-business.

Performance is further enhanced by improved backup and recovery capabilities. With a SAN, backup and recovery can take place without involving either the existing LAN or WAN or individual application or transaction servers.

In addition, with information no longer tied to any one server in particular, failure of a single server is less likely to degrade information availability. SANs will support advanced multi-server clustering solutions for new levels of information availability and business continuity. And SANs permit near-real-time updates of remote disaster recovery sites for higher levels of disaster tolerance.

Management is also greatly simplified. A SAN permits the use of a common set of tools and a single point of control to manage a centralized pool of information. As a technology marrying storage, servers, networking, and systems management, SAN requires an unprecedented level of cross-discipline expertise.

Finally, SANs today are where e-business was just a few years ago. It is clear that they can play a critical part in establishing a competitive edge in today's dynamic global business environment; but many organizations regard them with confusion or outright skepticism.

Like e-business, the promise of SANs is compelling; a SAN offers the ability to connect to more people, handle the incredible growth of business data, and respond more quickly to customer wants and needs. But like e-business, it will require a holistic, multidisciplinary approach to deliver the full benefits of SANs in the least amount of time.

FROM HERE...

This chapter showed you how to deploy a SAN, get started on a SAN, use storage switch technology to accelerate the next phase of SAN deployment, and put data to work for e-businesses. The next chapter covers SAN testing and troubleshooting, documenting and testing SANs, and certifying SAN performance.

END NOTES...

[1] The Home Depot, 2455 Paces Ferry Road, Atlanta, GA 30339, 2001.

[2] Blanks Color Imaging, MediaFlex, 900 East Hamilton Avenue, Suite 350, Campbell, CA 95008, 2001.

[3] Blanks Color Imaging, 2343 N. Beckley Avenue, Dallas, TX 75208, 2001.

[4] Banta Digital Group, 18790 West 78th Street, Chanhassen, MN 55317-0426, 2001.

[5] Erik Ottem, *Getting the Most from Your Storage*, Gadzoox Networks, Inc., 5850 Hellyer Avenue, San Jose, CA 95138, 2001.

[6] Joel Warford, *Storage Switch Technology Accelerates Next Phase of SAN Deployment*, Gadzoox Networks, Inc., 5850 Hellyer Avenue, San Jose, CA 95138, USA, 2001.

[7] *Storage Area Networks: Putting Data to Work for E-Businesses*, IBM Corporation, Marketing Communications, Servers, Route 100, Somers, NY 10589, 2001.

14 Certification of SAN Performance

IT professionals have a big headache—and it's got storage written all over it. Storage complications facing IT professionals are growing exponentially as users demand more storage. Data centers must satisfy the demand for storage, back up all their data on the network in ever-shrinking timeframes, and manage storage devices without growing the personnel pool at the rate of their capacity growth. Solving these problems with today's budgets is a demanding and almost impossible task called the *IT Storage Conundrum.*

On today's networks, 70% of the data is inactive and eating up valuable online storage capacity. However, this data must be available on demand and it is cost-prohibitive to store it in the online RAID system. Imagine if you could migrate inactive data to a nearline storage device that offered high performance, random access, better reliability, easier scalability, and field upgradability than your online RAID system.

> **Note**
>
> **The performance of a SAN depends on the components of the SAN. SAN performance depends on HBA, host drivers, FC fabric components (hubs and switches), and their interaction with the storage management software.**

SAN TESTING AND TROUBLESHOOTING.................

BlueArc [1], a new Silicon Valley company that promises to provide significantly better data storage performance, testing, and troubleshooting, is proving that the technology sector has not lost its appetite for speculation about the next great thing. BlueArc indicates it has completed design work and initial testing with customers of a new storage device that fetches data 5 to 10 times as fast as similar equipment from companies like EMC and Network Appliance. BlueArc also says that each of its specialized servers can handle 100 times as many simultaneous connections as its potential rivals and manage 200 terabytes of data—30 times the capacity of any rival.

The devices start at about $100,000 each. But everything the audience of high technology executives, investors, and reporters will hear has been carefully leaked to influential analysts in recent months with the kind of results marketers dream of.

Although benchmark tests like those cited by BlueArc do not translate directly into real-world advantages in every data storage application, they point to a real breakthrough. It's 2 to 10 times as good as today's products.

Nevertheless, the BlueArc *revolution* could take a bite out of not just the leading storage vendors, but also companies like Cisco Systems, Alteon, and Extreme Networks that sell gear to balance loads on storage networks. The industry analysts indicate that BlueArc's achievement is its design of new hardware that allows data to move in and out of storage systems at roughly the same high speeds it moves across the optical networks that link computers. Today's market leaders cannot match that without adding equipment or elaborate software.

BlueArc's solution has been to design new chips that are programmed specifically for the kinds of demands placed on them by storage management. The basic approach is not novel. Indeed, Cisco and others transformed the telecommunications business by replacing software-based switching systems with new hardware specifically tailored to the task.

However, established storage companies noted that most start-ups betting on specialized hardware solutions to technology problems fail, even in the best of times. They are going to have trouble getting chief information officers to take their systems, even for a free look. People aren't going to experiment with companies that have no global support and no track record at a time like this.

Note

Budgets are under pressure.

Next, let's discuss the theoretical performance differences between all Finite State Machine (FSM)-based Fibre Channel controller versus an embedded-microprocessor approach. Actual documentation of testing and performance results will then be presented.

DOCUMENTING AND TESTING SANS......................

An FSM can be thought of as a fully-custom microprocessor, cycling through a hard-coded execution path. Inputs to the FSM, both from external signals and from other

FSMs, allow it to make branching decisions, and since branches are hard-coded, no performance penalties (related to code fetches) are introduced. Outputs of the FSM allow it to control surrounding data-path and control logic, and to communicate status and commands to other FSMs.

FSM Performance

Since an FSM can be thought of as a custom microprocessor, all decisions are made and commands are executed once each clock cycle. Thus, any one single FSM running at 33 MHz is executing at an equivalent rate of 33 million instructions per second (MIPS). When combined with the fact that a critical Tachyon family protocol chip contains over 30 significant master and slave FSMs, it is evident that a FSM-based Tachyon controller executes the equivalent of over 1 billion instructions per second. It is this base level of processing power that provides the performance foundation for the Tachyon family of protocol ICs.

In addition, an FSM can be made to execute "commands" or "decisions" that cannot generally be accommodated by an embedded microprocessor in a single instruction cycle. FSM conditional statements can be virtually any length (a function of gates), as can signal assertions (commands). A microprocessor typically requires not only instruction fetches, but numerous instruction cycles in order to implement complex commands.

Direct FSM Advantages

A Fibre Channel controller must function at many different levels; and it must manage data words at the FC-1 layer; frames, sequences, and exchanges at the FC-2 layer; protocol mappings at the FC-4 layer. Moreover, for maximum performance, both inbound and outbound channels must be able to operate independently. The Tachyon FSM architecture is ideally suited for this multilevel concurrent operation, as no one portion of the chip ever need wait on other portions, unless absolutely required by the protocol itself. Furthermore, an FSM architecture allows tile control requirements of I/Os to be handled concurrently with the movement of data, again increasing the amount of parallelism and performance.

Scalability

With 1 Gb/s Fibre Channel, the Tachyon family of chips is limited by that rate of 200 MB/s full-duplex—the internal architecture of Tachyon ICs is designed to operate in much faster rates. Thus, as multigigabit Fibre Channel is adopted, Tachyon performance is expected to scale directly. And, as the next generation of backplane is defined and implemented, the Tachyon architecture will again present the necessary level of processing power to be able to take full advantage of the higher speeds.

Performance Results

A comparison of maximum sequential read and write I/Os per second (IOPS) between a Tachyon Tape Library (TL)-based HBA and a Brand-X (ISP2100-based) HBA is shown in Figure 14.1 [2]. IOMeter™ results show that the HHBA-5100A and HHBA-5101A Fibre Channel HBAs deliver sequential read IOPS up to 30 K and sequential write IOPS up to 25 K, while Brand-X is limited to 9.5 K and 7.5 K IOPS, respectively.

Thus, in the basic Fibre Channel configurations described in this part of the chapter, performance measurements of Sequential Read IOPS of up to 30 K and Sequential Write IOPS of 25 K, were achieved using *HHBA-5100A* Fibre Channel HBA. This performance data is shown in Figures 14.2 and 14.3 [2]. Brand-X's performance, in the same environment, is shown in Figures 14.4 and 14.5 [2].

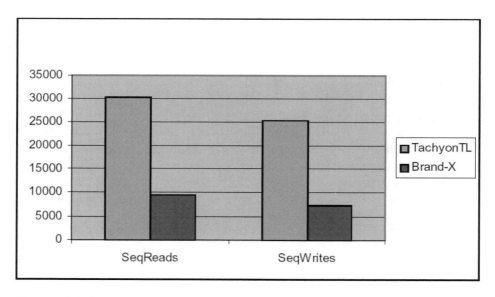

Figure 14.1
Maximum IOPS.

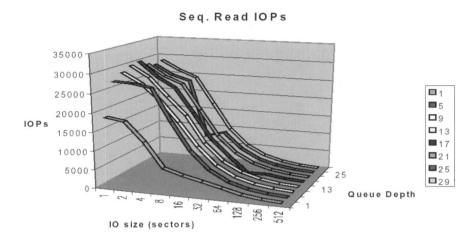

Figure 14.2
Test Type—100% Sequential Reads. Performance results (in IOPS) of HHBA-5100A Fibre Channel HBA.

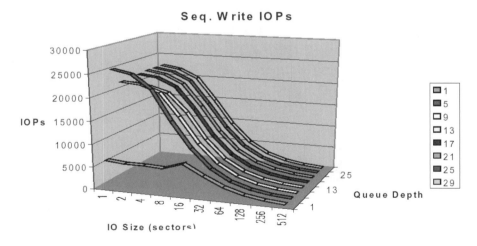

Figure 14.3
Test Type—100% Sequential Writes. Performance results (in IOPS) of HHBA-5100A Fibre Channel HBA.

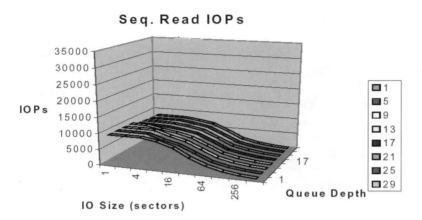

Figure 14.4
Test Type—100% Sequential Reads. Performance results (in IOPS) of Brand-X
Fibre Channel HBA.

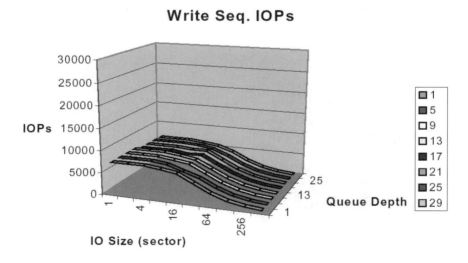

Figure 14.5
Test Type—100% Sequential Write. Performance results (in IOPS) of Brand-X
Fibre Channel HBA.

Additional performance points are as follows:

- Tachyon TL has 30–46% better IO Efficiency (IOPS/% CPU).
- Tachyon TL demonstrates lower CPU Utilization in TPC-C-like testing.
- Tachyon TL maintains high BW when connected to a switched configuration, while Brand-X's drops to 30% of TL's [2].

Therefore, the FSM-based architecture of the Tachyon protocol chips implements the required amount of processing power not only for today's Fibre Channel speeds, but provides the foundation for even greater performance in the future.

Test Configuration

The *HHBA-5100A* is a 32/64-bit PCI, Gigabit capable Fibre Channel Host Adapter focused on mass storage applications that require FC-AL, Class 3, and SCSI upper layer protocol handling. The heart of the *HHBA-5100A* is the HPFC-5100 TachyonTL Fibre Channel Interface Controller IC based on an FSM Architecture.

Consisting of a Peripheral Component Interconnect (PCI) short card form factor PCB and drivers for Windows NT, Novell NetWare, and SCO UNIXWare and 120, the HHBA-5100A provides Fibre Channel capability in a flexible add-in card format by interfacing the Fibre Channel protocol and cable media to PCI through a standard DB-9 copper interface [3]. The *HHBA-510IA* is a Gigabit Interface Converter (GBIC) variant of the HHBA-5100A Fibre Channel HBA (see Figure 14.6) [2].

Unisys JBOD with   Dell 2300 Server
8 Seagate Cheetah 9LP   Dual Pentium II 350 MHz

Figure 14.6

Performance Data

Tables 14.1 and 14.2 present a summary comparison of the two tested controllers during sequential read and write operation [2].

Table 14.1 Sequential Reads.

	Tachyon TL	Brand-X
Max IOPS	30,273	9,472
IOPS block size (bytes)	512	512
Max transfer rate (MBps)	93	88
Transfer rate block size (kB)	64	64
Max CPU	97%	42%
Max IOPS at 42% CPU	13,944	9,472
Max IO/% CPU	332	255

Note

The "Max IOPS at 42% CPU" is shown to demonstrate that if the Tachyon TL-based HBA is throttled in order to consume an equal percentage of the CPU resources as the Brand-X card, the maximum IOPS is still considerably higher.

Table 14.2 Sequential Writes.

	Tachyon TL	Brand-X
Max IOPS	25,306	7,286
IOPS block size (bytes)	512	512
Max transfer rate (MBps)	91	92
Transfer rate block size (kB)	64	256
Max CPU	87%	31%
Max IOPS at 31% CPU	12,462	7,286
Max IO/% CPU	402	276

TPC-C-like testing was performed using an 8 K I/O size with a 2:1 read/write ratio. In this limited testing, Tachyon TL outperforms Brand-X with lower CPU utilization (see Table 14.3) [2].

Table 14.3 TPC-C Type Configuration Results.

	Tachyon TL		Brand-X
Queue Depth	16	32	32
IOPS	1248.2	1411.2	1405.6
CPU Utilization	9.48%	10.14%	12.4%
IOPS/% CPU	131.7	139.3	113.3

SANs are forecast to provide higher availability of storage data and better server performance. With that in mind, let's see why.

CERTIFYING SAN PERFORMANCE............................

The stalwarts of the storage industry have come under fire from a newcomer to the market which claims the old guards' technology is *slow and cumbersome and uncertifiable*. Rather unsurprisingly, the industry giants have hit back at the latest addition to this increasingly crowded market, saying users would be 'foolish' to rely on untested and uncertified technology.

For example, BlueArc [1], which was recently launched, has claimed that rivals EMC and NetApps are out of date and slow and slammed their *cumbersome uncertifiable network performance* (see sidebar, "Certification Program for Storage Managers Set Up by EMC"). BlueArc has made a range of extravagant claims, including a statement that its NAS product, the Si7500, will fetch data 10 times faster than its competitors' products, while its specialized server can handle 100 times as many simultaneous connections and manage 200 TB of data—30 times more than the industry standard.

CERTIFICATION PROGRAM FOR STORAGE MANAGERS SET UP BY EMC

EMC Corporation recently announced a certification program for IT workers involved in managing storage devices. Analysts indicated the rollout could go a long way toward creating training standards in a part of the technology market that's sorely lacking in highly qualified support personnel.

The new certification program expands on an earlier set of training classes that were offered only to EMC's own employees and some of the Hopkinton, Massachusetts-based company's business partners. While rivals Network Appliance and Compaq Computer have also recently announced storage-related certification programs, EMC's offering is significant because its training regimen is very robust and equipment-neutral.

EMC is trying to fulfill two basic goals with the new program: improve the capabilities of IT technicians involved in implementing storage devices and create increased loyalty to its products. But, beyond the obvious potential benefits for EMC, the program could help set professional standards for storage networking equipment as a whole.

Certification is a key element that had been missing in EMC's ability to measure whether or not technicians at customer sites could manage its storage systems. EMC just wasn't able to put their arms around who could do what.

The Proven Professional Certification Program is aimed at building skills to support methods and operations, instead of (specific) products. The courses will include a combination of live Web-based training and instruction at 13 training facilities and 21 data centers in North America, Europe, and Asia, according to EMC.

EMC expects to put about 4,000 workers from customers and business partners through the training in 2002. IT workers can also choose to bypass the training classes and immediately take the certification tests, which are being administered by ProMetrics Consulting in Wayne, Pennsylvania. The certification programs being announced by EMC and other storage vendors come at a time when the available pool of trained storage managers isn't keeping up with demand created by the exploding volumes of information being generated by companies.

BlueArc has built its storage server architecture and based it on networking technologies. Their rivals are still working on the old-fashioned PC-based architecture which causes major problems. BlueArc has applied the same technology which is used in network architecture to rebuild their NAS servers to improve the performance (see sidebar, "SAN Certification Being Offered by SNIA").

SAN Certification Being Offered by SNIA

The Storage Networking Industry Association recently unveiled a program aimed at certifying IT professionals and solution providers in the SAN field. The SNIA certification will not focus on particular technologies and will be vendor-neutral.

Instead, the certification will focus on skills related to the assessment, troubleshooting, and deployment of SANs, as well as a variety of different technologies used with SANs. Technologies to be covered include Fibre Channel, Gigabit Ethernet, and direct access file system (DAFS).

SNIA will not provide the training related to the certification. Instead, potential testers can get the necessary training from a number of organizations such as Half Moon Bay, California-based Infinity I/O, or via storage vendors. With vendor training, there's a reasonable chance to pass. But, it's more than just the technology.

BlueArc's competitors were quick to hit back. BlueArc is focusing too much on the performance issue.

No company in their right mind would want to rely on BlueArc's technology. They have no disaster recovery, no database support, and they lack publicly approved benchmarks. Successful storage operation is not about the data's fast movement at the center of the network, but also at the periphery of it (see sidebar, "SSPs for SunTone Certified by Sun").

SSPs for SunTone Certified by Sun

Sun Microsystems is assisting its storage service provider partners by extending its SunTone Certification and Branding Program to cover the Storage Service Provider (SSP) space. At the recent SunTone++ iForce Service Provider Conference, Sun executives indicated the company will start certifying SSPs under the SunTone program.

Two SSPs, Arsenal Digital, Durham, North Carolina and StorageNetworks, Waltham, Massachusetts, have already been SunTone-certified. For SSPs, SunTone certification makes it easier for Sun clients looking for managed storage services partners to work with them, and lets SSPs take advantage of SunTone-related advertising and sales initiatives.

SSPs who have gone through the certification process have proven that their storage configurations work, making it easier to work with both Sun customers and Sun salespeople. Arsenal Digital has storage points in hosting partners such as Verio and AT&T; and Sun salespeople get compensated for bringing in customers looking for hosted services. For the customer side, Arsenal Digital becomes part of Verio and AT&T's program as a partner of Sun, and they know they are getting service and a program that works.

BlueArc's technology has not been through enough tests to back up the company's claims. A user would be foolish to rely on unproven technology in the current economic climate (see sidebar, "KeyLink Launches Certification Program").

KeyLink Launches Certification Program

KeyLink Systems recently launched a certification program for solution providers to develop expertise in selling and servicing storage solutions. KeyLink, a division of Pioneer-Standard Electronics, developed the program, called SPACE, or Solution Providers Achieving Certifications in Excellence, after identifying a *huge shortage* in storage expertise among solution providers.

SPACE gives solution providers specialized certifications and tools to help them beat competitors in nine storage niches, such as tape, high-end disk, and optical. It's a high bar to be a good storage solution provider.

Through SPACE, solution providers can target areas such as network design and management, software development and upgrades. The margins here have not particularly eroded like other services have.

The storage market is flourishing under four main drivers: e-business growth; business intelligence and data warehousing; high demand for network availability; and server and storage consolidation. And, storage product pricing is dropping on average at about 35% per year. In other words, you can't just take a solution provider that knows little about storage and survive.

Finally, BlueArc is entering an increasingly crowded marketplace with few collaborators. Because the NAS space has become very crowded, there is a need for aggressive competition. But, they should look into channel partnering because selling directly to corporations will be hard for them.

FROM HERE ....

This chapter covered SAN testing and troubleshooting, documenting and testing SANs, and certifying SAN performance. The next chapter discusses the data management solution, virtual Storage Area Networks, and a management strategy for the FC-AL.

END NOTES...

[1] BlueArc Corporation, Corporate Headquarters, 339 Bernardo Ave, Mountain View, CA 94043, 2001.

[2] "Performance Advantages of a Finite State Machine-based Fibre Channel Controller," Agilent Technologies Company, Headquarters, 395 Page Mill Rd., P.O. Box #10395, Palo Alto, CA 94303, 2001.

[3] John R. Vacca, *The Cabling Handbook (2nd Edition),* Prentice Hall PTR, 2001.

Part 5

Maintaining SANs

15   Management of Storage Area Networks

If you have spent any time thinking about storage, odds are, you have thought about SANs recently. SANs are rising in prominence as more shops look to them to solve storage problems and more vendors jump on the bandwagon. But how do you manage SANs and what can they do for you?

According to IDC research, SANs and the Fibre Channel technology that connects them, will become the preferred storage solution in enterprise data centers. Furthermore, Fibre Channel-based storage revenue will hit $26 billion by 2003, according to IDC reports. These numbers cannot be ignored.

Clearly, there is some substance behind this craze. Several factors help make the SAN so attractive to the enterprise: performance, reliability, and ease of management. A SAN functions like a specialized network within the enterprise and allows unrestricted information exchange between hosts and storage devices, which can bring substantial storage relief.

Storage is perhaps the supreme dilemma of distributed computing. In the rush to empower the end-user by decentralizing computing resources, IT managers lost control over storage. This may seem like the goal of distributed computing (putting data in the hands of those who use it), but that is not the case. In fact, the goal is to give users more control over their environment and the tools they use to turn data into information. There's a big difference between this and decentralized storage of data.

By decentralizing data storage, distributed computing places the responsibility for reliably maintaining data on the shoulders of the folks least able to effectively carry out the task—the typical end-user. Users love the freedom to find new tools and new ways to look at the data stored on their systems. But for the most part, they ignore the responsibility of managing this data.

Data can be found on end-user systems, end-user-managed *servers*, workgroup and departmental servers, and the servers on the back end that make up the fabric of enterprise IT. As one can imagine, backups, version control, performance monitoring, and all the other aspects of a good storage strategy take place on these systems in varying degrees—from not at all to nearly always.

It is easy to see what problems may occur. Critical data residing on end-user systems is not backed up or, at best, it is backed up irregularly. Redundant copies of files consume disk space and network bandwidth. Multiple versions of files create reconciliation headaches. Performance issues abound as servers with popular data and applications bog down, while less-used ones rack up idle CPU ticks. This scenario virtually cries out for a centralized approach to storage management that provides fault-tolerant, regularly backed-up, high-performance, and flexible storage of the data that fuels enterprises today—something a SAN can provide.

The Web also creates glorious storage problems. The rapid pace of Web application development and deployment consumes infrastructure at an alarming rate. And your Web site may have 40,000 hits today and 400,000 hits tomorrow when the latest update to your software is available, a big news story breaks, or a hot new stock debuts. In this frenzied world, several constants emerge. Vast quantities of data need to be instantly and reliably available to servers and applications across the enterprise. Decoupling storage and servers by employing a SAN can alleviate capacity bottlenecks by allowing for dynamic reconfiguration of storage resources and the systems that access them.

These were the problems faced by iSearch, a company that specializes in maintaining resume databases for employers and job-search Web sites in Los Angeles. With 4 million resumes in dozens of databases and the performance demands of intelligent Web-based search applications, the company knew they would face a nightmare if they did not get their storage right the first time. The solution from Storage Technology that iSearch implemented on its Compaq Alpha server farm provides centralized storage for iSearch's databases. The SAN is fault-tolerant, high-performance, and (most importantly) dynamically reconfigurable to meet changing customer needs.

But to no avail, even if your company's SAN is reconfigurable to meet customer needs, the unforeseen can still happen. For example, what happens when a hiring outsource firm dies? Does your company have a back-up plan? When iSearch went belly-up recently, it left a lot of big-name companies scrambling to recover lost resumes.

Now, let's look at the pieces of a SAN and how they come together to solve problems such as iSearch's. Perhaps the best place to start is to define a SAN again: It is a high-speed interconnection that links storage devices and servers in a shared environment. It is, essentially, its own network in which data travels over a SAN independently of the LAN. It completely bypasses any bandwidth conflicts that may arise in the enterprise.

You can't have a discussion about SANs without having a discussion about Fibre Channel, the de facto technology that provides the interconnection for the SAN. One way to look at Fibre Channel is as a cross between a SCSI and Ethernet, only faster and with the potential to span much greater distances.

Like SCSI, Fibre Channel provides a robust connection between storage devices and servers or clients. Like Ethernet, Fibre Channel supports many devices on one network and can support different topologies, including loops and switched environments. Unlike SCSI or 100 MBps Ethernet, Fibre Channel provides extremely fast connections up to 1 GBps, with 4 GBps speeds on the drawing board.

Also, Fibre Channel can span 10-kilometer distances and, more commonly, the distances found in campus environments—or up to 45 kilometers via the use of the latest technology. This means that components on a SAN can be distributed more freely than can devices on a SCSI bus, facilitating space, security, and disaster-recovery requirements.

On a Fibre Channel SAN, you might find devices such as Fibre Channel hubs and switches, which provide the kind of functionality that Ethernet hubs and switches provide. You might also find bridges from Fibre Channel to SCSI and Fibre Channel to Ethernet, facilitating the inclusion of more conventional devices on the SAN.

Of course, a SAN without servers and storage devices would not be a SAN. Servers can be attached to a SAN via Fibre Channel host bus adapters (HBAs). If a server does not support a Fibre Channel HBA, it can be attached via a SCSI or Ethernet to Fibre Channel bridges to give it access to the SAN. As with servers, storage devices may or may not be Fibre Channel-enabled, but can be attached to a SAN either way. Major storage vendors offer Fibre Channel-enabled disk drives, disk arrays, optical libraries, and tape libraries. Legacy SCSI devices are not left out in the cold either, as a Fibre Channel-to-SCSI bridge will bring them into the SAN fold.

Of course, a SAN without software would be an expensive furnace. When you get to the software piece of the puzzle, you reach the frontier of today's SAN technology. The technical foundation provided by SAN hardware and the Fibre Channel interconnection opens the door for amazing storage capabilities, but current software support for the SAN is quite rudimentary.

With today's software, you can expect a SAN to provide servers with access to data stored on SAN-attached disk and tape. You will also be able to make better use of resources, such as tape libraries, by sharing them across multiple servers. Soon, you will have tools to complete backups across a SAN, without the need for a server, and to give network clients better access to SAN resources.

So, how do these pieces come together to make a SAN a valuable addition to your storage strategy? Simply put, they provide a reliable, high-performance, dynamically reconfigurable storage architecture. Because of the shared nature of Fibre Channel, devices connected to it are not dependent on a single host as they are with a SCSI.

Disk arrays, for example, can be shared by a number of hosts on the SAN. The number of hosts accessing a given disk resource can be increased or decreased dynamically depending on the capacity requirements of the resource. And tape drives, often the most expensive parts in a storage architecture, can be shared efficiently by a number of hosts without a dedicated tape server.

A SAN provides a truly centralized storage solution. The upside is that centralized storage is easier to manage than distributed storage. Backing up a large disk array is far less painful in a SAN environment than backing up dozens or hundreds of clients and servers in a more traditional environment.

And with the distance spans possible with Fibre Channel, you get centralized storage with the flexibility of physical location. For example, you can locate a tape library near users who need access to it and keep the servers and disks in a secure data center. Likewise, offsite backups linked directly to SAN-attached storage are possible, decreasing the logistical demands of a full-fledged disaster-recovery strategy.

Today's SAN solution solves some fundamental storage management problems. As SAN hardware and software technology continues to advance, even greater storage management possibilities will be realized.

DATA MANAGEMENT SOLUTION ....

As organizations seek out cost-effective ways to manage the virtual explosion of information created by e-business and other initiatives, they are turning to SANs. As previously explained, SANs are a networked storage infrastructure designed to provide a flexible environment that decouples servers from their storage devices. SANs accomplish this by providing any-server-to-any-storage connectivity through the use of Fibre Channel switch fabric technology (commonly referred to as the SAN fabric). SANs address today's most challenging business requirements: how to protect and access critical data, how to utilize computing resources more efficiently, and how to ensure the highest levels of business continuance. For example, at the center of the SAN fabric, are solutions such as Brocade Fibre Channel switches, which provide the reliable high-performance data transfer that is critical to efficient SAN operations. Today, the Brocade SilkWorm family of switches delivers high performance while enabling a wide variety of scalable SAN configurations.

The Growing Need for More Efficient Information Management

During the last decade, a multitude of changes in computing technology and the globalization of business via the Internet have created a tremendous growth in storage requirements—forcing many organizations to reassess the way they view their storage environment. Clearly, ever-increasing information access requirements have had a profound effect on most data centers. For instance, the windows of time available for data backup and recovery have virtually disappeared. Storage capacity requirements have skyrocketed. IT staffs have faced increased pressure to keep pace with growth—while cutting costs. As a result, many organizations are searching for cost-effective ways to ensure high data availability and reliability.

To remain successful in such a dynamic marketplace, organizations need reliable storage systems that can effectively manage and protect critical business information. These systems must be able to scale quickly to manage anticipated data growth—a difficult problem for many traditional storage approaches. As a result, organizations are now accessing and managing the ever-increasing amount of enterprise data through innovative SANs.

SANs are networked environments that provide a scalable, reliable IT infrastructure to meet the high-availability, high-performance requirements of today's most demanding applications. More importantly, SANs are strategic solutions that give organizations a fast, centralized way to manage their information assets.

Today, the standard protocol for SANs is Fibre Channel technology, which supports high levels of scalability, performance, and manageability and helps overcome the distance limitations of previous connectivity protocols such as SCSI. Fibre Channel technology enables a flexible networked environment optimized for server-to-storage data communications and high-speed server-to-server interconnectivity.

The Advantages of a SAN Infrastructure

By migrating to a strategic SAN model, organizations can revitalize their IT infrastructure to significantly improve information management (see sidebar, "Emerging Storage Model"). In particular, SANs are ideal for addressing some of the most challenging business requirements, including:

- How to ensure that all data is protected and accessible across the enterprise
- How to improve the efficiency of IT resource management
- How to maximize system and data availability
- How to develop a reliable disaster recovery solution [1]

EMERGING STORAGE MODEL

LeftHand Networks, a newcomer to the storage market, was among the companies touting new products and services at the first Storewidth industry conference, which took place recently in Laguna Niguel, California. LeftHand indicated it has secured a $10 million initial round of funding from several venture capital groups and highlighted its use of Network Unified Storage (NUS), which it is promoting as an alternative to the more widely used NAS model.

The Boulder, Colorado-based company claimed it can help companies eliminate data bottlenecks by using its NUS products to create clusters of storage systems in parallel configurations, linked together using Ethernet connections. With NAS systems, additional controllers and disk drives are connected to the same CPU, which can slow data rates, because too much data must pass through a single, central point, according to LeftHand. In addition, vendors must use Fibre Channel products or some other type of connectors to link the storage hardware to the rest of a network.

LeftHand's NUS products eliminate the need for Fibre Channel or other connection technologies by allowing storage products to talk directly to the network and to each other via an existing Ethernet network. LeftHand will target online service providers, financial institutions, and storage service providers with its product roll out, which is expected in the first quarter of 2002. The products are currently being beta tested.

Each NUS module includes a CPU, network connection, system controllers, and up to four swappable disk drives. The systems will start at less than $15,000.

A number of companies are moving toward NUS as a storage option. NUS eases the management burden, and management costs tend to dominate the total cost of ownership with storage.

In addition, LeftHand's NUS products make use of standard Internet protocols, rather than requiring administrators to become familiar with Fibre Channel technologies. There is a tremendous benefit right there, because there are people who don't understand how to use Fibre Channel [4].

Greater Data Protection for Improved Backup and Recovery

As enterprise data becomes a much more valuable business asset, ensuring its stability and protection is more critical than ever. Many organizations have faced the challenge of having to back up more and more data even as backup windows have continued to shrink. In fact, many organizations have discovered that they cannot cost-effectively back up all their data as consistently as they would prefer. Instead, they have been forced to devise different backup strategies for the various types of enterprise data, depending on how mission-critical the data is.

Traditionally, backup and recovery models have featured dedicated disk and tape systems for each particular host server, with each host backing up its own data to its own locally attached tape drives or library (see Figure 15.1) [1]. This design is a relatively poor utilization of tape resources because, even though one server's tape drive might be idle, another server cannot use it. In addition, each operating system platform tends to use unique backup and recovery software applications, which complicates the overall management of the resources as well as the backup and recovery process itself. The disk and tape systems also tend to be slower, less reliable, and much smaller than today's enterprise storage systems, because most organizations cannot afford faster, more reliable storage resources for each particular server.

A more advanced, traditional approach to backup and recovery that alleviates some of the drawbacks of the dedicated tape approach involves implementing a more enterprise-oriented backup and recovery solution (see Figure 15.2) [1]. This typically

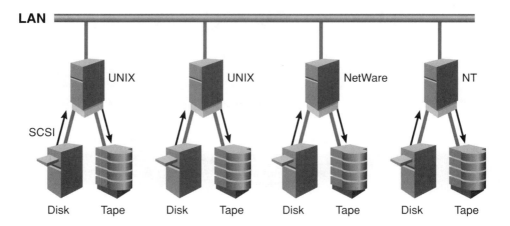

Figure 15.1
A traditional backup and recovery model with dedicated storage resources for each server.

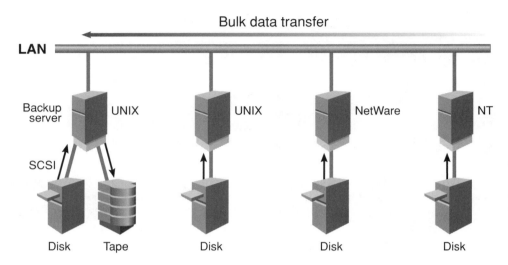

Figure 15.2
A traditional backup and recovery model over a LAN with a primary server to control storage resources.

involves a primary backup and recovery server that controls tape resources. Sophisti-cated applications—such as VERITAS NetBackup, Legato NetWorker, and Tivoli Storage Manager—control the backup and recovery process. The backup server re-ceives data from other servers across a LAN or WAN, then stores that data on central-ly owned disk and tape resources. This centralized approach provides much better utilization of tape resources while making the deployment of faster, more reliable tape drives and libraries much more cost-effective.

The primary drawback to this approach is that the network introduces potential bottlenecks for the backup and recovery process—and potentially impacts the sys-tem's ability to meet backup and recovery windows. In addition, using the primary LAN or WAN to perform backup and recovery can potentially degrade performance for production workloads running on the same network.

In contrast, SANs can simplify the data backup and recovery process and help ensure the fast backup and recovery of all enterprise data in a timely manner. SANs are ideal for backup-intensive environments, especially when there are clearly defined areas for isolating backup workloads.

The switched 100 MBps full duplex capabilities of Fibre Channel fabrics can significantly improve backup and recovery performance. Moreover, Fibre Channel is designed to transport large blocks of data with greater efficiency and reliability than IP-based networks. Two popular models for SAN-based backup and recovery are typ-ically referred to as *LAN-free* and *server-free* backup and recovery.

Removing the LAN from the backup and recovery process provides a variety of advantages. SAN-attached tape drives and libraries can be implemented so that each server sends its own backup data directly to the shared tape resources instead of through the network to the backup server. Sophisticated backup and recovery software applications still control the process, tracking the backup and recovery data. The SAN enables bulk data transfer from each server to shared SAN storage, but the LAN is used only for communication (not data) traffic between the servers (see Figure 15.3) [1]. The result is a faster, more scalable, and more reliable backup and recovery solution—with more effective utilization of storage, server, and LAN resources.

A still-evolving SAN backup and recovery implementation is known as server-free backup and recovery. Data is transferred directly between storage devices (for example, from disk to tape) without using host servers. This process is enabled by an evolving technology called 3rd-Party Copy, which is implemented in SAN appliances (such as Crossroads or Pathlight bridges), host systems (such as Legato Celestra), or storage devices themselves (in the future). Server-free backup and recovery significantly reduces application host CPU cycles—freeing up valuable CPU cycles to improve operating efficiency and enable higher workloads across the enterprise (see Figure 15.4) [1]. This, however, is still an evolving technology. Further integration with operating systems, databases, and applications is necessary to support production-level backup and recovery.

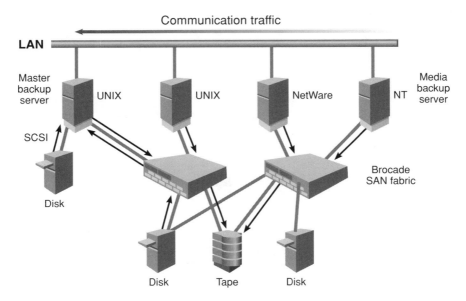

Figure 15.3
A SAN-based LAN-free backup and recovery model.

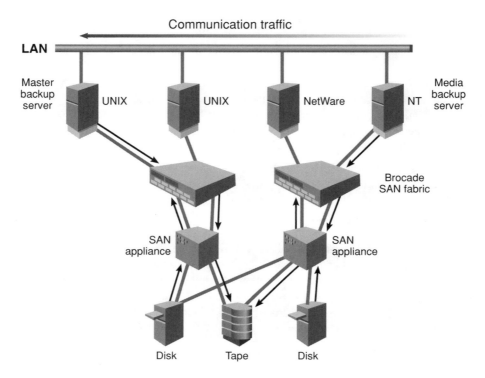

Figure 15.4
A SAN-based server-free backup and recovery model.

The advantages of a LAN- or server-free backup and recovery environment can be dramatic. For instance, after it deployed a LAN-free backup solution for its Windows NT Exchange server environment, a large North American hospital was able to reduce its backup window from 18 hours to just 4 to 6 hours. Other companies have experienced similar results.

More Efficient Utilization of IT Resources through Server and Storage Consolidation

Traditionally, organizations have paired specific storage resources with servers, primarily due to technical restrictions. This implementation results in poor utilization of storage resources, because the storage is dedicated to each server—not shared among servers. For example, free disk space on one server's disk subsystem cannot be used by other storage-constrained servers. Simply adding more servers and storage resources as requirements grow, typically results in a very difficult environment to manage, with poor utilization of resources.

In addition, because organizations are implementing so many server and storage devices, they tend to implement less expensive but typically slower and less reliable devices. This paired server-device model has proven to be especially inflexible during periods of expansion.

To help avoid such disruption and cost, SANs provide the advantages of flexible connectivity, more efficient use of storage and server resources, enhanced scalability, and increased manageability. In fact, SANs provide unprecedented flexibility for storage environments—changing the way storage resources can be purchased and managed. By enabling any-to-any server and storage connectivity via switches, SANs decouple specific devices to improve storage resource sharing. This cost-effective open systems approach enables the *virtualization* of resources and the selection of best-of-breed heterogeneous server and storage equipment (see Figure 15.5) [1].

SANs can help organizations grow their storage and server environments much more quickly, since storage capacity can grow independent of server usage. This approach provides a high degree of efficiency in utilizing resources while simultaneously enabling growth without system disruption.

For example, after deploying a SAN, a large hospital reduced the number of its primary Windows NT servers from 50 to 7—with significantly improved automation and administration to lower operating costs. In addition, a large telecommunications company that recently implemented a SAN was able to slice its previous storage requirements in half while reducing its server allocation by one-third.

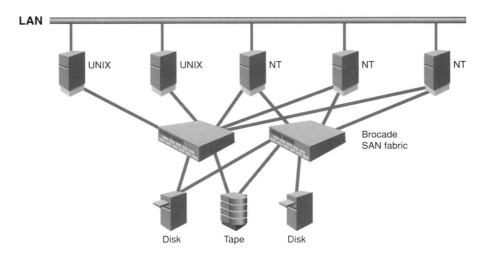

Figure 15.5
A simplified best-of-breed SAN infrastructure with heterogeneous server and storage resources.

Advanced Scalability and Manageability

SANs also provide a framework for indefinitely scaling up the server and storage infrastructure as the number of users increases—without necessarily inhibiting performance. This approach enables the deployment of new storage resources without disrupting operations on the rest of the system. Many organizations start with a relatively modest server configuration and add new servers with or without associated storage. As the number of nodes in the network grows, more switches are added to the network. To simplify administration, the fabric automatically learns the network topology.

SANs also improve storage resource management through centralization, even within distributed IT architectures. For example, SAN software tools enable organizations to allocate storage to various hosts, replicate that data, back it up, and monitor it on a continual basis. These capabilities are critical in facilitating storage growth while maintaining system uptime requirements and controlling administrative costs. Moreover, building a SAN fabric that leverages enterprise storage management software applications—from such vendors as VERITAS, Tivoli, and Computer Associates—can further increase the manageability and benefits of SANs.

For example, a leading storage services provider is currently building the world's largest dedicated data storage network designed to support multiple terabytes of business-critical data. To accomplish this goal quickly and efficiently, the company is implementing a network of hundreds of SANs built on Brocade SilkWorm 2800 fabric switches. The Brocade solution provides scalable, managed storage services that provide virtually unlimited data storage on a *pay-as-you-grow* basis.

Business Continuance through High Availability

Due to service-level agreements, industry regulations, or other business needs, today's organizations demand the highest possible system availability. In fact, incidents that were previously viewed as minor unplanned outages can now severely impact business operations. To address this requirement, SANs are designed to facilitate a high-availability environment that can help prevent (or better tolerate) system outages.

Some of the key availability benefits of SANs include built-in redundancy, dynamic failover protection, and automatic traffic rerouting capabilities. For instance, flexible connectivity options enable the development of SANs that have no single points of failure. In addition, Brocade Fabric OS software can automatically detect network problems and route traffic around any failed links to help ensure a continuous reliable path for data. Lastly, SANs provide hot-plugging capabilities that enable organizations to install, configure, and bring storage online without experiencing server downtime. By combining multiple networked switches with a Fabric OS, organizations can build scalable, strategic SANs that provide extremely high availability.

SANs can also support high-availability operations by enhancing clustering implementations. Clustering is typically used to ensure that applications continue to run in the event of a host server failure. Traditional, non-SAN clustered environments typically include two servers sharing disk storage. If one server fails, the other server assumes the failed server's workload and continues running the application. The failover server accesses the data through the shared disk. This represents a relatively inflexible design, because it is usually limited to two servers sharing storage—with the failover server often remaining idle until pressed into duty. In addition, the servers and storage devices are usually located near each other—a configuration that provides only limited protection against disasters.

With SAN clustering, many more servers can share SAN-attached storage. In some implementations, any server can handle the additional workload when one server is unavailable—ensuring that there are no idle server resources (see Figure 15.6) [1]. Longer distances between devices also facilitate a more effective disaster recovery plan.

The large telecommunications company (described previously) employed a SAN infrastructure with a VERITAS Cluster Server and Brocade SilkWorm switches to create an environment with extremely high data and application availability. Before the SAN was deployed, the implementation included three clusters, each with two SUN servers. Resources were being wasted because there were three idle failover servers and neither the application load nor data was shared between clusters. After

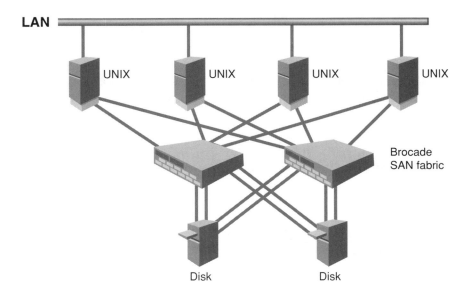

Figure 15.6
A high-availability clustering model with switch failover capabilities.

the SAN implementation, only three servers (instead of six) were required, and only half the storage resources were required. Any of the three servers can now assume a failing server's workload. Today, the company can efficiently manage its SAN by dynamically allocating storage and applications, and by performing nondisruptive server and storage maintenance.

Remote Disaster Recovery Capabilities

A critical factor in any high-availability networking model is the ability to protect and recover data—and quickly get systems back online—following a disaster. SANs provide a solid foundation to support environments where data must be automatically transferred to a remote facility for disaster recovery purposes. As a result, SAN-based disaster recovery configurations can provide more efficient backup and recovery, extended distance connectivity, and additional fault tolerance.

A disaster recovery solution depends greatly on the organization's specific requirements of how long systems can be unavailable and how *back-level* the data can be after reinstating applications following a disaster. Obviously, many types of businesses cannot afford even minutes of downtime without significant consequences. Other organizations might be able to tolerate downtime of a day or longer. As a result, disaster recovery plans need to account for particular availability requirements as well as IT equipment, network configuration, staffing, and the overall process.

SANs provide a key component of the disaster recovery solution by protecting data over long distances in hot-standby or mirrored configurations and by enabling long-distance electronic tape vaulting solutions. Native Fibre Channel technology provides the 10 km or greater link extended distance connectivity required to maintain geographically separate disaster recovery facilities or mirroring operations. When used in Large Fabric configurations, SANs can utilize WANs or MANs to cover even longer distances.

For instance, remote switches can provide virtually unlimited distance connections through the ATM protocol over existing WANs (see Figure 15.7) [1]. Brocade has partnered with CNT Corporation [2] to provide an Open Systems Gateway between Brocade switches. Brocade also offers Extended Fabrics support to provide native Fibre Channel connectivity over distances up to 100 kilometers.

Brocade accomplishes this by leveraging either extended wavelength gigabit interface converters or dense wave division multiplexing from providers such as ONI Systems Corporation [3] to interweave data traffic over Fibre Channel. These Fibre Channel networks not only provide long-distance configuration, but also help speed up the recovery process to reduce the amount of lost productivity and revenue.

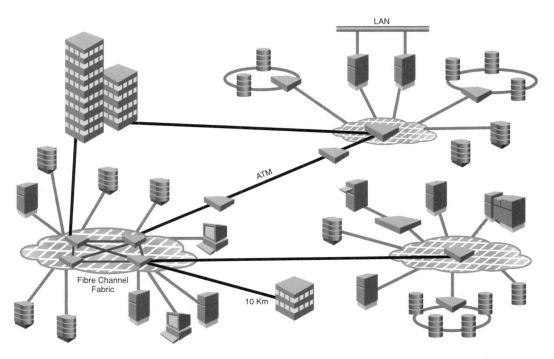

Figure 15.7
A MAN with native Fibre Channel connections over longer distances.

For example, a large private-sector bank recently implemented one of Europe's largest fully redundant, heterogeneous SAN environments based entirely on 20 Brocade SilkWorm 2800 16-port fabric switches. The result is a high-availability computing system that networks more than 320 Fibre Channel devices. The SAN deployment features extended distance connectivity, which enables the disaster-ready backup site to be located 35 kilometers from the main data center.

A Strategic Technology for the Future

Although SAN environments continue to evolve, their rapid widespread acceptance reflects their unlimited value in the efficient management of information. Today, SANs are providing an unprecedented way to manage explosive data growth—improving storage management, configuration flexibility, and cost-effectiveness. Thus, the future of SANs appears to be just as bright. By demonstrating the flexibility to scale incrementally, SANs are proving to be an excellent way to achieve a high return on storage investments—providing a strategic infrastructure for years to come.

VIRTUAL STORAGE AREA NETWORKS.....................

Data management solutions providing seamless access to primary and secondary storage will grow in importance over the coming years. They will enable system administrators to manage and control their ever-increasing stored resources more comfortably. You are currently witnessing several forces in the IT landscape that point to a new and significantly more important role for secondary storage. New integrated primary/secondary storage solutions will ensure that the increasing volumes of critical business data are easily available and accessible to users while providing solid data protection that has not been addressed by traditional approaches.

In today's Internet driven economy, a variety of factors are creating an unprecedented demand for information access:

- Digital convergence, as more image, audio, and video data makes their way to the computer.
- An increasing demand for round-the-clock data availability, driven by the Internet.
- An increase in the mission-criticality of applications running in distributed-computing environments.
- A trend towards recentralization to ensure 100% uptime, which is resulting in more servers per site, all with steadily increasing hard disk capacities. At the same time, there is a growing awareness that traditional storage management approaches are failing and a new approach is needed.
- The need for secondary storage is increasing because of the following factors: Traditional data protection approaches do not adequately protect critical business data. Conventional approaches such as backup force excessive server downtime and provide minimal support for seamless, on-demand access to data resources.
- Backup windows are shrinking as the average server hard disk grows in size and as the organizational demand for 24x7 availability becomes ever more urgent.
- There is an increasingly heterogeneous and complex computing environment, requiring ever-greater system-management expertise.
- Most seriously, there is a growing shortage of trained, competent systems administrators [5].

Today, primary storage is growing at an 82% compound average rate, according to IDC. The average number of servers per site is tripling every year. Although average capacities per server are increasing dramatically, data loss is common and can result in business failure. Moreover, businesses are facing an extremely severe shortage of skilled people to keep these mission-critical systems running efficiently. Network system administrators and software developers are in short supply the world over. Today qualified IT workers represent the largest category of skilled labor imported to the United States.

While the raw cost of digital storage keeps dropping, the cost of managing that storage is falling much more slowly. In fact, the cost of managing additional network storage is a multiple of the cost of the actual hardware involved. Indeed, according to Strategic Research Center (SRC) of Santa Barbara, California, every $1 spent on primary storage costs $5 in management expense. Thus, primary storage needs are growing, and storage management has become a critical problem. To understand how secondary storage can alleviate this situation, it is useful to look at two simple storage dynamics: The majority of the data stored on a server hard disk (as much as 80%) is infrequently accessed, with the frequency of access diminishing over time; and as primary disk capacity increases, the volume of older data that requires occasional access builds exponentially.

Storage solutions that integrate primary and secondary storage volumes into a single logical volume provide a new approach to these problems. They offer intelligent automation of data migration and provide cost-effective long-term data retention to ensure that digital data assets are viable beyond the life of the current hardware. Specifically, secondary storage provides:

- Solutions that increase the overall availability and accessibility of data with minimal administrative involvement, providing rapid and easy retrieval of data to users and applications, regardless of location.

- Solutions that automatically move data from primary storage to more cost-effective secondary-storage media with minimal administrator involvement.

- Solutions that efficiently manage data flow to and from different media in a multiple-media storage structure.

- Solutions that provide capacity expansion and protection without requiring frequent and excessive downtime.

- Solutions that provide system administration tools that allow policy- and rules-based management and support a *setup-and-walk-away* usage paradigm [5].

The remainder of this part of the chapter will provide the reader with an analysis of storage and information access trends; then summarize data management requirements; and finally, propose a next generation storage management solution, SmartStor InfiNet, which addresses these issues.

Requirements for Storage and Access

There are three converging factors driving the need for integrated primary/secondary storage solutions:

- *Massive Growth in Networked Storage Capacity:* There are a number of factors driving storage growth, including an increase in the typical size of files stored and the proliferation of e-commerce [9] and data-intensive email. Industry analysts estimate that storage capacity will grow at a rate of 82% per year requiring a need for highly scalable and more cost-effective storage management solutions.

- *The Need for 24 × 7 × Forever Access to Data:* The emergence of the Internet and Intranet is requiring mission-critical applications to be continually available without any downtime. The traditional online/offline model is no longer a viable solution in most cases, as these applications are requiring all data to be kept online for longer periods of time. There is no longer any such thing as *end-of-life* for data.

- *Current Inefficiencies in Storage Management:* This massive storage growth and need for continuous access is revealing a number of inefficiencies in today's storage management options. It is estimated that approximately 82% of overall storage costs are being spent on simply managing the storage.

Each of the preceding factors is discussed in detail next.

Massive Growth in Networked Storage Capacity

As a result of the widespread use of data-intensive applications, businesses are accumulating significantly greater amounts of data than in the past. Improvements in technology are increasing the value of accumulated data, making it a strategic asset that enterprises seek to leverage for competitive advantage. International Data Corporation, an independent information technology research firm, estimates that multi-user disk storage grew from more than 7,000 terabytes in 1993 to more than 184,000 terabytes in 1999, and will reach more than 1.9 million terabytes in 2003. A byte is the amount of computer memory required to store one number, letter, or symbol. A terabyte is equal to one trillion bytes. The following factors are driving the growth in the value and volume of stored data:

- The increase in the typical size of files stored, especially from data rich applications such as digital video and other multimedia applications

- The widespread adoption of data mining, data-intensive email, and enterprise resource planning applications
- The proliferation of e-commerce and the use of the Internet for critical business functions
- The increase in the number of users requesting access to large databases of information
- The need to store redundant copies of enterprise data for mission-critical applications. The last five years has seen unprecedented growth in the amount of networked data stored by companies [5]

Figure 15.8 presents a forecast from Strategic Research Corporation [6] of the typical capacity per server for centralized networks, and Figure 15.9 presents a forecast of the typical total server capacity per site for centralized networks from 1997 to 2003 [5]. Because sites are growing in both capacity per server and number of servers, the total site server capacity increases at a faster rate than the average server capacity. By 2003, SRC forecasts that the average capacity per server will be over 170 GB and the average capacity per site will approach 2 TB. And the total network storage market for client-server networks (PC and UNIX servers) is estimated to be over 600 petabytes (PB) in 2000 growing to nearly 2,000 PB in 2003.

TYPICAL CAPACITY PER SERVER

in Gigabytes

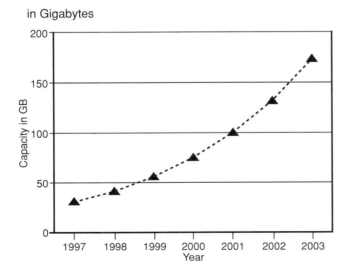

Figure 15.8
Capacity per server.

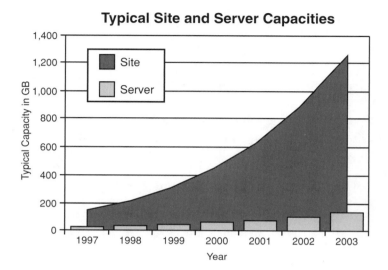

Figure 15.9
Capacity per site.

The Need for 24 × 7 × Forever Access to Data

While storage capacity is expanding, corporations are faced with the mandate to improve accessibility to information. The connectivity provided by LANs and the Internet has created the requirement that companies maintain the availability of information online for 24 × 7 × forever access. In the past, the lack of direct access meant that data was often taken offline with requests for this type of data being handled at high cost through human intervention. However, the emergence of the Internet and Intranet is requiring mission-critical applications to be continually available without any downtime. One example of an application that is driving this demand is airline reservation systems.

Airline Reservation Systems • Airline reservation systems are well suited for secondary storage management software. Before the Internet, airlines would typically use RAID arrays to manage their ticketing process and then move the data offline to tape. Manual processes were employed if access to the offline data was required. Today, an airline company is required to maintain the information for a longer period of time in order to analyze customer preferences (data warehousing) or provide Internet access to customers for frequent flier programs, mitigating the need to pay customer support personnel. With storage expansion, the company's airline reservation system continues to use high performance RAID disk storage during the ticketing process, but moves the information to secondary media once the ticket is used. Applications and customers can then access this information within seconds, albeit at a reduced performance, should the need arise. Storage expansion thus increases the availability of the information to its employees and customers at a fraction of the cost of maintaining it on RAID systems. This type of application is now the norm driving storage and $24 \times 7 \times$ forever accessibility demand, resulting in the need for terabytes of storage to keep all data online.

Current Inefficiencies in Storage Management

With the rampant growth in networked storage and applications requiring unlimited access to data, resources such as disk capacity, number of connected workstations, and number of LAN segments are escalating out of control. Administrators are faced with the endless process of purchasing and installing more disk drives and systems while attempting to ensure that systems are up and running. Many people underestimate the cost of this amount of storage and storage management, yet industry analysts calculate storage cost at approximately \$0.20/MB for hardware and about \$0.80/MB/ year for data management. With that, administrators are facing a number of challenges, including:

- Mission criticality
- Shortage of IT personnel
- Escalating cost of operations
- Inadequate data protection
- Excessive downtime and productivity losses

Mission Criticality • The most significant development affecting the future of distributed computing is the deployment of mission-critical applications within a distributed environment. As network applications provide services to distributed clients on the LAN and the Internet, these application servers are no longer just simply data repositories, they are now crucial to the success of the corporation.

Shortage of IT Personnel • It is important to note that the capacity per site and the number of network administrators managing that capacity is not growing at the same rate. Network capacities are growing faster than companies' ability to hire network administrators. The growing gap between capacity and the number of administrators means that significant improvement in storage management tools is a necessity. As depicted in Figure 15.10, a typical administrator will be responsible for managing almost 200 GB of network storage in 2003 [5]. When one factors in the workstations for which these administrators are also responsible, the capacity under their control is enormous. IDC estimates that the overall market for storage management software will grow from \$3.5 billion in 1998 to \$6.7 billion in 2003.

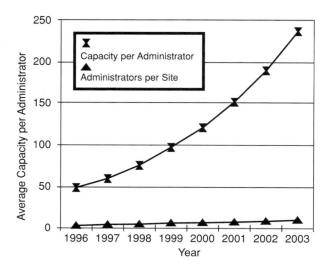

Figure 15.10
Capacity under management per administrator.

Escalating Cost of Operations • The out of control growth of storage and processing needs coupled with the severe shortage of trained network administrators has resulted in escalating costs of operations for many sites. Network administration tools have failed to keep up with this growth and many sites continue to use manual processes to keep systems running. Administrators are looking for system management products that automate key administration functions while preserving data access.

Inadequate Data Protection • Traditionally, enterprises have adopted backup processes to ensure against loss of data by creating and storing duplicates of existing data files, primarily on tape. While backup solutions are generally well-architected for data loss and business continuance, they do not provide seamless on-demand file availability for users and applications, an important requirement in today's Internet-enabled world. Backup programs are architected to maximize backup speed and not for data access. As such, they are not well suited as tools for data accessibility and management.

Excessive Downtime and Productivity Losses • A major problem associated with backup is that as the amount of data increases, backups take longer to perform and consume increasing amounts of network transmission capacity, or bandwidth. Computer networks have a limited amount of bandwidth, and most of this capacity is consumed during business hours by the demands of the network's users. As a result, backup is traditionally performed outside business hours. However, the need to provide 24×7 availability exacerbates this problem, since the number of hours available each day for backup are significantly reduced. As storage capacity explodes, network administrators have even smaller windows of time in which they can back up increasing amounts of data without impairing the performance or accessibility of the network.

So, what is the answer to the preceding dilemma? Let's take a look. Keep in mind though, for demonstration purposes, the following product is only one possible answer. There are many others.

Possible Answer: SmartStor InfiNet

The storage trends and the inevitable administrative problems they create translate into a specific product need; and as the user community is coming to recognize and understand these problems better, it is demanding solutions that place prominence on long-term, technology-independent data accessibility and automated data management.

For example, Smart Storage's SmartStor InfiNet is built on a standards-based architecture and provides a cost-effective, scalable, and automated solution that increases accessibility and availability of enterprise data, while reducing management overhead. The product has been designed by Smart Storage to address storage management issues by focusing on two general principals in regard to storage capacity and file usage: The majority of data (about 80%) stored on networked hard disk is infrequently accessed, with the frequency of access diminishing over time, and as primary disk capacity grows, the volume of older data that requires occasional access increases exponentially.

Note

SmartStor InfiNet is only one of many products that have exactly the same features. This product is mentioned here for demonstration purposes only. Prentice Hall and this author are not promoting one product over another.

Based upon these principals, InfiNet has been developed to virtually and seamlessly expand primary storage, using secondary storage libraries to store the less frequently accessed data. In doing this, InfiNet minimizes the need for an administrator to add and manage more and more primary storage for files that will be accessed less and less often over time. For example, the product can virtually expand a server's hard disk from 100 gigabytes to 20 terabytes seamlessly and simply, just by adding one or more optical or tape libraries to the server with InfiNet software. SmartStor InfiNet monitors file activity on the hard disk and moves data between hard disk and the secondary storage system depending upon system administrator policies and file usage.

The file migration operation is performed in the background and is completely transparent to any user or application accessing the data. All of the data, whether it's on primary or secondary storage, appears to the user as a single drive letter. SmartStor

InfiNet allows users to access data immediately from the hard disk and within seconds from the secondary storage libraries.

The Benefits of InfiNet

Storage virtualization will be the key for all successful companies in your e-business environment. Imagine trying to individually administer a collection of storage devices covering an entire football field by using the traditional data management software. Users are required to manage the computing environment based on manual intervention and are expected to manage each storage device by physical address. It is no surprise that user error has been rated consistently as the primary reason for system outage. InfiNet's policy-based data management removes the burden of knowing the physical location of data and storage resources. Easily modified, assigned, or changed, this logical connection between virtual and physical address is a powerful tool for implementing complex enterprise data protection strategies. Once InfiNet is implemented, administrators will realize a number of storage management benefits including:

- Scalability
- Online accessibility
- Automated storage administration
- Reduced reliance on backup/restore
- Cost-effective storage media
- Data/investment protection
- Reduced training cost

Scalability

Administrators are no longer limited to their primary storage capacity. InfiNet allows customers to expand their storage needs to accommodate their growing network easily and seamlessly. Using InfiNet, customers' storage capacity can grow incrementally from a system with just 100 gigabytes to as many as 20 terabytes on the same server.

Online Accessibility

Smart Storage's solution provides one comprehensive view of data regardless of the type of storage device. InfiNet allows customers direct and seamless access from the operating system to secondary storage devices held in libraries. From their desktops, the end-users can access data from the libraries directly from their applications. This technological approach enables most applications to operate seamlessly with the customer's storage devices.

Automated Storage Administration

InfiNet eliminates much of the manual processes involved in data management by automatically monitoring file access on hard disks (primary storage) and migrating infrequently accessed data to secondary storage libraries, while still providing access to the information through the operating system. Smart Storage's storage expansion software products automatically migrate infrequently accessed data to less expensive media and libraries that do not require further backup, thereby reducing administration costs.

Reduced Reliance on Backup/Restore

Since InfiNet enables administrators to move old data onto secondary storage to make room for new data on the primary hard disk storage, the software essentially enables administrators to maintain a fixed backup window because only the data that resides on hard disk needs to be included in the backup cycles. In addition, since all data (old and new) is kept online, your need to restore old data from a backup tape is significantly reduced.

Cost Effective Storage Media

As storage capacity is increasing at a rate of 82% per year, administrators are looking for more and more ways to find more efficient storage. Although the cost of hard disk has decreased significantly, DVD and/or tape storage still costs less than 25% of the cost of RAID at 500 GB capacity levels. And this fraction falls further as capacity increases [5].

Data/Investment Protection

By leveraging industry-standard hardware and operating system platforms, InfiNet can be scaled to fit the requirements of anything from a departmental workgroup to a global corporate enterprise. InfiNet supports a wide range of removable disk, MO and tape libraries, as well as standalone drives and even fixed disks and arrays. InfiNet can exploit SANs for high-bandwidth LAN-free storage operations and resource sharing. Most important of all, InfiNet can lower the Total Cost of Ownership (TCO) by automating and streamlining backup, archiving, and recovery operations throughout the enterprise. In addition, InfiNet's nonproprietary, standard-based UDF file system ensures that your data will be accessible well into the future, regardless of hardware and technology changes.

Reduced Training Cost

The InfiNet user interface provides an Internet Explorer-like, easy-to-use unified console to manage all your storage resources. Intelligent wizards, context-sensitive right-clicks virtually eliminate the usual time-consuming training needed to implement and monitor complex data protection strategies. By using the built-in configuration wizards, a novice system administrator can have InfiNet up and running within minutes. By digging deeper into the advanced features of the interface, expert users will find that InfiNet offers powerful, detailed control over data access parameters and some unique options not found in other data management packages. By reducing operator error, the InfiNet GUI prevents the typical problems associated with managing growing storage resources.

Return on Investment

The InfiNet solution streamlines and automates key data management functions, eliminating the need to add to your IT staff to handle growing data volumes. Gartner Group estimates the $6 out of every $10 in storage costs is spent on administrative labor.

Given the expected 82% Compound Annual Growth Rate (CAGR) determined by Strategic Research Corporation (SRC), any organization managing a 100 GB of storage today, will be managing over a terabyte of data in five years. Although primary RAID or hard disk storage is becoming less and less expensive, this amount of primary storage will still come with a hefty price tag. But more importantly, the nature of magnetic hard disk is volatile and therefore incurs a significant amount of management overhead, as administrators must ensure that the data is accessible and protected, in addition to making sure that there is enough storage space available.

In the preceding, there was a discussion about the secondary storage media at 500 gigabytes—costing only 25% of the same amount of RAID storage; yet the media cost is only part of the overall total cost of ownership. The management of that storage makes up for the majority.

Figure 15.11 illustrates the hardware cost saving breakdown of RAID versus magneto optical (MO), DVD, and tape [5]. The calculation is based on 500 GB storage capacity with 60% data growth rate.

When using the traditional method of keeping all data on either primary storage or tape backups, industry analysts have determined that for every dollar spent on the

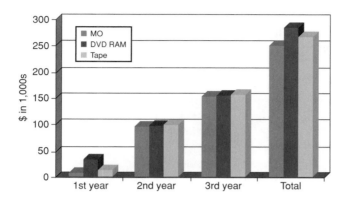

Figure 15.11
InfiNet Direct savings based on hardware cost reduction (300 employees with 60% data growth rate).

hard disk storage itself, organizations will spend four dollars on managing it. The more hard disk storage accumulated by an organization, the more time administrators will spend backing up, adding hard disk space, diagnosing problems, swapping out drives, and restoring data—all of which are manual activities that result in significant administrative costs. Figure 15.12 illustrates a much more dramatic difference between RAID and DVD and tape storage when factoring in the cost of storage management [5]. The lower total cost of ownership offered by InfiNet and secondary storage yields a significant cost savings over a 3-year period as illustrated in Figure 15.12.

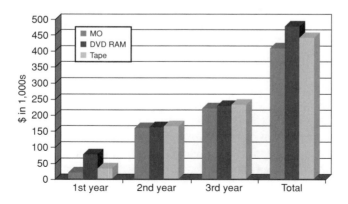

Figure 15.12
Direct savings based on hardware and data management cost reduction (300 employees with 60% data growth rate).

SmartStor InfiNet accomplishes this significant savings in storage management overhead by minimizing or eliminating some of the most costly and time consuming management related procedures, including:

- Backup and restore
- File management
- Adding drives

Backup and Restore

Approximately one third of storage management costs can be attributed to the backup/ restore process. The more primary storage an organization accumulates, the more data that needs to be backed up, increasing the time to backup and reducing productivity. In addition, the process of restoring data can be a very cumbersome and manual process. InfiNet can significantly reduce management costs associated with backup by enabling administrators to maintain a fixed backup window.

File Management

InfiNet eliminates much of the manual processes involved in data management by automatically monitoring file access on hard disks (primary storage) and migrating infrequently accessed data to secondary storage libraries, while still providing access to the information through the operating system. Smart Storage's storage expansion software products automatically migrate infrequently accessed data to less expensive media and libraries that do not require further backup, thereby reducing administration costs.

Adding Drives

Keeping up with an 82% annual growth rate of storage capacity can be very taxing on IT resources, and can result in excessive (and expensive) downtime. SmartStor InfiNet reduces the management costs associated with this process as it enables administrators to add a terabyte or more of virtual storage by adding a secondary storage library to the server. Adding more storage is just a matter of adding another library with no or minimal downtime required.

Indirect Business Value: Customer Satisfaction For E-Business

On average, each e-business customer generates about $20,000 per year (service/merchandise purchase plus customer profile plus stock value). Since it costs thousands of dollars to acquire each new customer, e-business must focus on high user satisfaction to bring the customer back for a second purchase. The information technology challenges presented by such sudden, rapid growth in an industry with highly demanding customers are staggering.

Compounding these requirements, e-retailers must also be cost conscious. The fight to gain market share in this space can drain capital in short order, and many e-businesses have nowhere near the resources of industry giants (Wal-Mart for example). A traditional IT model will keep frequently accessed data in the primary storage and all other information in an offline data vault. In order for a customer to access offline information such as their 18 months-old purchase history, email or phone messages are the only options available. This process will require a *runner* to physically retrieve the offline data, which would often take many hours and require the representative to call or email the customer back. SmartStor InfiNet can optimize this traditional IT model by seamlessly migrating the infrequently accessed data from primary storage to secondary storage instead of to the offline data vault. This solution allows employees and customers to view all information over the corporate intranet or Internet via their familiar and easy-to-use Web browser. By virtualizing the primary storage with lower-cost optical disks and tape storage, users and applications can access all data regardless of physical location. The importance of this capability could be exemplified in handling peak activities of e-commerce Web sites. Storage resources can be added seamlessly to the enterprise without any system interruption. As the company serves up increasing volumes of data to customers, you need the storage infrastructure to support that data level. SmartStor InfiNet is a product that can grow and scale, as your business requires.

Efficiency Gain in the Financial Industry

The financial industry continues to grow exponentially with the dynamic economy. Each company must put in place a technical infrastructure robust enough to handle high volumes of business-critical transactions, yet resilient enough for flex with the breathless pace of changes. Aside from producing monthly account statements for its customers, the company must also download thousands of pages daily of in-clearing and transit data for check, stock/bond certificates, ATM transactions, and other financial services. Payroll reports alone amount to over hundreds of pages per day. The barrage of information is routinely catalogued on microfiche, printed, and hand-delivered to employees and customers. The staff hour and storage space required are both tremendous and out of control. The cost of microfiche and paper alone is $400,000 for a typical financial company with 600,000 customers. With the SmarStor InfiNet solution, all digitized documents can be indexed for easy retrieval from nearline storage media that uses a fraction of the space of paper or microfiche, without the need for human intervention or error. Employees and customers can freely access the reports they need, retrieving, viewing, and printing them as needed directly from their desktops. In this age of the Internet economy, technology forms a critical element to differentiate a company from its competitors. SmartStor InfiNet provides standards-based multiplatform support with unlimited scalability within a comprehensive architectural framework. With Smart Storage's virtual storage technology and the expertise of valuable channel partners, the InfiNet solution will significantly enhance your ability to meet present and future business demand.

> **Note**
>
> **Remember, SmartStor InfiNet is only one of many products that does exactly the same thing. This product is only mentioned here for demonstration purposes. Prentice Hall and this author are not promoting one product over another.**

How Does InfiNet Work?

InfiNet expands a server's storage capacity by integrating the primary hard disk and secondary storage libraries into one file system, presenting all data as a single drive letter as shown in Figure 15.13 [5]. Once the software is installed, the administrator can easily configure and manage secondary storage devices and the expanded primary volume(s) through an intuitive, graphical user interface.

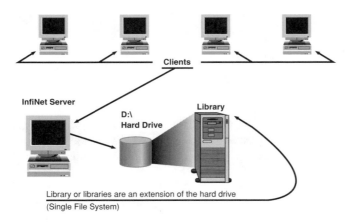

Figure 15.13
Storage expansion.

Navigating views and invoking commands through InfiNet's main application window is done in much the same way one would navigate Windows NT Explorer (see Figure 15.14) [5]. Primary Volumes, Media, Devices, and *Jobs* are presented in *Explorer-like* tree view. All commands can be executed through right-click menus as shown in Figure 15.15 [5].

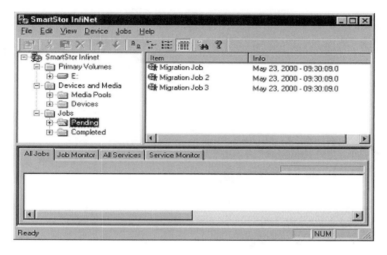

Figure 15.14
SmartStor InfiNet Application Window.

Figure 15.15
Right-click menu options for a Migration Job.

When you run the product for the first time, an automatic device configuration wizard appears and walks you through the process of installing your secondary storage library(ies). Once the devices are installed, the administrator can set up one or more migration jobs, which define which files to migrate from primary to secondary, and when the migration should take place. A Migration Job Wizard walks the administrator through this process as shown in Figure 15.16 [5]. Using the Migration Job Wizard, the administrator can choose to migrate files based upon type and location. Then, the administrator can choose files to be migrated by age, size, attribute, or any combination of the three as shown in Figure 15.17 [5]. The last step in creating a migration job is to schedule when it should run as shown in Figure 15.18 [5].

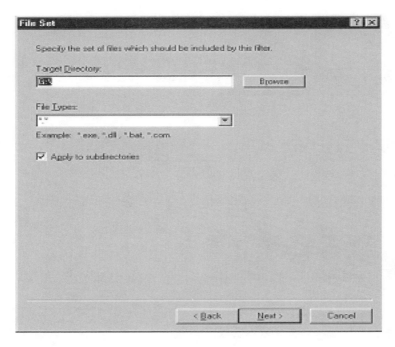

Figure 15.16
Selecting a file set in the Migration Job Wizard.

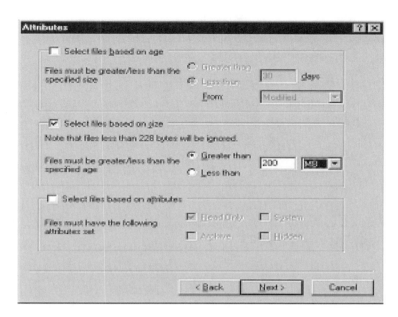

Figure 15.17
Filtering selected file set by attributes.

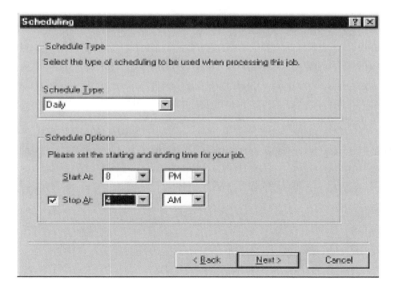

Figure 15.18
Scheduling the migration job to run daily.

An administrator might want a migration job to run at a specific time each day, or at a couple of times throughout the week. InfiNet offers both daily and weekly scheduling options. Once the migration job is triggered at the scheduled time, all files that meet the criteria defined in the migration job are automatically and seamlessly migrated from the primary hard disk to the secondary media. The next time a user or application goes to access the migrated files, InfiNet delivers it to the user as if it still remained in its original location—absolutely no manual intervention by the administrator is required. The space on the primary hard disk is now available for new data to be stored.

Finally, let's look at another SAN management product that does something entirely different: A comprehensive management strategy for the FC-AL.

FIBRE CHANNEL-ARBITRATED LOOP: A MANAGEMENT STRATEGY ....

Among the many benefits it offers for storage networking, Fibre Channel can provide a much higher level of visibility and control than was previously available in parallel SCSI bus configurations. Leveraging Fibre Channel's advantages to create innovative management and diagnostic tools requires a comprehensive strategy and consistent implementation in product design. These new toolsets will be essential for integrating network management platforms with storage, and for building a foundation for predictive management.

This part of the chapter examines the layers that compose a comprehensive management strategy for FC-AL: device management, problem detection, problem isolation, recovery, and predictive (proactive) management as shown in Figure 15.19 [7].

Although Fibre Channel architecture facilitates sophisticated management strategies, few Fibre Channel vendors have implemented more than the most rudimentary features of *device management*, the lowest level of the management hierarchy. For example, Vixel has accomplished the first four layers of this model in its Rapport 2000 managed hub, and has designed its managed products to be software upgradeable to the top layer, *predictive management*. Fulfillment of this strategy offers customers a single system view of the storage network and qualitatively higher levels of operational control.

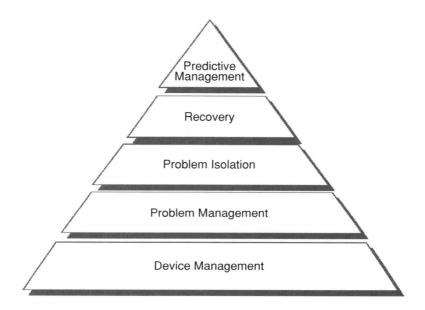

Figure 15.19
Comprehensive management strategy for Fibre Channel Arbitrated Loop.

When is Management Required?

Management capability in any network device requires additional circuitry, microcode, and application software which necessarily raises the per-port cost. Manageability is always desirable, but is a tradeoff between cost and functionality. The more complex a storage network configuration becomes, the higher the requirement for manageability.

Vixel's Rapport 1000, for example, is an unmanaged, low-cost seven-port hub. It is a popular choice for configurations where lower port populations and single vendor sourcing may not justify higher levels of control. Status LED's at each port and auto-bypass circuitry (which verifies the signal integrity of an attached node) is often sufficient for small homogeneous storage networks.

As port density increases, a storage network's added population pushes management issues to the forefront. A larger, 10–50 node Arbitrated Loop may have Host Bus Adapters (HBA's) and storage arrays from a variety of vendors. The storage network may be running Wolfpack or other server clustering applications. Cable plants may involve a mix of copper, multimode, and single-mode fiber [8]. The same loop topology may be transporting both IP and SCSI-3 protocols. All of these factors bring added complexity to the storage network and make management capability an essential part of a user's business decision when selecting a hub vendor.

In LAN/WAN internetworking, companies often mandate SNMP support, even for the smallest configurations. Support of SNMP management is now assumed for every network device, from ethernet hubs and switches to routers to Channel Service Unit/Data Service Units (CSU/DSUs). This requirement is driven by the desire of Network Operating Centers (NOCs) to have complete visibility and control throughout the network. As storage networking evolves on a Fibre Channel infrastructure and becomes more closely tied to internetworking, a comprehensive management strategy will be essential.

Management Definitions: Simple Network Management Protocol (SNMP)

The common language of multivendor network management is SNMP. An IP-based protocol, SNMP has a reduced set of commands for soliciting status or setting operational parameters of target devices. An SNMP management platform is typically run as a graphical interface on a large UNIX or NT workstation and may poll thousands of devices throughout a routed network. The management platform is the SNMP manager; the managed device contains an SNMP agent.

Device status information may include a variety of data points: serial number, vendor ID, enclosure status, port type, port operational state, traffic volumes, error conditions, and so forth. This information is organized in an MIB that is maintained by both the management workstation and the device agent. There are several standard MIBs that have been sanctioned by the internetworking community through a series of Requests for Comments (RFCs). If a vendor wishes to include additional device information that is not specified in a standard MIB, vendor-specific parameters or status can be compiled in an Enterprise MIB or MIB extension. Since there is currently no standard MIB for Arbitrated Loop hubs, SNMP data for an Arbitrated Loop hub may be available via both standard MIB-II structures and vendor-specific MIB extensions.

Device information and status within a MIB is organized in a hierarchical data structure, the Structure of Management Information (SMI). SMI defines an information tree whose branches lead to various management information bases and whose leaves are discrete data about a device's functionality. SMI notation, which is part of the payload of an SNMP query, is essentially an address pointing to the location of the data requested by the management workstation.

While providing the ability to actively poll a device for status, SNMP allows a device to generate unsolicited status information (a trap). If a preconfigured error condition or threshold is reached, the device will initiate an SNMP message to the manager workstation as an alert. On the management platform, the icon representing the device typically turns yellow or red, and the application may send a page to the network operator.

In addition to multivendor SNMP management platforms (HP OpenView, Cabletron Spectrum, etc.), hardware vendors often provide their own graphical configuration utilities. These utilities are *element* managers, in that their focus is a specific vendor's product set, and the parameters and real-time diagnostics specific to the hardware elements of that product set. Part of a comprehensive management strategy for providing a single system view involves integrating the element manager into more global management platforms.

As TCP/IP has increasingly become the Esperanto of data communications, SNMP has become the favored management protocol and is supported by nearly all hardware and software networking vendors. Storage is the last area of data networking to feel the onslaught of IP, and is consequently the most recent recipient of SNMP capability. This evolution works out quite well for storage networking management, since SNMP now offers proven, stable, standards-based functionality and is widely supported by the rest of the networking world.

SCSI-3 Enclosure Services (SES)

The most prevalent server-to-storage protocol is Small Computer Systems Interface, or SCSI. In legacy SCSI systems, SCSI protocol is run over limited-length parallel cables, with up to 15 devices in a chain. The latest version(s) of SCSI (SCSI-3 or higher) offers the same disk read/write command set in a serial format, which enables Fibre Channel as a more flexible replacement for parallel SCSI. SCSI-3 over Fibre Channel allows server and storage vendors to offer higher speed, longer distances, and greater population for storage networks with fewer changes to upper level protocols.

The ANSI SCSI-3 Enclosure Services (SES) proposal defines a command set for soliciting basic device status from storage enclosures. Similar to SNMP Get and Set commands, SES provides SCSI SEND DIAGNOSTIC and RECEIVE DIAGNOSTIC RESULTS commands to query a device. SES may be used to retrieve power supply status, temperature, fan speed, UPS, and other parameters from both SCSI and proxy-managed non-SCSI devices.

SES is significant for FC-AL management, since it is a potential source of overhead within loop data traffic (it is *in-band* management). An Arbitrated Loop hub may be neutral in the deployment of SES within storage networks, since it simply facilitates movement of all SCSI-3 transactions. If the hub itself supports SES queries, it becomes a participant (a node) in the loop. A management strategy for FC-AL should, as required, accommodate non-SNMP management protocols, but exercise caution in introducing management traffic into the loop.

General Issues in Arbitrated Loop Management

Arbitrated Loop for storage networks is analogous to shared media LAN topologies like FDDI and Token Ring, but presents unique features and definitions. Understanding these distinctions from traditional LAN management implementations is necessary for appreciating the challenge that a comprehensive Fibre Channel management strategy poses.

In-Band and Out-of-Band Management

In traditional LAN/WAN terminology, *out-of-band* management is provided via an alternate data path, typically a serial RS-232 or SLIP connection. An out-of-band managed Ethernet hub or router, for example, is typically accessed through a command line (text) interface over a dial-in modem or direct connect serial cable. Management traffic is *out-of-band* since it does not flow through the primary LAN or WAN interface. Current router, LAN hub, and LAN switch technology provides an out-of-band interface only for worst-case situations: the primary interface is down and SNMP management is not possible through the network.

In-band management, in LAN/WAN environments, is the preferred access method. Management traffic (SNMP commands via IP) is intermixed with data traffic along the primary (Ethernet, Token Ring, Frame Relay, etc) interface. Providing there is no catastrophic condition in the network, normal device configuration, status, and monitoring information can be performed from management stations anywhere in the network. Network managers rely on the devices they are managing to route both user data and the management traffic itself. And since routers and switches provide multiple paths through a meshed network, management queries have less overhead impact than would be incurred over a single link.

Things are somewhat different in the Fibre Channel world. In-band management in an Arbitrated Loop, for example, necessarily incurs traffic overhead, since the initiating manager would have to arbitrate, open, and close repeatedly to solicit information from the loop's nodes. Server-to-storage conversations (the most critical exchanges in datacentric networks) would be repeatedly punctuated with management traffic. So, although there are some valid functions that could be performed by in-band management in an Arbitrated Loop environment (soliciting SCSI Enclosure Services data), in-band management is not the preferred access method and should be employed sparingly.

Out-of-band management in Fibre Channel is typically accomplished through an Ethernet interface on the switch or hub, although a serial, console interface may also be provided. Out-of-band management via Ethernet has three main advantages: it keeps management traffic off the loop where it will not burden business-critical data, it makes management of an Arbitrated Loop possible even if the loop is down, and it is accessible from anywhere in a routed network. In this sense, it is *in-band* in LAN/WAN terms.

Hub-to-Hub Management

For overall cost reduction, it is useful to have a single management card in one hub be able to manage multiple hubs in a stack. Vixel's Rapport 2000, for example, provides an external management bus to extend management from a single card to up to eight hubs. Since the management bus is separate from the hub's loop ports, this solution preserves the customer's investment in ports that are available for nodes.

An alternative hub-to-hub management scheme, however, is implemented by introducing side-band traffic across a hub-to-hub cascade link. This scheme claims to be *out-of-band*, since the management traffic does not arbitrate for possession of the loop when management data is sent from one hub to another. Instead, the management data is transported as low frequency *jitter* across the same link that is being used by end-user traffic. By introducing jitter into an active Arbitrated Loop, this management strategy poses a risk to loop integrity and does not provide management visibility if the hub-to-hub link is down. Given that the entire Fibre Channel industry is attempting to *reduce* the amount of jitter in Fibre Channel storage networks, it is ironic that anyone would conceive and implement a management scheme that *introduces* jitter into customer environments.

Reactive versus Proactive Management

The focus of traditional network management platforms is to provide the tools to monitor, troubleshoot, and reconfigure network components *in real time*. If a device errors, the error is detected and reported to the management platform immediately, which results (depending on how the management platform is configured) in a visual notification (the device icon turns yellow or red), an audible alarm, or a page being sent to the network operator. The network operator can then use standard SNMP tools, the vendor's MIB extensions, or the vendor's management application to diagnose the problem.

This management practice is *reactive*, in that remedial action is always a reaction to a problem that has already occurred. Reactive management is essential for day to day network operations, but is insufficient for maintaining network stability and preventing lost revenues.

Vendors of more sophisticated management platforms have, over the past few years, successfully engineered applications that can predict and resolve problems *be-*

fore they impact the network. Proactive management platforms use the same SNMP data that reactive platforms employ, and so require no changes to network devices. The predictive capability is accomplished by periodically rolling SNMP statistics into relational databases and then trending that data over time. Proactive management can thus trend utilization, track marginal performance of a device, and provide statistical justification for capacity planning and network upgrades.

As storage networks evolve on Fibre Channel architecture, it is critical that Fibre Channel vendors provide a path from reactive, operational management to proactive, fault preventative management. This strategy implies a feature-rich Management Information Base (MIB) extension that provides more useful information to a proactive management application, and product designs that allow selective queries of attached nodes.

Trouble-Shooting Arbitrated Loops

Arbitrated Loop offers unique challenges for diagnosing operational problems. Unlike Token Ring or other shared media, transactions on an Arbitrated Loop are not always visible to all nodes.

In Token Ring, for example, a data frame is sent from source to destination, the destination copies the data, marks the frame as copied, and returns the frame to the source. Once the source verifies the data has been copied, it is responsible for removing the frame from the ring. Since the data must traverse the entire ring, any intervening node can view it. All that is required to troubleshoot a Token Ring transaction, then, is to insert a Network General Sniffer anywhere on the ring and observe.

In an Arbitrated Loop, a data frame is sent from source to destination, but the destination *removes* the frame from the loop. Other nodes are unaware of the transaction. Troubleshooting an Arbitrated Loop may therefore require a data trace at *each* suspect port. This is typically accomplished by inserting data analyzers on either side of a port, and capturing the transaction as it arrives to or leaves the port. This is not only an expensive diagnostic that requires considerable Fibre Channel expertise, but by inserting and deinserting data analyzers (which sometimes requires removing active nodes), it may alter the topology of the loop and actually hide the problem under investigation.

A management strategy that addresses this unique feature of Arbitrated Loop solves the most pressing operational issue for storage network managers: eliminating the 80/20 rule for problem identification and recovery. If 80% of downtime spent simply identifying the source of a problem can be eliminated or dramatically reduced, then the customer's exposure to lost revenue is dramatically reduced, the disruption to users is dramatically reduced, and operational staffing requirements are dramatically reduced. Vixel's management strategy solves this problem with the Rapport 2000.

Note

Again, Rapport 2000 is only one of many products that have exactly the same features. This product is only mentioned here for demonstration purposes. Prentice Hall and this author are not promoting one product over another.

Device Management

The first level of a management strategy is device management. *Device* refers to the hub enclosure, power supply, fans, and hub ports. This level may incorporate basic control features if the hub supports configurable parameters (port enabled/bypassed), inventory/asset support (serial number, identifying name), type of port or GBIC, microcode version reporting, and management topology mapping (identifying multiple hubs in a managed configuration).

If the vendor supplies a management GUI, device management is typically displayed as a graphical rendering of the hub and ports, with color-coded status for power, fans, and ports. In one vendor's implementation, fan status is represented by an animated icon of a turning fan, while temperature is represented by an animated icon of a thermometer pulsing up and down. For device level management, Vixel has elected to use straightforward, color-coded indicators and text for these components (see Figure 15.20) [7].

Device management is the *minimal* criteria for declaring a product *managed*. Device management is useful for obvious low-level hub status, but while providing useful information on the health of a fan or power supply, it cannot provide useful information on the *health of the loop*. To extend management beyond the enclosure components and basic port state to the entire loop (or multiple loops), requires extending the management strategy to higher levels.

Unfortunately, some vendors have been satisfied to produce products that meet only the minimal SNMP management criteria, and yet market them as the most comprehensive management systems for storage networking. Imagine the frustration of a storage manager who, when the loop unexpectedly goes down, brings up the management GUI, clicks on a button to display the hub status and sees only cute animated icons of twirling fans and burbling thermometers, but has *no useful tools for diagnosing or recovering the loop.*

Figure 15.20
The Rapport 2000 hub view provides a color-coded management card, enclosure, loop state, port and Gigabit Interface Converter (GBIC) status at a glance.

Problem Detection

Useful management tools should enable the storage manager to quickly detect a problem, isolate it from the loop, and recover loop activity. These higher levels of management require a carefully conceived design of both hardware and software components, and reflect a commitment to and understanding of what the customer requires for stable storage network operation.

Problem detection in an Arbitrated Loop is a difficult but resolvable engineering task. As outlined above, since Arbitrated Loop is not a broadcast media, identifying the source of a problem may require a port by port interrogation. Observing Fibre Channel activity at each port, however, should not interfere with normal loop traffic (it should be performed out-of-loop). This implies a means to eavesdrop on a port's activity without incurring delays or interference in user transactions.

In addition, the collective observations at each port should be aggregated to a *loop status.* When a device is inserted into an Arbitrated Loop hub, for example, it will initiate a loop initialization sequence and momentarily pass through an *OpenInit* state in the process of acquiring a loop address. If a single port is in an OpenInit state, that may reflect normal loop initialization activity. If all ports are hung in an OpenInit state, however, it indicates that the loop is in an unsuccessful initialization sequence and requires further diagnostics.

By combining a port level diagnostic that observes each port's activity with a loop level diagnostic, Vixel is able to provide problem detection tools to quickly identify an offending node and describe the specific failure. Figure 15.21 shows normal loop activity [7]. Problem detection in Arbitrated Loop should readily identify a number of conditions:

- Physical connection (signal integrity, transmitter and receiver status, GBIC status)

- Presence of valid Fibre Channel characters
- Identification of Fibre Channel ordered sets issued from any port
- Identification of Start of Frame sequences (indicating data transactions)
- Identification of Arbitrated Loop-Port Addresses (AL-PAs)
- Recognition of port insertion and removal
- Recognition of loop initialization sequences
- Recognition of loop normal operation
- Recognition of loop failure [7]

By monitoring these conditions, it is possible not only to detect that a problem exists, but to pinpoint the exact cause to the port and node level. This, in turn, provides the basis for quickly isolating the problem from the loop and recovering from it.

Vixel's Rapport 2000 is engineered for rapid problem detection, and includes an event log which records any significant change in loop status. This feature is especially useful for unattended or off-hours operation. If a misbehaving HBA, for example, intermittently goes out of service, the event log will record that activity over time.

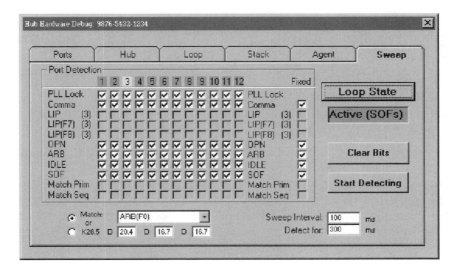

Figure 15.21
The Rapport 2000 sweep screen provides both port and loop detection. Detected problems are instantly reported with color-coded indicators on loop, stack, hub, and port views.

Problem Isolation

A prerequisite for meaningful hub management is to provide a means to take a problem device offline and run diagnostics against it. This allows the loop to regain normal activity while a potentially more lengthy troubleshooting process continues.

Most Arbitrated Loop hubs provide a means to automatically isolate (bypass) a node if it loses valid signal. Loss of signal, however, is not the most common cause of loop disruption. It is more common for a problem node to have a valid Fibre Channel signal, but invalid or inappropriate Fibre Channel characters. A useful automatic isolation of a problem node should trigger inappropriate Fibre Channel characters (or the absence of expected characters) and sequences (streaming LIP F8s—a loop down sequence) that are disruptive to the loop.

The management application should also provide graphical tools for manually bypassing or inserting a node, and the capacity to run diagnostics from the end node to the hub and back (loopback mode). These facilities give the operator the ability to selectively perform non-disruptive tests on the lobe (port, cable, and end node) and determine corrective action before the port is reintroduced to the loop.

Recovery

Recovery from an error condition involves two components: recovery of loop activity and recovery of a node's participation in the loop. Automating the recovery process insures high availability of data and facilitates unattended operation of the storage network.

Isolating an errant node from the loop will restore loop operation. But, if the problem node represents gigabytes of business-critical data (a RAID array), recovery of the entire loop mandates the most rapid restoration of that node to service.

If, for example, a storage array is generating valid Fibre Channel signal, but its state machine has become confused, it would be useful to *wake* the device by sending it a specific Fibre Channel ordered set instead of physically power-cycling the array or replacing its interface. Quickly restoring the array to service would give the operator the opportunity to monitor the device and, if necessary, schedule maintenance during offpeak hours.

The Vixel Rapport 2000 provides automated recovery features to bring confused nodes back to service as shown in Figure 15.22 [7]. If the node cannot be recovered, it is automatically removed from the loop so that the loop itself can recover. If the loop is brought down by a node's persistent attempt to initialize (streaming Loop Initialization Process [LIP] F8, or *loop down* sequences), the Rapport 2000 automatically bypasses all ports and reinserts them into the loop one by one. As each port is inserted, it is checked to see if it is the offender. If not, it is allowed into the loop to resume normal operation. If a node is the source of LIP F8 streaming, an attempt is made to recover it. Only if it fails to respond to the recovery attempt is it then bypassed from the loop.

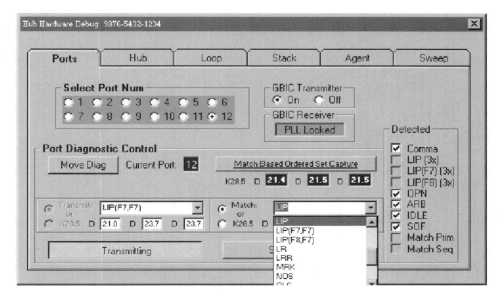

Figure 15.22
The Rapport 2000's automatic recovery features and port level diagnostic can be used to recover an attached node without disrupting normal loop operation.

The ability to rapidly recover loop operation and to recover attached nodes promotes server/storage interconnect to a much higher level of reliability and accelerates the migration from legacy SCSI to storage networking. To deploy large server and storage configurations on Fibre Channel, customers need confidence that this topology will not only overcome bandwidth, distance, and population issues, but will keep downtime to an absolute minimum. Vixel's Rapport 2000 has been engineered with that business priority at the forefront.

Predictive Management

At the highest stage of the management hierarchy, the goal of predictive management is to eliminate downtime (lost revenues) and provide valid data on traffic volumes and patterns for capacity planning.

Predictive management is accomplished with both hardware and software components. The features described previously for problem detection, isolation, and recovery all contribute to predictive management, since they focus on minimizing downtime. The ability to proactively verify the status of a port, cable plant, and end node before introducing it into the loop, is a significant contribution to the predictable operation of the storage network. The next step toward eliminating downtime is to accumulate loop and port statistics on a periodic basis via a predictive management platform (Concord Network Health, ClearStats, HP-EASE, etc.) trend activity over time.

In Arbitrated Loop, it is not unusual for a node to issue a loop initialization. In normal loop operation, the loop would quickly pass through the initialization sequence and return to its previous activity. If the node is sporadically issuing loop initializations, however, it may indicate that the HBA is marginal and needs to be replaced. Observing that activity over time provides the basis to schedule nondisruptive service on the device and address a problem proactively before it becomes severe.

The Rapport 2000 incorporates additional proactive tools to maximize loop operation. If a new RAID array is being introduced into an active loop, the operator can first put the port in bypass mode, attach the cable and end node, and issue Fibre Channel ordered sets to the node to verify that it is operational. Once that verification is complete, the operator can then enable the port for insertion into the loop. If the HBA supports loopback mode, the operator could set the hub port into loopback and run diagnostics from the node to the hub. Since most Arbitrated Loop problems occur when a new device is introduced, proactive management tools provide significant control over the storage network. Thus, Vixel's long-term management strategy is to simplify storage network configuration, extend both hardware and software product capabilities toward fault-tolerant management, forge partnerships with the leading standards-based proactive application vendors, and continue broadening and deepening the definition of storage network management.

Finally, a coherent, knowledgeable, well-conceived and consistently implemented management strategy is essential for creating robust storage network solutions. The evolutionary path from the first LAN connection to today's Enterprise Networking is littered with vendors who underestimated the customer's requirements or were satisfied to produce products that met only minimal standards. As you consider migration from SCSI to a new storage network topology, look for vendors whose products make Fibre Channel the most reliable, scalable, and manageable choice for a long-term solution.

FROM HERE...

This chapter covered the data management solution, virtual SANs, and a management strategy for the FC-AL. The next chapter discusses the facts about SAN software, documentation standards, and increasing efficiency in the prepress market.

END NOTES...

[1] "Brocade SAN Solutions: A More Effective Approach to Information Storage and Management," Brocade Communications Systems, Inc., 1745 Technology Drive, San Jose, CA 95110, 2001.

[2] CNT Headquarters, 6000 Nathan Lane North, Minneapolis, MN 55442, 2001.

[3] ONI Systems Corp., 166 Baypointe Parkway, San Jose, CA 95134, 2001.

[4] Ashlee Vance, "LeftHand Pushes Emerging Storage Model At Show," LeftHand Networks, 6185 Arapahoe Road, Boulder, CO 80301, 2001.

[5] "OTG DiskXtender 2000: Virtual Storage for Today's E-economy," OTG, Corporate Place 93, 100 Burtt/300 Ballardvale, first floor, Boston, MA, 2001.

[6] Strategic Research Corp., 350 S. Hope Ave. Suite A-103, Santa Barbara, CA 93105, 2001.

[7] Tom Clark, "A Management Strategy for Fibre Channel-Arbitrated Loop," Vixel Corporation, Corporate Headquarters, 11911 North Creek Parkway South, Bothell, WA 98011, 2001.

[8] John R. Vacca, *The Cabling Handbook (2nd Edition),* Prentice Hall PTR, 2001.

16 Ongoing Maintenance

Storage service providers (SSPs) hit the scene in a big way in 2001, hawking such services as ongoing maintenance in the form of outsourced tape and disk backup and recovery, and storage consolidation among corporate offices. Now SSPs and infrastructure service providers are working with vendors to improve the fine-tuning (ongoing maintenance) of storage networking through availability and accessibility of data over these new SANs.

The year 2000 was a big year for SSPs. As the concept matures, SSPs are differentiating themselves by offering different ongoing maintenance service-level agreements (SLAs) for storage, and also applications on top of storage. Usually SLAs are tied to availability. In the networking world, you're very familiar with that; it's a new concept for storage. But best effort is very scary for storage. In storage you care about ongoing maintenance, availability, latency (how quickly can you get at it), and backup.

The SSP model typically starts with the concept of a SAN. As previously noted, SANs are specialized, high-speed networks interconnecting data storage devices. But sharing goes against the basic architecture of most storage systems, so new devices were needed to make the model work.

Traditionally, since storage has not been capable of sharing between systems it's been storage and server as a tightly coupled sale. However, SANs first enable you to put a switch between the server and storage to let the customer have a choice of vendors—use HP (Hewlett-Packard Co., *www.hp.com*) for servers, and storage from Compaq (Compaq Computer Corp., *www.compaq.com*), for example.

But, although the switch now allows the SSP or customer to get to any server from any storage, the server still thinks it owns any storage it can discover because that's how it was built. So, a SAN appliance is inserted between server and storage to assign logical volumes to the physical storage that lives on the disk drives. This capability is known as virtualization or SAN management.

SANs, which both SSPs and enterprises employ, are broadly offered in storage subsystems. But, managing a SAN is fairly involved, so for most customers, it's not really a build-it-yourself type of network; therefore, they use an SSP.

The emergence of SANs has given rise to a discussion about how to more quickly configure additional storage as needed and how storage should tie in with the new IP-centric world. The new trend people are wondering about is taking block storage and running it over Ethernet. The Internet Engineering Task Force (IETF, *www.ietf.org*) is considering a new way to get to block I/O, or data input/output, using a protocol called IP-based small computer system interface (iSCSI).

There are two general types of storage: file and block. Normally, you get at data over a network with file I/O. Files are secure and have names. Block storage, meanwhile, doesn't have a particular data type, name, or owner; it's more like raw storage. Block is like an empty file system—it's capacity space, but with nothing in it yet. The mechanisms for security, naming, and ownership that exist with files don't exist with blocks. So that's something the industry would need to create for blocks. However, going to block storage and iSCSI would bring about several benefits, including the ability to easily add capacity, faster data access, and the ability to benefit from equipment economies of scale.

Today, if you want more capacity for files, you get more disk drives. But with iSCSI, you could dial up your SSP and get more capacity—part of the ongoing maintenance. Of course, SSPs can do that today with files, but they build the capacity behind the files themselves rather than having existing storage that can be made available on the fly.

Also, files are perceived as being too slow because there's a lot of operating system overhead with files. Files are secure, named, and typed, but are slow to access and are tied very specifically to an OS.

To date, Fibre Channel (a standard developed by ANSI to provide an inexpensive way of rapidly transferring data between computers, storage devices, and other peripherals) delivers blocks to I/O, while Ethernet cannot. You want to move to iSCSI/Ethernet because there are more switches and adapters and more choices with Ethernet. Fibre Channel use is limited and, thus, more expensive. But, it will take four to six years before iSCSI is practical, because the software has to catch up.

But, that doesn't necessarily mean Fibre Channel is on its way out. The industry recently settled on standards for Fibre Channel, and those products are coming to market in 2002.

There are lots of problems with iSCSI and it has not yet been standardized. It's not clear where it will fit in the marketplace.

Note

The SAN industry is trying to figure out where iSCSI makes sense.

For example, Brocade is working with Cisco Systems Inc. (*www.cisco.com*) instead, on Fibre Channel tunneling over IP. That method supports end-to-end management, unlike iSCSI, which has no available applications to manage end-to-end configuration of such systems. Plus, iSCSI chews up a lot of Customer Premise(s) Equipment (CPE). TCP is in software on computers, so if you're running a database and need to access storage, it can take up to 40% of the CPU just to access the network interface card (NIC), only leaving 60% to run database inquiries. However, some companies, such as Emulex Corporation (*www.emulex.com*), have come out with TCP offload engines to take TCP off the CPU and put it on a separate NIC.

With all the recent interest in storage over the public network, optical equipment vendors are partnering with storage vendors to capitalize on the opportunity. Among such partnerships are those between Coriolis Networks (*www.coriolisnet.com*) and Crossroads Systems (*www. crossroads.com*); ONI Systems (*www.oni.com*); Brocade; ADVA Optical Networking (*www.advaoptical.com*); and INRANGE Technologies (*www.inrange.com*), a storage networking vendor.

More than an interoperability deal, ONI and Brocade have joined forces to deliver three end-to-end, application-specific storage solutions, which may also include additional vendors such as Compaq. The first of the three solutions ONI and Brocade are delivering does storage consolidation, meaning that it allows two sites to access the same pool of storage, with a Sun Microsystems Inc. (*www.sun.com*) Solaris environment at one site and an NT-based solution at the other. The second is a remote backup application in which heterogeneous environments access shared test storage. The third is for disaster recovery and uses synchronous mirroring. All three applications use optical nodes from ONI and Brocade switches.

The Coriolis/Crossroads deal was spurred by interest from traditional carriers wanting to offer SANs in a more efficient way. SAN traffic tends to be big chunks of data across the network. It tends to be somewhat bursty. Because of that bursty nature of data, it's very inefficient for a carrier to allocate data at peak rates because it creates over-provisioning and idle bandwidth, and creates waste.

So, Coriolis joined with Crossroads to provide access to SANs using Crossroads' SAN interfaces. But, Coriolis has a mechanism to transport data across the shared transport that carriers provide. So, they can take an OC-48, for example, and make it look more like an OC-768. When the SAN is not transmitting data, the carrier can use the transport mechanism to transfer data to someone else.

While these carriers themselves don't want to be in the business of outsourcing storage, they do want to have SAN transport ability so they can offer enterprises a Fibre Channel interface; a modem that takes Fibre Channel in; and the ability to offer an SLA from the SAN location.

THE FACTS ABOUT SAN SOFTWARE.......................

Of about 300 TB of data stored in three separate SANs at the Boeing Company (Chicago, Illinois), only 2 TB to 3 TB can be shared in a SAN with products from different vendors because the SAN software available to manage them is unreliable—a real ongoing maintenance problem. Every vendor is deploying their own flavor. They're not interoperable.

Vendors bring technology, deliver it, and scratch their heads as to why no one wants it. You should try to encourage and let vendors know, if they don't have tools, then you don't want the product. You aren't alone here.

While storage vendors continue to hype storage manageability and open standards, users say the applications they've seen fall far short of what they need, such as automated load balancing and storage virtualization or the pooling of storage capacity from mixed vendor environments. In reaction to customer pressure, Hopkinton, Massachusetts-based EMC Corporation announced recently that it would be releasing ESN Manager, which promises to join disk storage systems made by Compaq, Hewlett-Packard, and Hitachi, and tape devices from Storage Technology (see sidebar, "Storage Software").

STORAGE SOFTWARE

Hitachi Data Systems recently announced the release of its NAS *head* appliance. The head sits on top of its Lightning and Thunder arrays, providing access to data from IP networks. With the hardware product lines in place, HDS figures that with refreshes, they're good for a year or two. Building a SAN software business is HDS's chief goal.

The company did $50 million in software sales in the first quarter of 2001, and it plans to introduce new software every quarter for the next 12 months. Its strategic partners are Veritas Software and, to a lesser extent, Microsoft.

HDS's aim is to be first to market with a virtualization product that enables a user to not only see, but also to manage any storage devices on a network, be it HDS's or third-party equipment. That vision is 18–24 months off. The company will buy where it needs to and is currently scooping out startups to add value to the micro code it's developing in conjunction with Veritas.

First out of the block, HDS will address usability, where it admits it trails behind EMC. The leaping off point for much of the work is its High

Command management protocol product, which enables users to see and use all of their storage management applications from a single, graphical console.

HDS claims it continues to pick up competitive wins against market leader EMC, and touts ABN Ambro, Qwest, Morgan Stanley, SBC Services, Credit Suisse First Boston, and Zurich Insurance as its latest scalps. Most were IBM replacements, HDS indicated, which it won in bake-offs against EMC.

The company declined to comment on reports that it has ousted Sun Microsystems's T3 storage at Sun poster child customer eBay, which is said to have installed HDS Thunder arrays. HDS indicated it doesn't comment until its customers do.

HDS, which in 2000 lost German reseller Comparex to EMC, indicated it's the best thing that could have happened. HDS did more business through its own German sales in the month of March 2001, than Comparex did in the entire year 2000.

It's widely held that HDS's increasing exposure to Wall Street is the preamble to being spun out from parent Hitachi. HDS claims that no formal decision has been taken yet.

In its year to March 31, HDS did $1.2 billion in revenue in storage, or 75% of the US group's $1.6 billion in total revenue. This compares with $774 million out of $1.5 billion in 2000. The company indicated it recorded over $100 million more profit this year than last. Indirect sales, including Hewlett-Packard, account for 25% of business.

Revenue growth should come in at between 25% and 30% overall for 2002, while storage will achieve 80% to 100% growth. HDS estimates its enterprise market share to be between 20% and 25%. It claims it has ousted IBM to become the number two enterprise storage vendor, behind EMC. As for future technology such as SCSI-over-IP, HDS indicated its enterprise customers have told it there's no way they are going to be putting their mission-critical data onto their corporate Web networks [1].

IBM also recently said its corporate strategy is shifting toward one of networked storage management. IBM currently sells Tivoli Storage Network Manager, but the company plans to improve interoperability with other vendors' products with its Storage Tank software, which it said will be rolled out in stages in the second half of 2002.

IBM sees its newest software product as the *Holy Grail* of open connectivity, allowing interoperability with any other product. Ultimately, it will even be able to handle EMC's stuff.

Heterogeneity and interoperability are the big words in 2001. EMC and IBM have it now. Will it get better? Yes, as far as heterogeneity and connectivity are concerned.

In 1999, IBM's storage and server sales were split. In 2001, it's a 70/30 split in favor of storage, with 75% of that on storage networking.

All agree that interoperability and storage virtualization drives down the cost of storage by allowing an organization to use all of its networked storage as if it came from a single source. IBM has also promised the availability of iSCSI, or storage over IP, for midmarket customers that can't afford Fibre-Channel SANs by 2002. But, past promises by vendors have nurtured a healthy skepticism among IT managers who are reluctant to spend money on new technology without seeing a successful track record.

Nevertheless, Fibre-Channel networks are complicated enough without having to worry about wrapping them in an additional layer of connectivity such as IP. It's always shocked this author that network vendors didn't seem to get that storage networking was about network switching. They thought it was just going away—that it was a fad.

For example, Gordon Food Services' (Grand Rapids, Michigan) SAN, now at 3.5 TB, is expected to grow two- or three-fold by 2002. Networked storage tools are available, such as EMC's Volume Logix application, which maps storage networks and monitors individual switches and routers. Using them, however, creates vendor lock-in. While vendors are certainly willing to be open with server platforms and switches, they're not necessarily willing to extend it to their storage.

Now, let's look at how SANs offer a welcome solution to the prepress industry's ongoing maintenance networking problems.

INCREASING EFFICIENCY IN THE PREPRESS MARKET ....

Finally, today's graphic arts industry is creating increasingly large image files to handle increasingly large and higher-resolution printed images. Computer networks that have served the prepress industry so well over the past ten years need to be reexamined in the light of this greater demand from the prepress market.

Computer networking plays a vital role in prepress facilities operation. Networks provide the production environment with access to data locally (within the facility) and over wider areas that connect other facilities, advertising agencies, graphic designers, and clients. Yet, with increasing size of files used in prepress, Local Area Networks (LANs) are proving inadequate for many tasks.

The direct-to phenomenon could be the biggest reason. Raster image processors (RIPs) and open prepress interface (OPI) applications that feed new computer-to-plate (CTP) devices now often generate gigabyte-size files. At that size, even gigabit Ethernet is inadequate for reasonable file transfer and copy times.

To make matters worse, many of today's prepress production environments employ multiple computer platforms. High-end graphics workstations are typically Apple Macintosh computers or computers running some version of UNIX® or Microsoft® Windows NT®. But file and application servers tend to be limited to Windows NT or a version of UNIX. While ordinary LANs can handle such a mix of computers transparently, files must still be copied and transferred among these various computers for work to be accomplished.

SANs offer a welcome solution to the prepress industry's ongoing maintenance networking problems. SANs can be used to easily transfer gigabyte-size files in a reasonable amount of time between computers. SANs can work transparently with the same mix of computers that LANs can. And SANs can even eliminate the need for transferring and copying files among multiple computers.

The Problem of Performance

Computer networking technology has been built for the masses. The typical corporate LAN handles relatively tiny files—how large is a word processor document or spreadsheet? LAN equipment manufacturers have been focusing on requirements of the larger, corporate computing market, not the greater bandwidth requirements of the smaller graphics arts industry. While there have been real improvements in LAN performance over the last 20 years, these have amounted to only two orders of magnitude improvement in throughput—100 times faster. Compare this to the million-times increase in computing speed and even to the increase in print resolution from 60 dpi to 1,200 dpi—a resolution increase of 400 times.

In today's prepress client/server networks, storage is normally not connected directly to the devices that need the data, but rather to a general purpose network server running a general-purpose operating system, such as Windows NT, some version of UNIX, or Novell NetWare. These servers are connected to the computers that need the data using standard LAN technology, such as Ethernet. This indirect access to storage over a limited size pipe (the LAN) is the root of the I/O performance problem.

For example, in a modern prepress environment, the processing of data generally revolves around an OPI application, which prints files to PostScript using a server-based workflow. As the pages are printed to PostScript, the low resolution images are replaced with the high-resolution images using the OPI application. All these images, both low and high resolution, are stored on the file server's RAID storage subsystem. The resultant large PostScript files and high-resolution images are also kept on the server's RAID for further processing by RIP applications and image manipulation programs, such as Photoshop.

Several separate computers, connected by a LAN, are used for each of these applications (OPI, RIP, Photoshop), and files are constantly being transferred from the application's computer to the server fronting the storage. While this workflow wasn't a problem ten years ago when the typical printer handled only 300 dpi resolution and nothing larger than a poster, today's 1,200 dpi full-color printers are being used to create house-size images that require house-size image files from many hundreds of megabytes up to a few gigabytes in size.

Many prepress facilities have tried various data management tools and hardware storage solutions in an attempt to handle such large files with their present equipment. For most, the solution becomes apparent only when they realize their LAN is the bottleneck and nothing but a faster network will solve their problems.

Storage Area Networks

SANS are a relatively new invention, created in an attempt to simplify the management of disk storage for multiple computers. SANs are similar to LANs in that they both connect multiple computers together through cables [3]. SANs go a step farther than LANs, however, by also connecting directly to disk storage. In fact, SANs use standard disk storage interface technologies to create the network—SCSI, SSA, and Fibre Channel. Therefore, a SAN cable can actually be a SCSI cable, an SSA cable, or a Fibre Channel cable, and plug directly from a computer's SCSI, SSA, or Fibre Channel interface board (called a host bus adapter, or HBA) to a disk drive's connection port.

Because of connection number and length limitations of SCSI and the general market failure of SSA, Fibre Channel has been the SAN connection medium of choice. Fibre Channel typically uses an optical connection (fiber optic cables) that allows it to extend many miles and enables easy and troublefree cable insertions and removals. To allow multiple computers to connect to multiple disk drives, fibre channel switches and hubs (functionally, like Ethernet switches and hubs) are inserted between the computers and the storage. A properly built SAN can connect many computers (workstations and servers) to many disk drives, which are usually arranged in a fault-tolerant configuration, or RAID.

With a SAN, computers now have a high bandwidth connection between each other and their disk storage. Fibre Channel provides as much as 100 megabytes per second of bandwidth. Compare that to 100BaseT Ethernet at about 5 megabytes per second and you'll find the possible potential for twenty-times the speed improvement. But, SANs also have an added benefit of requiring many times-less processor power to transmit the same amount of data as a LAN. LAN communication protocols were built to use less-than-perfect connections and, because of that, much error checking and rechecking is built into the software that controls the data flow over the LAN. SANs use disk media channels that provide hardware error checking and eliminate much of the processor overhead required to move data over them. While 100BaseT Ethernet could use 30% of the processing power of a typical computer to move some data at 5 megabytes per second, a SAN would use less than 5% of the same processor's power to move the same data at nearly 100 megabytes per second.

Even though the SAN connects multiple computers to storage, some software is still needed to make the SAN and the computers work together. Unfortunately, the operating systems used on today's computers expect to have any storage accessible to them through their HBAs available for their exclusive use. Should multiple computers be connected to the same disk volumes at the same time as the hardware of a SAN allows, data on those disks will be scrambled.

The easiest way to overcome this problem is to use what is generally called LUN masking. LUN masking allows a disk across a SAN to be assigned to one computer connected to the SAN and effectively hides or masks that disk from the view of the other computers. If you use LUN masking, a single RAID could be partitioned into multiple logical disks (LUNs) with each assigned to a specific computer. While this would allow multiple computers in a prepress facility to share a single RAID, it wouldn't allow multiple computers to share the files on that RAID. Each computer could access only its own disk and would still require the LAN to transfer files between those disks. LUN masking is not a good solution for SANs in prepress facilities.

The Power to Share

A better solution is to use software that allows multiple computers to all use the same disks across the SAN at the same time. If multiple computers are allowed to work in this way, some method of arbitrating between the computers that are reading and writing the same disks at the same time is required. For many facilities, some sort of password protection and disk, directory, and/or file locking is needed to keep unauthorized users from accidentally accessing (or damaging) information they don't need. Methods to prevent this from happening have already been invented (in the LAN) which are being used everyday by prepress facilities around the world. Standard LANs permit a system administrator to assign particular disks, folders, directories, and even individual files to particular users. LANs, or more accurately, LAN software allows some users to only read files, while others can read and write files. LAN software also arbitrates among multiple users who try to read the same file simultaneously, effectively helping them to share the same file. If only it were possible to mix the sharing capabilities and technical maturity of LAN software with the high bandwidth and low processor overhead of SANs.

File Sharing of a LAN at the Speed of a SAN

For example, Tivoli® SANergy®, from Tivoli Systems [2], does exactly that. Running on each of the computers connected to the SAN, Tivoli SANergy tricks the applications running on these computers into thinking they are accessing files from a server across the LAN. Actually, the files the computers are accessing are coming directly over the SAN at much higher bandwidths.

Tivoli SANergy is implemented as a SAN redirector. One or more servers on the SAN act as the Meta Data Controllers (MDCs) for SANergy.

These MDCs mount the logical disks on the RAIDs across the SAN, format them with their native file systems, and act as ordinary servers to the other computers connected to the SAN that are also running Tivoli SANergy—the hosts.

SANergy, running on the host computers, hides a computer's direct SAN connection from the computer's operating system. When an application wants to access a file across the SAN, it recognizes that file residing behind the server (the MDC) and so makes a request of the MDC for the file—exactly as it would if it were NOT connected to the SAN. SANergy intercepts the request and rather than let the MDC provide the file, it provides the low-level disk file pointers to the file. With the file pointers in hand, SANergy, running on the host computer, allows the computer to recognize that there is a direct connection to the disk through the SAN and lets the computer get the file. While this sounds like a complex process, the file comes to the host computer many times faster than a server and LAN could have provided it, because of the greater speed of the SAN and the lower processor overhead of handling the data.

Just as important is that all the normal file access permissions and security were still used, because the file request went out over the LAN to a regular server that is acting as the MDC. A system administrator, assigning permissions to SANergy users across a SAN, does nothing different when users are only connected to the LAN. From the point of view of applications running on the SANergy host computers and the users operating these applications, it appears that they have a normal LAN connection to a server. The only exception is that this LAN connection seems to provide data at 100 megabytes per second!

A Mix of Operating Systems

Because Tivoli SANergy uses the inherent sharing abilities built into LAN technology (just like a LAN), SANergy allows a mix of computers running different operating systems to all access the same disk partitions and even the same files at the same time.

While the MDC, running Window NT, or Windows® 2000, or the new Windows XP, will format the mounted SAN storage with its native file systems (NTFS)—it can share that storage with computers running different operating systems—Macintosh OS, Sun Solaris™, IBM® AIX®, Tru64, and Irix. Similar to a Windows server sharing files across the LAN with many kinds of computers, SANergy enables the sharing of files across the SAN with many kinds of computers. Tivoli SANergy not only provides a high-bandwidth and low processor-overhead network that works transparently (exactly like a LAN), but it also provides the network for many different types of computers running many different operating systems.

A Slightly Different Workflow

Because LANs were slow, graphic artists were forced to copy the entire file they were working on from the storage behind the server to their local workstations. Not only did this require many seconds or even minutes to produce the copy, but it introduced many other potential problems—multiple simultaneous users, duplicate file names, and overwriting of intermediate versions.

With a SAN and Tivoli SANergy, the workstation can work on a file in SAN RAID storage without copying it. It is easier and faster to work on the file as it resides on the SAN's RAID, because the SAN connection to storage is just as fast or faster than the workstation's connection to its internal disk drive. If a graphics application can use a file that appears to be across the LAN, the designer can simply open the file and work on it—as though it were on a local disk. When the work is complete, the designer closes the file or resaves it under a new name. The next person to work on the file will only need the name the file is saved under so processing can continue.

A system administrator can designate some files as read-only for some users and other files as read-and-write for other users. In this way, everyone can observe the process, but only those authorized can change it. With a SAN, many of the problems of LAN-based workflow go away.

Finally, with the increase in print resolution and the physical size of printed materials today, prepress facilities are experiencing an explosion in the size of the file to be manipulated and moved through their facilities. LAN technologies that served them so well in the past can't keep up with today's files ranging from hundreds of megabytes to gigabytes in size.

SANs provide a direct, high-bandwidth, and low processor-overhead connection between storage subsystems and servers and workstations. Like the LAN, this new network wires multiple computers together. But, it also directly connects to centralized disk storage. With Tivoli SANergy running on all the computers connected to the SAN, this new network even seems to operate exactly like the familiar LAN (but much, much faster) up to 100 megabytes per second, twenty-times faster than 100BaseT Ethernet.

With Tivoli SANergy and a SAN, the best parts of the LAN are still maintained—the same administration, the same security, the same sharing abilities, and the same mixing of computers with different operating systems. But, because this new network is as fast as or faster than every computer's internal disk connection, the need to move or copy files between storage and computer is eliminated, simplifying workflow and preventing potential sharing problems. Tivoli SANergy and a SAN is the only combination of software and hardware that works transparently with the networks that prepress facilities have been using, and it provides the high bandwidth that today's printing industry needs.

FROM HERE..

This chapter discussed the facts about SAN software, documentation standards, and increasing efficiency in the prepress market. The next chapter covers present and future SAN management standards.

END NOTES..

[1] the 451, "HDS Focuses on Storage Software," searchStorage.com, TechTarget.com, 117 Kendrick Street, Needham, MA 02494, 2001.

[2] "Shared Storage Area Networking for the Prepress Market," Tivoli Systems Inc., 9442 Capital of Texas Highway North, Arboretum Plaza One, Austin, TX 78759, 2001.

[3] John R. Vacca, *The Cabling Handbook (2nd Edition),* Prentice Hall PTR, 2001.

17 Standards Development

The Storage Networking Industry Association (SNIA) needs to change the way it thinks about standards development [1]. The SNIA needs to be chastised for thinking too narrowly. For thinking only within the computer center. They need to think around the world.

Interoperability in a data center environment is a baby step. SNIA needs to go beyond and reach for a bigger solution, one that is on a global scale and broader in scope than the data center.

As previously explained in earlier chapters, the SNIA is a nonprofit trade association that promotes storage standards development through forming and sponsoring technical work groups, maintaining a vendor neutral Technology Center in Colorado Springs, and by promoting activities that expand the breadth and quality of the storage networking market.

Interoperability is no longer just a basic interconnect problem. Standards are wonderful things—there are so many of them. We need more.

SNIA is not doing enough fast enough. The lack of standards often leaves customers stuck within a single vendor's solution in a homogeneous environment, and not altogether happy.

Among the predictions for the future of storage are the convergence of SANs and NAS and a flip-flop in the overall makeup of the IT environment where servers would become the peripherals to storage devices. In 2000, no one thought anybody would be concerned about cost of ownership. SNIA thought there was an infinitely elastic market. SAN vendors have hit tough economic times and issues are no longer focused on speed, but rather return on investment, and total cost of ownership.

Nevertheless, storage is a commodity, a simple container that is rapidly disassociating itself from the computer. Storage has very little intrinsic value. The value is in the data inside those containers.

SAN MANAGEMENT STANDARDS ....

Assuming you can get a Storage Area Network up and running, the next problem is managing your SAN. You not only need to manage storage over the SAN, which means managing backup and restore, disaster recovery, data movement, and data sharing. You also need to administer the SAN infrastructure itself, including device management and resource management, despite the lack of industry standards development.

EMC, Legato, Tivoli, and Veritas offer storage management targeted at SANs. All have bulked up by making major acquisitions during the last few years. EMC acquired Data General and its Clariion storage division along with some smaller storage software companies. Veritas bought Seagate Software. Legato countered by acquiring Vinca, Intelliguard, and several smaller companies. Tivoli acquired a division of Mercury Systems to obtain the SANergy data-sharing system. While supplying point solutions such as backup, data movement, and clustering over a SAN, the four companies have also developed more comprehensive strategies that feature integrated suites of products.

For example, Showtime Networks, has been using SANergy from Tivoli [2]. Showtime studios produces outdoor advertisements which appear on billboards, phone booths, and bus shelters as well as magazine pages, newspapers, and posters.

Showtime's graphic artists use Macintosh workstations, which are connected to a Clariion Storage array (containing 350 GB of storage) via a Vixel Fibre Channel switch and a Gadzoox Fibre Channel hub. A Windows NT server on the SAN runs the SANergy software.

Prior to the introduction of SANergy, Showtime's artists were spending too much time on tasks not directly involved with their design work. Showtime found that people were spending about 50% to 60% of their time doing disk access functions like opening, saving, printing, and copying files. The actual work being done was a very small part of their day.

Every day, Showtime deals with a huge amount of data in the form of 1- to 2-GB files. These files have to be moved from one artist to another in the course of a day's work. Prior to the SANergy deployment, these large files had to be copied over the messaging network—a time-consuming procedure that reduced productivity. At the same time, this traffic degraded the performance of the network. With SANergy and fiber-optic cabling that was already in the building [6], Showtime has reduced the time it took to move files from 30 minutes to a few seconds.

By using a SAN, Showtime Networks has been able to reduce costs even though their workload has increased by 500% in 2000. Showtime indicates SANergy was well worth the investment of $150,000. The system paid for itself in less than six months because of the increase in productivity.

Managing the Infrastructure

In addition to management over the SAN, the management of the SAN infrastructure is also important. The major vendors are Computer Associates (CA), EMC, Hewlett-Packard, and Vixel.

All the vendors offer similar functionality. Primarily, they are management products that feature topology mapping with some sort of alerting mechanism that is activated when a device has a problem, and they usually drill down into the devices' own management tool.

The only problem with these SAN management solutions is they are not based on industry standards. A case in point is CA [3]. CA could not wait for the relevant organizations to create an appropriate management standard. CA is very happy to adopt standards as they emerge, but they are not going to wait for standards bodies to deliver customer solutions when their customers are screaming at them for standards development.

As a result, CA provided an extension to its Unicenter TNG systems management platform so its customers could manage their SANs from the same console as their messaging networks and systems. The management products offered by CA, EMC, HP, and Vixel go beyond other management products in offering multivendor capability. For example, SAN device vendors Ancor, Brocade, Chapparal, Crossroads, and Gadzoox have their own software products, but they provide management only for their own devices.

To prevent this bifurcation of management software, an industry group called the Fibre Channel Alliance is working with the Storage Networking Industry Association to develop a SAN management information base, which the vendors have pledged to adopt. The standard is in the final phases of being formulated and submitted to the Internet Engineering Task Force for ratification. Once it is ratified, adopted, and implemented by vendors, any interoperability issues that now exist will be eliminated. The SAN will have overcome another major hurdle.

THE FUTURE OF SAN STANDARDS ....

It is said that the good thing about standards is there are so many of them to choose from, many of them being proprietary. Storage is certainly no exception to this rule. Companies looking for ways to consolidate rapidly expanding storage volumes are, in many cases, eyeing Storage Area Networks. But potential users should be advised: The technology is still maturing and storage vendors have been fighting among themselves about how best to set those standards.

Luckily, it seems likely that storage vendors, including the major players Network Appliance, EMC, and IBM, are starting to react to the demands of their corporate customers and are developing stronger cross-vendor standards. There is still a lack of agreed standards and it will take until 2003 before there is any coherent model from the major vendors.

There are big egos and vested interests in all the proposed standards, but the sheer volume of the market means momentum will gather to push through an agreed standard. This market will dictate how standards will evolve in the future.

The most important standards will be those for communications and interfaces because they will be the fundamentals on which future business systems are built. However, it is likely to take until 2004 or longer before the technologies will be suitably established; and until then, the standards wars between the vendors will continue.

Standards Wars: The Contenders

In the blue corner stands IBM, the company that used to dominate the market for large data center storage before it lost most of its share to EMC. In the other corner stands EMC. As a dominant storage vendor, EMC had, in the past, taken both standard and RAID product initiatives in the SANs area. EMC is the de facto leader of the Fibre Alliance, an assemblage of storage vendors seeking to implement SANs as Fibre Channel-based networks.

EMC formed the Fibre Alliance in February 1999 for the purpose of submitting its version of an MIB to the Internet Engineering Task Force, the body that has determined several key internet standards. EMC and Hewlett Packard were two of the more prominent backers of the proposal. The MIB is a group of parameters, or variables, whose values define and describe the status of a network and its components. The MIB provides a heterogeneous method of managing multiple Connectivity Units across a SAN.

However, the SNIA had planned to author an MIB proposal of its own. The Fibre Alliance was not interested in taking the initiative in other areas of SAN specification. The ball remained in the SNIA's court on many of them.

At a meeting of its working group in May 1999, SNIA decided the best way for it to participate in the MIB standards-setting process was to comment extensively on the Fibre Alliance's proposal. But to many, the exchange between the two groups was indicative of a standards leadership void. And many thought that no one was setting any standards at all, despite protestations from the key players.

It also became more apparent that the speed of the network had increased faster than the speed of the data channel. The Fibre Alliance and SNIA were struggling with setting standards for Fibre Channel technology that doubled in speed from 100 megabytes per second to 200 megabytes per second. That, coupled with Gigabit Ethernet soon to jump to 10 Gbps, made the need to concentrate on one evolving standard more necessary than ever.

Standards Depend on the Customer

That was then, and a lot of bridge building has been done since. Storage vendors should be in a better position to meet a wide range of requirements just so long as new standards are adopted—quickly.

Standards have to be driven by customers' needs. There aren't a lot of Storage Area Networks in place at the moment, and that has meant standardization has been driven by technology rather than by what is wanted by customers. It will be another five years before we see the move to true open standards and not ones defined by vendors' proprietary systems.

A major step was taken at the end of 2000 at the Storage Networking World Conference in Orlando, Florida when the SNIA agreed on the specification of the interface for the all-important Fibre Channel Host Bus Adapter (HBA). This is a critical component needed to make different Storage Area Network (SAN) systems interoperate. In addition, it will allow innovative independent software vendors to add greater functionality to SAN-based systems.

The SNIA also aims to be an independent arbiter of SAN interoperability, having grabbed the nettle of establishing an independent test facility. The organization has worked with Compaq to produce what it claims is the largest independent storage network in the world, designed specifically as a testing environment for all SAN systems.

Many SAN vendors have already set up their own testing facilities, but these have been limited in scope and have tended to test interoperability of only a few systems. The rate of growth in storage and SAN systems means that customers want all systems from all vendors to interoperate.

Such interoperability is far more important than the brute performance of any one vendor's systems, though this has not stopped many vendors trying to convince users that their Fibre Channel systems can run at 2 Gbps transfer speed, while the reality is that most manage barely half that.

Two Gigabits and Beyond

But, the appearance of standards that improve interoperability will encourage the development of technology that can reach 2 Gbps and beyond. This process will in turn be aided by the appearance of standards in another area of IT processor-to-processor communications.

The proposed InfiniBand interprocessor communication standard, which is being developed by such server specialists as IBM, Sun, Compaq, and Dell, could have a leading role (see sidebar, "I/O Standard Enhances Storage Networking") [5]. The idea is to overcome what will soon be a major bottleneck in systems design, by increasing the speed with which data can move in and out of the processor.

I/O STANDARD DEVELOPMENT ENHANCES STORAGE NETWORKING

The demand for greater speed across network connections has been restricted by a number of bottlenecks. Arguably, the greatest restriction to data flow is the nature of the I/O architecture. While data can buzz around the world with astonishing speed, it must still have a point of organization and delivery. In many cases, an organization may have tremendous amounts of bandwidth, yet have systems with extremely slow and primitive I/O buses.

InfiniBand technology addresses the shortfall of current I/O buses. The performance gains could range from 500 Mbps to 6 Gbps per link. The implications for storage networking are enormous.

The InfiniBand Trade Association (IBTA) [5] developed and published the specification for the InfiniBand architecture in the fall of 2000. The development of this specification had industry-wide support, with over 326 companies participating. The new point-to-point linking technology is expected to be transformed into a variety of interconnect and computer server commercial products by the end of 2002. Companies like Intel, for example, already have InfiniBand prototype devices in development and have established dedicated interoperability labs.

InfiniBand enables increasing data flow rates on servers, storage devices, and interconnect devices through the I/O fabric. The term fabric is used in order to illustrate the nature of the architecture that relies on communication strands or links. As with any fabric, these strands can be interwoven to provide different patterns of data flow. In theory, the I/O throughput with InfiniBand technology should be increased initially by two to four times. The simple design offers increased system performance, enhanced reliability, and greater availability. It also provides independent scalability of fabric elements.

Cram Course on Infiniband Architecture Technology

A fabric of InfiniBand switches and links is used to provide connections between servers, remote storage, and networking devices. The InfiniBand fabric will both coexist with, and replace, existing I/O technology standards. While *standards* such as Ethernet, Fibre Channel, and Peripheral Component Interconnect (PCI) have existed side by side and continue to evolve, none of them effectively provide true interoperability or manageability. The InfiniBand architecture can theoretically provide operating system and hardware platform interoperability while improving system configurations.

The key to InfiniBand is switching technology that links high-channel adapters (HCA) to target channel adapters (TCA). The switch operates between the HCA and TCA to manage and direct data packets. Architecturally, the high-channel adapter typically resides near the CPU and memory as shown in Figure17.1 [4]. In contrast, the target channel adapter supports the storage and peripheral device I/O.

InfiniBand switching technology offers manageability that does not exist in traditional buses. With InfiniBand, it is possible to utilize variables on data packets that include service levels and other identifiers. And through the InfiniBand fabric, it is also possible to configure InfiniBand links between multiple tiers of servers. The objective is to more appropriately allocate the resources of the entire system and connected devices.

InfiniBand was created to dramatically increase the speeds of n-tier architectures. InfiniBand links will transcend connections between first-tier Web servers, second-tier application servers, and third-tier database servers. The multiple data strands that comprise the InfiniBand fabric can be combined in 1x, 4x, and 12x strands in order to achieve higher-speed interconnects. This technology will be particularly valuable when used in clustering environments for classic failover, workload adjustments, and general manageability. Each of the three levels of fabric strands will be applied to specific technology needs:

- The 1x link will most likely be used for simple connectivity. For example, front-end devices like Web hosting, file, or print services can effectively utilize the throughput of a single 1x link.

- The two-tier computing environment could find the 4x link particularly beneficial. On this level, it is common to find multiple processor systems on which workload balancing is an underlying requirement. Therefore, the ability to configure the data flow accordingly could dramatically impact overall performance.

- The 12x link will be best used for third-tier and n-tier environments. Latency is always a concern in heavy-transactional environments and cannot be tolerated. The InfiniBand architecture helps eliminate data flow latency by virtue of the availability of multiple link strands.

InfiniBand replaces shared bus architectures. As a result, I/O can be removed from the server chassis itself. This will enable significantly greater server chassis design density. Moreover, it will result in less physical space being needed to host more computing power. Freed from strictly confining shared I/O buses, data centers can be constructed with more scalable and flexible infrastructure configuration.

Driving Forces behind Infiniband Technology Adoption

InfiniBand technology connects servers to remote storage and networking devices, and other servers. In addition, it can be used inside servers for interprocessor communication (IPC) in parallel clusters. Internet Service Providers (ISPs) and other enterprise users that require dense server deployments will benefit from the small form factors of InfiniBand devices. Industry supporters of InfiniBand believe that many other potential benefits exist, including enhanced performance, reduced system latency, streamlined data sharing, built-in security, and quality of service and advanced usability features.

The problem InfiniBand is resolving involves mismatched technologies combined with lagging, outmoded components. With processors eclipsing 1GHz, and server farms scaling as needs require, speed is being achieved safely in peer environments. However, when these environments have to push data outside their confines, the issue of interoperability immediately raises its ugly head. Dealing with mixed equipment, operating systems, storage methodologies, and data streams, all play a part in the current slowdown.

Revolutionizing Internet Data Centers

As a new server I/O technology specification, InfiniBand is expected to revolutionize Internet data centers. It simplifies and expedites server-to-server connections. It also makes links to other server-related systems such as remote storage and networking devices less cumbersome.

The InfiniBand specification is designed to overcome current interoperability limitations. In so doing, InfiniBand will address traditional bandwidth hogs like streaming video, graphics, and multimedia bandwidth like any other data transmission.

InfiniBand positively overcomes hardware bottlenecks. The speed of server virtual memory and storage memory communications has always been an issue. The bus technology in servers simply has not been up to the task. InfiniBand link-based technology will reduce this problem.

An interesting and possibly major advance made possible by InfiniBand is the innovation of remote clustering. Scalable and highly available clusters could conceivably exist through the interconnection of servers in remote locations. The current requirement to colocate all clustered servers could be eliminated.

Another important factor in the adoption of InfiniBand technology is cost. According to Framingham, Massachusetts-based International Data Corporation (IDC), cost will play a significant role in promoting InfiniBand adoption. IDC analysts expect that InfiniBand will drive down the cost of servers, interconnects, bridges, and switches. Users of these products will need to refocus on providing highly available solutions that take full advantage of this new system architecture.

SAN Implications

The potential for InfiniBand to transform computing is tremendous. The first significant change is that the CPU and memory can be separated from storage. This will permit the individual management of application loading on the CPU, memory, and storage. The system will no longer be a monolithic beast, but a highly configurable set of components in which data flow can move with appropriately defined speed.

The initial use of InfiniBand will probably be traditional and restricted to bus improvement within the same server. However, this should rapidly evolve into clustering environments and first-tier Web server applications. The next likely utilization will occur with Storage Area Networks (SANs) where data retrieval is critical. The next wave will include radical new designs of computer systems that embrace more specialized functionality and are not constrained by the current *everything-in-the-same-box* architecture.

IDC View of Infiniband

IDC is bullish on the future of InfiniBand. They have defined a number of markets in which InfiniBand should have the greatest impact. IDC envisions the following computing marketplace activity:

General Purpose Entry Server Market

IDC foresees a substantial adoption of InfiniBand for general purpose server utilization. As a segment that constitutes 90% of all server units, it is believed that migration can occur to InfiniBand without major impacts on existing infrastructures.

Application Server Market

A rapidly growing segment of the server market (projected by IDC to top $22 billion by 2005) includes special purpose servers that are usually preconfigured and preinstalled. Since these systems have narrowly defined computing purposes, they are ideal for factory-based InfiniBand installation. Arrays of systems could be installed using InfiniBand fabric.

RISC Server Market

Vendors of proprietary RISC systems will probably be slow to adopt InfiniBand technology. IDC believes that these vendors are at least in part locked into the ASIC-controlled subsystems that are *burned into* silicon. When adoption does take place, look for it on the lower end of the RISC based offerings first.

Server Provider Adoption

The emerging service provider segment should be among the earliest wide-scale adopters of InfiniBand. In part, this will occur because service providers do not have significant legacy system investments. They will also benefit for the flexibility, dense server designs, performances, and cost of ownership that is promised with the InfiniBand technology fabric.

The Role of the InfiniBand Trade Association

The IBTA was created to ensure that industry I/O standards could address costly computing environment bottlenecks. The IBTA has three primary objectives:

1. Plan and develop comprehensive specifications that meet current and future requirements.

2. Draw on existing technology to advance the concept of peer-to-peer interconnection.

3. Utilize its governance authority to balance the development process in an open and fair manner.

The goals of the IBTA are broader than mere administrative objectives. Ultimately, the group hopes the resulting technical specification will result in a number of solid benefits for the computing and networking industry. These include:

- InfiniBand technology will be initially used to connect servers with remote storage networking devices and with other peer servers. The technology will also be used within servers for Internet protocol communication (IPC) in parallel clusters. This will benefit organizations such as ISPs.

- Greater performance, reduced latency, enhanced built-in security, and improved quality of service.

- Total cost of ownership. By addressing issues of speed, reliability, and configuration, costs can be lowered and performance increased.

- Scalability to increase in two areas. First, the fabric is designed to eliminate latency in I/O transmission. Second, the physical modularity will result in a reduced need to purchase extra capacity upfront. Scaling can occur in what the IBTA calls a *pay-as-they-grow* approach.

Finally, new software and hardware industry standards appear so often that it is difficult to evaluate them all. Many standards die before giving birth to commercial products. InfiniBand will likely not fall into that category. In fact, its high level acceptance seems already assured by endorsements from Compaq, Dell, Hewlett-Packard, Microsoft, and Sun Microsystems. The technology appears to have both technological and economic merits.

Challenges still lie ahead for InfiniBand. This is one of many I/O industry standards. The investment already made in bus architectures is tremendous, and therefore resistance to change could be significant. Regardless of the technical value-add associated with InfiniBand, change takes time and legacy environments will not quickly be altered [4].

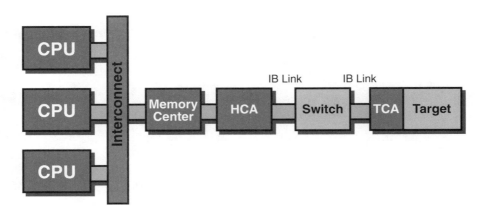

Figure 17.1
Simplified view of InfiniBand architectural model.

With the probability of Fibre Channel-based SANs delivering data at 2 Gbps, processors will need to match that performance level. This is what InfiniBand could do. The sponsors are targeting 2.5 Gbps transfer rates, and are pitching at 6 Gbps in the longer term. And, while network administrators wait for Fibre Channel standards to be developed, Internet Protocol is rapidly gaining ground as an alternative storage interface.

One reason is that administrators are beginning to get the tools to make storage over IP, or SoIP, a reality (see sidebar, "IP Storage Standards Development"). Nishan Systems has already released a complete set of SoIP products, comprising several switches and management software. However, some experts question using such a protocol because storage systems don't tolerate latency and lost data packets.

IP Storage Standards Development

When it comes to embarking into the relatively uncharted waters of IP storage standards, some users might be hesitant to take a chance on mapping out future directions. For example, Measurisk, an independent, New York City-based application service provider (ASP) offers advanced risk measurement analysis to capital market participants worldwide. Measurisk's storage compass points to iSCSI—and this ASP is ready to set sail.

When it comes to standards, good price/performance ratios and high marks in ease-of-use/speed of implementation usually produce a winner. Right now, those criteria work against Fibre Channel. Both SCSI and IP are well established standards, so iSCSI will do quite well.

Measurisk is a beta user of IPStor, an IP software solution for SAN and NAS environments offered by FalconStor of Melville, New York. IPStor (designed to work with iSCSI when it becomes available) allows users to construct an IP-based network storage infrastructure using off-the-shelf technologies such as Gigabit Ethernet, SCSI, and Fibre Channel.

Measurisk is starting to deploy high-density servers that primarily provide operating system storage. Thus, the systems are in need of external storage. Measurisk has learned from their older servers that internal or direct-attached external storage is not manageable across the enterprise and has the potential to be underutilized. These two factors led them to pursue SAN-based solutions in 2000. They soon came to learn that SANs are expensive, proprietary, and lack interoperability standards. These attributes effectively put them on the sideline in terms of implementing a SAN solution.

Measurisk can address the preceding issues by using IP-based storage. The company purchased its first NAS device in 2000, which confirmed their theories regarding the usefulness of these appliances. Measurisk indicates IPStor saves them from having to wait for SAN interoperability issues to be resolved. It also means they are able to leverage their existing investment in Gigabit Ethernet and will not have to learn about Fibre Channel.

IPStor is hardware-independent and directly supports standard storage interfaces such as SCSI and Fibre Channel without converter boxes. The solution's full suite of storage services include mirroring, replication, snapshot, zero impact backup, and restore.

IP Debate Heating Up

As vendors begin to promise more IP-based storage solutions, the debate over proposed IP storage standards development is becoming more strident. An assortment of players in the storage industry are hard at work on a variety of specifications for IP storage. Three proposals include the draft for SCSI over IP (iSCSI) submitted to the Internet Engineering Task Force (IETF); Fibre Channel over Internet Protocol (FCIP); and Internet Fibre Channel Protocol (iFCP), a gateway-to-gateway protocol to interconnect SANs based on existing SCSI and Fibre Channel devices over TCP/IP. An additional proposal, Fibre Channel Backbone, is also before ANSI.

The SCSI protocol that appears to be strongest is iSCSI. This layers SCSI on top of IP, and uses all of the IP advantages, such as flow control and congestion control to give high data integrity and traffic control. If the data is being sent over the Internet, this kind of traffic control is really necessary, and will be demanded by the Internet community.

In an effort to show unity in the storage industry, the Storage Networking Industry Association (SNIA) announced recently the formation of the SNIA IP Storage Forum. As previously mentioned, SNIA is a not-for-profit organization, made up of more than 300 companies and individuals spanning the storage and networking industry.

The purpose of the SNIA IP Storage Forum is to market and promote standards-based block storage networking solutions using IP networks. In addition to expanding market awareness of IP storage, the Forum will also work with standards bodies to help bring IP standards-based solutions to market. IP storage technologies will allow new storage solutions that exploit the use of the industry-standard Internet Protocol: Applications for IP storage that include remote mirroring and backup, distributed Internet data centers, storage service provisioning, transparent Local Metropolitan, and Wide Area Network storage networks.

Industry Unity over Standards?

The SNIA IP Storage Forum itself is evidence that the industry players are working together to educate and illuminate the future customers of IP storage solutions. It is important to realize that most storage is still directly attached to servers. Many customers would like the benefits of pooled storage, but don't want a second network. Everybody has an Ethernet. Everybody knows it. It's plug-and-play and incredibly affordable.

Still, not everyone is as prepared or eager to travel the IP storage route. Storage buyers are trying to make sense out of what they can do in 2002, without committing to the future, where many of the wars are yet to be fought. It has more to do with preserving potential than getting it right, because what's right can change within the course of a year. Most buyers are not on the bleeding edge. They will wait for larger vendors to present them with strategies for deploying *ultimate* IP storage solutions. This is where it gets interesting. There may not be consensus among the big players, giving new definition to *competing alternatives*.

In fact, camps do exist. Backers of iSCSI include Cisco, Hewlett-Packard, and IBM. The FCIP proposal is backed by vendors such as Brocade Communications Systems, Gadzoox Networks, and Lucent Technologies. By 2004, 28% of an IT budget will be storage. 2002 is the year of getting it ready. The standards need to be completed (iSCSI is slated for 2002) and proof of concept products will be available during 2002 toward the end of the year.

Despite the various proprietary interests, there are signs of vendor cooperation and partnership. In the SAN arena, for instance, vendors continue teaming up to offer SAN-designed applications. Brocade Communications Systems, of San Jose, California, and HighGround Systems, of Marlborough, Massachusetts, recently announced that they are expanding their partnership to deliver enhanced storage resource management solutions for Brocade-based SANs. High Ground is now utilizing the Brocade application programming interface (API) to achieve better interoperability with the Brocade SilkWorm infrastructure. Users will be able to use Highground's Storage Resource Manager (SRM) solutions to proactively manage Brocade-based heterogeneous SANs. Management capabilities will include real-time *layered views* of the SAN topography.

Customer Considerations

It makes sense that vendors want to demonstrate to customers that they are getting value for their storage dollar. Most buyers are additionally hindered right now by budgetary constraints due to the slowing economy. The focus may change from easiest to deploy and manage to best ROI.

Some users are already heavily invested in Fibre Channel technology, and thus don't see a pressing need for further investments in IP storage solutions. The principle advantage of Fibre Channel technology is the ability to present disk resources to multiple servers and platforms.

Instead of being forced to buy proprietary IBM disks to cover that requirement, you can allocate disk to those servers from a Hewlett-Packard XP256, which offers roughly 3 terabytes of storage. Once those servers are retired, the disk can be reallocated elsewhere. Along the same lines, you can allocate large amounts of disk to a given server and then take it back and allocate it to another server all via logical assignment versus physical connections. You can appreciate that flexibility.

One vendor touting the benefits of IP storage is Nishan Systems of San Jose, California. The company's SoIP solutions encompass iFCP and iSCSI along with Internet Storage Name Service (iSNS), a companion name service protocol designed to meet the requirements of iFCP and iSCSI.

The SoIP approach does not have the flow control and congestion control which will be necessary for transferring SCSI data over the Internet, but would be fine for use on one's own network or in a data center. Since this is the target of much of the early need for IP Storage, it is a fine protocol, but it doesn't stand up to the long term needs of allowing Internet data transfers.

An encapsulation approach to sending data over IP looks promising, but is also not without technical hurdles. This is easier to do and to visualize than a layering scheme but has some performance and overhead drawbacks. It is also easier to understand than layering and will definitely be used by many companies. iSCSI will be dominant in layering, and FCIP will be the strongest for encapsulation; both will be widely used.

No Winning Protocol Likely

Despite early predictions for strong iSCSI acceptance, there is likely to be no single *winning* protocol in the storage standards arena. Multiple protocols will exist and the adapter cards will automatically handle all of the most popular approaches. The real winner is IP. The power of Ethernet yet again comes to bear. Tunneling, encapsulation, and layering will all be used, depending on the application.

Today's enterprise largely runs Fibre Channel, and will continue to embrace it. They will use IP to tie SAN islands together, and to create SAN to WAN connections. The mass market for IP storage is in the small to medium business—those that have yet to implement a fiber channel SAN but who want/need a storage network. They are more price sensitive and less performance sensitive, therefore making them a perfect match.

Of course, certain wrinkles are still being ironed out. The main technical issues in the IP storage arena currently focus around ordered messaging and the ability to deal with dropped packets. These are really TCP/IP issues and are being worked out. In storage, like life, there is no magic bullet. There will continue to be a mix of new and legacy technologies, ad infinitum. The issue isn't one of cannibalization, but how do we make all these things work together cohesively?

Finally, let's keep pushing ahead on everything that you can agree on, while keeping your mind open to new ideas. Right now, this part of the industry is in its infancy. They need more of almost everything. IP storage today has limited speed and needs a higher guarantee of integrity. For these reasons, the initial implementations are going to be in areas where performance and other needs are not so critical—backup, for example. But, as the industry solves problems and increases performance for IP Storage, the potential exists to use it anywhere.

FROM HERE ....

This chapter discussed the present and future SAN management standards. The next chapter covers the causes of data unavailability; cost tradeoffs; high availability objectives; and the SAN, including the single building, campus cluster, and metro cluster.

END NOTES..

[1] SNIA, 2570 West El Camino Real, Suite 304, Mountain View, CA 94040-1313, 2001.

[2] Viacom, Inc., New York, NY, 2001.

[3] Computer Associates International, Inc., One Computer Associates Plaza, Islandia, NY 11749, 2001.

[4] Robert Williams, "InfiniBand I/O Standard Will Enhance Storage Networking," Enterprise Certified Corporation, 180 Sunrise Lane Boulder, CO 80302, 2001.

[5] InfiniBand℠ Trade Association Administration, 5440 SW Westgate Drive, Suite 217, Portland OR, 97221, 2001.

[6] John R. Vacca, *The Cabling Handbook (2nd Edition)*, Prentice Hall PTR, 2001.

Part 6

SAN Solutions and Future Directions

18 High Availability Business Systems: The Role of SANs

$\mathbf{A}$s always, in today's business environment, time is money. However, it is no longer an eight-hour a day, five-day-a-week affair. Today's businesses run twenty-four hours a day, seven days a week, fifty-two weeks a year. Whenever data is not available, it costs businesses money in terms of lost transactions, lost management opportunities, and lost customer relationships. While this has long been the case for large global enterprises, it is now also increasingly true for even small and medium sized organizations—lack of access to data at any time is painful, often disruptive, and occasionally fatal to such organizations. Thus, this chapter examines the causes of data unavailability, the costs and solutions for HA systems, and the applicability of the SAN architecture to this issue.

THE CAUSES OF DATA UNAVAILABILITY.................

There are several factors that affect downtime or unavailability of data as shown in Figure 18.1 [1]. The results are not surprising.

While most data unavailability is due to unexpected systems outages, such as hardware and software problems, a significant amount of data unavailability is due to planned downtime. Altogether, systems outages of all kinds account for about 80% of the total. Environmental issues such as power outages, fires, floods, or people errors such as the man on a backhoe digging in the wrong place, cause the remaining 20% of the downtime.

There are many ways to manage these problems. For example, data unavailability due to people errors and software problems can be managed with improved procedures and processes, but nevertheless will probably not be completely eliminated. Hardware problems can be managed with redundancy and other techniques, but likewise cannot be completely eliminated. Things will break, regardless.

Data Unavailability

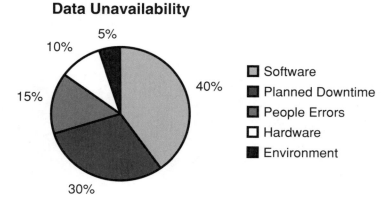

Figure 18.1
Causes of data unavailability.

Certainly, you can increase protection by increasing the safeguards, but such protection can be expensive. The question is, how much guaranteed data availability can you afford? The answer is: *It depends.*

Cost Trade-Offs

Given twenty-four hour, seven-days a week utilization, 99% availability translates to data being unavailable the equivalent 3.9 days per year. Critical applications would generally not accept this amount of downtime, whereas some applications would find this acceptable. Think of your manufacturing management application not being available for almost four days a year. Could your business afford it? Probably not.

Moving to 99.9% availability translates to a more acceptable 8.8 hours of downtime in a year. But it might also cost ten times as much for such a system. Is it worth it?

The reason that an application is important to a business is the economic value per hour it has to that business. For example, at a major financial center it might cost $5 million per hour for such downtime, but noncritical applications may cost only $40,000 per hour or less.

Thus, there is a gradient of trade-offs that must be assessed. This, in turn, has lead to a gradient of High Availability options, each with its own cost/benefit ratio.

HIGH AVAILABILITY OBJECTIVES ....

The traditional solution to data unavailability has been HA systems. This is a catchall phrase that covers many different approaches to increasing data availability. But generically, an HA system is designed to do several things:

- First, it must reduce downtime due to planned maintenance.
- Second, it must be resilient to unexpected hardware and software failure.
- Third, it must also deal with problems such as disaster recovery in case of fire, earthquake, flood, or even the errant backhoe operator [1].

Traditionally, the solution to an HA requirement has been the fault tolerant system, a term that is often applied to a hardware configuration that allows redundant or otherwise protected components to failover (or switch) to a new component or set of components so that downtime is minimized. A simplified example is given in Figure 18.2 [1]. Generally, these cost two to ten times as much as the equivalent nonfault tolerant system.

The system diagramed in Figure 18.2 consists of a number of client workstations, each with connectivity to the database servers A and B. Normally, only one system is active, while the other mirrors the activities of the online system. Should the online system fail, then the backup system takes over. There are many variants of this configu-

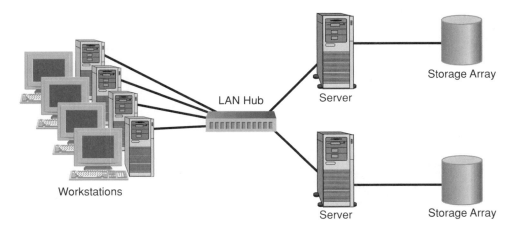

Figure 18.2
A Simplified Fault Tolerant System.

ration, some with complex heartbeat monitors, while others operate with a simple timeout of a request from a client. However, they all have several features in common:

- Generally, all the equipment is in one room, increasing risk in case of a fire or flood.
- These systems are redundant. Because they are redundant, only half of the equipment is actually working productively.
- The entire database is connected to one system (or the other). This causes a choke point as the number of clients increases.
- There are complex software problems involved in insuring that the updated data from a client is properly posted in both systems.
- Recovery from a failure often requires downtime to update the failed system to the status of the still active system. This increases maintenance downtime [1].

However, until recently, these systems were the only satisfactory solution to data availability issues. But that has changed.

Nowadays, this is another meaning to the term *data availability* that is rapidly growing in significance, and that is data's availability not just to the central system, but to all the other users of that data. No longer are computer systems unitary and located in just one site. They are rapidly becoming collections of systems often located kilometers from each other, all connected together in a mesh or fabric of interconnecting systems that communicate continuously not only with each other, but with the corporate-wide repository of data as well. This has lead to a new paradigm that deals with both sets of data availability issues. It is the Storage Area Network.

THE SAN ....

A new architecture called the SAN was developed in response to the requirements of High Availability of data, scalable growth, and system performance. Not only does it increase the availability of data to the central system, but throughout the enterprise.

SAN employs FC technology to allow innovative ways to protect and distribute important data. The key to a SAN is that large volumes of data can be located independent of any one computer system and yet be available to all that have need of it. The data can also be spread out geographically; it does not need to be all in the same room to have acceptable performance. And as you shall see, there is safety in distance. In addition, the architecture permits both mirrored and RAID configurations of disk storage for the added protection those technologies afford. Redundancy of connectivity is also supported to guard against the errant backhoe operator. And finally, SAN offers data transfers in the gigabit per second range compared with the commonly used SCSI interface that usually connects at 160 megabits to 320 megabits per second.

The SAN architecture can provide new options for reliability in a distributed environment. SAN can greatly lower the cost and improve the scalability of HA solutions, thus enabling a wider range of applications to benefit. Now, let's review a series of possible topologies using SAN architecture to illustrate the SAN's flexibility for HA designs, starting with a small company occupying a single building and proceed up to large corporations with buildings spread all over a city.

The Single Building

The simplest scenario for an HA configuration is one that it is contained in a single building. This arrangement is typical of small companies. The SAN system shown in Figure 18.3 is a simple extension of the redundant system shown in Figure18.2, except all the storage is now Fibre Channel based and thus available to all the systems on the SAN [1]. In this case, both servers are now active, allowing a larger number of clients access.

While external people errors such as the backhoe operator are minimized, other concerns such as catastrophic fire or flood are increased. Loss of the building might cause considerable downtime unless a redundant remote standby site exists. Clearly, there is much to be said for a geographic distribution of such assets.

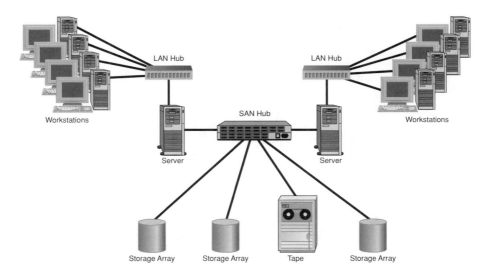

Figure 18.3
A typical SAN system.

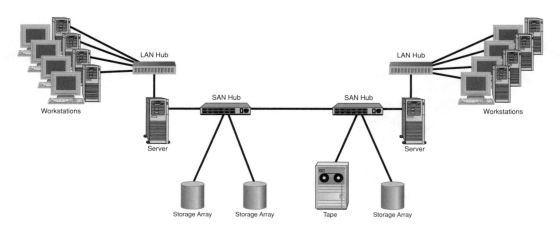

Figure 18.4
The cascaded multiple hub SAN.

However, even here, the individual components of a SAN HA configuration such as shown in Figure 18.4 can be spread out through that building, either on opposite ends of the same floor, or on different floors [1]. However, the cascaded hub design shown in Figure 18.4 is a more typical solution. As shown, various database components are now attached to more than one hub, with the hubs interconnected. This design still permits all clients equal access to all components in the database, while still offering some residual capability even if one of the hubs is destroyed.

The Campus Cluster

The cascaded hub SAN also has an application in the campus cluster. A campus cluster is usually found in medium-sized corporations and offers greater protection by using multiple buildings. A campus cluster usually consists of buildings in the same area, often no more than a few hundred meters apart, so employees can walk among the buildings. Most disaster planning could be easily accommodated in this environment. For instance, fire loss is easily contained. And while the errant backhoe operator is now of slightly greater concern, even he can be controlled simply by visual observation of the campus.

However, a second issue arises as the number of clients increase, and that is bandwidth. Even though a Gigabit per second is a very fairly substantial bandwidth, it can be used up with enough clients. The SAN solution to this problem is the area switch as shown in Figure 18.5 [1]. The connection has been replaced between the two hubs in Figure 18.4 with area switches. This device is fairly new, but it promises to revolutionize the design of SANs because unlike Hubs which transmit all the data

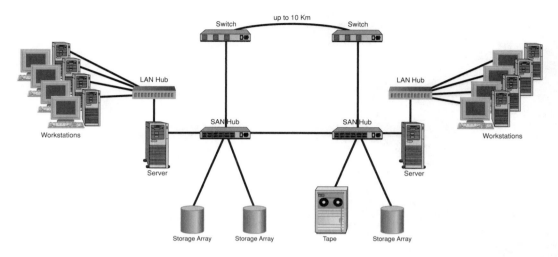

Figure 18.5
The Area Switched SAN.

they receive to the entire SAN, the area switch localizes data transfers whenever possible. Data requested by a local client is kept local and only data requested by a client on the other side of the link is sent across. Since most traffic on any network is local, this greatly reduces data sent needlessly to the remote systems.

An additional feature of the area switch is that the link can be up to 10 kilometers with single mode fiber optics and as much as 30 kilometers with special repeaters. This makes the area switch not only a natural for the campus cluster, but also for the metro cluster as well.

The Metro Cluster

While the campus cluster affords protection from fires, other natural hazards such as earthquake, tornado, and flood could adversely affect an enter campus. Although metro clusters increase the costs of management and interoffice travel, they also reduce risks to most natural hazards.

As noted, the SAN FC technology allows up to 10-kilometer distances, and, with special additional hardware, up to 30 kilometers. And, the use of area switches as shown in Figure 18.6 reduces the traffic between the remote sites to just what is needed [1]. While this provides protection against a greater range of disasters, such as flooding, explosions, and most power outages, there is still that man on the backhoe. Even then, SAN has an answer as shown in Figure 18.6.

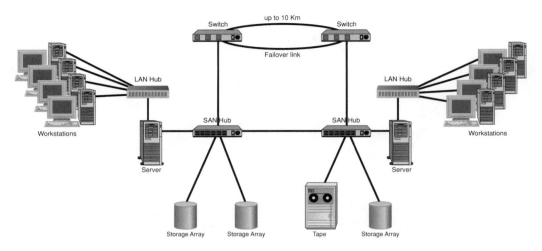

Figure 18.6
The failover area switched SAN.

This configuration is exactly like the one in Figure 18.5 but with the addition of a second fiber optic cable between the two switches [2]. These work in the same manner of failover redundant systems of yesterday but only as far as the cable is concerned. The two switches know that they have two independent cables to use for communications and, therefore, use just one until it fails. Then, they automatically switch to the second. Thus, even the human risks of a metro cluster can easily be contained into acceptable levels of risk.

Finally, in today's global economy, data availability is more important than ever. As enterprises and applications grow, the ability to grow a data infrastructure is critical.

FROM HERE...

This chapter discussed the causes of data unavailability; cost tradeoffs; high availability objectives; and the SAN, including the single building, campus cluster, and metro cluster. The next chapter examines solutions to making SAN work.

END NOTES...

[1] Erik Ottem, "The Role of SANs in High Availability Business Systems," Gadzoox Networks, Inc., 5850 Hellyer Avenue, San Jose, CA 95138, 2001.

[2] John R. Vacca, *The Cabling Handbook (2nd Edition),* Prentice Hall PTR, 2001.

19 SAN Solutions for Considerations

In the storage arena, terms such as *state-of-the-art* haven't been used as often as in other areas of networking technology. When this phrase has been used regarding storage, it was usually referring to a disk with exceptional speed. Today, it can be applied much more often due to the rapid pace at which new, innovative products are being developed.

As previously discussed in earlier chapters, at the center of today's storage area is network storage SANs and NAS. One of the most important components in the new storage paradigm is the networking switch, which is divided into two classes: directors and fabric switches. In the director class, McData, Qlogic (*www.qlogic.com*), and IN-RANGE Technologies (*www.inrange.com/main.php*) are leaders. In the fabric switch area, Brocade Communications (*www.brocade.com*) dominates with a 90% market share, according to IDC.

Caution

URLs are subject to change without notice.

The director-class switch is a high-port-count switch that provides higher reliability than a fabric switch because of its total redundancy, including software redundancy. This was true until Brocade introduced a 64-port fabric switch, the SilkWorm 6400, in October 2000. The SilkWorm 6400 offers impressive reliability based on parameters such as MTBF and MTTR.

Brocade has combined four of its 16-port switches and placed them in a prewired chassis. Previously, high port counts were synonymous with director-class switches that sold for very high prices. For example, QLogic supplies a 32-, 64-, and 128-port SANbox Fibre Channel Director. This switch, in its various configurations, consists of 8-port, hot-swappable, plug-in modules that expand the director to 64 ports per chassis.

Building a 128-port switch requires joining two cabinets with a backplane intercon-nect module. The QLogic 64-port switch costs approximately $250,000; the Brocade SilkWorm 6400 costs $155,000.

Using this modular approach to building Fibre Channel fabric switches, Brocade provides a fabric switch with a port count as high as the monolithic director switches, but at a lower cost. Brocade provides a port count as high as the monolithic director, but at a lower cost (director vendors dispute this). This modular approach demon-strates how storage networking is becoming more like traditional networking in terms of scalability.

Another significant breakthrough is the ratification of the ANSI standard for in-tercommunication between Fibre Channel switches (the ANSI FC-SW-2 standard) in October 2000. It will probably take four to six months for switch vendors to implement it. If the standard functions as intended, users won't have to stick with one vendor when purchasing Fibre Channel switches for their SANs; different vendors' switches will be interoperable, allowing users to take advantage of new technology and lower prices that would be unavailable in the absence of this level of interoperability.

In addition to switches, the controller is another important component of net-work storage, and state-of-the-art in this arena means providing for multiprotocol data movement. For example, Troika Networks' (*www.troika.com*) Zentai controller per-mits three different protocols—Virtual Interface (VI) Architecture, SCSI, and IP—to operate simultaneously over the same wire.

This feature consolidates multiple functions onto one network and offloads data traffic from the LAN during backup operations. The controller also creates a high-availability environment through its dynamic multipathing capability, and eliminates any single point of failure with server clustering. Hitachi uses the Zentai controller in its flagship Lightning 9900 storage array system.

In the storage array category, the Hitachi Data Systems (HDS) Lightning 9900 (*www.hds.com*) is one of the most innovative products on the market. Rather than just an upgrade that replaces a few components (such as chips and buses), the 9900 is a completely new design. Hitachi changed the system from the industry-standard bus architecture to a crossbar-switch architecture, which resulted in an internal bandwidth of 6.4 Gbps—the highest bandwidth of any storage data array currently available. In addition, seek times were reduced to 5.7 milliseconds (ms) for read operations and 6.5 ms for write operations.

EMC (*www.emc.com*) focuses on integrating existing hardware into an ESN (*www.enterprisestoragegroup.com*) in both its high-end Symmetrix line and its midrange Clariion line. In practical terms, EMC has combined NAS and SAN tech-nologies, viewing them as complementary, rather than competing, approaches.

EMC also has midrange storage arrays in its Clariion line, and uses Clariion as an edge technology and Symmetrix as the core technology of an ESN. EMC uses the ESN concept to pursue business in specific vertical markets. For example, the company uses a combination of NAS and SAN technologies to pursue the media distribution market. The company uses NAS technology, in the form of its Celerra server, in conjunction with Symmetrix-based SANs for this application.

The ESN concept is put to use by the Shoah Foundation, a nonprofit organization founded by Steven Spielberg to educate people on the Holocaust by providing them with videotaped testimonies of Holocaust survivors. Located in Los Angeles, the foundation has a library of videotapes stored on a Symmetrix-based SAN and served to the viewer by means of a Celerra File Server that feeds a group of kiosks at the foundation's home base. The foundation has deployed Symmetrix storage, Celerra, and kiosks in sites throughout the world, all of which connect over a WAN to the main site in Los Angeles. If a visitor to a remote site cannot find a particular videotape at that site, he or she can order the tape directly from the main library and have it delivered over the WAN to the remote-location kiosk.

Compaq Computer, Dell Computer, IBM, Sun Microsystems (*www.sun.com*), Hewlett-Packard (*www.hp.com*), and XIOtech (*www.xiotech.com*) also have recent product advances. Of these vendors, Compaq has progressed most in closing the gap with EMC. Since 1999, the company convinced many IT executives that it could deliver software functionality equivalent to that of EMC with its SANworks storage management suite. Compaq acquired the storage assets of Digital Equipment and developed software that can compete with anything in this industry. Compaq offers data replication, remote copy, and virtualization software (software that permits the establishment of a storage pool in a heterogeneous environment that can be divided and allocated to specific servers on demand); in short, all of the software that EMC offers.

Its most recent introduction is a SAN appliance called VersaStor, a dedicated server that provides virtualization and management within a SAN. The VersaStor implementation of virtualization uses asymmetrical pooling (in other words, the virtualization box is not in the data path). With VersaStor's asymmetrical pooling, there is no single point of failure at the storage pool level and no inherent latency is introduced.

Dell competes effectively in the midrange of the SAN market with its Power Vault line. It offers a very affordable SAN (around $200,000 for one terabyte) and, through its storage appliance (an OEM version of a box from StorageApps), it delivers most, if not all, of the functionality of EMC's Symmetrix system at a much lower price—$50,000. The company delivers a 1.5 TB SAN with high-end functionality for $250,000, compared to $1.5 million for a comparable Symmetrix-based SAN from EMC or $500,000 for a comparable Compaq SAN.

IBM (*www.ibm.com*) is betting its future in the SAN marketplace on its Shark disk array, formally known as the Enterprise Storage Server, Models F10 and F20.

Model F10 offers a maximum storage capacity of 1.68 TB, 8 TB, or 16 TB of cache, and up to 16 Fibre Channel ports. Model F20 offers a maximum storage capacity of 11.2 TB, 8 TB, or 16 TB of cache, and up to 16 Fibre Channel ports. Additionally, the Enterprise Storage Server offers flash copy, remote copy, and extended remote copy software.

Sun Microsystems lost its way early in the SAN revolution and is also trying to get back in the race with its Sun StorEdge T3 array. The T3 has a wide capacity range (from 162 GB to 88 TB). Armed with the T3, a competitive software set, a new storage appliance for management, and an alliance with VERITAS (*www.veritas.com*), Sun plans to provide both midrange and high-end systems.

Hewlett-Packard is another giant that faltered in the SAN era. It formerly resold the EMC Symmetrix line, but discontinued that relationship about 18 months ago. It replaced Symmetrix with the Hitachi Freedom line and is reselling the Hitachi 7700e and 9900 Lightning as the HP XP256 and XP512, respectively. These arrays, complemented with numerous software products, provide the basis for Hewlett-Packard's midrange and high-end SAN offerings. Hewlett-Packard has established a new division that integrates its storage, networking, and software operations.

XIOtech, a wholly owned subsidiary of Seagate, offers high-end SAN features for around $250,000. XIOtech offers virtualization across multiple Magnitude data arrays in a SAN. XIOtech Magnitude-based SANs feature functionality such as replication and easy-to-use management tools for $200,000.

Despite several impressive technological developments in the field of storage, some storage management functions that proved troublesome in the past continue to plague users today. For example, the backup function still poses a difficult problem for today's users. Because of serverless backup's potential ability to solve the backup problem, it may be the most important development in storage.

The importance of backup is also reflected in the efforts of storage software vendors to solve problems in this space. VERITAS' Vertex Initiative is this vendor's focus on backup development. This effort consists of snapshot technology that eliminates the backup window and minimizes recovery time.

VERITAS' ServerFree Agent, working with NetBackup 4.0, provides the snapshot technology and combines it with server-free data movement for SANs. Phase one of this initiative includes software snapshot, hardware snapshot, and SAN snapshot solutions. In the software snapshot category, VERITAS offers two products: NetBackup FlashBackup and VERITAS for Oracle Advanced BLI agent. In the hardware snapshot category, the company offers NetBackup for EMC Symmetrix and NetBackup for HP XP256. In the SAN snapshot area, VERITAS offers NetBackup ServerFree Agent, which is used with NetBackup 4.0.

Legato (*www.legato.com*) and Computer Associates (*www.ca.com*) also have serverless backup products that use agent technology. The agent basically creates a snapshot of the file system or database the user wants to back up, directs the snapshot file system to copy directly from disk to tape, and keeps the backup software informed about what happens.

If vendors deliver on their claims, they could really have something. It's not certain yet that you can do the *outboard backup* things yet, which are being announced and promised as wonderful. But if it's there, it's certainly state-of-the-art.

A major barrier to widespread acceptance of SANs has been the cost of the hardware and SAN software applications. In addition, the SAN has never really delivered on its promise of interoperability in a truly heterogeneous environment.

The storage appliance reduces SAN application costs and, through virtualization, allows the SAN to function in a heterogeneous environment. The virtualization provided by the storage appliance makes the Fibre Channel SANs usable in a true heterogeneous environment—both heterogeneous operating systems and heterogeneous storage.

StorageApps (*www.storageapps.com*) is the current leader in this space with its SANLink SAN Appliance. The SANLink appliance (a dedicated server that performs virtualization and management within a SAN) supports data mirroring, snapshot, and virtualization, and provides security through LUN mapping and masking.

Note

A LUN is a unique identifier located on a SCSI bus that enables the management software to differentiate among multiple devices. It performs all of these functions at a cost of $50,000, as opposed to $100,000 or more for some so-called high-end systems.

In addition, the SANLink appliance reduces costs by simplifying SAN management and allowing users to build more elaborate SANs using their existing storage equipment. Other SAN appliance vendors include Compaq, Sun Microsystems, StoreAge, DataCore Software, VERITAS, and Vicom (*www.vicom.com*).

Another significant addition to SAN technology is the use of optical technology to extend the distance covered by a SAN in metropolitan areas. Using optical technologies such as Wavelength Division Multiplexing (WDM) and Dense WDM (DWDM), vendors extended the distance over which storage data is transported to 120 kilometers.

Fibre Channel switch vendors and service providers, such as StorageNetworks (*www.storagenetworks.com*) found it necessary to extend the distance over which they could transport data in metropolitan areas (see sidebar, "Gap Bridging"). This need arose primarily because of customer desire to transport data to disaster-recovery sites in outlying areas. For example, in New York City, brokerage firms and other financial services companies have been shipping their data, on tape and by truck, from Manhattan to disaster-recovery or business-continuance centers in New Jersey for years.

GAP BRIDGING

As SSPs gain more and larger customers, the complexity of the problems they are asked to solve grows proportionately. Sometimes, SSPs must use technologies not initially considered when SANs were first devised.

Such was the case when StorageNetworks began to receive requests from some of its large New York customers for the capability to transport data from their Manhattan data centers to facilities in New Jersey. For years, these customers relied on manual methods to ship data to New Jersey as part of their disaster-recovery plans. In other cases, customers wanted a business-continuance plan in the event of an outage.

The metro optical ring that StorageNetworks implemented with ONI Systems equipment goes from New York City through the Lincoln Tunnel to Weehauken, south to Jersey City, and back to New York City through the Holland Tunnel. The network links Storage Networks' SANs, located at Exodus colocation facilities in each of these cities. This optical MAN permits StorageNetworks to expand capacity and provide services such as replication, remote backup, and disaster recovery for customers in Manhattan.

StorageNetworks is deploying similar optical metropolitan networks in other cities throughout the country. Other SSPs will follow suit.

With the advent of SSPs, these customers wanted to take advantage of SANs to perform this operation electronically rather than physically. One problem: The enabling Fibre Channel technology didn't allow data to traverse the required distances. Optical MANs helped solve this problem.

Another SSP problem that optical MANs help solve is the SSPs' need for more space. SSPs initially purchased space in the form of *pods* in colocation facilities, such as those owned by Exodus. As their business expanded, many SSPs found that the space around them had been taken up. Optical extenders (optical networking components such as DWD multiplexers) provided an easy means of accomplishing this expansion because they could go over required distances to other locations where facilities could be built out. The SSPs, in turn, were able to provide their end-user customers with a *virtual pod* to meet their storage requirements.

Three major vendors in this market are ONI Systems (*www.oni.com/home.jsp*), ADVA Optical Networking (*www.advaoptical.com/adva_home.asp?ID=2*), and Nortel Networks (*www.nortelnetworks.com/index.html*). ONI Systems is relatively new to the SAN space, but has forged alliances with several companies, including Brocade, EMC, and Compaq. ONI has deployed a metro optical ring for an SSP called StorageNetworks (see sidebar, "Gap Bridging").

ADVA has been in the optical networking market since 1997, but is relatively new to the SAN extender space. The company purchased SANs in February 2000 and has allied itself with some major storage and networking vendors. ADVA supplies EMC with optical equipment for internal use and partners with it to solve distance-extension problems for SANs. Working with Verizon and INRANGE, ADVA has deployed a number of optical MANs.

Nortel is the market leader in both the DWDM long-haul and metro markets, according to the Dell'Oro Group (*www.dell.com/us/en/gen/default.htm*), an independent consultancy. Nortel works with such partners as Brocade, Compaq, EMC, HDS, IBM, and QLogic. Nortel has applied its experience in optical networking to the SAN extension problem with its OPTera Metro 5200 Multiservice Platform. Initially, Nortel plans to focus on the SSP market.

Industry analysts expect optical MANs to become more ubiquitous in the SAN space, as more SSPs begin to supply storage services in metropolitan areas—and as more corporations begin to modernize their backup- and disaster-recovery procedures over distances via SANs.

According to Enterprise Storage Group, storage over IP is one of the two most significant recent developments in the storage field (the other being virtualization made possible by storage appliances). The reason that storage over IP is an important technology, is that it's ultimately going to enable users to have a choice between building storage networks on an Ethernet infrastructure that they already have, or building a separate storage network based on Fibre Channel. Up until now, there has been no choice for users (they had to build a Fibre Channel-based storage network).

Storage-over-IP systems offer a number of advantages: they protect more data than was possible before, deploy more information anywhere, and leverage user investments in existing IP network infrastructures. The major players in this space are Cisco Systems (through its purchase of NuSpeed), SAN Valley (*www.sanvalley.com*), Gadzoox, Nishon, SanCastle (*www.sancastle.com*), Computer Networking Technology (CNT) (*www.cnt.com*), Lucent Technologies (*www.lucent.com*), Entrada, and Pirus (*www.pirus.com*). Cisco (*www.cisco.com*) expects to introduce a storage-over-IP product in January 2002, and Lucent expects to follow suit shortly thereafter. Currently, however, CNT is the most active participant in storage over IP.

CNT has a long history of working with IBM on ESCON channel extenders for the S/390 and its predecessor mainframes, and this experience paid off when the company was called upon to provide similar capabilities for SANs. Since 1997, CNT has evolved into working with large storage vendors and offering solutions for remote disk mirroring, remote tape, and virtual tape. CNT has worked with Compaq (*www.compaq.com*) to provide Fibre Channel over ATM and has successfully tested this solution over long distances.

CNT works with EchoStar Communications/DISH Network, a direct broadcast satellite television company. Using a phased approach, EchoStar deployed a SAN based on CNT's UltraNet Open Systems Director technology. In phase one, the company began using the CNT SAN for server consolidation. In phases two and three, EchoStar will perform remote disk mirroring and remote tape vaulting over its existing IP infrastructure. In phase one of the SAN deployment, EchoStar experienced a 500% improvement in backup speed.

For its data replication over IP solution, CNT is working with EMC and Compaq. EMC supplies the data replication software, which creates images of storage data between storage systems by means of Symmetrix Remote Data Facility (SRDF). SRDF contains the intelligence to implement data mirroring's copy/recovery.

To deliver the SRDF over IP, CNT's UltraNet Storage Director software converts SRDF data frames to IP packets. This results in data transport with increased reliability and scalability. CNT has a similar relationship with Compaq, in which it uses its UltraNet Storage Director with Compaq's Data Replication Manager (DRM, the equivalent of SRDF) for remote mirroring. For remote backup/recovery over IP, CNT is working with VERITAS' NetBackup product and its own UltraNet Storage Director to provide remote backup/restore and disaster-recovery solutions.

With the many innovations brought about by storage networking (SAN and NAS), the term *state-of-the-art* is becoming commonplace. And the result of these innovations has been a true paradigm shift in the way storage is used. Storage and its management no longer play a minor role in computing; rather, in many cases, storage networking supplies solutions to many of today's most pressing problems—how to accomplish backups in a 24×7 environment; how to ensure 100% uptime; how to increase performance; and how to control computing costs amid explosive growth.

So far, storage technology is keeping pace with the staggering growth in computing. Based on the imaginative solutions that vendors have introduced so far, there is every reason to believe that new solutions will continue to emerge to meet the aforementioned needs for at least the next few years.

Nevertheless, whether you are implementing a SAN solution today or are looking towards the future, what are the solutions to making a SAN work? The next part of the chapter looks at various solutions via a SAN architecture that makes a SAN work.

SOLUTIONS TO MAKING A SAN WORK ....

As previously explained, a SAN is a high-speed subnet that establishes a direct connection between heterogeneous storage resources and servers. One can think of a
SAN as an extended and shared storage bus. SANs liberate storage devices, so they
are not on any one particular server bus, and attach them directly on the network via
network processors. The result is a SAN architecture that makes all storage devices
accessible to all servers within the network. This sharing of components is an alternative to expensive investments in additional equipment and eliminates the bottleneck
between the server and storage (see Figure19.1) [1]. At the same time, it is increasing
efficiencies and allowing more megabytes into the pipe. The following are solutions
(or ways) to make SAN work:

- The way to get gigabit speed (100 MBps), highly reliable, managed server-to-storage connectivity
- The way to build an easily scalable, multiterabyte storage network—never
  before possible
- The way to deploy high availability server/storage clusters and free up
  your LAN from lengthy backup tasks by moving it onto the SAN [1]

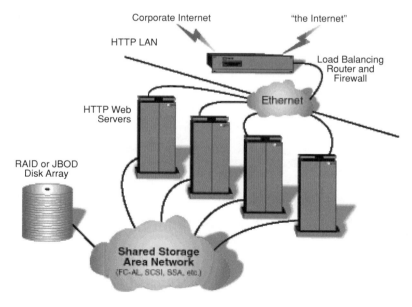

Figure 19.1
The sharing of components.

Making SAN Work

SANs or Storage Area Networks are getting a lot of people talking. Unfortunately many of those talking like SUN, IBM, HP, StorageWorks, and MTI would have us believe that a SAN is some sort of *Magic Sauce* that they have secretly concocted that no one else knows how to replicate. And, if you just buy their *Magic Sauce,* the big dream of sharing data and storage easily and economically will be yours.

Vendors say that they actually manufacture from scratch all of the myriad hardware and software pieces that make up the storage evolution that is SANs. They would have us believe that they

- Are masters at everything.
- Have mastered the art of SAN-enabling management software for byte level file locking.
- Have designed, built, tested, and shipped three to four generations of intelligent Fibre Channel hubs or switches.
- Have done the same for Fibre Channel Host Bus Adapter cards.
- Manufacture their own RAID controllers, backplanes, power supplies, cables [6], drives, fans, LEDs, touchscreens, and drive chassis.
- Somehow *branded* their own products as being better than anyone else's and that if you do not buy their bag of goods nothing else will work.
- Have made their's more expensive because you are paying for brand name and service (read: marketing and huge profits). Of course, that's why they have such huge profits [1].

Nevertheless, the aforementioned is not the best way to provide solutions to a fast growing, value-adding business in today's web-centric world. The days of monolithic corporations telling us that they have all the answers, as we follow blindly like sheep, are over. The Internet has leveled the playing field. It has created more rags to riches stories and success than the corporate world ever did. On the Internet, everyone has the opportunity to have more—more information, more choices, more time, and more power.

So, why all the ranting on about the beauty and power of the Internet, and how does this all relate back to your companies need for a better solution for your data and web applications? How can this help your company grow? Simple: More. More information, more choices, more time, and more power.

ENTERPRISE SAN SOLUTIONS ....

Providing a range of preconfigured and customized solutions is the theme of this part of the chapter. Now, let's look at how IBM offers a SAN portfolio that is designed to meet your storage needs today—and well into the future. For example, the following portfolio offers:

SAN Solutions for Consolidation: Improve asset utilization, lower your operating costs by centralizing capital and people. Automatically reallocate storage resources as your business needs dictate.

SAN Solutions for Data Protection: Free up your server cycles, offload your data network, provide mission-critical backup, and better utilize your storage resources.

SAN Solutions for Sharing: Increase network response time, improve your hardware and software utilization, reduce data duplication, and improve information availability.

SAN Solutions for Disaster Tolerance: A strategy that can easily and flexibly accommodate your business as it evolves.

SAN Solutions for Consolidation

If your business is like most, your distributed enterprise is populated with fragmented storage environments. As a result, storage capacity is often underutilized, and reallocating or reconfiguring storage resources often causes both disruptions and downtime. How do you improve asset utilization, lower operating costs by centralizing capital and people, and automatically reallocate storage resources as your business needs dictate? It's simple.

The Power of SANs

Storage area networks offer a powerful solution for consolidating storage resources to boost storage management, flexibility, and cost effectiveness (see Figure 19.2) [2]. Serving as an indispensable part of every business e-infrastructure, SANs link multiple storage systems and servers over a secure, high-speed network that is data (rather than server) centric. They enable storage devices, such as tape libraries and disk arrays, to be shared. They improve data availability, reduce downtime costs, can significantly decrease management and administrative costs, and improve asset utilization. Simply put, SANs are the leading storage infrastructure for the world of e-business and beyond.

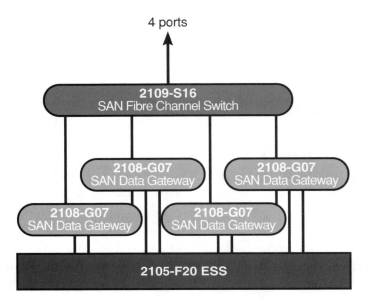

Figure 19.2
Enterprise—SAN solution for consolidation.

The SAN Revolution

Recognizing the need to consolidate the multiple, isolated islands of storage in today's environment, IBM was one of many vendors who pioneered the SAN solution for "consolidation family" (see sidebar, "Consolidation"). These powerful offerings of products and services reduce the costs and risks of deploying a SAN-based storage consolidation strategy in your enterprise.

CONSOLIDATION

IBM's Netfinity server and storage consolidation steps:

- Allocate and reallocate disk chunks to specific servers without rebooting the system—a real value when IS resources are tight.

- Share storage resources in a clustered and nonclustered environment across multiple servers in diverse locations.

- Back up data from server to tape to reduce backup time, minimize LAN disruption, improve performance of the LAN, and maintain availability of applications and data for the end user.

- Implement existing Netfinity servers and storage products without having to replace the technology.

- Enjoy the benefits of fibre technology in a tape environment by maintaining a high level of performance over long distances (up to 10 km) and implementing better disaster protection with automatic tape backup in remote locations.

- An industry-standard solution that interoperates with the major tape backup software applications.

- Allows centralized management of backup operations.

- This Netfinity SAN configuration is a template for consolidation [2].

The SAN Solutions provide better utilization of storage resources, resulting in improved productivity. They also enable IT managers to more effectively monitor and manage data growth.

SAN Smart Paks for Consolidation

Each SAN solution consists of two main parts. First is an interoperability-tested template that provides a starting point for creating a customized solution designed to satisfy your unique requirements. Second is a set of service offerings that includes a SAN assessment to help tune the solution, as well as implementation services to ensure a quick, smooth deployment.

Recognizing that one size does not fit all, the SAN solution family of solutions offers a comprehensive range of network and storage options to best suit your needs. By deploying a SAN Smart Pak for Consolidation, you are not only leveraging SAN technology to solve critical IT challenges, but you also are investing in a scalable, flexible storage infrastructure, an Enterprise SAN, that will support your on-demand business growth today and tomorrow.

Controlling Who's Got Access

A SAN's any-to-any connectivity enables multihost access to a centrally managed pool of storage, providing better management, flexibility, and cost effectiveness. Sharing storage is one thing, but sharing storage securely is another. In order to prevent multiple hosts from clobbering each other's storage, a mechanism is needed to control access to the physical storage itself. And customers have choices, depending on the level of control needed. Channel zoning is a function provided by Fibre Channel switches that creates virtual point-to-point connections between servers and storage ports. Zoning cannot, however, limit access to individual logical units, or LUNs. For example, if more granular access is required, then LUN masking is available in selected disk systems such as the IBM Enterprise Storage Server and the storage partition feature of the FASt500 Fibre Channel Storage Subsystem. LUN masking filters all available storage from the hosts except for those portions (LUNs) specified by the administrator.

SAN Solution for Data Protection

As the value of strategic information rises, so too does the value of fast, reliable backup (see sidebar, "Enterprise Backup Solution"). In today's nonstop business environment, solving this escalating storage challenge is critical to ongoing success. How do you free up server cycles, offload your data network, provide mission-critical backup, and better utilize expensive storage resources? It's simple.

ENTERPRISE BACKUP SOLUTION

This sidebar describes data flow in an Enterprise backup solution and how it is affected by the introduction of SAN technology. The specific intent is to describe the use and function of LAN-free SAN technology and Server-free backups in an Enterprise backup solution to reduce backup windows and improve data throughput.

Enterprise Backup

The goal of Enterprise SAN backup operations is to address the decreasing windows of opportune time and the increasing magnitude of data to be managed within a limited time frame. In the last ten years, almost every enterprise has seen at least a ten-fold increase in data volume in the enterprise. Some web companies have seen data growth as high as 50 GB in a single six-month period. At the same time, opportune times for backup are being further constrained by the change in enterprise business hours. There have also been changes in the types of businesses moving data, such as e-commerce [5] and Internet-based enterprises that require differing hours of operation than many traditional businesses. Additionally, as the global economy becomes pervasive, an enterprise's international operations drive access requirements around the clock. Also, things as simple as the way you view computers have changed your data availability requirements. Enterprise personnel who would have never used a computer five years ago are now storing volumes of data that must be accessed at ever increasing business hours. Digital data, whether traditional computer data, image, or sound, is proliferated at rates that exceed the bandwidth of traditional backup means by large margins. Backups have always been recognized as a critical part of data center operations, but how do you continue backups without affecting your enterprise operations in light of these growing concerns? Many years ago, IT organizations began battling these problems by dedicating backup servers to performing CPU and I/O intensive enterprise backups, or often by creating a completely separate LAN just for backup traffic to reduce the ever-growing volume on the corporate LAN. Inevitably, IT departments have had to spend many man-hours tracing throughput bottlenecks as these backup solutions have grown more and more complex.

All these events have caused IT managers to look for a cost-effective solution that meets the needs of the enterprise's growing data volume and decreasing time windows. What is really needed is a giant leap in technology, a method of doing backups without using a LAN and I/O intensive *window*. SAN technology allows the Enterprise to fully leverage the utility and bandwidth of the automated library and tape drives they have already invested in and provide for maximum efficiency in accessing all of the drives in the library. The goal is to *free* the LAN from backup traffic. To demonstrate how backup methods have evolved, let's look at the scenarios that follow.

Throughput Issues

Enterprises long ago began doing backups through a scheme of tape drives attached directly to machines that served as application servers. This solution provided excellent throughput, but the growing volume of data and need for increasing data availability quickly showed this solution's limits in scalability. This schema also shows another weakness. As data volume grows, the I/O intensive *window* must increase. A very simple backup scenario is depicted in Figure 19.3 with only three Application Servers [3]. This example depicts one of the simplest backup schemes that you could have. Each server in this scheme must be directly attached through a SCSI chain to a number of tape drives, in this case two. Since the slowest element is the tape drive, the server's throughput will be the aggregate bandwidth of these two drives. To increase throughput, you would theoretically add tape drives. Since 1/2-inch tape drives and DLT both have a theoretical burst bandwidth limit of about 7 to 10 MBps, you are now certain that the SCSI bus can handle higher throughputs than just two tape drives. When backing up the three servers themselves, you will get pretty good throughput with a schema like this (on the order of about 14 to 20 MBps burst rate for two tape drives). You will also have pretty good functionality and connectivity. You can back up more than one server at a time, but the tape drives are always associated with the same server. Backing up to a drive attached to another server would be impossible without using the enterprise LAN. Also, since our robot is almost full of drives, what happens when we add new servers? Also, you cannot recable this scenario easily if you decide that one server needs more tape drives than another to handle an increase in data. Even when building a small scenario like this, you can look back and see how the direction of enterprise data over the last ten years would have affected this scheme. The growing number of business hours means that you have a smaller amount of time (or no time) to use the application servers in order to back up their data. In addition, as your data volume grows, adding servers would prove expensive and would interfere with your increasing business hours. You will probably have used up most of your drive slots in the robot, and reducing the number of drives per server would cut your throughput almost in half. The next obvious step was to use the enterprise LAN as a transportation method, as depicted in the second scenario as shown in Figure 19.4 [3].

A few years ago data volume was lower and LAN pipes seemed to have huge amounts of bandwidth that you'd never be able to use. When the time came to choose how best to dedicate more bandwidth to your ever-growing data problems, it seemed obvious to simply use the enterprise LAN. You could then dedicate machines to being solely backup servers and remove the direct connections to your application servers. Unfortunately, in doing this, you are using CPU and I/O cycles on the application server, pushing data across a LAN at about 17 MBps (For ATM OC-3), and using CPU and I/O bandwidth on a backup server in order to move the data further across a SCSI bus to your tape drives at a burst rate of about 14 to 20 MBps. During this process, you may also be taking CPU cycles and bandwidth from one or more network routers sitting between the application server and the backup server. You may also be reducing the bandwidth available on the LAN to the application servers to move data to clients. Also, even though you may have a fast, expensive LAN pipe such as OC-3, its high overhead does not let you reach your highest burst rate on the tape drives, essentially throttling your throughput on your backup server. Even though you may have purchased extra hardware for use as the backup servers and increased the amount of hardware which successful backups were dependent on, sadly you probably have not really solved your problems. Not only do you have more data now than you had five years ago, but the Enterprise's *data movement* capacity is limited to the bandwidth of a congested enterprise LAN. However, with SCSI's cabling technology, it was impossible to alleviate your throughput issues by dynamically attaching the tape drives without the use of the LAN. You are probably also limited in your ability to do simultaneous backups on multiple machines, because your LAN pipe is being stretched to its limits even with relatively new technology for your LAN backbone. To support your growing data volume, today you are forced to wait for faster data pipes to emerge on the mainstream market, such as gigabit Ethernet. Even then, you cannot be sure that the protocol overhead will allow you to get the throughput you need from your backup servers using newer LAN technology. This probably added to your expense in tape drives, more memory, or more CPU for your backup server to increase bandwidth and make for a relatively complicated future for your backups. Your average amount of man-hours spent troubleshooting bottleneck issues has probably increased, which also increases your IT budget with this scheme. In addition, with your decreasing business hours, you have even less time (or no time) to put all of these issues together to try to make everything work together for a successful backup of critical data.

Direction Of Data Management

Fortunately, SAN technology is now providing you with new answers for these issues. If data trends continue, you will be able to predict that your data volume will continue to increase tremendously. The first thought when addressing a data management problem like this might be that you need more speed or throughput. On the contrary, LAN pipes, SCSI technology, and CPU power are increasing in speed, but that does not necessarily mean that your volume of data will not also increase. It also does not mean that you will be able to do backups without using business processing and I/O time. Instead, let's consider an increase in *connectivity*. LAN-free backup solutions allow all tape drives to be dynamically attached to any Fibre Channel attached machine at any time, creating a new concept occasionally referred to as *moveable bandwidth*. This has the effect of reducing the backup layers to a single layer that is a Fibre Channel attachment capable of up to 100 MBps per link

(200 MBps full duplex). Scalability in a LAN-free solution, like a network attachment, becomes an issue of simply putting a Host Bus Adapter (HBA) in the machine and attaching it to the SAN Network. Throughput becomes simply a matter of tape drive throughput and scheduling for the backup. Tape drives can be moved dynamically from machine to machine, reducing idle time. This also reduces the total number of drives needed to get the same throughput, since your drives are being used on multiple machines. Data is also moved off the Enterprise LAN, eliminating worries of saturating data-serving LANs. New functionality is also added, such as the possibility of redundant connections to tape and disk, increasing backup reliability.

Now, let's revisit the issues just talked about in the preceding—using your new example: all five servers can share the bandwidth of the tape drives dynamically as shown in Figure 19.5. The software administrator controls bandwidth allocation. If one server has twice as much to backup as the others, then bandwidth can be increased on that machine by allocating more tape drives to it. If you assume that you will not backup more than two servers simultaneously, then in this example you would have two *spare* drives. You could dynamically allocate four in any combination to any of the servers backing up. This means that you already have enough tape drives to begin scaling your system without reducing bandwidth at all. If backup window reduction is your main concern, you can backup three machines simultaneously to two drives each or all five to five drives (leaving one spare for high availability), and you have almost eliminated your backup *window*. More importantly, you can change your mind at any time without having to recable the solution. Also, you no longer have to work with a bus that is half-duplex. You can both send and receive data simultaneously making SCSI a much more efficient protocol over fibre channel. You have at least 100 MBps of bandwidth that you can use for both send and receive. You will almost certainly not be able to use the full 200 MBps, but these two factors still help to increase your throughput which means that the tape drives will be able to reach their burst rate more often and sustain their burst rate for longer periods of time. You no longer have to direct traffic through one overutilized server and network link, and removing the backup traffic from the Enterprise LAN allows improved data movement from the application servers across the LAN while backups are executing. In addition to increasing the speed of your backups, you have regained all of the benefits of the first solution without having to sacrifice the scalability that the first solution lacked. You will be able to effectively cope with your increasing data volume, and the number of critical business hours that you use to do backups has decreased. This is not the perfect solution, however. What about data centers that must run around the clock and do not have *any* nonbusiness hours with which to do backups?

The next step in SAN LAN-free backups will be implementing the new standard for a SCSI Extended Copy command that has emerged. As software that supports the new Extended Copy becomes available, external disk array devices will be able to move data in blocks directly from the array to tape, bypassing completely any CPU and I/O cycles on the application servers. Since the data will no longer be moving across the enterprise LAN or be using CPU cycles on application servers, this will effectively eliminate the need to use nonbusiness hours to do backups.

With this knowledge, if you would like to add more optional components, then you could add one or two RAID arrays to hold the data from the application servers. Now that you can see the storage as a separate entity (with upcoming functionality that storage can be replicated to a second disk array), you can also backup one array using Extended Copy commands while the other continues serving data to the application servers. Data movement will occur directly from the array to the drives in the robot without using CPU or I/O cycles on the application servers. And since you do not have any conceptual length limit on Fibre Channel cabling, you can put the replicated disk array in any location that you can run a dedicated cable to. Your data volume can be allowed to increase to the capacity of the array without affecting your ability to do backups. Furthermore, you should no longer be concerned with data backup, since the backing up of data should not interfere with your production data. These two RAID arrays do not, however, replace the functionality of the backup utility. You could not search archives of data to find a deleted file without the tape solution. Instead, you've added functionality. Now, you will not only have a tape archival service running independent of your enterprise data, but you also will have a disaster recovery method that can be implemented within minutes of a fatal loss of hardware.

In today's IT environment, it's critical to be able to handle your increases in the volume of digital data in your environment and the reduced number of hours with which that data can be replicated. Replicating your data and providing business assurance only adds volume to your congested enterprise LANs. With Storage Area Networks, you can now remove that data from the enterprise LAN and even remove backups as an application that would run on your congested enterprise servers. Engineered SAN solutions provide IT environments with tested, proven methods of solving the enterprise's common, everyday business needs. Turnkey SAN solutions build on previous technology to make it more flexible and maximize your business investment [3].

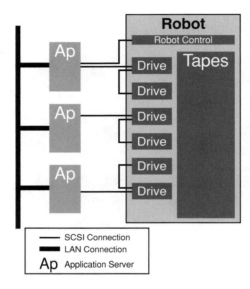

Figure 19.3
Simple backup scenario.

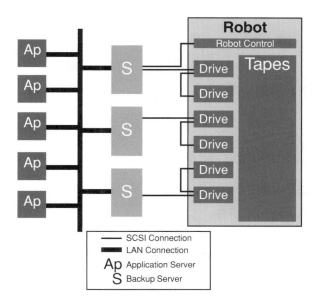

Figure 19.4
Using the enterprise LAN as a transportation method.

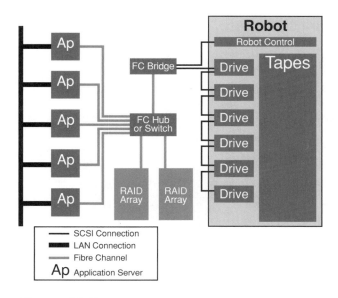

Figure 19.5
All five servers can share the bandwidth of the tape dynamically.

Because SANs provide a dedicated data network, they enable a five to 20 times reduction in backup time. Better yet, industry consultant ITcentrix projects that over time, you'll be able to achieve a sizable reduction (up to 57%) in management costs as you consolidate distributed backup islands, better utilize tape resources, and centrally manage all backup processes from one central location.

The Backup

For example, Tivoli Storage Manager's Tape Resource Pooling feature enables multiple Tivoli Storage Manager servers to share tape drives and libraries in a SAN environment in an automated and secure manner. Rather than having each Tivoli Storage Manager server *own* its own tape device, one of the Tivoli Storage Manager servers acts as the tape manager or traffic cop controlling the mounting, dismounting, and allocation of tape drives to the other requesting Tivoli Storage Manager servers on demand, as required. Tape pooling enables tape resource sharing, as well as provides enhanced automation and improved tape management and security. In addition, by flowing the backup data over the SAN rather than the LAN, backup data is no longer competing for bandwidth with application data on the LAN increasing the responsiveness and performance of the LAN.

So, how do you free up server cycles, offload your data network, provide mission-critical backup and better utilize expensive storage resources? Let's take a look at sidebar, "Data Protection."

DATA PROTECTION

Netfinity SAN with data protection offers the following:

- The benefits of fibre technology in a tape environment by maintaining a high level of performance over long distances (up to 10 km) and implementing better disaster protection with automatic tape backup in remote locations.

- An industry-standard solution that interoperates with the major tape backup software applications.

- A highly scalable SAN building block that allows implementing more robust SAN solutions with additional servers and storage without having to *rip and replace* existing technology investments.

- Allows centralized management of backup operations.

- Allows sharing of tape assets in a clustered and nonclustered environment across multiple servers in diverse locations.

- Back up data from server to tape to reduce backup time, minimize LAN disruption, improve performance of the LAN, and maintain availability of applications and data for the end user.
- When using multi-drive tape libraries, concurrent backups can improve overall efficiency of the system [2].

SAN SOLUTIONS FOR SHARING ....

In today's e-commerce-driven business climate, information is stockpiling at an unprecedented pace. The challenge is not only to store this information, but also to make it available on-demand regardless of who in your enterprise needs it.

Share Storage, File Systems, and Files

For example, Tivoli SANergy File Sharing allows you to share SAN-based storage arrays, file systems, and files across multiple systems simultaneously. Tivoli SANergy File Sharing uses the maturity, security, and inherent sharing abilities of industry-standard LANs and enhances them with high-bandwidth and low-processor overhead of SANs to provide high-performance and heterogeneous file sharing. SANergy File Sharing is unique in that it is based on the standard file systems and network services provided by the operating systems that it supports today (Windows NT, Windows 2000, Windows XP, MacOS, Solaris, Irix, AIX, and Tru-64).

Again, how do you increase network response time, improve hardware and software utilization, reduce data duplication, and improve information availability and data currency? Let's take a look at sidebar, "Sharing."

....

SHARING

Netfinity servers and SANergy solutions provide the following:

The File Sharing of a LAN

- Transparent file sharing
- Full file and byte-range locking
- Robust access control
- Multiplatform Intel server support

The Speed of a SAN

- Shared, centralized storage
- High bandwidth, low latency Fibre Channel
- Direct media access
- Efficient, lightweight protocol

Compatible Open Standards

- Windows NT security with NTFS
- Network-aware application support [2]

SAN SOLUTIONS FOR DISASTER TOLERANCE ....

If you lose access to a key division or enterprise data repository because of a disaster, what does it cost your business short-term and long? In an era when strategic information drives success and business is conducted $24 \times 7 \times 365$, any downtime can be costly or catastrophic. So how do you architect a disaster tolerance strategy with no single point of failure; a strategy that can easily and flexibly accommodate your business as it evolves? Again, it's simple.

Clustering to Achieve True Availability

A cluster is two or more interconnected servers (sometimes called nodes) that create a solution to provide higher availability, higher scalability, or both. The advantage of clustering servers for high availability is seen if one node fails, another node in the cluster can assume the workload of the failed node, and users see no interruption of access. The advantages of clustering servers for scalability include increased application performance and a greater number of users that can be supported. You can think of a cluster of servers as if they were a single, unified computing resource. With the total redundancy of multiple servers, the cluster can help achieve greater system uptime.

Clustering can be implemented at different levels of the system, including hardware, operating systems, middleware, systems management, and applications. The more layers that incorporate clustering technology, the more reliable, scalable, and manageable the cluster.

Finally, how do you architect a disaster tolerance strategy with no single point of failure; a strategy that can easily and flexibly accomodate your business as it evolves? Let's take a look at sidebar "Disaster Tolerance."

Disaster Tolerance

Netfinity cluster with tape pooling includes the following:

- Increase the availability of Windows NT-based applications through managed failover in a clustered environment.

- Add tape storage to a Microsoft Cluster without recertifying the configuration.

- Keep your data and applications highly available for end users in a clustered environment.

- Implement one tape library and share it across multiple servers (shared resources) in a clustered environment.

- Enjoy the benefits of fibre technology in a tape environment by maintaining a high level of performance over long distances (up to 10 km) and implementing better disaster protection with automatic tape backup in remote locations.

- Use an industry-standard solution that interoperates with the major tape backup software applications.

- Allow centralized management of backup operations.

Netfinity Advanced Cluster Enabler for OPS Provides:

- Advantages of the Oracle database for clustering solutions on Microsoft Windows NT for expansive scalabilty, redundancy, and fibre channel data protection.

- A high-availability, highly reliable implementation that allows up to eight clustered servers to share disk storage.

- Better, more balanced performance of the disk subsystem with 100 MBps throughput per channel.

- The benefits of fibre technology by maintaining a high level of performance over long distances (up to 10 km) and implementing better disaster protection.

- A highly scalable SAN building block that allows implementing more robust SAN solutions with additional servers and storage without having to *rip and replace* existing technology investments.

Legato Remote Mirroring Extensions for MSCS

- Eliminates a potential single point of data failure.
- Helps ensure data integrity.

- Allows MSCS clustered servers to be in different locations.
- Provides a mirrored disk configuration while eliminating the need for a shared disk.
- Allows proactive monitoring of server uptime.
- Can reduce total cost of clustered server ownership [2].

STORAGE MANAGEMENT SOLUTIONS: THE VISION ..

Today's business environment is undergoing tremendous change. Effective management of digital information is becoming the key to successful competition and continued growth. The storage industry is responding with the rapid-fire introduction of new technologies that all promise to fix your problems. These technologies include Fibre Channel interconnects; Fibre Channel hubs; switches and bridges; the SAN topology; new magnetic disk and tape recording formats and densities; new file systems; new data fingerprinting and reduction techniques; meta-data controllers; resource sharing; and even data sharing. In total, these pieces combine to form what is called the *Information Grid.*

The Information Grid revolution carries with it extraordinary possibilities. It also comes with significant challenges. The Information Grid is full of emerging technologies providing storage management solutions to confidently deploy, access, share, and protect information.

HOLO-VISION STORAGE MANAGEMENT SOLUTIONS OF THE FUTURE ....

Finally, for all of their digital sophistication, CD-ROMs, hard drives, DVDs, and all other computer storage media share one trait with the tin foil cylinder that Thomas Edison first used to capture his recitation of *Mary Had a Little Lamb.* They all use only their surfaces to record information.

So it's not surprising that holography, with its ability to create and store images in three dimensions, has long been seen as a way to create high-capacity, but physically compact, systems for digital storage. A system that could store information throughout a disk, from top to bottom and side to side, could (in theory, at least) hold huge amounts of data. It's a very old idea indeed.

Turning holographic data storage into a product has been a struggle. Decades of research, much of it in the United States and Japan, created systems that lived only in laboratories because they were too costly or too unreliable for the real world.

Hopefully, holographic storage technologies partly developed by Bell Labs will change all that—and Bell Labs may not be alone. Two other research groups that include International Business Machines, Kodak, Lucent Technologies, and other companies, along with several colleges, may also be close to conquering the problems of holographic storage.

For example, a plastic disc, the size of a DVD or CD-ROM, will initially be able to hold roughly 400 gigabytes, enough to store 100 full-length feature films. That capacity could be increased to trillions of bytes (or terabytes) over time. If you think of a CD as a two-bedroom apartment, a terabyte disk would be the entire Empire State Building.

Perhaps the most familiar holograms are the shiny security images on credit cards or the representation of Princess Leia that was shown by R2-D2 in the initial *Star Wars* movie in 1977 [4]. To create a hologram of an object, light from a single laser is split into two beams. Laser light is used because of its uniform wavelength and phase. One beam goes straight to the target, often photographic film, but in this case, a disc. That is the reference beam. The other, known as the signal beam, is usually reflected off the object that is to be transformed into a holographic photograph.

Because pieces of computer data have no physical form that can be photographed, turning them into a hologram requires a preliminary step. The ones and zeroes of the data bits must be turned into black and white squares, using a type of liquid crystal display. That LCD, called a spatial light modulator, displays black and white images of the bits that need to be recorded. The signal beam passes through that display on its way to the disc.

Whether the hologram is being used to record data or an image, the signal beam is modified by what it encounters. When it reaches its target, the modified signal beam collides with the reference beam, causing an interference pattern that is recorded to produce the hologram. To store data, the interference pattern is recorded within a disc containing chemicals that change form in response to light. Before writing the next chunk of data, the system waits for disk to rotate slightly.

One of the biggest problems surrounding early attempts at holographic storage had more to do with materials than physics or computer science. Many of those systems used crystals that reacted to light to create and store data as holograms, but such crystals proved to be both expensive and difficult to work with.

Finding a substitute was not easy. To avoid data errors, the medium had to have a very high optical quality and, above all, be close to perfectly flat. To make things even more difficult, the Bell Labs team was looking for something that could allow discs to be manufactured for about the same cost as a blank DVD.

Eventually, the group produced a plastic composed of two polymers. One creates the transparent and flat base. Suspended within it is a second polymer that reacts to specific colors of laser light.

Of course, the discs are just a small part of the problem. While the materials scientists fiddled with polymers, others working on the project worked on faster ways to transfer data.

Other data discs, like DVDs, CDs, and hard drives, transfer data to computers literally bit by bit. Those drives generally accelerate the process of moving the ones and zeroes of digital information one at a time by spinning more quickly. Some hard disks now run at just under the speed of sound.

To avoid that mechanical complexity, the Bell Labs system takes data from a computer and lumps it into blocks of one million bits apiece. Those chunks, in turn, are what the spatial light modulator displays for the transfer to the hologram. Once the hologram is created, the bits are scattered throughout the disk, which is transparent, in the roughly cylindrical patterns formed by the meeting of the two laser beams.

Since the hologram image reappears only when the two beams realign along an extremely precise point in the disk, the chunks of data can actually overlap without interfering with one another. When the computer needs to restore a specific piece of retrieved data, a digital table of contents spins the disk to the correct position to recreate the required chunk of data. A digital camera within the holographic disk system captures the resulting holographic image and zaps one million bits of data to the computer in a single flash, rather than serving up a feeble string of ones and zeroes. That is fast enough, by Bell Labs' estimate, to download an entire digitized movie in 30 seconds. With a 56 K modem, that would take several days. The super-jumbo discs, holding terabytes, will alter the color and other properties of the laser beam to pack in even more chunks of data.

Cases must be developed to keep the discs absolutely flat. An even slightly warped disc can alter the laser light enough to produce useless patterns rather than tidy holograms.

That is not to say, however, that hologram storage will always rely on spinning disks. Users with storage needs that are not measured in terabytes might be satisfied by tiny cards. You can probably put 20 gigabytes on a postage-stamp size card.

By using lasers developed for DVD drives, full product development would take a few years. The partial sponsorship of the work at Bell Labs by the National Imagery and Mapping Agency, part of the Defense Department, suggests the identity of one potential customer.

Nonetheless, the Pentagon would not be the only user if all worked according to plan. Bell Labs had also been approached by some consumer electronics makers. There are a number of potential consumer applications. High on the list, no doubt, is the military's civilian next-of-kin: gaming.

FROM HERE

This chapter examined solutions on how to make SANs work. The next chapter takes a look at the role of SANs in computer forensics with regards to computer and data storage of evidence collection and forensic analysis.

END NOTES

[1] "SANergy Enables Scalable Web Hosting," Cutting Edge Bridgette Inc., 8191 Center St., La Mesa, CA 91942, 2001.

[2] "IBM SAN Solutions for Consolidation," IBM Corporation, 1133 Westchester Avenue, White Plains, NY 10604, 2001.

[3] Kevin Trotman, "Reducing Enterprise Backup Windows," Storage Area Networks Corporation, 900 W. Castleton Road, Castle Rock, CO 80104, 2001.

[4] John R. Vacca, *Holograms and Holography: Design Techniques and Commercial Applications (with CD-ROM)*, Charles River Media, 2001.

[5] John R. Vacca, *Electronic Commerce: Online Ordering and Digital Money with CDROM, 3rd Edition*, Charles River Media, 2001.

[6] John R. Vacca, *The Cabling Handbook, 2nd Edition*, Prentice Hall PTR, 2001.

20 Role of SANs in Computer Forensics

Forensic computing is the science of capturing, processing, storing, and investigating data from computers using a methodology whereby any evidence discovered is acceptable in a court of law. Imaging on the other hand is the process used by police and law enforcement agencies in the United States, United Kingdom, Europe, and around the world to secure and store computer evidence. Imaging is an evidentially sound method of making a perfect duplicate of computer media and has the advantage of being system independent. The case for imaging as the preferred method for capturing and storing computer evidence (see sidebar, "Capturing and Storing Computer Evidence") has developed, in computer terms at least, over a long period of time.

CAPTURING AND STORING COMPUTER EVIDENCE

Little did Sir Charles Babbage, Alan Turing, and Von Neumann realize the consequences of their actions as forefathers of the modern computer. In the not too distant past, everything of any importance was recorded on paper. Copies were laboriously written out by a myriad of clerks, and alterations were relatively easy to spot when compared with the original. Next came the typewriter and then the photocopier, great labor saving devices, but spotting false documents became more difficult. A whole branch of forensic Science arose from this to deal with the matter of *Questioned Documents*.

The arrival of mass storage devices created even more problems as far as copies were concerned. Information was no longer stored in easily readable words, but as a series of magnetic impulses recorded on tape and disk. How then was this to be copied or produced in readable form? There were two simple answers:

First, the answer to creating a copy was to take a *bit* image of the drive which recorded all of the data on a disk. This proved to be a fairly reliable but cumbersome method, as the image had to be restored to the original or identical disk and only really existed in the world of the mainframe and minicomputer.

Second, the most obvious way to produce data in a readable form was the printout. Simple? Yes; but how then to check the information in its original form? The answer was to call upon the services of a multitude of "experts" to recreate the original system and reproduce the printouts (at what cost?).

Luckily for the investigator, access to computers in the early days was limited to large companies and the incidence of computer data during investigations was sparse. The advent of the IBM PC and its many variants introduced new problems into the world of investigation: the volume of data, the ability to change data without trace, and the ability to hide or delete data. Computing was made available to the masses which naturally included the criminal fraternity. It was apparent that specialist knowledge was needed to investigate this new technology and thus was born the art of *Forensic Computer Examination.*

Initially, the only method available to the investigator was to obtain a backup of the files on a disk, restore those files to another disk, and go through them one at a time. Many early backup packages used the *imaging* method, but by the mid-to-late 1980s, they were being replaced by software which allowed the user to backup and restore selected files. This was a leap forward as far as the user was concerned, but not much use for investigators. This is because selective backup operates at the file system level and consequently does not copy free and slack space (residual data)—not very satisfactory when you are looking for that elusive deleted file. The next step was to examine the original media with a disk editor.

Many a long hour has been spent with a disk editor going through each sector of the original disk, only to be met at the end of the day with the allegation the investigator has somehow tampered with the original media. A principle that emerged from these allegations (which is now being widely adopted by law enforcement agencies) is: *No action taken by anybody performing an investigation on a computer should change data held on that computer or other media which may subsequently be used as evidence.*

While it seems to be common sense, it is surprising how many people do not realize the consequences of just *booting* a PC under its own operating system. Date and time stamps (which may be crucial) will change and allegations of tampering will be made.

This is where taking an *image*, and working solely on that image, preserves the data in its original form. The adaptation of imaging to the investigation of magnetic media, together with the appropriate software, now allows the forensic computer examiner free range to all of the data on a disk without fear of corrupting the original.

The untrained or inexperienced user will fall into traps and cause problems—perhaps even invalidating any evidential data found. Today, there are accepted guidelines for good practice [1].

The importance of taking a sound image is fundamental to all subsequent investigation work and cannot be overemphasized. Examination of a computer by the technically inexperienced (see sidebar, "Pitfalls and Risks") will almost certainly result in rendering any evidence found inadmissible in a court of law. With the aforementioned in mind, this chapter examines the role of SANs or data storage in computer forensics with regards to evidence collection and forensic analysis to reconstruct the past.

PITFALLS AND RISKS

The task of imaging a simple desktop PC may superficially seem quite trivial. However, for the data produced from the investigation to be of much use in a court of law, certain criteria must be met. For example:

- Can you be sure that you haven't changed any of the time and date stamps of the files contained on the SAN media?
- Can you be sure that you haven't changed the contents of the data itself?
- Have you maintained an audit trail of the steps that you have taken?
- Do you know what operations the computer performs when you turn it on or off?

Generally, unless you have been specifically trained to investigate computer systems, the answer to these questions will be a resounding no. Special techniques and procedures have been developed in association with the police and other law enforcement agencies to ensure that you are able to produce evidential images of computer material without compromising the evidential integrity of the data.

The techniques employed vary from system to system. However, it is essential to know the consequences of your actions before carrying them out. Some of the problems that your customers probably have experienced in the past include:

- Time and date stamps relating to critical files changed when booting the machine
- Information in the *free space* of the disk overwritten during the boot up
- During an investigation, a virus was spread corrupting many files on the system, resulting in a claim for damages being brought against the investigator
- A server-based system was unable to be brought back to life after being inappropriately turned off, resulting in a law suit and a claim for consequential damages against the firm of investigators
- While investigating a machine, a virus was found and then removed to prevent infection of the investigating software. The act of removing the virus changed many times, including date stamps on the machine; and of course, changed the contents of the file containing the virus [1].

EVIDENCE COLLECTION ....

Most storage vendors offer a complete range of computer forensic services from providing the initial investigation on site to processing, storing, and investigating the captured evidence.

Securing the Computer Evidence

Questioning a computer must be done thoroughly, carefully, and without changing anything on that computer. The following procedures and techniques have been developed to do just that:

- Take an exact copy of everything on the computer.

- Maintain an audit trail so that the investigation process can be recreated.
- Verify actions taken at every point of the investigation.
- Enable quick identification of information and evidence from the computer [1].

This is done by taking an exact copy or image of the suspect computer. The image contains all the information that existed on the original machine without exception. The image contains information which is not possible to access by normal means, such as:

- Data which may have been deleted.
- Information hidden outside of the usual storage areas.
- Partially overwritten areas of older data [1].

These vital snippets of data may form crucial evidential links and often lie hidden away in the depths of the computer's filing system. The image is an exact replica or clone of the suspect computer. Therefore, it can be investigated in place of the original computer. By using the image, investigators can explore all areas of the data looking for evidence or clues without changing, or compromising, the original. The investigator can view the last accessed Internet sites, read saved email files, and navigate around the image as if it were the original computer—a vital step forward in tackling computer crime.

The image is used by law enforcement officers to put computer evidence into court. It has been accepted as being as good as the original computer data.

FORENSIC ANALYSIS.......................................

Hidden or deleted data can be found—quickly, reliably, and efficiently. If computer evidence lies in hidden system files, deleted or partially overwritten areas anywhere on the SAN medium, Evidential Systems will find it. These systems are designed for use by professional investigators such as police, IT security staff, and customs officials.

Evidential Systems comply to the best practice guidelines for the capture of computer evidence and comprises Imager, Disk Emulator, and Forensic Software. They integrate seamlessly with normal investigative procedures and have a proven track record in court. To ensure a successful prosecution, the target or suspect computer remains unaffected by the imaging process and a full audit trail (procedural record) is automatically maintained. The specialist hardware is complemented by uniquely powerful search and analysis software tools which are run to index all the information on the image.

Now, let's illustrate the reconstruction of past events with as little distortion or bias as possible. There won't be a discussion of real crimes here, however (other than a few technical homicides inflicted on code by vendors); in fact, there will rarely be a discussion of computer crimes at all.

RECONSTRUCTING PAST EVENTS...........................

Many analogies can be drawn from the physical to the virtual realms of detective work—anyone who has seen a slaying on a police show can probably give a reasonably good account of the initial steps in an investigation. First, you might protect and isolate the crime scene from outside disturbances. Next comes recording the area via photographs and note taking. Finally, a search is conducted to collect, package, and store any evidence found. The digital analogs to these steps are precisely what is recommended when faced with a computer investigation.

Becoming A Digital Detective

If you want to solve a computer mystery effectively, you need to examine the system as a detective, not as a user. Fortunately for programmers, many of the skills required are the same used when creating or debugging software—logical thinking, uncovering and understanding the cause and effect of a computer's actions, and possessing an open mind. There are a few significant differences between chasing down a bug and trying to solve a mystery, however. As a programmer, you're often only working against yourself—trying to fix problems of your own making. Debugging takes time, testing, and repeated effort to ensure that the bugs are squashed. Solving a computer crime is more akin to working against rival programmers who are attempting to subvert your code and hide their crafty work.

Other than that, solving computer mysteries has much in common with its physical counterpart. You generally don't have a lot of time to solve a mystery. Evidence vanishes over time, either as the result of normal system activity or as the result of acts by users. Likewise, every step that you take destroys information, so whatever you do has to be right the first time or valuable information is lost. Repetition is not an option.

Fortunately, you can have one major advantage over your opponent—knowing your system better than anyone else. Many computer forensic mysteries are fairly basic and are caused by relatively inexperienced people.

More than ever, understanding cause and effect are absolutely crucial—any opponent has lots of opportunities to change or subvert your machine. An in-depth technical understanding of the system and what it does on a day-to-day basis is vital. How can you trust a compromised system to produce valid data and results?

Let's start with a simple example. Here are some of the basic steps involved when running a command:

- The shell first parses what is typed in, then forks and executes the command (environment and path variables can have a significant effect on exactly which command gets executed with what arguments, libraries, and so on).
- The kernel then needs to validate that it has an executable. It talks to the media device driver, which then speaks to the medium itself. The inode is accessed and the kernel reads the file headers to verify that it can execute.
- Memory is allocated for the program and the text, data, and stack regions are read.
- Unless the file is a statically linked executable (that is, fully contains all the necessary code to execute), appropriate dynamic libraries are read in as needed.
- The command is finally executed [2].

As you can see, there are a lot of places in the system that work together when a command is executed—and a lot of places where things can be compromised, go wrong, or otherwise be of forensic interest. If you are working against someone and you cannot trust these components, is there any hope of drawing valid conclusions?

Much of the challenge of forensic computing is trying to make sense of a system when the data you're looking at is of uncertain heritage. In this part of the chapter, let's focus on several aspects of this process and see how to draw valid conclusions in spite of the problems associated with it.

Frankenstein

Given a collection of logfiles, wouldn't it be great if you could use those stored records to replay past events, just like watching a video tape? Of course, logfiles record stored system activity with relatively low time resolution. The reconstructed behavior would be a little stiff and jerky, like the monster in Frankenstein.

Most computer systems do not record sufficient stored information for Frankenstein-like experiments. Still, computers produce numerous logs in the course of their activities. For example, UNIX systems routinely maintain stored records of logins and logouts, of commands executed on the system, and of network connections made to the system. Individual subsystems maintain their own logging. Mail delivery software, for instance, maintains a stored record of delivery attempts, and the cron daemon for unattended command execution has its own activity logs. Some privileged commands, such as switch userid (su), log every invocation regardless of its success or failure. Each individual logfile gives its own limited view of what happened on a system, and that view may be completely wrong when an intruder has had opportunity to tamper with the stored record.

The next couple of paragraphs focus on how multiple sources of information must be correlated before one can make a sensible judgment. The examples are UNIX specific, but that is hardly relevant.

Figure 20.1 shows information about a login session from three different sources: from TCP Wrapper, logging from login accounting, and from process accounting [2]. Each source of information is shown at a different indentation level. Time proceeds from top to bottom.

The TCP wrapper logging (outer indentation level) shows that on May 25, at 10:12:46 local time, machine spike received a telnet connection from machine hades.porcupine.org. The TCP Wrapper logs connection events only, so there is no corresponding stored record for the end of the telnet connection.

The last command output (middle indentation level) shows that user wietse was logged in on port ttyp1 from host hades.porcupine.org and that the login session lasted from 10:12 until 10:13, for a total amount of time of less than one minute. For convenience, the stored record is shown at the two times that correspond with the beginning and the end of the login session.

May 25 10:12:46 spike telnetd[13626]: connect from hades.porcupine.org

wietse	ttyp1	hades	Thu May 25 10:12 - 10:13 (00:00)

hostname	-		wietse	ttyp1	0.00 secs Thu May 25 10:12
sed	-	wietse	ttyp1	0.00 secs Thu May 25 10:12
stty	-	wietse	ttyp1	0.00 secs Thu May 25 10:12
mesg	-	wietse	ttyp1	0.00 secs Thu May 25 10:12
who	-	wietse	ttyp1	0.00 secs Thu May 25 10:12
w	-	wietse	ttyp1	0.00 secs Thu May 25 10:12
ps	-	wietse	ttyp1	0.00 secs Thu May 25 10:13
ls	-	wietse	ttyp1	0.00 secs Thu May 25 10:13
w	-	wietse	ttyp1	0.00 secs Thu May 25 10:13
csh	-S	wietse	ttyp1	0.00 secs Thu May 25 10:12
telnetd	-S	root	___	0.00 secs Thu May 25 10:12

wietse	ttyp1	hades	Thu May 25 10:12 - 10:13 (00:00)

Figure 20.1
Information about a login session from three different sources.

Output from the *lastcomm* command (inner indentation level) shows what commands user wietse executed, how much CPU time each command consumed, and at what time each command started. The order of the stored records is the order in which each process terminated. The last two stored records were written at the end of the login session, when the command interpreter (csh) and the telnet server (telnetd) terminated.

How trustworthy is information from logfiles when an intruder has had opportunity to tamper with the stored record? This question will come up again and again in the course of SAN management. Intruders routinely attempt to cover their tracks. For example, it is common to find process accounting stored records from user activity that have no corresponding login accounting stored records. Fortunately, perfect forgeries are still rare. And, a job done too well should raise suspicion too (*What do you mean, our web server was completely idle for 20 hours?*).

The stored records in the example (see Figure 20.1) give a nice consistent picture: Someone connects to a machine, logs in, executes a few commands, and goes away. This is the kind of logging that you should expect to find for login sessions. Each stored record by itself does not prove that an event actually happened. Nor does the absence of a stored record prove that something didn't happen. But when the picture is consistent across multiple sources of information, it becomes more and more plausible that someone logged into wietse's account at the indicated time. Information is power, and when you're investigating an incident, you just can't have too much of it.

Beauty is More than Skin Deep

As Figure 20.2 illustrates, computers present one with layers and layers of illusions [2]. The purpose of these illusions is to make computers more convenient to use than the bare hardware from which they are built. But the same illusions impact investigations in several interesting ways.

Computer file systems typically store files as contiguous sequences of bytes and organize files within a directory hierarchy. In addition to names and contents, files and directories have attributes such as ownership, access permissions, time of last modification, and so on.

The perception of files and directories with attributes is one of the illusions that computer systems create for us, just like the underlying illusion of data blocks and metadata (inode) blocks. In reality, computer file systems allocate space from a linear array of equal-size disk blocks, and reserve some of that SAN capacity for their own purposes. However, the illusion of files and of directories with attributes is much more useful for application programs and their users.

And, the perception of a linear array of equal-sized disk blocks is an illusion as well. Real disks are made up from heads and platters. They store information as magnetic domains and reserve some of the SAN capacity for their own purposes. Howev-

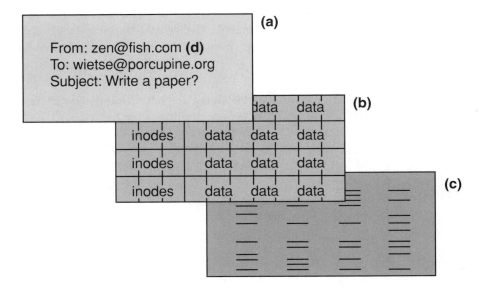

Figure 20.2
Simplified picture of files as seen by: (a) users and applications; (b) file-system software in the operating system; (c) hardware.

er, the illusion of a linear sequence of equal-sized disk blocks is much more useful for the implementation of file systems.

The layering of illusions limits how much you can trust information from a computer file system. Only the physical level with the magnetic domains is real; this level is also the least accessible. The abstractions of disk blocks, contiguous files, and of directory hierarchies are illusions created by software that may or may not have been tampered with. The more levels of abstraction, the more opportunities for mistakes.

The layering of illusions also limits the possibilities for both data destruction and data recovery. Deleting a file from the file system is relatively easy, but is not sufficient to destroy its contents or attributes. Information about the deleted file is still present in the disk blocks that were once allocated to that file. Program and other tools are currently being developed by other storage vendors that recover files and file attributes from unallocated disk blocks.

There is concern within the storage industry community with regards to the storage and security of sensitive information such as cryptographic keys and unencrypted data. Unless you use equipment that protects data by self destruction, it is necessary to erase sensitive data adequately to prevent it from falling into the wrong hands.

Destroying information turns out to be surprisingly difficult. Memory chips can be read even after a machine is turned off. Although designed to only read 1s and 0s, memory chips have undocumented diagnostic modes that allow access to tiny leftover fragments of bits. Data on a magnetic disk can be recovered even after it is overwritten multiple times. Although disk drives are designed to only read the 1s and 0s that were written last, traces of older magnetic patterns still exist on the physical media. You can find spectacular images of semiconductors and of magnetic patterns online in the Digital Instruments Nanotheater (*www.di.com*).

In the future, the term *electronic dumpster diving* will be used when talking about the recovery of partially destroyed stored information. The challenge of electronic dumpster diving is to make sense out of trash. Without assistance from a file system, disk blocks are no longer grouped together into more useful objects such as files, so reconstruction can be like solving a puzzle. As more and more layers of illusion are impacted by data destruction, the remaining information becomes more and more ambiguous.

This leads to the paradoxical conclusion that stored information can be volatile and persistent at the same time. The important thing to know is this: The volatility of stored information is largely due to the abstractions that make the information useful.

What's Going On?

So far, this part of the chapter touched upon how long stored data stays around after being deleted, but how about the bits that are currently being used on your system? Intruders and other problem makers are most likely going to be interested in what is on your computer, not what isn't. For example, let's look at some stored data on various UNIX servers on the Internet to see how frequently their files were accessed. While this isn't meant to be the last word on the subject (systems may vary widely in the numbers of files they have, the usage patterns, and so on), they are indicative of system behavior.

For example, Table 20.1 shows file utilization patterns of typical systems [2]. These numbers are obtained by gathering timestamps on files.

Table 20.1 Percentages of typical file utilization patterns

Time Range	*www.things.org*	*www.fish.com*	*news.earthlink.net*
Over a year	76.6	75.9	10.9
6 months–year	7.6	18.6	7.2
1–6 months	9.3	0.7	72.2
Day–month	3.6	3.1	7.4
Within 24 hours	2.9	1.7	2.3

The vast majority of files on two fairly typical web servers have not been used at all in the last year. What is important to note here is that, even on an extraordinarily heavily used (and extensively customized) Usenet news server, less than 10% of the files were touched within the last 30 days. There are lots of files gathering electronic dust on a typical system, whether they are:

- Seldom used or archived/stored data
- Programs that users install, test, and forget about
- System programs and configuration files that are never touched
- Archives of mail, news, and data, and so on [2]

Similar patterns emerge from PCs that run Windows 9x, NT, XP, and the like. Research shows that often over 90% of the files haven't been touched in the last year. Microsoft systems are often even more one-dimensional in their functionality—being primarily used for wordprocessing, spreadsheets, and the like, and not as Internet servers or general-purpose systems. This is the case even though Microsoft operating systems are as complex (if not significantly more so) than the servers in Table 20.1.

Why is this? Even a 1-MIPS machine could generate enough new data to fill a terabyte drive in a very short time. Computers are busy enough, certainly, but most activity accesses the same data, programs, and other parts of the machine over and over again. In practice, every computer has substantial numbers of files and commands that are rarely (if ever) used. And any modern computer will have at least hundreds (if not thousands) of commands at its disposal. Computers have evolved over time to either be all things for all users or to be full of specialized little programs that no one has the heart to throw away. Fine, you may say, but why does any of this matter?

Now, a few words on looking for things. When you go looking for something specific, your chances of finding it are very bad. Because, of all the things in the world, you're only looking for one of them. When you go looking for anything at all, your chances of finding it are very good. Because, of all the things in the world, you're sure to find some of them.

Looking for Things

When looking for specific items, not only is the task difficult but often painfully time consuming. And, just as an example, a search for a lost sock will usually turn up many other hidden and lost items before uncovering your target.

So, rather than looking for a particular thing on a computer, you'll want to examine everything. Intruders and other miscreants (almost by definition) display atypical behavior—utilizing odd commands, looking in strange places, or doing things that normal users don't. And, problems usually consist of either anomalous actions or typical behavior gone bad—either of which cut down the search tremendously. Finding the results of this activity is especially simple if you know what the system normally looks like. In general, if actions and changes in data are indeed concentrated, when the locus changes, it is often easy to spot. Intruders also often modify or damage the systems they're on, whether it is simply eliminating or modifying audit or log evidence, putting in back doors for easy access to the system later on, or engaging in artistic WWW defacement.

Interestingly, however, destroying or modifying data to hide evidence can leave significant marks as well—sometimes more telling than if they had left the system alone. Consider the physical world—anyone walking on a snowy walkway will obviously leave footprints. If you see the walkway clear of any tracks, it might make you suspicious: Did someone brush away all traces of activity? As we all know from programming experience, it is significantly easier to find a problem or bug if we know something is wrong than if we're simply presented with a program. Like the old joke—*It's quiet. Yeah, too quiet!*—seeing a system devoid of activity should make your forensic hackles rise.

FROM HERE ....

This chapter examined the role of SANs in computer forensics with regards to computer and data storage of evidence collection and forensic analysis. The final chapter presents a summary, current conclusions, and recommendations for the future of SAN development and implementation.

END NOTES..

[1] "The Evolution of Evidence Capture," Vogon International Limited, Talisman Business Centre, Talisman Road, Bicester OX26 6HR, UK, 2001.

[2] Dan Farmer and Wietse Vinema, "Reconstructing Past Events," T.J. Watson Research Center, IBM Corporation, 1133 Westchester Avenue, White Plains, New York 10604, 2001.

21 Summary, Conclusions, and Recommendations

As enterprise data becomes more important to the success of competitive and customer service initiatives, making room for the storage of burgeoning amounts of data will become more critical over time. Organizations are storing 11 to 12 times as much data now than they were only a few years ago, according to Winter Corporation of Waltham, Massachusetts, and International Data Corp. That growth is expected to rise to 30 to 60 times the current rate in the next few years.

While the needs for storage are increasing, storage recording density is increasing 200% every 17 months and the price of storage is dropping about 40% annually. These advancements mean that storage capacity is no longer a limiting factor even as the volume of data is growing.

With the rate of growth in storage and information needs, attention to your organization's storage methodologies is becoming a critical success factor. The problem here, and the greatest limiting factor, is not acquiring storage, but managing it.

Most organizations are still adding storage, typically NAS, unless the benefit of a SAN is obvious. This is particularly true for smaller organizations, but they can expect to experience the same storage growth problems as larger organizations.

The benefits of managing storage will become apparent to large and small organizations when they discover that not managing storage will increase their costs of doing business four to 11 times. Storage might not be the most exciting of topics, but that will change as organizations learn of its importance.

THE STORAGE NETWORK BEHIND THE SERVER.....

The rapid growth in data intensive applications continues to fuel the demand for raw data storage capacity. Applications such as data warehousing, data mining, online transaction processing, and multimedia Internet and intranet browsing are resulting in the near doubling of the total storage capacity shipped on an annual basis. Further fueling the demand for network storage, analysts have predicted that the number of network connections for server-storage subsystems will exceed the number of client connections by 2002.

The Problem: Limitations Loom over Surge of Data

With the rise of client networking, data-centric computing applications, and electronic communications applications, virtually all network stored data has become mission-critical in nature. This increasing reliance on the access to enterprise data is challenging the limitations of traditional server-storage solutions. As a result, the ongoing need to add more storage, service more users, and back up more data has become a monumental task.

Having endured for nearly two decades, the parallel SCSI bus that has facilitated server-storage connectivity for LAN servers is imposing severe limits on network storage. Compounding these limits is the traditional use of LAN connections for server storage backup which detracts from usable client bandwidth. To contend with these limitations, network managers are often forced to compromise on critical aspects of system availability, reliability, and efficiency. To address the debilitating and potentially costly effects of these constraints, an infrastructure for server-storage connectivity which can support current and future demands is badly needed. Thus, impending limitations of existing network server connectivity consists of the following:

- Bandwidth to service clients and maintain data availability
- Scalability for long term, rapid growth
- Flexibility to provide optimum balance of server and storage capacity
- Manageability for ease of installation and maintainability [1]

The Solution: Storage Area Networking

The SAN is an emerging data communications platform which interconnects servers and storage at Gigabaud speeds. By combining LAN networking models with the core

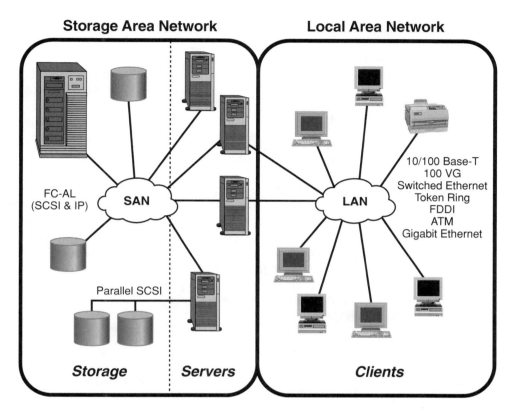

Storage Area Network   **Local Area Network**

FC-AL
(SCSI & IP)   **SAN**

Parallel SCSI

10/100 Base-T
100 VG
Switched Ethernet
Token Ring
FDDI
ATM
Gigabit Ethernet

LAN

Storage   *Servers*   *Clients*

Figure 21.1
The Storage Area Network environment.

building blocks of server performance and mass storage capacity, SAN eliminates the bandwidth bottlenecks and scalability limitations imposed by previous SCSI bus-based architectures (see Figure 21.1) [1].

   In addition to the fundamental connectivity benefits of SAN, the new capabilities, facilitated by its networking approach, enhance its value as a long term infrastructure. These capabilities, which include compute clustering, topological flexibility, fault tolerance, high availability, and remote management, further elevate SAN's ability to address the growing challenges of data-intensive, mission-critical applications. From a client network perspective, the SAN environment complements the ongoing advancements in LAN and WAN technologies by extending the benefits of improved performance and capabilities all the way from the client and backbone through to servers and storage. Thus, benefits of the storage area network environment include:

- High Bandwidth
- Modular Scalability
- High Availability & Fault Tolerance
- Manageability
- Ease of Integration
- Total Cost of Ownership [1]

Fibre Channel: The Open SAN Solution

Fibre Channel-Arbitrated Loop has emerged as the high-speed, serial technology of choice for server-storage connectivity (see Table 21.1) [1]. With over 70 companies, including industry leading disk drive, disk array, server, and networking connectivity suppliers, supporting FC-AL, it has become the most widely endorsed open standard for the SAN environment. This broad acceptance is attributed not only to FC-AL's high bandwidth and high scalability, but also to it's unique ability to support multiple protocols, such as SCSI and IP, over a single physical connection. This enables the SAN infrastructure to serve as both a server interconnect and as a direct interface to storage devices and storage arrays.

Table 21.1 Complementary SAN, LAN, and WAN technologies

Technology	Current Bandwidth	Future Bandwidth	Applications
ATM	622 Mbps	1+ Gbps	LAN and WAN
Ethernet	100 Mbps	1 Gbps	LAN and WAN
FC-AL	1 Gbps	4 Gbps	SAN

High Bandwidth

FC-AL provides a 2.5 to 10 fold increase in effective data bandwidth over the traditional parallel SCSI storage interface (see Table 21.2) [1]. Additionally, FC-AL offers future expandability. While the current FC-AL standard for bandwidth is 1 Gigabaud, planned enhancements to 2 and 4 Gigabaud give FC-AL a solid platform to address longer term bandwidth requirements.

Table 21.2 Comparison of FC-AL and UltraSCSI.

Attribute	UltraSCSI Limit*	FC-AL SAN
Data Transmission	Half-Duplex	Full-Duplex
Effective Data Bandwidth**	40 MBps	200 MBps
Protocol Support	SCSI	SCSI, IP, others
Connection Scalability	15 drives per bus	126 nodes per loop
Connection Distance	25 m	10 km
Relative Storage Capacity***	136 GB	9,172 GB

Based on wide differential UltraSCSI parallel interface standards

**Under FC-AL's 8b/10b encoding, 1 Gbaud = 100 MBps data rate*

***Based on 9.1 GB disk drives and one, eight drive disk array per node for SAN*

Server and Storage Scalability

The modular scalability of FC-AL is key to enabling an infrastructure for long term growth and manageability. Traditional parallel SCSI bus connections have been limited to a total of 7 or 15 storage devices. As bus bandwidth is pushed further and further, this limit is compressed to even fewer devices per bus. In contrast, FC-AL supports up to 126 nodes per loop with a typical configuration consisting of a combination of servers and multidisk arrays per node. By adding multiple loops, the overall scalability is limitless.

Scalability in terms of capacity management and capacity balancing is an area of significant differentiation between FC-AL and SCSI. Largely dictated by the limits on physical cable length, parallel SCSI storage connectivity requires close proximity to its host system, typically a server. This translates to a single, integrated server-storage enclosure that contains both server processing power and one or two SCSI buses of limited scalability as shown in Figure 21.2 [1].

Under this single server-storage enclosure model, the scaling of server capacity and storage capacity becomes inflexible and inefficient. Single enclosures typically hold only 4–10 drives. In order to scale the storage capacity beyond this limit, additional server-storage enclosures, including the cost of the server processor board and peripherals, is required. The interdependence between the server and storage capacity in this single enclosure model leads to inefficient and costly scaling. With a diverse combination of data-intensive applications and server processing-intensive applications running concurrently in the enterprise, the need for more flexible and efficient scaling is needed as shown in Figure 21.3 [1].

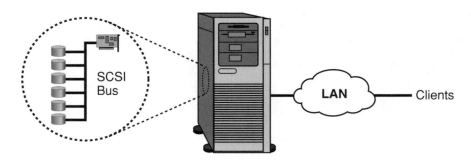

Figure 21.2
Traditional integrated server-storage model.

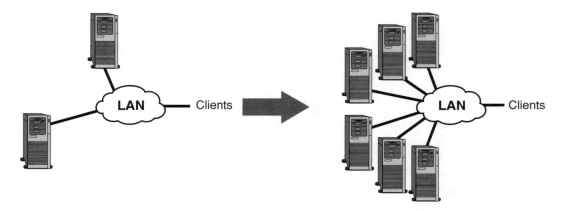

Figure 21.3
Interdependent capacity scaling with integrated server-storage model.

With less stringent cable length limitations, FC-AL enables the networking of separate server and storage enclosures within the SAN environment (see Figure 21.4 [1]. Also, this capability provides a more flexible and cost-effective path for the independent scaling of server performance and storage capacity where either may be expanded independently to achieve an optimum balance as shown in Figure 21.5 [1].

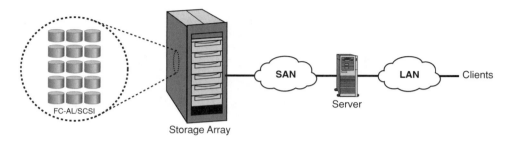

Figure 21.4
Server-storage networking model of SAN.

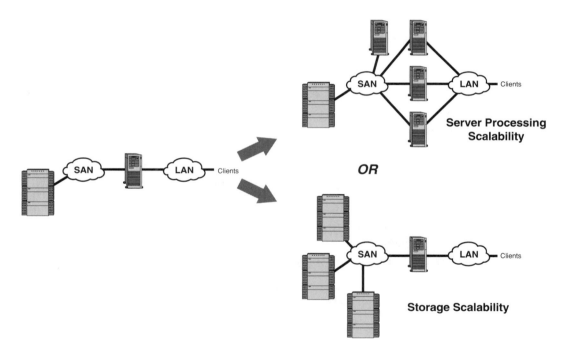

Figure 21.5
Independent capacity scaling with server-storage networking model.

Modular Connectivity

In addition to superior flexibility in scaling server processing capacity and data storage capacity, the networking approach of FC-AL introduces aspects of interconnect scalability that have not been possible with previous architectures (see Figure 21.6) [1].

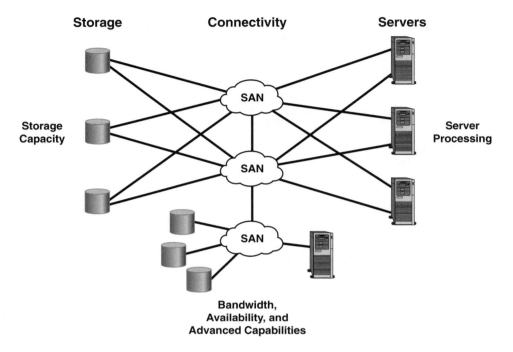

Figure 21.6
Scalability of storage, connectivity, and servers.

Through the use of modular networking devices such as hubs, switches, bridges, and routers, advanced SAN topologies can be created to scale overall bandwidth, enhance availability, and enable advanced SAN application capabilities in storage management (see sidebar, "SAN Tips") and load balancing.

SAN TIPS

In addition to seeking product features that meet your requirements, here's a short checklist of questions you should ask every storage management software firm before dedicating your time and resources toward any SRM solution.

1. *Customer References:* Does anyone even use the product? Look carefully. Some SRM companies disguise their storage management references with users of other products the company makes. Look for recent case studies from reputable organizations.

2. *Independent, Unedited Lab Reviews:* Does the product even work? Ask for unedited copies of independent, third-party lab reviews by trusted sources such as eWeek labs, Windows 2000 Magazine, and others. If they don't have any positive lab reviews, the company may be hiding something.

3. *Real-Time Monitoring:* What good is a storage management software solution that only monitors your storage part of the time? You need a solution with a real-time finger on the pulse of your storage, without incurring unnecessary delays. It's only real time if you're monitoring it before the data touches the storage device.

4. *Storage Management Control:* Many storage management products can only provide reactive storage management. At the end of the day, you need something that is proactive, allowing you to control the problem before it becomes a problem. Ask the ISVs if they can do anything to prevent the storage problem. After all, it really isn't management if you can only be in reactive mode all the time. Management means preventing the problem, not just reacting to it.

5. *Outstanding Support:* Put the company's support to the test. Was it responsive? How was its Web support? Don't overlook this important factor in your buying decision.

6. *Patented Technologies:* Look for innovative products that have patented technologies. Those that don't have patented technology could be either offering a cheap substitute for the real thing, or could be in the middle of a lawsuit. If the latter is the case, buying from them would be extremely risky (particularly if they have to turn over their code and ask their customers to de-install the illegal product).

7. *Product Awards:* Save yourself from having to reinvent the wheel. Which products have won industry awards in side-by-side comparisons and customers' choice awards? Steer clear of any that haven't.

8. *Track Record:* Good products make good news. Lousy products get little coverage. The trade rags want to tell their readers about proven, successful technologies, not lemons. Scan the ISVs' websites for lots of good news stories. Sites that lack these are probably hiding something, or the press doesn't see the products as mature enough to deserve valuable ink.

9. *Global Presence:* If you're not global now, you probably will be some time in the future in this global economy. Look for an ISV with local offices around the world.

10. *Reputable Partners:* Look for solid partnerships with reputable organizations. Who is licensing the company's technology? Who is distributing it? Who is bundling it? If nobody will partner with them, there may be a reason [2].

High Availability and Fault Tolerance

In addition to the high availability and fault tolerance provided by specific storage management and clustering configurations, many FC-AL devices provide features that ease the general deployment of fault tolerant SANs. One example of these on-board capabilities is the feature of dual porting, which has become standard on FC-AL disk drives, to facilitate dual loop configurations. These dual loops provide a redundant path to each storage device in the array in the event that one of the loops is down or is busy as shown in Figure 21.7 [1].

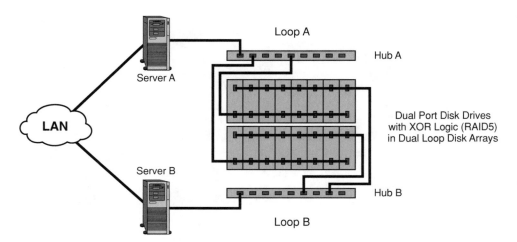

Figure 21.7
Dual loop array configuration.

The implementation of RAID configurations in storage arrays has become a standard approach for fault tolerance and is fully supported by the SAN environment. In fact, to even further embrace the RAID approach, FC-AL disk drives provide internal exclusive-or (XOR) logic which effectively provides Level 5 RAID capabilities from within the disk drive itself. This addition facilitates robust, proven fault tolerance—while reducing the requirement for more complex and costly RAID controllers.

Manageability

Visibility down to the node and device level is essential to easing the efforts of installation, deployment, and maintenance of any network. By embracing a network management approach, SAN connectivity devices, such as hubs and switches, have integrated highly evolved management capabilities modeled after proven LAN and WAN management techniques. A fully managed SAN platform can offer monitoring and bypass control of individual nodes, loops, enclosures, storage devices, and connectivity devices. Thus, open standards platforms for SAN management are as follows:

- SCSI command set
- SCSI Enclosure Services (SES)
- SCSI Self Monitoring Analysis and Reporting Technology (S.M.A.R.T.)
- SAF-TE (SCSI Accessed Fault-Tolerant Enclosures)
- Simple Network Management Protocol (SNMP)
- Web-Based Enterprise Management (WBEM) [1]

By embracing the best-practice network management standards established by LAN and WAN platforms, information regarding SAN topology, status, and alerts can be easily accessed by system administrators. This high visibility management not only helps reduce unplanned downtime, but can also simplify remote system recovery and restoration in the event of a failure. Traffic monitoring capabilities can also be embedded into the SAN management system to facilitate sophisticated, cost-effective load balancing and capacity planning.

Ease of Integration

Just as compelling as its ability to advance the capabilities of networked servers and storage, the ability to integrate SAN solutions into an existing network provides tremendous value in ease-of-integration. Since the SAN environment exists behind the server, existing server–LAN connections can easily be leveraged to facilitate a gateway between LAN and SAN, and allow utilization of legacy servers.

The broad cabling options supported by FC-AL also ease the introduction of SANs into existing campus networks [4]. By leveraging preexisting twisted pair, coax, and optical cabling, SAN connection distances of up to 10 kilometers can be achieved without the need to pull new cable.

As a key building block of SAN deployment, SAN connectivity devices offer dynamically-configurable, hot-plugging capabilities. Combined with a graphical management interface, these features simplify troubleshooting and accelerate installation.

Total Cost of Ownership

Offering an infrastructure for cost-effective, long-term growth, fault tolerance, and manageability, the SAN environment provides Total Cost of Ownership (TCO) advantages which have never before been possible with servers, storage, or server-storage connectivity (see Table 21.3) [1].

Table 21.3 Total Cost of Ownership (TCO) advantages provided by SAN environment.

SAN Feature	TCO Benefit
Connects to existing LANs	Optimizes existing investment
Fully managed environment	Minimized support costs
Integrated fault tolerance	Minimized down time
Distributes server-storage resources	Complements Network Computer (NC) paradigm
Independently scalable servers and storage	Highly efficient scaling of resources

Advanced Application Capabilities

As an alternative to the traditional parallel SCSI storage interface, FC-AL's bandwidth and scalability provide highly compelling advantages for change. However, it is not until the more advanced facets of FC-AL are explored that the innovative strength of SAN comes into focus. By introducing the network-like features of extended connection distance, IP support, and use of hubs, bridges, switches, and routers for complex topologies, the SAN infrastructure enables a broad range of new capabilities that were not previously possible for servers or storage. Examples of these capabilities include: advanced storage management and server-storage clustering.

Advanced Storage Management

The problem of advanced storage management is increasing amounts of network-stored data which have become cumbersome, if not impossible to maintain in a timely, secure, fault tolerant, and restorable manner. The solution to this would be the high bandwidth and topological flexibility offered by the SAN environment as it accelerates the data backup process and facilitates new, innovative platforms for remote backup, mirroring, and hierarchical storage.

Perhaps the biggest challenge facing storage management is the need to provide efficient, secure, high availability access to critical data. To effectively overcome these challenges, a number of fundamental issues must be addressed as shown in Table 21.4 [1]:

Table 21.4 Fundamental issues must be addressed to address challenges.

Storage Management Challenge	SAN Solution
Length of time required to backup data	Bandwidth and protocol efficiency accelerate backup
Inability to backup, mirror, or restore remotely	Cable lengths up to 10 km support remote operation
Lack of alternatives to local backup and mirroring	Ideal platform for distributed hierarchical storage management (HSM)
Use of LAN connections for server backup consumes client network capacity	Separation of server-storage connections from LAN connections reduces LAN traffic

The bandwidth and connectivity limitations imposed by server-to-storage parallel SCSI connections and server–LAN connections offer little to address these formidable tasks. Through its bandwidth, extended connectivity, and transport efficiency, the SAN environment uniquely offers a broad range of solutions for storage management, including remote backup (see Figure 21.8) [1], mirroring, recovery, and distributed hierarchical storage management using a broad range of online and nearline storage devices.

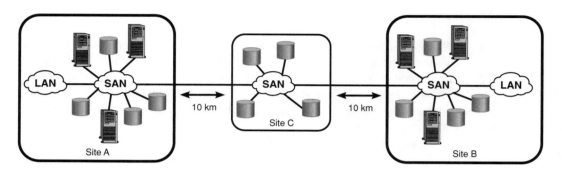

Figure 21.8
Remote backup.

Server-Storage Clustering

The problem with server-storage clustering is fault tolerance for server or disk array failures that requires costly redundant systems. The solution would be server-storage clusters facilitated by SAN that provide high availability and fault tolerance using cost-effective, mainstream server and storage subsystems.

Once considered a solution for high-end distributed processing, server-storage clustering is quickly approaching mainstream markets as shown in Figure 21.9 [1]. With the growing need for high bandwidth and high availability, fault tolerant servers for real-time applications (such as online transaction processing, and the distributed processing and automatic failover features of clustering) are increasing in demand. The connectivity and performance benefits of the Storage Area Network make it the ideal open platform for mainstream clustering configurations such as those based on Microsoft's Windows NT Server.

Thus, with the increasing complexity of networked computing systems and global enterprise solutions, it is refreshing when a single technology yields both unmatched performance and exceptional Total Cost of Ownership benefits. In the case of Fibre Channel-Arbitrated Loop and the rapidly developing Storage Area Network, an evolutionary open technology promises to revolutionize the networkcentric, data intensive computing era through a new, innovative market space. Open system SAN solutions and products are now available from leading OEMs, integrators, resellers, and independent suppliers of FC-AL host adapters, intelligent hubs, disk drives, and disk array enclosures.

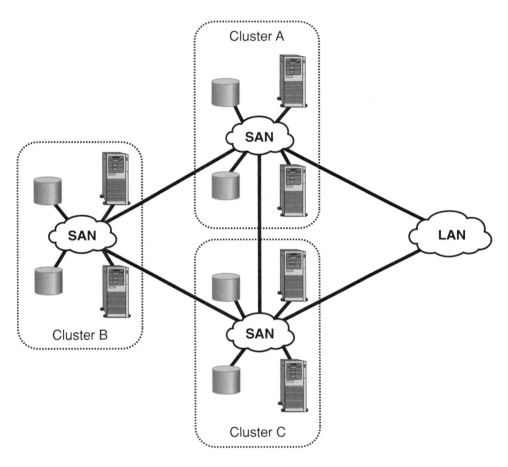

Figure 21.9
Clustering.

So, what is the future for mixed SCSI and Fibre Channel networks? Let's take a look!

SAN FUTURE ....

SCSI will continue for a long time. There are a number of enterprise customers who are comfortable with it. SCSI will continue to ship until probably 2008. There are also a lot of problems being solved by Fibre Channel. The technologies are complementary, and vendors intend to route between them for a long time.

Yet, the SAN will evolve to a more networking feel. For example, Infiniband routing is a specification for next-generation system I/O that uses multiple switched paths to route data between peripherals and the processor.

Great Uses for Fibre Channel

One of the first great uses for fibre channel is LAN-free backup, where customers can move bulk backup data and recovery from the LAN to the storage network and free up 40 to 50% of the bandwidth on the LAN. They move the data to media that can do the backup typically 20 times faster.

Server-free backup are seen as the next step in that movement. Customers can use their SAN investment and give greater efficiencies and throughput to the process of backup and recovery. You'll need to migrate existing storage and servers into the SAN. With the advances in optical networking, you can have remote copies of your data thousands of miles away.

Advancements

Certain advancements must occur before SAN equipment becomes a commodity so that consultants don't need to plan, install, and manage it. In other words, *interoperability* is the key word here. Solutions must work together out of the box and be relatively simple to configure. Online configuration tools that are easy to use will also be critical. Finally, management of the SAN infrastructure is key to making this new enterprise storage architecture functional once installed. IT managers need to get comfortable with SANs and their continuing function. SAN management software will help immensely.

Service Differentiation

With the popularity of the Internet, users need to differentiate between the services they receive from a local data center and an Internet-accessed data center. SANs will be a key enabler for the Internet to continue its rapid growth. As companies look at handling growth, internal and external sources for storage growth and management should be considered. The differentiation will be based upon elements such as the business model and the cost desired by the customer. The differentiation most likely will come down to a business decision, an analysis that yields the best solution for each business.

Return-on-Investment (ROI) Business Case

What is the ROI business case that will convince senior management to authorize the purchase of a SAN? There are a number of points to consider, each of which comes down to managing the rapid growth of storage. As you know, the amount of storage purchased is doubling every year. This is placing a huge burden on IT staff as they attempt to manage this storage.

The ROI in this case is: do you want to stay in business? Moving beyond this point, take the example of LAN-free backup. What are your information assets worth? Keeping them protected and accessible via backup is a requirement.

With SANs, backup can be improved in speed by a factor of 20, and the cost can be distributed over a larger population of servers, making it much cheaper to purchase and operate. SANs bring more manageable gigabytes per IT staff-person and enable organizations to scale with the growth in storage at much less than linear cost increases. Otherwise, the growth of storage will drive a management cost model that no one can afford.

Finally, let's look at the real storage future—Holograms! Briefly discussed in Chapter 19, a more detailed discussion of their future use will ensue in this final chapter.

STORAGE ENTERS THE THIRD DIMENSION: WHERE NO SAN HAS GONE BEFORE......................

To many, holograms are either those silver pictures of William Shakespeare on your credit card or something off Star Trek. But the technology may finally move out of the realms of sci-fi novelty and into storage.

The demand for storage in the enterprise is increasing rapidly, as is the need for cheaper technology with more capacity. Until now, improvements made in magnetic storage technologies have met the mounting requirements, but some experts are suggesting that holographic storage could provide a cheaper solution (see sidebar, "Are Holograms Too Pricey?").

ARE HOLOGRAMS TOO PRICEY?

A new storage technique that taps the technology behind the familiar hologram stickers on credit cards promises to put entire libraries and weeks worth of motion pictures on a couple of CD-size discs. But with an expected price tag of nearly $100,000, hologram storage remains little more than an apparition.

Still, that hasn't stopped high-tech powerhouses such as IBM Corporation and Lucent Technologies' spin-off InPhase Technologies from racing to develop the new technology, which they see as the natural next step in cramming more data into ever-smaller spaces. Current storage technologies have natural physical limits, but the appetite for higher capacity is always increasing. InPhase Technologies envision this to be a very mass-market, high-volume technology.

Storage needs are growing at 80% a year, driven mostly by the rapidly expanding Internet. And, the needs of Internet companies alone are doubling every 100 days.

That bursting demand doesn't even count the storage crunch felt by the video and film industries or businesses like hospitals, insurance firms, and department stores that keep ever-increasing piles of data. When it comes to storage space, holograms don't disappoint. InPhase's prototype CD-size hologram disc can hold up to 400 gigabytes of information and retrieve it at speeds of roughly 30 megabytes per second. At that speed, people could download a DVD movie in about 30 seconds.

IBM is working on a system that stores 250 gigabytes in a square inch of hologram space. A prototype hologram storage machine exhibited recently at CeBIT, the world's largest computer and technology trade show, can hold 1 terabyte, or 1,000 gigabytes of information in a hologram crystal chip the size of a watch face, according to German creators Optostor AG.

Using the Whole Area

The secret is storing data in three dimensions throughout the entire thickness of the storage medium, be it a disc, a card, or a wafer-thin chip. Current magnetic and optical storage devices, such as computer hard drives or CD-ROMs, store data on their surfaces only.

Hologram storage media also have lifetimes of up to 100 years, compared with the typical 4-year span of the typical hard drive, because they are more resistant to temperature swings, water, acid, and electrical fields. Companies are working on a number of different approaches to the experimental technology, but most systems use dual lasers to change the molecular structure of a polymer or crystal storage medium. This creates microscopic holograms that represent data.

The idea is for the lasers to hit the medium at thousands of different angles and depths, using the medium's entire thickness. By recalling data in packets of millions of bits, downloading from hologram storage is also envisioned as being at least 30 times faster than current storage methods, which read back data one bit at a time.

Despite its technological appeal, hologram storage, which has experimental roots stretching back 30 years, still faces roadblocks. The storage material itself has long been a problem. It needs to be sensitive enough that a low power laser can write and read on it. But if it is too sensitive, the laser can actually wipe out stored data as it's being retrieved. There is no recording medium that meets all the criteria right now.

Price is also a big hurdle. Optostor hopes to begin selling its hologram storage device in 2002 for $93,000. At that price, the technology will be within reach only for high-end companies that have massive storage needs.

Proceeding with Caution

IBM is taking the same approach, focusing its research on storage devices for so-called data warehouses. IBM's version could be ready by 2002, but the company may not rush this product to market.

Technically, it can be done right now, but one should wonder about its viability as a business. IBM has a reputation that they don't want to jeopardize by bringing out something that's not ready for prime time.

At the same time, InPhase is working to make hologram storage a mass medium that people can use in their homes like floppy discs and CDs. Analysts indicate that, despite the virtues of three-dimensional storage, hologram memory will see steep competition from good old-fashioned floppies, zip disks, and hard drives, where $1 can buy well over 100 megabytes. If it can't come to market at rock-bottom prices in comparison to magnetic storage, which is really cheap, then it's going to struggle [3].

The advantage of holographic storage is that unlike magnetic technologies, which store data in a two-dimensional plane using the magnetic coating on a disk platter, holographic technologies store data in three dimensions. As it is a three-dimensional technology, increasing the thickness can also increase the storage capacity of a disk.

Storing information in a hologram is just one aspect of a move towards making faster, more powerful computer systems that process data using light rather than electricity. In a holographic optical memory, information is recorded using two laser beams.

One beam carries data encoded in a pattern of light and dark regions, like the pixels of a monitor. The second *reference* beam traverses the first at right angles, and the interference between the two beams produces a three-dimensional pattern of light and dark. This pattern is imprinted in a block of material that acts as the storage medium, rather than as photographic film that records the distribution of light and dark in a scene to which it is exposed.

The key point about a holographic memory is that numerous sets of data can be recorded into the same block of material, superimposed atop one another. Each set is recorded using a reference beam crossing the *write* beam at a slightly different angle. It's like taking several photos on the same exposure, but still being able to view each one individually.

Storage Goes Holographic

Some companies are trying to develop commercial holographic storage systems. Lucent launched a joint venture called InPhase Technologies, with storage firm Imation. InPhase will work on photopolymer and manufacturing technology that has been developed by the two parent companies to develop holographic data storage systems (HDSS).

These two partners have improved materials and systems technology enough to launch a business around it. It is claimed that the company has used DVD-developed lasers to reach storage densities of 300 gigabits per square inch and transfer rates of many tens of megabits per second.

InPhase's challenge involves technology that has been researched for more than 20 years, but which has yet to realize its promise. Lucent has indicated in the past that problems involving systems, materials, and funding have delayed development over the years and prevented the technology's commercial fruition.

In addition, the technology has been overshadowed by swift advances in magnetic technology, which has achieved better than expected speed and capacity improvements by exceeding what were once thought to be its physical limits. At the same time, progress in holographic data storage (HDS) proved more difficult than imagined.

InPhase is not the only company trying to turn HDS dreams into commercial reality. Its rivals include Holoplex, founded by Demetric Psaltis, a professor of electrical engineering at the California Institute of Technology [3]. Also, IBM has invested considerably in holographic technology over the years, and was a major player in the United States government-funded Holographic Data Storage System consortium in the mid-1990s, along with Rockwell Science Centre and Stanford University.

This consortium had managed to increase storage density and data rates beyond anything that was achieved before. IBM is still continuing research, but is taking a wait-and-see approach to product development. It will sit on the sidelines and see whether the startups make the technology cost-effective before it enters the market.

Advanced System from NASA

But some of the research projects on holographic storage point to what might be possible. NASA, for example, has been working on an Advanced Holographic Memory system that would be capable of storing 1 TB of data and have a data transfer rate of up to 1 Gbps, with power consumption of just 0.01W/Gb. It would also require no moving parts. The power consumption alone could provide major benefits for firms, especially as power demands from more and more storage and hardware threaten to push power stations to the limits of their capacity.

However, all does not bode well for holographic technology. The United States government, a long-time proponent of the potential of holographic systems, recently decided to stop investment in the technology. In November 2000, the United States Defense Advanced Research Projects Agency (DARPA) cancelled all government funding of holographic storage research.

The advances already seen in holographic storage will boost the amount of information that can be stored on, for example, a DVD. However, price, as well as capacity, is a major consideration for firms buying storage systems. The next couple of years will see a huge increase in demand for storage and more competition between vendors. This competition will hopefully result in lower prices all round and more storage whatever the technology.

END NOTES..

[1] Dave Tang, "Storage Area Networking: The Network Behind the Server," Gadzoox Networks, Inc., 5850 Hellyer Avenue, San Jose, CA 95138, 2001.

[2] Steven Toole, "SRM Vendor Checklist," searchStorage.com, TechTarget.com, 117 Kendrick Street, Needham, MA 02494, 2001.

[3] John R. Vacca, *Holograms and Holography: Design Techniques and Commercial Applications (with CD-ROM)*, Charles River Media, 2001.

[4] John R. Vacca, *The Cabling Handbook, 2nd Edition*, Prentice Hall PTR, 2001.

Appendix A
Online Storage Management Checklist

Online storage management systems manage the logical and physical flow of data from one media or device to another over time. The online storage management system should be capable of representing the environment at many different levels of granularity: from the file system and device level, to the more granular formatting options, and to scheduling. It should be easy to use, incorporate, and remain in synch with the wide variety of vendors and standards constantly changing in the marketplace. Some features to look for in developing a storage management approach include the following:

- Powerful Administration

- Flexible File Migration

- Quick Access to Data

- Automated Scheduling

- Advanced Diagnostics

POWERFUL ADMINISTRATION ....

Administration allows configuration of the virtual file system from any Windows NT server or workstation on your network. Using this simple, Explorer-style GUI, users can control all aspects of the storage system, including hardware devices, media, migration rules, task scheduling, and extended drives.

FLEXIBLE FILE MIGRATION ....

Migration rules determine which files are moved to which hardware device and media. Rules can be defined to migrate entire directories or particular files by extension, size, or attribute. Schedules allow migration to take place at off-peak times, improving system performance during periods of high activity.

QUICK ACCESS TO DATA ....

Applications require quick access to files when they are needed. File data is *cached* on extended drives for a configured period of time for faster retrieval. By caching files, media swapping is minimized, significantly improving system performance. Options are also generally available for defining when files are purged from extended drives. Additionally, the system should support direct read for read-only applications that do not require caching.

AUTOMATED SCHEDULING ....

Automated scheduling reduces the time for many time-consuming events such as file move to media, prefetch, and media tasks (format, label, copy, compaction, and file report). Flexible scheduling allows these events to occur at convenient times (nights and weekends), maximizing productivity during regular operating hours.

ADVANCED DIAGNOSTICS ....

If you encounter errors during server operation, online viewers in the Administrator report error conditions. Standard Windows NT application logging and network broadcasting should be supported. Lower level software provides low-level SCSI device and jukebox diagnostics. These powerful tools assist you in identifying and solving media and hardware problems.

Appendix B
List of Top SANs Implementation and Deployment Companies

$\mathbf{A}$ gang of new top SAN implementation and deployment companies is readying hardware, software, and services that will make it easier for customers to manage and access storage resources across corporate networks. With names like 3ware and Data-Core, the firms have rolled out products ranging from Windows NT-based SANs-in-a-can to storage management tools and Fibre Channel devices.

The companies are readying products meant to fill the gaps left by first-generation SAN and network storage vendors, including Brocade Communications, Cross-roads Systems, and Gadzoox. What follows in Table B.1, is a list of the present top SAN implementation and deployment companies (with corresponding URLs)—first, second, and next generation.

Table B.1 *SAN implementation and deployment companies*

Company	URLs
3Ware	www.3ware.com
Advanced Media Services	www.amssiorage.com
Alacritech	www.alacritech.com
Arsenal Digital Solutions	www.arsenaldigital.com
Articulent	www.articulent.com
Auspex Systems, Inc	www.auspex.com
Bakbone Software, Inc.	www.bakbone.com

Table B.1   SAN implementation and deployment companies (Continued)

Company	URLs
Berbee	www.berbee.com/enterprise/san.html
Brocade Communication	www.brocade.com
CaminoSoft	www.caminosoft.com
Centennial	www.centennial.co.uk
Champion Computer Corporation	www.championcc.com/html/san.htm
CISCO SYSTEMS	www.cisco.com
CNT	www.cnt.com
Compaq Computer Corp.	www.compaq.com
Computer Associates	www.computerassociates.com
DataCore	www.datacore.com
Dot Hill Systems Corp.	www.dothill.com
EMC CORP	www.emc.com
Exybyte	www.exybyte.com
Gadzoox	www.gadzoox.com
Hitachi Data Systems	www.hds.com
IBM Corp.	www.storage.ibm.com
ITPRC	www.itprc.com/san.html
JNI	www.jni.com
I-TECH Corp.	www.i-tech.com
Lucent Technologies	www.lucent.com
McDATA Corp.	www.mcdata.com
Neartek, Inc.	www.neartek.com
Net Convergence	www.netconvergence.com
Nishan	www.nishan.com
OTG Software	www.otgsoftware.com
Quantum|ATL	www.quantumatl.com

Table B.1   *SAN implementation and deployment companies (Continued)*

Company	URLs
SAN Solutions	www.sansolutions.com
Smart Storage, Inc.	www.smartstorage.com
Solid Data	www.soliddata.com
Sony	www.aittape.com
St. Bernard Software	www.stbernard.com
Storability	www.storability.com
Tivoli	www.tivoli.com
Transoft	www.transoft.net
TrelliSoft, Inc.	www.trellisoft.com
VA Linux Systems	www.valinux.com
Verbatim Corp.	www.verbatim.com
Veritas	www.veritas.com/us/products/san
Vitesse	www.vitesse.com/news/010400.htm
Vixel Corporation	www.vixel.com
Worldstor	www.worldstar.com
XIOtech Corp.	www.xiotech.com
Xyratex	www.xyratex.com/technology/san.htm

Warning

URLs are subject to change without notice.

Appendix C
SAN Product Offerings

$\mathbf{T}$he rapid growth in data intensive applications continue the demand for raw data storage capacity. Applications such as modeling, Internet and intranet browsing, multimedia, processing, data warehousing, and mining are resulting in the doubling of the total storage capacity.

With the growth of networking in organizations today network-stored data has become mission-critical. However, with regards to the access to the enterprise, data is challenging the limit of traditional server-storage solutions. As a result, the ongoing effort to add more storage, service more users, and back up more data, has become a monumental task. What follows in Tables C.1 to C.5 [1], are SAN product offerings for:

- Consolidation

- Sharing

- SAN Servers

- SAN Storage

- Data Protection

- Disaster Tolerance

- SAN Software

Table C.1   Product offerings for consolidation

Enterprise Solutions		UNIX Solutions	Intel Solutions		
			Entry Level	**Mid Range**	**High Performance**
Data Center with Director	**Data Center with FC Switch**	**UNIX**	**Intel—entry level full FC**	**Intel—mid range SCSI**	**Intel—high performance full FC**
McDATA ED5000	SAN Fibre Channel Switch 2109-S16	SAN Fibre Channel Switch 2109-S16	SAN Fibre Channel Managed Hub 35341RU	2109S-08 SAN Fibre Channel Switch	2109S-16 SAN Fibre Channel Switch
SAN Data Gateway 2108-G07	SAN Data Gateway 2108-G07	SAN Data Gateway 7139-11	FAStT200	FC RAID subsystem	FAStT500
2105-F20 ESS— Shark	2105-F20 ESS— Shark	7133-D40— IBM Serial Disk System			

Table C.2   Product offerings for data protection

Enterprise Solutions		UNIX Solutions	Intel Solutions		
			Entry Level	**Mid Level**	**High Performance**
Data Center with Director	**Data Center with FC Switch**	**UNIX**	**Intel—entry level full FC**	**Intel—mid range SCSI**	**Intel—high performance full FC 3502**
Magstar 3494 Tape library	Magstar 3494 Tape library	Magstar 3575 Tape library	3502	Magstar 3575 Tape library or 3502	Magstar 3575 Tape library or 3502
SAN Data Gateway 2108-G07	SAN Data Gateway 2108-G07	SAN Data Gateway 2108-G07	SDG Router 2108-R03	SDG Router 2108-R03	SDG Router 2108-R03

Table C.2 Product offerings for data protection (Continued)

Enterprise Solutions		UNIX Solutions	Intel Solutions		
			Entry Level	Mid Level	High Performance
Data Center with Director	Data Center with FC Switch	UNIX	Intel—entry level full FC	Intel—mid range SCSI	Intel—high performance full FC 3502
McDATA ED5000	SAN Fibre Channel Switch 2109-S16	SAN Fibre Channel Switch 2109-S16	SAN Fibre Channel Managed Hub 35341RU	SAN Fibre Channel Switch 2109S-08	SAN Fibre Channel Switch 2109-S16
Tivoli Storage Manager	Tivoli Storage Manager	SAN Data Gateway 7139-11	Tivoli Storage Manager and industry standard backup application software	Tivoli Storage Manager and industry standard backup application software	Tivoli Storage Manager and industry standard backup application software
2105-F20 ESS— Shark	2105-F20 ESS— Shark	Tivoli Storage Manager	FAStT200	FC RAID subsystem	FAStT500
		7133-D40— IBM Serial Disk System			

Table C.3   Product offerings for sharing

Enterprise Solutions		UNIX Solutions	Intel Solutions		
			Entry Level	Mid Level	High Performance
Data Center with Director	Data Center with FC Switch	UNIX	Intel—entry level full FC	Intel—mid range SCSI	Intel—high performance full FC 3502
Magstar 3494 Tape library	SAN Fibre Channel Switch 2109-S16	SAN Fibre Channel Switch 2109-S16	SAN Fibre Channel Managed Hub 35341RU	SAN Fibre Channel Switch 2109S-08	SAN Fibre Channel Switch 2109-S16
SAN Data Gateway 2108-G07	SAN Data Gateway 2108-G07	SDG Router 2108-R03	Tivoli Storage Manager	Tivoli Storage Manager	Tivoli Storage Manager
McDATA ED5000	Tivoli Storage Manager	SAN Data Gateway 7139-11	FAStT200	FC RAID subsystem	FAStT500
Tivoli Storage Manager	2105-F20 ESS—Shark	Tivoli Storage Manager			
2105-F20 ESS—Shark		7133-D40—IBM Serial Disk System			

Table C.4   Product offerings for disaster tolerance

Intel—utilizing MSCS	Intel—utilizing OPS	Intel—utilizing LME
SAN Fibre Channel Switch	SAN Fibre Channel Switch	Legato mirroring extension for MSCS
MSCS	Oracle Parallel Server	Finisar GB Ethernet optical link extender
FAStT500	FAStT500	FAStT500

Table C.5   SAN Product offerings of servers

Description	Servers
SAN servers: The engines of e-business and the right solution for your SAN	S/390
	RS/6000
	Netfinity
	AS/400
	NUMA

SAN STORAGE ....

Data is the basis for most of the business value created by information technology, and the storage infrastructure is the foundation upon which data relies (see sidebar, "SAN Product Offerings of Storage").

SAN PRODUCT OFFERINGS OF STORAGE

Features

- Flexible & heterogenous connectivity
- Secure transactions & data transfer
- 24x7 response
- Scalability for fast-growing environments

Products

- Enterprise Storage Solutions
- Magstar MP (Multi-Purpose) 3570 Tape Subsystem
- Enterprise Storage Server
- Magstar MP 3575 Tape Library Dataserver
- Modular Storage Server
- Magstar 3590 Tape Subsystem
- 7133 Serial Disk System
- Magstar 3590 Silo Compatible Tape Subsystem
- Magstar 3494 Tape Library

Netfinity Storage Solutions

Enterprise Storage Solutions: IBM provides a wide range of tested, easy-to-install, high-capacity storage products to support Netfinity servers.

Disk Storage Solutions

- *Enterprise Storage Server:* ESS provides superior storage sharing for UNIX, Windows NT, AS/400, and S/390 servers.

- *Modular Storage Server:* MSS provides multiplatform support for major UNIX, Windows NT, Windows 2000, Windows XP, Novell NetWare, and OpenVMS platforms in homogeneous or heterogeneous multihost environments.

- *7133 Serial Disk System:* The 7133 Serial Disk System provides outstanding disk storage performance with advanced SSA bandwidth for UNIX and Windows NT servers.

Tape Storage Systems and Libraries

- *Magstar 3494 Tape Library:* Magstar 3494 has a capacity of up to 374 terabytes and is modular, flexible, reliable, and has a low entry price.

- *Magstar MP (Multi-Purpose) 3570 Tape Subsystem:* Magstar 3570 is ideal for traditional backup and for applications where fast access to mass data is important.

- *Magstar MP 3575 Tape Library Dataserver:* Magstar 3575 provides unattended storage for the mid-range systems and network servers.

- *Magstar 3590 Tape Subsystem:* Magstar 3590 provides the highest levels of capacity, performance, and reliability of any IBM tape subsystem.

- *Magstar 3590 Silo Compatible Tape Subsystem:* Magstar 3590 enables owners of many StorageTek (STK) Automated Cartridge Systems (ACS) to dramatically increase performance and reduce floor space without having to replace their entire library system [1].

SAN SOFTWARE ....

As an example of SAN Software, IBM and Tivoli Systems (an IBM company and a developer of management systems) help users meet the complex systems and storage management challenges involved in designing, implementing, maintaining, and protecting SANs. IBM and Tivoli offer users the following SAN software solutions (see sidebar, "SAN Product Offerings of Software").

SAN PRODUCT OFFERINGS OF SOFTWARE

Tivoli SAN Management Software

- Tivoli Storage Network Manager

Tivoli Future SAN Software

- Tivoli Storage Manager Enhancements

Tivoli SAN Protection Software

- Tivoli Storage Manager
- Tivoli Data Protection for applications
- Tivoli Data Protection for workgroups

IBM Storwatch Software

- IBM StorWatch Serial Storage Expert
- IBM StorWatch Specialists
- IBM StorWatch Enterprise Storage Server (ESS) Expert

Tivoli SAN File Sharing Software

- Tivoli SANergy

Tivoli SAN Management Software

Tivoli Storage Network Manager: Tivoli Storage Network Manager offers a comprehensive SAN management solution that discovers, displays, allocates, monitors, automates, and manages SAN fabric components and disk storage resources.

Tivoli SAN Protection Software

- *Tivoli Storage Manager:* Tivoli Storage Manager is the enterprise storage management solution. Tivoli Storage Manager, along with its complementary products, offers SAN-enabled integrated enterprise-wide network backup, archive, storage management, and disaster recovery capabilities.

- *Tivoli Data Protection for applications:* Tivoli Data Protection products utilize vendor certified interfaces to provide online and incremental backup and restore of popular e-business applications. These include Microsoft SQL Server and Exchange, Lotus Notes and Domino, Oracle, Informix, and SAP R/3.

Tivoli SAN File Sharing Software

Tivoli SANergy™: Tivoli SANergy gives you the ability to share SAN-based storage arrays, file systems, and files across multiple systems simultaneously. Using the maturity, security, and inherent sharing abilities of industry-standard LANs, Tivoli SANergy enhances them with high bandwidth and low-processor overhead you expect of SANs. The result is high-performance, heterogenous file sharing. Tivoli SANergy is based on the standard file systems and network services provided by supported operating systems. Today, these include Windows NT, Windows 2000 and XP, MacOS, Solaris, Irix, AIX, and Tru-64.

Future Tivoli SAN Software

Tivoli Storage Manager is planned to be enhanced with the following SAN functionality:

Server-free Data Movement

Tivoli Storage Manager servers and clients will drive SAN based, Server-free data movement. This technique off-loads all data movement into the SAN. Data transfers will be done from source media across the SAN directly to the target media without flowing through any server. By removing all servers from the data path, customers will see improved data throughput as well as reduced CPU and I/O load on their servers. (Planned availability to be determined [TBD]).

IBM StorWatch Software

IBM StorWatch Enterprise Storage Server (ESS) Expert

IBM StorWatch ESS Expert gathers and presents information that can significantly help storage administrators manage the Enterprise Storage Server (ESS). Capabilities are provided for performance management, asset management, and capacity management.

IBM StorWatch Serial Storage Expert

IBM StorWatch Serial Storage Expert (StorX) simplifies the planning and management of SANs implemented on Serial Storage Architecture (SSA) loops, thereby improving productivity and saving time for storage administrators. Capabilities include SAN element discovery, element configuration, topology mapping, disk logical name information, and monitoring for disk hardware errors and RAID events.

IBM StorWatch Specialists

IBM StorWatch Specialists are storage management tools that are integrated into specific IBM storage products. The IBM StorWatch Enterprise Storage Server Specialist is an integrated storage management tool that enables storage administrators to centrally monitor and manage IBM Enterprise Storage Servers.

The IBM StorWatch Fibre Channel RAID Specialist simplifies the management of clustered storage with the IBM Fibre Channel RAID Storage Server. As a network-based integrated storage management tool, it lets storage administrators configure, monitor, dynamically change, and manage multiple Fibre Channel RAID Storage Servers from a single Windows 95 or NT Workstation. High availability and full redundancy are provided with the host-specific Fibre Channel Storage Manager tool that resides on the host system providing automatic I/O path failover when a host adapter, IBM Fibre Channel Storage Hub, or a storage server controller fails.

IBM StorWatch SAN Data Gateway Specialist simplifies the management of SAN Data Gateways by providing a graphical user interface to centrally configure, manage, and service multiple SAN Data Gateways across the enterprise. The IBM StorWatch SAN Data Gateway Specialist runs on attached host servers and network-attached Windows NT workstations. It simplifies migration to Fibre Channel technology for IBM SCSI-attached disk and tape systems and devices while accelerating Storage Area Network implementation.

Finally, the IBM StorWatch SAN Data Gateway S20 Specialist is a Windows NT-based management tool that provides configuration and service functions (including mirror group definition, creation of composite drives, and Instant Copy disk management), and can also manage multiple SAN Data Gateways across the enterprise. [1].

END NOTES...

[1] "Enterprise Storage Area Networks," IBM Corporation, 1133 Westchester Avenue, White Plains, New York 10604.

Appendix D
Standards for SANs

Storage industry leaders Brocade Communications Systems, Compaq Computer Corporation, EMC Corporation, Hitachi Data Systems Corporation, International Business Machines Corporation, and McDATA Corporation, recently announced several industry-changing initiatives intended to provide storage product customers with the first qualified crossvendor, interoperable storage networking solutions to come from the Storage Networking Industry Association. The initiative also provides improved cooperative support among storage product vendors. The six companies have completed joint qualification of two open Storage Area Network solutions that enable the coexistence of data zones containing Compaq (recently merged with HP), EMC, Hitachi Data Systems, and IBM storage system products on a single, shared Fibre Channel fabric; and the four storage system vendors have signed bilateral cooperative support agreements intended to simplify joint customer support in multivendor environments.

SNIA INITIATIVES

Based on the groundbreaking cooperation among the six companies, the SNIA (see sidebar "About SAN Standards") has also recently announced the new Supported Solutions Forum which will expand upon these initiatives. The six companies will serve as founding members of the forum.

ABOUT SAN STANDARDS

FCA—Fibre Channel Association

FCA is organized as a not-for-profit, mutual benefit corporation. The FCA, since its inception, has grown to encompass more than 190 members including companies located and managed in the United States and through its affiliate organizations in Europe and Japan.

In other words, FCIA is an international organization of manufacturers, systems integrators, developers, systems vendors, industry professionals, and end users. With more than 190 members and affiliates in the United States, Europe, and Japan, the FCIA is committed to delivering a broad base of Fibre Channel infrastructure to support a wide array of industry applications within the mass storage and IT-based arenas. FCIA Working Groups focus on specific aspects of the technology that target both vertical and horizontal markets, including storage, video, networking, and SAN Management.

NSIC—National Storage Industry Consortium

NSIC membership consists of over fifty corporations, universities, and national labs with common interests in the field of digital information storage. Corporate membership includes most major U.S. storage product manufacturers and many other companies from the storage industry infrastructure. NSIC has its headquarters in San Diego and was incorporated in April 1991 as a non-profit mutual benefit corporation.

SNIA—Storage Networking Industry Association

SNIA is an international computer system industry forum of developers, integrators, and IT professionals who evolve and promote storage networking technology and solutions. The SNIA was incorporated in December 1997 and is a registered 501-C6 non-profit trade association. Their members are dedicated to ensuring that storage networks become complete and trusted solutions across the IT community.

The SNIA works towards this goal by forming and sponsoring technical work groups, by producing the Storage Networking World Conference series, by building and maintaining a vendor neutral Technology Center in Colorado Springs, and by promoting activities that expand the breadth and quality of the storage networking market. The SNIA's ability to accomplish its goals is directly attributed to the dedication and hard work of hundreds of volunteers from their member companies.

SNIA is also a not-for-profit organization, made up of over 200 companies and individuals spanning virtually the entire storage industry. SNIA members share a common goal: to set the pace of the industry by ensuring that storage networks become efficient, complete, and trusted solutions across the IT community. To this end, the SNIA is uniquely committed to delivering standards, education, and services that will propel open storage networking solutions into the broader market.

Open SAN solutions are standards-based storage networks that provide tested interoperability of products supplied by multiple vendors. Intended benefits include increased flexibility for networked storage infrastructures, reduced costs from consolidating SAN islands, greater investment protection, and maximized value of storage networking technology. Storage networking customers are now able to deploy heterogeneous SANs from multiple suppliers with interoperability and improved support.

The fact that competing storage vendors have been able to agree on configurations and software levels to jointly qualify and have entered into cooperative support agreements, is remarkable. Even more remarkable is the fact that this initiative has already permeated the storage industry through the SNIA. The storage market is entering an exciting new world of multivendor cooperation.

Initial Open SAN Solutions

The open SAN solutions qualified by the six companies consists of 128-port Fibre Channel fabrics that allow a variety of server platforms to access data residing on Compaq StorageWorks®, EMC Enterprise Storage™, Hitachi Data Systems Freedom Storage™, and IBM Enterprise Storage Server™. One solution uses Brocade Silk-Worm® Fabric Switches and the other uses McDATA ED-5000 Directors. Each storage system and its associated servers are logically partitioned into a vendor-specific data zone. The Fibre Channel fabric is shared by all four data zones. Detailed information about the configurations can be found at *www.snia.org/ssf.*

Streamlined Customer Support

The bilateral cooperative support agreements recently announced are intended to provide procedures for handling customer service calls seamlessly and expeditiously in a multivendor environment. Customers will receive support in accordance with the terms of their support agreements with individual vendors, and the individual vendor's obligation to provide the specified level of support under those agreements will remain unchanged. Under the new cooperative support agreements, vendors will be able to contact each other and share information to streamline the troubleshooting of issues arising in multivendor storage environments.

Next Steps by the SNIA

Future work of the SNIA Supported Solutions Forum will bring enhancements to the initial open SAN solutions. Planned enhancements include expanding the size of the configurations, involving additional vendors, adding more components, increasing the level of component interoperability, adding multivendor switch interoperability, and integrating popular storage networking applications.

This announcement by the founding members of the SNIA Supported Solutions Forum advances previous standards and Plug-Fest work accomplished in the industry. Storage customers can now implement open SAN solutions with greater flexibility than ever before. With this announcement, the storage networking industry has made a quantum leap toward mutually supported open SAN interoperability. Until now, the chances of a SAN user being able to have one host interface talk to several different vendors' storage products were next to none.

Next, iSCSI is a new connectivity standard that may offer a lower-cost approach to building flexible, scalable SANs. But, is it ready for enterprisewide deployment.

SETTING A NEW STANDARD FOR SANS ....

Finally, in an era of rapidly expanding storage demands and increasingly distributed enterprises, SANs have emerged as the most flexible, scalable way to meet big-league storage demands. The trouble is, SANs are expensive: Up until now, they've been built on fibre channel hardware that can cost as much as $1,000 per port.

Enter iSCSI, a new approach to building SANs due to be adopted as a standard by the fourth quarter of 2002. Promoted by such heavy hitters as Cisco and IBM, iSCSI replaces fibre channel's tightly integrated hardware and software network protocol with a software protocol, TCP/IP, which can be carried by a wider variety of networking hardware.

Combining existing hardware, lower-cost networking components, and easily understood Internet protocols, iSCSI is expected to make SANs affordable even for smaller enterprises. iSCSI has yet to prove itself, with standardization work and testing still in progress, but for those contemplating or building SANs today, the technology demands consideration.

How iSCSI Works

iSCSI isn't complicated; it wraps SCSI commands inside IP packets. In theory, the technique is similar to that used by fibre channel, where SCSI commands are wrapped inside fibre channel frames. IP networking, however, is more well known and functions on a wider variety of networking hardware, including ordinary Ethernet LANs, corporate WANs, and the Internet.

Any network capable of supporting IP can be pressed into service for iSCSI, including asynchronous transfer mode (ATM) or frame relay connections (two of the most popular protocols for corporate WANs), optical carrier or leased T1 or T3 digital lines, or even digital subscriber lines (DSL).

One of the only genuinely new hardware items needed for iSCSI SANs is a network interface card (NIC), which can extract the SCSI commands from incoming IP packets for the storage devices. This special NIC needs no software or general-purpose CPU and no hard drives or interfaces other than Ethernet and SCSI, making it the thinnest of thin servers.

Storage devices equipped with NICs are called IP storage; they are equipped with just enough electronics to get on a network and communicate with a server. Features commonly found on NAS devices (file and user management, security, and a Web or FTP interface) are absent from IP storage. Instead, the relationship between a server and IP storage is exactly the same as with traditional Server Attached Storage; the only difference is that the devices are connected to each other over the network.

Just as with conventional Server Attached Storage, the server takes on the responsibilities of user and file management. Hard drives and RAID systems are formatted using the server's native disk format, while optical jukeboxes and tape libraries are managed by library management systems.

Development Milestones

Before SANs offering all these advantages can be deployed, the iSCSI standard has to be adopted by the Internet Engineering Task Force (*www.ietf.org*), the advisory committee that recommends standards for the Internet and its technologies. Only then can advances, including iSCSI NICs (for storage devices) and accelerated Ethernet cards (for servers), be introduced.

Note

Servers can be connected with conventional Ethernet cards, but vendors are already developing accelerated Ethernet cards designed to improve server performance.

Realistically, iSCSI devices should start shipping in quantity in the first quarter of 2002. Even if the equipment becomes available on this schedule, it will be 12 to 24 months before iSCSI gets widely adopted.

Accelerated Ethernet cards will have to incorporate special processors to maintain a TCP/IP stack. iSCSI has been demonstrated with regular Ethernet cards, using the server's CPU to do the work of encapsulating SCSI commands in IP packets, but it's a processor-intensive task and very slow. Early iSCSI shipments will mainly familiarize developers and users with the protocol while the hardware matures.

The cost will not be a limiting factor in the adoption of iSCSI. Because iSCSI is based on Ethernet technology, it can be deployed on both clients and servers. The high volume required for client-side installation of accelerated Ethernet cards should bring costs down.

While accelerated Ethernet cards may not reach the commodity prices of conventional Ethernet ports (which now sell for less than $20 each), costs could fall a few hundred dollars per port within a year. This figure is less than (though not much less than) fibre channel's price range of $500 to $1,000 per port. In addition, iSCSI SANs can use existing Ethernet routers and hubs, while fibre channel requires special hardware throughout.

Potential iSCSI Roadblocks

Citing questions about iSCSI performance, some storage vendors are less enthusiastic about iSCSI. It remains to be seen how much performance users will get out of iSCSI systems in real-world applications. It will be at least 12 months before iSCSI will be competitive with fibre channel in terms of performance and latency. If the price of iSCSI-capable ports remains high, most users will not want to install them on every client in an enterprise.

Most client computers don't need high-speed access to centralized storage, and most of a SAN's cost is in management, not hardware. SAN hardware accounts for about a third of system costs. Cutting hardware costs by choosing iSCSI over fibre channel saves only a small fraction of total system costs.

Another potential pitfall for iSCSI users is that it requires high-quality network service. Except for in-house corporate LANs and WANs, IP networks don't usually have the same quality of service you get with fibre channel. IP networks are usually designed for general-purpose networking, not for storage infrastructure. Those who plan to rely on commercial network bandwidth to support a SAN must ensure that it is up to the task.

Both fibre channel and SCSI took seven to eight years development each before they were ready for widespread deployment. iSCSI has just three years development behind it and is five years behind fibre channel.

Performance, quality of service, and cost issues with IP networks have to be solved before iSCSI will be a serious contender in enterprise storage networks. These are engineering issues and are solvable, but it will take time. Still, there is the possibility that iSCSI will replace fibre channel for most storage network architectures within about five years.

If iSCSI can truly replace fibre channel, SANs may change from being exotic, high-end storage solutions to systems that can be deployed at all but the smallest organizations. iSCSI can also encompass a much wider variety of storage devices, including magneto-optical and low-end CD/DVD jukeboxes. If the rosiest predictions for iSCSI come true, the technology may turn out to be the preferred method of adding storage to networks and transform SANs into mainstream storage infrastructures.

Appendix E
SCSI versus Fibre Channel Storage

Some industry analysts indicate SCSI over TCP/IP is the best fit; others tout the benefits of Fibre Channel over IP. Which argument has the most merit? Let's take a look.

SCSI..

Implementing SCSI over TCP for IP storage leverages existing network hardware, software, and technical know-how. SCSI over TCP will enable the use of Gigabit Ethernet, a proven industry standard, as an infrastructure for SANs. TCP/IP and Ethernet are dominant technologies in networking, and analysts see this trend continuing with SANs [1].

Using Gigabit Ethernet and SCSI over TCP offers significant economic benefits. The vast number of Ethernet equipment manufacturers, coupled with the technology's maturity, mean Ethernet equipment will always be more readily available than Fibre Channel equipment and at a lower price. SCSI over TCP SANs also will be less expensive to support than Fibre Channel-based SANs, which require additional training for the IT staff. In addition, the limited number of management tools for Fibre Channel SANs means an IT department will have to spend more time supporting the network [1].

There are also technical advantages to deploying Gigabit Ethernet and SCSI over TCP SANs. SCSI over TCP will let companies use existing management platforms that provide advanced levels of support. TCP/IP and Ethernet have been around for decades, and duplicating their technical achievements is counterproductive. Fibre Channel's chief technical problem is that it is attempting to reinvent the wheel. Issues such as security and quality of service have already been dealt with (and continue to be improved) in TCP/IP networks, while Fibre Channel vendors are just beginning to scratch the surface [1].

Fibre Channel is the only viable solution for implementing a SAN until SCSI over TCP becomes available. Some Fibre Channel switch vendors are developing routers that will let Ethernet networks attach to Fibre Channel SANs. This will give customers a choice between deploying an end-to-end Fibre Channel SAN and using a router to minimize the amount of Fibre Channel that must be installed. Fibre Channel/Ethernet routers may be a decent interim solution, but they don't have long-term potential because extra overhead is added, encapsulating and de-encapsulating packets back and forth across the router. An end-to-end Gigabit Ethernet SAN using SCSI over TCP won't have this added overhead and therefore will outperform a Fibre Channel/Ethernet SAN [1].

Fibre Channel vendors argue that Fibre Channel is optimized for storage applications and provides much higher performance than the combination of TCP/IP and Ethernet. This is debatable, especially because TCP accelerators are being developed and TCP/IP stacks are being embedded in silicon. Should you start planning for SCSI over TCP for your SAN? Consider the fate of other technologies that have attempted to compete with Ethernet, such as token ring and LAN-based ATM, and the answer will be clear [1].

FIBRE CHANNEL..

Fibre Channel over IP leverages IP-based network services to connect SAN islands over LANs, WANs, or MANs, independent of link-level transport protocols. It solves a real user problem, is available today, and has no ready substitutes. By contrast, SCSI over TCP/IP is still in the embryonic stages, faces significant technical obstacles, and for the near future, is a solution in search of a problem [2].

Fibre Channel over IP's main advantage is it needs no modifications to the storage subsystem or the server operating system. SCSI over TCP/IP, on the other hand, requires filter drivers, so the server operating system can do IP-network to SAN emulation. Unless Microsoft and other operating system vendors sign up for this mapping effort, practical implementations will be limited [2].

But why would anyone want SCSI over TCP/IP? The idea is positioned to connect servers (SCSI initiators) to disk drives or storage controllers (SCSI targets) using TCP/IP over Ethernet and WAN connections. A possible vision of the future has LAN-based storage protocols supplementing existing SAN and Network Attached Storage models—globally accessible net-attached disks, instant capacity scaling from LAN-connected storage service providers, and raw data sharing over the Internet at close to wire speeds [2].

But do we really need SCSI over TCP/IP to do this? Storage over IP is here today. That's what file systems such as Network File System do [2].

Fibre Channel over IP solves real problems associated with building geographically remote storage subsystems. One of these problems is that Fibre Channel, which efficiently maps the SCSI storage protocol, typically supports links of 50 kilometers or less. In addition, distributed file protocols that can be bridged and routed over existing LANs and WANs need an extra remote server, can't be synchronized below the file level, and must be independently implemented for each file system. Fibre Channel over IP solves these problems by supporting synchronized block I/O operations over long distances [2].

Furthermore, the network interface at the Fibre Channel/LAN boundary can be tuned for performance by locking a path, using SONET, or assigning a dedicated wave division multiplexing channel. Security issues can be addressed by connecting over an IP-based VPN. While an end-to-end IP network transport cannot cost-effectively provide this level of service today, Fibre Channel over IP partitions the problem, so the storage aspect is contained within the SAN, while the wide-area connectivity challenges (security, latency, bandwidth, and reliability) are handled by mature WAN and IP technologies. Fibre Channel-to-LAN routers are ready now to drop into existing topologies and create real value for high-availability systems [2].

END NOTES...

[1]   Alex Winokur, "SCSI Over TCP/IP," SANgate Systems, Inc., 144 Turnpike Road, Route 9, Southborough, MA 01772, 2001.

[2]   Wayne Rickard, "Fibre Channel Over IP," Gadzoox Networks, Inc., 5850 Hellyer Avenue, San Jose, CA 95138, 2001.

Appendix F
List of Miscellaneous SAN Resources

The many facets of implementing SAN technology can be confusing and unclear as an IT group works through the issues of how to best implement a SAN architecture or even how to best build a mission-critical capable network environment. To solve this problem, let's look at the following SAN resources:

FIBRE CHANNEL

- **FibreChannel Association** (*www.fibrechannel.com*): News, information, and product guides on Fibre Channel.

INDUSTRY ASSOCIATIONS

- **Storage Networking Industry Association (SNIA)** *(www.snia.org):* Organization for promoting storage solutions and technologies. SNIA offers a comprehensive library of white papers and general information on both SANs and NAS on its Web site.

MISCELLANEOUS SAN RESOURCES

- **Cutting Edge** (*www.storage-network.com/contact.htm*): Links to several SAN related white papers

- **SAN Overview** (*www.sresearch.com/wp_9801.htm*): An introduction to SANs, prepared by Strategic Research

- **SAN Resource Center** (*www.gadzoox.com/sanresourcecenter*): Gadzooks Networks' information on SANs

- The book, *Introduction to DWDM Technology*, by Stamatios V. Kartalopoulos, provides a good basic introduction to the Dense Wavelength Division Multiplexing technology used to extend SANs in metropolitan areas.

- ONI Systems offers a very helpful white paper entitled "Storage Area Network Transport Over the Metro Optical Network," which explains how optical networking technology, particularly DWDM, applies to SANs. This white paper can be found at the ONI Systems Web site.

- Hitachi Data Systems (HDS) offers white papers on its Lightning 9900 and on Multiprotocol Fibre Channel at its Web site.

- Computer Network Technology (CNT) offers some valuable information on storage over IP at its Web site.

SCSI

- **Ultra160** (*www.ultra160-scsi.com*): An industry alliance focused on the160 MBps SCSI Standard.

VENDORS

The following is a list of some new products in areas such as enterprise messaging, partnerships, storage resource management, and Fibre Channel.

Enterprise Messaging

Sun Microsystems recently announced that it would join more than 60 other storage networking vendors in demonstrating its enterprise messaging solutions at the SNW Interoperability Lab. This lab is a featured event at conferences and is organized by SNIA, a cosponsor of SNW.

Sun demonstrated storage policies in its HighGround Storage Resource Manager (SRM), which is important for mission-critical applications such as messaging. In the lab, Sun showed how HighGround SRM allows IT professionals to develop a map of their global storage stacks. SRM's global view of heterogeneous storage resources and associated trending histories help IT implement more effective storage practices and plan for additional storage capacities and supporting technologies.

StorageProvider has also joined the 60-plus vendors in the Interoperability lab. One of the themes at the interoperability lab was Data Storage Utility/Storage Service Provider (SSP) and StorageProvider. The purpose of the SSP theme demo was to show that service providers can give users solid, secure, and flexible storage management services.

Partnerships

Brocade Communications Systems and Computer Associates International (CA) recently announced they are expanding their relationship so they can deliver storage management for Brocade-based SANs. This partnership brings better interoperability between the Brocade SAN infrastructure and CA's open storage management and data protection solution.

CA's storage management software solutions represent a new generation of world class SAN management applications that will give customers advanced protection and management of their enterprise data. The CA solutions will leverage the rich features of Brocade's distributed Fabric Operating System to expand the SAN management options available to Brocade customers.

Another area that the two companies promise to focus on is security. Brocade and CA are working together to ensure that their security development efforts are integrated and complement each other's solutions. CA's eTrust security solutions promises high security compatibility with Brocade Secure Fabric Operating System, part of the Brocade fabric architecture.

Another piece of this fabric architecture is Brocade's SilkWorm 1200, a high-port density, multiprotocol core fabric switch that was recently announced at SNW. It is designed to support next-generation storage applications and services. It expands the capabilities of Fibre Channel storage environments and promises to support IP and InfiniBand networks. It further provides scalability and availability and reportedly reduces the overall cost of storage management. The SilkWorm 1200 has forward and backward compatibility and will be available in the fourth quarter of 2002.

In another announcement, Adaptec indicated it will begin shipping samples of its new iSCSI HBA, called the AEA-7110C, to OEMs later in 2002. The AEA-7110C allows users to build SANs on their existing IP/Ethernet networks.

The AEA-7110C was unveiled in conjunction with a recently introduced line of IBM iSCSI storage servers. The two companies showed how their products worked together in an interoperability demonstration.

Developing products that adhere to the iSCSI standard is an important building block for the future of the standard. Access to block-level data over common IP networks is a growing requirement, and a high performance iSCSI HBA which operates over existing IP networking infrastructures, will enable customers to maximize their investments in existing storage networking environments.

The AEA-7110C is a 64-bit, 66-MHz Ethernet controller that off-loads TCP/IP processing from the server and enables block-level storage data to be sent from the server to storage devices. It operates over an existing Category 5 cabling infrastructure. This type of cabling allows companies moving to Gigabit Ethernet for storage networking to do so without having to install new copper cables or fiber optic environments.

Storage Resource Management

Announcements made in the SRM category include a general availability release of StorageAlert/OS by TrelliSoft. The vendor claims StorageAlert/OS is the industry's first Java- and Web-based SRM solution suite. The suite provides lower storage costs because (from a single Web browser-based interface) it tracks application availability and monitors storage assets and usage across UNIX and Windows environments.

Fibre Channel

Lucent Technologies recently demonstrated Opti EdgeSwitch, a Fibre Channel over IP (FCIP) product. FCIP is a standards-based technology coauthored by Lucent and other storage networking vendors. It allows storage networking over IP networks and gives a single device high-speed SAN interconnections over regional and long-distance backbones.

OptiStar EdgeSwitch uses FCIP to deliver Fibre Channel to data centers and storage facilities that are geographically dispersed. This allows carriers and enterprises to offer storage applications such as data backup, disaster recovery, data replication, storage hosting, and storage trading over existing carrier networks. For example, a data center in Northern California could easily back up its critical data at storage facilities located in other areas across North America.

OptiStar EdgeSwitch gives SANs a direct optical link to IP-based Metropolitan and Wide Area Networks. FCIP technology in the switch solves the problem of Fibre Channel traffic traveling only 10 kilometers in a network when working alone. Because of these distance limits, Lucent claims, Fibre Channel previously could not be used for wide-area service delivery.

OptiStar EdgeSwitch sits at the intersection of the SAN and WAN and sends Fibre Channel data into IP packets for both block- and file-level storage traffic. The traffic is then routed over the IP WAN along with IP data traffic. This approach makes it possible to share a high-capacity WAN link between both IP storage and data traffic.

I-Tech also made a Fibre Channel announcement. The company introduced the Satellite IFC-8202 Fibre Channel Analyzing Hub, an interface testing solution. The Satellite IFC-8202 combines a two-channel analyzer and an eight-port hub within a compact unit. Multiple networked users can access the device via a standard Ethernet TCP/IP connection.

Also making a Fibre Channel announcement was McDATA, which released ED-6064, its Fibre Channel Galaxy-Class Director. The ED-6064 Director is a SAN backbone that offers scalability, flexibility, and provides guaranteed 99.999% data availability, which translates into less than five minutes of downtime each year.

The Galaxy-Class Director defines the basis that SAN platforms are built upon. The ED-6064 is the core of McDATA's advanced SAN architecture and delivers a previously unobtainable level of flexibility. When customers consolidate their servers and storage, they also consolidate their access. The ED-6064 Director provides bullet proof access and allows for a truly complete, open SAN.

In assessing the ED-6064, large users desire scalable, manageable, and available director-class switches for their SAN backbones. Fewer is always better and easier to manage.

Miscellaneous Announcements

Troika Networks recently announced the SAN Command Enterprise family of network management solutions for its Zentai Controllers. Also, BakBone Software and Seagate Removable Storage Solutions recently announced an OEM software bundle under which Seagate will use a copy of BakBone's NetVault backup and restore software with its Viper 200 Ultrium tape drive and Viper 2000 autoloader.

Computer Network Technology recently introduced a new storage networking router to its UltraNet family of storage networking solutions. The new UltraNet Edge Storage Router will support high-speed network architectures including FCIP, InfiniBand, and iSCSI.

Glossary

8b/10b encoding

An encoding scheme that converts an 8-bit byte into two possible 10-bit characters; used for balancing 1s and 0s in high-speed transports.

ABTS

Abort Basic Link Service.

ACC

Accept link service reply; the normal reply to an Extended Link Service request (such as FLOGI) indicating that the request has been completed.

Access arm

The device in a disk or disc drive that holds the read/write heads and moves them into position.

Access fairness

A process by which contending nodes are guaranteed access to an Arbitrated Loop.

Access method

The method used to access a physical medium in order to transmit data.

Access time

How long it takes a magnetic or optical drive to find data. It is the sum of the average latency and average seek time. In optical drives, seek time is often expressed in "aver-age seek time 1/3 stroke." This means the average time it takes the drive to find a file within 1/3 of the disc's radius. Since optical discs hold 325 megabytes per side, 1/3 stroke is the time it takes to seek from about 107.25 megs. It is *not* 1/3 the time it takes for a full stroke. The two are not directly proportional.

ACK

Acknowledgement frame; used for end-to-end flow control; verifies receipt of one or more frames from Class-1 or Class-2 services.

Active copper

A fibre channel connection that allows copper cabling up to 33 meters (100 yards) in length between devices.

Address identifier

A 24-bit number used to indicate the link-level address of communicating devices. In a frame header, the address identifier indicates the source ID (S_ID) and the destination ID (D_ID) of the frame respectively.

ADPCM (Adaptive Delta Pulse Code Modulation)

An audio encoding compression technique which encodes the difference between the predicted value of the signal instead of the absolute value of the original waveform so that the compression efficiency is improved. This difference is usually small and can thus be encoded in fewer bits than the sample itself. Used in CD-I and CD-ROM XA recording.

Alias server

A proposed standard as part of FC-PH-3; it will use the well-known address FFFFF8 and will maintain identifier mappings to support multicast group management.

AL_PA

Arbitrated Loop Physical Address; an 8-bit value used to identify a device participating in an Arbitrated Loop.

AL_TIME

Arbitrated Loop Timeout value; twice the amount of time it would take for a transmission word to propagate around a worst-case loop. The default value is 15 milliseconds (ms).

American Standard Code for Information Interchange (ASCII) sort

A means of alphabetizing that accounts for capital letters and numbers. To arrange something in an ASCII sort, numbers (digits) come first in numerical order, followed by capital letters in alphabetical order, followed by lower case characters in alphabetical order.

ANSI

American National Standards Institute; the governing body for standards in the U.S.

Application Program Interface (API)

Generic term for any language and format used by one program to help it communicate with another program. Specifically, an imaging vendor can provide an API that enables programmers to repackage or recombine parts of the vendor's imaging system, or integrate the imaging systems with other applications, or to customize the user interface to the imaging system.

ARB

Arbitrative Primitive Signal; this applies only to an Arbitrated Loop topology, and is transmitted as the fill word by an L_Port to indicate the port is arbitrating access to the loop.

Arbitrated Loop

A shared 100 MBps fibre channel transport supporting up to a maximum of 126 devices and 1 attachment to a fabric. Ports with lower AL_PAs have higher priorities.

Arbitration

A method of gaining orderly access to a shared-loop topology.

Archival quality

The extent to which a reproduced image will (or won't) last "forever."

Archive

A copy of data on disks, CD-ROM, magtape, etc., for long-term storage and later possible access. Archived files are often compressed to save storage space.

ARP

Address Resolution Protocol; a TCP/IP function for translating an IP address to an Ethernet (link-level MAC address).

ASIC

Application-Specific Integrated Circuit.

ATM

Asynchronous Transfer Mode; a high-speed packet-switching transport used for transmitting data over LANs or WANs that transmits fixed-length units of data. It provides any-to-any connectivity and nodes can transmit simultaneously.

Automated retrieval

Using a computer to identify and locate a stored image of some kind. Generally requires the use of key words or codes in an indexing scheme.

Automated Tape Library (ATL)

Large-scale tape storage system, which uses multiple tape drives and mechanism to address 50 or more cassettes.

Bandwidth

The transmission capacity of the cable, link, or system.

BB_Credit

Buffer-to-buffer credit; used to determine how many frames can be sent to the recipient.

BCA (Burst Cutting Area)

A zone near the hub of a DVD reserved for a bar code that can be etched into the disc by a laser. Since bar code cutting is independent of the stamping process, each disc can have unique data recorded on it, such as a serialized ID. DVD readers can use the laser pickup head to read the BCA.

Blue Book

The new standard for combining audio and data seamlessly on one CD. Also known as CD-Extra or CD-Plus.

Blue Laser

A type of laser capable of writing bits with up to five times greater density than the infrared lasers commonly used. In 1993, IBM demonstrated a recording density of 2.5 billion bits per square inch on a magneto-optic disk. It is expected that blue lasers will be commercially used within a few years.

Broadcast

Sending a transmission to all N_Ports on a fabric.

Burn

Generating a CD-ROM on a specialized writer (CD-R); "burn" comes from the heat generated by the high-powered laser needed to make the pits.

Bypass circuitry

Circuits that automatically remove a device from the data path when valid signals are dropped.

Byte

Eight bits of data grouped together to represent a character or some other computing data.

Cache (Memory & Magnetic)

Small portion of high-speed memory used for temporary storage of frequently used data. Reduces the time it would take to access the data, since it no longer has to be retrieved from the disk.

Caddy

The plastic and metal carrier into which a CD must be inserted before it is loaded into some CD-ROM drives or CD recorders and which is a highly controversial feature of DVD-RAM media. Also called cartridge.

CAM

Content addressable memories.

Camp on

Proposed as an optimization for fabric queue connect requests so that they are satisfied in the order received.

Cascade

Connecting two or more fibre channel hubs or switches to increase port capacity or distance.

CAV (Constant Angular Velocity)

CD-ROM drive method in which a steady spin speed is maintained, resulting in increased data transfer rates and reduced seek times as the head moves towards its outside edge. Has largely superseded CLV.

CD-Compatible

CD-R discs written that can be read in either a CD-DA player or in a CD-ROM reader.

CD-DA (Compact Disc-Digital Audio)

Jointly developed by Philips and Sony and launched in October 1982, CD-DA was the first incarnation of the compact disc, used to digitally record and play back music at unprecedented quality. The standard under which CD-DA discs are recorded is known as the Red Book.

CD-Extra

A multisession disc containing a number of audio tracks in the first session, and one CD-ROM XA data track in the second session. Additional characteristics are defined in the Blue Book standard. An alternative to mixed-mode for combining standard CD-D audio (which can be played in a normal audio player), and a computer application, on a single disc. Also known as CD-Plus.

CD-I (Compact Disc-Interactive)

A compact disc format (developed by Philips and Sony) designed to allow interactive multimedia applications to be played through a computer/disc player attached to a television. The CD-i standard is called the Green Book.

CD-i Bridge

A set of specifications defining a way of recording CD-i information on a CD-ROM XA disc. Used for Photo CD and Video CD.

CD-R

Recordable CD disc.

CDR

Clock and data recovery circuitry.

CD-ROM (Compact Disc-Read Only Memory)

A standard for compact disc to be used as a digital memory medium for personal computers. The 4.75" laser-encoded optical memory storage medium can hold about 650 MB of data, sound, and limited stills and motion video. A CD-ROM player will typically play CD-DA discs, but a CD-DA player will not play CD-ROMs. The standard used for most CD-ROM formats is known as Yellow Book, based on the standard published by Philips.

CD-ROM XA (CD-ROM Extended Architecture)

A hybrid format, promoted by Sony and Microsoft, that combines CD-ROM and CD-i capabilities. The extension adds ADPCM audio to permit the interleaving of sound and video data to animation and with sound synchronization. It is an essential component of Microsoft's plan for multimedia computers and also the physical format for Kodak's Photo CD format.

CD-RW (Compact Disc-Rewritable)

Once known as CD-Erasable, or CD-E.

CD WORM

Compact Disc Write-Once Read-Many.

CE

Conformité Européenne.

Channel

A point-to-point link whose task is to transport data from one point to another.

CIM

Common Information Model; a management structure enabling disparate resources to be managed by a common application.

CIRC (Cross-Interleaved Reed-Solomon Code)

The first level of error correction used in every compact disc, and the only one used for audio CDs. It consists of two Reed-Solomon codes interleaved crosswise.

Class 1

A connection-oriented class of service that requires acknowledgment of frame delivery.

Class 2

A connectionless class of service that requires acknowledgment of frame delivery between N_Ports.

Class 3

A connectionless class of service that requires no acknowledgment of frame delivery between N_Ports.

Class 4

A connection-oriented service that allows fractional parts of the bandwidth to be used in a virtual circuit.

Class 6

A connection-oriented multicast service geared toward video broadcasts between a central server and clients.

Class F

A connectionless class of service that gives notification of delivery or nondelivery between E_Ports, used for control, coordination, and configuration of the Fabric.

CLS

Close Primitive Signal; only in an Arbitrated Loop; sent by an L_Port that is currently communicating on the loop, to close communication to another L_Port.

CLV (Constant Linear Velocity)

The traditional CD-ROM drive method in which motor speed is regulated to keep the track passing under the read head at a steady speed. See also CAV.

Common Object Model

The Common Object Model is the functional equivalent of the Component Object Model for UNIX-based platforms that today include SunOS, OBM, AIX, HP-UX, ULTRIX, OSF/1, and OpenVMS. The Common Object Model defines a Storage Management.

Community

A relationship in SNMP between an SNMP agent and a set of SNMP managers that defines authentication, access control, and proxy characteristics.

Compact Disc (CD)

A standard medium for storage of digital data in a machine-readable form, accessible with a laser-based reader. CDs are 4 1/4" in diameter. CDs are faster and more accurate than magnetic tape for data storage. Faster, because even though data is generally written on a CD contiguously within each track, the tracks themselves are directly accessible. This means the tracks can be accessed and played back in any order. They are more accurate because data is recorded directly into binary code; magtape requires data to be translated into analog form. Also, extraneous noise (tape hiss) associated with magtape is absent from CDs.

Compact Disc-Digital Audio (CD-DA)

Jointly developed by Philips and Sony and launched in October, 1982, CD-DA is the first and most popular incarnation of the compact disc, used to digitally record and play back music at unprecedented quality. It has gained worldwide acceptance as a standard to which all digital audio CD disc and CD drives adhere. Philips/Sony's CD-DA standard is known as the Red Book.

Compact Disc-Interactive (CD-I)

A compact disc format, developed by Philips and Sony, which provides audio, digital data, still graphics, and limited motion video. Designed to be played through a small computer/disc player on a home television screen. The CD-I standard is also known as the Green Book.

Compact Disc Read-only Data eXchange (CD-RDx)

A proposed standard for full-text retrieval from CD-ROMs.

Compact Disc-Read Only Memory (CD-ROM)

A data storage system using CDs as the medium. CD-ROMs hold more than 600 megabytes of data.

Compact Disc-Write Once (CD-WO)

ISO/IEC 13490 (ECMA 168); Volume and file structure for Read-Only and Write-Once disk media for information interchange.

Component Object Model

The Component Object Model, or COM, is a standard mechanism for objects written by different companies in different programming languages to interact. COM is the basic "wiring and plumbing" for all OLE features. For instance, COM allows component software applications to be integrated into larger business systems through OLE Automation.

Compressed pattern storage

The storage that holds the double-byte fonts for the IBM 3800 printer.

Compression

A software or hardware process that "shrinks" images so they occupy less storage space and can be transmitted faster and easier. Generally accomplished by removing the bits that define blank spaces and other redundant data and replacing them with a smaller algorithm that represents the removed bits.

Compression ratio

The ratio of a file's original size over its compressed size. A compression ratio of 16:1 means the compressed file is 1/16 as large as the original file. An 800 K file compressed with this ratio would be reduced to roughly 50 K.

Computer Output to Laser Disk (COLD)

Technique used to transfer computer-generated output to optical disk.

Constant Angular Velocity (CAV)

Technique enabling data recorded with a variable linear density to be read, whereby the speed of rotation of the disk remains constant.

Constant Linear Velocity (CLV)

The technique of adjusting the speed of a disk's spinning, so that the larger outer tracks (which normally would spin faster) can be slowed down and thus hold more data than the smaller inner tracks. Used in CD-ROM. Storage Management head as it reads data from or writes data to the disk.

Controller

A computer module that interprets signals between a host and a peripheral device. The controller typically is part of the peripheral device.

COS

Class of service.

CRC

Cyclic Redundancy Check; a self-test for error detection and correction.

Credit

A numeric value that represents the maximum number of receive buffers provided by an F/FL_Port to its attached N/NL_Port such that the N/NL_Port may transmit frames without overrunning the F/FL_Port.

Cue Sheet

A list of audio files which are to be recorded to a CD in Red Book format. Also referred to as a compilation list.

Curie Point

The temperature at which the molecules of a material can be altered when subjected to a magnetic field. In optical material, it is approximately 200 degrees centigrade.

Cut-through

A switching technique that allows a routing decision to be made as soon as the destination address of the frame is received.

DAT Auto Loader (DAL)

Device that accepts a magazine of five or so DAT tapes, which are each addressable.

Data compression

Reducing the amount of electronic "space" data takes up. Methods include replacing blank spaces with a character count, or replacing redundant data with shorter stand-in "codes." No matter how data is compressed, it must be decompressed before it can be used.

Data decompression

The regeneration of a bit-map from a compressed representation.

Datagram

A Class 3 Fibre Channel service that allows data to be sent quickly to multiple devices attached to the fabric, with no confirmation of receipt.

Decompress

To reverse the procedure conducted by compression software, and thereby return compressed data to its original size and condition.

Dedicated simplex

A means that permits a single N_Port to simultaneously initiate a session with another N_Port as an initiator, and have a separate Class 1 connection to another N_Port as a recipient.

Demigration

The most common way to cache from optical storage is to prefetch images from an optical server and move them to magnetic media, either on a file server or at the workstation, before they are requested by the user. Some vendors call this "demigration" (migration is moving data to optical storage).

Device drivers

Small programs that tell the computer how to communicate with particular types of peripheral devices.

Diagnostic code

An alphanumeric or word display that signals a system condition such as a malfunction. The code is either self-explanatory or refers to further instructions that are explained in an operator guide.

Digital Audio Tape (DAT)

A technology that records noise-free digital data on magnetic tape. Generally used for audio, a DAT cassette can hold zero to two gigabytes when adapted for data storage.

Digital Data Storage (DDS)

A DAT format for storing data. It is sequential; all data that is recorded to the tape falls after the previous block of data.

Direct Access Storage Device (DASD)

Any online data storage device. A disc, drive, or CD-ROM player that can be addressed is a DASD.

Direct Read After Write (DRAW)

A method that ensures that data written on recordable media is error free.

Direct Read During Write (DRDW)

A method of error correction on an optical disc that reads new data immediately during the same disc rotation.

Directory service

The facility within networking software that provides information on resources available on the network, including files, users, printers, data sources, applications, and so on.

Disc

A digital storage medium. Optical discs are made of a metal alloy recording surface sandwiched between a rigid substrate and a plastic protective coating. Lasers record data in the metal alloy by either creating tiny pits (ablation technique) or by causing small bubbles to form in the "negative" area, thereby reflecting the laser away. Generally, disk with a "c" means optical disc. Disk with a "k" means magnetic hard or floppy disk.

Disc-At-Once

In Disc-at-Once mode, the whole disc is written without turning off the recording laser. All of the information to be recorded needs to be staged on the computer's hard disk prior to recording. The mode is especially useful for creating a master disc for subsequent mass production via a replicator since it eliminates the linking and run-in and run-out blocks associated with multisession and packet recording modes, which often are interpreted as uncorrectable errors during the mastering process. It requires the premastering software to send a "cue sheet" to the CD-R/DVD-R drive that describes the disc layout.

Disk

A round, flat recording medium which consists of a substrate(s) with one or more layers deposited on the surface(s) onto which information can be recorded and played back when the disk is loaded in a disk drive.

Disk array

Combining redundant disk or disc drives for more capacity, or for disaster recovery.

Disk array controller

Acts as a manager between the host and the drives. Comprised of a main computer module, channels for each drive, and a host channel for each host input. Adding memory modules increases performance.

Disk cache

Place in memory where frequently recalled data is stored while you're working. It makes retrievals much faster.

Disk controller

A hardware device that controls how data is written to and retrieved from the disk drive. The disk controller sends signals to the disk drive's logic board to regulate the movement of the Storage Management.

Disk drive

A device containing motors, electronics, and other gadgetry for storing (writing) and retrieving (reading) data on a disk. A hard disk drive is generally not removable from the machine. A floppy disk drive accepts the removable disk cartridges.

Disk duplexing

A method of fail-safe protection, occasionally used on file servers on LANs. Disk duplexing involves copying data onto two hard disks simultaneously, each through a separate disk channel. The idea is, if one disk or channel is faulty, the other will most likely continue to operate normally.

Disk management

Refers to the control of information stored on a disk—the logical relationship of subdirectories to root directories, for instance.

Disk mirroring

A fault-tolerant technique that writes data simultaneously to two hard disks using the same hard disk controller. The disks operate in tandem, constantly storing and updating the same files. Mirroring alone does not ensure data protection. If both hard disks fail at the same time, you will lose data.

Disk pack

A cartridge of hard disk platters arranged as a single unit. A disk pack contains more space for storing and retrieving information than one single disk.

Disk sector

Magnetic disks are typically divided into tracks, each of which contains a number of sectors. A sector typically contains a predetermined amount of data, such as 256 bytes.

Disk (file) server

A mass storage device that can be accessed by several computers, usually through a LAN.

Disk storage

A method of storing data on rotating circular magnetic platters called disks.

Disk striping

Spreading data over multiple disk drives. Data is interleaved by bytes or by sectors across the drives.

Disparity

The relationship of 1s and 0s in an encoded character; positive disparity contains more 1s, negative disparity contains more 0s, neutral disparity contains an equal number of 1s and 0s.

Distributed file system

A type of file system in which the file system itself manages and transparently locates pieces of information from remote files and distributes files across a network.

DIVX (DIgital Video eXpress)

A proprietary extension to the DVD-Video standard which effectively turns it into a pay-per-view system. Introduced in the second half of 1998, its backers—led by the Circuit City electronics chain—abandoned the technology in mid-1999.

DLS

Dynamic Load Sharing; allows for recomputing of routes when an Fx or E_Port comes up or down.

Document retrieval

The ability to search for, select, and display a document or its facsimile from storage.

Domain ID

A unique number between 1 and 239 on a switch that identifies the switch to a fabric.

DOW (Direct OverWrite)

With CD-RW, the traditional concept of erasure does not exist. New data is simply written over existing data in a single-pass. CD-RW is therefore known as a Direct Over-Write (DOW) system.

DVD (Digital Versatile Disk)

The replacement for the ubiquitous compact disc. Like the CD it is available in a number of different formats. Unlike the CD, it is available with a number of capacities ranging from 4.7 GB to 17 GB.

DVD-R (DVD Recordable)

The write-once DVD format. DVD-R discs are the DVD counterpart to CD-R discs.

DVD-RAM

A new type of rewritable compact disc that provides much greater data storage than today's CD-RW systems. The caddy-mounted discs will initially provide 2.6 GB per side on single or double-sided discs.

DVD-ROM

The read-only format supports discs with capacities of from 4.7 GB (enough for an MPEG-2 compressed full-length movie) to 17 GB and access rates of 600 KBps to 1.3 MBps. Backward-compatible with CD-ROMs.

DVD+RW

A competing (to DVD-RAM) rewritable DVD standard being promoted by Hewlett-Packard, Philips, and Sony. Unlike the DVD-RAM standard, +RW allows the use of bare discs. The two standards are incompatible. At one time the DVD-Forum were insisting on the name being changed to "+RW"—but this appears to have had little effect.

DVD-Video

A consumer DVD format for displaying full-length digital movies. DVD-Video players attach to a television like a videocassette player. Unlike DVD-ROMs, the Digital-Video format includes a Content Scrambling System (CSS) to prevent users from copying discs. This means that today's DVD-ROM players cannot play DVD-Video discs without a software or hardware upgrade to decode the encrypted discs.

DWDM

Dense Wave Digital Multiplexing; see WDM. Allows more wavelengths to use the same fiber.

Dynamic Random Access Memory (DRAM)

The kind of RAM used in SIMMS. The data stored in Dynamic RAM (as opposed to "Static RAM") fades away over time, so the information has to be refreshed (rewritten) every few thousandths of a second. Although this consumes much more power than the static design, each memory cell can be built from just one transistor instead of the four required for static RAM, so higher memory capacities can be built economically.

E_D_TOV

Error-Detect Time Out Value; the maximum round-trip time that an operation could require before declaring an error condition.

EE_Credit

End-to-end credit; used to manage the exchange of frames by two communicating devices and set the maximum number of frames that may remain unacknowledged.

EIA
Electronic Industries Association.

ELP
Extended Link Process.

Emulex
A brand of host bus adapter.

EOF
End Of Frame; a group of ordered sets used to mark the end of a frame.

E_Port
An expansion port connecting two switches to make a fabric.

Erasable optical
Another word for rewritable. An optical disc that does not mark its data permanently into the disc surface.

Erasable storage
A storage device whose contents can be changed, i.e. random access memory, or RAM.

Erase head
On a magnetic tape recorder—voice or video—this is the "head" which erases the tape by demagnetizing it immediately before a new recording is placed on the tape by the adjacent record head.

Exchange
The highest-level fibre channel mechanism used for communication between N_Ports. They are composed of 1+ related sequences and work either uni- or bidirectionally.

Fabric
One or more fibre channel switches in some networked topologies. One of three fibre channel topologies, when N_Ports are connected to F_Ports on a switch.

FAN
Fabric Address Notification; keeps the AL_PA and fabric address when loop reinitializes if the switch supports FAN.

F_BSY
Fabric Port Busy Frame; a frame issued by the fabric to indicate that a frame cannot be delivered because the fabric or destination N_Port is busy.

FCA
Fibre Channel Association.

FC-0
Lowest layer on fibre channel transport; represents the physical media.

FC-1
This layer contains the 8b/10b encoding scheme.

FC-2
This layer handles framing and protocol, frame format, sequence/exchange management, and ordered set usage.

FC-3
This layer contains common services used by multiple N_Ports in a node.

FC-4
This layer handles standards and profiles for mapping upper-level protocols such as SCSI and IP onto the Fibre Channel Protocol.

FC-AL
Fibre Channel Arbitrated Loop.

FC-AV
Fibre Channel Audio Visual.

FC-CT
Fibre Channel Common Transport.

FC-FG
Fibre Channel Generic requirements.

FC-FLA

Fibre Channel Fabric Loop Attachment.

FC-GS

Fibre Channel generic services.

FC-GS-2

Fibre Channel second-generation generic services.

FC_IP

Fibre channel over IP protocol.

FC-PH

The fibre channel physical and signaling standard for FC-0, FC-1, and FC-2 layers of the Fibre Channel Protocol, and also indicates signaling used for cable plants, media types, and transmission speeds.

FC-PH-2

Second-generation physical interface.

FC-PH-3

Third-generation physical interface.

F_RJT

Fabric Port Reject Frame; a frame issued by the fabric to indicate that delivery of a frame is being denied, maybe because class is not supported, or there is an invalid header, or no N_Port is available.

FC_SB

Fibre Channel Single Bytes.

FC-SW

Fibre Channel Switch Fabric; specifies tools and algorithms for interconnection and initialization of Fibre Channel switches to create a multiswitch Fibre Channel Fabric.

FC-SW-2

Fibre Channel Switch Fabric (second generation); specifies tools and algorithms for interconnection and initialization of Fibre Channel switches to create a multiswitch Fibre Channel Fabric.

FC_VI

Fibre Channel Virtual Interface.

FCC

Federal Communications Commission.

FCIA

Fibre Channel Industry Association; its mission is to nurture and help develop the broadest market for Fibre Channel products.

FCLC

Fibre Channel Loop Community.

FCP

Fibre Channel Protocol; SCSI to Fibre Channel mapping.

FDDI

Fibre Distributed Data Interface; ANSI architecture for a MAN; a network based on the use of optical-fibre cable to transmit data at 100 megabits per second.

FFFFF5

Well-known Fibre Channel address for a Class 6 multicast server.

FFFFF6

Well-known Fibre Channel address for a clock synchronization server.

FFFFF7

Well-known Fibre Channel address for a security key distribution server.

FFFFF8

Well-known Fibre Channel address for an alias server.

FFFFF9

Well-known Fibre Channel address for a QoS facilitator.

FFFFFA

Well-known Fibre Channel address for a management server.

FFFFFB

Well-known Fibre Channel address for a time server.

FFFFFC

Well-known Fibre Channel address for a directory server.

FFFFFD

Well-known Fibre Channel address for a fabric controller.

FFFFFE

Well-known Fibre Channel address for a fabric F_Port.

FFFFFF

Well-known address for a broadcast alias-ID.

File Allocation Table (FAT)

Data written to a magnetic disk is not necessarily placed in contiguous tracks. It is usually divided into many clusters of data in many locations on the disk surface. The FAT is the special area on a disk which keeps track of where clusters of data have been written for retrieval later.

File server

LANs were invented to allow users on the LAN to share and thereby conserve the cost of peripherals (printers, modems, scanners) and to likewise share software. The file server is the machine on the LAN where the shared software is stored.

Fill word

The primitive signal used by L_Ports to be transmitted between frames.

Fixed disk

Another name for hard disk. So-called because it is installed in a computer and not meant to be removed.

FL_Port

A fabric loop port to which a loop attaches; needs FL card LED turned on. It is the gateway to the fabric for NL_Ports on a loop.

Flash

Programmable NVRAM memory that maintains its contents.

FLOGI

Fabric Login; a process by which a node makes a logical connection to a fabric switch.

F_Port

A fabric port to which an N_Port attaches.

Fractional Bandwidth

The partial use of a link to send data back and forth, with a maximum of 254 Class 4 connections per N_Port.

Frame

A data unit containing a start-of-frame (SOF) delimiter, header, payload, cyclic redundancy check (CRC), and an end-of-frame (EOF) delimiter. The payload can be 0-2112 bytes, and the CRC is 4 bytes.

FRU

Field Replaceable Unit; a component that can be swapped out upon failure.

FSP

Fibre Channel Service Protocol; The common FC-4 level protocol for all services, transparent to the fabric type or topology.

FSPF

Fibre Shortest Path First; a routing protocol used by fibre channel switches.

Full duplex

Concurrent transmission and reception of data on a link.

Full fabric citizenship

A loop device that has an entry in name server. Gateway hardware that connects incompatible networks by providing the necessary translation, both for hardware and software.

GBIC

Gigabit Interface Converter; a removable transceiver module permitting fibre channel and Gigabit Ethernet physical-layer transport.

Gbps

Gigabits per second.

GBps

Gigabytes per second.

Gigabit

1,062,500,000 bits per second in Fibre Channel.

GLM

Gigabit Link Module; a semitransparent transceiver that incorporates serializing/deserializing functions.

G_Port

A generic port that supports either E_Port or F_Port functionality.

GUI

Graphical User Interface.

Hard disk

A storage device that uses a magnetic recording material. Generally, hard disks are fixed inside a PC. Hard disks store anywhere from five to hundreds of megabytes.

HBA

Host Bus Adapter; an interface between a server or workstation bus and the fibre channel network.

Hierarchical File System (HFS)

In DOS, the file management system that allows directories to have subdirectories and sub-subdirectories. In Macintoshes, files may be placed into folders, and folders placed within other folders.

HiPPI

High-performance Parallel Interface; an 800 Mbpsinterface normally used in supercomputer environments.

Hot swappable

A component that can be replaced while under power.

HSSDC

High Speed Serial Data Connection; a form factor that allows quick connections for copper interfaces.

HTTP

HyperText Transfer Protocol; the standard TCP/IP transfer protocol used on the World Wide Web.

Hub

A fibre channel wiring concentrator that collapses a loop topology into a physical star topology. A hub automatically recognizes an active node and inserts it into the loop. A node that is not functioning is automatically removed from the loop.

Hunt Group

A number of N_Ports registered as a single Alias_ID, so the fabric can route it to a port that is free.

Idle

An ordered set transmitted continuously over a link when no data is being transmitted, to maintain an active link over fibre. It also helps maintain bit, byte, and word synchronization.

In-band

Transmission of management protocol over the Fibre Channel transport.

Initiator

A server or workstation on a fibre channel network that initiates transactions to tapes or disks.

Intercabinet

A specification for copper cabling that allows up to 33-meter (100-yard) distances between cabinets.

Intermix

Allows any unused bandwidth in a Class 1 connection to be used by Class 2 or Class 3.

Intracabinet

A specification for copper cabling that allows up to a 13-meter (42-foot) distance within a single cabinet.

IOD

In Order Delivery; a parameter that when set, guarantees that frames get delivered in order, or they are dropped.

IP

Internet Protocol; the addressing part of TCP/IP.

IPI

Intelligent Peripheral Interface.

ISL

Interswitch Link; a connection between two switches using the E_Port.

Isolated E_Port

This occurs when an ISL is online but not operational between switches because of overlapping domain IDs or no identical parameters such as E_D_TOVs.

ISP

Internet Service Provider.

Jaycor

A brand of host bus adapter.

JBOD

Just a Bunch of Disks; a term for disks typically configured as an Arbitrated Loop segment in a single chassis.

Jitter

A deviation in timing for a bit stream as it flows through a physical medium.

Jukebox Management

In a network, tasks like retrieval and writes to a jukebox come randomly from all the users. These tasks vary in urgency—retrievals are higher priority than writes, for example. Jukebox management software sorts out requests from the network by priority.

Jukebox Management Software (JMS)

The software that controls the writing, geographic placement, and ultimate retrieval of data in an optical jukebox.

K28.5

A special 10-bit character used to indicate the beginning of a Fibre Channel command.

LAN

Local Area Network; a network where transmissions are typically under 5 kilometers (3.4 miles).

Latency

The period of time that a frame is held by a network device before it is forwarded.

LED

Light Emitting Diode; a status indicator on a switch, typically yellow or green.

LIFA

Loop Initialization Fabric Assigned frame; contains bitmap of all fabric assigned AL_PAs and is the first frame transmitted in the loop initialization process after a temporary loop master has been selected.

LIHA

Loop Initialization Hard Assigned frame; a hard assigned AL_PA that is indicated by a bit set and is the third frame transmitted in the loop initialization process after a temporary loop master has been selected.

LILP

Loop Initialization Loop Position frame; the final frame transmitted in a loop initialization process. A returned LIRP contains an accumulation of all of the AL_PA position maps. This allows all loop members to determine their relative loop position. This is an optional frame and is not transmitted unless the LIRP is also transmitted.

Link

A bidirectional point-to-point serial data channel.

Link control facility

A termination card handling physical and logical control of the fibre channel link for each mode.

LIP

Loop Initialization Process; a means to get an AL_PA address, to indicate a loop failure or to reset a node.

LIPA

Loop Initialization Previously Assigned; where the device marks a bit in the bitmap if it had not logged in with the fabric in a previous loop initialization.

LIRP

Loop Initialization Report Position frame; the first frame transmitted in the loop initialization process after all L_Ports have selected an AL_PA. It gets transmitted around the loop so all L_Ports can report their relative physical position. This is an optional frame.

LISA

Loop Initialization Soft Assigned frame; the fourth frame transmitted in the loop initialization process after a temporary loop master has been selected. L_Ports that have not selected an AL_PA in a LIFA, LIPA, or LIHA frame will select their AL_PA here.

LISM

Loop Initialization Select Master frame; the first frame transmitted in the initialization process when L_Ports select an AL_PA. It is used to select a temporary loop master or the L_Port that will subsequently start transmission of the LIFA, LIPA, LIHA, LISA, LIRP, or LILP frames.

Login server

The unit that responds to login requests.

Looplet

Private Arbitrated Loops connected by a fabric.

LPB

Loop Port Bypass; a primitive sequence transmitted by an L_Port to bypass the L_Port to which it is directed. It is used only in Arbitrated Loops.

LPE

Loop Port Enable; a primitive sequence transmitted by an L_Port to enable an L_Port that has been bypassed with the LPB. It is used only in Arbitrated Loops.

L_Port

Node Loop port; a port supporting the Arbitrated Loop protocol. It appears as the part of the output of a switchShow Telnet command.

LPSM

Loop Port State Machine; logic that monitors and performs the tasks required for initialization and access to the loop. It is maintained by an L_Port to track behavior through different phases of loop operations.

LR

Link Reset; a primitive sequence used during link initialization between two N_Ports in point-to-point topology, or an N_Port and an F_Port in fabric topology. The expected response is an LRR.

LRR

Link Reset Response; a primitive sequence during link initialization between two N_Ports in point-to-point topology, or an N_Port and an F_Port in fabric topology. It is sent in response to an LR, and expects a response of "Idle."

LWL

Long wavelength fiber-optic; connector is color-coded blue, and is based on 1,300-millimeter lasers supporting 1.0625-Gbps link speeds.

Magnetic media

Variety of magnetically coated materials used by computers for data program storage.

Magnetic recording

A technique of recording analog or digital signals or data on a medium of specially prepared grains of iron oxide; old-fashioned tape recording (although floppy and hard disks use basically the same technology).

Magnetic tape

Storage medium that uses a thin plastic ribbon coated with iron oxide compound to record data with electrical pulses. Mag tape is a sequential storage medium, the next bit of data is recorded after the last bit. In order to locate a specific bit of data, you have to look through the whole tape until you find it. The standard for data recording is nine-track mag tap; one byte (eight bits plus a parity bit) fits across the tape width-wise.

Magneto-Optic (MO) Recording

Recording data using optical means to change the polarity of a magnetic field in the recording medium. Data is erasable and/or rewritable.

Magneto-optic recording layer

A layer of rare earth transition metals which is of high coercivity at normal temperatures but can be easily oriented in the presence of an external magnetic field when heated to the Curie Point temperature.

Magneto-optical (MO)

A high-density, erasable recording method. A laser heats a grain of a rare earth element, which makes it susceptible to magnetic influence. The write head passes over the grain while it's still susceptible. The data can then be read by another laser, whose light is not hot enough to change the grain's polarity.

Magneto-resistant (MR)

Newish Quarter Inch Tape (QIC) technology that increases the capacity by 2-1/2 times. Uses the magnetic resistance of the gaps between magnetic spots, not the size of the gap. The gaps can be smaller, hence allowing more data in the same space.

MAN

Metropolitan Area Network.

Mass storage

Applications, such as imaging, and processing-intensive operating systems, such as Windows, pushed the demand for mass storage options—optical discs, tape drives, and arrayed hard drives. Recently, the ante has been upped further with libraries and changers—multiple arrays of already-quite-large devices like tape drives. It's not uncommon for a typical office worker to be connected to (or have access to in sub-second times) multiple gigabytes of storage.

Mbps

Megabits per second.

MBps

Megabytes per second.

Metric

A relative value assigned to a route to aid in calculating the shortest path.

MIA

Media Interface Adapter; a device that converts optical connections to copper ones.

MIB

Management Information Base; an SNMP structure for device management that contains an abstraction of configuration and device information.

Modified Constant Angular Velocity (MCAV)

Qualifies an optical disk which includes several centric zones. Each zone is read at constant angular velocity, crossing from one zone to another involves modifying the velocity.

Modified Constant Linear Velocity (MCLV)

Describes a disk on which tracks are divided into bands. Within a band, the disk spins at constant angular velocity, but that velocity is different for each band. The relation between velocity and band location is similar to velocity radius curve for CLV operation.

MRK

Mark Primitive Signal; used only in Arbitrated Loop, it is transmitted by an L_Port for synchronization and is vendor specific.

MTBF

Mean Time Between Failures; an expression of a unit of time indicating the longevity of a device.

Multicast

A restricted broadcast to a subset of the N_Ports on the network.

Multifunction drive

An optical drive which can use both WORM and rewritable media.

Multilayer CD

A proposed means of increasing the storage capacity of CDs and CD-ROMs. The idea is to sandwich several translucent recording layers atop one another with small gaps in between. The reading laser can move in and move out to put each layer in focus for reading. The translucency of the layers allows the laser to see through and not be affected by other layers.

Multimode

A fiber-optic cabling specification that allows up to 500-meter distances between devices.

NAS

Network Attached Storage; a disk array connected to a controller that gives access to a LAN Transport.

NDMP

Network Data Management Protocol; used for tape backups without using server resources.

NIC

Network Interconnect Card.

NL_Port

Node Loop port; a port supporting the Arbitrated Loop protocol.

Node

A fibre channel device that supports one or more ports.

Node name

A 64-bit unique identifier assigned to a Fibre Channel node.

Non-OFC

A category of laser transceiver that does not require open fibre control due to its low intensity.

Nonparticipating Mode

This mode is entered if there are more than 127 devices on a loop, and an AL_PA cannot be acquired.

NOS

Non-Operational Primitive Sequence; used during link initialization between two N_Ports in the point-to-point topology, or an N_Port and F_Port in the fabric topology. It is sent to indicate that the transmitting port

has detected a link failure or is offline. An OLS is the expected response.

N_Port

A fibre channel port in a fabric or point-to-point connection.

OFC

Open Fiber Control; a method used to enable and disable laser signaling for higher-intensity laser transceivers.

Offline storage

Archival storage not directly accessible to your computer. Requires manually finding and inserting the medium (usually tape) into a drive. Upside: inexpensive, removable, high-capacity media. Generally refers to quarter-inch cartridges (QIC), digital audio tape (DAT), or helical scan backup (8 mm, 4 mm, and videocassette), but actually means any media stored on a shelf. Downside: s-l-o-w. And, it requires careful file management.

OLS

Offline Primitive Sequence; this is used during link initialization between two N_Ports in a point-to-point topology or an F_Port and an N_Port in a fabric. It is sent to indicate that the transmitting port is attempting to initialize a link, has recognized the NOS primitive sequence, or is going offline. The expected response to an OLS is an LR.

OLTP

OnLine Transaction Processing.

Online

Data that is available on a primary storage device so that it is readily accessible to the user.

Operation

An FC-2 term that refers to building blocks.

OPN

Open Primitive Signal; this applies only to Arbitrated Loop, and is sent by an L_Port that has won the arbitration process to open communication with one or more ports on the loop.

Optical

(1) Containing lenses mirrors, etc., as in optical view-finder and optical printer. (2) In general, having to do with light and its behavior and control, as in optical properties, optical rotation. (3) Pertaining to the science of light and vision.

Optical disc storage and retrieval

The combination of an optical drive or juke-box and software to manage the search and retrieval.

Optical disk

A storage device that is written and read by laser light. Certain optical disks are considered.

Optical drive

Machine for reading or writing a data storage medium (disk, tape, card, etc.) that uses light for examining patterns.

Optical Hard Drive (OHD)

A term pioneered by Pinnacle Micro, Irvine, CA. OHD technology, according to Pinnacle, combines the advantages of magneto-optical technology with speeds approaching those of hard drives.

Optical tape

A storage medium that works with the same technologies as optical discs (M-O, phase change) but the substrate is in the physical form of tape, like regular mag tape. In fact, I'm told there will soon be a viable optical tape product, based on phase change, that can hold one terabyte in a standard IBM 3480-style cartridge. A regular magnetic 3480 now holds about 500 megabytes.

Ordered set

A group of low-level protocols used to manage frame transport, initialization, and media access, and to distinguish fibre channel control information from data.

Originator

The N_Port that originated an exchange.

Out-of-band

Transmission of management protocol outside of the fibre channel network, usually over Ethernet.

OX_ID

Originator Exchange Identifier; a 2-byte field in the frame header used by the originator of an exchange to identify frames as being part of an exchange.

Parallel

The simultaneous transmission of data bits over multiple lines.

Participating Mode

The normal operating mode for an L_Port that has acquired an AL_PA on a loop.

Passive copper

A low-cost copper Fibre Channel connection allowing distances up to 13 meters (14 yards) between devices.

PBC

Port Bypass Circuit; a circuit in hubs or a disk enclosure to open or close a loop to add or remove nodes.

Picker

In jukeboxes, the "hand" on the robotic "arm" that grasps and moves the disc to or from the storage slot, disc drive, or mailslot.

More boringly called the "carriage." Some jukes are "dual-picker."

PLDA
Private Loop Direct Attached; a logical loop.

PLOGI
A port-to-port login process where initiators establish sessions with targets.

Point-to-Point
A dedicated Fibre Channel connection between two devices.

Port
A Fibre Channel entity that connects a node to the network.

Port Log
A record of all activity on a switch, kept in volatile memory.

Port Log Dump
A view of what happens on a switch from the switch's point of view. This is the command used to read the Port Log.

Port name
A unique 64-bit character identifier assigned to a Fibre Channel port.

POST
Power On Self Test; a routine that the switch performs to test its components.

Primitive sequence
Ordered sets that indicate or start state changes on the transport medium and require at least three consecutive occurrences to trigger a response.

Primitive signals
Ordered sets that indicate actions or events and require just one occurrence to trigger a response. Idle and R_RDY are used in all three topologies, ARB, OPN CLS, and MRK are in Arbitrated Loop.

Private device
A device that supports loop and can understand 8-bit addresses but cannot log into the fabric.

Private loop
An Arbitrated Loop with no fabric attachment.

Private loop device
An Arbitrated Loop device with no fabric attachment.

Private NL_Port
An NL_Port on a public or private loop; it only communicates with other ports on the loop, not with the fabric.

PSU
Power Supply Unit.

Public device
A device that supports loop and can also log into the fabric.

Public loop
An Arbitrated Loop attached to a fabric switch.

Public loop device
An Arbitrated Loop device that supports fabric login and services.

Public NL_Port
An NL_Port that may communicate with other ports on the loop as well as through an FL_Port to other N_Ports on the fabric.

Qlogic
A brand of host bus adapter.

QoS
Quality of Service.

Queue

A mechanism for each AL_PA address that allows for collecting frames prior to sending them to the loop.

RAID

Redundant Array of Independent Disks; disks look like a single volume to the server, and are fault-tolerant either through mirroring or parity checking.

RAID levels

Level 1 mirrors data—all data is written on two or more separate disk drives for redundant back up.

RAID rank

Group of drives managed by the disk array controller and configured to work as a defined set in host I/O operations.

Random Access Memory (RAM)

The primary memory in a computer. Memory that can be overwritten with new information. The "random access" part of its name comes from the fact that all information in RAM can be located, no matter where it is, in an equal amount of time. This means that access to and from RAM memory is extraordinarily fast. By contrast, other storage media, like magnetic tape, requires searching for the information, and therefore takes longer.

Random storage

Direct access storage devices, such as hard drives and floppies, write data anywhere on the disk that is free and quick to get to. They even break up contiguous files into scattered chunks of data all over the disk. The whereabouts of all these chunks is registered on a file allocation table (FAT). Random storage is much faster to retrieve from than linear storage, such as that used in magnetic tape.

R_A_TOV

Resource Allocation Time Out Value; used to timeout operations that depend on the maximum allowable time a frame could be delayed in the fabric and still be delivered.

Read cache

The cache is used to accelerate read operations by retaining data which has been previously read, written, or erased, based on the prediction that it will be reread.

Read Only Memory (ROM)

Data stored in a medium that allows it to be accessed but not erased or altered.

Receiver

A device that does detection and signal processing.

Redundancy

Having multiple occurrences of a component to maintain high availability.

Redundant Arrays of Inexpensive or Independent Discs (RAID)

A storage device that uses several optical discs working in tandem to increase bandwidth output and to provide redundant backup.

Redundant Array of Inexpensive Tape drives (RAIT)

It had to happen. Innovative Storage in Concord, CA, makes a tape changer that behaves like a RAID Level 1 and Level 3.

Remote Procedure Call (RPC)

A mechanism through which applications can invoke procedures and object methods remotely across a network. Using RPC, an application on one machine can call a routine or invoke a method belonging to an application running on another machine.

Remote switch

An optional product using a Computer Network Technology gateway over ATM.

Repeater

A circuit that uses recovered clock to regenerate and transmit an outbound signal.

Responder

The N_Port with which an Exchange originator wishes to communicate.

Retimer

A circuit that uses an independent clock to generate outbound signals.

Rewritable optical

Optical media from which data can be erased and new data added. Magneto-optical and phase change are the two main types of rewritable optical disks.

Rewritable optical disk

Optical disk on which data is recorded. The data in specified areas can subsequently be deleted and other data can be recorded.

Route

A path between two switches.

R_RDY

Receiver Ready; a primitive signal indicating that the port is ready to receive a frame.

RSCN

Registered State Change Notification; a switch function that allows notification to registered nodes if a change occurs either with or within the fabric.

R_T_TOV

Receiver Transmitter Time Out Value; used by the receiver logic to detect loss of synchronization between transmitters and receivers.

RX_ID

Responder Exchange Identifier; A 2-byte field in the frame header used by the responder of the Exchange to identify frames as being part of a particular exchange.

S_ID

Source Identifier; A 3-byte field in the frame header used to indicate the address identifier of the N_Port from which the frame was sent.

SAN

Server Storage or Area Network; a network linking computing devices to disk or tape arrays and other devices over fibre channel.

SCR

State Change Registration; the command used by devices to register to receive RSCNs.

SCSI

Small Computer Systems Interface; a parallel bus architecture and a protocol for transmitting large data blocks to a distance of 15–25 meters.

SCSI-2

An updated version of the SCSI bus architecture.

SCSI-3

A SCSI standard that defines transmission of SCSI protocol data over serial links.

SEQ_ID

Sequence Identifier; a 1-byte field in the frame header used by the responder of the Exchange to identify frames as being part of a particular Exchange.

Sequence

A group of related frames transmitted unidirectionally from one N_Port to another.

Sequence initiator

The N_Port that begins a new Sequence and transmits frames to another N_Port.

Sequence recipient

The N_Port to which a particular Sequence of data frames is directed.

SERDES

SERializing/DESerializing circuitry; a circuit that converts a serial bit stream into parallel characters, and vice-versa.

Serial

The transmission of data bits in sequential order over a single line.

Server

A central computer that processes end-user applications or requests.

SES

SCSI Enclosure Services; a subset of the SCSI protocol used to monitor temperature, power, and fan status for enclosed devices.

Single mode

A fiber-optic cabling specification that provides up to 10-km (6.8-mile) distances between devices.

sLink service

Facilities used between an N_Port and the fabric, or between two N_Ports for login, sequence/exchange management, and maintaining connections.

Small Computer System Interface (SCSI)

An industry standard for connecting peripheral devices and their controllers to a microprocessor. SCSI defines both hardware and software standards for communication between a host computer and a peripheral. Computers and peripheral devices designed to meet SCSI specifications should work together. A single SCSI adapter card plugged into an internal IBM PS/2 micro channel PC slot can control as many as seven different hard disks, optical disks, tape drives, and scanners, without siphoning power away from the computer's main processor. Formerly known as SASI (Shugart Associates Systems Interface).

Small Computer System Interface-2 (SCSI-2)

A 16-bit implementation of the 8-bit SCSI bus. Using a superset of the SCSI commands, the SCSI-2 maintains downward compatibility with other standard SCSI devices while improving reliability and data throughput.

SMI

Structure of Management Information; a notation for setting or retrieving SNMP management variables.

SNMP

Simple Network Management Protocol; A TCP/IP protocol that was designed for management of networks over TCP/IP, using agents and stations.

SNS

Simple Name Server (or Service); the service provided by a fabric switch that stores names, addresses, and attributes related to Fibre Channel objects, and can cache the information for up to 15 minutes. This is also known as a directory service.

SOF

Start Of Frame; a group of ordered sets that marks the beginning of a frame and indicates the class of service the frame will use.

SoIP

SCSI over IP.

SONET

Synchronous Optical Network; a standard for optical networks providing building blocks and flexible payload mappings.

Special character

A special 10-bit character that does not have a corresponding 8-bit value but is still considered valid. The special character is used to indicate that a particular transmission word is an ordered set. This is the only character to have five 1s or 0s in a row.

SRM

Storage Resource Management; the management of disk volumes and any file resources.

Storage

A device used to store data; such as a disk or tape.

Storage and retrieval system

An imaging system implemented to allow users to search and gather large numbers of documents. See workflow system.

Storage capacity

Amount of data that can be contained in an information holding device or main memory, generally expressed in terms of bytes, characters, or words.

Storage media

The physical device itself, onto which data is recorded. Magnetic tape, optical disks, and floppy disks are all storage media.

Store-and-forward

A switching technique that requires buffering an entire frame before a routing decision is made.

Stripe

The data and parity from the associated chunks of each member of the RAID set.

Striping

A RAID technique for writing a file to multiple disks on a block-by-block basis, with or without parity.

Switch

A fabric device providing full bandwidth per port and high-speed routing of data via link-level addressing.

SWL

Short WaveLength fiber optic; connector is color-coded black, and is based on 850-mm lasers supporting 1. 0625-Gbps link speeds.

T11

A standards committee chartered with creating standards for data movement to and from central computers.

Tachyon

A chip developed by Hewlett-Packard, and used in various devices. This chip has FC-0 through FC-2 on one chip.

Tape

A magnetic storage media. Comes in rolls or cassettes, and in standard widths: 8 mm, 1/8", 1/4", 1/2". Analog music recording uses mag tape up to 2 inches wide.

Tape Archive and Retrieval (TAR)

A file scheme to produce tapes on one system which are erasable on other systems. For example, UNIX can read tapes produced by an MS-DOS TAR program.

Tape drive

The machine, actually a collection of devices, that transports, reads, and/or writes a magnetic tape.

Target

A disk array or a tape on a Fibre Channel network.

TCP/IP
Transmission Control Protocol over Internet Protocol.

Telnet
A virtual terminal emulation used with TCP/IP.

Tenancy
Possession of an Arbitrated Loop by a device to conduct a transaction.

Terabyte (TB)
From "tera," which means trillion, although it actually means 1,099,511,627,776 bytes in a computer's binary system. A terabyte is 1,024 gigabytes.

Time server
A Fibre Channel service that allows for the management of all timers.

Topology
The physical or logical arrangement of devices in a networked configuration.

TPC
Third Party Copy; a protocol for performing tape backups without using server resources.

Transceiver
A device that converts one form of signaling to another for transmission and reception; in fiber optics it means optical to electrical.

Translative mode
Allows public devices to communicate with private devices across a fabric.

Transmission character
A valid or invalid character transmitted serially over fibre.

Transmission word
A string of four consecutive transmission characters.

Trap
An SNMP mechanism for agents to notify the SNMP management station of significant events.

TTL
Time To Live; the number of seconds an entry exists in cache before it expires.

Tunneling
A technique for making two different networks interact where the source and destination hosts are on the same type of network, but there is a different network in between.

U_Port
Universal Port; a port that can operate as a G/E/F/FL_Port.

ULP
Upper Level Protocol; the protocol that runs on top of Fibre Channel through the FC-4 layer. Typical protocols are SCSI, IP, HiPPI, and IPI.

Unicast
A routing method that provides one or more optimal path(s) between any two switches in the fabric.

VAR
Value Added Reseller.

VCSEL
Vertical Cavity Surface Emitting Laser; an improved and more reliable type of laser.

Vertical recording
A magnetic disk recording technique that increases the available storage space.

Very High Density (VHD)
Techniques of recording 20 megabytes and more on a 3-1/2" magnetic disk.

Virtual circuit

A one-way path between N_Ports that allows fractional bandwidth.

Virtual DISK (VDISK)

Part of the computer's Random Access Memory assigned to simulate a disk. VDISK is a feature of the MS-DOS operating system.

Virtual drive

A portion of RAM used as if it were a hard disk drive. Virtual drives are much faster than hard disks because your computer can read information faster from memory than from a hard disk. Information on a virtual drive is lost when you turn off or restart your computer. Also known as RAM drive.

Virtual storage

Your total storage capacity equals your fixed-drive capacity, combined with the capacity of removable storage devices. This gives an illusion of unlimited storage capacity.

Volume label

A name assigned to a floppy or hard disk in MS-DOS. The name can be up to 11 characters in length. You assign a label when you format a disk or, at a later time, using the LABEL command.

WAN

Wide Area Network.

Warm and hot spares

Drives that are electronically connected and powered on (hot spare) or powered-off (warm spare). When a drive fails, the controller automatically uses the hot or warm spare.

WDM

Wavelength Division Multiplexer; allows multiple wavelengths to be combined or filtered on a single cable.

World-Wide Name

A registered 64-bit unique identifier for nodes and ports in a fabric.

Write back Cache

A cache write strategy that writes to the cache memory, then may flush the data to the primary media at some future time. The user sees the operation as complete when the data has reached the cache. The intent of this strategy is to avoid unnecessary accesses to the primary media.

Write Once Read Many (WORM)

Optical storage device on which data is permanently recorded. Data can be erased, but not altered, and no additional data can be added.

Write Protect

Using various hardware and software techniques to prohibit the computer from recording (writing) on storage medium, like a floppy or hard disk. You can write protect a 5-1/4" diskette by simply covering the little notch with a small metal tag (physical write protect). You write protect a hard disk file with software (logical write protect).

Zoning

A feature in fabric switches or hubs that allows segmentation of a node by physical port, name, or address.

Index